Center for Modern Oriental Studies



# Changing Identities

# The transformation of Asian and African societies under colonialism

Papers of a symposium held at the Centre for Modern Oriental Studies, Berlin, 21-22 October 1993

Ed. by Joachim Heidrich

**Studien 1**

Verlag Das Arabische Buch

**Die Deutsche Bibliothek - CIP-Einheitsaufnahme**

**Heidrich, Joachim (Hg):**
Changing Identities. The Transformation of Asian and African Societies under colonialism / Joachim Heidrich. - Berlin: Verl. Das Arabische Buch, 1994
(Studien / Forschungsschwerpunkt Moderner Orient, Förderungsgesellschaft Wissenschaftliche Neuvorhaben mbH; Nr. 1)
ISBN 3-86093-062-1
NE: Förderungsgesellschaft Wissenschaftliche Neuvorhaben <München> / Forschungsschwerpunkt Moderner Orient: Studien

Forschungsschwerpunkt Moderner Orient
Förderungsgesellschaft Wissenschaftliche Neuvorhaben mbH

Kommissarischer Leiter:
Prof. Dr. Peter Heine

Prenzlauer Promenade 149-152
13189 Berlin
Tel. 030 / 4797319

ISBN 3-86093-062-1
STUDIEN

Bestellungen:
Das Arabische Buch
Horstweg 2
14059 Berlin
Tel. 030 / 3228523

Redaktion und Satz: Margret Liepach, Helga Reher

Druck: Druckerei Weinert, Berlin
Printed in Germany 1994

# Contents

Introduction 5

**Colonialism, Transcultural Interaction, Modernization**

*Anouar Abdel-Malek*: Identity, Alterity, Reductionism - Positions 11

*Reinhard Schulze*: Zur Geschichte der Islamischen Moderne. Probleme und Perspektiven der Forschung 25

*Joachim Heidrich*: Orient und Okzident als Zivilisationsräume der Moderne 41

*Barun De*: Imperialism, Nationalism, and the Dialectics of Changing Identity in the Indian Subcontinent 61

*Subrata K. Mitra*: Caste and the Politics of Identity: Beyond the Orientalist Discourse 79

**Foci of Identity Construction**

*Peter Heine*: Kultur, Identität und Politik in Saudi-Arabien 97

*Bipan Chandra*: The Historical Process of the Formation of the Indian Nation 109

*Tapan Raychaudhuri*: The Construction of a Hindu Identity in 19th Century India. A Synopsis 119

*Dietrich Reetz*: Community Concepts and Community-Building: Exploring Ethnic Political Identity in Colonial India 123

*Erik Komarov*: Specificities of Emergence of Modern Social Classes in India in the 19th and Early 20th Centuries 149

*Miloslav Krása*: A Note on the Impact of Europeans as Reflected in the Traditional Art of Bengal. A Historian's View 165

*Terence Ranger*: African Identities: Ethnicity, Nationality and History. The Case of Matabeleland, 1893 - 1993 177

*Achim von Oppen*: Mobile Practice and Local Identity. Changing Market Moralities in Rural Northern Rhodesia (Zambia), 1930s to 1960s 197

*Jan-Georg Deutsch*: Slavery, Coastal Identity and the End of Slavery in German and British East Africa 215

*Ulrich van der Heyden*: Die Entstehung der Unabhängigen Afrikanischen Kirchen in Südafrika - kirchliche Emanzipationsbestrebungen oder Ausdruck eines frühen Nationalismus? 225

**Indigenous Premises, Change and Modes of Response**

*J. V. Naik*: Intellectual Basis and Ideological Premises of Maharashtrian Response to British Colonial Rule 241

*Dick Kooiman*: Separate Electorates: Separate Identities? Experiences from Colonial India 255

*Annemarie Hafner*: Gab es eine Arbeiterkultur im kolonialen Indien? 273

*Petra Heidrich*: N. G. Ranga und Swami Sahajanand Saraswati - Bauernführer zwischen Tradition und Moderne 289

*Heike Liebau/Margret Liepach*: Christliche Hindus - indische Christen? Die "Nationalarbeiter" der Dänisch-Halleschen Mission in Südindien im 18. Jahrhundert 307

*Dagmar Glaß*: Popularizing Sciences through Arabic Journals in the Late 19th Century: How al-Muqtaṭaf Transformed Western Patterns 323

*Milos Mendel*: The Concept of "shura" as an Example of Islam's Response to the Impact of European Values 365

*Hervé Bleuchot*: Le droit penal colonial et les reactions Soudanaises 375

*Wolfgang Schwanitz*: Changing or Unknown Identities? The example of the Deutsche Orientbank AG in Cairo and Alexandria (1906 - 1931) 401

# Introduction

The present volume grew out of a symposium on *Changing Identities in Asian and African Societies under Colonialism*. The symposium was arranged by the Centre for Modern Oriental Studies and held in Berlin on 21 and 22 October, 1993. Scholars who specialise in areas which are covered by the research conducted at the Centre - that is, Africa, Near and Middle East, and South Asia - were invited to contribute papers. Professor Peter Heine, the Acting Director, welcomed the gathering. Professor Dietmar Rothermund, who spoke on behalf of the Board of Advisers, reviewed the growth of the Centre since its inception in 1992 and outlined the scope of its future research.

The symposium intended to stimulate discussion on a subject which currently engages scholars of several disciplines. The choice of the subject has been occasioned by academic, but also by more immediate considerations. The recent decades witnessed a remarkable and politically relevant proliferation of group identities of various kinds and at different levels - ethnic, social, religious, national and subnational - as well as a crisis of long-established ones in diverse parts of the globe, leading to sometimes rather dramatic consequences. The underlying idea in arranging the symposium was to venture a fresh look at the transformation of Asian and African societies by focussing on the issue of changing identities and making this the point of departure. It was suggested to the invitees that the task could be achieved by drawing attention to external as well as internal factors which contributed to identity-building, by singling out factors which determined and changed the role of identities in different historical situations under colonialism, and finally, by attempting a cross-cultural comparison of events bearing similarity but which could possibly have been generated by disparate processes.

The developments ever since decolonization in the erstwhile colonised countries of Asia and Africa necessitate a thorough rethinking. Apart from the need to expand the factual knowledge about what actually occurred within the societies under colonialism and thereafter, the multilinear trends which have surfaced in the modern period of world history constitute a major topic for studies devoted to these continents. The preliminary findings in this respect lend support to critiques of earlier simplified notions of a unilinear universal evolution. Moreover, as we stand at the threshold of a new millenium, the experiences gained in course of the twentieth century should be taken into consideration. The outgoing century witnessed the emergence on the part of former colonial countries of a strong urge to change a largely European-dominated world order towards a new type of universal relations without any form of hegemonic domination. Against this background, the dialectic relations between Europe or, for that matter, "the West", and non-European societies and cultures, including the perception of such relations, are bound to play a predominant role for examining societal transformations and putting individual events in a proper historical perspective. Simultaneously, the transformation of Asian and African societies requires to be perceived as a continuing process which comprises the precolonial, colonial, and postcolonial phases.

The participants of the symposium responded to the challenge by addressing in their papers aspects of the transformation of societies in Asia and Africa chiefly during the colonial and partly the postcolonial period, with particular reference to concepts, construction and changing roles of identities. Drawing on the findings obtained by various scientific disciplines as a frame of reference, the contributions shed light on the internal history of countries under colonialism and delineated factors and trends which to a considerable degree predetermined the course of postcolonial societies. The authors visualized their individual topics mainly as constituants or manifestations of larger and more comprehensive processes of the modern and contemporary periods of history. Some of the papers addressed the premises of further research explicitly.

Several authors included the configuration of linkages which resulted from the transcontinental and transcultural interaction. As a result, the interpretations offered in the contributions tend to transgress the limits of particular countries or regions as well as the frontiers of the colonial period. The investigations into the complexities of the construction of perceptions of "the other" provide new insights into the dimensions of confrontation, rejection or transcultural assimilation as documented by the histories of Asian and African countries.

The contributions approached historical change as the product of interaction in the ideological, political, social and economic spheres. They isolated elements of change which is significant as this enables us to inquire about cause. By implication, the papers supported the idea of a comparative study of societies which underwent transformation in conditions created by colonialism as most useful in leading to a sharper sense of understanding of the mode and direction of basic changes which are generally covered by the disputed term of modernization. Closely linked to this aspect is the question about the relevance of genetic relationship of modernizing trends and the derivative discourse as vehicles of change and of establishing new identities.

The deliberations favored the idea of a multi- or interdisciplinary approach as well as cross-cultural and cross-regional comparison. The symposium could naturally deal only with a limited number of aspects of the vast and multifaceted subject raised and with a few only of its accompanying cognitive questions. Yet it dealt with a wide range of issues.

Most of the contributions published in this volume are extended versions of papers which were actually submitted to the symposium. They have been roughly grouped under three captions. The topics chosen by the authors as also the regional orientation of the participants and their papers reflect a certain imbalance which, of course, was not by design. The authors emphasised different perceptions of the theme which they took up in the context of the historical specificities of their respective fields of studies. The subject itself could not provide a common denominator, so far as the theoretical or methodological approaches were concerned. Differing or even contradicting views held by individual authors are too obvious and need not be pointed out here. They figured also in the debate which followed the presentation of papers.

It is not possible to cover the discussion adequately and to reproduce the entire substance of the deliberations. Only a few of the issues may be mentioned.

In course of the tour d'horizon of world history accomplished by Anouar Abdel-Malek in his introductory address, the author pointed to a "crescent of renaissance" of global significance which he believes to be currently discernible in the dynamic region of Eastern Asia. From that region he expects a wind of change that is likely to reshape today's world. This thesis and the conclusion derived from it regarding the future preeminent role of developing countries or of the "East" as a source of global change met with a guarded response.

One of the debated issues centred on the role of colonialism or colonial administration in "creating" traditions and loci of identity formation, chiefly motivated by the objective of guaranteeing the governability of the subordinated country. Colonialism tended not only to wipe out the past of the people ruled by the alien power, it also deprived them of their future (Jan Breman). In the context of the prevailing preconditions for self-identification and the emergence of an anticolonial "counter-consciousness", the nature of nationalism both as a criterion of self-reference and as an instrument of political mobilization was hotly disputed. Barun De insisted on deeper empirical studies and cautioned against an inclination to overlook the over-centralizing nature of nationalism in colonial situations.

Different arguments were brought forward as to whether the traditional or the newly emerging identities would exercise a stronger impact on contemporary social and political affairs. Attempts at homogenizing different identities might be explained as a design to subvert them for a particular hegemony. But the option of establishing a democratic identity of heterogenous and only loosely interlinked groups cannot be excluded altogether. On the other hand, moves invoking a particular cultural or ethnic identity may be targeted at counterposing an alternative cultural identity which chooses to keep a specific domination in place.

Another intervention called for examining the reasons of the unequal capacity of individual cultures to embrace various ethnic or religious identities or to tolerate their coexistence (Subrata Mitra). Attention was drawn to the different roles which identities could assume in various circumstances. Observations suggest an obvious shift - over time - from a more centripetal to a more centrifugal tendency underlying the process of identity building, or towards a trend to differentiate and separate the components of already existing entities in recent time (as reflected by "new" ethno-religious nationalisms or subnationalisms), in contrast to the older trend to primarily establish larger and more homogeneous entities out of a conglomerate or a variety of components (Georg Elwert).

Considerable exchange of arguments ensued the reference to levels and foci of identity formation. Terence Ranger took exception to the preponderance of ethnicity-related topics in the contributions by the Africanists, compared to the near absence of the same topic in the papers of Indianists. He felt this to be a misrepresentation of the actual state of scholarship. Ranger elaborates his views in a lengthy introduction to his paper printed in this volume.

Another major issue of the debate concerned the relationship between universal and particular features or the validity of the concept of world history vis-a-vis the necessity to recognize multiple forms and paths of historical evolution in the modern and contemporary world. While the need to support a differentiating attitude remained basically undisputed, Bipan Chandra argued that on factual and epistemological grounds a conceptual frameworks will be indispensible which sustains the very notion of universal history. That problem was, in substance, followed up by the call for evolving identifying concepts which are applicable to non-European situations, or else, of establishing adequate instruments of cognition through a process of "cultural translation" (Reinhard Schulze). The discussants broadly agreed on the necessity to specify the meaning of modernity and modernization and felt that both terms should be delinked from the notion of "modern times". According to Sami Zubaida, modernity always became Western modernity, but rather many different streams and movements owe their origin to the historical process called modernization. In addition, attention was drawn to the issue of an endogenous modernization, the chances of which need to be studied also in the context of the preconditions for developing underdeveloped countries. The deliberations, in a passing reference, touched upon the capacity of self-transformation of societies or the scope of endogenously generated changes in a colonial situation. But due to shortage of time this question had to be left inconclusive.

It is hoped the publication of the papers will further the objective of the symposium to which they had been submitted.

Joachim Heidrich

# Colonialism, Transcultural Interaction, Modernization

# Identity, Alterity, Reductionism - Positions

Anouar Abdel-Malek

I

As we are called upon to explore the theme of 'changing identities', there is need to clarify the historical moment of the position of the problem.

The 'identity' problématique belongs to the 1950-1970 period, i.e. the culmination of the independence processes (from the early 1900s to 1945) coupled, and converging with, the national liberation movements and revolutions of the 1949-1973 period. By end 19th century already, colonialism had been superseded by classical imperialism; itself leading to hegemonic imperialism, as from 1947, and, more so, around the 1989-1992 implosion of the hitherto prevailing Western-centered bi-polar order.

History, re-visited? This could be one approach, attempting to sum up and refine what has been attempted and oft achieved.

History is on the move, impetuously, with unforeseen tempi, raising a disconcerting panoply of issues, suggesting hitherto uncharted paths, bringing marginalized factors and actors to the limelight, shaking well-established theses and beliefs. The winds of change: the transition from the transformation of the world to, literally, the making of a new world.

Hence, the relevance of taking stock of what has been achieved in major problem areas, beyond the feeling of déjà vu; and prospecting novation: both new substantive formulations of classical and ongoing problems and processes; and, more so, prospecting new factors and visions that are shapint historical dialectics at then onset of the 21st century.

II

Why should 'identity' - either posited; or changing - constitute a problem area? And, if so: when did it take shape in the realm of thought?

A first, convenient, entry point can be located in the perplexity of the Western mind reflecting upon its encounter with, or discovery of, the 'other': Bartholemeo de Las Casas plea for the sameness, the humanity, of Indians in Central and South America after 1492 and the ensuing massacres; Montesquieu's feigned surprise, facing the Orient: 'Comment peut-on être Persan?'

Convenient - yet vastly inadequate, emanating from the well-documented history of European, then Western, expansion in the world. The world of the 'other'. The world of other civilizations, cultures, nations, ethnic groups, societal formations. The world from which, precisely, the question of, and quest for 'identity', identities and their recognition have taken shape, and are deploying with ever-growing and oft-perplexing strength.

Could we attempt to trace the itineraries of thought and action pursued in each of the two sides of our common river?

## III

In times ancient, the great civilizational empires - Egypt, China, Persia; the separate circles of the Mayas, Aztecs and Incas; parallel to the African circles - viewed the otherness of subject populations as the wider, widening, parameter(s) of their own civilizational identity, to be assimilated; rather than distinct, enduring 'identities' - with few exceptions, in operational terms.

These ancient civilizational empires were succeded by several centuries, more often than not occulted in the dominant perception of the world. An yet, 'in the centuries immediately preceding Europe's expansion, the most important regional international systems, alongside medieval Latin Christendom from which the modern European states-system developed, were: the Arab-Islamic system, which stretched from Spain to Persia; the international system of the Indian subcontinent and its extensions eastward, founded upon a traditional Hindu culture but with predominant power in the hands of Muslim rulers; the Mongol-Tatar dominion of Eurasian steppes, which had also become Muslim; and the Chinese system, long under Mongol domination' while sub-Saharan Africa, Mexico and Peru, in the Americas, and Australasia did not enjoy a comparable degree of coalescence and continuity.[1]

Within these ancient civilizational empires, the three major monotheistic religions recognized their either across civilizational boundaries respective communities of believers (Christianity and Islam), or centering on a chosen people (Judaism). While the concept of citizenship in the Roman empire was posited facing the mass of the foreign subject peoples, literally the barbarians.

## IV

The age of maritime discoveries leading to the age of revolutions - scientific; industrial; bourgeois democratic - was also the age where historical surplus value converged in the hands of the rising bourgeoisies of Europe, the end result of the domination of the Three Continents: the looting of Indian Central and South America; the human hemorrage inflicted by slavery upon Africa; the marginalization of the central Islamic area as from the Crusades; the belated domination of South, South East, Central, and finally East Asia.

From the Renaissance to hegemonic imperialism, such is the path that led the West-Europe mainly; the U.S.A. since mid-20th century - to centrality in modern times. Centrality and hegemonism: hence the need to seek new conceptions of the 'other', to develop a new vision of the two sides of the river.

1. 'Universalism', based the high ground of the Aufklärung and the Encyclopaedism, posited the unity of mankind, the rights of man, the ideals of liberty, equality, fraternity. These noble ideals, proclaimed as the essential message of Europe and Western civilization, could thus inspire and justify the colonial and imperialist dominance and exploitation of the non-Western peoples, cultures and nations, invited to welcome the 'white man's burden'.

Salvation however could obtain as from linking the two circles in the ethos of universalism: if principles were proclaimed, enshrined in so many official documents, they could help the downtrodden to feel part and parcel of the human condition. A time would come when lofty principles would take flesh.

2. Yet, within the centre - the hegemonic core area - contradictions were taking shape, essentially between the new capitalist oligarchies, commercial, industrial, financial, and the working people. Injustice struck at the very heart of the virtuous centre. Class struggles, sometimes leading to class war, within each capitalist country; intra-national wars between different countries eager to expand their sphere in the outer circle (the 'peripheries'), leading to world wars.

The stage was thus set for a more refined definition of the differences obtaining within the inner circle of social dialectics, the major contribution of Marxian thought to the science of human societies. The time had come to provide a novel unifying mould to the exploited and oppressed majority, in the very heart of the core area itself. Hence the emergence of 'universalism', bringing together the exploited working people of capitalist societies at a universalist level, precisely, against the league of their exploiters. An approach which extended much later, after the October 1917 revolution and the rise of national liberation movements and national communism in the Orient, to the 'peoples of the East', the basis for the new world alliance against protracted injustice, towards social justice and socialism.

3. The 1939-1945 World War, and its aftermath, was to give rise to a third, this time all-encompassing, vision. The weakening of the former dominant Western colonial and imperial powers coupled with the visible rise of the U.S.A. as the leading hegemonic power in the capitalist-imperialist camp, coupled with the bipolar balance of power based on nuclear deterrence (1947-49), incited the leading economic-strategic power to think in terms of its centrality within the new universe.

Hence the thesis of the 'global reach' during the Truman presidency, which led to the formulation of 'globalism' as the third, final, stage of the interrelations between the different units of the outer circle of social dialectics in the world. The world conceived as a global village, whose centre (i.e. capital city) was none other than the central hegemonic imperialist power in the post-Yalta period.

V

On the other side of the river, reactions to this protracted penetration of the West was inevitably of a strategic defensive tonality, till the recent perception of the civilizational dimensions of the whole range of crises, world transformation, the prolegomena to the making of the new world.

1. At the time of 'universalism', dependent nations and societies stressed their 'alterity', or 'otherness', i.e. their feeling of being distinct from the new world centre. While at the same time asserting their willingness, or even assertive wish in the case of nations, to emulate Europe, in the hope of being accepted in the concert of nations. This position of the problem was seen as a direct challenge to the centrality of the West: from Mohamed-Aly's Egypt to the Meiji restoration in Japan; from Morocco to India; from the Taiping to the Kuomintang and Mao Tsetung's Long March in China.

'Universalism' had no place for otherness, in the realconcrete world of Realpolitik. Only compradores were sought. Hence the 'alterity'/'otherness' stage in the assertion of distinct identities from mid-18th till mid-19th centuries.

2. During the 19th and 20th centuries, this vision evolved gradually towards 'sovereignty' and 'independence' - in political terms, coupled with the economic dimension as the true nature of imperialism came to be recognized.

'Internationalism', welcome as it was, remained distant from the area of direct confrontations. These were to be tackled as from the national ground: the nation as crucible, wherefore the essentially political (cum economic) nature of national independentist and national liberation movements.

3. The global reach - combining advanced technologies with nuclear weaponry and the hegemonic mass media - raised the challenge at a much higher level. This time, the very existence of distinct identities was at stake.

Hence the move from the mainly political vision of identity to the cultural, rather the national-cultural position of the problem around the key concept of 'specificity'.

The three stages of this itinerary have been briefly sketched, to signalize the path. The formative elements will be analyzed after taking stock of the profound transformational processes now under way, towards shaping our new world.

World transformation can be analyzed in three domains/levels, a deeply interwoven web of networks, acting at different tempi, acuity, efficacy - with momentous consequences.

## VI

The concept and vision of 'power' itself:

- The centre of gravity of power is changing: from the military-strategic, to the economic-scientific-technological factors. In the last instance, while military might can maintain hegemony, and the control of major sources of energy and raw materials, it can neither develop new areas into valuable allies, nor break the resolve of peoples, let alone nations.
- The centre of gravity of power is shifting: from the Atlantic Euro-North American world, to East Asia, at the heart of the Asian continent and its Pacific rim. Still perceived in economistic terms, this momentous movement is now seen to reflect a fundamentally different set of value systems, in the realms of beliefs and societal organization alike. Wherefore the perception that historical creative novation can obtain, in lieu and place of the imposition of a new 'order'.

## VII

The converging pressure of new, or newly perceived, menaces:

- Natural resources - raw materials; energy sources, essentially oil; water - seen as a non renewable stock, the 'limits to growth' along the patterns set by the advanced industrial capitalist countries.
- The spread of drugs and deadly diseases, spreading mainly among the youth and the poor.
- The relentless rise of demographic curves, mainly in the agrarian regions, China excepted.
- The ever-increasing rate of unemployment in the advanced industrial countries, except Japan, thus bringing to the fore the very nature of work in modern societies.
- The disruption of the balance between man and nature: the rise of the environmental menaces, of the new deep concern with ecology.

Facing these converging negative factors, discussion is now centering on the respective efficacy of: either taming them via the application of more sophisticated technologies; or, rather, the critical revision of the major, Western, civilizational project itself - an altogether different matter, of immense relevance and magnitude.

## VIII

Last but ot least, the growing influence of formative factors which were deemed to be an the downward curve, or even withering away, now described as emerging, or re-emerging:

1. The national factor: the nation as crucible across the whole range of its manifestations in world cultures and societal formations. From the oldest nations to the new national states; ethnic groups striving for nationhood; ancient peoples imposing their presence through protracted struggles; the implosion of empires across national, or multi-ethnic, boundaries; the growing wave of claims to nationhood by small and/or isolated territories; even talk of the 'disuniting of America', Jefferson's 'only true new nation', this time under the centrifugal influence of national-cultural and ethnic huge component elements.

2. The state, oft considered as the hegemonic instrument of one or more social classes or groups in the larger, national, society, condemned either to irrelevance (by the 'global village' vision) or oblivion (after the advent of classless societies); now re-visited, as the central actor in the economic-technological upsurge of East Asia, as well as the regulator-protector of all advanced market economies. The shield of cultural identity, during the interlude of the unipolar hegemony.

3. The resurgence of tanscendance, at world level. Both: major world religions traditions (mainly Confucianism and Taoism, in China, East and South East Asia; syncretic Shintoism in Japan; Hinduism), parallel to the revitalizing of liberalism, pragmatism, positivism, coupled with the negative mind and nihilism in the West. To be sure, 'man does not live by bread'. The major interrogations of philosophia perennis, at the onset of a new world in the making.

4. The civilizational quest, bringing together all the threads of challenge, novation, continuity, resurgence. If so much ist challenged, if so many paths open anew, it seems natural to assume that the ongoing 'project', by its essence civilizational be questioned; while a new set of projects, linking in one major convergence circle, take shape as a new civilizational project inspiring the making of the new world.

## IX

The fateful 1989-1992 turning point acted as a trigger. For the first time since the making of international society, in the 16th century, the frame and sense of equilibrium was lost. The world - often viewed from the systems analysis viewpoint - could no more be approached with the usual tools of political analysis: 'rationality', 'order', 'system', 'equilibrium', et all. The systematic implosion of the socialist states system in East Europe and the former Soviet Union, the demise of the Western socialist alternative, coupled with the rupture of the Afro-Arab-Asian intercontinental intertwined civilizational-circles of the Orient as a result of the two Gulf wars are now seen to represent the most dangerous development in modern times. Chaos and gloom seem menacing, symbolized by the Bosnian tragedy, with growing levels of confrontation in large sectors of the Eurasian former Soviet Union, the rising tide of demographic potential migrations. While the unipolar centre gradually draws back from its purported role as the sole ruler and regulator. Now gearing itself to confront both Japan, China, the new Asia, as well as the new Europe-in-the-making, its former vassal during the defunct Cold War.

## X

In this maelstrom, the assertion of identity is being raised to new levels. The first and last trench. The ultimate resource and reassurance in times of unpredictable massive change, oft seen as menacing in the hitherto central area.

At this point, it seems proper to take note of a central dichotomy: while the 'arc of crisis' strikes at the heart of the centre - mainly, from East-Central Europe to the Middle East and South West Asia -, another arc, rather a 'circle of resurgence and renaissance' is fast rising in the major part of the Orient, in Asia, around China and East Asia. About which more later as we address the identity problématique at this new level, at the time of the making of the new world.

How can the dialectics of the relentless globalization pressures with the revival of identities be addressed in a meaningful way?

Several factors, as so many variables, can be useful as entry points to analysis, and action.

## XI

Speaking of identities, facing globalism and hegemonism, it is essential to distinguish between the capacity of different units/actors to comprehend and take action. All units of the international society, or international system, are formally, i.e. legally, identical: thus, the smallest island state has equal status with, say, the U.S.

and China, within the U.N. system. 'States' are thus units of analysis, being all legally equal members of the same larger world community.

Yet, the action field is open to such 'units of analysis' as are capable to take action. 'Units of analysis and action' comprise: the major superpower(s); the major world powers; major regional powers; a number of nation states possessing a high degree of efficacy, and therefore influence, in select areas (e.g. economic; religious); or occupying exceptional geopolitical position in the interplay of continents, geo-cultural areas, channels of trade and communication.

Other units are less capable of going beyond asserting their identity; and can thus be expected to accept more readily the relentless pressures of reductionism.

## XII

Thus defined, the main actors in the dialectics between globalization and the maintenance of identity can call upon two major set of resources, both rooted in the depth of their specific historical field.

First and foremost, each and every main actor (main 'unit of analysis and action') relies on his own potential. The usual positivest-quantiative analysis dwells on the economic, political, societal variables (e.g. GDP; state and parties; defence and security; the army; education, literacy, cultural life, religion, demography, inter all).

The missing factors are usually ignored, or dubbed under the derisive labels of 'national character', tradition' - specificity understood as exceptionalism, a mix of Idealtypus with exoticism. Since mid-20th century, the question of tradition has occupied centre-place. At the time when this dimension plays a growing role, day after day, across the world, at the very centre of the dialectics between specificy and universality, globalism and identity, reductionist modernization and national-cultural modernity, a concerted counter-offensive unfolds, via the deconstructivist new wave (in fact, the aggiornamento of the neo-positivist structuralism-functionalism) to deride the 'invention' of tradition, the viciated nature of the nation as such - in fact, the mainstay of the maintenance of identify-through-transformation, facing reductionism and hegemonism.

On 'the other side of the river', generations of research and action now converge to consider tradition as the cumulative legacy of the most resilient foundations of a given societal, national-cultural formation, that have stood the erosion of time. In fact, in truth: the living legacy of endonenous creativity in all fields essential to the maintenance of identity, through the long march of history.

The maintenance of identity, capable of providing its creative inputs to the commonweal of the growingly intertwined interactive linkage circles that are shaping our new world.

The basic potential, the ultimate resource. As distinct from the more influential (tactical) actors, more influent during the shorter range of history.

## XIII

The second set of factors reach for the outer dimension, the geo-historical environment of a given actor ('unit of analysis and action'). Three major macro-societal levels can be distinguished:

1. Nations (or socio-economic national formations) comprising one or more ethnic groups, within a unified economic ensemble structured in social classes, around a recognized national culture (or network of composite cultures), centering around one central locus of social power, unitary, federal or confederal: the state.

2. Geo-cultural area: the major 'regional' ensembles, bringing together a number of nations, ethnic groups and societal formations, around one or a limited number of major common languages and their acompanying cultural traditions.

3. Civilizations (or civilizational circles/moulds) defined as of a distinct vision of time, of the human condition in the long duration. Thus, the going-through-time vision of the Orient - as expressed in its religions and philosophies - develops into the symbiotic approach of existence and action, the basis of the communitarian, group, spirit as distinct from the analytic mind of Western civilization, the basis of individualism, systemic organization, reductionism.

A cursory review of the list of meaningful actors in the dialectics of identity and globalism shows a very wide typologycal spectrum. From China, the one unit which is at one and the same time the centre of a major civilizational circle, combined with an integrated set of geo-cultural areas, and its continuity as one nation state through millineries, to the more frequent category of medium nations within their own geo-cultural and civilizational circle, there are several varieties, notably such nations that occupy a pivotal place both in their respective geo-cultural area, and between different such areas, or continental ensembles; while a few can take stock of their unique religious centrality.

The capacity of different actors to take meaningful action, to maintain identity through world transformation, specificity as a creative component of the new universality(ies) depends, essentially, on the understanding of these complex networks, linkages and potentials by the political class as a whole, its leadership, addressing the structural basis of socio-political action at this crucial juncture in the history of our humankind.

## XIV

In this context, the primacy of the political may incline to seek such conceptual tools as can refine the understanding of the maintenance and change of identities. Thus, the 1970 position of the concept of specificity can be evoked: The analysis of the concept of specificity can be attempted at three levels/moments:

1. The level/moment of general definition, as from the origin. In order to reach for the specificity of a given society, one should seek what has been the pattern of societal maintenance obtained in a given socio-economic national formation, as from the critical study of its historical development. This particular pattern of this societal maintenance is nothing else but the pattern of structuration and interaction of/between the four key factors which constitute every societal maintenance:

- the production of material life in the geographic and ecologic framework (the mode of production stricto sensu);
- the reproduction of life (sexuality);
- social order (power and the State);
- the relation with the time-dimension (the limitedness of human life, religions and philosophies).

In that ensemble, the production of material life occupies the decisive place in the structuration of the whole pattern of maintenance, but only so in the last instance. By applying this model to different societies, we would be in a better position to clarify the gerenal picture, to qualify and to give colour - through the introduction of dominant touches - the first analysis undertaken as from socio-economic criteria.

2. The level/moment of the mergence of spation-temporal factors to conscious awareness. The study of specificity is not undertaken in the outer world of pure epistemology - but within the framework of the concrete evolution of given societies. This evolution puts the time factor in the forefront: wherefore the central importance of the notion of 'Depth of the historical field'. There ist no question of seeking a specificity in the case of an occaional society - a jamboree, student movements, a State artificially put together for the show (another Biafra), etc. To talk of societal maintenance is to address oneself to the long duration of history which moulds - not to contingency. By that we mean that one could validly speak of specificity in the old social-national formations - the ideal terrain for specificity - in those formations which have not yet reached the national level of evolution stricto sensu, in the 'new nations' also, after the word of Thomas Jefferson speaking of the United States of America. One can thus see how vast ist the field: the immense majority of nationa and peoples in our time. The social sciences will feel less at ease with the 'space' factor - because of the falling out of favour of one form of geo-politics. However, the historical evolution of societies does not take

place in the abstract space of the dialectics of the mind - 'History', in place of 'history' - neither does it unfold itself in the secluded field of epistemology. Societies - but only within the framework of their geographical conditions, considered under two aspects:

- the aspect of localization, which leads to the appreciation of the place thus assigned by this localization, to each society and its State as compared to others, i.e., geo-politics;
- the aspect of the internal conditioning, i.e., ecology, which indicates and quantifies resources and potentials which have then to be tempered by taking into consideration the demographic factor.

3. The moment-dimension of the dialectics of the factors of maintenance with the factors of transformation, as from the action, ultimately decisive, of the mode of production, and, at extreme limit, of the progress of techniques of production. To disentangle that which is maintained, from that which maintains (this is an altogether different thing than to speak of 'invariables' - of a posterior origin), that which is maintained, that which maintains according to a certain pattern, from that which was not, and becomes, from that which ist, and shall be no more: to distinguish the four link factors, whatever be the relative weight of such factors at such and such stage of historical evolution.

4. The concept of specificity will be used both in the hegemonic area and in the dependent area.[2]

## XV

The heartland of the idendity problématique in our changing time and world lies in the feasibility of shaping alternatives to the pressures of the hegemonic civilizational project and strategy. Already, perceptive powerful voices are warning against the deadly perils of the triumphalism-nihilism combinatory, grounded in the market ethos, the end point of the productivist-consumerist-hedonist build up - now proclaiming the 'end of history', the attempted imposition of the iron-clad central hegemonism via the two-pronged arsenal of the control of advanced technologies and mass media.

## XVI

The major forces capable of taking creative action, i.e. shapint a new set of theses leading to the formation of a new civilizational project, or set of converging projects, can be recognized:

1. The Orient, resurgent, occupies centre place. Essentially, East Asia (the 'Kanji Culture Sphere', or Chinese civilizational circle) extending towards North East, South East, Southern, Central and West Asia. Attention is focussing on the hitherto unheard of exponential rates of economic growth (China and Malaysia leading the field, one generation after Japan - amidst the flowering of NICs and 'new tigers'). Yet, the vaery basis of this mighty process mut surely lie elswhere - the market exigencies and economic variables being common to all regions. Precisely in the socio-cultural factors deep at work since long, now being given the possibility to deploy thanks to the combined effects of the liberation of Asia at the time of the weakening of the global reach of the Western cental forces.

The code word, 'Confucianism', oft linked, and/or opposed, to 'political Islam', opens the path to serious analysis of the socio-cultural basis, the formative factors of the new civilizational project now in its formative stage, beyond the economic-technological upsurge.

To sum up recent converging research, this project ist taking shape around four major orientations:

- Peace based on justice, as the global survival mission; making maximal use of endogenous intellectual creativity;
- Development conceived as human and social development, making maximal use of endogenous intellectual creativity;
- Solidarity: the united national front, in the inner (national) circle; cooperation towards complementarity in the regional and international circles;
- Spirituality - the revival of religions and major philosophical quest - providing for the normative approach to human activities, in all fields.

2. Europe, now seeking its path towards unity, as the centre of Western civilization, with various degrees of interaction with and influence upon Latin America, sectors of North America. Even though economic recession, ethnic conflicts and, essentially, the stock waves of the implosion of the former Soviet Union, beginning to unfold, concur to obscure the positive farces on the rise, which have yet to gather optimal momentum.

Two major orientations, in effect two major schools of thought and action, can be seen as the major actors, and orientations:

- The revival of Christian spirituality coupled with the national-cultural claim for distinct identities in major medium powers of the continent. The convergence of these normative approaches, different as they seem at a first level of analysis, is being turned into an imperative against the spread of nihilism, the disintegration of proud nations and cultures, faced with reductionism and vassality.

- Social justice, as the imperative principle of any viable democracy. Hence, the growth of reformist social market conservatism, the resilience of social-democracy, more so perhaps the growth of reformed democratic socialism in a wide range of former communist countries and parties.

## XVI

The interwoven, intricate set of action; their highly different levels of intensity, growth tempi, self-adjustment capabilities; as well as the resonance and impact of major actors and factors upon our changing world is in need of a guiding thread.

Hence, the concept of 'historical initiative' put forth as one contribution of major international-comparatist research achieved at The United Nation University (1978-82), now gradually expanding in a growing range of analyses of historical processes.

The main locus and major set of forces of historical initiative in our times, shapint the makind of the new world within the constraints and facing the challenges of world transformation, is located in, and represented by, the resurgence of the Orient, around its kernel, East Asia. The basic movement is towards convergence with the new Europe. This ist the new Eurasian heartland, with Asian-African Islam as its main central linking circle, firmly linked to Latin America via the two oceanic circles, a 'New Silk Road' - starting from the Orient.

## XVII

The path to approach the dialectics of identities facing reductionism, of specificities and universalities at the time of the making of our new world, delineated in the theses hereabove, calls upon all concerned to face rising turmoil with a clear vision and resolve.

Dialectical contradictions can in no way be tamed by forced reductionism. Nor should they be tackled in a confrontational spirit.

The basic, principled, approach here advocated is for the non-confrontational treatment of dialectical contradictions, geared towards complementarity. As against both reductionism and manichean dichotomies.

More than at any previous time in world history, the spirit of the enterprise as it were should steer clear of the apodictic, assertoric position(s) of the problem, while rooting itself in the interrogative, problematic, approach.[3]

If 'the future has not already been lived' (Aragon), we are invited to take stock of the potentials and perspectives offered to our new world in the making by 'time, the refreshing river', in the spirit of Joseph Needham, maître en l'art de civilisation.

## Notes

1 Bull/Hedley & Watson/Adam (eds.), The Expansion of International Society, Oxford 1984, p. 1-3.

2 Pour une sociologie de l'impérialisme. In: L'Homme et la Société (1971)21; La Dialectique Sociale, Paris 1972, pp. 389-392; Spécificité et Théorie Sociale, Paris 1977; The Concept of Specificity - Positions, The United Nations Univesity, Tokyo 1979, p. 3.

3 Positions, here succintly presented, as of the author's publications, mainly: Egypte, société militaire, Paris 1962 (Torino 1967; Madrid 1967; New York 1971; Frankfurt/M. 1971; Beirut 1968); Kûltur Emperyalizmi, Istanbul 1967; Dirâsât fî'l-Thaqâfah al-Wataniyyah (Studies in National Culture), Beirut 1967; Idéologie et Renaissance Nationale: l'Egypte moderne, Paris 1969, 1975; La Pensée politique arabe contemporaine, Paris 1970, 1975, 1980 (Ankara 1971; Roma 1978, London 1983; Tokyo in prep.); Sociologie de l'Impérialisme, Paris 1971 (Mexico 1975); La Dialectique Sociale, Paris 1972 (Tokyo, Mexico, Bari, Sao Paulo, Cairo 1975-1992); Al-Fikr al-'Arabî fî Ma'rakat al-Nahdah (Arab Thought in Struggle for Renaissance), Beirut 1974, 1978; L'Armée dans la Nation (Asie, Afrique, Amérique Latine), Alger 1975 (Beirut 1978); Spécificité et Théorie Sociale, Paris 1977; La Renaissance du monde arabe, Bruxelles 1982; Nahdat Misr (The Renaissance of Egypt), Cairo 1983; Rîh al-Sharq (East Wind), Cairo 1983; Taghyîr al-'Alam (The Transformation of the World), Kuwait 1985; Al-Share' al-Misrî wa'l-Fikr (Egyptian Street and Thought), Cairo 1989; Al-Ibdâ' wa'l-Mashru' al-Hadârî (Creativity and the Civilisational Project), Cairo 1991; (with A.N. Pandeya, co-ed.): Intellectual Creativity in Endogenous Culture, The U.N. University, Tokyo 1981. Project on 'Socio-Cultural Development Alternatives in a Changing World (SCA)' - 1978/1982, final report, abridged version, The U.N. University, Tokyo 1985; Historical Initiative - the 'New Silk Road', Kanji Culture Sphere Forum, 3rd International Conference 'East Asia in the 21st Century' (Yokohama, 13-14 November 1992); Inculturation - Beyond the 'Logic of Contempt', European Academy, Madrid, 6-9 November 1992).

# Zur Geschichte der islamischen Moderne
# Probleme und Perspektiven der Forschung

Reinhard Schulze

## Gibt es eine islamische Moderne?

Lange Zeit oszillierten die orientalistischen Forschungen insbesondere in den Bereichen der Islamwissenschaft und Arabistik zwischen zwei Polen: auf der einen Seite stand die eher philologisch orientierte Erforschung der "autochthonen" islamischen Geschichte, auf der anderen Seite die fachlich vielgestaltige Beschäftigung mit dem zeitgenössischen Orient. Als sich in den siebziger Jahren immer mehr Forscherinnen und Forscher zugunsten einer gegenwartsbezogenen Orientforschung aussprachen, die die klassische Orientalistik komplementär ergänzen und auch der Islamwissenschaft einen gebührenden Platz einräumen sollte, stand die Erforschung der neuzeitlichen, vorkolonialen Geschichte der islamischen Welt nicht zur Debatte. Denn während die autochthone Geschichte der islamischen Welt (allenfalls) bis in das späte Mittealter geführt wurde und die gegenwartsbezogene Orientforschung historisch (allenfalls) bis in das frühe 19. Jahrhundert zurückwies, fand die vorkoloniale Neuzeit in der islamischen Welt, also grob der Zeitraum von 1500 bis 1800 weder das Interesse der breiteren Orientforschung noch der orientalistischen Disziplinen im engeren Sinne. Diese "Zwischenzeit", vielfach als eine Epoche der Dekadenz und des kulturellen und sprachlichen Niedergangs bezeichnet, wurde lediglich von osmanistischen, safawidistischen und mogulistischen Disziplinen aufgegriffen. Dies entsprach natürlich der politischen Landkarte der islamischen Welt in der Neuzeit, die ja deutlich von eben diesen Reichen geprägt war. Der arabischen islamischen Welt wie auch der islamischen Kultur überhaupt wurde in der entsprechenden Forschungslandschaft hingegen kein prominenter Platz zugewiesen.

Begründet wurde die Vernachlässigung dieser "Zwischenzeit" meist nur mit dem Verweis darauf, daß der innovative Gehalt der islamischen Geschichte in jenen Jahrhunderten sehr gering und keinesfalls mit dem vergleichbar sei, was Europa zu einer "geschichtlichen Idee" gemacht haben.[1] Der "kulturelle Niedergang" der islamischen Welt habe den vormodernen Charakter seiner Kultur nachhaltig geprägt, ja, der Islam selbst wurde als Argument für die kulturelle Dekadenz ausgemacht. Mithin sprach man gerne vom Islam als einer vormodernen Kultur; als solche könne sie nur durch exogene, sprich westliche Faktoren "modernisiert" werden. Wenn also von islamischer Moderne gesprochen wurde, dann meinte man meist die "Modernisierung" der islamischen Welt durch die westliche Kultur.

Diese Sicht war schon früh zu einem Standardmodell in der Beschreibung der islamischen Welt geworden. Ja, es hat sogar die heftigen Kritiken an den Modernisierungstheorien[2] überlebt, die in den siebziger Jahren einsetzten und die zu einer vielfältigen, kontroversen Neubestimmung der Modernisierung geführt haben. Die Zählebigkeit der populären Niedergangsthese ist allerdings überraschend; denn letztere ist weder das Ergebnis einer wissenschaftlichen Grundlagenforschung (denn auch die Niedergangsthese müßte belegt werden) noch ist sie allein aus einem generalisierten Vorurteil heraus zu verstehen. Vielmehr müssen andere Aspekte berücksichtigt werden, welche unmittelbar die interkulturellen Beziehungen zwischen der islamischen und der europäischen Welt berühren; ja, es kann gefolgert werden, daß die Niedergangsthese selbst das Ergebnis eines "europäischen Monologs" über den islamischen Orient ist, der im Verlaufe der kolonialen Expansion auch in der islamischen Welt heimisch geworden ist und der die bis in das 19. Jahrhundert hinein wirkende kulturelle Übersetzung zwischen der islamischen und der europäische Welt zunichte gemacht hat.[3]

Hier soll nicht weiter über die möglichen Hintergründe der Niedergangsthese gesprochen werden.[4] Solange nicht ausführlichere Forschungen uns solide Kenntnisse zur Geschichte der Dekadenztheorien und ihrer Rezeption in der islamischen Welt (als *inḥiṭâṭ*[5]) gegeben haben, bleibt viel Raum für Spekulationen. Es scheint mir daher sinnvoll, den Spieß umzudrehen und zunächst von einer Gegenthese auszugehen, nämlich von der These, daß die islamische Welt in der vorkolonialen Neuzeit mit ihren kulturellen Traditionen eine Moderne vorbereitete, welche die Große Rezeption der westlichen Moderne im 19. Jahrhundert so ermöglichte wie einst die europäische Welt die islamischen Wissenstraditionen des Mittelalters ohne "Krise" rezipieren gekonnt hatte. Das "Krisenbewußtsein", also die kognitive Erörterung einer historischen Dekadenz, die die islamische Welt von einem bestimmten Zeitpunkt[6] an "befallen" hätte, müßte demnach als Resultat einer Integration des europäischen Diskurses über die islamische Geschichte in die islamischen Elitenkulturen gewertet werden.

## Anmerkungen zur Forschungsgeschichte

Beginnen möchte ich mit einigen Bemerkungen zur Forschungsgeschichte. Die wissenschaftliche Erforschung der vorkolonialen Neuzeit in der islamischen Welt (16. - 18. Jahrhundert) hat sich in der westlichen Orientalistik erst in den letzten vierzig Jahren entfaltet. Auch wenn es bislang noch keine ausgesprochene Forschungstradition zur islamischen Neuzeit[7] gibt und die wissenschaftliche Kooperation zwischen einzelnen Institutionen und Forschern als mangelhaft angesehen werden muß, können einige Publikationen als Wegmarken hin zur Etablierung einer an neuzeitlichen Fragestellungen interessierten Islamwissenschaft beziehungsweise Orientwissenschaft herangezogen werden. Sie stammen meist aus den USA (S. Shaw, H. A. R. Gibb), aus Großbritannien (P. M. Holt) und Frankreich (J. Berque, R. Mantran, A. Raymond); aus der deutschsprachigen Forschung kamen neue Impulse für eine Befassung mit der neuzeitlichen islamischen Geschichte bisher vor allem aus dem Bereich der Osmanistik und der Iranistik.[8] Diesem gemessen an der Zahl der Publikationen nur geringen Forschungsinteresse stand eine doch recht weitläufige, aus dem 18., 19. und frühen 20. Jahrhundert stammende europäische Literatur gegenüber, die aber kaum in der Orientalistik rezipiert wurde.[9]

Die in den fünfziger Jahren publizierte und weit bekannte, zweibändige, trotzdem aber nicht abgeschlossene Untersuchung zur "islamischen Gesellschaft" im 17. und 18. Jahrhundert von Gibb und Bowen[10] bildete den Auftakt zu einer "modernen" Erforschung der islamischen Neuzeit und diente lange Zeit als Wegweiser und wichtigste Sekundärquelle überhaupt. In einer auf Institutionen bezogenen Gesamtschau versuchten die Autoren, die Auswirkungen der Dezentralisierung des Osmanischen Reichs auf die arabische Welt zu erforschen und formulierten eine weitreichende Theorie zum Niedergang in der islamischen Welt, welcher vor allem durch die islamische Kultur als Faktor einer "Entwicklungsblockade" verursacht worden sei. Schon früh hatten Albert Hourani, Norman Itzkowitz und später Roger Owen[11] kritisch Stellung zum Werk von Gibb & Bowen genommen und gezeigt, daß das Konzept des "kulturellen Niedergangs" der islamischen Welt aus sozial- und wirtschaftsgeschichtlicher Sicht unhaltbar ist.[12] Eine politikgeschichtlich orientierte Gesamtschau, die sich generalisierender Aussagen weitgehend enthielt, legte 1969 Holt vor. Er hatte sich schon seit 1959 mit der Geschichte Ägyptens im 18. Jahrhundert befaßt und auch die wichtige Dissertation von Abdul-Karim Rafeq, The Province of Damascus 1723 - 1783[13], betreut.

1971 machten Th. Naff und R. Owen erstmals das 18. Jahrhundert zum Thema einer internationalen Fachtagung.[14] A. Houranis mehrfach nachgedruckter Beitrag zu dieser Tagung[15] dürfte eine der ersten systematischen Untersuchungen zur islamischen Kulturgeschichte im 18. Jahrhundert sein. Allerdings war Hourani angesichts des mangelhaften Forschungsstandes gezwungen, sich auf eine rein faktuelle Aufzählung von Beobachtungen zu beschränken und von jeder weiterführenden Deutung Abstand zu nehmen. Noch aber hielten die Herausgeber an der Sicht fest, daß der "Niedergang" ein bestimmendes Merkmal der islamischen Geschichte im 18. Jahrhundert gewesen sei, wiewohl jenes Jahrhundert auch als eine Epoche "des Erhaltens, der Kontinuität und Ausarbeitung"[16] angesehen werden könne.

Während nun in den späten siebziger und achtziger Jahren die Forschungen zur islamischen Kultur- und Wissensgeschichte in bezug auf das osmanische Kernland[17], auf Indien[18] und Iran beachtliche Fortschritte machte[19] und auch die Arbeiten zu Marokko im Anschluß an Jacques Berques grundlegende Untersuchungen gut vorankamen[20], fehlten entsprechende Forschungen zur islamischen Kultur in anderen Gebieten der islamischen Welt, insbesondere des arabischen Mašriq fast ganz. Lediglich die syrische Literaturgeschichte, und hier besonders der Mystiker ʿAbdalġanî an-Nâbulusî[21], fand ein gewisses Interesse[22]; für Ägypten war man lange einzig auf die kompilatorische Arbeit von Muḥammad Sayyid Kailânî[23] angewiesen.

Leitthemen der historischen Forschung waren wirtschafts- und sozialgeschichtliche Fragen, die es implizit erlaubten, von kulturgeschichtlichen Wertungen Abstand zu nehmen. Dank dieser Arbeiten, die vielfach die reich ausgestatteten Archive im ehemaligen Osmanischen Reich benutzen, sind wir recht gut über die sozial- und wirtschaftsgeschichtlichen Entwicklungen informiert. So gelang es André Raymond, mit seinem epochemachenden Werk zur Stadtgeschichte Kairos im 18. Jahrhundert (1973/74), eine Sozialgeschichte zu verfassen, welche ganz ohne die tradierten Kategorien "Verfall" oder "Dekadenz" auskam. Seiner Tradition folgten inzwischen Forscherinnen und Forscher, die sich u. a. der Stadtgeschichte von Aleppo, Damaskus und Algier widmeten.[24] All diese Arbeiten[25] aber haben bislang den kulturgeschichtlichen Aspekt weitgehend vernachlässigen müssen, da die literarischen und wissenschaftsgeschichtlichen Quellen kaum aufbereitet waren.[26] So wissen wir heute - mit Ausnahme des Osmanischen Reichs selbst (hierzu hatten sich schon im frühen 20. Jahrhundert türkische Autoren wie Rafîq Aḥmad ausführlich zu Wort gemeldet), Marokkos, Indiens[27] und Irans - nur wenig über die wissens- und kulturgeschichtlichen Traditionen der vorkolonialen Zeit.[28]

1979 veröffentlichte Peter Gran seine Studie zur ägyptischen Gesellschaft 1760 - 1840 und überschritt erstmals die Grenze zu einer vergleichenden Wissensgeschichte.[29] Seine Hypothesen zu einer endogenen Moderne in der ägyptischen Gesellschaft haben viel Widerspruch hervorgerufen, da sie auf einer oberflächlichen Aufarbeitung der Quellen, einer in die Quellen projizierten Interpretation und einer fast mechanistischen Gleichsetzung von sozialen Klassen und Wissenstypen aufbauten. Forscher wie Gabriel Baer, Ewald Wagner und Fred de Jong haben nachdrücklich auf diese methodischen und faktischen Mängel verwiesen, so daß kaum jemand noch bereit war, die Plausibilität der Granschen Hypothesen erneut und auf der Basis neuen Quellenmaterials zu überprüfen. Lediglich Michel Mazzauoi[30] wagte einen weiteren Versuch, die bislang genutzten Quellen neu zu interpretieren und in den Zusammenhang einer islamischen Moderne zu stellen. Immerhin hatte sich nun - vielfach mehr intuitiv als durch Quellenforschung belegt - die Ansicht breit gemacht, daß die alte These von der sozialen, wirtschaftlichen und kulturellen Dekadenz der islamischen Welt, die erst durch den europäischen Kolonialismus überwunden worden sei, nicht mehr haltbar ist und daß es in der islamischen Welt regional spezifische, oft disparitätische Prozesse gegeben hat, welche durchaus mit der Herausbildung einer Moderne bezeichnet werden können.

Die Arbeitsergebnisse einer Konferenz von Jerusalem 1985[31] stellten den ersten Versuch dar, eine Bestandsaufnahme der Forschungen zu einer vergleichenden und problemorientierten Erörterung der islamischen Kultur im 18. Jahrhundert zu machen. Die präsentierten Fallstudien aber geben nur beschränkt Auskunft über interaktive kulturgeschichtliche Prozesse. Das Buch hat insofern einen großen

Verdienst, als es das islamische 18. Jahrhundert unter einer neuen gemeinsamen ideengeschichtlichen Fragestellung betrachtet. Diese bezieht sich auf das Konzept der "Erneuerung" (renewal) und "Reform"; damit haben die Autoren zwar Abschied von der tradierten Dekadenztheorie genommen, aber gleichzeitig zu einer quasi zyklischen Geschichtsbetrachtung zurückgefunden. Als Hauptmerkmal kultureller Prozesse in der islamischen Welt wurde so die zyklische Erneuerung angenommen. Dies reflektiert natürlich die Sicht zahlloser Theologen jenes Jahrhunderts, die sich oder andere oft als "Erneuerer des Jahrhunderts" feierten. An die Stelle der "Dekadenz" war nun das Konzept der "Erneuerung" getreten. R. Peters faßte einige Merkmale dieser "Erneuerungsbewegungen" in einem vielbeachteten Aufsatz zusammen.[32]

## Erkenntnisinteresse und Erkenntnisziele

Die These, die diesem Bericht zugrunde liegt, besagt, daß das, was heute vorsichtig als "Erneuerung" oder "Reform" in der islamischen Welt des 18. Jahrhunderts bezeichnet wird, Teil eines umfassenderen sozial- und kulturgeschichtlichen Prozesses war. In ihm verbanden sich pietistische, mystische und kritisch-rationalistische[33] Traditionen zu einem neuen dynamischen, aber auch widersprüchlichen Gefüge, welches keineswegs mehr als lineare Fortschreibung mittelalterlicher Weltbilder gedeutet werden kann. Umrahmt von Stil-, Mode- und Denktraditionen, die provisorisch mit den Begriffen Renaissance und Barock bezeichnet werden sollen, mündeten die intellektuellen Auseinandersetzungen zwischen den drei Haupttraditionen in einem aufklärerischen Prozeß, welcher schließlich die tiefgreifende Rezeption westlicher Aufklärungstraditionen ermöglichen sollte.

Die drei genannten Traditionen Pietismus, Mystik und Rationalismus stellen natürlich an sich keine Neuerungen der Neuzeit dar, sondern folgen ihrerseits älteren, in der Islamwissenschaft sehr gut erforschten Traditionslinien. Entscheidend für die Neuzeit ist der ideengeschichtliche Wandel dieser einzelnen Traditionen, ihr soziales und kulturelles Zusammenspiel und ihre Entfaltung im politischen Prozeß. So kann angenommen werden, daß die drei dominanten großen Traditionen gemeinsam auf die Entfaltung eines neuen Weltbildes unter den Eliten reagierten und dieses mitgestalteten; gleichzeitig aber überdauerten in vielen sozialen Bereichen die älteren Weltbilder und prägten eine Vielfalt lokaler und regionaler Traditionen, die nur mittelbar auf das kulturelle Umfeld der Eliten reagierten.

Das islamische Gelehrtentum, das sich als Hüter der Wissenskulturen verstand, kann folglich nicht mehr (oder besser: wie zuvor auch nicht) als eine soziale und kulturelle Einheit angesehen werden; vielmehr gliederte sich das Gelehrtentum entsprechend der von ihm vertretenen Traditionen in pietistische, mystische und rationalistische Fraktionen, die sich jeweils eine eigene Klientel in der Gesellschaft suchten. Ein Merkmal der neuzeitlichen islamischen Kulturen scheint die Neubestimmung der sozialen Zuordnung der Gelehrten zu diesen Traditionen, wobei auffällig ist, daß diese jeweils zur Verabsolutierung ihrer spezifischen Kultur tendierten. Der sich hieraus entwickelnde Dogmenstreit war somit sehr viel deutlicher als früher mit sozialen Auseinandersetzungen verbunden.

Während die pietistischen und mystischen Traditionen schon sehr früh gruppenbildend waren (im Osmanischen Reich z. B. als *qâdîzâdeli, aqšbandîya, baktâšîya*) und vielfache Metamorphosen erlebten (bis hin zur arabischen *wahhâbîya* oder zur schiitischen *šaiîya*)[34], traten erst im Verlaufe des 18. Jahrhunderts die Anhänger einer kritisch-rationalistischen Tradition als - allerdings noch näher zu bestimmende - "Gruppe" auf. In der arabischen Kultur nannten sie sich teilweise selbst "Ideenträger" (Intellektuelle, *(ûlû l-fik(a)r)* und grenzten sich damit bewußt von den Gelehrten *(ûlû al-ᶜilm)* ab, indem sie sich (wie der Name anklingen läßt) das Poetische und die "Idee" als kulturelle Merkmale aneigneten.[35] Die Bestimmung der islamischen Moderne im 18. Jahrhundert hängt somit eng von dem Nachweis einer neuen islamischen Intellektuellenkultur ab, die ihrerseits wieder in einer merkwürdigen, noch zu deutenden Beziehung zu einem Bürgertum stand, auf das schon A. Raymond und ihm folgend G. Delanoue hingewiesen haben.[36] Nach den bisherigen Erkenntnissen waren die "Intellektuellen" als Kritiker des tiefgreifenden Disputs zwischen Pietisten und Mystikern schon im 17. Jahrhundert aufgetreten. Doch erst um 1740 hatten sie eine literarische Tradition begründet, welche um 1780 im islamischen Klassizismus einen Höhepunkt erreichen sollte.

Die islamischen Kulturen der vorkolonialen Neuzeit und vor allem des 18. Jahrhunderts waren - so läßt sich also vermuten - weitgehend von pietistischen, mystischen und rationalistisch-kritischen Traditionen geprägt. Ideengeschichtlich verfügten die islamischen Kulturen somit über jene Traditionen, welche im europäischen Kontext als Grundbausteine der Moderne und der Aufklärung gedeutet werden.[37] Diese Traditionen sind - insbesondere für Indien und das Osmanische Reich - ansatzweise, wenn auch als isolierte Phänomene beschrieben worden. Eine synthetische Sicht, welche diese Traditionen als ein interdependentes Epochenphänomen[38] deutet, ist aber bislang noch nicht entwickelt worden. Wiewohl sich diese Traditionen schon im islamischen Mittelalter entwickelt haben, bot das 18. Jahrhundert doch den Rahmen für eine besondere Konjunktur, da der sich nun deutlich abzeichnende sozialgeschichtliche Wandel - hierbei spielt die regionale Autonomie eine besondere Rolle - zur Herausbildung einer neuen Elitenkultur führte, für die das konzeptionelle Zusammengehen dieser Traditionen ein wichtiges Moment ihres Weltbildes ausmachte.

Die orientalistische Forschung könnte nun danach fragen, in welchem Umfang sich die Eliten in ausgewählten islamischen Ländern eine Weltsicht aneigneten, welche sich im Spannungsgefüge zwischen Pietismus, Mystik und wissenschaftlichem Rationalismus bewegte. Obwohl auch die Erforschung einzelner Regionen wichtige Erkenntnisse zur Kulturgeschichte verspricht, sollte auch die Komparatistik als wichtigstes Erkenntnisziel ausformuliert werden. Sie bezieht sich vor allem auf kulturgeschichtliche Erscheinungen, wobei Kultur folgenden als ein Netzwerk sozialer Beziehungen verstanden werden soll, das über Kommunikation vermittelt wird und über die ein gewisser Konsens besteht. Folglich sollten die Quellentexte als Ausdruck sozialer Kommunikation verstanden werden. Sie sollen in unterschiedlicher Gewichtung danach befragt werden, wie über Weltbilder und Lebenswelten kommuniziert wurde und welche Veränderungen sie über das 18. Jahrhundert hinweg dokumentieren. Ein weiteres Forschungsinteresse besteht daher auch in der Herausbildung einer vergleichenden Kulturgeschichte der islamischen Welt in der Neuzeit. Die Interpretationen der islamischen Geschichte haben nur selten Raum für eine Komparatistik geboten.[39] Verglichen werden allenfalls Herrschaftstypen oder Gesellschaftsordnungen;[40] da aber vielfach darauf verzichtet wurde, ein tertium comparationis herauszuarbeiten, das einen weitergehenden, qualifizierten Vergleich ermöglichen könnte, bleiben die Darstellungen zwangsläufig summarisch und erlauben kaum, weitergehende, kulturübergreifende Überlegungen anzustellen. Auf der Grundlage der Forschungshypothese sollen die drei ideengeschichtlichen Traditionen Pietismus, Mystik und Rationalismus ein solches tertium comparationis beschreiben.

## Kritische Stimmen und methodologische Schwierigkeiten

Die Überprüfung dieser Thesen allerdings gestaltet sich aus verschiedenen Gründen schwierig. So viel wir auch über einzelne wirtschafts- und sozialgeschichtliche Aspekte wissen (etwa zum besonders reichhaltig belegten islamischen Stiftungswesen, zur Handelsgeschichte und zur Institutionsgeschichte), so wenig wurden die viele tausend zählenden wissenschafts- und literaturgeschichtlichen Quellen gesichtet und bearbeitet, die über die Veränderungen von Weltsichten und Lebenswelten Auskunft geben könnten. Selbst in den neuesten Publikationen finden sich kaum Aussagen zur Wissens- und Kulturgeschichte.[41] Erschwerend kommt hinzu, daß der Buchdruck, ein wichtiges Merkmal der europäischen Moderne, in der islamischen Welt im 18. Jahrhundert noch praktisch keine Rolle spielte. Kulturgeschichtliche Forschungen zum 18. Jahrhundert haben es deshalb fast ausschließlich mit Handschriften zu tun. Dies allein schon läßt vermuten, daß wir nicht von den gewohnten (technischen) Merkmalen der europäischen Gestalt der Moderne ausgehen dürfen. Vielmehr muß für die islamische Welt eine Vielzahl von spezifischen ästhetischen Stil- und sozialen Kommunikationstraditionen sowie von entsprechenden Kulturmitteln zugrunde gelegt werden, die es noch im einzelnen zu bestimmen gilt. Allerdings sollten diese nicht mit den ideengeschichtlichen Traditionen gleichgesetzt werden, die ja durchaus in völlig anderen als den in Europa gewohnten Formen vermittelt werden konnten. Gerade dies dürfte die Spezifität wie Universalität der Moderne ausmachen, und folglich können auch Untersuchungen zu nichteuropäischen Traditionen der Moderne zu einem besseren Verstehen der Moderne überhaupt beitragen.

Die Lesung dieser literarischen, theologischen, historischen und mystischen Texte birgt zahlreiche Schwierigkeiten. Konventionell werden die islamischen Literaturen des 18. Jahrhunderts lediglich danach bewertet, in welcher Weise sie die "klassischen" islamischen Traditionen fortschrieben. Das heißt, die islamischen Literaturen werden nicht als Beleg für eine bestimmte Weltsicht im 18. Jahrhundert gelesen, sondern als Beleg für die Zeit der islamischen "Klassik". Diese Annahme schließt die Literaturen aus dem Forschungsinteresse aus, da die postulierte, allerdings kaum bestätigte "fehlende Innovativität" der Literaturen keinerlei Anreize für eine auf "Entdeckung" ausgerichtete Forschung bietet. M. Mazzaoui hat aber zeigen können, daß wir mit einem bislang kaum erfaßten Innovationsgehalt der islamischen Wissenskulturen im 18. Jahrhundert rechnen können.[42]

Zum anderen gibt es keinerlei Forschungstradition, die auch nur ansatzweise mit der über 150 Jahre währenden europäischen Beschäftigung mit dem 18. Jahrhundert gleichgesetzt werden kann. Aus verschiedenen Gründen wurde die islamische Geschichte der Neuzeit zunächst in der europäischen Orientalistik, dann auch in den einheimischen Historien zugunsten einer Rezeption der europäischen Moderne ausgeblendet und verdrängt. So wurde das, was als islamische Moderne bezeichnet werden kann, im 19. Jahrhundert vollkommen von dem Diskurs der europäischen Moderne überlagert. Der Diskurs über die Moderne in den islamischen Gesellschaften war folglich fortan immer ein Diskurs über die europäische Moderne in den islamischen Gesellschaften. Die autochthonen Grundlagen für die Große Rezeption (1820 - 1920) verschwanden schnell im Dunkel der Geschichte. Die Gründe hierfür müßten noch gesondert erforscht werden wie die Folgen für die hieraus resultierende Geschichtsauffassung.

Die Versuche einer Neubestimmung der islamischen Kulturgeschichte stehen damit in einem engen Zusammenhang zur zeitgenössischen Diskussion um die Interpretation der Moderne in der islamischen Welt. Von sehr unterschiedlichen Positionen aus wird der Anspruch erhoben, die Moderne auch als einen integralen Bestandteil der islamischen Geschichte zu verstehen. Die meisten Deutungen (von M. Arkoun, J. Kraemer, G. Makdisi u. a.) beziehen sich aber auf Einbeziehung des islamischen Mittelalters, um den historischen Kontext der Herausbildung eines modernen Weltbildes in Europa zu beschreiben. In diesem Zusammenhang werden Konzepte wie Humanismus oder Aufklärung als zeitlose Konstrukte benutzt. So werden heute zunehmend die "kritisch-rationalistischen" Traditionen des islamischen Mittelalters aufgegriffen, um der essentialistischen Ausdeutung des Islam entgegenzuwirken.[43] Das politische Ansinnen in der Rekonstruktion eines nicht-essentialistischen Geschichtsbildes tritt deutlich hervor: zum einen soll der heutigen islamischen Kultur ein eigenständiger Weg in die Moderne gewiesen werden, indem auf den genetischen Zusammenhang zwischen europäischer Neuzeit und islamischer Geistesgeschichte hingedeutet wird. Zum anderen soll gleichzeitig der

Spezifität der islamischen Kulturen Rechnung getragen werden, um so dem Vorwurf des Eurozentrismus und der "Verwestlichung" entgegenzuwirken.

Dieser Diskurs über Aufklärung und Moderne hat sicherlich eine wichtige Bedeutung in der zeitgenössischen Diskussion. Doch kann nicht übersehen werden, daß die alten Theoreme bezüglich eines "Niedergangs" der islamischen Kultur beibehalten werden, indem weiterhin die islamische Neuzeit aus der Forschung ausgeblendet wird. Selbst M. Arkoun attestierte der islamischen Kultur einen "Stillstand" nach dem Wirken von Averroes.[44] So bleibt auch die Frage, warum die islamische Kultur trotz des genetischen Zusammenhangs zur abendländischen Neuzeit "den Sprung in die Moderne" nicht nachvollzogen habe, offen.

Der konzeptionelle Mangel einer solchen Deutung liegt vor allem in der Ahistorizität, indem europäische Epochenbegriffe ihrer zeitlichen Gebundenheit enthoben und zu kulturgeschichtlichen Universalien verallgemeinert werden.[45] Sicherlich kann der Beitrag der islamischen Wissenschaften an der Ausformulierung des neuzeitlichen Weltbildes nicht überschätzt werden. Doch bleibt die Frage, ob die islamische Kulturgeschichte in gleicher Weise mit dem mittelalterlichen Weltbild gebrochen hat wie die christlichen Kulturen Europas. Die historisch-hermeneutische Befreiung von der "fundamentalistischen Situation" muß auch die wissensgeschichtlichen und soziologischen Probleme einbeziehen, welche zur Vorstellung von einer weitreichenden islamischen Dekadenz in der Neuzeit geführt haben.[46] Wenn dagegen von einem systematischen, zeitlosen Aufklärungsbegriff ausgegangen wird, ließe sich zwar die rationalistische Kritik mancher muslimischer Denker besser deuten; der für die islamische Geschichte aber wichtige Kontext zur vorkolonialen Neuzeit ginge dann verloren.

Die Bedeutung der Rekonstruktion der islamischen Neuzeit für die Gegenwart kann nicht überschätzt werden. Solange die islamische Geschichte nicht als ein dynamisches, offenes System heterogener Traditionen etabliert wird, bleibt die islamische Frühzeit - neben einer offenen Apologie westlicher Geschichte - das einzige identitätsstiftende Ideal der Gegenwart. Der Verlust der historischen Kontinuität wurde durch einen doppelten Essentialismus ausgeglichen: dem Wesen der westlichen Kultur wurde das Wesen des Islam gegenübergestellt. Geschichte in der islamischen Welt erhielt dann den Charakter eines "Flickenteppichs" (*bricolage*), der anderen Rückbezügen als auf "den Islam" (ist die idealisierte islamische Frühzeit) oder den "Westen" (ist die idealisierte europäische Gegenwart) keine Entfaltungsmöglichkeit bot. Letzten Endes wurde genau dies wiederum zu einem Merkmal islamischer Geschichtsauffassung gemacht.

Kritische Stimmen zu einer Erörterung der islamischen Moderne sollen nicht verschwiegen werden. So zweifeln Rudolph Peters[47] und R. S. O'Fahey & Bernd Radtke an der Herausbildung innovativer Tendenzen in den islamischen Kulturen des 18. Jahrhunderts; sie begründen ihre Ansicht vor allem mit dem Hinweis darauf, daß die Weltsichten des 18. Jahrhunderts lediglich als Fortführung islamischer Traditionen früherer Jahrhunderte interpretiert werden können. O'Fahey &

Radtke betonen hierbei besonders die Rolle der Mystik und kritisieren nachdrücklich die Bestimmung eines "Neo-Sufismus", während R. Peters deutliche Kritik an dem Konzept der Aufklärung in islamischen Gesellschaften selbst äußert. Tatsächlich scheint das Konzept des "Neo-Sufismus", dessen Geschichte O'Fahey & Radtke vorzüglich nachzeichnen und das auch ich zunächst übernommen hatte, kaum geeignet, die komplexen kulturgeschichtlichen Traditionen in der islamischen Moderne zu erfassen.[48]

Die Vorbehalte gegenüber einer Theorie zur islamischen Moderne sind allerdings nicht zwingend, da sie letzten Endes auf der gleichen mageren Quellenbasis entwickelt wurden wie die entsprechende Gegenthese. Auch scheint es mir keineswegs sinnvoll, ein Phänomen wie die mystische Tradition isoliert und nur philologisch zu betrachten, da hierdurch der die Elitenkulturen bestimmende Kontext verschiedener Traditionen verloren geht. Schließlich glaube ich, daß die Tatsache, daß bisher kaum philosophische Texte zu einer "Aufklärungstradition" gefunden wurden, nicht gegen die Moderne-These spricht. Da "Aufklärung" in diesem Kontext als soziales und gleichzeitig kulturell-ästhetisches Konzept verstanden werden soll, können sich entsprechende Weltsichten auch in anderen Literaturen als gerade der Philosophie verbergen. Und genau diesen gilt es nachzuspüren.

Eines aber läßt sich mit Bestimmtheit schon jetzt sagen: die aus der Geschichte außerislamischer Gesellschaften wie Europa gewohnten Mittel zur Bestimmung der Moderne (v. a. im Bereich der Technologie und Ökonomie) scheinen in der Kulturgeschichte der islamischen Gesellschaften eine untergeordnete Rolle gespielt zu haben, auch wenn sich immer wieder Hinweise auf eine Erörterung naturwissenschaftlicher und technologischer Fragen in arabischen, persischen und osmanischen Texten finden lassen. Einen Disput etwa in Analogie zu den Auseinandersetzungen um Newtonsche Erkenntnisse läßt sich kaum dokumentieren. Hier liegt wohl ein spezifischer "europäischer" Diskurs der Moderne vor. Gleichfalls muß aber der Tatsache Rechnung getragen werden, daß die naturwissenschaftlichen und technologischen Thesen der europäischen Moderne ohne große Widerstände in den islamischen Traditonen integriert werden konnten.[49] Auffällig ist auch, daß die wenigen kritischen Stellungnahmen islamischer Gelehrter meist aus der Zeit nach der Herstellung der kolonialen Situation (also etwa nach 1870) stammten[50]; frühere Kritiken beziehen sich durchweg auf die Macht, die mit den Technologien und Wissenschaften verbunden war, und weniger auf die Erkenntnisse beziehungsweise Techniken selbst.[51] Offensichtlich handelten die Kritiker hier tatsächlich als religiöse Gelehrte, die sich von nichtreligiösen Wissensformen kritisch abgrenzten.[52]

Wenn sich aber in der Ideengeschichte islamischer Kulturen Quellen für eine Weltsicht finden lassen, die sich in einem "strukturanalogen" Sinne nur unwesentlich von den europäischen Traditionen der Moderne[53] unterscheidet, dann stellt sich die Frage nach einer grundsätzlichen Neubewertung dessen, was die europäische Geschichte bislang als Moderne bezeichnet hat.

Ein sehr berechtigter Einwand betrifft die Terminologie, mit der die islamische Moderne beschrieben werden soll. Ist es überhaupt sinnvoll, die islamische Geschichte mit europäischen Epochenbegriffen zu belegen? Verbirgt sich nicht hierin unterschwellig eine Fortführung des Eurozentrismus mit anderen Mitteln? M. E. ist diese Frage von zweitrangiger Bedeutung; es ließen sich sicherlich (zu einem späteren Zeitpunkt) arabische, persische oder türkische Begriffe nutzen, um die neuzeitliche Geschichte der islamischen Gesellschaften zu erfassen. Diese aber hätten stets spezifischen Charakter und entsprächen eher der Beschreibung der spanischen Kultur im 18. Jahrhundert als "decadentismo".[54] Tatsächlich verfügt jede auch in der islamischen Welt beheimatete Nationalhistoriographie über tradierte spezifische Zeitbegriffe, die aber nicht isoliert gesehen, sondern im Kontext einer weitergehenden, global wirkenden Abstraktion gedeutet werden. So war auch Spaniens "decadentismo" Teil der "europäischen Geschichte der Moderne". Die in den vergangenen Jahrzehnten entwickelten Theorien zur Geschichte der Moderne gründeten so auf einer Verallgemeinerung einer Vielzahl von lokalen und regionalen Traditionen; die Grenzziehung Europa muß hierbei als willkürlich angesehen werden, denn nichts kann den Ausschluß islamischer Traditionen aus der Bestimmung der Moderne begründen als die Anschauung, daß die Moderne doch das Ergebnis einer christlichen Tradition sei.[55]

Betrachtet man die weitergehenden Kriterien zur Bestimmung der Moderne, so gelangt man zu einem Satz von Definitoren, denen kaum noch der (konstruierte) europäische Deutungshorizont anzumerken ist. So soll die Moderne historisierend, ästhetisierend und säkularisierend zugleich wirken, auf Schriftlichkeit, Universalismus, Globalität und Zeitlosigkeit gründen und sich in mannigfaltigen Weltsichten (Rationalismus, Monismus, Mystizismus, Pietismus, Anthropozentrismus etc.) äußern.[56] Je allgemeiner so die Moderne definiert wird, desto eher scheint eine Zuordnung der islamischen Kulturgeschichte zu diesen Definitoren erlaubt.

Die Theorie der islamischen Moderne wendet sich implizit auch gegen eine allzu leichtfertige Ausformulierung eines Kulturrelativismus. So werden manche Kritiker wohl vermerken, daß die Theorie der islamischen Moderne einen Rückschritt gegenüber der historischen Fallethik bedeutet, da sie die spezifischen Kulturerfahrungen zweitrangig zugunsten eines weitreichenden historischen Universalismus behandelt.

Tatsächlich liegt der Verdacht nahe, daß die globalisierenden Theorien des 19. und 20. Jahrhunderts, die in der westlichen Welt scheinbar überwunden sind, nun für den islamischen Raum fortgeschrieben werden. Am deutlichsten hat dies jüngst Patricia Crone vermerkt.[57] Crone zeichnet ein Bild gegen die klassischen Blockadetheorien. Demnach gab es keinen Wettlauf um die Moderne, den Europa gewann und den die anderen Kulturen wegen bestimmter Blockadefaktoren verloren, sondern jede Kultur entwickelte sich spezifisch und parallel zugleich. Die moderne Industriegesellschaft sei ein europäisches, mit all den beiläufigen kulturellen Erscheinungen ausgestattetes Spezifikum. Es resultierte aus sehr eigenständigen

Bedingungen europäischer Formation, die im Grunde aus dem Scheitern der Bewältigung der vorindustriellen Gesellschaft resultierten. Etwas anders formuliert und natürlich mit einer anderen Pointe hatte schon Buṭrus al-Bustânî dieses Problem gesehen. 1869 schrieb er: "Jeder, der sich beide Gruppen genauer besieht, wird feststellen, daß die Araber es sind, die aus einer Zivilisation hervorgegangen sind, während die Europäer aus einer Barbarei hervorgegangen sind."[58] Alle Kulturen, die die Probleme der vorindustriellen Gesellschaft gemeistert hatten, benötigten, so P. Crone, die Moderne nicht. Folgt man den Überlegungen von Patricia Crone, dann bräuchten wir uns nicht weiter um eine "islamische Moderne" zu bemühen, da die Moderne nichts anderes sei als das Ergebnis einer europäischen Verlegenheit. Dieses Postulat aber müßte dann revidiert werden, wenn die bislang kaum gelesenen, geschweige denn interpretierten Quellen zur Wissens- und Kulturgeschichte etwas anderes sagen.

## Anmerkungen

1 So vor allem Bassam Tibi, Im Namen Gottes? Der Islam, die Menschenrechte und die kulturelle Moderne. In: Michael Lüders (Hg.), Der Islam im Aufbruch? Perspektiven der arabischen Welt, München 1992, 144-161, hier 160.

2 Hier soll nochmals betont werden, daß der Klassiker der Modernisierungstheorien, Lerner, seine Thesen vor einem ägyptischen Hintergrund entwickelte, vgl. Daniel Lerner, The Passing of Traditional Society: Modernizing the Middle East, New York 1958.

3 Zum Problem der kulturellen Übersetzung vgl. Reinhard Schulze, Geschichte der islamischen Welt im 20. Jahrhundert, München 1994, 11ff.

4 Hierzu habe ich an anderer Stelle einige Anmerkungen gemacht, vgl. z.B. Im Banne des Islam: Anmerkungen zur islamischen Begeisterung. In: Hermann Forkl/Johannes Kalter et al. (Hg.), Die Gärten des Islam, Stuttgart 1993, 379-381; Orientalistik und Orientalismus. In: Werner Ende/Udo Steinbach, Der Islam in der Gegenwart, München [3]1994/95 (im Druck) und Alte und neue Feindbilder. Das Bild der Araber und des Islams im Westen. In: Georg Stein (Hg.), Nachgedanken zum Golfkrieg, Heidelberg 1991, 244-259, 259-260.

5 Die aktuelle Niedergangsthese, die in bezug auf die neuzeitliche Geschichte der islamischen Welt benutzt worden ist, hat nur wenig mit den zyklischen Abfolgemodellen Ibn Haldûns zu tun, auch wenn heute gerne eine fatale "Ibn Haldûnistische" Rückdeutung des Konzepts "Niedergang" vorgenommen wird, vgl. z.B. Abdulkader Irabi, Arabische Soziologie. Studien zur Geschichte und Gesellschaft des Islam, Darmstadt 1989, 34.

6 Der Zeitpunkt des Beginns des Niedergangs wurde u.a. mit dem Tod von Ibn Rušd 1198, mit der Eroberung Bagdad durch "die Mongolen" 1258 oder mit dem Beginn der "wirtschaftlichen und militärischen Überlegenheit Europas" zu Beginn des 16. Jahrhunderts in Verbindung gebracht.

7 Im folgenden ist unter "islamische Neuzeit" stets der Zeitraum von etwa 1500 bis 1820, unter "islamische Moderne" der Zeitraum von etwa 1650 bis heute zu verstehen. Im Rahmen dieses Berichts ist es nicht möglich, auf alle relevanten Publikationen einzugehen.

8 Z.B. Barbara Kellner-Heinkele, Der arabische Osten unter osmanischer Herrschaft. In: Ulrich Haarmann (Hg.), Geschichte der arabischen Welt, München 1987. Bis in die siebziger Jahre hinein wurde der allerdings selten benutzte Begriff "islamische Moderne" meist auf die Gegenwart bezogen, vgl. Ulrich Haarmann, Die islamische Moderne bei den deutschen Orientalisten. In: Friedrich H. Kochwasser/Hans Robert Roemer (Hg.), Araber und Deutsche. Begegnungen in einem Jahrtausend, Tübingen-Basel 1974, 56-91. Auffällig ist, daß sich die aus der Freiburger, von H.R. Roemer geprägten Tradition stammende iranistische Orientalistik (u.a. B. Fragner, B. Hoffmann) sich sehr viel deutlicher als anderswo um eine historiographische Erfassung der Neuzeit in Persien bemühte.

9 Eine Forschungsbibliographie zur Geschichte der islamischen Welt im 18. Jahrhundert ist in Vorbereitung; sie umfaßt zur Zeit etwa 3000 Einträge.

10 H.A.R. Gibb/H. Bowen, Islamic society and the West: a study of the impact of Western civilization on Moslem culture in the Near East. Volume I: Islamic society in the eighteenth century, I-II, London 1950, 1957.

11 Albert Hourani, The changing face of the Fertile Crescent in the 18th century. In: Studia Islamica *8*(1957), 91-118; Norman Itzkowitz, Eighteenth Century Ottoman Realities. In: Studia Islamica *16*(1962), 73-94; R. Owen, The Middle East in the 18th century - an 'Islamic' Society in decline: a critique of Gibb and Bowen's Islamic Society. In: Review of Middle East Studies *1*(1977), 113-134.

12 Die Kritik an Gibb & Bowen wurde nochmals aufgegriffen von Huri Islamoglu und Çaglar Keyder, Ein Interpretationsrahmen für die Analyse des Osmanischen Reiches. In: Dieter Senghaas (Hg.), Kapitalistische Weltökonomie. Kontroversen über ihren Ursprung und ihre Entwicklungsdynamik, Frankfurt/M. 1979, 201-234 (engl. The Agenda of Ottoman History, Review 1977, 101-134).

13 Beirut 1966.

14 Thomas Naff/Roger Owen (Hg.), Studies in the Eighteenth Century Islamic History, Carbondale, Ill, 1977.

15 Ebenda, 253-276.

16 Ebenda, 4.

17 Hierzu müßte eine gesonderte Bibliographie erstellt werden.

18 Allerdings handelt es sich zum großen Teil um Einzelstudien, z.B.: J.S. Baljon, Religion and Thought of Shah Wali Allah Dihlawi, 1705-1762, Leiden 1986; Sayyid Athar Abbas Rizvî, Shah Wali-Allah and his Times. A Study of Eighteenth Century Islam, Politics and Society in India, Canberra 1980. Eine erste vorsichtige Gesamtdeutung bietet Ahmed Ali, The Golden Tradition, New York 1973, 25ff.

19 Henri Corbin, La Philosophie iranienne islamique au XVIIe et XVIIIe siècles, Paris 1981.

20 Jean-Louis Michon, L'autobiographie (Fahrasa) du soufi marocain Ahmad ibn 'Agîba (1747-1809) et son Mi'rag, Leiden; [2]Paris 1969, [2]1973.

21 Aladdin Bakri, ʿAbdalġanî an-Nâbulusî (1143/1731). Oeuvre, vie et doctrine, (nichtpubl.) Thèse doct. ès-Lettres, Université de Paris I, 1985.

22 Usâma ʿAnûtî, al-ḥaraka al-adabîya fî bilâd aš-Šâm ḫilâl al-qarn at-tâmin ʿašar, Beirut 1971.

23 Muhammas SayyidKailani, al-adab al-miṣrî fî ẓill al-ḥukm al-ʿutmânî, Kairo 1965.

24 Ein zweites Thema war die Agrargeschichte; vgl. u.a. ʿAbdarraḥîm ʿAbdarraḥmân ʿAbdarraḥîm, ar-rîf al-miṣrî fî l-qarn at-tâmin ʿašar, Kairo 1974, [2]1986; Lucette Valensi, Fellahs tunisiens: l'économie rurale et la vie des campagnes aux XVIIIe et XIXe siècles, Lille 1975; Kenneth Cuno, The Pasha's peasants. Land, society, and economy in Lower Egypt, 1740-1858, Cambridge 1992.

25 Vgl. jetzt aber Abraham Marcus, The Middle East on the Eve of Modernity. Aleppo in the Eighteenth Century, New York 1989. Darin findet sich ein Kapitel zur Gelehrtenkultur, die vorrangig auf einer Auswertung von Muḥammad Râġib aṭ-Ṭabbâḫ, iʿlâm an-nubalâ' bi-târîḫ Ḥalab aš-šahbâ', I-VII, Aleppo 1923-1926 [²1988] und Alexander Russell, The Natural History of Aleppo, I-II, London ²1794, beruht.

26 Eine Ausnahme bildet Percy Kemp, Territoires d'Islam. Le monde vu de Mossoul au XVIIIe siècle, Paris 1982.

27 Hierzu die gerade eingereichte Habilitationsschrift von S. Jamal Malik, Islamische Gelehrtenkultur in Nordindien, die eine umfassende Bibliographie enthält.

28 Hierzu auch Albert Hourani, How should we write the history of the Middle East?, IJMES *23*(1991), 125-136. Der mangelhafte Stand der Quellenforschung machte es Hourani jedoch schwer, seinen hohen Anspruch, eine "collective mentality" in der Sozialgeschichte der islamischen Neuzeit zu berücksichtigen, in seinem Werk A History of the Arab Peoples (1991) einzulösen.

29 Peter Gran, Islamic Roots of Capitalism. Egypt 1760-1840, Austin, Tex. 1979.

30 Michel M. Mazzaoui, East and West: Moslem Intellectual History During the Eighteenth Century. In: Graeco-Arabica. First International Congress on Greek and Arabic Studies, vol. II, Athen 1983, 87-97.

31 Nehemia Levtzion, The Eighteenth Century, Background to the Islamic Revolutions in West Africa. In: Nehemia Levtzion/John O. Voll (Hg.), Eighteenth-Century Renewal and Reform in Islam, Syracuse, N.Y. 1987, 21-38.

32 Rudolph Peters, Erneuerungsbewegung im 18. und in der ersten Hälfte des 19. Jahrhunderts. In: Werner Ende/Udo Steinbach (Hg.), Der Islam in der Gegenwart, München 1984, 91-105.

33 Dies kann nur eine vorläufige Sammelbezeichnung sein; gemeint sind jene Wissenstraditionen, die der Kognition und Empirie einen eigenständigen Rang in der Erkenntnis neben (oder bisweilen gegen) Glauben und (mystischer) Erfahrung zuwiesen. Diese Traditionen waren im Mittelalter natürlich nicht zwangsläufig gegen die Theologie gerichtet, sondern statteten sie vielmehr mit einer im kalâm typisierten Argumentationsweise aus, welche die Traditionarier (und später die Pietisten) heftig attackierten.

34 Vgl. z.B. Madeline Zilfi (1988) und Esther Peskes (1994).

35 Reinhard Schulze, On the Culture of the Islamic Modern. Egyptian and Syrian Citoyens (aulâd al-balad) in the Second Half of the Eighteenth Century (in Vorbereitung). Der Begriff "Ideenträger" wurde im späten 18. Jahrhundert bewußt als Bezeichnung für jemanden benutzt, der sich außerhalb der tradierten Gelehrtenkulturen bewegte. Über die Einzelpersönlichkeiten, die so bezeichnet wurden, ist heute kaum noch etwas bekannt.

36 Für die sozialgeschichtliche Bestimmung des "Bürgertums" gibt es verschiedene Vorschläge; meist wird im Zusammenhang mit dem Osmanischen Reich der Begriff aʿyân (oder engl. "urban notables") benutzt, der im 18. Jahrhundert die herausragende Stellung der "neuen Familien" bezeichnet.

37 Panajotis Kondylis, Die Aufklärung im Rahmen des neuzeitlichen Rationalismus, Stuttgart 1986.

38 Epochen sollen als zeitlich begrenzte Einheiten von kommunikativem und ästhetischem Konsens bestimmter sozialer Gruppen über Wissen, Stil und Mode begriffen werden.

39 Vgl. einen Versuch bei Ira M. Lapidus, A History of Islamic Societies, Cambridge 1988, 239-548.

40 Albert Hourani, A History of the Arab Peoples, Cambridge, Mass. 1991, 249-262.

41 Vgl. zum Osmanischen Reich jüngst Michail Serafimovic'Mejer, Osmanskaja imperija v XVIII veke. C'erty strukturnogo krizisa. [thes.dokt. MGU, 1989] Moskau 1991; Rifa'at 'Ali Abou -el-Haj, Formation of the Modern State. The Ottoman Empire, sixteenth to eighteenth

centuries, Albany, NY 1991; Michael Winter, Egyptian Society under Ottoman rule, 1517-1798, London 1992.

42 Michel M. Mazzaoui, East and West: Moslem Intellectual History During the Eighteenth Century. In: Graeco-Arabica. First International Congress on Greek and Arabic Studies, vol. II, Athen 1983, 87-97.

43 Vgl. Anke von Kügelgen, Averroes und die arabische Moderne. Ansätze zu einer Neubegründung des Rationalismus im Islam, Leiden 1994; Armando Salvatore, The making (and unmaking) of political Islam, unpubl. PhD, European University Institut, Florenz 1994.

44 Vgl. z.B. Mohammed Arkoun, "Westliche" Vernunft kontra "islamische" Vernunft? Versuch einer kritischen Annäherung. In: Michael Lüders, Der Islam im Aufbruch. Perspektiven der arabischen Welt, München 1992, 261-274.

45 Sicherlich ist es heute üblicher, Aufklärung als Universalien zu handeln und sie nicht mehr im spezifischen epochengeschichtlichen Kontext des 17. und 18. Jahrhunderts zu belassen; Jochen Schmidt spricht von einer "Strukturanalogie", die etwa zwischen der Griechischen Aufklärung und der Aufklärung des 18. Jahrhunderts herrsche, vgl. Jochen Schmidt, Einleitung: Aufklärung, Gegenaufklärung, Dialektik der Aufklärung. In: ders. (Hg.), Aufklärung und Gegenaufklärung in der europäischen Literatur, Philosophie und Politik von der Antike bis zur Gegenwart, Darmstadt 1989, 1-31. Diese Anschauung wurde natürlich schon von Max Horkheimer/Theodor W. Adorno, Dialektik der Aufklärung, Frankfurt/M. 1971 (zuerst Amsterdam 1947) vorbereitet.

46 Hierzu Brunschvig/von Grunebaum (1957) und in Kritik daran Georg Stauth, Islam und westlicher Rationalismus, New York usw. 1993.

47 Rudolph Peters, Schulze's Quest for an Islamic Enlightenment. In: Die Welt des Islams *30*(1990), 160ff.; R. S. O'Fahey/Bernd Radtke, Neo-Sufism Reconsidered. In: Der Islam *70*(1993), 52-87.

48 Eine weitergehende Kritik von B. Radtke, auf die ich ausführlich antworten werde, soll demnächst [in: Die Welt des Islam, 34(1994)] erscheinen.

49 Vgl. z.B. Reinhard Schulze, Inquiries into Islamic Modernity prior to the 18th Century. The Reception of the Heliocentric World among Muslim Scholars. In: A. Harrak (ed.), Contacts between Cultures. West Asia and North Africa, Lampeter 1992, 423-428 (33rd International Congress of Asian and North African Studies, Toronto 1990, Selected Papers, Vol. 1.) und die Akten der Tagung Transfer of modern science and technology in the Muslim World. Proceedings of the international symposium on "Modern Science and the Muslim World": science and technology transfer from the West to the Muslim World from the Renaissance to the beginning of the XXth century, Istanbul 1992.

50 Vgl. R. Peters, Religious Attitudes Towards Modernization in the Ottoman Empire. A nineteenth century pious text on steamships, factories and the telegraph. In: Die Welt des Islams 26(1986), 76-105.

51 Z.B. Muḥammad Bâqir al-Mağlisî, iṯbât-i harakat-i šams, Hdschr. Kairo, dâr al-kutub, pers. I/206.

52 Eine schöne Diskussion dieses Problems am Beispiel Chinas bietet Joseph Needham, Wissenschaftlicher Universalismus. Über Bedeutung und Besonderheit der chinesischen Wissenschaft, Frankfurt/M. 1979, 120-165 [The Role of Europe and China in the Evolution of Oecumenical Science (1970)].

53 Zusammengefaßt u.a. bei Stephen Toulmin, Cosmopolis. The Hidden Agenda of Modernity, New York 1990 [dt. Frankfurt/M. 1994].

54 Dieser Begriff kennzeichnet ja im Gegensatz zu "Niedergang" den intentionalen Gebrauch der "Dekadenz" im literarischen Feld. Vgl. dagegen die Benennung der osmanischen

Hofkultur der ersten Hälfte des 18. Jahrhunderts als "Tulpenzeit" (*lâle devri*), z.B. Rafîq Aḥmad, Istanbul nâṣîl egleniyordu?, Istanbul 1927, 135ff.

55 Der umgekehrte Schluß, daß der Islam die Moderne verhindert habe, ist unlogisch, da sonst andere, nichtislamische und nichteuropäische Kulturen zum Bestandteil der Moderne gemacht werden müßten.

56 Vgl. Stephen Toulmin, Cosmopolis. The Hidden Agenda of Modernity, New York 1990.

57 Patricia Crone, Die vorindustrielle Gesellschaft. Eine Strukturanalyse, München 1992, 165ff.

58 Buṭrus al-Bustânî, ḫiṭâb fî l-hai'a al-iǧtimâᶜîya wa-l-muqâbala baina l-ᶜawâ'id al-ᶜarabîya wa-l-ifranǧîya, Beirut 1869, 37.

# Orient und Okzident als Zivilisationsräume der Moderne

Joachim Heidrich

## I

Jahrzehnte nach Überwindung der Kolonialreiche ist es gleichermaßen aktuell, über das Einwirken Europas auf andere Kontinente während des Bestehens moderner Kolonialsysteme wie über die Konsequenzen der gleichzeitigen Interaktion der Gesellschaften und Kulturen des "Westens" und des "Ostens" für die Menschheitsentwicklung nachzudenken. Die postkoloniale Phase brachte bislang nicht die erhoffte Annäherung der Kulturen oder ein tieferes Verständnis für Andersartiges. Eine dominierende Erscheinung wurde vielmehr die Proliferation von Identitäten. Als eine vordringliche Aufgabe der historischen Forschung ergibt sich im Rückblick auf die Vorgeschichte wie die Erfahrungen des 20. Jahrhunderts, methodische Instrumente zu schaffen, um "den Anderen" bzw. "das Andere" adäquat zu erfassen.[1]

Unmittelbaren Anlaß für die Überlegungen zur Problematik gaben die in der postkolonialen Situation angestellten geistigen wie politischen Bemühungen um die Begründung der Authentizität eigenständiger Entwicklungswege und der eigenen Identität in den selbständig gewordenen asiatischen und afrikanischen Ländern. Die neuen Subjekte der Geschichte betraten eigene Wege und suchten diese als authentisch zu legitimieren. Das europäische Beispiel erwies sich in der Praxis für die angestrebte Entwicklung bald als ungeeignet und konnte nicht länger als universaler Maßstab gelten. Zudem erwuchsen Zweifel an der Brauchbarkeit des Entwicklungsmodells, auf das der "Nordwesten" seine jahrhundertelange Dominanz gründete, für die Formulierung von globalen Zukunftsstrategien. Auf "europäischer" Seite wiederum veranlaßte die Kritik am "kolonialen Blick"[2] eine deutliche Distanzierung von Überlegenheitsansprüchen der (westlichen) industriellen Zivilisation. Der Paradigmenwechsel schuf eine Voraussetzung, um Anderes als ein gleichwertiges Anderssein zu begreifen und nicht bloß - wie im kolonialen Diskurs und älteren Universalismusvorstellungen angelegt - als ein "noch nicht Vollkommenes" oder "nicht Gleichwertiges." Der historische Entwicklungsprozeß ist neu zu analysieren und zu bewerten.

Der Realität, die in der postkolonialen Situation entstand, suchte Ernst Bloch frühzeitig mit einer originellen Interpretation gerecht zu werden. Er bezeichnete die historische Szenerie als ein "dynamisches Multiversum" und verwies schon in den fünfziger Jahren auf die sich abzeichnende Eigenheit der Entwicklungspfade in der ehemaligen kolonialen Welt, die sich von dem früher als "Norm" betrachteten europäisch-nordamerikanischen Typus abhob.[3] Blochs Konzept ließ Raum für die

Annahme verschiedener Formen oder Wege der Modernisierung. Es gestattet, unterschiedliche kulturell geprägte Manifestationen des historisch-gesellschaftlichen Prozesses ebenso zu erfassen wie dessen universale Dimension. Mit anderen Worten: Der Ansatz ermöglicht eine historische Sichtweise, die eine nach vorn offene, jedoch universale und zugleich multilineare Zivilisationsentwicklung gelten läßt.

Die Problematik erschöpft sich indes nicht in der gleichsam räumlichen Abgrenzung von gängigen Makroidentitäten wie Okzident und Orient. "Das Andere" existiert zweifellos nicht als statisches und epochenübergreifend unveränderliches Anderssein. Es erhält seine spezifische Prägung immer auch durch die Präsenz einer vergangenen Zeit im Rahmen der jeweiligen Kultur selbst. Das ist von vorrangigem Belang für das Selbstverständnis einer Gesellschaft. Die ständige Präsenz oder der "Schatten" der Vergangenheit ist als gestaltender Faktor der Identitätsbildung zwar erkannt[4], jedoch noch unzureichend untersucht worden. Es handelt sich um ein Phänomen, das Gadamer aus heuristischer Sicht "als Einrücken in ein Überlieferungsgeschehen, in dem sich Vergangenheit und Gegenwart beständig vermitteln", interpretierte.[5] Noch weniger Aufmerksamkeit fand bislang jene Dimension, in der "das Andere" nicht nur als Tradiertes aus einer vergangenen Epoche im Unterschied zur gelebten Zeit erscheint, sondern auch in Gestalt einer Vision der erstrebten Zukunft. Das betrifft die Vorstellung von der Zukunft der eigenen Gesellschaft wie die der Menschheit im allgemeinen. Solch theoretische Antizipation dient der Ableitung von Sozialstrategien zur Realisierung eines künftigen Zustandes. Das ist von praktischer Bedeutung gerade in "peripheren" Ländern, die von den tendenzbestimmenden Prozessen der Neuzeit an den entwicklungsgeschichtlichen Rand gedrängt worden sind. Vor dem Hintergrund der gesellschaftlichen Transformationsprozesse unter dem Kolonialismus geht es um ein bedeutsames konstitutives Element im Selbstverständnis oder im Zustandekommen des "Gegenbewußtseins" der Völker[6], für die emanzipatorische Anliegen im Vordergrund stehen.

Anhand von drei historischen Situationen aus Asien soll im folgenden eine Annäherung an die Problematik versucht werden. Die Thematik liegt jedoch im Spannungsfeld kontroverser Ansichten. Dazu einige Vorbemerkungen.

Ein ganzheitliches Konzept des zivilisatorischen Prozesses verlangt ein realistisches Bild der Dialektik in den Beziehungen zwischen Europa und Außereuropa in der neueren Geschichte, die wesentlich durch die Ausbreitung kapitalistischer Verhältnisse bestimmt worden sind. Deren dichotomischer Charakter widerspiegelt sich in der epistemologischen Diskussion des Gegenstandes. Eine Position, begründet von Intellektuellen aus Entwicklungsländern, betrachtet die postkoloniale Struktur des Wissens in der Dritten Welt vorwiegend negativ als "a peculiar form of imperialism of categories"[7] und verwirft "the old universalism within which the earlier critiques of colonialism were offered."[8] Diese Denkrichtung befürwortet eine besondere Epistemologie für die Untersuchung kolonialer und postkolonialer

Gesellschaften und hält das für die Aufgabe der noch unvollendeten "kulturellen Dekolonisation."

Gemäß der zugrundeliegenden Idee hätten wir es mit zwei separaten analytischen Feldern - dem Orient und dem Okzident - zu tun. Die Vorstellung impliziert die Existenz von zwei selbständigen und quasi transhistorischen Kategorien als Ausdruck verschiedener Identifikationsfelder. Die Betrachtungsweise führt zu zwei anfechtbaren Konsequenzen. Einerseits wird das in der Aufklärung wurzelnde Argumentieren mit Vernunftbegriffen auf eine lediglich durch Machtinteressen bedingte Rationalisierung reduziert. Weil im 19. Jahrhundert die Kolonialherrschaft europäischer Mächte über außereuropäische Völker vorwiegend rational (und nicht, wie in einer früheren Phase der Neuzeit, religiös-missionarisch) begründet wurde, geriet die Aufklärung selbst und gelegentlich sogar ihr Vorläufer, der europäische Humanismus, in den Verdacht, Magd des Kolonialismus und Instrument zur Errichtung der europäischen Suprematie gewesen zu sein. Die universale Gültigkeit kognitiver Begriffe wird geleugnet und letztlich die Hoffnung auf Vernunft als geschichtsgestaltende Kraft beiseite geschoben. Andererseits gerät auch die Idee des Nationalismus in den Kolonialländern und die sie begleitende antikoloniale Bewegung ins Zwielicht, weil deren Repräsentanten sich vorwiegend in dem der europäischen Aufklärung entstammenden Gedankenspektrum bewegten. Ihnen wird, soweit sie westliche Ideen oder Ideale übernahmen und sich der fremden Macht nicht ausdrücklich verweigerten, ohne Rücksicht auf die historische Situation sogar Kollaboration vorgeworfen.[9]

Die Problematik samt zugehörigen epistemologischen Aspekten ist u.a. durch die seit längerem andauernde "Orientalismusdebatte" thematisiert worden, deren Grundanliegen die Überwindung der eurozentrischen Welt- und Geschichtsbetrachtung und damit die Vollendung der kulturellen Dekolonisation ist. Doch auch aus anderem Blickwinkel sind methodisch relevante Argumente vorgetragen worden, so etwa in Form der Mahnung an die Sozialwissenschaften, konkrete Situationen in der außereuropäischen Welt nicht einfach mit Hilfe der aus europäischer Erfahrung gewonnenen Konzepte zu interpretieren, sondern empirisch mit Hilfe kontextualer Analyse bei gleichzeitigem translokalen Vergleich anzugehen.[10] Die Erörterung der Fragen ist nicht nur eine theoretische Angelegenheit, zumal nunmehr am Ende des 20. Jahrhunderts die Herstellung "einer Welt" als praktische Aufgabe gilt, d.h. einer Welt, in der zumindest formal gleichberechtigte und gleichrangige Partner interagieren und transkultureller Austausch eine hohe Intensität erreicht, und darüber hinaus - gewissermaßen als "Gegenprojekt" zur geopolitischen Strategie aus der Periode des kalten Krieges - auch die Verwirklichung einer globalen Zivilgesellschaft auf der Basis universal gültiger Prinzipien ins Auge gefaßt wird.[11] Solchen Tendenzen werden jene Ansichten nicht gerecht, die nichteuropäisches Anderssein als konstante Größe hin- und einem ebenso statisch begriffenen "Europäertum" gegenüberstellen. Das aber prägt gleichermaßen das ältere Konzept der Negritude, das eine "schwarze Kultur" postulierte, Technik und

Wissenschaft als afrikafremd und den Afrikaner 'von Natur aus' zum Bauern erklärte[12], wie die durch Edward Said's Auseinandersetzung mit dem anglo-französischen Orientalismus des 19. und 20. Jahrhunderts ausgelöste Kritik am westlichen Orientbild.[13]

Wenngleich inzwischen von "post-orientalistischer Historiographie der Dritten Welt" die Rede ist[14], bleiben die mit dem alten Schlagwort aufgeworfenen Fragen auch unter "postmodernen" Vorzeichen weiterhin relevant. Sie sind eine Herausforderung für die Geschichtsschreibung, und zwar nicht nur jene zu Asien und Afrika.

Die entwicklungsgeschichtliche Gebundenheit von Begriffen und die begrenzte Brauchbarkeit universalistischer Konzepte für das Verständnis neuzeitlicher weltgeschichtlicher Vorgänge ist hinlänglich begründet worden. Zurecht wurde hervorgehoben, daß Max Webers häufig zitierte, auf Indien bezogene Gesellschaftsanalyse nicht an "Kategorien der indischen Tradition (ansetzt) und den darin zum Ausdruck kommenden Relationen (nachspürt), sondern sogleich allein mit den Begriffen der westlichen Tradition arbeitet."[15] Das ist indessen kein zureichender Grund, die Existenz universaler Kausalität und transkultureller Rationalität zu verneinen.

Auch in diesem Punkt muß das Zustandekommen aus der Geschichte erklärt werden.

## II

Konzepte, die das nichteuropäische Anderssein mit dem nivellierenden Terminus des Orientalischen bezeichnen, reflektieren vor allem eine intellektuelle Dichtomie, die wiederum auf die dichotome Weltentwicklung im kapitalistischen Zeitalter und die durch den Kolonialismus geschaffene Wirklichkeit zurückzuführen ist. Obgleich hier angesprochene Vorstellungen erst in der postkolonialen Phase feste Gestalt annahmen und Einfluß gewannen, haben sie eine längere Vorgeschichte.
Mit der seit dem 17. Jahrhundert im Nordwesten Europas einsetzenden Herausbildung der "modernen Gesellschaft" entstand auch jener Eurozentrismus, der "mehr als eine Variante traditioneller Ethnozentrismen" verkörpert.[16] In ihm widerspiegelt sich eine neue historische Etappe, die auch dem seit der Antike geformten Orientbegriff einen neuen Sinngehalt verlieh.[17]

In der gegenwärtigen Orientalismusdebatte spielt jedoch die Frage, wie das Orientmodell zustande gekommen ist, keine vorrangige Rolle. Dabei wurde die Notwendigkeit, den historiographischen Aspekt als Mittel zum Erfassen der unterschiedlichen Situationen im Gesamtbereich des Orients zu beachten, nachdrücklich angemahnt.[18] Historisches Herangehen erscheint auch geboten, um zu klären, welche Rolle das europazentrierte Orientverständnis unter kolonialen Verhältnissen in der Geistesgeschichte auf der "anderen Seite" spielte.

## III

Das 16., 17. und noch das 18. Jahrhundert kannten keinen überlegenen Okzident, noch einen sich selbst isolierenden Orient, der mit ersterem nicht mehr Schritt hielt, wie van Leur feststellte.[19] Die Wahrnehmung des Anderen seit Beginn der "entfalteten Moderne" (Habermas) verlief als ein aktiver Diskurs auf beiden Seiten. Europäische Beobachter nutzten die Beschreibung "orientalischer" Gesellschaften oder deren Geschichte zur Kritik an Mängeln der eigenen. Aus europäischer Sicht wurden im allgemeinen Werte hervorgehoben, die Idealen sozialer Assoziationsformen und individueller Denkhaltungen im Zeitalter der Aufklärung und der bürgerlichen Umwälzung zu entsprechen schienen oder deren Abwesenheit in den westlichen feudalen Gesellschaften als Mangel empfunden wurde. Als kritischer Spiegel diente dabei das Wissen über China und Indien ebenso wie solches über Afrika.[20] Doch hierbei gab es keine Einbahnstraße.

Ein Beispiel auf der anderen Seite ist Mirza Abu Taleb Khan, ein muslimischer Inder türkischer Abstammung und mit einem persisch geprägten kulturellen Hintergrund aus Lakhnau (1752 - 1806).[21] Auf einer mehrjährigen Reise zwischen 1799 und 1803 lernte er auch Westeuropa kennen. In seinem ausführlichen Bericht wahrte er zwar eine kritische Distanz und äußerte sein Erstaunen über den westlichen Glauben an Perfektion und Progreß, andererseits bewunderte er aber besonders alles Britische und bekundete die Absicht, durch die Schilderung der "Befindlichkeit der Künste und Wissenschaften in Europa" das Wissen seiner Landsleute auf treffliche Weise zu befördern.[22] Ihm ging es gewiß nicht um die Übernahme fremder Wertesysteme. Doch Abu Taleb schätzte die Errungenschaften der industriellen Revolution ebenso wie gewisse bürgerliche Freiheiten, das Bildungs- und das Justizsystem in England.

Etwa zur selben Zeit erörterten Vertreter der fremden Hegemonialmacht in Südasien die möglichen Folgen der Einführung westlicher Formen von Bildung sowie moderner bürgerlicher Institutionen in ein orientalisches Land im Hinblick auf praktisch-politische Konsequenzen. Einerseits fühlten sie sich als Repräsentanten einer überlegenen und "weiter entwickelten" Nation und Zivilisation. Andererseits dachten sie in den Kategorien der Zeit, gemäß denen die beherrschten und von anderen Völkern bewohnten Territorien in Übersee - auch wenn sie wie die britischen in Asien damals nur von einer Handelskompanie kontrolliert wurden - nicht als Kolonie, sondern gleich eroberten Gebieten als Bestandteil des Empire galten. Tatsächlich erschien in den gängigen Vorstellungen das Empire als ein Gemeinwesen, in dem das Wohlergehen des einen Teils vom Schicksal des anderen abhing.[23] Im ersten Viertel des 19. Jahrhunderts gewannen die Ansichten der britischen Utilitaristen und des politischen Liberalismus in der praktischen Politik endgültig die Oberhand. Die von den Vertretern des "klassischen" Orientalismus im ausgehenden 18.Jahrhundert gerade in bezug auf die Kultur und Gesellschaft

Indiens entwickelten Ansichten blieben fortan hauptsächlich in der geistigen Sphäre wirksam.

Die Erörterungen über den Umgang mit jenen Besitzungen waren stark von den Erfahrungen aus der antikolonialen nordamerikanischen wie dem Wissen über die bürgerliche französische Revolution von 1789 beeinflußt. Das zeigen die geäußerten Befürchtungen offizieller Repräsentanten der britischen Macht in Asien. Mountstuart Elphinstone, ein profunder Kenner der indischen Szene und erster Generalgouverneur der Provinz Bombay, befürwortete in seiner privaten Korrespondenz die Einführung der christlichen Religion, weil er den Hinduismus für eine Ursache der "Rückständigkeit" der Einheimischen "in laws and morals" hielt, gab aber zugleich zu bedenken, daß "some false prophet" den Plan für eine Reform der bestehenden Religion mit dem für die "deliverance of the country from foreigners" verbinden könnte.[24] Er setzte sich für die Vermittlung moderner Bildung an die Untertanen im Land ein, verwies aber gleichzeitig darauf, daß die Aneignung von Bildung durch Einheimische die Franzosen Haiti und die Spanier Südamerika gekostet habe. Nichtsdestoweniger schien ihm Bildung bei der Überwindung tyrannischer und der Aufrechterhaltung gemäßigter Regierungen nützlich zu sein, und "it is therefore to be hoped it may strengthen ours..."[25]

Hier haben wir die von Embree charakterisierte spezifische historische Konstellation: Die Briten kamen als " the inheritors of political and cultural revolutions that had already profoundly modified Western life".[26] Das minderte die Schärfe der kulturellen Konfrontation, begünstigte zugleich objektiv die Errichtung der fremden Vorherrschaft sowie danach deren Stabilisierung. Im Unterschied zu Portugiesen, Spaniern oder expandierenden islamischen Mächten "the British did not articulate the values and attitudes of their culture in religious terms. Instead, they used a vocabulary that made it possible for Indians to accept new ideas without any apparent infringement on the central core of the religious and cultural tradition they had so long guarded from alien intrusion."[27]

Gebildeten Einheimischen, die westlichen Ideen aufgeschlossen waren, wurde die Entwicklungsdistanz zwischen ihrem Land und der Metropole bewußt. Gleichzeitig keimte in ihnen die Erwartung auf, die Einführung demokratischer Institutionen könnte der eigenen Gesellschaft neues Leben einhauchen. Wie die Aufklärungsideologen in Europa suchten sie die Gesellschaft von oben zu reformieren. Daher erwarteten sie zuerst Hilfe von der Metropole.[28]

Die zeitgenössische Debatte wurde von europäischer Seite auch in Publikationsorganen liberaler Provenienz in dem fremdbeherrschten Land selbst öffentlich geführt. Man glaubte an den Aufstieg Indiens zu einer der ersten Nationen durch die Verbreitung moderner Bildung unter der indischen Bevölkerung und durch die "colonization from home".[29] Die materielle und geistig-moralische Entwicklung sollte Anliegen und Ziel der britischen Politik in Asien sein und zum Ruhme Britanniens beitragen: "Upon the British Asiatic policy, in the development of the unbounded resources of British Asia, depends the ascendency of the British name." [30]

Der Glaube an die progressive Rolle wie die transkulturelle Gültigkeit zivilgesellschaftlicher Institutionen war seinerzeit fast unbegrenzt. Als ungleichartig wurden jedoch die Voraussetzungen für deren Verbreitung eingeschätzt. Gerade Indien verfüge aber über günstige Bedingungen für eine freie Presse unter der Leitung von Einheimischen und frei von störenden politischen Einflüssen, einer Presse, der man eine wichtige Rolle bei der Entwicklung des Landes und der Mobilisierung seiner menschlichen Ressourcen zuschrieb. Im *Calcutta Journal* vom 21. September 1820 heißt es: "India is not involved in complete barbarism like many nations of the American, or the African continent... India has already made so considerable a progress in refinement that we may rank it among the foremost of the nations likely to profit by the press.... The magnitude of the task of enlightening India, is such...that without the aid of a native press, there would have been little hope of its being speedily accomplished."[31]

Im Zusammenhang mit den Erwägungen über die Ansiedlung von Europäern tauchten allerdings Bedenken auf, ob eine solche Kolonisierung nicht auch eine Gefahr für die britische Herrschaft in sich bergen könnte. "...the indiscriminate admission of Europeans into the country might tend to alienate the minds of the inhabitants from Britain,or possibly lead to its disruption from Britain in a way similar to that of America."[32] Andererseits bliebe die Zahl der Siedler wahrscheinlich begrenzt. Und vor allem: "Those who in any country wish for changes and revolutions, are seldom such as possess a great portion of landed property therein". Ein Europäer würde sich vernünftigerweise schon gar nicht gegen die Schutzmacht wenden, die seine Existenz in dem fremden Land allein garantieren könnte.[33] Die Diskussion setzte sich fort, wobei später auch die Frage nach gleichen Rechten für "Indo-Briten" und Einheimische aufgeworfen wurde.[34] Indien wurde bekanntlich weder eine Siedlungs- noch eine Plantagenkolonie.

In der durchaus als konfliktträchtig empfundenen Lage sollte die freie Presse die Herrschenden auf Mißbräuche oder Gesetzesübertretungen hinweisen und somit das Funktionieren der Administration garantieren helfen. Dies sei umso notwendiger, als keiner der Untertanen über mehr politischen Einfluß verfüge als andere und vor allem, weil im Lande keine Mittelklasse existiere, die als entscheidender oder eigentlicher Änderungsfaktor angesehen wurde.[35] Wahrscheinlich schimmert hier die im England des 18. Jahrhunderts aufgekommene Vorstellung von einer "civil society" durch. Der Vorstellung gemäß schien eine prä-bourgeoise und sozial wie ideologisch amorphe Schicht - sie verkörperte jenes Segment der Gesellschaft, in der wirkliche Veränderungen stattfanden - in der Lage zu sein, die Anliegen einer Mehrheit der "Nation" zu repräsentieren und zu vertreten.[36]

Die Diskussion über Reformen griffen indische Intellektuelle auf. Sie nahmen unter den obwaltenden Bedingungen in mancher Hinsicht die Funktion einer "neuen Mittelklasse" wahr. Sie sahen in der Verbreitung moderner Bildung sowie in religiösen und sozialen Reformen Garantien für die Erneuerung ihres Landes und Volkes. Im Grunde traten sie für die Anpassung sozio-religiöser Institutionen der eigenen Kultur an die neuen Gegebenheiten des Zeitalters ein, keinesfalls jedoch für eine Unterwerfung unter die kulturelle Dominanz "des Westens". Sie reagierten innovativ, indem sie sich mit den überkommenen Zuständen ihrer Gesellschaft auseinandersetzten und diese zu ändern trachteten, weil sie in ihnen Ursachen für die Unterlegenheit sahen. Sie waren weder bloße Epigonen noch Kollaborateure, wenngleich geleitet von den Idealen der bewunderten "westlichen" Gesellschaft und voller Illusion über die Möglichkeit eines harmonischen Zusammenwirkens von Herrschern und Beherrschten.

Die Erwartung einer gemeinsam getragenen gesellschaftlichen Erneuerung ihres Landes dämpfte allerdings die Praxis der Kolonialbehörden. Diese traten selbst ihren eigenen Landsleuten entgegen, die solchen Gedanken nahestanden. So wurde der britische Herausgeber des liberalen *Calcutta Journal* wegen seiner Ansichten und deren Verbreitung bereits 1823 des Landes verwiesen. 1826 verbot ein Zirkular des Gouverneurs den Angestellten der Ostindien-Kompanie den Kontakt mit der Presse. Jede Person "who advocated reforms, however desirable, was regarded more or less a dangerous innovator."[37] Über das Denkschema, dem die Vertreter der Kolonialmacht damals anhingen, traf neuerdings in einem ganz anderen Zusammenhang A.O.Hirschman eine erhellende Aussage. Er verwies darauf, daß trotz des im 18.Jahrhundert in Europa allgemein verbreiteten Glaubens an Fortschritt ältere Wertvorstellungen noch längere Zeit im wesentlichen unverändert weiter tradiert wurden.[38] Die Idee der Innovation erhielt ihre positive Bedeutung erst viel später, nämlich mit der Durchsetzung der industriellen Revolution. Es sind deshalb durchaus Zweifel angebracht, wie tief die in einem Teil der historiographischen Literatur hervorgehobene "Modernisierung" des südasiatischen Subkontinents "von oben" unter dem Einfluß liberaler Ideen zwischen 1830 und 1850 tatsächlich griff. Abgesehen von direkten und zerstörerischen Folgewirkungen der industriellen Umwälzung in England war von der eingeschlagenen Politik auf lokaler Ebene wenig zu spüren. Die einheimische Gesellschaft "was not changing in any important sense, but adapting itself to the new situations in the traditional Indian way."[39]

Neues wurde implantiert, eröffnete durchaus neue Chancen und wurde von einigen im Lande auch so begriffen. Doch eine strukturelle Veränderung innerhalb der Gesellschaft fand nicht statt. Zwar garantierte ein Gesetz von 1835 die Pressefreiheit und eine grundsätzliche Gleichstellung der indischen und englischen Presseorgane, doch wurde im Justizsystem die schon lange praktizierte Ungleichbehandlung nach rassischen Gesichtspunkten festgeschrieben. Die Behörden stemmten sich gegen die Ideen der Erneuerung der indischen Gesellschaft wie gegen reale Veränderungen oder suchten sie allenfalls auf eine vorsichtige "Verwestlichung" zu begrenzen. Die auf britischer Seite vorherrschende Meinung lautete so: "The danger to India is not, in the present day, *external,* but *internal;* and, so long as we promote the well-being of the nations of British India, preserve their social and religious institutiuons, and do not interfere with their laws of inheritance and adoption, which are part and parcel of their religion, we shall have nothing to fear internally. Education is the stepping-stone to all knowledge."[40]

Die indischen Reformer der jüngeren Generation "criticised the acts of oppression and extortion carried out by the local government in India and tried to inculcate a sense of national dignity and self-respect among the Indians."[41] Sie waren erfüllt von "love for the twin gods of liberty and rationalism."[42] Doch für die Verwurzelung der Ideale okzidentalen Ursprungs fehlte es in der anderen Umgebung an jenem institutionellen Rahmen, der sich in Europa im Laufe der frühen Neuzeit herausgebildet hatte. Seit Ram Mohan Roy blieb das Wirkungsfeld aller Reformer in der ersten Hälfte des 19. Jahrhunderts auf enge Kreise in urbanen Zentren beschränkt; sie erhielten keine Unterstützung durch Volksbewegungen. Die Reformer verband andererseits nichts mit den gegen Ende des Zeitabschnitts eingepflanzten Elementen einer neuen Produktionsweise. "Moreover, all these reformers suffered from a serious illusion that British Parliament, once they knew the grim realities of India, would respond to their grievances."[43] Diese Faktoren setzten den schwachen Ansätzen in Richtung auf eine "Indisierung" enge Grenzen. Die Umstände beförderten nicht gerade die Neigung unter den sozial (Kastenschranken) und intellektuell ohnehin elitären Repräsentanten der neuen Mittelschicht, ihrerseits um Hilfe bei der Umsetzung ihrer Ideen oder für die Veränderung des als änderungsbedürftig empfunden Zustandes der Gesellschaft bei den eigenen Landsleuten nachzusuchen. Der Verlauf der Ereignisse begünstigte letztlich das Aufkommen eines in der Literatur zählebigen Vorurteils, wonach die Reformer aufgrund ihrer "englischen Bildung" lediglich als "verwestlichte" oder "koloniale" Intellektuelle anzusehen seien.

## IV

Die ausreifende koloniale Situation oder die "Formalisierung" der imperialistischen Kolonialherrschaft in der zweiten Hälfte des 19. Jahrhunderts schuf ein für Ideen der Reform und Modernisierung der indischen Gesellschaft ungünstiges Klima. Nach Errichten der direkten Herrschaft der britischen Krone stützte sich ihre Kolonialadministration auf konservative soziale Kräfte im Lande und lehnte Reformen direkt ab. Als Folge dessen kam eine andere Konstellation als in selbständig gebliebenen Ländern Asiens zustande. Ein kontrastierender Vergleich mag das verdeutlichen.

Am Beginn des Weges zur selbstbestimmten Entwicklung des modernen Japan stand der im Namen des Meiji-Kaisers 1868 verkündete Grundsatz: "Knowledge should be sought throughout the world so as to strengthen the foundations of imperial rule."[44] Mit dem Ziel, die politische Einheit und soziale Harmonie herzustellen oder zu stabilisieren wurde Modernisierungsideen aus dem Westen die Tür geöffnet, obwohl die industriell fortgeschrittenen westlichen Nationen die potentiell größte Gefahr für Japans Souveränität darstellten. Als "Modell" diente nicht das benachbarte und kulturverwandte China.[45]

Im kolonialen Indien der zweiten Hälfte des 19. Jahrhunderts ließen patriotische Intellektuelle angesichts praktischer Erfahrungen von der ideologischen Prämisse ab, daß Britanniens Herrschaft "wohltuend" sei und der Bevölkerung Indiens zum Nutzen gereiche, weil sie die Entwicklung und Modernisierung des Landes fördere.[46] Stattdessen wurde die fundamentale Diskrepanz zwischen (liberal-zivilisatorischem) Anspruch und kolonialer Praxis erkannt und herausgestellt. Dadabhai Naoroji meinte 1867, einerseits hätten materielle Fortschritte (z.B. Eisenbahnen) und eingebrachte politische Ideen dazu beigetragen, "a new national life" ins Leben zu rufen und die Hoffnung auf politische und geistige Erneuerung zu wecken. Andererseits hinge es jetzt vom Verhalten der Behörden ab, wieweit sich der Patriotismus der Gebildeten unter den Einheimischen mit Loyalität zur britischen Herrschaft verbinden ließe oder sich gegen diese richten werde.[47] Die Repräsentanten der herrschenden Macht wurden nun gewissermaßen bei ihrem Wort genommen und aus indischer Sicht "Englands Verpflichtungen gegenüber Indien" eingefordert.[48]

Naoroji hielt damals wie andere Intellektuelle seiner Generation die "Regeneration der (indischen) Nation" und ihre Entwicklung im Einklang mit dem Menschheitsfortschritt und nach dem Muster des industriell wie politisch fortgeschrittenen "Westens" auch unter britischer Oberhoheit noch für möglich. Er setzte allerdings voraus, daß die Regierenden ihr "Empire-Verhalten" aufgäben. Ähnlich dachten die Gründer der gesamtindischen politischen Bewegung, des Indischen Nationalkongresses, sowie deren britische Parteigänger, die "Dissidenten" aus dem Beamtenapparat der Kolonialbehörden (A.O.Hume, William Wedderburn, Henry J.S.Cotton).[49] Während die Abschaffung der britischen Herrschaft zunächst noch nicht auf der Tagesordnung stand, führten Naoroji und die meisten anderen Nationalisten ihre Kritik am ökonomischen System der Kolonialherrschaft allmählich bis zu politischen Schlußfolgerungen weiter. Sie legten damit das Fundament für eine antikolonialistische Ideologie und formulierten teils auch selbst die Forderung nach Beendigung der politischen Kontrolle der inneren Angelegenheiten durch eine fremde Macht.[50]

Die nationalistischen Intellektuellen beanspruchten, die Anliegen "der Nation" zu artikulieren und im Namen des Volkes zu sprechen. Das ist eine bis heute kontrovers diskutierte Thematik. Reduktionistische Auffassungen tendieren dazu, diesen Personenkreis hauptsächlich als Sprachrohr besitzender Oberschichten zu betrachten, oder - eine stärker verbreitete Sicht - das Motiv ihres Handelns allein in ihrem westlichen Bildungshintergrund zu sehen und lediglich selbstsüchtige Interessen dahinter zu vermuten. Dem stellte M. Torri unter Hinweis auf die koloniale Realität eine andere Argumentation entgegen. Der Anspruch, Bannerträger von Aufklärung, Freiheit und Fortschritt zu sein, enthielt eine polemische Spitze und ermöglichte den Nationalisten zu begründen, daß "according to key principles of the English political tradition itself, they were entitled to a growing role in the government of their own country, along the path already taken by white dominions." [51] Politische Reformen - zunächst noch unter fremder Oberhoheit - sollten die aktive Mitwirkung bei der Regenerierung des Landes mit Hilfe von Modernisierung ermöglichen, die eine kulturelle Erneuerung einschloß, zugleich aber nationalen kulturellen Traditionen entsprach.

In der Folgezeit nahm der Modernisierungsprozeß aufgrund der heterogenen Bevölkerungsstruktur und der pluralistischen wie hierarchischen Gesellschaftsverfassung Indiens spezifische Züge an. Die Formierung von Organisationen zur Vertretung politischer Interessen verlief nicht durchweg entlang einer Trennlinie zwischen Einheimischen und Fremden. Vielmehr kam es infolge der herkömmlichen sozialen Segmentierung und dem inhärenten Konfliktpotential sowie auf der Grundlage von funktionierenden "traditionellen" Loyalitäten zur sozialen Organisation kommunaler Identitäten.[52] "Korporative Identitäten" formierten sich vorwiegend auf Basis sozial-kultureller, religiös-kultureller und ethnisch-territorialer Gemeinschaftsbindungen. Die Reaktion auf die Fremdherrschaft und deren Folgen variierte folglich von Gruppe zu Gruppe und in bezug auf einzelne Regionen.[53] Auch deutlich politische Interessen traten vorerst in territorialem oder lokalen Gewand zutage.[54] Die koloniale Rechts- und Verwaltungspraxis festigte die vorhandenen oder im Laufe des 19. Jahrhunderts neu aufkommenden sozialen Identitäten[55] und territorialisierte sie obendrein. Dadurch wurde sogar jene Gruppenmobilität eingeschränkt, die bereits in der vorkolonialen Gesellschaft innerhalb der hierarchischen Sozialordnung möglich gewesen war. Gleichzeitig förderte die Kolonialadministration die politische Instrumentalisierung von Gruppeninteressen. Unter diesen Umständen wurden "Modernisierungsschritte" wie beispielsweise Bildungsmaßnahmen in erster Linie im Rahmen von sozialen Gemeinschaften oder Gruppen unternommen, was wiederum eher die Verstetigung und Abgrenzung der Gruppen begünstigte und dem Aufkommen der antikolonialen politischen Bewegung beträchtliche Hindernisse in den Weg legte. Die gleiche Tendenz behinderte auch die endogenen Bemühungen um eine kulturelle Erneuerung und die Evolution einer gruppen- und territorienübergreifenden kulturellen Identität. Erschwerend kam hinzu, daß der unter der Fremdherrschaft eingeleitete gesamtgesellschaftliche Kulturwandel für die Masse der Bevölkerung vor allem eine Kulturentfremdung bedeutete.[56] Denn in der kolonialen Lebenswelt wurden alltagskulturelle Traditionen marginalisiert oder im Verhältnis zur Kultur der sozialen und geistigen Elite herabgesetzt, was eher zur Unterminierung des Selbstbewußtseins und der kulturellen Identität des Volkes beitrug.

Die künstliche Verfestigung traditioneller Institutionen wie der Kaste durch die Kolonialpraxis im Interesse der Machtstabilisierung wurde durch den Mythos von der stagnierenden, unveränderlichen Gesellschaft und der allein auf Beharrung gerichteten Denkhaltung gestützt. Die europäische "orientalistische" intellektuelle Tradition trug ihren Teil bei, indem sie die Rolle der Texte und Epen sowie der in ihnen niedergelegten Werte zum Maßstab der zeitgenössischen Verhältnisse machte und den Blick nicht auf die realen Verhältnisse lenkte. Von dieser Wissenschaftstradition blieben zunächst auch die nicht unerheblichen Veränderungen fast unbeachtet, die in der vorkolonialen Gesellschaft stattgefunden hatten, ebenso wie die über Jahrhunderte nachweisbaren, gegen die rigide Kastenhierarchie oder das brahmanische Ritual gerichteten Bewegungen, die - hervorragend verkörpert in der Bhakti-Bewegung - das Ideal menschlicher Gleichheit propagierten.[57] Der "kolonialistische Traditionalismus" verfestigte Vorurteile, gegen die Reformer und Nationalisten angehen mußten. In dieser geistigen Auseinandersetzung begründeten und formulierten sie humanistische wie universalistische Ideen und Wertvorstellungen, die zu Kernbestandteilen der Ideologie des Nationalismus und im weiteren Sinne der Nationalbewegung wurden.

Nach K.N. Panikkar betraf das vor allem zwei Problemfelder.[58] Einerseits gab es das Bemühen, die einseitige Hinwendung zum Außerweltlichen und Übernatürlichen zu überwinden und den Problemen der weltlichen Existenz größere Aufmerksamkeit zu widmen. Daraus folgten Überlegungen, wie die Religion bei der Lösung realer sozialer und politischer Probleme, bei der Bewältigung zeitgenössischer "humanitärer" Anliegen zu nutzen sei. Der andere Aspekt bestand in der bewußten Wahrnehmung der bedrückenden Armut und des menschlichen Elends. Es wuchs das Verständnis für die Manifestationen von Ungleichheit und deren soziale Folgen. Auf der Suche nach Lösungen wurden relevante Ideen anderer Herkunft aufgespürt und auch im zeitgenössischen "Westen" entwickelte Konzepte aufgegriffen, die in der eigenen Gesellschaft keinen Nährboden hatten.

Anregend könnte auch hier ein Vergleich mit einer andersartigen Situation, nämlich der im China des späten 19. Jahrhunderts sein. Das Land war selbständig, hatte sich aber des europäisch-imperialistischen Ansturms zu erwehren und stand gleichzeitig zunehmend ernsten wirtschaftlichen Problemen gegenüber, die seine Eigenständigkeit bedrohten. Jedoch: "China under her indigenous government did not have the crisis of cultural identity as India did under the British rule. The impact of imperialism was more political and economic than cultural."[59] Die identitätsbestimmenden kulturellen Merkmale waren hier - noch begünstigt durch eine relativ homogene Bevölkerungszusammensetzung - mit der politischen Struktur eng verflochten. Politische Neuerungen und Reformen mußten deshalb sofort an Grundfesten der eigenen Kultur rütteln.[60] Obwohl es durchaus faktische Kenntnis über die Entwicklung in westlich-industrialisierten Länder wie über dort herrschende ökonomische Lehrmeinungen gab, fanden "westliche" Doktrinen in China bis ins 20. Jahrhundert hinein kaum Akzeptanz.[61]

V

Für Indiens Nationalisten wurde am Beginn des 20. Jahrhunderts die nationale Wiedergeburt zum Hauptanliegen. Die soziale Reform stellten sie im Interesse der Einheit der patriotischen Kräfte zurück. Chinas Perspektive sah Sun Yatsen hingegen damals bereits in einer Revolution, die "nicht nur einen nationalen, sondern auch einen sozialen Staat hervorbringen" würde, obwohl seiner Meinung nach die soziale Frage aufgrund des allgemeinen sozioökonomischen Entwicklungsstandes noch nicht zur brennendsten Angelegenheit herangereift war.[62]

Für eine 1922 veröffentlichte Aufsatzsammlung mit dem programmatischen Titel *The Futurism of Young Asia* fand der Autor, Benoy Kumar Sarkar, das Leitmotiv: Krieg dem Kolonialismus in der Politik und dem Orientalismus in der Wissenschaft.[63] Der Verfasser war ein publikationsfreudiger und vielseitiger indischer Ökonom und Soziologe mit reichen persönlichen Erfahrungen im Umgang mit den metropolitanen Gesellschaften im Westen wie mit Gesellschaften in Ostasien.[64] In der Einleitung des Buches sprach der Autor seine Hoffnung auf eine Erneuerung der Welt aus. Nach reichlich einem Jahrhundert westlicher Vorherrschaft über Asien fordere nun - wie Japans Sieg über Rußland bei Port Arthur 19o5 gezeigt habe - dieser Kontinent seinerseits "Eur-Amerika" heraus. Das eröffne zugleich die Chance, die Welt von "okzidentalen Idolen" zu befreien und eine globale geistige Erneuerung einzuleiten.

Sarkars Darstellung reflektierte indessen nur exemplarisch eine seinerzeit zumindest in Asien aufkommende Kritik am europäischen Bild von der außereuropäischen Geschichte, wie es im 19. Jahrhundert aus kolonialistischer Sicht konstruiert worden war. Diese Kritik ist Bestandteil des ideengeschichtlichen Reflexes einer Zäsur im realgeschichtlichen Verlauf. Die historische Herausforderung wurde auch in weitsichtigen Kreisen Europas zur Kenntnis genommen.[65] Der langgehegte Mythos von der Unbesiegbarkeit und Überlegenheit Europas oder "des Westens" war erschüttert, der Zenith der europäischen Suprematie zumindest über den asiatischen Kontinent schien überschritten. Asien forderte Europa jetzt auch durch die sich abzeichnende Entwicklungsperspektive seiner Wirtschaft und seiner Militärmacht heraus. Die Interaktion der Gesellschaften beider Kontinente begann neue Formen anzunehmen und motivierte Überlegungen zur Gestaltung der künftigen Beziehungen. Zugleich wurden die bisherigen kolonialzeitlichen Vorstellungen unhaltbar, die auf dem Glauben beruhten, daß "the superiority of British power and culture was an inherent rather than a historical phenomenon."[66] Asiens geistige und politische Repräsentanten meldeten sich mit eigenen Vorstellungen zur künftigen Gestaltung ihrer Länder wie der Welt zu Wort. Der bisher vorwiegend nach innen gerichtete Nationalismus zog fortan stärker die zeitgenössischen globalen Prozesse in Betracht.In deren Rahmen wurde der künftige Platz des eigenen Landes und dessen weiterer Weg bestimmt.[67]

Jetzt gewannen universalistische Gesichtspunkte an Gewicht. Sie dienten als Ausgangsbasis für die Kritik am "westlichen" Anspruch auf Suprematie, auf politische und kulturelle Hegemonie. Kritisiert wurde ebenfalls das westliche Bild vom Orient. Das veränderte Herangehen bewog selbst die Befürworter eines an den industrialisierten Nationalstaaten des Westens orientierten Fortschrittsstrebens, den Eigenwert und die kulturell-zivilisatorische Eigenständigkeit ihres Landes zu betonen. Das von M. Visvesvaraya 1920 für Indien vorlegte umfassende Entwicklungsprogramm wollte trotz der ausdrücklichen Bejahung des industriegestützten "modernen" Fortschritts nach dem Vorbild Japans und westlicher Länder eine Alternative zur kolonialen Modernisierung darbieten. Als Ziel formulierte der Autor eine der eigenen Kraft vertrauende nationale Gemeinschaft und die Gestaltung eines wahren nationalen Lebens.[68] Das Beispiel Japan erlangte solch großes Gewicht, weil sich das asiatische Land "westliche" Technik erfolgreich anzueignen verstand und damit zugleich seine japanische Eigenart behauptete. Visvesvaraya riet, in Indien die negativen Folgeerscheinungen der Industrialisierung zu vermeiden und einen Weg der Modernisierung zu beschreiten, der bei allem technologischen Fortschritt die dem Kapitalismus des "Westens" anhaftenden Gebrechen ausschließen und u.a. auch sozialen Frieden gewährleisten würde.

Auch Sun Yatsen stellte sich das moderne China nicht als Kopie des Westens, sondern als eine bessere Gesellschaft chinesischer Prägung vor, die er Sozialismus nannte. Er wollte nicht einfach "dem alten Pfad der westlichen Zivilisation folgen".[69]

Ein Grundanliegen der Visionen war die Mobilisierung und Nutzung endogenen geistigen wie materiellen Potentials unter Verwendung exogener Ideen und Impulse, wofür adäquate (politische) Rahmenbedingungen erforderlich wären.

Wenngleich die historischen Veränderungen in Asien durchaus im zeitgenössischen Denken Europas zur Kenntnis genommen wurden, überwog hier doch weiterhin eine andere Interpretation. Die europazentrierte Geschichtsschreibung, die zögerlich die Vorgänge in Asien wahrnahm, subsumierte sie lediglich als eine Variante unter das übliche unilineare Entwicklungskonzept. Für sie war "der Wandel des orientalischen Menschen im 20. Jahrhundert ... nur Teilerscheinung eines allgemeinen Prozesses, der Europäisierung der Menschheit... Diese Europäisierung ist eine Erziehungs- und Abwehrtätigkeit zugleich. Sie kann von außen an die Völker herangetragen werden; sie kleidet sich dann in die Formen des Imperialismus, der die Völker in seinem Interesse und nur, soweit es seinem Interesse entspricht, in Wirtschaft, Technik und Weltanschauung Europas einbezieht... Die Europäisierung kann aber auch nach anfänglichem Widerstreben von den Völkern selbst ausgehen; sie kleidet sich dann in die Formen des Nationalismus und greift viel tiefer in das gesamte Volksleben ein."[70]

Eine solche Interpretation des gesellschaftlichen Strukturwandels blieb nicht nur europa-, sondern war zugleich stark technozentriert und nahm in gewissem Sinn die spätere Modernisierungstheorie mit ihrer Idee der nachholenden Entwicklung vorweg. Demgegenüber traten auf der "anderen Seite" universalistische Konzepte hervor, die sowohl die Zukunft des eigenen Landes oder dessen Erneuerung wie die Zukunft der Welt nicht einfach in einer "Europäisierung" oder Verwestlichung erblickten, sondern in einer Erneuerung, die materiell-technischen wie geistigen Fortschritt mit sozialer Umgestaltung auf Basis der neubelebten und auch durch Impulse von außen angereicherten indigenen Kultur verband.

Sarkar hielt die bestehenden asymmetrischen politischen Beziehungen zwischen "dem Westen" und dem Orient ebenso wie die Hegemonie der westlichen Kultur für eine historisch vorübergehende Erscheinung. Ihm jedenfalls galt Europa nicht als "ewiger" Quell von Veränderung und Fortschritt. Andererseits begriff er Asien und Europa nicht als Größen, die sich auf völlig getrennten Pfaden in der Geschichte bewegten oder einander ausschlossen. Er vertraute vielmehr auf einen neuen Prozeß der universal ausgreifenden Aufklärung im 20. Jahrhundert und plädierte für eine universale Theorie der Vernunft, die den realen Gegebenheiten gerecht werden und einer neuen Weltgesellschaft zum Entstehen verhelfen würde. Insofern reflektieren seine Ansichten zugleich jenen in globalen Dimensionen geführten Diskurs über die "moderne Gesellschaft" und universale Entwicklung, der von der Existenz einer "Weltgesellschaft" oder einer "globalen Ökumene" ausgeht und sich durchaus mit in Indien bodenständigen Vorstellungen stützen ließ.

Den Repräsentanten kolonialisierter Gesellschaften schwebte ein alternativer Universalimus vor.[71] Er war nicht ausschließlich gedacht, sondern anerkannte die Vielfalt kultureller Werte und Normen.

Die Akzente mochten im einzelnen unterschiedlich gesetzt sein. M.K.Gandhi erblickte den Kern des durch den Kolonialismus hereingetragenen Konflikts im Zusammenprall alter und moderner Zivilisationen und identifizierte den "Industrialismus" als eine Hauptgefahr oder Ursache moralischen Verfalls. Doch so wie Indien beim Kampf um seine politische Selbständigkeit nicht bloß eigene, sondern Menschheitsinteressen vertrete, sollte sich auch das künftige freie Indien für die wechselseitige Befruchtung der Kulturen einsetzen und seine eigene fremden Einflüssen öffnen. "I want the cultures of all lands to be blown about my house as freely as possible. But I refuse to be blown off my feet by any."[72] Gandhis Universalismus war ethisch begründet. Sein Rückgriff auf Vorstellungen oder Symbole der hinduistischen Tradition (ram rajya) gab ihm Metaphern in die Hand, um einen erstrebten besseren Zustand zu umschreiben. Er wollte sicherlich keinen Ausschließlichkeits- oder Überlegenheitsanspruch für den Hinduismus bzw. dessen Anhänger begründen. Rabindranath Tagore wiederum setzte sich für eine interkulturelle Ost-West-Synthese ein und sah darin einen Weg zur Vervollkommnung der Menschheit. Entschieden verurteilte er den aggressiven Nationalismus territorialer Nationalstaaten, wie er ihn in Gestalt des Nationalismus im "Westen" und in Japan kennengelernt hatte.[73]

## VI

Nach dem ersten Weltkrieg verdichteten sich in Asien Ideen der "nationalen Rekonstruktion" zu alternativen Entwicklungsvorstellungen, die selbst dann, wenn sie sich Errungenschaften der "westlichen" industriellen und bürgerlichen Gesellschaften zum Vorbild nahmen, nicht uneingeschränkt einem westlichen Modell nacheiferten. Historischer Optimismus und ein Universalismus kennzeichnete diese Haltung, der die Tendenz innewohnte, sowohl nationalistische Ausschließlichkeit wie die Entgegensetzung von Ost und West zu überwinden. Ein anderes Merkmal war eine gelegentlich artikulierte vage Vorstellungen von einer "asiatischen Persönlichkeit", die Sprecher der kolonialen und unterentwickelten Länder mit den Emanzipationsidealen ihrer Völker verbanden. Der lokale Nationalismus als Ausdruck des Strebens nach Selbstverwirklichung hatte auf intellektueller und politischer Ebene[74] sein Pendant in einer weltoffenen Haltung und seine Repräsentanten unterschieden ihn sehr wohl von der "selbstsüchtigen" europäischen Form, die aus dem 19. Jahrhundert stammte. Ein in Südasien vorherrschender Trend suchte auf dem Weg der selbstbestimmten Verbindung von nationalen kulturellen Traditionen und "neuen" Werten eine Identifikationsgrundlage für die Wiedergeburt der eigenen Gesellschaft in einer mehr humanen Weltordnung zu schaffen. Es war die Suche nach neuen Wegen.

## Anmerkungen

1 Vgl. Dietmar Rothermund, Kognitive Interaktion und die Hermeneutik der Fremde. Einleitungsreferat zum ersten Symposium des DFG-Schwerpunktprogramms "Transformation der europäischen Expansion vom 15. bis 20. Jahrhundert. Untersuchungen zur kognitiven Interaktion europäischer und außereuropäischer Gesellschaften", Heidelberg, 25.2.1993, vervielfältigtes Manuskript, 1ff.

2 Henning Melber/Gerhard Hauck, Kolonialer Blick und Rationalität der Aufklärung. In: Peripherie, (1989)37, 6ff.

3 Ernst Bloch, Differenzierungen im Begriff Fortschritt. Sitzungsberichte der Deutschen Akademie der Wissenschaften zu Berlin, Klasse für Philosophie, Geschichte, Staats-, Rechts- und Wirtschaftswissenschaften, Jg. 1955, Nr.5, Berlin $^{2}$1957, 43.

4 Siehe hierzu Ranajit Guha, An Indian Historiography of India: A Nineteenth-Century Agenda and its Implications, Calcutta/New Delhi 1988, 2.

5 Hans-Georg Gadamer, Wahrheit und Methode. Grundzüge einer philosophischen Hermeneutik, Tübingen 1965, 274f.

6 Istvan Meszaros (Hg.), Neocolonial Identity and Counter-Consciousness. Essays on Cultural Decolonization by Renato Constantino, London 1978, 9.

7 Ashis Nandy, The Politics of Secularism and the Recovery of Religion, in: Veena Das (Hg.), Mirrors of Violence. Communities, Riots and Survivors in South Asia, Delhi, 1992, 69.

8 Ashis Nandy, The Intimate Enemy. Loss and Recovery of Self Under Colonialism, Delhi [7]1993, X.

9 Vgl. Partha Chatterjee, Nationalist Thought and the Colonial World. A Derivative Discourse?, Delhi 1986, Kapitel 1 und 2.

10 Vgl. John Harris, A Review of South Asian Studies. In: Modern Asian Studies *22*(1988)1, 55.

11 Vgl. Richard Falk, Democratising, internationalising, and globalising: a collage of blurred images. In: Third World Quarterly *13*(1993)4, 627ff.

12 Vgl. Basan Tibi, Leopold Senghor's "Negritude". In: Das Argument, *9*(1967), 422ff.

13 Edward Said, Orientalism, New York 1978.

14 Gyan Praksh, Writing Post-Orientalist Histories of the Third World: Perspectives from Indian Historiography. In: Comparative Studies in Society and History *32*(1990)2, 383ff.

15 Martin Fuchs, Theorie und Verfremdung. Max Weber, Louis Dumont und die Analyse der indischen Gesellschaft, Frankfurt/M. 1988, 113.

16 Manfred Kossok, Das Jahr 1492. Christoph Kolumbus und der Übergang zur Moderne. In: asien, afrika, lateinamerika, *20*(1993), 586.

17 Vgl. David Kopf, A Macrohistoriographical Essay on the Idea of East and West from Herodotus to Edward Said. In: The Calcutta Historical Journal *XI*(1968-1987)1-2, 1ff.

18 Vgl. Review Symposium: Edward Said's Orientalism. In: Journal of Asian Studies XXXIX(1980)3, 481ff.

19 J.C. van Leur, Indonesian Trade and Society. Essays in Asian Social and Economic History, The Hague 1955, 289.

20 Vgl. Javed Majeed, Ungoverned Imaginings, Oxford 1992, 198, zur Haltung von James Mill in seiner History of British India von 1817 im Kontext der zeitgenössischen Erörterungen über die britische Gesellschaft; vgl. ferner Heinrich Loth, The Knowledge of Asia and Africa in the Age of Enlightenment. In: Joachim Heidrich (Hg.), The French Revolution of 1789. Its Impact on Latin America, Asia, and Africa, Berlin 1989, 39ff.

21 Mujeeb Ashraf, Muslim Attitudes Towards British Rule and Western Culture in India, Delhi 1982, 207, bezeichnet ihn als "perhaps the first outspoken educated Muslim to respond favourably to British rule and Western culture" in Indien.

22 Mirza Abu Taleb, Reisen in Asien, Afrika und Europa, hg. von Manfred Rudolph, Leipzig 1987, 19 (gekürzte deutsche Übersetzung von Abu Taleb, Travels, hg. von Charles Stewart, London 1814).

23 Vgl. Javed Majeed, a.a.O., 138.

24 M. Elphinstone to Captain Irvine, 10.1.1819, zit. in: Kenneth Ballhatchet, Social Policy and Social Change in Western India, 1817-1830, London 1957, 248f.

25 Elphinstone an Malcolm, 27.1.1819, zit. in: K. Ballhatchet, a.a.O., 249.

26 Ainslee T. Embree, Utopias in Conflict. Religion and Nationalism in Modern India, Berkeley etc. 1990, 33.

27 Ebenda.

28 Vgl. Joachim Heidrich, Entwicklung durch Reform im Orient. Das 19. Jahrhundert. In: Gerhard Höpp (Hg.), Entwicklung durch Reform. Asien und Afrika im 19. Jahrhundert (asien, afrika, lateinamerika, Sonderheft 3), Berlin 1991, 13.

29 Calcutta Journal, 20.10.1820. Nachgedruckt in: Selections from the Indian Journals, Vol. II: Calcutta Journal, Calcutta 1965, 420.

30 Calcutta Journal, 20.10.1818. In: Ebenda, vol.I, Calcutta 1963, 29.

31 Calcutta Journal, 21.9.1820. In: Ebenda, vol. II, Calcutta 1965, 336f.

32 Calcutta Journal, 24.9.1820. In: Ebenda, 353.

33 Ebenda, 355.

34 Vgl. On the Colonization of India by Europeans. In: The Kaleidoscope, Calcutta, No.2, September 1829. Nachgedruckt in: Gautam Chattopadhyay (Hg.), Bengal: Early nineteenth Century (Selected Documents), Calcutta 1978, 32ff.

35 Calcutta Journal, 18.10.1820. Nachgedruckt in: Selections..., a.a.O., vol.II, 416.

36 Vgl. Andreas Wirsching, Bürgertugend und Gemeinsinn. Zum Topos der "Mittelklassen" in England im späten 18. und frühen 19. Jahrhundert. In: Archiv für Kulturgeschichte, *72*(1990)1, 177f.

37 Zit.in: S.B. Singh, Growth of Public Opinion in India (1835-1861). In: N. R. Ray (Hg.), Growth of Public Opinion in India: 19th and Early 20th Centuries (1800-1914), Calcutta 1989, 4.

38 Albert O. Hirschman, Industrialization and Its Manifold Discontents: West, East and South. In: World Development, *20*(1992)9, 1227.

39 C.H.Philips/Mary Doreen Wainwright (Hg.), Indian Society and the Beginnings of Modernisation c. 1830-1850, London 1976, 3.

40 W. Hough, Political and Military Events in British India From the Years 1756 to 1849, vol.I, London 1953, X, zit. in: Philip Lawson, The East India Company. A History, London and New York 1993, 144.

41 Chattopadhyay (Hg.), Bengal..., a.a.O., XIX.

42 N.K. Bose, Modern Bengal, Calcutta 1959, 47.

43 Chattopadhyay, Bengal..., a.a.O., XIX.

44 Tsunoda Ryusaku/William Theodore de Bary/Donald Keene (Hg.), Sources of Japanese Tradition, New York 1958, 644.

45 Stephen N. Hay, Asian Ideas of East and West. Tagore and His Critics in Japan, China, and India, Cambridge, Mass. 1970, 83, machte auf diese Merkwürdigkeit aufmerksam.

46 Bipan Chandra, Ranade's Economic Writings, New Delhi 1990, Introduction, X.

47 Dadabhai Naoroji, England's Duties to India. In: Ders., Essays, Speeches, Addresses and Writings, hg. von C.L. Parekh, Bombay 1887, 28, 35.

48 Vgl. den Titel des Aufsatzes zit. in Anm. 47.

49 Vgl. Edward C. Moulton, Early Indian Nationalism: Henry Cotton and the British Positivist and Radical Connection, 1870-1915. In: Journal of Indian History *60*(1982), 125ff.

50 Vgl. Bipan Chandra, a.a.O., XIII.

51 Michelguglielmo Torri, "Westernised Middle Class", Intellectuals and Society in Late Colonial India. In: Economic and Political Weekly *XXV*(1990)4, PE-2.

52 Vgl. Satish Saberwal, Elements of Communalism. In: D.N. Panigrahi (Hg.), Economy, Society and Politics in Modern India, New Delhi 1985, 227.

53 Vgl. R. Suntharalingam, Politics and Nationalist Awakening in South India, 1852-1891, Tucson 1974, XIV.

54 Vgl. Rajat Ray, Urban Roots of Indian Nationalism. Pressure Groups and Conflict of Interests in Calcutta Politics, 1875-1939, New Delhi 1979, 35.

55 Vgl. J.C. Masselos, Towards Nationalism, Bombay 1974, 10f.

56 Vgl. Erwin Aschenbrenner, Kultur - Kolonialismus - Kreative Verweigerung. Elemente einer antikolonialistischen Kulturtheorie, Saarbrücken 1990, 29.

57 Vgl. M.N. Srinivas, Changing Values in India Today. In: Economic and Political Weekly *XXVIII*(1993)19, 933f.

58 K.N.Panikkar, Culture and Ideology. Contradictions in Intellectual Transformation of Colonial Society in India. In: Economic and Political Weekly *XXII*(1987)49, 2117.

59 Huiyun Wang, Comparative Discourses on Social Change in India and China. In: Gandhi Marg *14*(1993)4, 610.

60 Vgl. ebenda, 611.
61 Cheng-chung Lai, Types of Economic Ideas in Late Imperial China and the Role of Western Economic Thought. In: The Journal of European Economic History *20*(1991)2, 369.
62 Sun Yatsen, Die "Drei Volksprinzipien" und die Perspektive Chinas (21. Dezember 1906). In: Ders., Reden und Schriften, Leipig 1974, 103.
63 Benoy Kumar Sarkar, The Futurism of Young Asia and other essays on the relations between the East and the West, Berlin 1922, IIIf.
64 In einer späteren Erklärung an die Polizeibehörde zwecks Erlangen eines Visums behauptete er, nie an der antikolonialen Bewegung teilgenommen oder mit irgendeiner politischen Bewegung sympathisiert zu haben. Vgl. National Archives of India: Govt. of India, Home Department Political, File No. 24/LVI 1929, Subject: Grant of passport for Europe to Professor Benoy Kumar Sarkar provided he abstains from all political activities.
65 Vgl. Stanley Rice, The Challenge of Asia, London 1925, 11, 32, 104.
66 Susanne Hoeber Rudolph/Lloyd I. Rudolph, The Modernity of Tradition, Chicago-London 1967, 161.
67 Vgl. zur "Neuorientierung" der bengalischen Intelligenz im frühen 20. Jahrhundert Tapan Raychaudhuri, Europe Reconsidered. Perceptions of the West in Nineteenth Century Bengal, Delhi 1988, 332.
68 M. Visvesvaraya, Reconstructing India, London 1920, Vf., 3.
69 Sun Yatsen, Die internationale Entwicklung Chinas (1919). In: Ders., a.a.O., 223.
70 Hans Kohn, Die Europäisierung des Orients, Berlin 1934, 111.
71 Vgl. Bhikhu Parekh, Colonialism, Tradition and Reform, New Delhi 1989, 21, speziell zu M.K. Gandhis alternativem universalistischem Konzept.
72 Mahatma Gandhi in Young India, 1.6.1921. Zit. nach: M.K. Gandhi, Sarvodaya, Allahabad 1958, 144.
73 Vgl. Rabindranath Tagore, Nationalismus, München 1918, passim.
74 Vgl. zum Ideal des Nationalismus C.R. Das, Presidential Address, Jahrestagung des Indischen Nationalkongresses 1922. In: Prithwid Chandra Ray, Life and Times of C.R.Das, London 1927, Appendix, 265.

# Imperialism, Nationalism, and the Dialectics of Changing Identity in the Indian Subcontinent

Barun De

## Change and Continuity Today

The theme of changing identities resurfaced in popular consciousness during the 1989 -1992 crisis of world order. Before that, identities were generally encapsulated under rubrics such as statehood, nationalism, or class (already then, a concept seen to be complex and multifaceted), creed (or religion in vaguer parlance) denomination, sect, or community (in the contemporary usage of social groups with some specific bonds of solidarity).

The 1989 - 1992 crisis in Eastern Europe, the USSR, and the Arab world, as well as among Afghans and Kurds, meant a radical challenge to established ideas of non-violent protest. There was a democratic resurgence of such ideals, as opposed to established structures of authoritarianism in the name of populist representation of silent masses. The Bonapartism of Chinese Communist State power evidenced by Tienanmen was one such case. The Decisive historiogrpahical turn in Western Europe and the USA towards free market, right wing liberalism away from revolutionary ideals based on terror, counter-terror, and a neo-Jacobinism (which had been spawned by scarcity generated by class oppression), underlay the Thermidorian universalism' which marked the French Revolutionary Bicentennial s celebration. The *boulevarsements* of autumn 1989 in Eastern Europe were marked by the symbolism of the fallen wall in Berlin and of the 'velvet revolution in Prague. And then there was the return to violence and reprisal in Romania. The slide from a idyll of Eurasia, the 'opening of Central Asia to the West' as blurbs to contemporary English tourist guides to 'Great Game' stories about Central Asia, call the splitting of the USSR part of Central Asia into 5 separate states: all these mark a radical change, in European and Asian power structures.

Old nationalisms, sub-nationalisms and ethnicities have resurfaced across Eurasia. There is an alarming growth of civil war in scattered points all over the old US foreign policy construct of 'an arc of crisis'. This stretches now from Abkhazia on the Black Sea to Gorno-Badakshan in the Pamirs; and perhaps up, in the future, towards the even more recently surfacing heartland tensions against the Yeltsin regime among Tartars south of the Urals, Central Siberians around Omsk, and along Russia's old imperial Amur frontier. Often endogenous stresses have been exogenously broadened in other areas by new imperialist violence. Such are the ethnic and religious sectarian tensions released by the U.S. led attack on Iraq, and indeed by the earlier sponsorship of the Iraqi attack on Iran. Azari, Kurd and

Alawite Shia, Turkman and Kirghiz, Tatar and Uighur, are all fractals. Their divergences have far outstripped any initial similarities, whatever they may have been, of the incipient Pan-Islam or even Pan-Turanism of the 1980s. These are all changes in the structures of known identities, which lead to new consciousness and call for new modes of conceptualization, as well as of political activism.

In Europe, with its once vaunted affluence and mythically comfortable freedom from tension, the promise of 1992 and the 'borderless' continent in which the informatics revolution would build new frontiers for market panaceas, seems to be watered down. Ghosts have arisen once again, of religio-communal and ethnic violence in another arc, stretching as far afield as the Shankill Road quarter of Belfast across Belgium and Germany with their poor minorities, to Slovenia, Croatia, Bosnia, Serbia and Herzegovina. These are no less frightening than what has happened in Biafra, Bangladesh, Kashmir or Peru. Majoritarian nationalist concepts of stability of authority seek to browbeat minorities. This is now a factor of economic calculation, social cohesion and diplomatic negotiation in international arenas.

The nationalist ideology had risen to apogee in the eighteenth and nineteenth centuries. It represented a new conglomerate of state authoritarianism, using the rhetoric of mass representation and democratic pluralism which worked through the medium of the middle and then working classes. It had thrived most when accelerated by capitalist development. Nationalist state power hardened in the later nineteenth and twentieth centuries into neo-absolutist forms - for instance in the Fascist states of the northern hemisphere, Italy, Germany, Romania, Japan working, so to say, overtime, under the thrusts of latecomer capitalism.

To this nationalism in the post war era from 1947 to the 1980s was accreted, what US modernization theory called, the 'new nations'. Their forms of identity were forged in the stress of anti-colonial movements - in themselves varied - from the two, or one-and-half century, old nation states in the Americas - through West Asian arbitrary state-forms, as in Turkey, Iran, Afghanistan and Saudi Arabia, into the South, South East, and Far Eastern new states after 1947 as well as the more chaotic developments of the African political systems. This second half of the twentieth century nationalism relied more on *etatisme*.[1] It shied away from purely civil social endogenous growth and market freedom of the fully unrestricted variety. This further fortified the strong state character of the late 20th century new world order. The sovereignty of nation states, the domination over them by bourgeois or *nomenklaturs* socialist ruling classes, and an apparent historical stability, based on Liberal or Communist ideology, (disseminated either by free market or *etatiste* modes of production) all seemed to bear the promise of lasting well into the twenty-first century. Modernisation theory presumed that national sovereignty would act as a flexible carapace, within which the informatics revolution could ferment economic *perestroika*.

State sovereignty, the repressive force of strong states and media manipulation (by multinationals even more than the new warring power of states *per se*) of hegemonic mass consensus, have by no means been challenged yet as facts of life, in this last decade of the twentieth century. Yet there has been a remarkable fission of popular consensus about the contemporary order. Newly 'fragmented' groupings which are as often as not conjured up by Commonwealth and U.S. historians, tilling a lance at old windmills called by now-aging young radicals as 'foundation Marxism', are now in academic vogue.[2]

In any case, the speed of change has become a process as significant as the sluggish pace of continuity in the making and reformulation of social identities. Socio-economic and political cultural change begins to even challenge what used to appear to be the Tocquevillean verities of *plus ca change mais plus c'est la meme chose*. The process forges a world of new, manipulative identities, less inhibited by tradition, courtesies, or care, that parents of my own generation (born, as our parents were, at the turn of this century) are able hardly recognise, or have to stoically accept, as part of a totally changed world. The necessity now is to see whether the emerging formations of new consciousness are deeper than their appearances and rhetoric; and whether they are not merely a changed visage.

There is another aspect of this problem - how have imperial structures influenced changes in Indian identity? The theme has assumed renewed importance on a more global scale, now that the Russian Empire, and its reorganization during the USSR revolution on Soviet principles, has crumbled along Russia's western and southern flanks. Ethnicity has now replaced cold war as the new flashpoint for crisis in the world political order. Without going into the question of 'ethnic revivalism' or how ethnicity is constructed, or to be defined, today, I propose to look back in history. This paper considers the dialectics of imperial and national forces in the construction of all-India identity as it emerged by 1947. In conclusion, it will 'pan' forward the field of perspective to express certain personal vies about the resurrection of old values in a period of current crisis in the post-colonial state.

## The Innovation of British Indian Imperialist Consolidation

The Battle of Plassey led to the establishment of dual control by the East India Company in one part of India over the Nawabis of Bengal and Bihar, Awadh, and the Carnatic, i.e. the northern and western hinterland of the Bay of Bengal. After 1772, it was no more possible for the British nation, conscious of its oligarchical parliamentary, i.e. proto-democratic Whig grandee tradition of liberal balance of powers between executive, legislature and judiciary, to leave unshackled so far away such vast conquests by its merchants and by their back-up armed forces. The growth of its national profits required assertion of sovereign control over a monopolist organisation, that was exploiting the conquest in plundering fashion. Britons by the 1780s realised that if parliamentary control was not asserted, there was the danger of falling into the same *mores* of subject peasantry and mercantile-cum-professional subservience to robber baron, class dominance. Such mores were then practised, if not by Nadir Shah of Persia (who had destroyed the traditional Safavid equipoise so belauded by Montesquieu in his *Lettres Persanes*, then at least by established Maratha captains in the Indian heartland such as Sindhia or Holkar, or by Nawab Shuja-ud-daulah of Awadh, and by the later Afghan Emperors in the Indus valley.

Within half a century, *de jure* indigenous sovereignty into which the Company inserted itself in a *de facto* status had lost all meaning. The new process of government, by a Governor General - in - Council, became new model for south Asian governance, 'differentially diffused' (a term adapted in the mid-twentieth century by Daniel and Alice Thorner from the US demographer of India, Kingsley Davis)[3] in various parts of the subcontinents, over the next one and a half centuries. Between 1773 and 1853, the whole of what came to be known as British India followed, by and large with local variations based on provincial tradition, this model of western imperialist governance, first established by Parliament for Bengal and the other Presidencies of Madras and Bombay - by the Regulating Act of 1773, the Amending Acts of 1781, the India Act of 1784, and the Charter Renewal Acts of 1793, 1833 and 1853.

The British parliamentary control model set norms for new social identities. India till 1799 and the death of Tipu Sultan (the last truly autonomous freedom fighter of post-Mughal India, who died on his own ramparts of Seringapatam), was still ruled by and large by feudal-from-below-cum-bureaucratic communities or local patriotism (i.e. affinity to *watan* or patri/matri/mony). These included Kashmiris under Sukjiwanmal; Punjab under the Khalsa Misls; Rajasthan under a congeries of Rajput princes; Rohilkhand under the various Ruhela chieftains' lineages; Bengal is the land where Bengali was spoken; Assam as ruled by the Ahoms from beyond Kuch Bihar to where the Tsanpo debouches from Eastern Tibet to become the Brahmaputra; Orissa centring round the settled plains of Mughalbandi and the Garjat; Andhra (still dominated by the Chandragiri - post-Vijayanagara traditions); the Marathas, *splayed out* over Central India, the Western Deccan, Gujarat, eastern Rajasthan and even the Antarvedi-Delhi-Hariana region, *but tied together* by a network of kinship, affinity, and pilgrimage centres in the Maratha *desh* within the Ghats and the Sahyadri ranges; and Malabar and the Nayar chieftaincies of the south-west peninsula.

Such local subordinate elite identities had been microscopic in scale troughout the medieval period (what D. D. Kosambi has called the period of feudalism-from-above-and from below[4] - i.e. decomposing imperial bureaucratic outpost systems, and uptrusting, socially mobile, robber barons of the countryside outside such outposts which emulated their political culture). They were territorial, ethnic, with little traditions (what my late friend and colleague Dr. Hitesranjan Sanyal used to call *Laukika achar*, as distinct from *marg-sanskriti*, or classical culture), linguistic and, *by no means* emphasising only religious identity. To the conquerors from the northern hills - whether across Baluchistan (as in the days of the ancient Persians or early medieval Arabs in Sind) or across the Pathan Valleys (as in the case of the Ghaznavids, Ghorids, and later Turco-Afghans an early Mughals) or down the Lohit-Bramaputra defile and across the Patkoi Hills (as in the cases of the Ahoms of the thirteenth to fifteenth centuries or the brief Burmese occupation of the Assam Valley in the early nineteenth century), the people of the plains and beyond, up to the peninsula were lumped in a territorial category of "Hind - U" - people of Hind (Sindhu) with a variety of Hindavi folk practices, rituals, etc.

These communities were not seen in the modern European sense of 'religion'. The category rather was one of composite culture. These were cultures, similar to that of China across the Eastern Himalaya and Yunnan, rather than of the more contiguous Arab Muslims, or the Europeans of Christendom, or of Shinto Japan. It was defined by a mix, territorial, linguistic, ethnic (one of the dictionary meanings for which, my son Bikramjit De told me while I was drafting this paper, is "not Christian" or "pagan" or "tribal"). Confessional solidarity was not a crucial element in such a composite mix. The term 'Hindu' represents a northern perspective looking southwards into the plains, an imperial centralist, not a diversified, gaze. Even in the Peninsula, where religious solidarity has been greater and more uninterrupted and thus less conflictual than in the North, with only three major, but relatively briefer interludes of Muslim attacks, confessional solidarity was not old. Lingayet or Srivaishnava sectarianism did not permit religious hegemony of any centralised, churchlike character. Nor did rule by Islamic monarchs (Sultan or Padshah) ever attempt such consolidation, except in brief interludes, such as the seventeenth century. The orthodoxy of Brahmanical consolidation has had a chequered history in the south.

A mix of diversity, a looseness of socio-economic grain, marked the prereliosity of the South, East and Central Asian littoral. British rule in nineteenth century India dirctly challenged this diversity. It overdetermined, i.e. it overemphasised centralised unity. We too often forget that the colonial challenge was one of force and imposition of authority. The initial British military victories over Indians (and indeed Asians) were not of greater armed force, but of comparative advantage in use of firepower, organization, and political skills before and after the actual fithting encounters.[5] European colonial penetration in eighteenth century Asia used an indigenous crisis; in which the local ruling classes failed to assert themselves; and in which they could not give successful leadership to their masses. A more significant point to follow is: How did the indigenous classes and masses react?

## Indigenous Identities: Plebeian Patriotism and the Dilemmas of Sub-Imperialism

In the late eighteenth century, the bulk of the emergent 'professional middle class', the priests and scholars (*ulama* and *pandits*), the warrior and gentry captains of horse, and musketeers who fought for cash (as *naqdi* levies), the doctors (*hakims* and *vaidyas*), the writers (*kayasthas, karanas, mudaliars, khattris, prabhus* or *amla* in general) and deputies and men of affairs in estates and businesses (*naibs, diwans* or *qumasthaha*) became increasingly demoralised in the eighteenth century. Rural revolt grew against increased demands on the surplus by the ruling class and its parasitical bureaucracy. This coincidentially increased repression by the decomposing state poser of Emperors, regional Nawabs and Maratha vassals. As Empires fell apart, the power of the latter and of their peripheral chieftains in the south, north-east of India and in the Himalayas also increased.

This demoralisation was later in the nineteenth century to be rhetoricized as 'Muslim tyranny' by even as broadminded and secular-spirited an Indian as Raja Rammohan Roy.[6] Initially in the eighteenth and early nineteenth centuries, the Indian middle classes accepted an identity of merely autonomy from those indigenous governments, which could not afford them protection. The emergent middle class served a variety of masters. But it was loyal to the honour and self-interest of their families, their *wataniyyat* (if we may coin such a term). They maintained state forms, which were changeable according to the political will of their governors. Since the new British rulers supplied a consistency of political will, the new middle class acted in consonance with British Indian consistency of political will.

Like the *havildars* and *jemadars* of the British Indian armies of the eighteenth century (a classic example of whom, in Madura, is chronicled by S. C. Hill in his old book *Yusuf Khan, The Rebel Commandant*, as the title being accorded to the latter of *Kumadan Baghi* by the admiring rising 'Tiger of Mysore' Haidar Ali)[7], the new middle classes,military as well as professional and not the peasantry were the true 'subalterns' of the Indian subcontinent - subordinate, hoping to be alternative rulers, yet ultimately subservient to colonialism. Those whom Ranajit Guha first called *nimnabarga* (lower orders, a pre-class term) were *not* subaltern in this more common sense of the English usage. Rather they were plebeians, *plebs* in the even older Italian, Roman sense of class struggle against patricians, evoked by Marx and Engels in the opening lines of the *Communist Manifesto*.[8]

'Havildari consciousness' (a term recently coined in private conversation by Dr. Tapan Raychaudhuri in Bengali *havildari chetanā* to translate subalternity) is quite contrary to the usage of 'people' or 'masses' ascribed to its coinage by the Oxford University Press series, so popular in Westernised Oriental Studies, which follows Hoare and Nowell-Smith's quaint terminology for the Italian 'subalterna', i.e. 'subordinate' borrowed from Gramsci's Aesopian language.[9] The intermediary Havildari-conscious class acquired a subordinate but relatively autonomous hegemonic identity, when British rule began to generalise the spread of British media of instruction, British Indian law and legal procedure codes and British revenue practices as well as British or Anglo-Indian dominated transportation and telecommunication systems all over nineteenth-century India.

Princely or chieftain identity waned in the high noon of nineteenth century empire. The Marathas, Sikhs, Rajputs, Jats, Gurkhas, the warrior castes of the South, Burmans were still in a phase of declining political power; they continued to be contumacious against imperial superordination - as indeed were Central Asians, Afghans, Caucasians, or Persian, Turks, Arabs and Maghrebis, or African tribesmen and Indonesian cultivators and fisherfolk, against Chinese, Russian, English, French, Dutch or German imperialism. These forces could not establish anti-imperialist solidarity, to help one another, or even to develop bonds of mutual respect, such as the later generation of Rashid Rida, Maulana Azad, Ho Chi Minh, Dzhou - En-Lai, Mustapha Nahas Pasha, Jawaharlal Nehru or Kwame Nkrumah were able to, a century later. However violent the manifestations of the 19th century non-European patriotism were (as in the case of the 1857 Indian Revolt and Sepoy Mutinies or the Zulu, Matabele or Mahdiyya was in Africa) or however it sought to differentiate indigenous (what the British called 'baboo' or 'native') autonomy, from the *herrenvolk* (i.e. supra-elite) imperial masters, whom the subalterns or compradores served as salariat and watchmen; patriots were still always subordinate, though quite often rebellious in their group identity vis-a-vis Western imperialism. This was the 'India of the Queen' after Victoria's 1858 proclamation declaring India as Crown territory after the 1857 Revolt.

Indian identity at that time can be understood in three segments. The plebeian elements were patriotic. An exception was the case when the push on the land and on their occupations was such that, depeasantised and driven into the sugar and coffee plantations of Mauritius, Ceylon, Fiji or the West Indies, they developed the first plebeian 'Non-Resident Indian' identities. Plebeian patriotism was localised in petty territorialities. It was social and community conscious, rather than nationalist. It was drawn into nationalism only in the twentieth century, when the Indian National Congress made efforts to first draw upon and later appropriate its support.

Secondly, there were the loyalists of British rule (rajbhakta or toadies as patriots later contemptuously dubbed them). These could be from all classes, from peasants and paupers to bureaucrats and princes. They were not necessarily motivated only by self-interest. They might consider British rule to be good for law and order in their own locality, or in the country as a whole - i.e. believe in the Pax Britannica without going too deeply into the circumstances of repression, counterinsurgency, and espionage among the subjects, by which Pax Britannica was continually represented. Or they might believe in an earlier version of what nowadays is frivolously called the TINA Factor (There Is No Alternative) - since no real alternative equivalent to British power indeed developed till second decade of the twentieth century.

Such people included Indian members of the Indian Civil Service, and other high bureaucratic echelons in the Medical or Engineering Services or Surveys of India. They were often patriots and moderate nationalists, but very cautiously Moderate and indeed like the early Fabians who came after this group in their critique of imperial malpractices or shortcomings. Romesh Chander Dutt, the economic historian, and retired ICS, President of the Congress, whose great *Economic History of India Under British Rule* exposed the exploitative character of colonialism, after retiring prematurely from the ICS, contested with Lord Curzon on his revenue policy and then joined the service of the moderate patriot Maharaja of Baroda, Sayajirao. Sir Surendranath Banerjee was dismissed from the ICS for a petty clerical oversight, but went on to weld all-India consciousness in the English language and become the archetypal Moderate loyalist. They were flip sides of the same Fabian-type of kaleidoscope. They were people who faith in the outcome, wither in the short or the long run, of efforts to use force against imperialism.[10] Indeed Dutt's Bengali novels, written in prose modelled on both Bankim Chandra Chatterjee historical and Sir Walter Scott's earlier 'Waverley' and resembling the plot of Pushkin's *Captain's Daughter* novels are romantic explications of the dilemmas of imperialist outpost captains of Rajput stock, working for Mughal superordinates - like Raja Todar Mal in Madhabi Kankan or Mirza Raja Jai Singh in Maharashtra Jeevan Prabhat. R. C. Dutt, ICS obviously saw himself in such roles. The greater litterateur Bankim, in life a more subaltern Deputy Magistrate writing *Kapalkundala* or *Durgeshnandini* about district rural life, cast himself as a more sober bystander, philosophically differentiated from the past, as much as he was from the hurlyburly of contemporary politics.

Or, the loyalists might actually be sub-imperialists - like the Maharajas of the Princely States and chieftains and landlords of various kinds who sought to aggrandize wealth, comfort as well as gain prestige and rank within the imperial system. British superiordinate politicians and bureaucrats from the times of Wellesley, Dalhousie and Disraeli to that of Risley, Hailey and Linlithgow carefully graded their rank ordering. There were the people on whom 'Raj' literature with its sacchavine sentimentalism nowadays thrives, the people evoked by the bulk of British rail-touring parties and American subaltern anthropologists all the way from Jaisalmer to Hyderabad, Trichur and Pudukkottai. Together the loyalists supplied the ideological superstructure for propagating the idea of Britain's civilising mission in the non-self-governing tropics.

## The Nationalist Variant

But there was a third class of evolving identity, which came dialectically, instead of lineally, out of imperial consolidation. Early middle class or gentry patriots like Raja Rammohan Roy in Bengal or Balshastri Jambhekar and Dadoba Pandurang in

Bombay, or Gazula Lakshminarasu Chettiar in Madras can be located on a saddle-point between patriotism and nationalism: where concern for maintenance and integrity of one's own regional values, such as religion, social norms, self-expressions though the media, language solidarities, etc., were facing challenges regarding their autonomous expression. The regional societies came in contact with new elements, such as domination of the polity by an alien power which worked through more advanced cultural technology, and organization. These new elements include printing of widely disseminated books, primary and secondary as well as collegiate education geared to bureaucratic employment, improved market and public health facilities, as well as fairly clearly defined civilizational ideological choices of a variety of European influences were available. These included Evangelical Christianity, as explicated by the Tanjore, Serampore and later Punjab and Nagaland and Lushai Hills Missions; Utilitarianism as expounded in the writings of Benthan and the Mills; later nationalism as modelled in the actions and thought of Mazzini, Garibaldi and Cavour etc.

This idea possessed, at the beginning of the present century, a force of composite identity, too often forgotten by those monochrome unitarian majoritarians who see nationalism as the only feature of what is actually a Trimurti. The image has three interfaces, like Elephanta, of resistance, loyalism, and political subalternity. Together, these make up the general features of British influence on Indian identity. The nationalist phenomenon becomes prominent only in the later years of the nineteenth century.

The moment was that of what has been compared to a saddle point and not necessarily, a particular path, clearly marked towards a determinate goal. Unlike David Kopf's over-deterministic elaboration of the sources of early nineteenth century Calcutta and Serampore of Carey, Marshman and Ward, or the behind-the-scenes bureaucratic activities and manipulation in generating Hindu College as a renaissance educational institution by men like the Supreme Court judge Sir Edward Hyde East, the Scots watch maker turned school teacher David Hare, the mercantile Debs of Sobhabazar, or Horace Hayman Wilson of the Calcutta Mint and later Oxford scholar,[11] renaissance of Bengali culture was parallel to the political economy of Britain's domination of the subcontinent by a mixture of force and consensus. It was also the ideology and social praxis of a subordinate elite in the Bengal towns attuning themselves to world capitalism as well as to landowner-literati-concentrated-villagers turning themselves into a new illuminati of British-veneered professionalism in the new rationalist, scientific, and also theological activities of the Victorian segment of the world system. Similar specificities of the coalition of interest between the alien forces from above, and the native urges for collaboration in the middle and lower reaches of state power that are common to all imperial systems of government (which have lasted for a century and more) were factors in the Indian renaissance. It is these specificities that are so central to progressive thought in twentieth century India about its present identity. It is their dialectical element that leads to complexities, which resurface whenever there is cultural crisis.

The national element, i.e. the desire for cultural authority over a state was the superordinate factor in the lives of all who identified themselves as British Indians or were subject to the paramountcy of its Governor-General (of India, no more Bengal, be it noted, from 1833 in the time of Lord William Bentinck and Thomas Babington Macaulay) or later (from 1858 after the abolition of the Company) of the Viceroy in Calcutta's Government House. This desire for cultural authority, and at least of socio-political rank equality with the British *Herrenvolk* came fresh from a sense of new cultural and home market federation. This arose in the 1860s and 1870s - after the decisive subordination of the Indian peasantry, as well as of the refractory, old elites, Sikh, Muslim and Rajput in the North, Maratha, Karnataki in the West. This new subordination was in the interests of post-Mutiny stern governance by a new middle class as well merchant-cum-usurer, and plantation-owner forces, Indian as well as British. They went all out to integrate not only South Asia but also other lobes of the Asia-Pacific region from Aden to Sydney and of the heartland from Baghdad and Astrakhan to Tientsin (in competition with Russians, French and Germans, and in the twentieth century, Japanese) into the world capitalist economy.

Such forces did not necessarily seek to build a strong or autonomous capitalism in India. The South Asian subcontinent as part of colonial capitalism was always seen as imperial market reserve bank. There could be reserves of raw materials or semi-processed commodities, exported out eastwards for dumping on its neighbour's markets (not just opium, but also Bombay yarn in China, for instance), but even more than that, westwards for grading and blending (like spices and tea) or manufacture (like cotton and manganese) for British stockholder profits. Or it could be as a stock of cheap labour to develop plantations in tropical islands and peninsulas like Mauritius, Fiji, the Malay States etc. for foodstuff or rubber or tin in world markets. Or ultimately it could be as ballast for an atrophying sterling balance of trade, and currency system. When it came to a conflict of interest, the British metropolitan one always prevailed. This meant that the middle class merchant-prince, lawyer, bureaucrat, medical, or straight politician subordinate elites - by the early twentieth century, polished in ways, sneered at by Englishmen in the acronym 'Wog' (Western Oriental Gentleman) - could not identify in their urges for fortune or prestige, with, the capitalist system at its most European *bourgeois conquerante* phase. The identification became a dialectical one-culturally torn between *watan* and westernised civilization, economically aspiring for protected markets, politically desirous of freedom from what now came to be condemned as alien nationality and arbitrary governance.

In a piece written a few years before he passed away, John Plamenatz, a Montenegrin by birth, educated and settled in England, explicated his earlier somewhat less clear views *On Alien Rule and Self-Government* in a more acceptable format in an article entitled 'Two Types of Nationalism'.

'... nationalism is a reaction of peoples who are culturally at a disadvantage... This ist not to set it down as merely a kind of envy ... it is to be found only among people who are, or are coming to be, sharers in an international culture whose goals are worldly ... critics of nationalism often speak of it as if it were essentially illiberal. Acton did so in the last century and Kedourie has done so in this. For my part I must say that ... nationalists have been liberal and also illiberal, according to the circumstances in which they have found themselves.'

Professor Plamenatz, in this lecture devlivered at Canberra in 1972, explained that Western or first-type nationalism could be more endogenous, with 'little need to equip (itself) culturally by appropriating what was alien ... (but there were) two kinds of nationalism...'

In the second type, of Slavs, Africans and Asians, which may be termed an 'Eastern or Orient' type, 'drawn gradually, as a result of the diffusion among them of western ideas and practices, into a civilization not of their own making, they have had, as it were, to make themselves anew, to create new identities for themselves. No doubt they already had some sense of identity or separateness when nationalism first began to take root among them. But there was an awareness also that the skills, ideas and customs acquired form their ancestors were inadequte, if they were to raise to the level of the peoples, who by the standards of the civilization into which they were being drawn, were more advanced than they were. This has made their nationalism in some ways profoundly different from that of the Germans, the Italians and other western peoples.'[12]

Elaborating on this point, Plamenatz calls the second or Oriental type (his Orient begins from the Slavic heritage from which he sought to extricate his thoughts) as *the nationalism of the poor and the weak.*

Today, such a position can be seen as a arch-Orientalist patronage of anti-colonialist positions taken since 1848, the year of what Plamenatz's intellectual forbear, Sir Lewis Bernstein Namier dissected, somewhat maliciously as *The Revolution of the Intellectuals*, in particularly Central Europe from which Namier's own parents had migrated. Orientalist it certainly is: and differentiated from the genuine fervour that anti-imperialism generates among its true believer. However, a positive understanding is to be found here about the sort of dilemma - let us call it dialectic - faced by many early nationalists in India.

Such were Justice Ranade, R. C. Dutt, Sivanath Sastri, Gopal Krishna Gokhale, Bipin Chandra Pal, Sardar Ajit Singh (of the Punjab Canal Colony agitations of 1907/08), V. O. Chidambaram Pillai of Tuticorin, Motilal Nehru, and over-shadowing this galaxy, figures like Swami Vivekananda and Mahatma Gandhi. Whether Moderate or Extremist in their Congress affiliations, or sometimes not even with such political affiliations, the Indian nationalists' identity reconstructed not only the regional patriotism of pre-British state forms and cultural traditions, but also the federative aspirations of the nineteenth century, as well as the rhetoric of British conquering integration. Each of these elements were there, in different measures and specificities in the identity of *Swadesh* (homeland, which is how *watan* translates in the Sanskritised tongues). But each was transcended in 'swelling pride' of all-India consciousness.

This finds its apogee, not in the Hindu chauvinism of Bankim Chandra Chatterjee's all-too fallible celibate monks of Ananda Math singing *Vande Mataram* (Mother, I bow to thee), nor in the provincialism of *Amar Sonar Bangla Ami Tomay Bhalobashi* (My golden Bengal, I love you) which Bangladeshis have taken as their national anthem from Rabindranath, but in the evocation of composite culture that Indians have taken as their natural anthem also from Tagore, *Jana Gana Mana Adhinayaka Jaya Hey Bharata Bhagya Vidhata* (victory to the leader of popular consciousness, the arbiter of India's destiny). Such anthems as *O Amar Desher Mati Tomar Parey Thekai Matha* (Oh, my country's soil, I rest my head on you) or *Dhana Dhanyey Pushpey Bhara Amader Ei Vasundhara Tahar Majhey Achey Desh Ek, Smriti Diyey Ghera* (our earth, filled with wealth, harvests, and flowers, within it is a country, surrounded by memories) evoke the same sense of all-encompassing national territoriality.

These Bengali songs come to my mind, since I think in Bengali as well as in English. But as soon as they come to my mind, there also crops up Subramanian Bharati, who presented Tamils with similar songs, which I know of, but failed to learn as I did not know Tamil, or Ram Prasad Bismil who went to the gallows, convicted of anti-imperialist revolutionary militancy, singing in Urdu - common to Muslim and Hindu alike - *Sarfaroshi Key Tamanna Ab Hamarey Dil Mein Hai, Dekhan Hai Zor Kitna Baain-e-Katil Mein Hain* (the desire for laying down my head is in my heart, it remains to be seen what strength there is in the executioner's arm) or the cadence of the title of a book about 'The Glorious Future of Indian Muslims' (*Hindustani Musalmanon Ki Raushan Mustagbil*) written to counter the Muslim League's raising of the Pakistan Demand, by a Deobandi maulvi, Tufail Ahmed Manglauri. No doubt, such evocations are possible in most Indian languages.

This transcendence from federation of communities into all-India consciousness represents one moment of the evolution of the new Indian identity, that I have been talking about, the moment of the first half of the twentieth century. This was when a concatenation of circumstances, a conjuncture of decolonization in the period of the two World Wars, an upsurge of Indian populist consciousness spanning bourgeoisie, peasant and workers, and even many otherwise loyalist Maharajas, swept across Britain's tropical colonial system. The 'success' of the Congress in this 'moment', which was by no means determinate, in taking only truncated power over the South Asian heartland and its north and north western peripheries, in an instant of the postwar collapse of British imperial political will in the 1940s, evoked a cultural freedom struggle, which ist too often forgotten by those who emphasise only the 'Transfer of Power in India', as the only event of the 1940s.

The memories of this cultural freedom struggle became enshrined in the hearts of people who had seen some elders suffering for this freedom struggle at its fag end in the student and workers upsurge and communal strife of the 1930s and 1940s (along with the failure of the Socialists and Forward Bloc in the 1942 Movement to energise the masses to an efficient armed War of Independence against imperialism). For such people it is not always easy to uncritically accept a historiography of nationalism as the only superordinate force replacing imperial state power. As D. D. Kosambi noted in his review of Jawaharlal Nehru's *Discovery of India*, 'the Indian Bourgeoisie Comes of Age' amidst mass backwardness and mass violence.[13] And as he noted in his historiographical critique of the first four volumes of the Bharatiya Vidya Bhavan's *History and Culture of the Indian People*, bourgeois communal historians like R. C. Majumdar merely inverted imperialist interpretations of the beneficial impact of the imperialism on India's manifold diversity into an overcentralizing shibboleth of nationalist unity rearing itself up from that diversity.[14] By the end of this century, such overcentralizing unity has come to be interpreted by majoritarien aspirants to vote bank control as Hindu unitarianism.

## The Present Ghosts of the Past

This note has not touched on many much more important elements in recent, i.e. 20th century, history: imperialist partitions, communalism, the construction of caste and ethnicity, the differential diffusion of a weak bourgeois industrialisation in the country, and the circulation of new elites, such as *mufassil* (or district) provincial professional people eager to capture State level ('State' as in the German *Länder*) power and influence, or rural landholding and contractor or food processing gentry and merchants (who find a Centre, overburdened with federal authority, unresponsive to their differential needs). All these forces have brought yet newer changes in identity which have not been adequately studied from the angle of contemporary history.

While as historians we neglect our contemporary historical experience, subordinate forces constructed within the dialectics of the colonial hegemony within the trimurti of resistance, loyalism and nationalism described above, have begun to revive the ghosts of the past. I have not left myself space to go now into how these reactionary forces of religious sectarianism, or casteist differentiation, or subcontinental disharmony, have been allowed to recoup themselves. But one may wind up with a little anecdote and its exegesis.

Wayfarers on South Calcutta homes and streets nowadays, i.e. in 1993, sometimes saw a curios sight. A blazon, which became unfamiliar from 1946/47 had reappeared proudly on the spindle chests or footbellies of the gangling youth, who crowd the narrow pavements between vendors' stalls and shopfronts. This is in the once-famous red-white-and-blue (still not as common as the Stars and Stripes) boldly etched in deep technicolour, the triple crosses of the British flag, sometimes recollected to the memories of those who are not even 'midnight's children', by a subtitle 'Union Jack, England'. Not the tricolour of the French Revolution, nor the rising sun of the Japanese Meiji Restoration, but British India's once very own imperial flag.

An apparently innocent T-shirt; meant ostensibly to signify just the petty cash to buy, or friends from whom to receive, imitations of Western imports. Why should this be disgusting and yet strip away illusions, cherished since the 1930s, about India's cultural independence from colonialisation's all pervasive seepage? The flag represents a monarchy whose aristocracy and middle classes migrated to climes, on all of which the sun never set at the same time. Yet it has exercised hegemonic charisma over Highlanders and bog Irish, decimated in previous centuries in the interests of an essentially Whig-cum-city magnate class, by bloody imperial warfare, or by sheep run enclosures or by potato blights.

In the early modern age, flags were the pennants of warfare. Now, as Eric Hobsbawm has pointed out about *The Invention of Tradition*, stadia sports are constructed, deconstructed, fused, and redisplayed over and over and over again, by masses of every class responding to, and bearing up in two hands the orchestrated manipulation of electronic media, by representing particles of devices to create organic wholes. Flags are very much integral to organicity. Colour television has given them new form and contemporary use.[15]

The hidden persuasion of the Union Jack on Indian chests in the 1990s is far from a return to tradition. The T-shirt culture is part of a recent craze, in sartorial matters, for the picturesque in miniature. In France, they print Impressionist masterpieces from the Musee de Orsay on T-shirts sold on the Heights of Montmartre. In India, the craze for the picturesque degenerates by a malapropism of usage, into 'ethnic chic'.

'Ethnicity' nowadays has come to mean the traditional, nativistic part of racial identity, the colourful, tribal primitive, as distinct from colourless, subfusc grey or white of blue-collar or white-collar workers. People who have little variety in their lives, whose human condition is too grey for words, or for depiction, generally seek to invert appearances by donning the sartorial version of peacock plumes. Beginning with the 'bleeding Madras' inculcated by *Vogue* and *New Yorker* in the 1960s, and available only to modernising, metropolitan middle classes, to today's fast colours, casual wear has become the badge of elegance: in the same way as the dark suit or/and *dhotikurta* in starched white or cream and gold seeks to give an appearance of solidity. And yet we are not talking only of the present. The motif we are discussing is of a flag that middle aged people wear, which their previous generation sought to fight or transcend: at least by what Gramsci called passive revolution, if not always freedom struggle, whole hog. Sartorial elegance is turned into a symbol of neocolonial culture - however deep beneath the pores of social structure, the neocolonial consciousness may fester.

In the political arena, on the other hand, by identifying the Indian national colours with its own party cause, the Congress (I) has led other parties to turn to alternative colours of their flags - the fast-fading red, now pale pink, the potential fiery cross in the already flaming saffron, the multihued favours of many creeds, and militant schisms in the north, the northeast, and the South. As India Independent's nation turns from its forty-seventh year, rent by strife of caste, creed and regional racial dominance, nationalism ossifies into a partisan term. Symbols may connote unity, diversities are the reality. Partisanism begins to infect the state, whether dominated at the Centre by one party, or in two peripheral states, by the CPI (M), or among the trader class high or low by the BJP intent on neo-Hinduizing a once-vibrant multi-racial, multi-ethnic, multi-religious, civilisational mosaic - or in yet other segments, by 'hurt psyche' or fanaticism or whatever, of Sikhs, Muslims, Eelam, Panun Kashmir, Kashmiriyat, etc. No satisfactory logo, theme-tune/anthem, or other statement of symbolism has been stated with sufficient authenticity, as '*Vande Mataram*' or '*Hindustan Hamara*' or '*Kadam Kadam Barhaeya Ja*' were in the days of Vivekananda, Tilak, Gandhi, Azad, Nehru or Patel. No alternative exists today to explicate, catchily enough, for the masses, an outlook of harmonious, and not conflictual, diversity.

This particular lacuna is represented by the apparent return of the Union Jack, and its association with England (and not even the rest of Britain). This is not the flag the wavers' parents challenged - for the last time, in the decade in the 1940-44, when the British Army held the ring, and Indian police and para-military forces broke peasant and worker militancy. Nor is it the flag which their peasants' leaders and peers hauled down in 1947. The present flag is an older insignia.

It is the symbol of merchants and their penetration backed by armed force into our subcontinental hinterlands, with innovative consumer goods triumphing over newer, imported or imitiated textile designs, machine-made products for quick communication (today the computer and its telephonic applications), more rapid fire armament (Bofors is now as outdated as the Exocets in the Malvinas of the early 1980s have become). This is not the Union Jack I was taught to revere and learned to ignore. It is a newcomer in the garb of a past tradition - the exact French for which is '*re-venent*' - one who comes back - from the past - but different in the present - a ghost, a spirit.

Writing a hundred and fifty or a bit less years ago in *The Eighteenth Brumaire of Louis Napoleon* about Bonapartist state power in France, Marx said: 'The tradition of all the dead generations weigh like a nightmare on the living. Just when they seem engaged in revolutionising themselves and things, in creating something new, they anxiously conjure up the spirits of the past to their service and borrow from their names battle slogans and costumes in order to present the new scene in time-honoured disguise.' In the same text, Karl Marx averred that history may repeat itself, but the first time as tragedy, the second time as farce.[16]

But even if we exorcise the Union Jack from designer shirts for the common man, will we be able to cast out other ghosts from the past. These are the images, legitimate in themselves, but fraught with horror in contemporary mythology, of Rama the bowman and his monkey hordes, or the Central Asian marauder Babur at Panipat and Khanua, and his captain raiding through Sharqi Jaunpur. Such images have proven potential for raising among common people far more fanaticism - what in Hindustani, may be called *Junoon* (being led by *jinn* or spirits). The Union Jack may be challenged by modern Indian History. But is ancient or medieval historiography alone sufficient to exorcise religions communalism of a nativistic variety, whether Hindu, Muslim, Sikh or Jain? If it is not, what are the appropriate constituents for an independent and federal outlook for India in, 1997, the forthcoming half century of our Independence. These are questions average citizens are asking.

## Notes

1 The statement in this and the previous paragraph is eleborated by the writer in two articles; Barun De, Complexities in the Relationships between Nationalism, Capitalism and Colonialism in Debiprasad Chattopadhyay, ed. History and Society, Essays in Honour of Prof. Niharranjan Ray, Calcutta 1976, pp. 479-512, and Nationalism as a Binding Force, The Dialectics of the Historical Course of Nationalism-I, Centre for Studies in The Social Sciences, Calcutta, Occasional Paper No. 93, July 1987.

2 See, for instance, the criticism of Sumit Sarkar, the present writer, and Asok Sen's critique of the implications of the concept of Bengal Renaissance written during the 1970s, by the Princeton historian Gyan Prakash, Writing Post-Orientalist Histories of the Third World, Perspectives from Indian Historiography. In: Comparative Studies in Society and History *32*(1990), particularly pp. 395/96, in a section devoted to 'Post-Nationalist Foundational Histories'. The specific critique of this phase of an apparent conjunction of Sarkar, De and Sen's work is that 'Without belittling the value of these interpretations, ... it is fair to say that the construction of India in term of ... failures represents a foundational view. While it highlights the paradoxes of 'renaissance' in a colonial context, the interpretation of these events as aborted or failed modernity defers the conclusion of the modernization narrative but does not eliminate the teleological vision. We are thus led to see the 'third worldness' of India in its incomplete narrative and unfulfilled promise, which invites complexity and fulfilment'.

3 Daniel Thorner/Alice Thorner, The Emergence of the Indian Economy. In: Land and Labour in India, Bombay 1962.

4 See Damodar Dharmanand Kosambi, An Introduction to the Study of Indian History, Bombay 1956 and 1973 (revised edition), chapters 9 and 10.

5 A variant of this view ist best argued by the finest of the historians of the British Indian imperial connection, Peter Marshall, Western Arms in Maritime Asia in the Early Phases of Expansion. In: Modern Asian Studies, *14*(1980), pp. 13-28. Marshall shows how the British-Indian coordination of military organization created a new imperial identity which gave the British a cutting edge over European and Indian competitors. He goes further and says 'Sometimes aided by European mercenaries, Indian states began to organise their infantry into disciplined formations and to improve their artillery. More and more guns came from Europe - 'hardly a ship came' in the 1960s 'that did not sell them cannon and small arms', and gun founding was further developed, especially in Southern India' (p. 27). The Awadh troope at Buxar and the Mysore formations gave British power a tough fight before defeat. 'The future Duke of Wellington's Victory at Assaye in 1803 was no more an easy triumph for superior western technology and organization than had been Francisco de Almeida's at Diu in 1509'. But Professor Marshall balances much too nicely in the direction of British Indian 'partnership in empire' in his last paragraph: 'The initiative for introducing new weapons and tactics had usually come from Europe, the professional standards of European soldiers and seamen were probably higher than those of their Asian contemporaries, and the European states and trading companies could plan and organize the use of force with a tenacity of purpose rarely matched on the Asian side. But these advantages had been to a large extent nullified by distance. The European challenge had not been on such a scale that Asians could not adapt to meet it.' (p. 28) In actual fact, maritime Asia was soundly subordinated and defeated in the century from 1757 to 1857.

6 The usage 'Muslim tyranny' as a category differentiated from 'British rule' was first pointed out by Tanika Sarkar, The Concept of Muslim Tyranny: An Unbroken Tradition. In: Presidency College Magazine, Dec. 1972.

7 See Samuel Charles Hill/Yusuf Khan, The Rebel Commandant, London 1914.

8 The actual text is hyperbolic, though arresting: 'The history of all hitherto existing society is the history of class struggles. Freeman and slave, patrician and plebeian, lord and serf, guild-master and journeyman, oppressor and oppressed stand in constant opposition to one another...' The qualifications to the sweeping generalisations are made in a footnote. Karl Marx/Friedrich Engels, Manifesto of the Communist Party (1848, printed according to the 1888 edition). In: Selected Works, Volume One, Moscow 1973, pp. 108/109.

9 The word 'subaltern' in standard English idiom is still used for 'juniormost officer' - archaic 'cornet or ensign, below the rank of lieutenant, but above the ranker class'. Its rather quirky translation from the Italian 'subalterna' to mean 'subordinate' or 'lower' was made by Quintin Hoare and Geoffrey Nowell Smith, Selections from the Prison Notebooks of Antonio Gramsci, New York 1971, who note on p.xiii-xiv, Questions of censorship (leading to 'circumlocution'): '...apart, Gramsci's terminology presents a number of difficulties to the translator: ... Non-hegemonic groups or classes are also called by Gramsci 'subordinate', 'subaltern' or sometimes 'instrumental' ... it is difficult to discern any systematic difference in Gramsci's usage between, for instance, subaltern and subordinate'. Ranajit Guha heralding his co-operative's bestselling series Subaltern Studies I, Oxford University Press, New Delhi 1982, without noting that 'subaltern' has many meanings in the Oxford Dictionary in its many versions, states flatly: 'The word 'subaltern' stands for the meaning as given in The Concise Oxford Dictionary, that is, 'of inferior rank'. It will be used in these pages as a name for the general attribute of subordination in South Asian society whether this is expressed in terms of class, caste, age, gender or office, or in any other way.' (Preface).

10 See Surendra Nath Banerji, A Nation in Making, Being the Reminiscences of Fifty Years of Public Life, London 1925.

11 For Britannocentric views of the impact of European influence on Indian thought, see David Kopf, British Orientalism and Bengal Renaissance. The Dynamics of Indian Modernisation, 1773-1835, Calcutta 1969.

12 John Plamenetz, Two Types of Nationalism. In: Eugene Kamenka (ed.), Nationalism, the Nature and Evolution of an Idea, London 1976, chapter 2, passim.

13 'The Indian Bourgeoisie Comes of Ages' was published in Kosambi's early collection, Exasperating Essays, which is not close to my hand at the moment of writing. A clear idea of Kosambi's social views will be found in: On the Class Structure of India. In: Monthly Review, New York *VDI*(1954), pp. 205-213, reprinted in A.J. Syed (ed.), D.D. Kosambi on History and Society. Problems of Interpretation, Bombay University 1985, pp. 133-142.

14 Ibid., pp. 65-71, What Constitutes Indian History, first published in: Annals of the Bhandarkar Oriental Research Institute, Poona *XXXV*(1954/55), pp. 194-201.

15 See Eric Hobsbawm, Mass-Producing Traditions: Europe 1870-1914. In: Eric Hobsbawm/Terence Ranger, The Invention of Tradition, Cambridge 1983, pp. 263-307, and Roland Barthes, Myth Today, edited and introduced by Susan Sontag. In: Roland Barthes, Selected Writings, Fontana 1983, pp. 101/102, for clues on these points.

16 Karl Marx, The Eighteenth Brunaire of Louis Bonaparte. In: Marx/Engels, Selected Works, I, loc. cit., p. 398.

# Caste and the Politics of Identity: Beyond the Orientalist Discourse[1]

Subrata Mitra

## The Problem defined

Why does caste, after four decades of social legislation, modern education and liberal democratic politics, continue to be a significant factor in India's public life? The question, posed to oriental circles at the turn of the century would have raised few eyebrows, because Indian society was meant to be like that, and, the thin modern coating added to it by British rule notwithstanding, could not behave in any other way. Today, an active electorate of five hundred million people questions some of the premises of the orientalist approach which considered Indian society incapable of selfdefinition or self-regulation. Nevertheless, as the spectre of 'caste war' and communal violence live up to a scenario all too familiar to the orientalists, there is the occasional throwback to the heady days of orientalism among 'essentialists', who present caste as the immutable essence of Indian society. Opposed to this is the instrumentalist approach which presents caste as merely a politically convenient self-classification for the purpose of material benefits. The paper explores the issue of the resilience of caste with reference to essence and agency, two views of caste that compete and occasionally conflate in the context of India's vibrant political process.

When Jawaharlal Nehru inaugurated the new republic of India with the famous speech on Freedom at Midnight, he gave voice to a section of the Indian elite that wished to see India transformed into a modern, secular state. Their aspirations were enshrined in the constitutional norms of equal citizenship, fundamental rights to equality and liberty, irrespective of caste, creed, religion or place of birth, and the judicial and bureaucratic apparatus of a modern state with which to implement these lofty ideals. Four decades after independence, some of these hopes lie shattered in the ruins of the Babri Mosque of Ayodhya and in the killing fields of Bihar and other places routinely afflicted with caste wars. The emergence of the politics of identity, where groups based on caste, religion, tribe and region appear as the main actors, once again raises an issue that gave rise to the original orientalist discourse: are the institutions of liberal democracy appropriate to India? Nehru, intensely aware of the dangers of communal violence, was familiar with the problem. Reproachful as they were, the modernist leadership of the Congress had watched with helpless fascination as the Muslim League, wielding religion as a vehicle of mass mobilisation, had fought for and won the right to have a separate homeland for Muslims. The stigma of the failure to resist the demand for the partition of India on the basis of religion, and the communal carnage that marked the birth of the new republic had convinced Nehru that the evils of caste and religion had to be firmly kept out of the public arena. In Nehru's view, shared by the ruling elite, drawn from a largely urban, professional and western educated background, the scientific spirit, technology, planning, social legislation and a rational bureaucracy were the answer.

**The resilience of caste**

In view of the aspirations of India's modernising elite, the ability of castes to survive large-scale social and economic change and to mutate into modern forms like caste associations continues to be a puzzle. That caste 'survives' is clear from several diachronic studies based on fieldwork.[2] What remains unclear is exactly which attributes of caste survive and why. Its protagonists constantly slip in and out of the two faces of caste - the traditional endogamous status groups organised around specific occupations - and caste associations where people come together using social ties for the purpose of promoting collective interest. Thanks to its liminality, caste appears as the quintessential Janus of Indian politics, with a jati face, turned towards the varna scheme and through it, to Indian tradition and identity, capable of moving people in ways and areas beyond the reach of modern institutions; and, an associational face which links it with the institutional fabric of the modern state. The political actor deftly manipulates both faces in order to generate power through this complex repertoire.

Interpreting caste therefore leads to the larger issue of how to relate the ontology of jati and varna (of which caste and the caste-system are but inadequate representations) to the moral basis of society and state in India. Here, the battle lines are clearly drawn. Essentialists and orientalists have a similar understanding of Indian tradition. Both views hold that castes, ensconced in the varna scheme, are the bedrock of Indian tradition. The secular modernists of India, on the other hand, view caste as synonymous with underdevelopment, hierarchy and prejudice. They wish to jettison it altogether. Essentialists, whose instinctive and political sympathies are for preserving the pure spirit of Indian civilisation in amber, ridicule such attempts as derivative, and, ultimately self-defeating. The fact, however, that in reality caste survives, and mutates, serves only to throw empirical doubts about both the rival schools.

While the larger issue helps relate endogenous institutions like caste to culture and identity in post-colonial societies, it is not possible within the limited space of an article to explore all aspects of the problem. The solution adopted here is to constitute the arguments and evidence into two parts. Part one will juxtapose an instrumental view of caste against the essentialist view that depicts it as the immutable essence of an ageless Indian society. Rather than being the essence of Hinduism, it will be argued, caste is a resource that political actors use in order to negotiate their status, wealth, power and identity. Evidence for this can be seen from the fact that castes are present outside the fold of Hinduism; that caste systems are based not on ideological consensus but social conformity maintained by force; and the continuous regeneration of caste is due to its instrumental value. Part two of the article will apply the instrumental view of caste to competitive politics since independence. Through these examples it would be shown that the inter-penetration of the traditional society and the modern state, brought about through the agency of caste, is the basis of its resilience. The conclusion will draw the broader implications of some of these arguments for an endogenous modernity.

## The Orientalist essence of Caste

Popular and scholarly perceptions of caste present it as an essentially Hindu institution. 'In its most literal interpretation', caste is perceived as 'an exclusively Indian phenomenon', not parallelled by any other institution elsewhere in its 'complexity, elaboration and inflexibility'. It 'moulds the psychology of the people', 'predetermines an individual's or family's pattern of behaviour in society' and 'plays a major role in the choice of leadership particularly in rural areas'. Further, 'from the individual's point of view, caste provides him with a fixed social status, limits his choice in marriage, determines his occupation and dictates to him the customs to be observed in the matter of diet, ceremonies and rituals at birth, initiation and death'[3]. This view of caste as a unique and enduring institution is reinforced by a long tradition in anthropology. 'Caste', as Hutton writes, 'no doubt keeps changing, and customs come and go; the pattern alters, but the principles that govern it, the frames that hold the pattern so to speak, are exceptionally constant for a human institution.'[4]

The popular perception of caste is informed by its depiction as a fixed presence, not contingent on the material basis of society, but, instead, exerting a decisive influence on it. It is supposed to derive its power from deeply ingrained beliefs in the Hindu psyche. These views were put together by Kroeber who defined caste as 'an endogamous and hereditary subdivision of an ethnic unit occupying a position of superior or inferior rank or social esteem in comparison with other such subdivisions'. Following this definition, he described the caste systems as systems of social stratification, examples of ranked aggregates of people, that are unusually rigid, birth-ascribed, and permit no individual mobility'[5]. Based on this definition of caste, a 'caste system can be said to occur when a society is composed of birth-ascribed, hierarchically ordered, and culturally distinct groups (castes). The hierarchy entails differential evaluations, differential rewards, and differential association. Castes are discrete, bounded and ranked entities. In a caste system, everyone belongs to a caste and no one belongs to more than one caste'[6].

Both the popular understanding of caste and its empirical description have been influenced by the theoretical explanations of its origin provided by writers who find a transcendent explanation for the existence of the social order in the ideology of caste. In terms of its composition, Hindu society is seen by them as uniquely based on caste, and, thus, necessarily different from their non-Hindu and the European counterparts. Quigley summarises the views of the writers of this genre in terms of the following basic premises:

'a) Traditional society is holistic: modern society is individualistic.
b) Because we [moderns] are individualistic, we always perceive hierarchy in terms of inequality: traditional society perceives hierarchy in terms of holism.
c) The principle of hierarchy is the *attribution* of a rank to each element in relation to the whole[7] (emphasis in original, S.M.). This is what 'holism' means.
d) In order to understand traditional society, we must transcend our individualistic ideology and embrace the holistic vision. Comparative sociology (anthropology) is impossible without this transcendence.'[8]

Seen thus, the political role of caste is theoretically unproblematic. Its existence is meant only to provide political reinforcement to a moral vision of Hindu society that is essentially hierarchic, based on the predominant concern of ridding oneself of pollution and consecrating the whole of material life to the search for moksha which can come from the pursuit of purity. It is easy to see why this essentialist view of caste, seen as a representation of Indian society, arouses such passionate debate. As an ideology of state-society relations, it is in many ways the opposite of the concept of equality that India's secular intellectuals consider to be the core value of the Indian state. For political reformers and intellectual advocates of modernity, caste comes across as a vestige of tradition irrevocably opposed to the modern world of democracy, social justice and economic growth.[9] This view of caste, ardently espoused by many educated Indians continues to underpin the debate on such contentious issues as religion, identity and, of course, the caste system itself.

### A Critique of the Essentialist View of Caste

Critical traditionalism, particularly the ideas of Gandhi, has had a significant though limited impact on the scholarly writings on Indian politics and the role of caste in it. In their *Modernity of Tradition* (1967) and the research on caste associations, the Rudolphs pointed in the direction of the ability of traditional institutions to act as a vehicle for modern functions.[10] However, the inability to specify caste actor as a hinge group who draws strength from both tradition and modernity and creates new norms in the process gave their findings an appearance of eclecticism, born out of an indulgence towards India's tradition rather than rigorous theoretical analysis.

Their assertion of the potential for modernity hidden within tradition was seen as an acknowledgement of India's fundamental difference from western societies and, thus, an affirmation of her uniqueness. Given a choice between ascriptive, hierarchy bound tradition and egalitarian and individualistic modernity, the Rudolphs gave the impression of arguing on both sides of the issue. Their position was severely criticised by Fox who referred pointedly to the tautological implications of their formulation. 'If aspects of the traditional survive', said Fox, 'it is because they had this potentiality; if they do not, it is because they lacked this potential ability.'[11]

Fox's criticism of the Rudolph's position gave a clear indication of the methodological difficulty of describing phenomena like caste that are endogenous to a culture in terms of categories extrinsic to it. When tradition and modernity are seen as dichotomous categories and caste is seen as the essence of Indian tradition as described by Dumont, the terms of social science discourse, informed as they are of the western values of individualism, limited government and secular state, would scarcely be in position to describe them empirically. Inden refers to this problem of cognition as typical to post-colonial societies where a traditional society and modern state face one another in mutual incomprehension. From this perspective, the roots of caste wars and communal conflicts go back to the manner in which the secular principle was enshrined within the constitution and the spirit in which it was implemented in practice. From the beginning, despite the end of foreign colonial rule, no consistent attempts were made to derive the principle of government from local and regional cultural and political traditions in India. The result, as Inden reminds us, was a 'nationstate that remains ontologically and politically inaccessible to its own citizens. Its government continues to be just like its immediate British Indian ancestor, merely a neutral enforcer of unity on a morselized society, continually in danger of being pulled apart by 'centrifugal' forces.'[12]

Caste associations, neo-castes, religious communities with a multi-plex role, whose anomalous presence at the heart of Indian politics inhibits the creation of a parsimonious theory are indicative of the ontological difficulty that Inden refers to. An anti-essentialist view which takes actors seriously and seeks to understand the political reality through categories intrinsic to the society will be of greater use in understanding the political evolution of Indian society. These issues can be discussed with reference to social stratification and the role of secular power in its maintenance and social interaction and the management of conflict.

The essentialist view paints the picture of a homeostatic society where different groups are organically linked. The anti-essentialist view does not deny the existence of society nor the complementarity of needs for which social transaction provides a mechanism of exchange. It only suggests that status inconsistency is an inevitable byproduct of this process, so that, at least in the short run, the role of force is indispensable for the maintenance of the caste system. Caste societies are not homeostatic; they generate enormous conflict and have to be maintained by force. Hence, politics becomes the cutting edge, society's method of 'self-correction'.[13]

The role of force in the maintenance of local caste systems and its collapse through the organisation of countervailing force can be seen in Robinson (1988), Beteille (1983), and Frankel and Rao (1989, 1990).[14]

Sociocultural change brought about through the instrumentality of caste provides further evidence of an anti-essentialist position. Within caste systems there is constant mobility striving. It is generally sought through 'status emulation' as groups attempt to imitate their social superiors. Mobility striving, while intrinsic in caste systems, is a constant threat to the status quo. It is suppressed whenever possible, but the process of suppression is difficult and never completely effective. Commenting on this process of constant contestation, Berreman suggests: 'They [the caste hierarchy] are maintained not by agreement but by sanctions. It takes much physical and psychic energy to maintain an inherently unstable, conflictive situation as a semblance of working order. The high-status groups must suppress mobility striving among others; rules restricting social interaction must be enforced; the purity and integrity of the group must be maintained; a myth of stability must be supported in the face of overt disconfirming evidence. On the part of low-status people, self-respect must be maintained despite constant denigration; resentment must be suppressed or carefully channelled.'[15]

Historical research reported by Professor Gould presents a contrasting picture of continuous change that differs radically from the essentialist image of unchanging Indian society. In the first of his three volumes he explores the origin of the caste system in terms of the 'sacralisation' of the occupational order and 'occupationalisation' of the sacred order in pre-industrial India, leading to the creation of an intricate social nexus. Professor Gould shows how urban professionals as well as rural politicians draw on the cohesive functions of caste in the course of their everyday political transactions. The result is a continuous creation of new social groups. These have been unsatisfactorily labelled as caste associations, because they are rarely formal enough to merit being called associations and while they might use the idiom of caste as a vehicle, caste is not the cause of their origin. It is best to understand the creation of new social groups in terms of political communities.'[16]

## Sacred Beliefs and Secular Power

The orientalist view of caste presented an essentialised version of Indian society where the desire for *moksha* and the avoidance of pollution provided a transcendental basis for the material organisation of society. A corollary of this view is the subordinate role that the repositories of secular power were expected to play with regard to those in charge of spiritual matters. Thus, the pure should rule the impure; the raja should be the inferior of the brahmin. A brief review of the literature shows that the situation was much more complex and regionally varied.

The first point that needs to be made here is that traditionally, belief was never considered absolute or in the abstract but only in reference to practice. 'There never was any question of a subject's being; entitled to put his beliefs into practice if society objected, for all *adhikaras* [which in its original usage implies both a right and a duty] came into existence within the sphere of a society and when societies became numerous or complex the king kept the balance within or between them. The king's failing to do this could not be contemplated: it meant the end of dharmas and the Rule of the Fish [*matsya-nyayal*].'[17] The holy text of Hinduism both ordained and approved of intervention by the temporal power and assemblies in the social and moral life of the community. 'When Manu tells us that different customs prevailed in different ages he suggests that the social code is not a fixed but a flexible one. Social customs and institutions are subject to change.' Derrett adds further that 'the state may determine what the law is within the general framework of dharma'. Political authority within the Indian state tradition required the mutual accommodation of the King and the Brahmin, responsible, respectively for secular power and sacred beliefs. In the Indian tradition, 'the regnum (*kshatra*) could not subsist on its own without the sacerdotium (*brahma*) which provided its principle of legitimacy.'[18] The role that the king as the representative of secular power plays in the interpretation of the codes of good conduct, sometimes in collusion and occasionally in competition with the Brahmin shows the position of neither was absolute or fixed within a social hierarchy. Referring to this, Quigley suggests that 'the entrenched ideal that 'Brahmans are the highest caste' has done most to hinder an alternative formulation of how caste system works.'[19]

## Macro Politics, Micro Society

The essentialist view summarised by Quigley (see page 4 above) presents Indian society as an internally undifferentiated whole which is politically self-sustaining. The anti-essentialist view which recognises the relative autonomy of politics, has been considerably reinforced since the growth of representative politics. The process started with the spread of British rule set in motion an inexorable process of change. Hardgrave's narrative of the 'breast cloth controversy' gives a vivid account of the transformation of the status of the untouchable toddy tappers of the Shanan caste as a consequence of the increase in the market value of their produce and the patronage extended to them by British troops stationed nearby.[20] The increase in wealth and relative decline in their dependence on local clients was reinforced by the influence of missionaries who encouraged Shanan women to cover the upper parts of their bodies like upper caste women. The departure from local norms of subordinate status and the resultant conflict which would have been severely dealt with within the local political arena now invited intervention by the police and courts of law leading to a settlement in favour of the Shanan women.

Subsequently, the Shanans took advantage of the recently introduced decennial census to have themselves recorded as Nadars. Within a few decades Kamraj Nadar, a member of this caste became the Chief Minister of the State who, as Congress President, was responsible for getting Indira Gandhi elected to the leadership of the Congress party and the Prime Minister of the country.

**Caste and Competitive Politics**

The introduction of limited franchise under British rule had already created a stir among the Indian electorate. The ensuing competition, and the differential mobilisation by untouchables had led to a strong reaction among the Congress leadership which saw the communal electorate as an attempt by the British to divide and rule. One of the legacies of the Poona Pact, which symbolised a historic rapproachment between the leaders of the untouchables and the Congress leadership was to set aside a quota for the representatives of the untouchables. The second legacy was the knowledge that local hierarchy could be renegotiated at the level of high politics through competitive electoral mobilisation. The lesson was not lost on the electorate, particularly among the less privileged sections after independence when universal adult suffrage was introduced in one fell swoop. After an initial interlude during which the locally dominant castes transformed the jajmani relations into a veritable vote bank through what the Rudolphs have called vertical mobilisation. However, intra-elite conflict and land reforms which helped further loosen the dependent relations between the locally dominant caste and those who worked for them quickly led to a situation of factional conflict and short term political alliances, called differential mobilisation. By the 1960s, electoral mobilisation had led to a new phenomena called horizontal mobilisation whereby people situated at comparable levels within the local caste hierarchy came together in caste associations. One consequence of horizontal mobilisation was the formation of new parties like the Republican Party, the Bahujan Samaj Party primarily supported by former untouchables or the various kisan parties and movements like the Lok Dal which draw their support mainly from the backward classes, which aggressively promoted sectional interest through the electoral arena.

One of the main consequences of four decades of competitive electoral politics on the local caste hierarchy has been to render all inherited relations of power necessarily contestable. The congruence of status, power and wealth, tenuous even at a period when little recourse for status negotiation was available outside the local arena has been further contested. As Washbrook reminds us, '...the merest sight or smell of privilege in any area of society instantly provokes antipathetic response among those who see or smell it. No privilege is inherently legitimate and no authority exists uncontested.'[21]

For the ease of presentation, we can conceptualise the role of caste as a factor in political behaviour in terms of an analytical scheme (table 1). Membership of a caste, ensconced within the local caste hierarchy can be perceived by some of its members as an obligation to support their social superiors. As the logic of political participation has spread through the Indian electorate, and the percentage of people taking part in elections has grown, 'vote banks' which functioned on the basis of vertical obligation have become progressively rare. As things stand now, it is common to find factions - short term political alliances - where one can find voters following their own interest and utilising all political resources at their command, including the membership of a caste.

Table 1
**Caste and Political Competition**

| *Value* | *Norm* | *Modality* | *Structure* | *Mobilisation Process* |
|---|---|---|---|---|
| Primordial (essence) | Obligation | Jajmani | Vote Banks | Vertical |
| Rational (agency) | Interest | Political orgainsation | Multi-caste Caste Associations | Differential Horizontal |

The scenario of contestation that Washbrook describes from the case of Tamil Nadu is repeated daily in all parts of India.[22] Underneath the violence and atrocities perpetrated in its name, caste is actively present as a factor in electoral mobilisation. Does caste consciousness perpetuate inherited caste related inequalities? What might sound counter-intuitive is in fact one of the enigmas of caste, for caste consciousness in fact destroys precisely those attributes of the caste system such as traditional social obligations, hierarchy and dominance which, the essentialist view presented as necessarily fixed in time and space. The point will be discussed at greater length below.

## Caste and the Politics of Positive Discrimination

Caste is conceptualised in the Indian constitution as the principal factor behind social hierarchy, inequality and social closure. Rather than banishing it altogether by a constitutional fiat, the constitution combats it in two distinct but related ways. The constitution specifically outlaws caste as a cause of discrimination along with gender, race, place of birth. Article 15, in laying down the norms of the right to equality for all citizens, provides for equal access to all aspects of political as well as civil life.

The practice of untouchability is prohibited by the constitution. 'The enforcement of any disability arising out of 'Untouchability' shall be an offence punishable in accordance with law' (article 17). The provision was given considerable force by the Untouchability Prohibition Act of 1955 which has subsequently been amended to give it even greater force. The new law, called the civil rights act is much more far reaching in its scope.

In the second place, the constitution provides for a range of political and legal instruments to combat past inequalities through positive discrimination in representation, public services, allocation of educational, economic and social facilities. A subsection of the fundamental provision for equal rights lays down categorically: 'Nothing in this article ... shall prevent the State from making any special provision for the advancement of any socially and educationally backward classes of citizens or for the Scheduled Castes and the Scheduled Tribes.' In addition, the constitution has provided for a number of administrative machinery to watch over the interests of the former untouchables, tribes and backward classes.

Not surprisingly, this has led to considerable political agitation by social groups who feel unjustly dispossessed of what they consider their fair share of the national wealth. The backlash against reservation policies has been fierce and widely spread. The rhetoric of the anti-reservation movement, couched in the abstract language of merit and equality both of which are supposedly violated by affirmative action should be familiar to those who have followed similar movements in other cultures. The unique element, which on the face of it appears eminently plausible is that while the idea of positive discrimination is both noble and necessary, by choosing caste as the basis of special privilege, a fresh lease of life is given to an institution which really ought to disappear. This argument, which has been discussed at length in the literature on reservation,[23] is based on an inadequate understanding of the dialectics of caste and caste consciousness.

The main achievement of the double instruments of legal equality and positive discrimination has been to sever the psychological link between jati and occupation. That some former untouchables do in fact succeed in securing high positions in public life gives credibility to the symbolic value of the policy. The instrumental role that caste plays both in raising consciousness and electoral mobilisation actually underlines the ideological basis of the varna scheme. Thus, 'while legitimizing caste at one level, it [the reservation policy] subtly underlined it at another level. Dissociated from its material roots, the consciousness of caste becomes purely formal, a badge of politically convenient self-classification to be manipulated and waved when necessary. [Now] A chamar does not automatically and instinctively think of himself as a chamar: rather he now presents himself as one to secure certain advantages. His being is detached from his self-consciousness, and that is a remarkable gain. Caste consciousness is a ladder he uses to climb out of a social cul-de-sac, and having got to the top he kicks it away. The dialectic of reservation is far more subtle than is generally appreciated.'[24]

## Caste, Community and Modern Politics

Formation of communities is the predictable outcome of the new atmosphere of competitive, modern politics where the logic of numbers and scarce resources is increasingly clear to social groups trying to acquire new privileges or to hold on to what once appeared securely theirs but is now coveted by other groups. The politics of community formation can be presented in terms of an analytical schema. (table 2) Unlike 'modern' or 'traditional' organisations, a community is a necessarily liminal structure, with a vernacular face turned towards local society to which it appeals in terms recognisable to the local arena; and, a universal associational face turned towards the modern state and the market. The caste association is the most frequent but not the only type of community one is likely to come across in contemporary Indian politics.

Table 2
**The Politics of Community Formation**

| | *Identity* | *Area* | *Strategy* |
|---|---|---|---|
| *Caste (jati)* | thick | insular | close |
| *community (sampradaya)* | thin | broad | open |

Seen as communities, castes are uniquely Indian in form but universal in content. Under the impact of four decades of electoral competition, social legislation and new economic opportunities and new political linkages have developed. Castes, as the analysis undertaken here has attempted to show, have never been the rigid, timeless essence of an unchanging India. The introduction of competitive politics and democratic institutions have quickened the pace of change in the social and political organisation of castes, increasingly perceived as communities in which people come together to promote collective interest. Castes are now perceived not as rigid but flexible by their members who treat them more as vehicles of self-promotion rather than a structure of domination by the powerful and self-censorship by the powerless. 'Scholars', as Inden argues, kept India 'eternally ancient' by attributing to her various 'essences, most notably that of caste'[25]. A new perspective which can depict India's institutions and political discourse as instruments through which her people seek to influence the course of their history therefore should start with a re-evaluation of caste.

## Conclusion

Simon Schama, in his widely acclaimed *Citizens: A Chronicle of the French Revolution* provides a broad range of historical evidence that modernisation theory has not taken into account in its prescriptive models about the transformation of traditional societies. Schama's criticism of these ahistorical presentation of modernisation in the sense of a great rupture, is scathing: 'Institutionally torpid, economically immobile, culturally atrophied and socially stratified, this 'old regime' was incapable of self-modernization. The Revolution needed to smash it to pieces before acting as a Great Accelerator on the highway to the nineteenth century. Beforehand, all was inertia; afterwards, all was energy; beforehand, there was corporatism and *Gemeinschaft*; afterwards, individualism and *Gesellschaft*. The Revolution, in short, was the permitting condition of modernity.'[26]
Following Shama's evidence, one can see how the *ancien regime* was not merely the decrepit and hollow political shell that it is often made out to be. Many of the financial and technological innovations of pre-revolutionary France were carried on to the new republic once the *interruption* of the Revolution was over. The other feature of the Revolution that modernisation theory does not take into account is the sacralisation of revolutionary symbols in a manner that conforms more to the mystique that surrounds authority in traditional societies rather than the rationality that modernity swears by. The invincible duo of the Goddess of Reason and the guillotine to which lesser mortals were to pay obeisance would outlive the revolutionary turmoil into recent times when the cry 'Republic in Danger' would bring out deeply seated reserves of communal will.

The cognitive problem of the ruling elites of post-colonial states with regard to their own societies as pointed out by Inden is the consequence of a double derivative. Their knowledge of modernity derives out of western sociological theories of social change which, themselves, as Schama points out, are empirically inadequate. The new politics of identity which draws both on pre-colonial values and the experience of countries other than the coloniser has produced a political agenda which the institutions of the postcolonial successor state cannot completely comprehend. By drawing on the specific example of the resilience of caste, this essay has tried to make a general point about the need for a comprehensive re-examination of the tools of our enquiry in a manner that would reflect the need for an endogenous modernity.

The article has argued that while castes are omnipresent and have been the subject of extensive field research, this general interest in caste is not matched by a general and parsimonious theory of its resilience.

Communities, drawing on the solidarity of caste networks are increasingly present in Indian politics where modern institutions compete for space with the traditional. The article has attempted to provide the groundwork for an explanation for these characters in search of an author, by first questioning the established view of caste as the essence of rigid, ageless India; and, then, formulating a conjecture that relates the resilience of caste to the search for identity, power and material benefits in India's competitive politics.

Whether one looks at the role of caste in elections, or its involvement with social and economic life in contemporary India, it becomes quite clear that the empirical complexity of caste is not reflected in its ontological perception by many educated Indians. Whereas the former points towards a social institution of enormous vitality, the latter dismisses it as a vestige of the past whose disappearance is a pre--condition for the great leap into the brave new world of modernity. The continuation of this 'orientalist' perception of caste, the article has argued, serves only to drive a wedge between the state and society. This intellectual stigma prevents law, bureaucracy and the media from doing precisely those things that would help transform caste from being an instrument of political oppression, hierarchy and social closure to the social basis of a plural and multi-cultural nation. 'A modern state, especially one as richly diverse as India, cannot be a collection of decommunalized individual atoms. It is and cannot but be a community of communities. Unless they are exclusive and politically divisive, corporate identities including healthy and suitable redefined caste identities are conducive to rather than hinder India's political integrity.'[27]

The analysis presented here seeks to describe the evolution of India's society and state in terms of a scheme that lays the baseline of analysis at the segmentary state whose dispersed authority structure was ensconced within a fragmented society where the jati formed the basic social unit.[28] The pan-Indian varna scheme provided a structure of ideological integration and social cohesion to these local jatis and regional varna schemes.[29] The relative power, status and rank of these social units was mediated by the 'enticing but enigmatic figure of the king.'[30] Authority within the Indian state tradition was the result of mutual legitimation of the raja and the brahmin, though, the specific nature of the balance of power depended on the local context.[31] The flux that characterised the system and in many parts of India, survived the arrival of Muslim rule.[32] It went into suspended animation once the British gained complete political supremacy. On their part, the British, after the bitter experience of the Mutiny, refrained from direct intervention with Indian society. The colonial prejudices against the ability of Indian society to be self-governing were complemented by the orientalist constructions of caste and Indian religion.

The arrival of independence and universal franchise greatly accelerated the competition for social status that had already started under British rule thanks to the slow extension of popular representation. The discussion of caste and competitive politics has shown how caste consciousness and multicaste factions served to challenge the domination of traditional social notables of upper castes. This dialectic of castes and democracy has produced communities that have emerged as the most vital link between the traditional society and the modern state and the market. The confluence of intense competition for benefits and the politics of identity has produced a fertile field, where new identities and norms are constantly produced as the necessary parameters within which transactional politics can be conducted.

Liberal democratic theory and the constitution of India consider the free interplay of voluntary associations as a legitimate method for the promotion of collective interest. In fact, the constitution, which is deeply committed to individual interest and representation, also makes symbolic overtures towards traditional values and symbols. Thus, the constitution itself introduces the dialectic between the individual and the society as the basis of nation and state formation in India. From this perspective, the uncomprehending polemics with which communities as political actors are greeted by India's secular intellectuals appears as a new form of orientalism in Indian guise. Further reflection would make it clear that the solution against the criminal activities that are conducted in the name of caste, is not to ban caste or for that matter religion constitutionally but to produce the political and institutional conditions under which they can function as legitimate social associations. The judicial and administrative institutions of the state should make sure that the organisation is accountable to its members, and that it functions within the parameters of the law. The Indian Constitution and Supreme Court provide the necessary institutional basis for this. There is still plenty of as yet unexplored potential for further social development within the ambit of India's social institutions for the creation of an endogenous modernity through which the society and state can be sure to gain mutual cognitive access.

## Notes

1 I wish to thank Marie-Thérèse O'Toole for her comments on an earlier draft.

2 Harold Gould, The Hindu Caste System, Delhi 1990; Subrata Mitra, Cast, Class and Conflict: Organization and Ideological Change in an Orissa Village. In: Purusartha 6(1982), p. 97-133.

3 Chambers Encyclopedia, p. 150.

4 J.H. Hutton, Caste in India, 1950, cited in: Chamber's Encyclopedia, p. 151.

5 A.L. Kroeber, Caste. In: Encyclopedia of the Social Scineces, New York 1930, vol. 3, p. 254.

6 Gerald Berreman, The Concept of Caste. In: International Encyclopedia of the Social Sciences, New York 1968, p. 334.

7 Louis Dumont, Homo Hierarchicus, The Caste System and its Implications, Chicago 1980, p. 91.

8 Quigley ascribes this part to A.M. Hocart, Caste: A Comparative Study, London 1950, but the main reference here is to the works of Dumont. See Declan Quigley, The Interpretation of Caste, Oxford 1993; Edward Said, Orientalism, London 1978.

9 Parekh talks about the efforts of India's modernist leadership, particularly Nehru which 'condemned caste, 'casteism' and 'caste-mindedness'. but did not know how to slay these demons.' See Bhikhu Parekh, Caste Wars. In: The Times Higher Education Supplement, 15 February 1991, p. 13.

10 Lloyd Rudolph/Susanne Rudolph, The Modernity of Tradition, Chicago 1967.

11 Richard Fox, The Avatars of Indian Research. In: Comparative Studies in Society and History *12*(1970)1.

12 Ronald Inden, Imagining India, Oxford 1990, p.197.

13 See Ashis Nandy, The Making and Unmaking of Political Cultures in India. In: Ashis Nandy, At the edge of Psychology: Essays in Politics and Culture , Delhi 1980, p. 50.

14 See Marguerite Robinson, Local Politics: The Law of the Fishes. Development through Political Change in Medak District, Andhra Pradesh (South India), Delhi 1988; André Beteille, The Idea of Natural Inequality and Other Essays, Delhi 1983; Francine Frankel/M.S.A. Rao (ed.), Dominance and State Power in Modern India: Decline of a Social Order, vols. I and II, Delhi 1989/1990.

15 Gerald Berreman, The Concept of Caste. In: International Encyclopaedia of Social Sciences, New York 1968, p. 338.

16 For a review of Gould, The Hindu Caste System, 3 vols., Delhi 1990, see Subrata Mitra, The Hindu Caste System. In: Contemporary South Asia, pp. 435-437.

17 Duncan Derrett, Religion, Law and the State in India, London 1968, p. 560.

18 Derrett quotes Coomasswamy to suggest the complementarity of sacred and secular power as follows: 'The King says to the priest: 'Turn thou unto me so that we may unite... I assign to you the precendence: quickened by by thee I shall perform deeds.'' Ananda Coomaraswamy, Spiritual Authority and Temporal Power in the Indian Theory of Government, New Delhi 1978, p. 81.

19 Quigley, The Interpretation..., p. 169.

20 Robert Hardgrave, The Breast Cloth Controversy. In: Indian Economic History Review (1982).

21 D.A. Washbrook, Caste, Class and Dominance in Modern Tamil Nadu: Non-Brahmism, Dravidianism and Tamil Nationalism. In: Frankel/Rao, Dominance and State Power..., vol. 1, p. 227.

22 See Douglas Haynes/Gyan Prakash (eds.), Contesting Power: Restistance and Everyday Social Relations in South Asia, Berkeley 1991.

23 See Rekha Kaul, Caste, Class and Education: Politics of the Capitation Fee Phenomenon in Karnataka, Delhi 1993; Mitra, Politics...

24 Parekh/Mitra, The Logic of Anti-reservation Discourse in India. In: Subrata Mitra (ed.), Politics of Positive Discrimination: A Cross National Perspective, Bombay 1990, p. 106-107.

25 Inden, Imagining..., p. 1.

26 Simon Schama, Citizens: A Chronicle of the French Revolution, London 1989, p. 184.

27 Parekh/Mitra, The Logic..., p. 107.

28 See Subrata Mitra (ed.), The Post-colonial State in Asia, Harvester 1991.

29 See R.G. Fox, Varna Schemes and Ideological Integration in Indian Society. In: Comparative Studies in Siociety and History, vol. 11, 1969, p. 27-44.

30 See D. Shulman, The King and Clown in South Indian Myth and Poetry, Princeton, N.Y. 1985, p. 15.

31 Ibid.

32 See Annecharlott Eschman/Hermann Kulke/Gaya Charan Tripathi (eds.), The Cult of Jagannath and the Regional Tradition of Orissa, Delhi 1986.

# Foci of Identity Construction

# Kultur, Identität und Politik in Saudi-Arabien

Peter Heine

Die Geschichte der Staatenbildung im Nahen und Mittleren Osten seit dem Zusammenbruch des Osmanischen Reiches als Ergebnis des Ersten Weltkriegs ist durch eine Vielzahl von Zufällen, kurzfristigen politischen, ökonomischen und strategischen Überlegungen und durch eine Vernachlässigung der ethnischen, religiösen und allgemein kulturellen Gegebenheiten in der Region gekennzeichnet. Eine Vielzahl der Konflikte, die den Nahen und Mittleren Osten seit dem Ende des Zweiten Weltkriegs erschüttert haben und auch heute erschüttern, sind auch Konsequenzen aus den Diktaten der europäischen Siegermächte des ersten großen Kriegs der Moderne. Auch wenn in einigen Fällen, vor allem bei der späteren Gründung der Vereinigten Arabischen Emirate oder des Sultanats Oman, die britische und französische Einflußnahme auf die endgültigen Grenzziehungen weniger direkt vor sich ging als bei der Schaffung des Iraq oder Kuweits, sind doch die Ergebnisse der Bemühungen hinter den Kulissen jedem Beobachter deutlich gewesen.

Auch das Königreich Saudi-Arabien hätte wohl keinen längeren Bestand gehabt, wenn es sich nicht zumindest auf die schweigende, doch wohlmeinende Zustimmung wenigstens eines Teils der britischen Kolonialverwaltung hätte verlassen können. Auch hier war ein Staat entstanden, der zwar eine größere kulturelle Einheit als z.B. der Iraq aufzuweisen hatte, aber dennoch aus sehr heterogenen kulturellen wie gesellschaftlichen Gruppen zusammengesetzt war. Mit der Verwendung des Begriffs von der "kulturellen Einheit" steht man vor einem Definitionsproblem. Es müssen hier nicht die mehr als 200 Definitionen von "Kultur" vorgetragen werden, die allein in einem Fach wie der Ethnologie bisher vorgeschlagen wurden,[1] so daß Clifford Geertz zu Recht feststellt, daß der Begriff "Kultur" "wegen seiner vielfältigen Bezüge und der geflissentlichen Verschwommenheit, in der er nur zu häufig verwendet wurde," in Verruf geraten ist.[2] Auf der anderen Seite ist ein Kulturbegriff, wie wir ihn bei Amatzia Baram finden, der sich mit Verweisen auf Begriffe wie Kunst, Poesie, Theater begnügt, in einem zeitgeschichtlichen Zusammenhang sicher nicht ausreichend.[3] Nach der Definition von Geertz ist Kultur ein "überliefertes System von Bedeutungen, die in symbolischer Gestalt auftreten, ein System überkommener Vorstellungen, die sich in symbolischen Formen ausdrücken, ein System, mit dessen Hilfe die Menschen ihr Wissen vom Leben und ihre Einstellung zum Leben mitteilen, erhalten und weiterentwikkeln"[4]. Auch wenn gegen diese Kultur-Definition kritische Einwände vorgetragen werden können, wird es sich herausstellen, daß diese Formulierung sich für den Kontext, der hier behandelt werden soll, als sehr praktikabel erweist.

Gemeinhin wird Saudi-Arabien in drei unterschiedliche Regionen aufgeteilt: Da ist zunächst der Nadjd, der als zentrale Region des Staates bezeichnet wird und sich durch die Tatsache auszeichnet, daß die Mehrzahl der großen tribalen Organisationen nomadischer Beduinengruppen - um das Wort "Stämme" zu vermeiden - in dieser Region ihre Basis haben. Lange Zeiträume der Geschichte des Nadjd sind gekennzeichnet durch einen hohen Grad von Autonomie von jeder zentralstaatlichen Kontrolle. Die wenigen permanenten Siedlungen wie Ha'il, Buraydah und 'Unayzah "were like islands in that they were surrounded by vast streches of desert that were controlled by autonomous Bedouin tribes. The basic bifurcation within the area was between the badiyah, "nomads" and the hadar, "sedentary folk""[5]. Trotz dieses grundsätzlichen Unterschieds verfügten die Einwohner des Nadjd über ein hohes Maß an kulturellen und sozialen Gemeinsamkeiten und bildeten damit, nach der Beobachtung von Altorki und Cole, eine Ausnahme gegenüber anderen Regionen der Arabischen Halbinsel.

Die zweite Region des Königreichs, der Hidjaz, wird dagegen als eine sehr heterogene, weniger hermetische Gesellschaft beschrieben, die sich durch ein gewisses Maß an multi-ethnischer, multi-kultureller, nahezu kosmopolitischer Haltung auszeichnete, was nicht zuletzt eine Folge der Anziehungskraft von Mekka und Medina, den großen Pilgerstätten, ist. Alles in allem handelt es sich um eine Region, in der das urbane, das seßhafte Bevölkerungselement nicht zuletzt wegen des Vorhandenseins von bedeutenden Städten wie Djidda, Mekka und Medina eine größere Rolle spielte und spielt als im Nadjd.[6]

Schließlich ist noch drittens die Oasenregion von al-Hasa am Persisch-Arabischen Golf zu nennen, die sich durch ihre schiitische Minderheit von den übrigen Teilen des Landes unterscheidet. Wir haben es also auch in Saudi-Arabien mit einem staatlichen Gebilde zu tun, daß sich durch eine gewisse kulturelle und soziale Heterogenität zwischen seinen einzelnen Regionen auszeichnet.

In mancher Hinsicht bestand in dem saudischen Königreich und den verschiedenen anderen Staaten der Arabischen Halbinsel allerdings eine größere Einheitlichkeit als beispielsweise im Iraq. Die Einwohner all dieser Staaten waren zumindest bei deren Entstehung in ihrer überwiegenden Mehrheit Araber oder verstanden sich zumindest als solche. Im Iraq dagegen lebte und lebt eine große ethnische bzw. nationale Minderheit, die sich einer Assimilierung gleich welcher Form immer widersetzt hat, nämlich die der Kurden. Um sie in den iraqischen Staat einzubinden, ist zumindest seit dem Beginn der Herrschaft der Baath-Partei im Jahre 1968 versucht worden, eine iraqische Nationalkultur zu entwickeln, die in starkem Maße auf die vorislamische und frühislamische Tradition des Zweistromlandes Bezug nimmt. Die Ideologen der Baath-Partei waren jedoch nicht die ersten, die sich auf diese Kulturen beriefen. Zuvor hatten arabische Nationalisten führende Heroen der orientalischen Geschichte von den alttestamentarischen Gestalten Abraham und Moses bis zu den Herrscherpersönlichkeiten des Alten Orients wie Hamurabbi, Sargon oder Nebukhadnezar als Araber vereinnahmt.[7] Vor allem in der bildenden

Kunst des modernen Iraq nach der Revolution von 1958 waren Anleihen bei Bildwerken des vorislamischen Mesopotamien gemacht worden. Am bekanntesten ist wohl das Halbrelief des Freiheitsmonuments von Djawad Salim am Bab Shardji in Baghdad, das in bemerkenswerter Weise alt-orientalische Stilelemente mit solchen aus der westlichen Moderne, vor allem dem sozialistischen Realismus, verbindet.[8] Im baathistischen Iraq geschieht diese Bezugnahme auf das vorislamische Mesopotamien in den unterschiedlichsten öffentlichen Bereichen. Die Namen der verschiedenen Verwaltungsbezirke des Landes wurden verändert. Aus Hilla wurde Babil, aus Kut wurde Wasit, aus Takrit wurde Salah al-Din, aus Mosul wurde Ninive. In der Kunst im öffentlichen Raum wurden Plastiken aufgestellt, die ganz deutliche Anklänge an die Plastik des Alten Orient haben. Man denke an die Darstellung der Shahrazadeh des Bildhauers Muhammad Ghani in der Abu Nuwas-Straße in Baghdad, die in den siebziger Jahren entstanden ist. Die Ausführung des Gesichts dieser künstlerisch sehr gelungenen Figur weist vor allem in der Augenbrauenpartie ganz deutliche Bezüge zu dem berühmten Frauenkopf aus dem 4. Jh. v. Chr. aus Uruk-Warka auf.[9] Derartige Beispiele auch aus der Malerei lassen sich beliebig vermehren. Die Verbindung von alt-orientalischen Herrschern mit dem iraqischen Präsidenten Saddam Husayn in den verschiedensten Formen der Staatspropaganda sind in vielen Beispielen während des zweiten Golfkrieges bekannt gemacht worden. Der Propaganda-Slogan, der manche Reisende auf dem Weg zum Saddam International Airport zum Schmunzeln brachte, *From Nebukhadnezar to Saddam Husayn Iraq rises again*, fand hier eine vielfältige bildnerische Umsetzung. Hinzuweisen wäre vielleicht noch auf die Tatsache, daß die verschiedenen Festivals des Landes, so in Mosul oder Babylon, auch Aufmärsche kennen, bei denen in vielfältiger Form durch Kleidung, mitgeführte Utensilien und Musik auf das altorientalische Erbe des Landes Bezug genommen wird. Mit dieser Anknüpfung an die vorislamische Tradition wird der Versuch unternommen, den arabischen und den kurdischen Iraqern das Gefühl einer gemeinsamen kulturellen Wurzel zu vermitteln. Gleiches wird auch auf eine andere, etwas extravagante Art getan, wenn das staatliche Modehaus (*Dar al-Azya'*) des Iraq, das 1970 gegründet wurde, die traditionelle Trachten der verschiedenen Teile des Iraq zu modernen Kleidungsstücken kombiniert. "Diese Kleidung soll die Gestalten und Landschaften, die in Mesopotamien vor tausenden von Jahren blühten, widerscheinen lassen. Diese Kleider sind eine Art von Aufruf, tief über unsere Geschichte und die Quellen unserer Zivilisation seit den ältesten Epochen bis in die Gegenwart nachzudenken."[10] Im übrigen kann es nicht überraschen, daß auch die Kochkunst in diese Aktivitäten eingebunden wurde. So erschien seit Mitte der achtziger Jahre in zahlreichen Auflagen im Iraq ein Kochbuch, das sich ganz besonders der heimischen Küche widmet.[11] All diese Bemühungen gehen im Iraq seit dem Beginn der siebziger Jahre vor sich. Sie sind, wie Amatzia Baram in seinem Buch *Culture, History and Ideology in the Formation of Ba'thi Iraq*[12] gezeigt hat, der interessante Versuch, einen Staat, der nicht nur, aber auch auf dem Reißbrett der Kolonial-verwaltungen entstanden war, in eine historisch tiefe, all die verschiedenen ethnischen Gruppen, religiösen Gemeinschaften und sozialen Klassen gleichermaßen betreffende kulturelle Tradition einzubinden.

All dem liegt die Vorstellung zugrunde, daß ein nationales Bewußtsein durch eine Anzahl von Annahmen wie den "gemeinsamen Kulturbesitz" geschaffen werden kann. H. Seton-Watson hat festgestellt, daß eine Nation entsteht, wenn "a significant number of people in a community consider themselves to form a nation, or behave as if they formed one"[13]. Man könnte hier auch anstelle des Begriffs der "Nation" einen wie "Club" oder "Religionsgemeinschaft" einsetzen. Daraus wird deutlich, daß eine politische oder religiöse Handlungseinheit immer eine Willensentscheidung, eine entsprechende Wahrnehmung und deren sprachliche Artikulation voraussetzt. Das bedeutet nicht, daß dies der Mehrheit der Mitglieder der "Nation" auch bewußt ist. Häufig gehen diese von einer in mythische Vorzeiten reichende Prä-Existenz ihrer Nation aus. Die iraqische Kulturpolitik nutzt dies auf geschickte Weise aus.

Es kann nicht erstaunen, daß in anderen Staaten der Region, die von vergleichbaren ethnischen und kulturellen Gegebenheiten geprägt sind, ähnliche Phänomene in unterschiedlicher Intensität zu beobachten sind. Dabei sagt der Beginn derartiger Entwicklungen etwas über den inneren Zustand der jeweiligen Staaten aus. Saudi-Arabien soll hier als Beispiel dienen. Bis zum Beginn der achtziger Jahre konnte man nicht den Eindruck haben, daß das Land unter einer erkennbaren Identitätskrise litt. Die verschiedenen Zeitungen des Landes sprachen von dem arabischen und dem islamischen Charakter des Landes. Das nationale Selbstverständnis wurde öffentlich durch die wahhabitische Form des sunnitischen Islams gekennzeichnet. Es gab wohl eine religiöse Opposition, die sich jedoch kaum offen artikulieren konnte. Vor allem in der Zeit eines aufstrebenden arabischen Nationalismus, wie des Panarabismus nasseristischer Prägung, entwickelten zumindest die führenden Kreise aus der Ablehnung dieser Ideologien ein hohes Maß an saudischer Identität.[14] Dem arabisch-islamischen Charakter schienen keine Gefahren zu drohen. Er war geprägt durch die wahhabitische Form des Islams, die durch das Königshaus, das dem Staat seinen Namen gegeben hatte, garantiert war. Die Al Sa'ud sahen sich als die Klammer, die die verschiedenen Landesteile mit ihren zahlreichen Unterschieden zusammenhielt. Dieser Staat war ohne die Königsfamilie nicht denkbar. Die Alternative war die Revolution, die wiederum mit der wahhabitischen Ideologie nicht in Übereinstimmung gebracht werden konnte. Von daher bestand aus saudischem Selbstverständnis heraus keine Notwendigkeit, sich um identitätsbildende Maßnahmen zu bemühen. Entstanden einmal Situationen, die ein Risiko für die Islamizität Saudi-Arabiens bedeuten konnten, wie etwa der Import von Video-Filmen pornografischen Inhalts, griffen die Religionsbehörden unter der Führung des prominenten Rechtsgelehrten Ibn Baz ein und veranlaßten Polizei und Sicherheitskräfte, derartige Gefahren auszuschalten.

Die islamische Einheit ging dabei selbstverständlich über den Bereich des Landes hinaus. Es gehörte zur veröffentlichten Meinung, daß die Muslime der Welt eine große zusammengehörige Gemeinschaft darstellen. Seit dem Beginn der neunziger Jahre kann man allerdings feststellen, daß in der saudischen Presse die verschiedenen regionalen Unterschiede, die der Islam kennt, durchaus nicht ohne eine gewisse Billigung ihrer Existenz zur Kenntnis genommen werden. So erschienen in den saudischen Tageszeitungen immer wieder Beiträge, in denen die unterschiedlichen Formen der Feiern des Ramadan in den verschiedenen Teilen der islamischen Welt dargesstellt wurden. Das geschieht durch Interviews, die mit Immigranten aus anderen islamischen Ländern geführt werden, oder in größeren Aufsätzen, in denen die Sitten und Gebräuche zum Ramadan geschildert werden, die von denen im eigenen Land abweichen.[15] Erste Verunsicherungen im offiziellen saudischen Selbstverständnis entstanden im Zusammenhang mit der Entsendung von einheimischen Studenten an Hochschulen des westlichen Auslandes, aber auch an die amerikanischen Universitäten im Nahen Osten. Man sorgte sich um die Charakterstärke der jungen Leute und ihre Fähigkeit, mit den auf sie einstürmenden Normen, Sitten und Gebräuchen in einer für das saudische Verständnis akzeptablen Weise umgehen zu können. Daher wurden Kurse für diese Studenten eingerichtet, in denen die Kenntnisse über den Islam und ihre eigene Kultur vertieft werden sollten.[16] Daß diese Bemühungen von unterschiedlich einzustufendem Erfolg gekrönt waren, zeigt der Bericht eines iranischen Studenten in den USA, der von einem saudischen Kommilitonen als Kommunist angesehen wurde, weil dieser *Shi'i* (Schiit) und *Shuyu'i* (Kommunist) nicht unterscheiden wollte.[17]

Saudi-Arabien ist ein Land, das durch eine beträchtliche Population von Arbeitsmigranten gekennzeichnet ist. Deren Bevölkerungsanteil ist zwar nicht so überwältigend wie in einigen anderen Golf-Staaten, in denen die sogenannten "locals" eine Minderheit von kaum mehr als 10 Prozent ausmachen, erweist sich in einer Reihe von Berufen jedoch als beträchtlich. Zu diesen Berufen gehört der tertitäre Bereich, vor allem die verschiedenen Dienstleistungsberufe. Daß die Behandlung von Dienstmädchen aus Indien, Pakistan, Bangladesh, Sri Lanka oder den Philippinen häufig zu kritischen Bemerkungen Anlaß gibt, wird in den saudischen Medien nur selten zur Kenntnis genommen. Worüber man sich in offiziellen Kreisen allerdings Sorgen macht, ist die Tatsache, daß diese jungen Frauen häufig als Kindermädchen eine sehr intensive Beziehung zu ihren Schützlingen haben, sie mit ihren Heimatsprachen und den Formen des Umgangs mit kleinen Kindern aus ihrer Heimat bekannt machen und so einen prägenden Einfluß auf sie ausüben. Die Mütter oder die weiblichen Verwandten kümmerten sich offensichtlich nicht intensiv um diese Kinder. Es bestanden an offizieller Stelle offensichtlich Befürchtungen, daß die Kinder so ihrer eigenen Kultur entfremdet würden. Es gab eine Reihe von Konferenzen, in denen Überlegungen über Möglichkeiten der Abhilfe angestellt wurden. Lösungen dieses offenkundigen Problems sind mir jedoch nicht bekannt geworden.

Zumindest Ansätze zu Lösungen fanden sich in einem anderen Bereich, in dem Dienstleistungskräfte in Saudi-Arabien besonders häufig Beschäftigung finden, nämlich in den Küchen und im Service-Bereich der Hotels, Restaurants und natürlich auch in den Küchen der Privathaushalte. Wenn man die Zeitungsannoncen der Restaurants in den großen Städten Saudi-Arabiens durchsieht, kann man leicht feststellen, daß einheimische arabische Küche in öffentlichen Lokalen praktisch nicht angeboten wird. An erster Stelle stehen indische und andere asiatische Restaurants, gefolgt von solchen mit Angeboten der italienischen und französischen Küche. Ferner finden sich die Angebote einiger libanesischer und türkischer Lokale. Nun mag man ohne Zweifel darüber streiten, ob es so etwas wie eine saudische Küche überhaupt gibt. Zumindest die Städte des Hidjaz verfügen allerdings über eine deutlich entwickelte kulinarische Tradition,[18] die durch den starken Einfluß der Migranten offensichtlich verloren zu gehen drohte. Auf Anregung der Prinzessin Muda bint Khalid ibn 'Abd al-'Aziz unternahm es die *Djam'iyyat al-nahda al-nisa'iyya al-khayriyya*, traditionelle Rezepte zu sammeln und zu publizieren. Nach öffentlichen Aufrufen wurden erfahrene saudische Hausfrauen, die sich gemeldet hatten, nach ihren Rezepten befragt. Die Ergebnisse dieser Befragungen wurden dann von professionellen Köchinnen oder Hauswirtschaftslehrerinnen ausgewertet und in die übliche Rezeptform, also mit genauer Angabe von Zutatenmengen und Kochzeiten, als Buch mit dem Titel *Min fann al-tabkh al-su'udi* herausgegeben. Im Jahr 1990 lag schon die 4. Auflage vor. Inzwischen sind weitere Kochbücher erschienen, die sich vor allem der saudischen Küche widmen. Vergleichbare Entwicklungen lassen sich auch in den anderen Golfstaaten und im Sultanat Oman feststellen.[19]

Während im Iraq die Bedeutung der Volkskunde (folklore) schon seit den siebzige erkannt worden war und man staatlicherseits auch die wissenschaftlichen Bemühungen und populären Veranstaltungen zu diesen Themen gefördert hatte, lassen sich entsprechende Tendenzen im öffentlichen Bereich für Saudi-Arabien erst seit 1992 konstatieren. Im Frühjahr dieses Jahres erschien eine Anzahl von entsprechenden Artikeln in Publikumszeitschriften und Tageszeitungen. Da finden sich Artikel über die *mishka* oder den *fanus ramadan* ebenso wie solche über die Vergnügungen des Rauchens einer Wasserpfeife.[20] In anderen geht es um den *dawraq*, das bauchige Tongefäß mit dem engen Hals, das sich so gut zum Kühlhalten des in ihm befindlichen Trinkwassers eignet[21], oder um *Mirashsh* und *Mibkhara*, das Gefäß mit dem Parfüm oder Orangenblütenessenz verspritzt wird bzw. das Räuchergefäß, in dem die "Düfte Arabiens" verbrannt werden[22]. Natürlich fehlt auch nicht der Artikel, der sich mit der traditionellen Form des Teebrauens befaßt.[23] All diese Zeitungsbeiträge sind bebildert. In der Regel handelt es sich dabei um Abbildungen von öffentlichen Brunnen u.ä., bei denen die entsprechenden Geräte als formales Vorbild gedient haben. Die Verwendung entsprechender Vorbilder der traditionellen Kultur findet man auch in dekorativen Brunnen anderer Golfstaaten.

Eine andere Gruppe von Artikeln befaßt sich mit Sitten und Gebräuchen wie dem Fest der Namensgebung am siebten Tag nach der Geburt eines Kindes[24] oder dem Musahharati, dem Mann, der die Fastenden im Monat Ramadan etwa eine Stunde vor dem ersten Gebet mit Trommelschlägen und lauten Rufen weckt, so daß sie Gelegenheit haben, vor Anbruch der täglichen Fastenperiode noch etwas zu sich zu nehmen.[25] In den Zusammenhang der Darstellung sozialer Regeln kann man auch die Beschreibung der Truhe für den Brautschatz (*sanduq al-saysam*) stellen, in der dann auch Teile des traditionellen Hochzeitsrituals referiert werden.[26] Im September 1993 erschien in der saudischen Tageszeitung al-Nahda eine Artikelserie von Faysal Iraqi, einem Bewohner Mekkas, der die dortigen Hochzeitsbräuche schildert.[27] Auch die ausführliche Beschreibung von ungewöhnlichen Marktformen, wie dem Markt der Frauen, müssen in diesem Kontext der Dokumentation traditioneller saudischer Lebensformen gesehen werden.[28] Schließlich finden sich Artikel, die sich mit Antiquitäten aus der arabischen Halbinsel, also Beduinenschmuck, alten Waffen u.ä. befassen. Dabei werden entweder die entsprechenden Geschäfte vorgestellt oder private Sammlungen und Sammler beschrieben.[29]

All diese Artikel wurden vor allem in der Ramadanzeit 1992 veröffentlicht. Alle befanden sich auf den Seiten von Arab News, die der Berichterstattung von Ereignissen aus dem Königreich vorbehalten sind. Spezielle Hinweise auf eine besondere lokale Herkunft dieser Sitten aus einem bestimmten Teil des Landes fehlten, so daß der Eindruck entstehen kann, als ob es sich um allgemein bekannte, für ganz Saudi-Arabien typische Dinge handelte, auch wenn sie nur in einem bestimmten Landesteil bekannt sind. Rituale und Artefakte werden so für die Konstituierung einer einheitlichen nationalen Kultur Saudi-Arabiens eingesetzt, auch wenn es sich um Produkte der materiellen Kultur oder um Bräuche handelt, die sich auch in anderen Teilen der arabischen wie der islamischen Welt finden.

Der Rückbezug auf Architekturzeugnisse als historische Dokumente, wie wir ihn im Iraq z.B. in der Renovierung, Rekonstruktion und Dokumentation von alten Baghdader Häusern finden[30], läßt sich inzwischen auch in Saudi-Arabien feststellen. So erschien in einer Tageszeitung eine mehrteilige Darstellung der Architektur in Saudi-Arabien[31], und auch die Rekonstruktion der Stadtmauern von Jiddah kann in diesem Zusammenhang gesehen werden[32]. Auch hinter dem in gleicher Weise von anderen Regimen der Region unternommene Versuch, archäologische Denkmäler aus vor-islamischer Zeit aufzufinden, mag die Bemühung gestanden haben, in Saudi-Arabien eine tiefer gehende gemeinsame Geschichte zu entdecken und so das historische Bewußtsein der Bewohner des Landes zu stärken. Werner Ende stellt dazu fest: "Wir haben es mit einem Problem zu tun, das für die Herausbildung bzw. historiographische Rechtfertigung des Nationalismus und Säkularismus in den Ländern der Dritten Welt von zentraler Bedeutung ist". Nach Hörensagen sind auch verschiedene Entdeckungen gemacht worden. Wissenschaftliche oder populäre Publikationen in diesem Zusammenhang lassen jedoch noch auf sich warten. Dies mag wiederum mit den säkularen Momenten dieser Suche nach der eigenen Vergangenheit zusammenhängen.[33]

Die beispielsweise im Iraq vorhandene Praxis, Festivals unterschiedlicher Thematik durchzuführen, um so die nationale Identität zu fördern, findet auch in Saudi-Arabien Nachahmungen. So wird im April 1993 zum achten Mal ein Festival des nationalen Erbes und der Kultur durchgeführt, das von der Nationalgarde organisiert und von König Fahd eröffnet wurde. Das Festival, das in Diandariyya, ca. 50 km nördlich von Riyad stattfindet, ist 1985 aus einem Kamelrennen hervorgegangen. Bei der Eröffnung des ersten Festivals hatte Kronprinz Abdullah als Kommandant der veranstaltenden Nationalgarde festgestellt, daß die Bevölkerung, geleitet durch den Islam, die Traditionen und das kulturelle Erbe der Nation in der Lage sei, den Herausforderungen der Gegenwart zu begegnen. "Der wahre Reichtum unseres Landes beruht auf seinem Erbe und seiner traditionellen Kultur." Der Organisator des Festivals von 1993, Dr. Abd al-Rahman Subayt Al Subayt, stellte fest: "Djanadariyya symbolisiert die glorreiche Vergangenheit des Königreichs, die auf dem Islam und der traditionellen Kultur beruht, die die Ideale unserer Vorväter waren. Daher ist die Bedeutung des Festivals in den vergangenen acht Jahren immer größer geworden." Auch 1993 war das Kamelrennen noch immer ein besonderer Anziehungspunkt des Festivals. Es hatte mehr als 300 000 Zuschauer. Alles in allem besuchten mehr als 1,5 Millionen Menschen die verschiedenen Veranstaltungen des Festivals. Ein besonderes Programm wurde für Frauen durchgeführt, an dem 120 000 Frauen und ebenso viele Kinder teilnahmen. Zu den Programmen gehören Wettbewerbe in Koranrezitation, Vorlesungen und Diskussionen über verschiedene Themen, Volkstänze, traditionelles Handwerk und Ausstellungen über das kulturelle, soziale und wirtschaftliche Leben der Menschen, die durch Generationen die arabische Halbinsel bewohnt haben. Auf diese Weise soll deutlich werden, daß die saudischen Traditionen und religiösen Überzeugungen trotz aller westlichen Einflüsse die bestimmenden und allgemein verbreiteten Faktoren für die saudische Gesellschaft bleiben. Es geht nach dem Selbstverständnis der Organisatoren des Festivals darum, die Prinzipien, Ideen und Werte des Islams und seine authentischen sozialen Traditionen, Lehren und Sitten, die tief in der saudischen Geschichte wurzeln, zu betonen. Darüber hinaus hat das Festival die Aufgabe, die Beziehung zwischen kulturellem Erbe und moderner kultureller und künstlerischer Arbeit zu bestimmen. Die Einbeziehung der Geschichte der Arabischen Halbinsel vor der Entstehung des saudischen Königreichs wird u.a. durch eine Ausstellung des Festivals deutlich. Die Sama (Saudi Arabian Monetary Agency) stellte Münzen und Banknoten aus, "including some rare coin collections of the currency in the Kingdom (sic) 1000 to 2000 years ago"[34]. Solche Aktivitäten sind nicht auf das Inland beschränkt. In Zusammenarbeit mit dem *Gulf Popular Heritage Centre* werden auch wissenschaftliche Untersuchungen der verschiedensten Bereiche saudischer Folklore durchgeführt. Besonderes Interesse hat dabei der Volkstanz gefunden. Inzwischen gibt es im Königreich mehr als 50 Tanzgruppen, die mit staatlicher Unterstützung die mehr als 160 traditionellen Tänze des Landes praktizieren.[35] Auch im Ausland wird auf die "saudische Kultur" hingewiesen. So beteiligte sich Saudi-Arabien mit einer Darstellung seiner Kultur und Tradition am Los Angeles Festival 1993.[36]

Auch bestimmte aktuelle Strömungen der Malerei in Saudi-Arabien können in diesem Zusammenhang genannt werden. Als Beispiel sei auf die seit mehr als 25 mit Ausstellungen ihrer Werke an die saudische Öffentlichkeit tretende Safiya Binzagr hingewiesen, zu deren thematischem Programm ausdrücklich die Darstellung saudischer Traditionen gehört. Sie sagt: "Es ist noch so viel zu zeigen und die Zeit fliegt dahin. Es ist traurig, daß wir dabei sind, unsere reiche Vergangenheit zu vergessen. Sehen sie sich andere Länder an, z.B. Indien. Dort trägt man noch die traditionellen Kleider, befolgt weiterhin einen traditionellen Lebensstil und folgt den alten Sitten. Wir Saudis dagegen übernehmen die moderne Art und vergessen unsere Kultur. Das ist traurig, weil wir uns dabei vergessen. Traditionen sind doch sehr wichtig, weil sie ein Teil der Zukunft sind". Sie fährt fort: "Ich habe es so eilig, weil die alten Leute, die die früheren Lebensumstände kennen, sterben. Als ich anfing zu malen, war alles einfacher. Meine Großmutter lebte noch und viele Tanten. Sie erzählten mir viel über die alten Traditionen und die Art der Kleidung, die sie damals trugen. Die Frau, die früher die Bräute geschmückt hat und mir sehr geholfen hat, als ich meine Bilder über Hochzeiten gemalt habe, ist nun ganz alt. Solche Frauen gibt es heute nicht mehr, und heutzutage sind alle Hochzeiten modernisiert. Die gegenwärtige Generation weiß nicht einmal mehr, wie es damals war. Darum male ich. Ich will unsere reiche Kultur für zukünftige Generationen bewahren." Daher ist es nicht erstaunlich, daß die Malerin ihre Bilder nicht verkauft, sondern in ihrem Privatbesitz behält, um später eine Art von Folkloremuseum mit den Bildern auszustatten.[37]

Als letztes Beispiel sei ferner noch angeführt, daß auch die Mode in diesem Kontext eine Rolle spielt. So berichtet "Arab News" im Mai 1992 von einem saudischen Couturier, Yahya al-Bishri, der eine Modeschau für saudische Mode in Moskau vorbereitet. Die von ihm entworfenen Modelle seien von arabischen und islamischen Vorbildern beeinflußt. Zuvor habe er seine Arbeiten schon auf Modeschauen in London, Paris und Amman gezeigt. Er erklärte dem ihn befragenden Journalisten: "Ich hoffe, daß meine Schau mit dazu beitragen wird, die arabisch-russischen Beziehungen, vor allem aber die russisch-saudischen Beziehungen, zu vertiefen."[38]

All diese Veröffentlichungen und die dahinter deutlich werdenden Bemühungen machen sichtbar, daß offenbar eine politische Notwendigkeit besteht, die Einheitlichkeit einer saudischen nationalen Identität zu betonen. Die in diesem Zusammenhang bedeutsame Frage, wie weit die Presse und die Einzelpublikationen durch zentrale Instanzen manipuliert werden bzw. in welchem Maß von staatlichen Stellen Zensur ausgeübt wird, läßt sich natürlich nicht in dem Maße beantworten, wie das bei Regimen der Fall ist, in denen Meinungsfreiheit in noch höherem

Maße als Gefahr für die bestehende Ordnung angesehen wird, als das z. Zt. noch in Saudi-Arabien der Fall ist.[39] Für die verschiedenen Bemühungen um eine Dokumentation der kulturellen Einheit des Landes mag es zwei Ursachen geben. Die erste ist wohl, daß die saudische Führung schon seit dem Ende der siebziger Jahre durch Vorgänge wie die Besetzung der großen Moschee in Mekka (1979), die Ermordung von König Faysal (1974), die ständigen Auseinandersetzungen mit der Islamischen Republik Iran und manches andere stärker verunsichert war, da diese spektakulären Ereignisse eine religiöse Konnotation hatten, also das Königshaus nicht mehr einhellig akzeptiert, vor allem aber öffentlich in seiner Islamizität angezweifelt worden war. Die Annahme des Titels "Hüter der beiden heiligen Stätten" durch König Khalid macht deutlich, daß hier der Grund für eine Gegensteuerung gesehen wurde.[40]

Der zeitliche Schwerpunkt von Artikeln und anderen Aktivitäten der geschilderten Art liegt im Frühjahr 1992. Es kann nicht ausgeschlossen werden, daß wir es hier mit den Nachwehen des zweiten Golfkrieges zu tun haben. Die Kritik in Teilen der islamischen Welt an der Anwesenheit von amerikanischen Truppen, also Nicht-Muslimen, in der Nähe der heiligen Städte des Islams auf Einladung des saudischen Königshauses einerseits und die nicht zu leugnende Tatsache des vorläufigen Scheiterns des arabischen nationalen Projekts in jeder Form andererseits ließen es für die herrschenden Kreise des Landes wohl ratsam erscheinen, eine nationale saudische Identität in den Vordergrund zu stellen.

Lange Zeit konnte man davon ausgehen, daß diese Betonung der engeren nationalen Identität in Saudi-Arabien nicht notwendig sein werde.[41] Die Entwicklungen haben es mit sich gebracht, daß auch dort die Tendenzen stärker werden, die regionale Kultur zu legitimieren bzw. eine solche Kultur künstlich zu schaffen, um die Individualität der saudischen Nation betonen zu können. Daß es sich hier um einen komplizierten Balanceakt handelt, bei dem sorgfältig auf die öffentliche Akzeptanz derartiger Neuerungen geachtet werden muß, liegt auf der Hand. Wichtig ist offenbar, daß das in der Kultur-Definition von Geertz angesprochene Moment der "Überlieferung" beachtet wird. Das reine Erfinden von Traditionen wird nicht akzeptiert. Zumindest Anklänge an die eigenen Traditionen müssen vorhanden sein. Dann ist das Ziel einer solchen Politik, nämlich das Entstehen einer Gemeinschaft - auch wenn es sich um eine "imaginierte Gemeinschaft" handelt - zu erreichen. Auf das saudische Beispiel bezogen, bedeutet das nicht, daß die arabischen und islamischen Aspekte des kulturellen Lebens in Saudi-Arabien aufgegeben werden. Aber es kommt doch zu einer Situation, in der die verschiedenen Facetten des kulturellen Lebens im Land in den Vordergrund gestellt werden, wenn dies die politischen Umstände notwendig erscheinen lassen. Gesellschaften sind allerdings nur bis zu einem gewissen Grad zu manipulieren. Wenn eine deutliche saudische nationale und kulturelle Identität hergestellt sein sollte, kann diese nicht ohne weiteres durch eine pan-islamische oder pan-arabische wieder abgelöst werden. Die in Ansätzen feststellbare Entstehung einer saudischen kulturellen Identität wird, falls dieser Prozeß noch einige Zeit anhält, irreversibel sein.

## Anmerkungen

1 S.A.L. Kroeber/Cl. Kluckhohn, Culture. A Critical Review of Concepts and Definitions, New York 1952.
2 C. Geertz, Dichte Beschreibung. Beiträge zum Verstehen kultureller Systeme, Frankfurt/M. 1983, 46.
3 A. Baram, Culture, History and Ideology in the Formation of Ba'thist Iraq, 1968-1989, New York 1991, 191.
4 Geertz, Dichte Beschreibung...
5 S. Altorki/D.P. Cole, Arabian Oasis City. The Transformation of 'Unayzah, Austin 1989, 17.
6 S. Altorki, Women in Saudi Arabia. Ideology and Behaviour among the Elite, New York 1986, 6-8.
7 S. Haim (ed.), Arab Nationslism. An Anthology, Berkeley 1967, 97ff., 105f., 139f.
8 Vgl. dazu Peter Heine, Malerei und Grafik in der islamischen Welt. In: Werner Ende/Udo Steinbach (ed)., Der Islam in der Gegenwart, München 1995 (im Druck).
9 Katalog "Schätze aus dem Irak von der Frühzeit bis zum Islam", Köln 1964, Katalog-Nr. 23 (Abb. auf dem Umschlag).
10 Culture and Art in Iraq, Baghdad 1978, 165.
11 Peter Heine, The Revivial of Traditional Cooking in Modern Arab Cookbooks. In: R. Tapper/S. Zubaida (ed.), Culinary Culture of the Middle East, London 1994.
12 Baram, Culture, History...
13 Seton-Watson, National and States, London 1977, 5.
14 Werner Ende, Religion, Politik und Literatur in Saudi-Arabien: Der geistesgeschichtliche Hintergrund der heutigen religiösen und kulturpolitischen Situation. In: Orient: *22*(1981), 389.
15 Arab News, 30.3.1992, 26.6.1992, 5.3.1993, 13.3.1993, 26.3.1993.
16 Werner Ende, Literatur, Politik... In: Orient *23*(1982), 389f.
17 M. Fischer/A. Abedi, Debating Muslims. Cultural Dialogues in Postmodernity and Tradition, Madison 1990.
18 Vgl. O. al-Sasi, Sprichwörter und andere volkskundliche Texte aus Mekka, Münster 1972.
19 Heine, The Revival of Traditional Cooking..., 57; vgl. auch Arab News, 19.3.1992, mit einem Artikel mit dem Titel: The ageless cuisine of iftar.
20 Arab News, 19.3.1992; 22.3.1992.
21 Arab News, 16.3.1992.
22 Arab News, 12.3.1992.
23 Arab News, 5.3.1992.
24 Arab News, 26.4.1992.
25 Arab News, 11.3.1992.
26 Arab News, 9.3.1992.
27 Arab News, 1.10.1993.

28 Ina Heine/Peter Heine, Oh ihr Musliminnen... Frauen in islamischen Gesellschaften, Freiburg-Basel-Wien 1993, 207-211.

29 Arab News, 22.10.1992, 27.10.1992, 25.2.1993.

30 Subhi al-Azzawi, Oriental Houses in Baghdad: Concepts, Types and Categories, parts 1-3. In: Ur. International Magazine of Arab Culture (1985)1, 2-14, (1985)2, 30-41, (1985)3, 7-21; Layth Raouf, Tradition and Continuity in the Modern Iraqi House. In: Ur. International Magazine of Arab Culture (1985)1, 15-24.

31 Arab News, 4.4.1992, 5.4.1993.

32 Vgl. Arab News, 4.3.1993.

33 Ende, Religion, Politik... In: Orient 23(1982), 190-193.

34 al-'Ukaz, 30.3.1993; Arab News, 9.4.1993, 20.4.1993, 21.4.1993.

35 Arab News, 11.9.1993, 2.

36 Arab News, 18.6.1993.

37 Arab News, 14.5.1993.

38 Arab News, 19.5.1992.

39 Vgl. dazu Ende, Religion, Politik... In: Orient *23*(1982), 29, 530-537.

40 Eine offiziöse Verdammung der Feiern aus Anlaß das Geburtstages des Propheten ist zu finden bei: 'Abd Allah b. Mani': Hiwar ma'a al-Maliki fi radd munkaratihi wa-dalalatihi, Riyad 1983. Die Polemik beginnt nach der Publikation eines Artikels in der Tageszeitung al-Madina al-munawwara vom 7.1.19982 von Muhammad 'Alawi al-Maliki, in dem der Autor zur Feier des Mawlid auffordert; Yamani 1992.

41 Baram Culture, History..., 141.

# The Historical Process of the Formation of the Indian Nation

Bipan Chandra

A nation is the product of a concrete historical process. Its formation can therefore be studied only by examining the concrete historical development. In case of India too both the Indian nation and nationalism were the products of its history. To study their evolution is to study the economic, political, social and ideological development of the Indian people. It also then becomes clear that the manner in which the Indian nation was formed was different from that of Europe's.

In India, nation and nationalism were not the products of ethnicity or common language or common culture or of a dominant position acquired by one ethnic or linguistic group, region or already formed nationality. Though aided by the centuries-old historical development, they were basically the products of the anti-colonial struggle for freedom. Resistance to colonialism took a national form because colonialism oppressed all classes and all sections of the Indian people. The Indian nation was formed in the course of and as a result of the struggle of the entire Indian people against colonialism and the colonial state.

The difference between the European paths and the Indian path of nation-formation also enables us to define the nation in the Indian context. The Indian nation means the coming into being of the Indian people as a historical entity. The Chinese, for example, do not use the word 'Chinese nation', but 'Chinese people' to express unity or describe the national entity. Because our national movement was born in the 19th century, we use the 19th century word 'nation' to mean the same thing, that is, the 'Indian people'.

What makes India a nation or a people is basically the historical development of common interests among Indians and the recognition of this fact. The nation or 'the people' were formed in India not because their society or culture became homogeneous but because their economic, political and cultural interests became one or the same, even when they continued to be differentiated by language and ethnicity and even culture. On the other hand, if these common interests had not developed, they would not have formed a nation, even if they had shared a common language and ethnie, as is the case of Arabs. Consequently, the question whether India is a nation or a federation of nationalities loses much of its relevance or analytical value. What we have to do is to recognize that the Indian people have historically simultaneously developed common economic, political, social and cultural interests as well as cultural, linguistic and ethnic heterogeneity. This was recognized by the leaders of India's freedom struggle when they based Indian nationalism on economic and political nationalism and not on cultural nationalism.

Nation is neither an inherent, a historical or trans-historical mystic all-time entity, possessing an eternal or immutable essence or nature, nor an artificial, ideological invention by a class or stratum or the elite to serve their narrow interests. Nation formation is both a historically objective and a subjective, that is emotional, intellectual, ideological historical process.

For a nation to be formed, its economy and polity and, to some extent, its cultures have to increasingly get integrated. But that is necessary but not sufficient, for the process of nation formation can be interrupted and disrupted by subjective political, cultural ideological and emotional factors. Hence, whether this process will be initiated or not and whether it will develop and grow or will break down depends on concrete historical development and concrete political and ideological practices.

Looked at from the historical point of view, the people of India have been getting unified into a people or a nation for centuries, especially since the middle 19th century.

## I

Let us first look at the objective factors in the making of the Indian nation.

Objectively, Indians were for centuries developing common interests and sharing common conditions of existence. Pre-colonial India had already acquired some elements of common existence and common consciousness. Despite India's immense cultural diversity, a certain cultural commonness, certain strands of a common cultural heritage, had developed. In particular, a great deal of commonness existed at the level of the Great Traditions or high literate cultures, though Small Traditions had also developed mutual linkages. There existed a certain shared literate Sanskrit-based culture in whole of India; similarly later Persian-based culture had also an all-India reach. Moreover, despite differences in languages and culture, there was enough cultural interaction and exchange for us to speak of the gradual formation over centuries of elements of a common, composite culture, including values, at different levels, whether geographical or social thus knitting the people of the subcontinent together. India was thus becoming, as Jawaharlal Nehru was to grasp, 'a durable entity' on the basis of commonality in culture. Common mythology, common pilgrimage centres and common religions and religious reform movements such as the Bhakti movement were an aspect of this phenomenon.

In India, the neighbouring cultures have so much in common that people can move around their neighbouring territories without friction, even when linguistic and cultural differences exist. Moreover, Indian cultures have historically functioned on the basis of cultural reconciliation and tolerance of belief rather than on the basis of domination and subordination. This has tended to lead to cultural synthesis rather than to cultural exclusiveness and cultural and ethnic 'cleansing'.

The politics of the rulers also cut across regions. The territorial reach of the more ambitious engulfed the subcontinent. Large kingdoms and empires set up state traditions on a regional as well as all-India basis to which the national movement could later appeal for territorial authentication. The concepts of Bharat Varsha and Hindustan were realities of Indian history. As S. Gopal has put it, 'The sense of unity was an emotional reality rooted in history even more than in geography'.

True, India was invaded and conquered on several occasions. But the successive waves of invaders invariably settled down here and became assimilated. The new ruling classes often integrated with the older ones, no longer remaining alien. In the 7th and 8th centuries, the invading Huns settled down and became Rajputs. The Mughals relied on the earlier zamindars, often Rajputs in North India and Marathas in Western India, and on the scribal castes, such as the Kayasthas, to collect revenue and administer the Empire. Neither the earlier ruling classes nor the common people identified the new rulers as foreigners, except perhaps the first generation.

There was, of course, resistance from the top and especially during the 17th and 18th centuries from popular rebellions, but neither involved ethnic, religious, linguistic or cultural grounds. It was the colonial historians who later invented the tradition of ethnic or religious resistance against the Mughals. But then they even invented the notion that because of ethnic and religious diversity, no national movement could endure in India or could even come into being!

Interestingly, even though many regional chieftains fought against the Mughal rulers and succeeded in setting up independent kingdoms, they continued to work within the framework of the Mughal revenue and administrative system and court etiquette and culture.

Also, economically, despite backward means of transport and communication, a great deal of India-wide trade, local and regional specialization in production and credit networks developed, especially during the late medieval period. For example, the rates of insurance on goods being transported from Ahmedabad to Delhi were perhaps lower during the 17th and 18th centuries than at present.

## II

The colonialization of the Indian economy, society and polity further strengthened the process of India's unification. The process of Indians developing into a unified people was very much quickened from about the middle of the 19th century. Growth of internal and external trade, destruction of the relative self-sufficiency of the rural economy and of different regions, creation of an all-India market and the development of modern industries, trade, banking and means of transport on an all-India scale, introduction of a uniform system of law, administration and education, and the creation of an all-India intelligentsia increasingly unified the country and created a single economic, administrative and political entity.

Colonialism did, of course, produce regional economic imbalances and disparity which encouraged divisive tendencies, but, despite the disparity, the economic linkages between the regions were more important. Moreover, regional imbalances were not the result of the evolution of different regional, regionally integrated, economies or of the economic domination of some regions by others, which would have led to separate economies or economic entities linked by colonial domination but basically separated if not mutually antagonistic.

## III

During the 19th and 20th centuries, the common enemy in the form of colonialism provided new uniting bonds to the Indian people. The very existence of foreign rule that oppressed all the people irrespective of their social class, caste, region, religion or language acted as a unifying factor.

Consequently, the prolonged anti-imperialist struggle and the feeling of solidarity engendered in its course, contributed powerfully to the making of the Indian nation. This aspect may be further dilated upon. Over time a basic contradiction developed between the interests of the Indian people and British colonialism as the latter began to hinder development in every area of Indian life an society. This contradiction and its cognition were basic to the formation of the Indian nation, for they generated national sentiments and created the material, moral, intellectual and political conditions for the rise and development of a powerful antiimperialist movement which in turn initiated and promoted the process of nation-making. Any understanding of Indian nation formation, therefore, inevitably involves an understanding and study of the anti-imperialist movement.

The consciousness of nationhood, of Indians being a people, did not flow automatically from the objective reality. The nation was created by the political choice and activity of the Indian people. The identity of Indians being a nation or one people came into existence as a result of the conscious ideological and political practices of the movement against colonialism. The nationalist intelligentsia, the 'new Indians' of the 19th century, realized that for national liberation and national development they must bring about the unification of the Indian people. They also saw that the previous, pre-colonial 'Indianess', Indian structures and institutions had not worked for Indian society or people when faced with the process of colonialization. Consequently, they set out to form the concepts of nation, nation-making, democracy, development and secularism around which to organize a national liberation struggle.

The founders of the Indian national movement frankly set out to create a new nation. They accepted that India was not yet a nation despite common history and geography and the elements of a common culture. But, they asserted, India had now entered the process of becoming a nation. India, they said, was a nation-in-the-making. The process faced many obstacles and was constantly challenged. It could not be taken for granted and had to be constantly developed and consolidated. Hence, one of the major objectives they set out before the national movement was that of welding Indians into a nation and the promotion of this process of nationmaking through intense ideological, political, economic and cultural efforts.

They also recognized that the size and diversity of India were such that special efforts different from those in other parts of the world would have to be made to carefully promote national unity. Their effort was to unify the Indian people on the basis of a common political and economic programme around which they could wage a common struggle. Consequently, only those issues, rights and demands were taken up which Indians had in common in relation to the colonial rulers. They also realized that India could be unified and its segmentation overcome only by recognizing and accepting its immense diversity . The differences in language, culture, religion, and ethny were then to be seen not as obstacles to be overcome but as positive features that were sources of strength to Indian culture, civilization and nation, and were, therefore, to be integrated with the merging common nationhood.

The Indian national movement was, therefore, committed to religious freedom, diversity of cultures, reorganization of Indian administrative and political units or states on linguistic lines, removal of economic disparity among regions, and full protection to and development of the cultures, life-styles, and economic autonomy of the tribal people. The movement accepted that a federal polity, a strong centre, a unified economy, and a composite culture had to be evolved on the basis of the principle of 'unity in diversity'.

We may also note that India was also increasingly getting divided into modern social classes and strata. Indian nationalism had little difficulty in coming to terms with the emerging class consciousness as also class organizations such as trade unions and kisan sabhas, on one side, and the Federation of Chambers of Commerce and Industry, etc., on the other side.

The social vision of the national movement encompassed a secular state. Secularism was defined in a comprehensive manner as the separation of religion from the state and politics, treatment of religion as a personal, private affair, state neutrality towards or equal respect for all religions, and refusal to discriminate between followers of different religions. Gandhi too in his later years underlined this definition of secularism. For example, he wrote in 1942: 'Religion is a personal matter which should have no place in politics'; and again in 1947: 'Religion is the personal affair of each individual. It must not be mixed up with politics or material affairs.'

A few other features of the national movement were equally relevant to the making of the Indian nation. For one, it was based on a well-developed critique of colonialism in its economic aspects and on a economic programme leading to independent economic development. In fact, as pointed out earlier, the nationalist leaders based the movement ideologically essentially on economic nationalism. They could not have based the movement on language or culture because most of the Indians were illiterate and lived within little folk cultures. Later, when the literate intellectuals raised issues of language their view point was accommodated. At cultural level also the movement incorporated literate high cultures and low cultures. But language and culture at no stage became central to the definition of the nation and nationalism in India. The movement was also fully committed to political democracy and civil liberties which were seen as basic building blocs of nation-making. A great champion of civil liberties, Tilak often proclaimed, to quote him in his own words, that 'liberty of the Press and liberty of speech give birth to a nation and nourish it.' Jawaharlal also repeatedly stressed that without democracy India could not be held together. What is even more important, the concepts of democracy and civil liberties were propagated among the mass of people, both in rural and urban areas, by the nationalist political workers during the Gandhian era.

The national movement was in many ways original and innovative. Basing itself on the historical experience and culture of the Indian people, it was also fully open to, and in fact related meaningfully to, contemporary world intellectual currents and mass movements. It also united broadest sections of the people and diverse ideological currents to struggle together for a common objective, through common forms of struggle even while encouraging open contention between different political-ideological trends and paradigms. Without such a consensual approach a diverse people like those of India could neither have been united into a powerful anti-imperialist mass movement, nor formed into a nation or a people.

The Indian national movement from the beginning, that is even when it was based primarily on the intelligentsia, defined the nation as nation-people. This was reflected in a broad pro-poor orientation. Moreover, the movement constantly defined itself in a more and more radical manner. The coming of Gandhiji strengthened the pro-poor orientation. It is the poor, the daridranarayan, he said, who constituted the nation, and consequently nationalism must be judged in terms of how it affected their life. In fact, no strand of the national movement supported the maintenance of social status quo, and increasingly, with the passage of time, the movement acquired, in the Gramscian sense, a 'National-Popular' character. This was also reflected in the fact that after 1935, the movement was primarily based on the Gandhi-Nehru paradigm, thus determining the political ethos of post-independence India.

It is also important to note that the Indian national movement was not initiated as a federation of regional national movements which joined to form an all-India movement which later formed regional and language-based units or branches.

The Indian National Congress was not founded in 1885 as a federation of pre-existing regional associations such as the Indian Association of Bengal, Madras Mahajan Sabha, Poona Sarvajanik Saha or the Bombay Presidency Association. Many of the leaders of these associations were among the founders of the National Congress, but they were not federating or merging their associations in it; they were founding a new all-India body. Later, when class associations such as the All India Trade Union Congress and the All India Kisan Sabha were founded, they too started as all-India bodies. The Communist Party, the Congress Socialist Party, the Women's Federation, the Muslim League, the Hindsu Mahasabha were all started as all-India organizations.

To sum up this aspect: Nation and nationalism are a historical phenomenon. Indian nation was not a datum prior to the national movement or provided to it. Indian nation was in part the result of the political and ideological struggle waged by the movement; it was during this movement that the Indian people acquired the necessary self-consciousness and identity of being one nation. Perhaps, without this movement, Indians would have remained nothing more than the inhabitants of a geographical region on the map.

I may point out that neither Europe nor the Soviet Union ever went through this experience. In Western Europe, the only similar experience could have been that of resistance against Nazi occupation. But this was not so: the resistance movements remained separate with British and American high commands providing the only linkage. Yugoslavia did go through the experience of national liberation struggle during World War II. But the experience was too brief to create a long-lasting national consciousness or construct a nation. The only historically comparative cases to that of India in this respect have been these of China, Indonesia, Egypts, Vietnam, Korea and Philippines.

## IV

The anti-colonial struggle had produced a New Nation. The task of consolidating it and of building it up was continued after 1947 by a highly imaginative and dedicated team of political leaders who had been earlier active in the national liberation struggle. Every one of the leaders had a contribution to make. For example, Sardar Partel's role in integrating hundreds of the princely states with the Indian Union and in facing up administratively to the trauma of the Partition and the partition-riots was outstanding. It is, however, with Jawaharlal Nehru's name that the post-1947 strategy of nation-building is associated. It was Nehru's fate to define and lay down the basic contours of the nation-building effort, for he, more than any other leader, was aware that independence had to be taken beyond mere political independence, the process of the making of the Indian nation had to be pushed forward, and the foundations of a democratic, equitable and socialist India had to be firmly laid.

Nehru had no ready-made blue-print for nation-building. Even while himself being a socialist, he did not believe that the party he headed or the country should be sharply divided on left-right lines. A newly liberated, underdeveloped country existing in a world dominated by developed capitalist countries could not be built up around a single rigid economic and political programme. Millions could be united around a common vision of nation-building but not around a clear-cut political-economic 'line'. Moreover, he saw nation-building as a process which would be defined as it moved forward. Nation-building required a broad societal consensus. Nehru would rather carry out a minimum programme which united the country rather than try to implement his own maximum programme which would divide the people. His success lay in the fact that by the time he departed, he had succeeded in evolving such a societal consensus and a minimum programme.

As is well known, Nehru's commitment to democracy and civil liberties was total. Democracy was, moreover, he believed a basic component of nation-building, for it was linked to the unity of the country.

Nehru and his generation of leaders had the farsight and the courage to commit themselves to two major innovations of world historical significance in nation-building and social engineering: to build a democratic and civil libertarian society among an illiterate people and to undertake economic development on the basis of a democratic political structure.

Nehru rejected capitalist economic development and bourgeois civilizational perspective and was committed to socialism, but he would not define socialism in rigid, schematic and statist terms. In broad, general terms socialism meant social justice and ending social and economic inequality and wide disparities in income. It also meant opposing the acquisitive instinct and capitalist competitiveness and promoting the cooperative tendency. It meant gradual ending of class distinctions and class domination, and increasing social ownership or control over the means of production.

At the same time, Nehru believed that for a long time to come India must have a mixed economy. Similarly, within the broad framework of planning, reliance will have to be placed for a long time on private enterprise and the market forces.

Nehru initiated the process of the rapid, independent and self-reliant economic development of India thus breaking the vicious circle of underdevelopment imposed on India by colonialism. His success can be measured by the fact that even those who accused him earlier of initiating neocolonial development today accept that under his leadership India made the structural transition from a colonial to an independent economy.

It was tragic that the national movement could not fully counter communalism and India was partitioned in 1947. But the founding fathers of independent India, led by Nehru, Sardar Patel and Rajendra Prasad, remained loyal to the secular vision and set out to build a secular society and state, undaunted by the partition and the partition riots.

One of Nehru's and his colleague's greatest achievements lay in the consolidation of the nation and the building of a strong state. The strong state alone could defend India's unity and independence and lay the foundations of an independent economy and a just society. 'We live in a dangerous age,' he wrote, 'where only the strong and united can survive or retain their freedom.'

## V

The making of the Indian nation was a slow, partial and highly differential process. It was and is moreover a prolonged historical process. The formation of new social classes and strata and the impact of colonialism also occurred in a differential manner. The result was the extremely uneven development, both in time and space, of national and antiimperialist consciousness among different social classes and strata as well as people belonging to different religious, castes, linguistic areas, etc.

The differential and partial character of nation-making created detours and divisions which were real but which can also be best understood and studied in the context of nation-in-the-making rather than as aspects of the denial of the emerging and growing nationhood or as separate nationalisms or even as sub-nationalisms.

Moreover, because nation-in-the-making was a prolonged historical process and not an event it was constantly challenged and was capable of being interrupted. This is what happened in 1947. While the national movement was able to overcome regionalism and casteism, it failed to fully overcome communalism which had emerged almost simultaneously with nationalism. But it is of some significance that the Indian part of partitioned India continued after 1947 on the previously chartered course of developing India as a secular, democratic nation. With every passing decade the process is becoming stronger, but so long as India does not form a fully structured nation the process is not only bound to face detours and divisions but is also capable of being interrupted and disrupted. Whether the process is interrupted or not depends on how it is viewed, defended and promoted.

## VI

What is the relevance of nationalism and a strong nation-state in today's India (or the ex-colonial societies). I believe that the potential of nation formation and nationalism is not yet exhausted here and they have a historical function to perform. Without entering into a long disputation I must express my disagreement with the view held by many Marxists which regards nation as a bourgeois construct and sees nationalism as an inherently negative ideology because it is basically a bourgeois class ideology. I, on the other hand, do no believe that nationalism has a distinct class essence. It is like democracy - it has no class content of its own; it can articulate with diverse ideological elements. Consequently, nationalism still does provide a real solution to the real problem of uniting the Indian people behind a strong nation-state in their struggle for modern social, economic, cultural and political development and for overcoming their peripheralization. Nor can the Indian people struggle for social change except as a people, as a nation.

Hence, given the centrality of nationalism in postcolonial societies, the debate should really centre on the definition and content of nationalism and the character of the nation-state today. Nationalism is inevitable; the question is what sort of political trends and ideological currents have to operate within its framework. Nationalism is here the site of struggle between historically progressive and historically reactionary forces. Nation state it the terrain on which different social classes and social forces fight for hegemony over the nation. The right-wing would retain the husk of nationalism, even while draining it of all progressive content. The more extreme right wing would give nationalism a jingoist and communal definition. On the other hand, there is the nationalism that represents powerful national-popular aspirations for democracy, social justice, equity, equality and for India occupying an honourable place in the comity of nations. In fact, the definition of nationalism is the ground on which different ideological, political and social forces are contending with each other today. And whichever political-ideological formation occupies the nationalist terrain will become the dominant force in India and will dominate or control the Indian state.

# The Construction of a Hindu Identity in 19th Century India. A Synopsis

Tapan Raychaudhuri

1. Hindu identity in pre-colonial times was a personal and locally relevant construct. It did not imply a sense of belonging to a larger group, certainly not a community covering the entire subcontinent. Besides, even in the definition of one's social identity it was not a primary referrent. Caste, the village of one's origin or domicile were the primary referrents. At a certain level, one would answer that one was a Hindu, if asked 'What are you?' but this was not the first likely answer to such a question.

2. 'Hindu' as a primary referrent of identity, emerged in the 19th century, was initially confined to sections of the western educated urban Hindus and the sense of belonging to a pan-Indian Hindu community emerged even later.

3. As ist often emphasised, the term 'Hindu' is of non-Indian origin and its original connotation referred simply to the people living in the geographical area of the subcontinent. In the Indo-Inslamic era, those Indians who believed in certain religious doctrines and observed certain ritual and devotional practices were identified as Hindus, though both in their beliefs and in their practices they covered a very wide range of variations. Interestingly, al-Biruni in his famous account of India, refers to the 'Brahminical religion', though he describes the Indian people as Hindus.

4. The construction of a self-conscious Hindu identity was a part of the phenomenon described in the literature as proto-nationalism. Its essential characteristic was the projection of an identity, based on social and cultural formations like social groups with similar or same religious beliefs, shared language, caste or habitation, and claims for that identity of a glorious past and specific shares in opportunities and material resources in the present. This self-conscious emphasis reflected an interaction between a selective perception of one's cultural characteristics, past and present, and an emerging awareness of political rights, in a specifically modern sense of the term. We see here a twofold process and each component interacting with the other: an articulation of social-cultural identities which had been taken for granted in the past and a politicisation of that identity. The caste associations of the nineteenth century are prime examples of such a development. If one can speak in terms of a hierarchy of identity formations, their highest and surely the most comprehensive manifestation was the idea of an Indian nation. Very often, the two were perceived to be coterminous, a persistent feature of irridentist Hindu nationalism to-day.

5. Arguably, the perception that the Hindus constituted a single cohesive, albeit diversified, community is of colonial origin. It is first clearly articulated in the writings of James Mill whose pradigm for Indian society was based on the notion of two mutually opposed and irreconcilable entities, Hindus and Muslims. Subsequent colonial discourses on India underlined the multi-ethnic nature of Indian society, partly as an argument to prove the impossibility of nationhood in India. At the same time, paradoxically, Hindus and Muslims continued to be projected as mutually irreconcilable monoliths. British historians' version of Indian history traced this record of conflict to the Indo-Islamic era, which they described as the period of Muslim rule. The conflicts between Rajput and other Indian chieftains on the one hand and the Turkish and Afghan invaders and their descendants on the other were presented as a record of Hindu-Muslim conflict.

6. Orientalist writings on Indian civilisation, past and present, also described the cultural inheritance in terms of particular religious traditions, particularly Hindu and Buddhist. The Indian great traditions thus came to be seen in popular discourse as the Hindu tradition.

7. The proto-nationalist discourse, in its emphasis on past glory, echoed this perception and projected a vision of Hindu India. The reform movements, Brahmo Samaj, Arya Samaj etc. were also geared to a quest for an essentialist Hindu faith, equally valid for all Hindus and their agenda for reform was similarly aimed at all Hindus. The past, as perceived in this discourse, challenged the colonial ascription that India had no patriotic tradition. It drew upon the colonial historiography of India to prove that their was a tradition of patriotic tradition. It drew upon the colonial historiography of India to prove that their was a tradition of patriotic resistance to the alien Muslim rulers in the history of conflicts between the Turko-Afghan and Mughal dynasts on the one hand and the Rajputs and Marathas on the other. These 'Hindu patriots' were then perceived to be the forebears of all Hindus, Bengalis, Gujaratis, Assamese and all. Individual thinkers focussed on particular features of the religious-cultural tradition to emphasise a hoary tradition of national unity. The fact that the sakta pithasthanas were scattered in all parts of the subcontinent was, for example, emphasised in this context. The alleged tradition of a nationalist identity became an exclusively Hindu tradition.

8. Some of the social-cultural movements in this period, aimed at raising community consciousness, actually had the effect of building up an exclusive and often confrontational identity. The record of the Arya Samaj, the Sanatana Dharmasabha and the movement glorifying Hindi, Hindu, Hindustan are instances in point. The latter's emphasis on cow protection sharpened the confrontational edge of this definition of identity. The contradictions within such definitions were not obvious at the time. The emphasis on Hindi and Hindustan excluded the bulk of the Hindu

population and had irridentist implications unacceptable to that majority. Such contradictions came to the fore only in the twentieth century.

9. The perception of a comprehensive and monolithic Hindu identity, which had no basis in social reality, persisted even in the maturer phase of nationalist consciousness when there was a conscious attempt to claim the Indo-Islamic past as a part of the national heritage and include the Muslims in the imagined community of the Indian nation. The basic colonial paradigm of two monoliths, Hindu and Muslim, was not rejected. Only, the Muslims, as the Hindus' foster brothers were now seen to be a part of the Indian nation.

10. The policies of the colonial state sharpened the sense of the Hindu identity. The Census operations accepted 'Hindus' as one basic category for enumeration, though there was a constant awareness of the difficulties of applying it in practice. Then in matters of allcation of resources, in appointments to government jobs and in the allocation of seats in the representative bodies at every level, Hindus and Muslims were treated as primary categories. The consciousness of identity was sharpened, fossilised and given an aggressive edge in consequence. Political parties and movements were to take advantage of this fact, but they did so mainly in the twentieth century.

# Community Concepts and Community-Building: Exploring Ethnic Political Identity in Colonial India

Dietrich Reetz

While the formation of political identity in India is most often associated with pan-Indian forces of the nationalist movement, regional identity-building before independence is often neglected or relegated to the background. Though the main political forces of the time, the Indian National Congress and the Muslim League, were themselves composed of different regional sub-groupings, both aimed at objectives comparable in their reach beyond a particular region and for the lure of power over the whole of India. To fill this gap, a comparative study of regional politics under colonial rule might be required. This paper focuses on ethnic and religious movements of an independent stature and a somewhat indigenous political nature before independence. It builds on a conceptual framework which was laid out in an earlier article on the subject.[1] The twenties and thirties of this century with their high tide of the nationalist movement gave a strong boost to mass support for regional political parties aiming at an ethnic or religious appeal. After independence their concepts, organisations and leadership networks extended right into the body politics of the young states of India and Pakistan.

For the purpose of comparison, I would distinguish between *three types of regional political reflexes* relying on ethnic and religious support: major activist, minor activist and loyalist movements. Their political status varied. At some time they were independent, on other occasions they belonged to one of the major pan-Indian movements, the Indian National Congress or the Muslim League and at times all three options applied simultaneously. When a local group championed a particular cause like the administrative amalgamation of the Oriya-speaking tracts of various provinces it lobbied for whatever support it could get, be it within Congress, any other party, or independently.

1. For the major activist movements it was characteristic that at some stage they became political parties, making full use of the techniques of mass politics. In the pursuit of their goals they would grow militant and clash with the colonial administration. But the Indian National Congress also attracted some of the fire. After Congress formed some of the provincial governments as a result of the elections of 1937 under the reformed constitution of 1935, smaller communities, more than ever before, regarded Congress as the *heir apparent* to British rule. As independence drew nearer, so grew the animosity these groups harboured for the Congress and the Muslim League who acted as the future masters of British India.

The 'Red Shirt' movement of the Pathans fell into this category. It started in 1930 and was closely connected with the Civil Disobedience movement. The Sikh movement of the early 1920s also belonged here. It grew out of a religious campaign to gain administrative control over the Sikh temples called the *gurdwaras*. The latter had almost changed into private property of the pro-British ministers, the *Mahants*.

The Madras-based Non-Brahmin movement from 1916 onwards has been included here as well. It was a social reform movement that aimed at the emancipation of all Hindus who were ranking lower than the Brahmans, the highest caste in Hinduism. In the late thirties it converted into an ethnopolitical Dravidian and Tamil movement which clashed with the first Congress Government of Madras Presidency under Rajagopalachari (1937-1939) over the language issue of Hindi vs. Tamil.

The Sikh, Pathan and Tamil cases serve as the major reference examples of the present study since they were the most extensive, coherent and sustained regional challenges. They represented a wide variety and broad sections of India's political and social geography.

2. Smaller activist movements of lesser extent and ferocity in Kashmir, Assam, Baluchistan and many more places which simmered sometimes in the underground or had only short peaks of prominence could be combined into a second group. They often did not succeed in creating a large impact on both the provincial and the national politics of India at the time. Yet, they created the first network of political activists, ethnopolitical concepts for their respective communities etc. and they usually continued after India and Pakistan gained independence.

3. The third type of movement mainly stuck to loyalist constitutional means. Here, first of all, one has to mention the various movements for the creation of linguistic provinces of the Andhra, of Sindh, of the Oriya, the Tamils, and the Kannarese. Some of their demands were granted through the reforms act of 1935. They usually had no spontaneous or militant mass following and were often confined to what one would call 'drawing-room politics.' At a later stage, they were partially incorporated into the Congress movement which was more receptive to regional sentiments and had shown the way by creating linguistic Congress provinces at its annual Nagpur session in 1920. On occasions when they did approach the public like the movements for the amalgamation of the Oriya and the Telugu areas, they were fairly successful in striking a sympathetic cord with the masses. Their legacy was substantial. Most of their leaders continued to work for ethno-nationalist causes of these communities once independence was achieved.

When the Pathans, the Sikhs and the south Indian Tamils developed sub-nationalisms of their own they often emulated the all-India nationalist movement since it was so successful with its campaigns of civil disobedience.

What was distinctive about Indian nationalism? Though it was inspired by Western concepts of territorial and political nationalism it was not identical with it. The cultural and religious factor was much stronger in India. More precisely, it was the system of intellectual and social norms within a particular religion rather than the belief in God that became the bedrock of infant nationalism. Influential Congress leaders like Gandhi (1869-1948) himself and, more pronounced, Aurobindo Ghosh (1872-1950), Gangadhar Tilak (1856-1920), Lala Lajpat Rai (1865-1928) and Madan Mohan Malaviya (1861-1946) used Hindu religious rhetoric, symbols and practices to reach the broad, illiterate masses. Nationalism was wedded to religion right from the very beginning whereas in Europe nationalism had been dissociated from religion, had after the Enlightenment and the French Revolution grown out of a negation of belief and the affirmation of reason. The Indian experiment was to reconcile reason with God. As Sayyid Ahmad Khan (1817-1898), a staunchly pro-British Muslim reformer, most radically speculated, God could not have given reason to man without wanting him to use it.[2] And Ramakrishna (1836-1886), when asked if God cannot be realised without giving up the world, answered, '... By living in the world you are enjoying the taste of both the pure crystallised sugar and of the molasses with all its impurities. ... Work with one hand and hold the Feet of the Lord with the other.'[3]

Modern political identity is no doubt a function of mobilisation. Groups of like-minded and interested activists, the famous élite, are as much involved in this process as the masses with their demands and expectations. In the early nineteenth century and prior to that political group identity had few opportunities to manifest itself in India, except in religion, in tribal, or clan affairs. Even the famous mutiny or uprising of 1857/58 was a largely spontaneous event which then was pushed in certain directions and utilised by local political and military leaders. It is true that there was a way of ascertaining the will of local village populations through councils, the traditional *panchayat* system. The hallmark of religious, tribal, caste or clan identity, however, was structural, largely indisputable authority which had not to be ascertained since it was either inherited or God-given. The very process of the transition from individual or local to group identity was one inseparable from the nationalist movement and the introduction of democratic political institutions, even if they were only partially or very minimally representative.

If all-India nationalism was moulded by religion from its inception, so was sub-nationalism, or ethnic politics. In that respect ethnic nationalism was even further apart from the Western model than Indian nationalism. It was much closer to traditional structures like caste, clan, tribe or religious community. In the cases under review here, ethnolinguistic identities could not be separated from religious aspects. Ethnic groups like the Pathans or the Tamils were equated with particular sub-divisions of religious communities. The Pathans were known as a Muslim people. The descent of their tribes from the Prophet and his times was always an important element in the group mythology of the Pathans.[4] Rejecting traditional

Brahmanical supremacy, Tamil religious reformers developed an egalitarian variant of Hinduism shifting emphasis to the worship of Shiva, one of the major incarnations of the Supreme Being in Hinduism, and the medieval Tamil *siddhi* teachers who questioned religious orthodoxies. Their religious hymns gave rise to the philosophical system of *Śaiva siddhanta* which acquire the status of indigenous revivalism.[5] In the Sikh case, the nexus between identity-building and religion was obvious and followed the opposite pattern with a religious community going ethnic. Fragmentation was another mark of distinction from the Western mould, both of the all-India and the regional variants. Where the social fabric betrayed a multitude of religious, caste, or tribal divisions it looked like a patchwork of multiple loyalties. Larger groups could be constructed in different ways with similar legitimacy out of the same material, the *jatis*, the basic units of Indian society. It was rather the rule than the exception that extra-regional movements like those of the lower-caste Non-Brahmins, the depressed classes, or religious orders of the Muslim *Naqshbandi* kind, were overlapping with linguistic movements of the Telugu, Tamils, Mahrattas, Sindhis etc., criss-crossing the political geography of India.

## Stages of Mobilization

At the same time, ethnic and all-India nationalism were modern concepts. They could hardly be regarded as a simple continuation of a well-worn pattern of society. Their appearance on the political stage involved drastic changes of conventional structures. The process of change through which social and cultural movements went to become nationalist was surprisingly similar for both the whole of India and its regional and ethnic components:

The shaping of political group concepts started with a drive for religious or cultural awakening and revival. Those movements bore the first traces of indigenous nationalism. Religious and ethnic community élites tried to redefine themselves against the alien influences of British authority and Christianity which had so successfully challenged their traditional hold over Indian society. The spiritual ancestor of Indian nationalism, Rammohan Roy (1772-1833), wrote the polemical pamphlet 'The Precepts of Jesus' in 1820 and the forebear of Muslim politics, Sayyid Ahmad Khan, joined in with the first Muslim commentary on the Bible, *Tabin al-Kalam,* in 1862. The 'Indian Renaissance' and the movement for better education of Muslims followed closely on the heels.

Revivalism also led to a renewed interest in the vernacular as an authentic medium of expression and instruction. At the same time, this was a response to the domination of English print and culture. Printing provided the vernacular languages with new avenues for dissemination of linguistic material and with the means for creating an indigenous intellectual élite. I here refer to Benedict Anderson's exposition of the influence of print capitalism on nationalist reflexes.[6] The vernaculars gained rising significance with the foundation of vernacular colleges and universities which became another hallmark of these movements.

At the second stage, loyalist parties emerged who were trying to plead the cause of the community they represented with the authorities on the lines of constitutional reforms and political representation. From the history of Congress loyalism is the known hallmark of its initial phase. And, when the Muslim League came into being in 1906, who could rival with its loyalism towards the authorities?

The third stage was characterised by a radicalisation of the pursuit of political goals of representation and power. While forces supporting the loyalist organisations often co-operated with the British because they owed their status to their patronage, they were now challenged by up-and-coming social classes connected with the general commercialisation of society. The new strata resorted to mass actions of a pronounced militancy along with the civil disobedience movement or following its suit. They positioned themselves for independence which since the end of the First World War was believed to be imminent in one form or the other. The Congress under Gandhi and Nehru and the Muslim League of the thirties and forties stand as obvious examples for this phase on the all-India stage.

Though these stages were no doubt mirrored by the regional movements under discussion their evolution showed significant variations. The clear sequence of time, leadership and organisation at different stages which was so typical of the all-India movements was blurred and sometimes reversed at the regional level. Be it for the lack or scarcity of leadership, structures and mobilisation in the region, fact is, that, unlike at the centre, ethnopolitical activists and organisations rather themselves passed through the different stages mentioned above displaying diverse attitudes at different times.

Religious reform efforts amongst the *Sikhs* started with the Singh Sabhas from 1873 onwards. The first well-known Sabha meeting gathered in Amritsar to protest derogatory remarks by some Hindus on the Sikh faith and the life of Guru Nanak, the founder of Sikhism. The Singh Sabha movement was driven by the desire to counteract conversions to Hinduism and Christianity. Other objectives were the preservation of the original teachings of the Sikhism of the Gurus against various accretions and the promotion of Western education.[7] The latter was symbolized by the foundation of a separate College for the Sikh community, the *Khalsa* College. The part of the loyalist party was played by the *Chief Khalsa Diwan* which was established in 1902. It continued to sponsor educational activities in the Sikh community. Sometimes its loyalty was overriding communal solidarity. When members of the *Ghadr* party, Sikh radicals and anarchists, returned to India in 1915, the Diwan supported the government's ruthless measures against them.[8] The Diwan continued and developed earlier educational activities. In 1917-18 when the next constitutional reforms act was being prepared, it started actively jockeying for the extension of the principle of communal representation [separating the electorates and the candidates on religious or communal lines] to the Sikhs. It was particularly feared that the Muhammadans who had been granted a statutory majority in the Punjab would use their bloc votes to 'tyrannise' the Sikhs.[9]

Radical politics in the Punjab started with the popular upsurge against the Land Colonisation Bill in 1907 in which the Sikhs were actively involved, although none of their community organisations participated. The Jallianwala Bagh massacre in the Punjab when Government troops were shooting defenceless and peaceful demonstrators on 13 April 1919 turned the tables on political fortunes across India. In December 1919, the inaugural session of the Central Sikh League in Amritsar heralded the radicalisation of Sikh politics. Leadership quickly passed into the hands of the more rebellious. Direct action was contemplated for the first time in October 1919 when the Sikh League gave a public call for 100 bands of martyrs - *shaheed jathas* - to proceed to Delhi and forcibly repair the wall of a Sikh Temple which had been demolished as a result of Government actions. They were to proceed at all costs - even of their lives. In December 1920, a movement was started to take over the Gurdwaras from the *mahants*. This campaign led to the revival of the *Akalis* not only as a religious sect but also as a political party after they had started out as the militant arm of the Temple Administration Committee, the *Shiromani Gurdwara Prabandhak Committee*.

The denial of constitutional reforms to the *Pathans* in the Frontier Province where elections were unknown even to the local bodies up to 1930 had significantly retarded the formation of Pathan political organisations. Educational concerns were taken up by religious leaders like the Haji of Turangzai (1858-1937) and Maulana Obeidullah Sindhi (1872-1944).[10] Their approach to education was aptly reflected by Maulana Sindhi who paid a stipend of 50 Rupies to English-educated students in Delhi so that they would attend his lectures on the Koran in the Fatehpuri Mosque in Delhi. 'He was of the view that the English-educated section of the community was ignorant of religion and if they got acquainted with the true spirit of Islam, they would serve the nation and the people better.'[11] The Haji started *Azad* schools, independent from government, in 1910, a programme in which Abdul Ghaffar Khan (1890-1988) was also involved. For this purpose Ghaffar Khan founded the *Anjuman Islah-ul-Afaghina* (Society for the Reform of the Afghans). The drive to induce villagers to boycott Government schools met only with limited success. In these *Azad Schools* the main elements of the curriculum were Islamic learning and Pakhtun culture. The Haji himself was a poet of note in Pashto.[12] The alternative schools programme was obviously started under the influence of the orthodox Muslim *Deoband* Seminar and its principal, Maulana Mohammad ul-Hasan, whom Ghaffur Khan held in high esteem. The seminar was not only the seat of Islamic tradition but also of anti-British feelings and activities.

In 1929, when Ghaffar Khan launched the *Red Shirt* movement, it was also called the 'Servants of God' Society or *Khudai-Khidmatgaran*, a name, indicative of the persisting strong concern for social and educational reform. One of his recurring demands was the foundation of a separate university for the Frontier Province.[13] In-between, loyalist political activity mainly took the form of deliberations on the advisability of the extension of constitutional reforms to the Frontier Province. It was the Frontier (Bray) Enquiry Committee formed in 1922 that was called upon to examine the question of reform.

By 1928, the Khans realised that an elected majority would eventually erode or do away with their revered status in the provincial body polity of the Frontier. The previous supporters of reform were frightened out of their cause during the interviews with the Simon commission touring India from 1928 for the revision of the Government of India Act.[14] When in the course of the civil disobedience movement the Frontier exploded in 1930, radical politics were forced on the province by the Red Shirts. They would not have gained widespread support in such a short span of time had they not made the revival of Muslim Pathan identity the focus of their campaign. Growing into a lower-middle class rural-based protest movement the Red Shirts surged to victory as a branch of the Indian National Congress during the first party-based elections to a provincial parliament in 1937. They captured 19 out of 50 seats in the new legislature and could eventually form a coalition ministry.

*Tamil* intellectual revival started in the late nineteenth century. *Tamil sangams* or associations were formed around the turn of the century sponsoring the publication of Tamil classics and scholarly analysis of Tamil literature. These efforts were generally non-sectarian which means that there was no particular reference to caste membership or religion. Both Brahmans and non-Brahmins participated in the movement. The most famous of modern Tamil poets, C. Subramania Bharati (1882-1921), was a Smartha Brahman. The religious element was added by the propagation of the *Śaiva Siddhānta* system. For this purpose, local organisations named *Śaiva Siddhānta Sabhas* were formed, the earliest of which could be traced back to Tuticorin in Tinnevelly district in 1883.[15] After that numerous *Śaiva Siddhānta* meetings were held in district towns of the Tamil areas. Intellectual interest in the Tamil tradition continued throughout the twenties and culminated in the foundation of a Tamil University, called the Annamalai University, at the temple center of Chidambaram in South Arcot district in 1929. When the ultra-loyalist South Indian Liberal Federation which came to be known as the *Justice Party* entered the public arena of Madras Presidency in 1916 it built on the foundations of the feeble and little known Madras Dravidian Association that had been formed in 1912. In South India, the exceptional plight of Hindus who were not Brahmins was prompted by a significant variation in Hinduism as compared to the north. Except for the Brahmans, all other caste groups were regarded to belong to the *Śūdras*, the lowest of the four major caste designations. Therefore, in south India, there were no intermediate caste groupings between the Brahmans and the Śūdras. Caste rules of avoiding marriage, social contact and inter-dining with lower castes were more rigid here and the Brahmans were considered to be much more arrogant and oppressive towards the lower castes than in the north. Brahmanism was equated with northern India and the non-Brahmins, originally quite an artificial term since it included all those who were not Brahmans, were supposed to be of Dravidian, i.e. south Indian origin. The Justice Party, therefore, started to pursue the aims of the non-Brahmins in a Dravidian context. The *Dravidian* cause emerged as proto-'Tamilism', i.e. ethnic nationalism of the Tamils, albeit in a more camouflaged and embryonic form. Addressing the first Justice Party Confederation in Madras in 1917, P. Tayagaraja Chetti stressed that 'the genius of Dravidian civilization does not recognize the difference between man and man by birth... It is the Aryans who have introduced this birth distinction ...'[16] Much longer than other loyalists, the Justice Party stuck to its pro-British policies encouraged by its relative success as the governing provincial party of Madras Presidency since the 1920 Legislative Assembly election till 1926 and from 1930 till 1936. Its electoral defeat of 1926 when it finished the race second with 22 seats after the Congress-Swarajists (41 seats) betrayed the signs of a deepening crisis in the party.

It was then that the Self-respect movement of Ramaswami Naicker, who had been a prominent non-Brahmin leader in Congress but left it over dissent on the caste issue, started to dominate the Justice Party until he was elected the leader of the party in December 1938. Naicker and his movement represented the kind of radical politics capable of reaching the masses. He felt no hesitation to resort to agitation in order to press for his demands. The movement 'went native' that is to say Tamil with its militant agitation against the compulsory introduction of the essentially North Indian Hindi language as a medium of instruction in the south Indian heartland of Dravidian culture and languages, advocated and tried by the first provincial Congress Government from 1937 onwards.

## Community of Belief

Interestingly, the movements under discussion all fostered and propagated notions of community which passed through similar stages. Goals and symbols were tied into concepts. They picked up prevailing trends and topped them with group interests of those leading the movements.

At the stage of revivalism religious reform groups counted on non-territorial and rather vague groups of adherents and believers. All Sikhs were members of the *Khalsa*, the Sikh community, living necessarily dispersed all over India with a higher density only in the Punjab. The reform efforts of the Non-Brahmin organisations were likewise directed at all Non-Brahmins irrespective of their place of residence, but with an emphasis on south India. The initial reform efforts amongst the Pathans were aimed at tribal loyalties. References to tribal allegiances were usually non-residential and extended also to their migration routes and their temporary Afghan homes although territories inhabited by a certain tribe became more meaningful during the period in question.

At this stage the perceived state of decay and degradation of the community constituted an important element of the emerging community ethos. They felt left behind in the race for education. They had allegedly degenerated in their social customs, had started betraying their religion or their traditional belief system. They therefore had to return to the Golden Age of their community or religion, had to free their belief system or religion from corrupting influences of the British, the Christians and/or the Hindus.

The *Sikhs* started to perceive these challenges very strongly after the annexation of Punjab by the British in 1849. The missionaries of various Christian orders were the first to establish their centres in different towns of the Punjab. They enjoyed the support of British officials and vied with each other in their proselytising pursuits. It was particularly Sikhs from the lower strata of society who were attracted to Christianity. The conversion of Maharaja Dalip Singh in 1853, followed by other aristocratic families, sounded a warning signal to Sikh orthodoxy. British administrators in the early 1850s had concluded that 'Sikhism' was on the decline since the number of Sikhs seemed to be on the decrease. Their census return of 1.2 million Sikhs in 1868 caused much controversy. It had followed a rather narrow definition of Sikhism keeping the number of its adherents fairly low.[17] The arrival of the Christians in the Punjab was closely followed by the emergence of the *Brahmo Samaj* and the *Arya Samaj*, Hindu reformist and revivalist movements. It was, therefore, considered high time when in 1873 with landed money support an organisation called *Singh Sabha* (society or chamber of Sikhs) was formed in Amritsar.[18] Under the guidance of the Maharaja of Faridkot and Baba Khem Singh Bedi, it focused on the education of their co-religionists. While Bedi was quite comfortable portraying Sikhs as a reformist element within greater Hinduism, another organisation, the Lahore Singh Sabha, championed the more aggressive assertion of Sikh separateness and attacked popular customs, such as respect for caste and Hindu influence in ceremonies and shrines.[19] Here was the Sikh variant of the all-India trend to restore the 'pure faith' and the 'true teaching' of religion. Its avowed objectives included the 'restoration of Sikh rituals', elimination of 'the other religious practices' and 'propagation of Sikh religion as desired by the Sikh Gurus.'[20] In addition to defending Sikhism against Arya Samaj attacks, the Singh Sabhas built schools and the aforementioned college, opened orphanages, established archives and historical societies and produced a flood of polemical and scholarly literature on Sikh tradition. By 1900, almost a hundred Singh Sabhas or related societies were scattered across the Punjab. Mainstream and majority revivalism was augmented by the increasing spread of the revivalist sects of the *Nirankaris* and the *Namdharis*, with the latter taking a violent turn in the Kuka rebellion.

If the arguments of degradation and decay were important to the Sikh movement, they were essential and central to the Non-Brahmin and the Self-Respect campaigns that foreshadowed *Tamil* activism. Their major intention was to raise awareness among the non-Brahmin caste groups of their downtrodden status in society. The credo of a movement of all non-Brahmins was formulated in Maharashtra as early as 1873 by Jyotiba Phule (1827-1890) and his *Satyashodhak Samaj*. He proclaimed the need to save the 'lower castes from the hypocritical Brahmans and their opportunistic scriptures'[21]. His major book published in the same year was ominously titled *Gulamgiri*, or 'Slavery'[22]. The activists of the self-respect movement led by E. V. Ramaswami Naicker believed that self-respect should come before self-rule. They wanted to increase their self-esteem and make the non-Brahmins realise that they could achieve everything in life without the Brahmans. It was the prevalent practices of Hinduism and the Brahmans who were supposed to be degraded. To remove the stigma of unworthiness from the non-Brahmins they wanted to give them a new sense of worth, the worth of their own tradition. Here the juxtaposition of the south Indian Dravidian languages and cultures to the north Indian seat of the Aryan civilization came in handy. Although the southern Hindus were part of the same centuries-old evolution of the Indian civilization and of Hinduism they were proclaimed the direct heirs to the indigenous Dravidian peoples who had allegedly been conquered by the North Indian Aryans.

Fighting degradation and decay was no less meaningful for the *Pathans*. This concerned both real and imagined degradation. The image of the Pathan even among the Indian political and religious élites was still portrayed as being savage and uncivilized. Hostage-taking and violent tribal warfare had instilled fear in many Indian hearts, in particular in those of the Hindu families who lived in or near the Frontier and who, with their considerable wealth were a favourite and easy target of Pathan trans-frontier raids from the formally independent belt of tribal territories beyond the settled districts of the Frontier Province.

The real degradation, however, concerned the social conditions of the Pathan tribes which were among the worse in India. Ghaffar Khan, the leader of the Pathans, exclaimed in 1931: 'Whose condition is worse today? Whose children are dying naked today? These are the children of the Pakhtun. Think, at least something, about this degraded state of yours.'[23]

The revival or rather the creation of a common Pathan or Pakhtun ethos was the foremost task of Ghaffar Khan, when he addressed thousands of village people across the frontier province in 1930-32. During those speeches which were simple in style and repetitive in content because they were addressed to a tribal audience he decried the lack of education, the disunity of the Pathans, the disregard for the Pashto language and the servility towards the *firangi*, the fair-haired Englishman. In the Shinkiari village on 7th November 1931, he argued: 'I say it is our country therefore the 'Maliki' [ownership, rule] will be that of the Pakhtun. The sovereignty will be that of the Pakhtun, no other nation has the right to come and rule over the country of the Pakhtun. This is my object and we want that the treasuries of our country should be used for the Pakhtun, the Firangi should not use it for making rivalry. We will satisfactorily feed our children and construct schools and hospitals. It is because of getting this country for the Pakhtuns that we have girded up our loins. If we do not get the country, we will lie down in the graves.'[24]

Ghaffar Khan liked to look upon himself first and foremost as a moral and social reformer. He claimed that his movement was a 'moral and spiritual' one and was aimed at eradicating the ills of Pakhtun society.[25] He tried to retract core values from the ethical system of the Pathans, the *Pakhtunwali* which allegedly had been forgotten and abandoned, particularly when resorting to violence in abductions and reprisals.

## Community of Need

In the times of loyalism the emerging ethnic and religious parties shifted the focal point of reference to issues of social status and political participation. Disabilities and deprivation became important catchwords of the day in order to evoke solidarity with demands for special communal or extended representation.

The *Chief Khalsa Diwan* contributed significantly to the codification and harmonisation of religious and political demands made on behalf of the Sikh community. After the Census of 1901, which had returned a rather low number of adherents to the Sikh faith in the Punjab (8.49 per cent), it negotiated with the British administration the redefinition of census criteria for Sikhism so that sects on the fringe like the lower-caste and *sahajdari* Sikhs could also be included in the community.[26] The recognition of a separate group identity assumed a critical importance for the Sikhs during the hearings of the Public Service Commission of 1913. While the representative of the *Diwan*, Sundar Singh Majithia, contended that Sikhs were separate from Hindus and deserved an employment quota of their own, Gurbakhsh Singh Bedi argued to the contrary that Hindus and Sikhs were inseparable and should be treated that way for the purposes of recruitment and other civil service arrangements.[27] Later, the Diwan thrived on the question of securing extra-proportional communal representation in the Punjab Legislative Assembly. The Muslims had been assured a quota of 50 per cent of the seats in the Punjab under separate Muslim electorates through the 1916 Lucknow *Compact*, as the agreement between the Congress and the Muslim League was called then. The Sikhs regarded the Muslim majority a statutory domination which it was apprehended would 'terrorise' the other communities. In order to offset this threat, the Sikhs who constituted 11.92 per cent of the population of British Punjab and the States in 1911,[28] demanded a share of one-third of the seats in the Punjab Legislature. The tremendous war effort and the large tax contribution of Sikh farmers and landholders were quoted in justification of the extra-proportional claim.[29] During the second Round-Table-Conference the Sikh memorandum of November 12, 1931 still demanded 30 per cent of the seats in the Punjab

Legislative Council if a communal solution in favour of the Muslims could not be avoided. Similarly, for the Punjab Cabinet and the Public Service Commission Sikh representation by one third was envisaged. In the Lower and Upper House of the future central parliament 5 per cent of the British Indian seats were to be reserved for Sikhs. Falling considerably short of Sikh demands, the Communal Award of August 16, 1932, retained the separate electorate for them in the Punjab and granted them a fixed quota of 31 plus one women's seat which amounted to a quota of 18.83 per cent. of the 175 seats in the new Punjab Council. This exceeded their population share by half or 50 per cent. Within the Punjab allotment of 30 seats in the Central Legislative Assembly Sikhs would be represented by 5 deputies amounting to 1.6 per cent.[30] The 1935 Government of India Act raised these figures only marginally to 33 in the Punjab Legislative Assembly and to 6 seats in the Central Legislature. It further provided them with 3 out of 50 seats in the North-West Frontier Province, and 4 out of 150 in the Federal Council of State, in case one came into existence. The Sikhs were particularly piqued at the refusal to grant them reserved seats in the legislatures of the United Provinces and Sindh where they formed sizable minorities.[31] In the meantime internal differences rapidly increased. The Akalis took to a more extremist position by which politically favouring complete independence from Britain which led them into an alliance with Congress. The Chief Khalsa Diwan found it necessary and promising to form its own party for the elections of 1937, the *Khalsa Nationalist Party*. As a confidential government report aptly observed the party had been formed 'with the object of getting back the influence which the Sikhs of the leading families in the province have lost' to the extremist faction of the Akalis.[32] In the 1937 elections, the loyalists succeeded. Out of the 33 Sikh seats they captured 18 and joined hands with the Muslim government of the Unionist Party under Sikander Hayat Khan which gained the absolute majority.[33]

The *non-Brahmin* movement was essentially a movement for the removal of disabilities. One of its first activities by its founding father, C. Natesa Mudaliar, was the creation of a hostel for non-Brahmin students in Madras to relieve their plight as they could not get access to other student accommodation due to caste restrictions. And, after it had been in office for two Council periods, the Justice Party was accused of running a 'jobocracy,' to which Ramaswami Mudaliar replied in an interesting twist: 'Yes, I am proud to be a job-hunter, only I hunt for jobs not for myself or my relations, ... but I ask openly and demand that jobs should be available to the hundreds of young men fully trained and equipped, who are now forced to remain idle, because they have not the fortuitous aids of other communities.'[34] Here again, it was the Public Service Commission of 1913 which threw up the issue in its full dimension. In 1912, of the appointments of Deputy Collectors, Sub-Judges, and District *Munsifs* [judges] in Madras Presidency, non-Brahmins held only 21.5, 16.7 and 19.5 per cent. of the posts respectively, while the Brahmans occupied 55, 82.3, and 72.6 per cent. of the jobs, with the Christians and the Muslims well behind. These figures were given by A. G. Cardew, the acting Chief Secretary to the Government of Madras. The fact that non-Brahmins as compared to 1896 had visibly lost ground added additional momentum to the dissatisfaction.[35] Shares in literacy and university graduates were equally uneven.[36] By 1926, this situation had drastically changed. Non-Brahmins had entered all spheres of public life and had in fact been dominating the politics of Madras Presidency for seven years.[37]

Communal representation in Parliament was considered to be one of the major remedies against their disadvantaged position. Yet here as in the case of the reservation of jobs in the administration heated arguments were exchanged over the advisability of reserving jobs and parliamentary seats for the majority which the non-Brahmins themselves claimed to represent. With the Brahmans making up 1.31 million in 1911,[38] all other groups were lumped together so that the non-Brahmin manifesto of 1916 and non-Brahmin leaders boasted of the support of 40 odd million non-Brahmins.[39] During the hearings of the 1919 Joint Select Committee of the British Parliament on the arrangements for constitutional reform of the same year non-Brahmin leaders succeeded to convince the committee members of the deep seated prejudice and bias against non-Brahmins and, more important, of the ability of the Brahmans, who practically held the monopoly of education and local administrative power, to manipulate the democratic process that was to be gradually introduced since people depending on them economically or spiritually would not dare voting against them. When the Brahman and non-Brahmin representatives could not agree over the share of communal representation for the non-Brahmins in the Legislative Council, the arbitrator, Lord Meston, decided in March 1920 they would be granted 28 reserved seats out of 63 which meant that in every constituency there would be one general seat, for which no caste or other qualifications applied, and one reserved for the non-Brahmins.[40] However, and this is interesting to note, significant communal reservation did not protect the Justice Party against electoral defeat in 1926 and 1937 when other parties and most notably Congress managed to court the non-Brahmin votes more successfully.

One significant reason for their decline was their increasing self-restriction to the interests of only selected non-Brahmin caste groups. At the core of the social concerns moving the non-Brahmins lay the non-Brahmin caste Hindu groups of the Mudaliars (Tamil Vellalas), the Naidus (Balijas), and the Reddys (Kapu, mainly from Telugu areas). The famous Non-Brahmin manifesto of 20 December 1916 which started the movement made a particular reference to these groups. Reading the manifesto carefully, one finds that from the very outset of the movement its chief aim was to provide these up-and-coming social groups with jobs and political power, to advance their status in the social hierarchy.[41]

Whether the *Pathans* and the Frontier Province were in need of reforms was hotly debated and disputed. The hearings of the Bray Committee made it clear that there existed a loyalist group of Khans which favoured constitutional reform for the

Frontier. The Committee report concluded: 'The Pathan of the districts is now keenly alive to the issues before us; and if mistrust of the Pathan is to override the Pathan's self-determination for self-development in a separate province, the danger of his turning westwards may become real.'[42]

But when pressed as to their readiness to accept the principle of election they insisted on nominated representation with special consideration for the Khans. K. B. Abdul Ghafur Khan was a case in point here. Khan Baz Mohammad Khan of Teri was rather an exception pleading for Khans to stand for elections along with the commoners. Another point of contention was the grant of certain privileges to the Hindu minority if a Council was introduced in the Frontier. The impression was that some of the Khans and elders questioned wanted the full range of reforms that were granted in the Punjab. In this, they were less guided by their intention to improve the situation in the Frontier Province than by their wish not to be seen as inferior to other groups and regions in India. It was a matter of tribal pride not to be considered lower than the neighbouring Punjabis.[43] When the Pathans pressed for reforms some were rather unsure what exactly the reforms would entail: 'If Reforms is a good thing, as all of them say it is a good thing, then it should be increased ... And if it is a good thing why should we be deprived of it?'[44] But the British failed to recognize the spirit of the time in the Frontier. When they extended the Montagu-Chelmsford reforms of 1919 to the province in 1932 they gave too little too late. With preparations for a new constitution after the findings of the Simon Commission in full swing, Pathan pride was deeply hurt at this minimalist concession. Only the 1935 Government of India Act treated the Frontier Province at par with the other provinces of British India.

Since the Pathans were not a minority or a disadvantaged group in any other aspect the reservation of seats as in the cases of the Sikhs and the Non-Brahmins was not a burning issue. Out of 50 seats which the Frontier legislature was to have, under the all-India scheme of communal representation 33 were rural Muslim seats. It further included three urban Muslim constituencies, nine general, *i.e.* mostly Hindu, three Sikh and two landholders seats.[45]

Though the Pathans did not argue over quotas in the legislature - they had rather graciously accepted that the minorities like the Sikhs, Hindus and the landholders were well overrepresented - public service employment became an important issue in the political debate. The very fact of the extension of the 1919 reforms to the province in 1932 had opened new job avenues to the aspiring local élite which were tremendously enhanced by the provincial autonomy introduced in 1937.

Presenting the case of constitutional reforms and employment opportunities to the Pathans, Ghaffar Khan decided to play on tribal instincts and conventional social norms. Arguing for reform he evoked envy and rivalry - feelings well-known from the Bray Committee hearings. He wondered whether the denial of reforms to the Frontier that had been granted to Madras, Punjab, the central and the united provinces, did not mean 'that the Pakhtun is not a capable man in his [British] opinion.'[46] Demanding the abrogation of special legislative powers for the Frontier, the *Frontier Crimes Regulation of 1901*, he was not averse against exploiting local superstition and religious prejudice. Protestation was not led on the ground of its undemocratic or discriminating character, but with reference to the fact that it curtailed the judicial powers of the tribes and gave certain limited rights to women to press their cases in courts of law.[47]

All this was massive evidence in support of the contention that at this point the communities of the Sikhs, Pathans, and non-Brahmins, later Tamils, had turned into communities of quotas and employment in the provincial services, the administration and the legislative councils. One has to remember, however, that only few people could hope to become provincial ministers or legislators. It was basically the English-speaking élite that stood to benefit from these movements. In 1931, literacy in English stood at roughly 1.22 per cent. which was a fairly select club (that still totalled up some 3.6 million people).[48] Right through the twenties and thirties voters who participated in the political process were likewise thinly spread. The provincial franchise of the population constituted 2.8 per cent in 1926.[49] This was indicative of the narrow social base political movements had at the time. Yet it was a necessary stage since for the first time it opened politics to participation by millions.

Since demands on behalf of the communities and ethnic groups had become more specific at this stage, territorial differentiation of their geographically amorphous group references also deepened. The rough borders of a homeland for their community became recognizable. The Sikhs established a sort of community government through the Gurdwara Act of 1925 which contrary to general politics granted universal suffrage in the elections for the organs of the Temple Administration of the whole community thereby making Amritsar and the Punjab their territorial seat of community administration. The 1931 Sikh memorandum at the Round-Table-Conference went even further. For the first time, it introduced the element of territorial readjustment to increase Sikh weightage within the Punjab province. If no agreement could be reached on Sikh demands for communal reservation, the boundaries of the Punjab should be altered by transferring predominantly Muhammadan areas either to the Frontier Province or to a separate, new province in order to 'produce a communal balance'. The Memo clearly strived to enhance the ethnic attributes of a redemarcated Punjab province by stipulating that the official language of the Province should be Punjabi and that it should be optional for Sikhs and others to use *Gurmukhi* script if they so desire.[50]

The Justice Party had also withdrawn to Madras Presidency supporting only casual contact with the Bombay Presidency Non-Brahmins. This became evident during the interviews by the Simon commission of non-Brahmins of one wing of the Justice Party, the South Indian Liberal Federation (Constitutionalists). Confronted with differences of opinion with non-Brahmins from Bombay Presidency who did not favour reserved seats they preferred to confine themselves to Madras.[51] And, while the Khans interviewed at the session of the Joint Select Committee 1919 rarely referred to the Pathans in general terms, these references became frequent by 1928 in the hearings of the Simon Commission. Reform-minded Khans started to identify their province, which had only been created in 1901 by way of separating five districts from the Province of Punjab, as the home for Pathan political aspirations in the ensuing all-India race for constitutional reforms and other 'goodies.'[52]

## Community of Deed

Yet, in spite of all the achievements of the constitutionalists which were embodied in the Government of India Act of 1935 and the ensuing elections, ethnic politicians and the masses were not satisfied. Those who advocated radical change on the political scene now associated themselves with the demands for both Indian independence and social reform for broader, mostly peasant masses. With the advent of radicalism politicians could rely on a much more diversified political network. Provincial administrations had been functioning more independently. For the 1937 elections, the 1932 Lothian Franchise Committee increased the provincial franchise to between 5 and 17 per cent. That was still not very representative of India's toiling millions. But it multiplied the electorate to 36 millions posing in itself a complex technical problem how to arrange elections under the conditions of India.[53] Political leaders made the present condition of the common masses their central topic to enhance their attraction. It was at this stage that for the first time ethnic and ethnoreligious movements gained a real mass following. The Shiromani Akali Dal in Punjab was said to have 80,000 members, according to British intelligence estimates.[54] Similar numerical estimates were given for the Red Shirts. The Self-Respect movement probably did not exceed several hundred, but its offspring, the anti-Hindustani movement, attracted crowds of 40 to 50 thousand people at the height of the campaign.

The perceived state of bondage and slavery became a major plank in their efforts to mobilise broader sections of people who led a miserable life. The Pathan leader Ghaffar Khan couched his political demands in similar words. When Stewart Pears, Chief Commissioner of the Frontier Province, received Ghaffar Khan for an interview on July 30, 1931, he was surprised that Ghaffar Khan took so little note of the constitutional reforms. The Frontier establishment had formed the opinion that the lack of participation of the emerging new Pathan élite in the governance of the province where the introduction of reforms had been considerably delayed was the chief cause of dissatisfaction. They had hoped that the extension of the Montague-Chelmsford reforms of 1919 would buy the Pathans off from the road of resistance and violence. Recording his impressions from the interview Spears could not conceal his contempt for Ghaffar Khan whom he considered a trouble maker, not a devout Muslim. Ghaffar Khan's 'harping on the present 'state of slavery' of the Afghan race Spears regarded as the reflection of a strong inferiority complex.[55] In the following years, the perceived state of slavery remained a recurrent theme with Ghaffar Khan's public pronouncements. When he toured the Frontier in 1945, he called on his listeners: 'We cannot continue to be slaves. The very idea is revolting, and it is a crime not to be free.'[56]

The events that occurred between 1930 and 1933 were almost a Pathan rebellion. Coinciding with the beginning of the Congress-led civil disobedience campaign on 30 April, 1930, which the Red Shirts had joined, the Pathans fiercely resisted attempts by the British to control political life in the province under a mainly security-related pretext. As allies of Congress the Red Shirts who ruled the province after the 1937 elections faced a similar dilemma of choice like the Sikhs. The Congress alliance could not protect them from the ascent of the conservative Muslim League in the course of its aggressive Pakistan campaign. The nearer independence drew the clearer it became that freedom from slavery for the Pathan movement of the Red Shirts didn't just mean freedom for India, but also emancipation of their community.

It was the related theme of suffering which was raised by the *Akali jathas*, volunteers of the Sikh movement, who courted arrest for the sake of their community. Writing to Mahatma Gandhi about the essentials of their movement on April 20, 1924, the Shiromani Gurdwara Prabandhak Committee explained its method of non-violent resistance: 'This method has been adopted with the conviction that it will lead to success by moving the callous heart of the oppressor by presenting to him the sight of suffering inflicted by him and that by cheerfully enduring this suffering strength will be evoked in us and the public will be convinced of the depth of our feeling and the sincerity of our cause. This suffering may take the form of imprisonment, fines, beating or death.'[57]

When Gandhi counselled in favour of a token individual protest of some volunteers, the SGPC in its letter defended the participation of Sikh masses in the activities: 'In your suggestion about the limitation of sathyagrahis to 'one or at the most two' you have not taken into account the significance of the institution of sangat in Sikhism and the principle of numbers involved in the Jaito struggle... The sangat is believed as the Guru incorporate. From the times of Guru Nanak onwards, Sikhs in large numbers have been proceeding to Gurdwaras and congregating therein. The freedom of temples would mean nothing without the free and unfettered exercise of this right.'[58]

After the passage of the Gurdwara Reforms Act of 1925 the temple movement died down. Though the act did not completely satisfy the Sikhs, attention reverted back to ordinary politics. But the equation of Sikh political forces had dramatically changed. The temple movement had established the Akalis as a new and radical political body whose leader Master Tara Singh (1885-1967)[59] was determined and willing to use its influence with the Sikh masses for permanently steering the course of Sikh politics into more stormy waters. Their temporary alliance with Congress from 1936 onwards showed the pitfalls of such policy. Though the Akalis supported the quest for complete independence, Congress as a national party had a different agenda. The Akali leaders who had fought so hard to attain their strong position in the Sikh community would only accept such actions and policies on behalf of the Congress high-command which did not clash with significant communal interests. In 1939 Congress decided not to join the British war efforts because India and their newly elected provincial governments were not consulted when India was declared a belligerent party and because it still hoped it could exert pressure on Britain to advance India's release into independence so that it could support Britain as a free nation. The Sikhs, however, had always maintained a special relationship with the army. Army service was the social basis for the existence of many a Sikh family. The Akalis, therefore, contrary to Congress policy, went for a wholehearted support to the recruitment effort. Gandhi was outraged and wrote to Master Tara Singh quite pointedly on August 16, 1940: 'As I have told you, in my opinion you have nothing in common with Congress nor the Congress with you. You believe in the rule of sword; the Congress does not. You have all the time 'my community' in mind. The Congress has no community but the whole nation. Your civil disobedience is purely a branch of violence.'[60]

Master Tara Singh resigned from the All-India Congress Committee but the Akalis did not leave the Congress. They tried to play both sides. Through the recruitment effort they hoped to win government support and to strengthen their bargaining position towards the Muslim League. But the Akalis grew increasingly frustrated over what they regarded was an attitude of appeasement when Congress declined to resist the Pakistan scheme by force. They feared that under the Pakistan scheme or any other communal solution that was based on the Muslim majority of the Punjab its rule would permanently remain with the Muslims reducing the Sikhs in their major home place to a position of obedience. When the Muslim League appeared to be unwilling to give the Sikhs comprehensive guarantees the Akalis decided to resist the inclusion of their main settlement areas into Pakistan tooth and nail. As a last remedy, the partition of the Punjab (along with Bengal) was effected in order to secure the non-Muslim areas for India. At this stage the Akalis again were in fair command of the Sikh masses who were ready to join them in opposing the original partition scheme. Though the Akalis remained with Congress for some time after independence was achieved they again parted ways when the Akalis felt in need of a communal solution for the Indian Punjab as well which rekindled the fire of hatred and terror.

The Justice Party found it difficult to approach broader sections of society. It was electoral failure in 1926 and later in 1937 that prompted some soul searching on the part of the non-Brahmin leaders. Given its staunchly anti-Congress politics in the preceding decades, one of the more surprising moves of the Justice Party leadership were attempts to forge a quasi-alliance with Congress. This in itself was not unusual since Congress claimed to be an umbrella organisation for all nationalist forces which it wanted to unite and to represent. Though the alliance did not materialise, in 1926 Justice Party activists were allowed concurrent membership of Congress. Then it was clear that renewal of the party would not come from within. The well-known non-Brahmin politician E.V.R. Naicker who had been with Congress represented the type of leader needed to gain a real mass following. Capturing the leadership of the Justice Party he acted from outside. With his Self-Respect movement that gained momentum after 1926 he created a political base of his own. His language was straight and kept in simple Tamil. Like other radical politicians of the time he reflected on the deplorable state of the masses whose plight he wanted to alleviate. The theme of degradation and bondage also resounded from him. In 1931, in the preamble to the party constitution he recalled the efforts of his party to rouse 'the attention of the mass people to the enormity of their superstitious habits, customs, and practices of their religion and caste, and of their degraded economic conditions of life,' and he decried 'that the various political, social and religious bodies and institutions are ever more determined to hold the masses in social, religious and economic bondage and degradation, through their political organisation all over the country.'[61]

Ramaswamy Naicker tried various weapons of mass politics before he finally made ethnic Tamil nationalism his major political abode. He vigorously attacked religious customs and superstition, the role of the Brahmans, the caste system and prevalent Vedic interpretation. For instance, he demanded a re-evaluation of major characters of one of the main scriptures of Hinduism. To him, the positive hero Rama was less important and more telling of his Aryan arrogance than Ravana whom he made the embodiment of a Dravidian hero. His followers resorted to burning the religious 'Book of Manu' which contained the major caste principles. Communal representation, that means continued reservation of seats for non-Brahmins, remained of utmost importance for him.

In 1931 Naicker started to come under the influence of socialist and communist ideas. After he made a tour of Russia and some European countries in 1931-2, he began to propagate the Russian experience in applying the principles of communism. He even translated Frederik Engels' 'Principles of Communism' into Tamil. In order to give the Justice Party and his own movement more depth and strength he started to train professional propagandists. But all to no avail. In the 1937 provincial elections, the Justice Party was left with only 17 seats out of 215 in the lower house of the Provincial Legislative Assembly while Congress took 159 seats.[62]

When in 1937 the Congress-led government under C. Rajagopalachari decided to introduce compulsory teaching of Hindi as a political symbol of the nationalist unity of India it provided Naicker with a long-sought after cause for political agitation. After the government began its Hindi programme in 125 selected secondary schools in June 1938, the agitators started picketing these. The main focus of the campaign, however, was on picketing the residence of the Chief Minister and of the Madras Hindi Theological High School. The agitators also tried to raise bands of volunteers, the famous *jathas*, but the right response from the public was somewhat wanting. Some of the agitation did create a public disturbance, particularly, when women joined in the campaign in November 1938. The number of prisoners in the whole course of the agitation went little over 1,000. Some of the better-attended meetings pulled crowds of 50,000 people showing a real mass concern for the aims of the anti-Hindustani movement, if only a temporary one. The agitation died down in 1939 and became irrelevant when the Congress ministry stepped down in October of the same year. In 1944 the Justice Party changed its name to Dravidian League (*Dravida Kazhagam*). The new party and its various offsprings, the *Dravida Munetra Kazhagam* and the *Anna-Dravida Munetra Kazhagam* were still to play their most important role in Tamil nationalism and Indian politics after independence was achieved.

## Claims and Realities: the Obstinate Balance of Independence

By 1947 group identity building had advanced a long way. Their leaders, however, did not receive the final blessing of the masses for their separate schemes of partial independence. All-India forces had been equally successful in shaping public opinion and identity perceptions.

Independence which had created the two sovereign states of India and Pakistan through a painful partition process did not fulfil the expectations of its major regional movements. The freedom of the nation states they did not consider their own freedom. All three movements met their Waterloo if only temporarily through the independence and its related factors. The Pakistan movement was probably the single most important political factor which had contributed to their dilemma since it had induced and incited a deadly and mutually exclusive competition for power and political representation. But beneath that there were several long-term factors at work which had strengthened regional élites and brought up the basically democratic demand for the emancipation of regional traditions and cultures. The failure to accommodate them more fully during the preparation of the Government of India Act of 1935 and during the transfer of power to the independent governments did cost the body polity of both India and Pakistan dearly. The movements were paralysed temporarily but within years could be seen fighting back causing an excruciating process of administrative and political adjustment to the multi-ethnic and multi-religious character of their societies.

The group concepts deployed after independence had been finalised during the period under review. They resolutely ascended from the ambiguous to the definite. They gradually became more territorial and power-oriented. At the same time moral rigour increased tremendously taking strength mainly from religious injunctions and the perceived need to return purity and morality to the belief system.

All the three movements under review banked on the moral example of their leader, on the personal sacrifice of their activists. The theme of sacrifice was obviously influenced by the ethics of Gandhi who repeatedly argued that Indians had to purify their souls and to make sacrifice. Here the topic of moral improvement was attached which resurfaced in the Sikh, Pathan and Non-Brahmin movements - a value obviously common to the whole Indian civilisation irrespective of religions or caste membership.

Possibly it was this linkage between morality and territorial power what tells the Indian nation or sub-nation concept from the Western model. In the Indian context religion and morality would and could not be distilled from national identity. I see two major reasons for that:

*First*, the need to reassert oneself against the real and perceived continued domination by the West which did not recede or diminish. The domination took different forms and shapes sometimes expressing itself in values and sometimes in economic relations. Whether this feeling was implanted or nourished by the colonial agent it was based on real inequality which persists even today. The morality-power connection may have been thought of as a partial remedy for that.

*Second*, and may be even more important: Where European nations for the reaffirmation of their identity can allow themselves to fall back on ethnic histories, constructed or real, ethnic histories in India were yet to emerge at the time of the foundation of Indian nationalism and its sub-nationalisms. It was this new sequence of historical events which returned the searching looks of Indian leaders time and again to religious and moral traditions. And it was this changed sequence of intellectual history which turned religious and moral tradition into a major part of the new ethnic histories which have been shaped since the last century.

At least during the 1920s and 1930s it was moral ethnicity that we encountered as the favourite community concept.

Contemporary developments in ethnic politics of the subcontinent confirm that the reorientation of community concepts to modernist economic development needs in a way was a passing one. The re-emergence of moral rigour in today's sub-nationalisms of South Asia is not new or surprising. If it is often attributed to disappointment with modern capitalism and political liberalism it can be equally explained through its formative roots in the period under review.

## Notes

1 Dietrich Reetz, Ethnic and religious identities in colonial India: a conceptual debate. In: Contemporary South Asia, Oxford 2(1993)2, pp. 109-122.

2 Cf. Dietrich Reetz, Enlightenment and Islam: Sayyid Ahmad Khan's Plea to Indian Muslims for Reason. In: The Indian Historical Review, New Delhi *XIV*(1988)1-2 (July 1987 & January 1988), pp. 206-218.

3 From the Gospel of Ramakrishna, pp. 158-60, quoted in: Steven Hay (ed), Sources of Indian Tradition, Second edition, vol 2: Modern India and Pakistan, New York 1988, pp. 66-67.

4 'The putative ancestor, Qais, lived at the time of the Prophet. He sought the Prophet out in Medina, embraced the faith, and was given the name of Abdur-Rashid. Thus, Pathans have no infidel past, nor do they carry in their history the blemish of defeat and forcible conversion' (meaning unlike others whose ancestors converted to Islam, D.R.). F. Barth, Pathan identity and its maintenance. In: Features of Person and Society in Swat: Collected Essays on Pathans. Selected Essays of Frederik Barth, vol. II, London 1981, p. 105.

5 Cf. John H. Piet, A Logical Presentation of the Śaiva Siddhānta Philosophy (India Research Series, VIII), Madras 1952, pp. 3-4ff.

6 Benedict Anderson, Imagined Communities, London-New York 1991 (rev. & ext. ed.), pp. 33-36 and chapter 3, pp. 37-46.

7 Cf. Harbans Singh, Origin and Development of the Singh Sabha. In: Punjab Past and Present, vol. VII, part I, April 1973, pp. 21-30, here: pp. 28-29; Harbans Singh, The Heritage of the Sikhs, Delhi 1983, pp. 232-239; G. S. Chhabra, Advanced History of the Punjab, Vol. II, Ludhiana 1973, pp. 454-465.

8 Kailash Gulati, The Akalis Past and Present, Delhi 1974, p. 19.

9 Memorandum on Sikh Representation submitted by the Chief Khalsa Diwan, Amritsar, in Indian Statutory Commission [I.S.C.], Selections from the Memoranda and Oral Evidence by Non-Officials (part I), London 1930, pp. 135-137.

10 For the biography of Maulana Sindhi, see Francis Robinson, Separatism among Indian Muslims: the politics of the Unites Provinces' Muslims, 1860-1923 (Cambridge South Asian studies, 16), London 1974, p. 425.

11 D. G. Tendulkar, Faith is a Battle, Bombay 1967, p. 22.

12 For the Haji of Turangzai see Government of India. Who's who in the Peshawar District. Corrected up to 1 January 1931, Peshawar 1931, p. 12. Confidential. Shelf Mark IORL L/P&S/20B.296/10. His civil name was Fazl-i-Wahid: 'In June 1915 he left British Territory and started on Rustam in August. He subsequently moved to Bagh in Mohmand (Kandahari) country and has since been unplacably hostile to Government losing no opportunity to suborn the assured clans.'

13 P. S. Ramu, Momentous Speeches of Badshah Khan: Khudai Khidmatgar (Servants of God) and National Movement, Delhi 1992, p. 38.

14 'The sudden introduction into the Province of an elective system for filling the seats in the Council will, in our opinion, disorganise relations of trust and confidence between the Khans and the people, and will also lead to discord. We have, therefore, proposed the constitution of the Council in the above-mentioned manner so as to preserve the influence of the Khans who, according to their merit, will be largely nominated by the Head of the administration, and their majority will be thus assured.' Memorandum submitted by the Khans of the North-West Frontier Province. In: I.S.C., Selections (part I), p. 248. See also evidence by the Khans' Deputation to the Simon Commission on 19 November 1928, ibid., pp. 249ff.

15 K. Nambi Arooran, Tamil Renaissance and Dravidian Nationalism, 1905-1944, Madurai 1980, pp. 20-21.

16 R. Varadarajulu Naidu (comp.), The Justice Movement, 1917, Madras 1932, section II, p. 139, quoted in: Eugene Irschick, Politics and Social Conflict in South India, Berkeley 1969, p. 289.

17 Quoted in J. S. Grewal, Legacies of the Sikh Past for the Twentieth Century. In: J.T. O'Connell et al. (eds.), Sikh History and Religion in the Twentieth Century, Delhi 1990, pp. 25-26.

18 Cf. Gobinder Singh, Religion and Politics in the Punjab, Delhi 1986, pp. 57ff.

19 N. Gerald Barrier, Sikh Politics in British Punjab prior to the Gurdwara Reform Movement. In: 'Connell et al. (eds.), Sikh History..., pp. 170-172.

20 Ajit Singh Sarhadi, Nationalisms in India and the Problem, Delhi (n. d.), p. 34, quoted in: Gobinder, Religion and Politics..., p. 58.

21 Quoted in: Sumit Sarkar, Modern India, Delhi 1983, p. 57.

22 Cf. Rosalind O'Hanlon, Caste, Conflict and Ideology: Mahatma Jyotirao Phule and Low Caste Protest in Nineteenth-Century Western India (Cambridge South Asian Studies, 30), Cambridge 1985; Gail Omvedt, Cultural Revolt in a Colonial Society: The Non-Brahmin Movement in Western India: 1873-1930, Bombay 1976, pp. 107ff.

23 Ghaffar Khan at a Red Shirt meeting at Khairmaidan on 6th November 1931. Quoted in: Ramu, Momentous Speeches..., p. 26.

24 Ramu, Momentous Speeches..., p. 33.

25 Erland Jansson, India, Pakistan or Pakhtunistan? The Nationalist Movement in the North-West Frontier Province, 1937-1947 (Studia Historica Upsaliensia 119), Uppsala 1981, p. 49.

26 Barrier, Sikh Politics..., p. 182.

27 Sundar Singh claimed beliefs were primary and outward appearances less important. For his evidence, see United Kingdom, Parliamentary Papers, Royal Commission on the Public Services in India: appendix vol. X, London 1914, Cd. 7582, p. 71-75. Gurbakhsh Singh Bedi who represents the established section of Sikh élite held the opinion that the emphasis on the separateness of Sikhs from Hindus is only 20-25 years old. Ibid., pp. 125-127.

28 Government of India, Census of India, 1911, Punjab, vol XIV, part I, subsidiary table i: General distribution of the population by religion, p. 193.

29 See, for instance, Great Britain, Parliamentary Papers, Joint Select Committee on the Government of India Bill, London 1919, cmd. 203, vol. 2: Minutes of Evidence, Evidence by Sardar Thaker Singh, p. 2726. For a thorough account of the representation demand and the exchange of respective arguments, see Memorandum on Sikh representation submitted by the Chief Khalsa Diwan, Amritsar, and the following interview in: I.S.C., Selections, (part I), pp. 135ff.

30 Christine Effenberg, The Political Status of the Sikhs during the Indian National Movement, Delhi 1989, pp. 53-57.

31 See Great Britain. Parliament, Government of India Act, 1935, London 1935, First Schedule: Composition of the Federal Legislature, pp. 218-219, Fifth Schedule: Composition of Provincial Legislatures, p. 245. The latter still showed 32 seats for the Sikhs in the provincial legislature. The addition of one seat was made after the publication of the Act.

32 Emmerson to Linlithgow, 19 October 1936, Linlithgow Papers, NMML. In: K.L. Tuteja, Sikh Politics 1920-1940, Kurukushetra 1984, p. 176.

33 Of the 175 seats, the Muslim Unionist Party got 96, Congress 18 (of which 5 were Sikh seats), the Muslim League got only 2. Of the Sikh seats, the Khalsa National Party secured 18, the Akalis 10, and the Congress 5. The rest were Independents. Ibid., p. 179.

34 Hindu, weekly edition, 1 January 1925, quoted in: Irschick, Politics and Social Conflict..., p. 263.

35 United Kingdom, Parliamentary Papers, Royal Commission on the Public Services, appendix vol. II, Minutes of Evidence ... taken in Madras from the 8th to the 17th of January, 1913, Cd. 7293, London 1914, pp. 103-104.

36 For further details see Arooran, Tamil Renaissance..., pp. 35-40.

37 The figures of comparative increase of general literacy and literacy in English released in the 1931 census for Madras Presidency proved convincingly that the non-Brahmin groups had made considerable advances. With general literacy of all ages in Madras Presidency standing at 9.26 per cent in 1931, general literacy of non-Brahmin caste Hindus varied between 7 and 40 per cent. which was a twofold increase over 1901. During the same period, their English literacy had increased up to ten times. Government of India, Census of India, 1931, Madras, vol. XIV, part I, Report, Subsidiary table v. Literacy by communities, Madras 1932, pp. 281-282.

38 India. Government of India. Census of India, 1911. Madras, volume XII, part II, Madras 1912, table XIII, part I: Caste, tribe, race or nationality, p. 112.

39 Hindu, 20 December 1916.

40 Irschick, Politics and Social Conflict..., p. 165.

41 The non-Brahmin manifesto stated that, '...though rather late in the field, the non-Brahmin communities have begun to move. They now represent various stages of progress. Some of them such as the Chetty, the Komati, the Mudaliar, the Naidu, and the Nayar, have been making rapid progress; and even the least advanced, like those who are ahead of them, are manfully exerting themselves to come up to the standards of the new times... In a variety of ways and in different walks of life non-Brahmins will now be found unostentatiously and yet effectively contributing to the moral and material progress of this Presidency. But they and their brethren have so far been groping helplessly in the background, because of the subtle and manifold ways in which political power and official influences are often exercised by the Brahmin caste.' Hindu, 20 December 1916. In: Irschick, Politics and Social Conflict..., p. 362-363.

42 Report of the North-West Frontier Enquiry Committee and Minutes of Dissent by Mr. T. Rangachariar and Mr. N. M. Samarth, Delhi 1924, p. 17.

43 Cf. Report and Evidence of the North-West Frontier Enquiry Committee,

44 See evidence to the Simon Commission in November 1928: I.S.C., *Selections*, (Part I), op. cit., p. 269.

45 Erland Jansson, *India, Pakistan or Pakhtunistan?*, op. cit., p. 54.

46 P. S. Ramu, *Momentous Speeches of Badshah Khan*, op. cit., p. 37.

47 'These laws are such that under them, our sisters and mothers go to the courts which is a cause of disgrace to us.' Ghaffar Khan at a meeting in Shinkiari on 7 November, 1931. In: Ramu, Momentous Speeches..., p. 36-37.

48 Government of India, Census of India, 1931, vol I. India, part II: Imperial Tables, pp. 424-425, calculated on the population aged 5 years and over.

49 I.S.C., Survey , London 1930, part III, Working of the reformed constitution, p. 197.

50 See the memorandum on Sikhs and the New Constitution for India, presented by Sardar Ujjal Singh and Sardar Sampuran Singh. In: United Kingdom. Parliamentary Papers. Cmd. 3997, Indian Round Table Conference, 2nd session, 7 September 1931 - 1 December 1931, proceedings, London 1932, pp. 74-75.

51 I.S.C., Selections, part II, p. 225.

52 When meeting continued resistance on the part of the Simon commission to extend complete reforms to the Frontier Province, Khan Sahib Sardar Gulhan Khan of the Advanced Muhammadan Party fumed: 'If we are wanted to be a part of India, in that case we want reforms: and if we are not wanted, if this manly and virile race is not wanted, then we can be told at once, and in that case I would suggest that we may be left alone. I.S.C., Selections, part I, p. 272.

53 Franchise (Lothian) Committee 1932. In: Indian Annual Register 1932, vol. I, Delhi 1990 (repr.), pp. 437-471, here: p. 455.

54 Cf. secret government memo on Akali Dal. In: Papers of Sir Evan Jenkins, Governor of the Punjab, Record of disturbances and constitutional affairs, confidential letters, interview notes etc., Mar-Aug 1947. India Office Library and Records R/3/1/176, file pages 75-80.
Kerr doubts that the mass participation was really massive. Mohinder Singh (The Akali Movement, Delhi 1978, pp. 100-101, table note) gives the number of 25,000 which even if doubled would amount to only 1.6 per cent of the Sikhs in the Punjab (3,110,060) in 1921. Ian J. Kerr, Fox and the Lions: The Akali Movement Revisited. In: O'Connell et al. (eds.), Sikh History..., p. 222, footnote 46.

55 Quoted in: Tendulkar, Faith is a Battle, p. 110.

56 Quoted in: Attar Chand, India, Pakistan and Afghanistan: a study of freedom struggle and Abdul Ghaffar Khan, Delhi 1989, p. 67. Another, similar quotation see ibid., p. 64.

57 Ganda Singh (ed.), Some confidential papers of the Akali movement, Amritsar 1965, p. 66.

58 Singh (ed.), Some confidential papers..., pp. 65-66.

59 He was the president of the temple administration committee SGPC from 1936 till 1944, and he also remained the president of the Shiromani Akali Dal for most of this period. Except for a short period in 1944, he remained the most prominent Akali leader of the time.

60 M. K. Gandhi, The Collected Works, vol. LXXII, Delhi 1978, pp. 395.

61 Quoted from: Arooran, Tamil Renaissance..., p. 269.

62 Madras Mail, 23, 27 February 1937. In: Arooran, Tamil Renaissance..., p. 184.

# Specifities of Emergence of Modern Social Classes in India in the 19th and Early 20th Centuries

Erik Komarov

The protracted process of formation of modern social classes and groups, i. e. the bourgeoisie and other 'middle classes', and the working class, started in India in the second half of the 19th century. Certain 'bourgeois elements' of society surfaced already in its first quarter, yet in very small numbers and at a few places only.

In India as elsewhere the emergence of modern classes resulted from and reflected the gradual disintegration of precapitalist (medieval) relations and the rise of bourgeois ones. The pronounced Indian specificities were conditioned by both indigenous and external factors. The major indigenous factor was the specific traditional social nature epitomized in the caste system and relatively high level of precapitalist market in medieval times. It largely conditioned the peculiar social shape of the emergent modern classes. The most important external factor was the British colonial rule which transmitted to India the brunt of rising world capitalism with its highly contradictory consequences. It largely determined the specific way of modern class formation.

## The Extreme Unevenness as the Major Specificity

The traditional mercantile and intellectual communities from among whom the emergent bourgeoisie and other middle classes were initially recruited in colonial times were quite substantial in late medieval India. However, they had evolved within the caste system and were much more rigidly separated from the lower social strata than was usually the case elsewhere, especially in the West, while a large section of the lower orders were subject to exceptionally severe social and economic oppression.

When colonial India came to be drawn in the world trade of the rising industrial capitalism of the West quite a few members of her traditional mercantile and intellectual elites proved able rather early and quickly, already in the 19th century, to master modern forms and means of economic activities up to industrial investment, as well as of education, social and political articulation and organization. Already in the 19th century their socially and politically active elements began identifying themselves as 'a new class of society' hitherto unknown in the country. Meanwhile the masses, even the emergent factory workers, yet remained essentially a medieval folk. The first signs of their awakening appeared during the times of the Swadeshi movement in 1906 - 1908. However, more or less organized struggles of industrial workers in the major centres and partially of the peasantry in some places started mainly from the 1920s, while the awakening of the vast mass of the rural and even urban poor began as a rule only after Independence and that too mostly not before the 1960s. There was very little, if any, modern class self identification even among the industrial workers, leave alone the peasantry and the rural poor, in spite of the efforts of the left in the freedom movement.

This type of social development, which largely prevailed throughout the colonial period has been defined by the present author as elitist modernization.[1]

## Some Specific Features of the Emergence of Bourgeoisie and the 'Middle Classes'

The emergence of the bourgeoisie in colonial India, especially at its initial stage, was caused by the relatively weak development of capitalist industry, both factory and prefactory in India itself, but rather by a partial but increasing transformation of the traditionally developed Indian mercantile capital into commercial capital which supported the industrial capital of Britain in the process of the colonial exploitation of India. This transformation actually preceded, and for some time overtook, the rise of industrial enterprise in India. Meanwhile, the formation of the industrial working class was dependent precisely on the rise and growth of capitalist production in India itself. This situation constituted the economic or material background of the extremely uneven growth of modern classes and strata in colonial India. The formation and development of the bourgeoisie and the 'middle classes' in general proceeded faster than the comparable process in the West and in comparison with the relatively retarded formation and growth of the industrial working class in India.

The nascent bourgeoisie came to acquire, along with the of readymade modern forms and methods of commercial and subsequently industrial entrepreneurial activitiy, also ready-made modern ideological, political and organisational perceptions from the West. This obviously accelerated the identification and articulation of the emergent bourgeoisie and middle classes in general.

When in 1829 Bengal Harkaru enthusiastically hailed the emergence of 'a class of society ... placed between the aristocracy and the poor and daily forming a most influencial class,'[2] this class comprised of hardly more, if not less, than just a few thousand persons in Bengal.

The limited and protracted transformation of the medieval society during a process of elitist modernization under colonial rule resulted in the formation of modern classes and groups mostly, and for quite some time nearly exclusively, within the framework of traditional social structure in the shape of caste system. The rising bourgeoisie, not to speak of bourgeoisified landholders as well as the intelligentsia and the educated middle classes, stemmed mostly or even almost exclusively from certain traditionally privileged castes and social communities. This signified the continuation of the traditional, medieval social gap between them and the masses fixed by the caste system. It also meant the continuation of traditional caste and communal cleavages among the emergent middle classes themselves which was accentuated in course of the bourgeois development and by the competition which facilitated the divisive policies of colonial rulers.

## Economic Changes

Yet the major fact of decisive historical significance was the very formation of the middle classes resulting from the economic changes in colonial society.

By the beginning of the 20th century India was drawn into the world trade to a much larger degree than any other major undeveloped country of Asia. In 1913 India, comprising about one third of the population, provided about half of the exports and possessed more than two thirds of the railway mileage of Asia (minus Russia and Japan). The shipment tonnage between England and India equalled almost that between England and the USA.[3]

Obviously no tangible connection of such a vast country with the world market would have been possible without the substantial participation of the Indian merchants turning into commercial traders and dealers. Acting as the agents and partners of the British commercial firms they appropriated not only financial resources but acquired also modern methods of commerce and banking. This evidently enabled the more enterprising among them to subsequently become the mill owners already from the second half of the 19th century onwards.

The minimum taxable income was Rs 500, i. e. Rs 41 per month, which exceeded at least by 5 to 6 times the wages of jute mill workers in Bengal in 1890.[4] In 1886 there were nearly 300,000 income and licence tax-payers of whom 220,000 were traders and dealers and the remaining 80,000 were for the most part members of public services and the learned professions.[5] Together with their families these tax-payers accounted for about 1 per cent of the population of British India, a tiny fraction indeed, but not so insignificant in absolute terms at that time. The data contradict a rather common notion and prove that the bulk of those who may be taken largely, if not wholly, as bourgeois elements or middle classes was made up primarily of the traders. but not of the intelligentsia. However, besides the 80,000 'public servants' who did not hail from the lowest ranks and the members of learned professions there were also about 8 000 college students (in 1887) and 214,000 pupils in secondary schools (in 1881).[6] Mainly from these years onwards the educated sections of the emergent middle classes distinctly identified themselves as the 'educated Indians' or the 'educated middle class'. Even though not all the members of the rising bourgeoisie and other medium groups were educated, which actually meant English educated (from the secondary level and above), the educated were those who mostly opted for the modernization of the country in fact for its bourgeois development.

In the second half of the 19th century India became a major sphere of British capital investments in Asia. In 1914 41 per cent of the total foreign and 66 per cent of the British investments in underdeveloped countries of Asia were made in India and Ceylon. However, as is well known the factory industry accounted for only tiny fraction of British investments in India: about 2 per cent were invested in mining and only 0,72 per cent in 'commerce and industry'. Moreover, the capital invested in British-owned or controlled private enterprises was made up mostly of the financial resources raised in India itself.[7] The capital goods were sold by respective concerns in England to commercial establishments in India, both English-owned and Indian-owned, which took up industrial business having to share profit in some way or other with the suppliers. Thus the British and Indian entrepreneurs do not seem to typologically differ from each other as founders of factories in India - both were commercial traders servicing the industrial capital of England and now they both were taking up industrial enterprises also. The colonialist privileges of British-owned business in India is here another matter. The share of India-owned capital in the total capital investments in India in the early 20th century was usually estimated at 25 - 30 per cent.

However there was a marked difference between the Indian-owned and the British-owned factory industries in regard to their orientation of production, and this is of major importance. Working mainly for the internal market since the early 20th century, the Indian-owned factory played an essentially greater transformative socio-economic role, particularly by creating conditions for further industrial development, than the British-owned industries which were mostly export-oriented. Hence it was mainly the rise of Indian enterprises which in spite of colonialist constraints initiated a relatively more pronounced industrial development in colonial India than in other major colonial and dependent countries of Asia. By 1921/22 the output of Indian cotton mills contributed over 60 per cent of the domestic production of cotton piece-goods and exceeded their import by nearly two times.[8]

Since the emergence of the internal market oriented factory industry, i. e. mainly since the early 20th century, the development of capitalism in India was becoming increasingly selfpropelled, albeit yet far from selfrelient. From that time the further growth of factory industry was accompanied by a tangible rise of pre-factory (early) forms of capitalist production. Consequently the numerical strength of the rising bourgeoisie markedly increased and the social sources of recruitment broadened, however in case of smaller entrepreneurs, the bigger ones almost exclusively belonging to traditional mercantile communities as before and the bigger investors included landlords, princes, etc. In 1947/48 (after Partition) there were about 23,000 joint stock companies. Nearly 75 per cent of capital invested in private industries was Indian-owned while about 2 per cent remained under direct control of foreign capital which also held about 27 - 28 per cent of the internal market.[9]

Almost one hundred years after the establishment of the first factories in India, however, the industrial revolution was yet very far from being completed, whereas in the West it took some 40 to 50 years. The emergent modern sector of the economy comprised hardly more than some 10 per cent of the active population. And this sector evolved a peculair hierarchic structure.

A corporate elite emerged from among the bourgeoisie which itself was still in the process of formation. The business community was constituted mostly by members of certain traditional mercantile castes. At the same, time according to B. B. Misra, the elite inside this community 'even earlier formed a separate caste by itself, and those who carried on business under them did so as their subordinate and service agents not as free merchants'. He generally classified 'the directors of Indian industries' at the end of colonial period as 'members of the upper rather than middle classes'[10]. Nevertheless by the time of Independence the Indian middle classes as a whole, although largely separated from the masses by traditional social barriers, were more developed than in most of other colonial and dependent countries. Being still a small fraction of the teeming population they represented an impressive section in absolute terms. The educated people (matriculation and above) counted for some 5 million individuals. And this mattered a lot.

## Education

In 1951 the literacy rate in India stood at 16,6 per cent (about 15 per cent in 1941 before partition) of the total population and at 24 per cent for the population of the age group of 15 and above. This was evidently not more if not less than in France in 1787 - 1790 (at the time of the French Revolution) when the estimated literacy rate of the newly married couples in that country was about 37 per cent. In Russia in 1897, not long before the Revolution of 1905 - 1907, the literacy rate of the total population was 21 per cent and that of the population above 9 years was 27 per cent (in European Russia - 30 per cent).

The elitist nature of the educational development in India was reflected among other things by the tremendous gap between growth rates of the secondary (2nd level) and higher (3rd level) education on the one hand and the primary (1st level) education on the other: 6 to 9 times, as against 3 times respectively between 1901 and 1906. The result was that according to the present author's calculation[11] the spread of the 3rd level education (number of students per unit of population) in India in 1951 equalled that in the major developed countries before the World War I, while the spread of the 2nd level education in India in 1951 even exceeded (by 1.4 times) that in the latter before World War I (Tables 1 and 2).[12] But it should be remembered that in the early 20th century in the above developed countries primary education and literacy became practically universal while in India even in 1951 the majority of population was illiterate and more than a half (58 per cent) of children remained outside primary school. Finally, in India in 1946 (before partition) the spread of 2nd level education among the general population was 1.6 times and the spread of 3rd level education was 1.5 times higher than in Russia in 1914. In India of 1951 both these indices were about 3 times higher than in pre-revolutionary Russia where, however, the literacy rate was markedly higher than in India after World War II.

Table 1

**Spread of secondary and higher education**

**Number of students per 10 000 of the total population and per the same unit of the literate***

| Country, Year | *Secondary Education* | | *Higher Education* | |
|---|---|---|---|---|
| | *Total population*** | *Literate* | *Total population**** | *Literate* |
| India | | | | |
| 1911 | 30 | 500 | 1 | 20 |
| 1946 | 80 | 480 | 5 | 42 |
| 1950/51 | | | | |
| a) all age groups | 150 | 930 | 11 | 71 |
| b) age 15 and above | 280 | 1180 | 23 | 97 |
| 4 developed countries**** | | | | |
| circa 1910 | 110 | 120 | 10 | 12 |
| 1950 | 510 | 560 | 32 | 36 |
| West Europe (all countries), 1950 age 15 and above | 540 | 540 | 50 | 50 |
| Russia, 1914 | 50 | 220 | 4 | 17 |

* All age groups if not otherwise indicated

** Rounded up to tens

*** Rounded up to unite

**** England, France, Germany (for 1950 - the FRG) and Japan. Mean values.

Table 2
**Relative Spread of Secondary and Higher Education**
**Ratios of numbers of students per 10 000 of the total population and per the same unit of the literate* in India to those in other countries**

| *Country, Year* | *Secondary Education* | | *Higher Education* | |
|---|---|---|---|---|
| | *Total population* | *Literate* | *Total population* | *Literate* |
| India - 4 developed countries** circa 1910 | 0.3 | 4.2 | 0.1 | 1.7 |
| 1951 | 0.3 | 1.7 | 0.3 | 2.0 |
| India, 1991 - 4 developed countries circa 1910 | 1.4 | 7.8 | 1.1 | 5.9 |
| India - West Europe (all countries) 1950 age: 15 and above | 0.5 | 2.2 | 0.9 | 1.9 |
| India, 1911 - Russia, 1914 | 0.6 | 2.3 | 0.3 | 1.2 |
| India, 1951 - Russia, 1914 | 3.0 | 4.2 | 2.8 | 4.2 |

* All age groups if not otherwise indicated
** England, France, Germany (1959 - the FRG) and Japan

Meanwhile it may be useful to compare the number of the 2nd and 3rd-level students in colonial India and in the above countries not per unit of the total population but per unit of the literate i. e. the 'spreads' of education of the 2nd and 3rd levels among the literate only, as is also shown in the above Tables 1 and 2.

The comparison leads to the seemingly paradoxical conclusion that in 1951 the literate in India received a much better 2nd- and 3rd-level education several times bitter than the literate in the developed countries both in 1911 and in 1951. However the literate in India comprising only a small section of the population belonged mostly if not wholly to the propertied classes (especially in 1911) as against practically universal literacy in the developed countries. Yet the number of the literate in India in 1911 (18.5 million) equalled about half of the total population of England or France and about one third of that of Germany. In 1951 their number in India (53.3 million) exceeded the total population of any major West European country and was equal to three fourth of the total population of Japan.

Be that as it may, one can well assume not only that the 2nd- and 3rd-levels education in India was exclusively or almost exclusively concentrated within the propertied classes which is rather self-evident but also that since the early 20th century the propertied classes, particularly their uppercrust, in India were provided with the secondary and higher education at least not to a much lesser extent than those in developed countries. In India of 1951 they appeared to enjoy it to a much greater extentthan in Russia of 1914. It can be argued that more often than not the standard of both the upper levels of education in India, especially in 1911 was lower than in developed countries and pre-revolutionary Russia. However, it was in any case a modern education.

A similar situation prevailed in India regarding the provision of the literate with periodicals and books, in comparison with the developed countries made by the same method as above.[13]

## Organization

The rise of a number of regional associations of modern type since the middle of the 19th century ultimately led to the founding of the Indian National Congress in 1885, which demonstrated the ability to build a national political organization on the scale of a vast and highly diverse country already at that time. The establishment of the Congress was practically simultaneous with the rise of business associations. Among them were the Bombay Native Piecegoods Merchant's Association (1882), the Bombay Millowner's Association and the Native Merchants Chamber of Coconda (1885), the Bengal National Chamber of Commerce (1887). The newly formed Congress provided 'a direct political background'[14] to such sectional organizations particularly of business and landed interests. Landlord's or landholder's associations, etc. were also formed in some provinces at that time.

The Indian Merchant's Chamber founded in 1907 was a sort of a forerunner of the Federation of Indian Chambers of Commerce and Industry established in 1927. Thousands of joint stock companies also reflected in their way the level of organization of the bourgeoisie and other propertied classes. To a large extent the same can be said of many of the cooperative societies which emerged in the early 20th century. In 1938 they numbered over 120,000 and had 5.6 million members.[15]

Besides modern organizations, there was a large variety of traditional bodies mostly of the propertied classes or led by them. They were often already somewhat modernised and intervowen with modern organizations. This increased organizational strength of the propertied classes simultaneously tended to or actually did result in a communal or casteist turn of their organizations and politics.

A kind of multiparty system gradually evolved particularly since the 1920s. The Congress itself became a specific combination of a national association and a dominant political party and received the biggest mass support. With the exception of the Communists and small left-oriented formations, the other parties outside the Congress were either communal and casteist, if they had any tangible mass following, or purely elitist, practically without mass support, but they nevertheless played no small political role under British colonial rule.

The quasi-parliamentary institutions (the Legislative Councils and Assemblies and also local self-government bodies) which came into being under the British rule since the late 19th and the early 20th centuries were avowedly elitist. The electoral system envisaged an electorate both extremely limited and divided on communal and social lines (separate electorates). Initially only an infinite small part of the population was enfranchised. In the 1930s the electorate, communally and otherwise divided as it was, was enlarged to a mere 14 per cent of the adult population (above 20) and that too only for the elections to the Provincial Assemblies. Incidentally only 54 per cent of this meagre electorate voted in the elections in 1937.[16]

The membership of national leaders in the legislative and local elected bodies who utilised this platform for a critique of the colonial rule, and more over the fact that the Congress after participation in the elections to Provincial Assemblies in 1937 formed provincial governments, even though for a brief spell, evidently contributed to creating democratic traditions, to training people for a parliamentary democracy. This was, however, only one aspect of the history of political democracy in the country. The democratic traditions were created first and foremost during the long and arduous course of the freedom movement which increasingly involved the masses under the leadership of Mahatma Gandhi. It was largely under his leadership that the freedom movement in fact implanted modern democratic norms of political action and behaviour. As early as 1916 Gandhi urged to demand Swaraj relying on 'our democracy'.[17] In 1925 he pointed out that Swaraj was to be attained 'by educating masses to a sense of their capacity to regulate and control authority[18]'.

## The Working Class

The workers of organized industries and transport numbering about 4.4 million in 1946 (by itself quite a tangible number) comprised less than 2 per cent of the active population. But the industrial workers were the first among the Indian masses to awake and to get organized. Because of the much higher productivity of their labour as well as their increasingly organized struggles the industrial workers were better off than the other poor. Nevertheless their living conditions were bound to be also determined by, and reflect, the state of the masses in general.

In 1913, according to an estimate by the present author, the statistically recorded wages of textile mill workers in Bombay, Ahmedabad (cotton) and in Calcutta (jute), which were higher than the wages of workers in a city like Cawnpore as well as of those in other industries, were 2.5 times lower than the average wages of the Russian industrial workers as a whole (both regarding the currency exchange rates and the purchasing power in respect of major foodgrains). The wages of industrial workers in Russia before World War I were 2.3 times lower than in Britain and 4 times lower than in the USA (on currency rates).

Between 1913 and 1939, according to the index compiled by K. Mukerji, the real wages of textile mill workers in Bombay and Ahmedabad increased about 2.5 times and in Calcutta 1.6 times.[19] Nevertheless the difference between the wages of industrial workers in India and those in developed capitalist countries did not shrink but, on the contrary, it rather widened.[20]

The increased statistically recorded average wages of factory workers in India in 1939 approximated those of the industrial workers in Russia in 1913 (in terms of purchasing power in respect of major foodgrains). In 1939 the wages of Indian textile mill workers in Bombay, who were better paid than the Indian factory labour on average, notably exceeded the wages of their Russian counterparts in 1913 who were worse paid than the average factory worker in Russia.[21]

However, in reality. the Indian worker would have in his hands at least a quarter less cash than his statistically recorded wages. One of the reasons of this difference was the exceptionally widespread and intensive 'secondary' (as Marx called it) exploitation of the industrial worker, particularly his exploitation by the money-lender. The surveys in the 1920s - 1940s revealed that over a half and frequently 70 - 90 per cent of Indian factory workers were indebted, the debt incured at 75 per cent interest if not more, exceeded monthly wages 2 to 4 times. Nothing of this kind was there particularly in Russia, although Russian workers also suffered from the 'secondary' exploitation but certainly not to such an extent. The spread and intensity of the secondary exploitation of Indian factory workers, especially their bondage to the money-lender actually reflected the state of oppression under which the vast mass of the Indian poor lived.

Nevertheless in India the gap between the wages of factory workers and agricultural labourers was truly striking and unheard of. According to our estimate in Russia in 1911 - 1913 the average daily wages of agricultural labourers of both sexes together amounted to over three quarters of the average daily wages of factory workers. Due to seasonal unemployment of agricultural labourers their annual wages were only slightly more than half of the annual wages of factory workers. In India before World War I, however, the daily earnings of male agricultural labourers were on average two times lower than the daily wages of textile mill workers in Bombay, Ahmedabad and Calcutta. By 1937 - 1939 this gap widened steeply - to 6 times in the case of cotton mill workers of Bombay and Ahmedabad and to 4 times in the case of Indian factory labour on average.[22]

The widening of the gap was due to the increase of wages of factory workers while those of agricultural labourers even tended to decrease on an all-India average, although the regional disparities of the wages of the latter somewhat diminished. The gap itself evidently resulted from the weakness of agriculture in colonial India and from the particularly depressed state of the agricultural labourers, usually bonded to their employers and who almost exclusively hailed from the low castes and especially from the Harijans. Meanwhile the caste and communal composition of the factory workers resembled more that of the population at large (as distinct from the caste composition of the middle classes), although the share of the low castes and untouchables in the industrial work force was bigger and the share of high castes was smaller than their respective shares in the region's population.[23]

The wage hike in the 1930s could not immediately and essentially change the specific medieval-cum-colonial state of oppression suffered by industrial workers too. Although in 1937 their statistically recorded wages were closer to the wages of their counterparts in pre-revolutionary Russia and by the same calculation Bombay cotton mill workers even drew more than the latter, the literacy rate of Bombay workers in 1940 was only just 30 per cent (30 per cent among men and more 3 per cent among women)[24], whereas in Russia on the even of October Revolution of 1917 64 per cent of factory workers were literate (76 per cent men and 38 per cent women)[25]. It can be presumed that the literacy rate among Indian industrial workers in general was lower, even much lower than that among Bombay mill workers who were better paid and had a longer and brighter story of struggle and organization.

## A Unique Ratio

It is particularly revealing to compare the ratios of the numbers of educated persons or of the 2nd and 3rd level students to the number of the industrial workers in India and in developed countries and in prerevolutionary Russia. In India before World War I there were not more than one million workers in mechanized enterprises and mechanized transport. Even they were almost totally illiterate. At the same time the number of persons literate in English reached also one million and the number of students of secondary schools and colleges totalled to about 950 000. Thus before World War I both the number of educated persons and the number of the 2nd- and 3rd-level students were actually not less than the number of industrial workers who formally had to be defined as 'modern' but were illiterate. Thus both the ratios were roughly 1 to 1.

Meanwhile in Russia in 1913 there were only two 2nd- and 3rd-level students for every ten workers of modern industry and transport. About two thirds of the workers were literate. In Britain this ratio in 1911 - 1914 was roughly 1 to 10 and in 1951 1.5 to 10; in Germany it was 1 to 10 and 2 to 10 respectively (in 1951 - in the FRG). In undivided India in 1946 this ratio was 7 to 10 against approximately 1 to 1 in 1911, i. e. it changed but little. In 1955 in India there were 4.7 million educated persons (matriculation or higher standard)[26] as against 5 million (or less) workers of organized industry and transport.

The near equality in numbers of educated persons belonging almost totally to propertied classes on the one hand and workers in modern industries, mainly illiterate, on the other is one of the most glaring manifestations of what has been called here elitist modernization in colonial India.

## Strike Struggles and the Organization

It may be surprising to find that already after World War I Indian industrial workers were not lagging behind but were rather ahead of their Western brethren in the strike struggle, at least quantitatively, and they were definitely ahead, often much ahead, of the industrial workers of other colonial and dependent countries. Arguably this resulted from a combination of the following factors: a) ruthless exploitation, b) a rather tangible absolute number of industrial workers and their very high concentration factorywise, c) stimulating atmosphere and role of the rising national freedom movement which increasingly involved the industrial workers as the most active and mobilizable component of the masses.

From 1921 to 1947 the annual average number of strikers in India (about 490,000) was comparable to that in Britain (510,000 between 1921 and 1947) and France (480,000 between 1920 and 1938), lagging behind substantially only to annual averages in the USA (1,210,000 between 1921 and 1947) and in Germany (840,000 between 1921 and 1932, i. e. before the Fascist regime), but it exceeded many times those in other countries both developed and underdeveloped (colonial and dependent), with the possible partial exception of China where statistics of industrial disputes were available only for Shanghai.[27]

The average percentage of strikers among workers of organized industry and transport between 1921 and 1947 was definitely higher in India than in practically all other major countries where it did not exceed 10 per cent (17 per cent in Italy as an exception though for a brief period of 1919 to 1925), but as a rule reached some 5 to 6 per cent, while in India it was not less than 12 per cent. In terms of the average scale and duration the strikes in India between 1921 and 1947 were as a rule much more powerful and prolonged than in other countries: workers involved per one strike - 1,600, mandays lost per one strike - 34,200 and per one striker - 19.

The results of strikes in India were, however, rather different. Till the middle of the 1930s more than a half of strikes in India were unsuccessful whereas in developed countries most of strikes ended either with a victory of workers or with a compromise. Poor organization of worker in India was obviously one of the reasons.

Attempts to defend and represent workers dated from the late 19th century. Calls and efforts for launching trade unions were made as early as 1906. But only after World War I the first trade union came into being. Although in 1920 already the All-India Trade Union Congress was founded, most of the trade unions, particularly in the 1920s, were very unstable and functioned rather as strike committees. Many strikes were obviously more spontaneous rather than organized actions. As R. Palme Dutt pointed out, the assistance of the so-called 'outsiders' or helpers 'was in fact indispensable'[28]. Freedom fighters who were motivated by the national political struggle and often inspired by the ideal of socialism under the impact of October Revolution in Russia approached the workers. But there were also very many others of various political and non-political orientations. Yet it should be noted that leaders of national movement harbouring dissimilar views began paying attention to the prospective TU movement as early as 1906 and 1907, i. e. in its embryonic stages, and even competed among themselves for its leadership when it was hardly born.[29]

However, even in 1939 the TU membership totalled only to about 400,000[30] i. e. comprised less than 10 per cent of the workers in organized industries - certainly not a small figure for a colonial country but also not commensurate with the scale and intensity of the workers' struggles.

The rather poor organisation or even its total absence from the struggles obviously reflected a highly specific situation of a labour movement at its early stage which rose in big industries of the 20th century.

During and immediately after World War II the situation in India changed markedly in different respects including the state of the industrial workers. Their numerical strength increased at least by one fourth, and the TU membership reached 1.3 million, as was claimed, while the living conditions drastically worsened. The explosion of the strikes in 1946 and 1947 led mostly by the Communists and the Congress Socialists 'threatened the whole economy of the country'.

The scale of the strike explosion in India was quite comparable to the unprecedented working class strike struggles in Russia during the 1905 - 1907 Revolution. The number of strikers in India in 1946 and 1947 and in Russia in 1905 and 1906 (1.7 million and 2 million per year respectively) was similar. The participants in India comprised about two fifth and in Russia nearly half of the workers in organized industries and transport. The number of workers in organized industries and transport in India in 1946 (about 4.4 million) was nearly the same as in Russia before World War I (about 4 million). However, India's population was 2.4 times bigger.

## Notes


1 Eric Komarov, Elitist Modernization in Colonial India: Some Specific Feature of Generation and Distribution of Politically Relevant Resources. In: Democracy in Modern World. Essays for Tatu Vanhanen. University of Tampere, Tampere 1989, pp. 247-278.

2 T.L.Majumdar (ed.), Indian Speeches and Documents on British Rule. 1821-1918, Calcutta 1937, p. 36.

3 A.T.Latham, The International Economy and the Underdeveloped World. 1965-1914, London 1978, p. 31.

4 Wages quoted from: Ranjit Das Gupta, Material Conditions and Behavioral Aspects of Calcutta Working Class. 1875-1899. Occasional Paper No. 22, Centre for Studies in Social Sciences, Calcutta 1979.

5 B.B.Misra, The Indian Middle Classes. Their Growth in Modern Times, Oxford University Press, Delhi 1978, p. 336.

6 S.N. Mukerji, History of Education in India, Baroda 1974, pp. 152-154.

7 A.K. Bagchi, Private Investment in India. 1900-1939, Cambridge University Press 1972, p. 159.

8 Ibid., p. 226, Table 7, 1.

9 Ekonomika Indii. Obtchaja kharakteristika, Moscow 1984, p. 36 (Russian).

10 Misra, The Indian Middle Classes..., p. 251.

11 The original data on education in India for calculation of the indicies here and below: Abstracts of Statistics for British India, London 1900-1939; Progress of Education in India 1902-1907, Calcutta 1909; Statistics of British India, Calcutta 1947; The Statistical Abstract for India 1946; India. Reference Annual 1970-71, Publication Division, New Delhi 1972; S. Nurullah/T.P.Haik, A Student's History of Education in India (1806-1847), Bombay 1951; S.Mukherjee, istory of Education... Data on Education in Russia: I.M. Bogdanov, Gramotnost i obrazovanie v dorevolutionnoy Rossii, Moscow 1964, p. 98 (Russian); B.R. Leikina-Svirskaya, Russkaya intelligentsia v 1900-1917 godakh, Moscow 1981 (Russian). Data on West European countries and Japan: Statesman Year-Books, London; UNESCO Statistical Year Book, 1965; The Role of Education in the Social and Economic Development of Japan. Ministry of Education, Tokyo 1946.

12 Erik Komarov, Elitist Modernization...

13 B.R. Sabade/N.V. Namjoshi, Chambers of Commerce and Trade Associations in India, Poona 1977, p. 35.

14 Statistical Abstract for British India 1929/30 - 1938/39, p. 466, 468.

15 Ibid., p. 73; Statistical Abstract for 1946/47..., p. 1.

16 M.K. Gandhi, Writings and Speeches, Madras 1922, p. 255.

17 R.K. Prabhu/U.R. Rao (eds.), The Mind of Mahatma Gandhi, Ahmedabad 1967, p. 317.

18 Quoted by: A.K. Bagchi, Private Investment in India..., p. 122, Table 5.1.

19 L.A. Gordon, In istorii rabochego klassa Indii, Moscow 1961, p. 60-61 (Russian).

20 Data on industrial wages in Russia: S.C. Strumilin, Izbrannyie proizvedenija, vol. 3, Problemy ekonomiki truda, Moscow 1962, p. 321; Zarabotnaya plata i proizvoditelnost truda v russkoi promyshlennosti za 1913-1922 g.g., Moscow 1923, p. 44 (Russian). Data on industrial Wages in India: Report of the Indian Factory Labour Commission, 1908, London 1908; Mukherji's series, quoted by: A.K. Bagchi, Private Investment..., p. 122; D.S. Bajpai, Our Labour Problem, Lucknow 1953, p. 26.

21 Data on agricultural wages in India: Prices and Wages in India, Calcutta 1923; Radhakamal Mukerjee, The Indian Working Class, Bombay 1948, p. 179; K.K. Ghose, Agricultural Labourers in India. A Study in History of Their Growth and Economic Conditions, Calcutta 1969, p. 123, Table VI: 2; p. 182, Table VII: 2; p. 18, Table VII: 4.

22 Ranjit Das Gupta, Factory Labour in Eastern India: Sources of Supply. 1856-1940. Some Preliminary Findings V-c. In: The Indian Economic and Social History Review *XII*(1977); Morris D. Morris, The Emergence of an Industrial Labour in India, Berkeley 1969, pp. 71-83.

23 B.G.Cokhale, The Bombay Cotton Mill Worker. Bombay Mill Owners Association, Bombay 1957, pp. 22-23.

24 A.G. Rashin, Formirovanija promyshlennogo proletariata v Rossi, Moscow 1940, p. 438 (Russian).

25 Pitambar Pant/T.P.Chandhuri, Educated Persons in India. Planning Commission, GOI, Indian Statistical Institute, Calcutta 1969, p. 2.

26 Here and below calculations relating to strikes are based on data presented in: Zabastovochnaya borba trudjatchikhsja. Konets XIX v.- 70ye gody XX v. Statistika, Moscow 1903 (Russian).

27 R. Palm Dutt, India Today, Calcutta 1979, p. 406 (reprint).

28 Vide Sumit Sarkar, The Swadashi Movement in Bengal. 1903-1908, New Delhi 1973.

29 Statistical Abstract for British India. 1929/30 - 1938/39, p. 505.

30 The Transfer of Power. 1943-47, vol. IX, London 1980, p. 597, 1947. A Note by the Joint Planning Committee, Jan. 31. See also vol. VIII, pp. 161-194.

# A Note on the Impact of Europeans as Reflected in the Traditional Art of Bengal. A Historian's View

Miloslav Krása

Contact with the penetrating Europeans in India was first experienced by the local inhabitants in and around the foreign factories dispersed along the maritime coast. However, it was most intensive in the Eastern part of the subcontinent where the real bridge-head for territorial expansion of the English East India Company was established after Palasi and the granting of *dīvānī* during the second half of 18th century. As the military and administrative centre of the new colonial power it enabled constant intercourse, including confrontation, between the indigenous population and the white sahibs at various social levels and for succeeding generations.

In Bengal in particular such mutual contacts had existed for much longer, from the time of the nawabship of Murshid Quli Khan especially, both in the towns and the countryside. Indians engaged in business with the Company or in the service in the Company's agents gradually developed into a new social stratum, familiar with the English language, fully depending upon their European masters and closely connected with the new establishment. Out of this stratum, in due course, there germinated the modern Bengali intelligentsia.

The colonial pattern of revenue collecting, the administrative structure, the judiciary, etc. became a prototype which, subject to local modification, was subsequently copied in other territories conquered during the next century. Thus, the European impact and the tradition of colonial institutions in Bengal was the longest and met with an appropriate response within contemporary Indian society. It was evidently one of the main reasons why the process of modern intellectual emancipation and political awakening among the Bengalis, known as the 'Bengali Renaissance', emerged in this region as early as the first half of 19th century. The socio-economic and political transformation was well reflected in the general public atmosphere and amply documented in many outstanding works of modern Bengali literature and in consequent investigations devoted to this topic by a host of Indian and foreign historian.

It was also precisely in this geographic region that the impact of the European element, along with the influence of Western culture in the Indian milieu, left a sketchy and transient but nevertheless definite trace in the local traditional art. Scattered specimens have survived portraying Europeans in the Indian environment, foreign soldiers, officers and merchants or scenes typical of the changing life under the British. These were produced on paper, modelled in terracotta panels or woven as designs into silk saris. They appeared in towns and still more in rural areas and were well known to contemporaries and even occasionally collected by them as curiosities. But for a long time they were neglected by the 20th century's art historians, who were interested above all and almost exclusively in Indian monumental architecture, classical sculpture and miniature paintings.

Single instances of similar endeavours by traditional artists to render account of the new situation, or to express prevailing attitudes towards the different reality, may have been preserved in other parts of India, but the Bengali examples seem to be unequalled in their spontaneity and unsophisticated charm. It is as if they have been endowed with the faculty to cross freely the bounds of the surrounding ocean of omnipresent and anonymous folk art.

The roots of the traditional art schools, at least in some cases, reached back to the period prior to European dominance. However, with the decline of the classical Indian art which accompanied the sudden disintegration of the old elites and the disappearance of generous patrons of art after the British conquest, the folk and traditional artists, with their undying creative activity acquired a new dimension. Throughout difficult times, marked by a forced interruption of the natural development of Indian society, they were destined to became the conservators of cultural continuity and guardians of the country's past heritage. Though originally strictly religious in their inspiration, they nevertheless were not blind to life around them and contemporary events, and quite often allowed secular motifs and scenes to enter into their creations.

It is no wonder that sooner or later the European element caught the imagination of some artists, and pictures of the foreign lords - strange in their appearance, curious in their habits and quite different in their manners - found their way into the traditional art of Bengal. Its obvious tendency towards secular extemporisation, allowing for the penetration of divers European motifs, has preserved for us today a marginal but unique and interesting source of Bengali social history. At the same time it reflects much of the contemporary atmosphere as well as many of the attitudes and feelings towards the Europeans, mainly those of the lower strata of Indian society.

Three genres of traditional Bengali art-work can be considered as typical from this point of view: the coloured drawings of the *Kālīghāt* style, the figurative terracotta reliefs on the brick temples of today's West Bengal (India) and Bangladesh, and the Baluchari saris woven from pure Murshidabad silk, also known as *bālūcar būṭīdār* (flowered baluchar). All these forms still flourished during the last century as an incidental corollary of the changes maturing in the Bengali socio-economic and political life. None of them survived for very long after 1900.

**Kalighat paintings**

The highly stylized coloured drawings or brush drawings were produced by traditional painters called *patuā* or citrakār, living as families or in groups in the Western part of Bengal. The expansion of this genre was greatly enhanced by the introduction of the first machine production of paper by William Carey in Serampore. From about the middle of the 19th century the artists settled mainly in and around Calcutta, particularly in the neighbourhood of Kalighat, the famous temple of the popular Hindu goddess Kālī. Their paintings of the Hindu deities and mythological motifs, and of Islamic motifs and secular portraits and scenes - varying and steadily declining in quality - were sold at village and city bazaars and beside Hindu temples and Muslim religious processions. The paper sheets on which their paintings were done were available on the streets around Kalighat until the early twenties, when this art definitely succumbed to the competition of modern prints and cheap lithographs.

The Kalighat paintings circulated among the broadest strata of Bengali society, adorned the interiors of both village and simple urban houses and seemed to be very near to the hearts of the common people, as their style clearly corresponded to the intimately known canons of the Bengali art tradition. But of hundreds of thousands of originals only a mere fraction was preserved in India and some other countries. Over ninehundred of them, originating mostly in the second half of the 19th century, are kept in museums in London, Oxford, Moscow and Prague. As a rule, the paintings are anonymous, although few of the artist's names are on record.

The first information about the Kalighat paintings can be gleaned from authors writing more than a hundred years ago. Ajit Ghose (1926) and Mukul Dey (1932) are among those who have aroused public interest in this genre with their articles in the more recent period. But the most competent monographs were published in the 50th and 70th by W. G. Archer and Hana Knížková.[1]

If we are to believe the Bengali art historian Ashok Mitra[2], the interest of the patuas in European motifs developed as early as 1820 - 1830. Though not documented by concrete examples this is not improbable, considering the agitated atmosphere in Bengal in those years. Scrutiny of the available extant paintings discloses ample instances of the indirect impact of European influence side by side with the direct portrayal of British officers either as representatives of administration in typical situations or as actors in secular scenes depicting contemporary events of general interest. The sole surviving instance of the latter is a series of paintings whose theme was the so-called Tarakeshvar scandal - involving the criminal prosecution and conviction of the priest of a temple of the Hooghly district, who seduced and violated a married woman, and of her husband who killed her after learning about it. The trial and sentences continued to stir the Calcutta public for a long time and the story stimulated the imagination of many

Bengali authors, who wrote songs, ballads and even prosaic and dramatic works performed on the stage.[3] Quickly accommodating themselves to the needs of the market, the artists could evidently deal easily with topical subjects and adapt their traditional style to any required theme.

The depicted life of the white sahib as seen through Indian eyes often includes dramatic hunting scenes, episodes from horse-races and figures of army officers in action. Quite in accordance with the stylistic conception, there is no trace of individuality in the portrayed persons, all being subsumed to one stereotypical pattern hardly changing from decade to decade. Foreign influence betrays itself in the representation of Indian men and women sitting on chairs, for example, in the European way or wearing Western accoutrements like the male shoe-buckle. There is a small selection of paintings in the Kalighat style, almost exclusively limited to portraits of animals and birds, in which the artists themselves, intentionally or subconsciously, took over much of the style of those of their colleagues employed in the service of the Company Bahadur. They were the last representatives of another distinctive artistic school, successors of the once glorious tradition of Mughal miniatures.

From the historical point of view the most interesting paintings are those documenting the new spirit of the time. Illustrating the mentality of the population, they express contempt for the wholesale imitation of Western manners, ridicule servility towards European masters and include scenes with explicit or implicit allegorical meaning. One can also come across portraits presenting Indian historical figures, generally venerated if not worshipped as heroes of the anti-British resistance, like the first mature ruler to fight for India's sovereignty, Sultan Tipu, or Lakhsmi Bai, Rani of Jhansi, the hero of the Great Indian Uprising in 1857 - 1859.

## Terracotta temple reliefs

The Bengal terracotta temples - Hindu shrines built mostly of well-fired bricks and covered with terracotta plaques featuring ornamental and figurative sculptures modelled in shallow or high relief - are perhaps the only Indian monumental art which survived and more or less prospered during the colonial era until the beginning of the 20th century. As an immortal testimony to the creative exertions of generation of wandering artists and craftsmen, predominantly from the *sūtradhārā* community, they came to symbolize Bengali cultural individuality in the best sense of the term.

The terracotta work on the temples naturally bears testimony to the local millenary tradition, but the wide range of motifs presenting the Hindu world of myths and deities developed vigorously only in the 17th century. It started first in Bankura and spread generally during the next century to dominate the temple walls entirely henceforth. The secular motifs appeared almost simultaneously. They were the artist's response to the prevalent atmosphere of religious and social upheaval which the Vaishnava message of Chaitanya had prepared the way for and which culminated in the renascent Bengali movement.

Hundreds of big temples and small shrines scattered across the vast alluvial plains of the Gangetic delta, were adorned with kilometres of scenes and stories on terracotta friezes and panels. These appealed to broad masses of people and extended to them an everyday source of inspiration. There is a striking similarity between the artistic styles of the terracotta sculpture and other Bengali forms of art, like paintings (including the Kalighat style), textiles, wood-carving and metalwork including folk art. In such mutual influences the terracotta artists had possibly played the dominating role. Because of the unfavourable monsoon climate and neglect by the society, many terracotta temples vanished or deteriorated. Today more than a thousand of them still survive, partly under protection. A great number of excellent terracotta plaques are no longer in situ, some of them being kept in museums, mostly in Calcutta, Dacca, Rajshahi, etc.

Archaeologists and other authors reported several times on the terracotta temples during the 19th and early 20th century. In Prague in the 1870th the Czech palaeontologist Otakar Feistmantel exhibited his own copies of their drawings he executed in Bengal. S. K. Saraswati (1933 - 1969), S. P. Roy Chaudhury (1942), S. Mukherji (1953), O. C. Gangoly and Mukul Dey (1959), S. C. Mukherjee (1960), Hitesh Sanyal (1963 - 1977), P. C. Das Gupta (1966 - 1971) and Prodosh Dasgupta (1971) were among the authors who contributed more elaborate treatments of the subject. However, thorough research on terracotta temples was available only in the 1980th after the appearance of the monograph by Zulekha Haque[4] and the posthumous publication of the richly-endowed archives of David McCutchion, edited and completed along with others by George Michell.[5]

The impact of the British, Portuguese and other Europeans on the Bengali sculptors and, through their meditation, on the predominantly rural population was quite substantial but still, some thirty years ago, could have been only vaguely guessed.[6] Painstaking examination of the terracotta panels revealed in the last decades innumerable portraits and scenes containing additional traces of European influence. From the numerous preserved temple foundation inscriptions disclosing names not only of the architects but also of the founders-cum-donors, we may assume their social status and possible European connections. The mere fact of how easily and naturally the Europeans inhabited the walls of temples in close proximity to Hindu deities and legends is worthy of note and testifies to the undiscriminating approach of the sculptor. On the other hand, his treatment of figures may be both dispassionate and expressive of deep concern and strong feelings.

We come across Europeans as cruel pirates and intruders, as heavily armed warriors and drunken soldiers, soldiers charging a gun, clutching daggers or waving swords. Pistols, bayonet and even details of guns can be exactly ascertained. Infantry men are seen to fix a mobile cannon on wheels and sailors on merchant ships are armed with cannons too. Very frequently found on terracotta plaques - placed like most of the secular scenes, outside the main front panels - are hunting motifs with Europeans killing tigers, for example, or pursuing boars (sometimes with spears) and hunting deer. Figures with European dress can be recognized on ships (apparently galleons) loaded with goods, live animals and slaves. On Shridhara temple in Sonamukhi, which dates from about the middle of the 19th century, a terracotta plaque was discovered depicting a bound Indian prisoner, being led by a European.[7]

A number of scenes refer to either professional or social communication between Europeans and the new Indian rural elite of merchants, zamindars and the like. They are presenting British visitors at dancing and musical performances in the company of Indian patrons. Frequent plaques show boating trips, pleasure ships built for officials or indigo planters, Europeans at drinking parties with Indian women and various intimate scenes. Some others depict European ladies in their garments and men smoking hookah, or being carried by Indians in palanquines.

The sculptured 'pantheon' of these strangers on the walls of Hindu temples excels in Hetampur in Birbhum district, where one is surprised to find on the walls of Chandranatha Shiva temple foreign and even historical personalities copied probably from Western originals. They have been identified as representations of figures ranging from Moses to Jesus and from Robert Clive to Queen Victoria. Another curiosity is a late 19th century terracotta plaque showing a railway train and documenting thus the introduction of this modern system of transport in Bengal. And again, here and there, there is an obvious satire or critical opinion implicit in the scene.

European influence reveal itself also in many minor details - like an Indian girl playing a violin (the Indian way, of course), storeyed buildings in the Western style, columns with classical Greek capitals or bungalows with porches and pillars. Especially on the 19th century terracotta temples in the region to the North-West and South-West of Calcutta, 'there is distinct evidence of European influences, particularly in the ornamental motifs and the rounded modelling of the figures, and the tendency toward illusionistic representation'[8].

## Baluchari saris

The third genre of this category is totally different in the subtlety of its material, yet it still cannot be said to be completely unrelated to the art of the terracotta sculpture, at least as far as its stylistic character and pattern are concerned. Originating in the very region of the ancient and world famous tradition of textile manufacture in the sericulture area, it was restricted to a mere ten villages with Baluchar as the founding centre, about ten kilometres to the north of Murshidabad. In close proximity to Baluchar (forming nowadays the eastern outskirts of the twin-township of Jiaganj-Azimganj), at a short distance across the Bhagirathi river, was situated a group of beautiful 18th century terracotta temples in Baranagar, and also one of the first local railway lines, constructed by the Indian Branch Railway Company in the 1860th, between Azimganj and the East India Railway network in Nalhati. Both must have left a strong impression on the imagination of the weavers in the near Baluchar.

The Baluchari saris are valued as by far the most artistic and precious textile products in Bengal, being made of silk. Also because they require the most intricate setting system of weaving programme (*nakśā*) and loom adjustment. One master weaver with his draw-boy needed up to six months to complete a single piece. The art flourished in the 18th and 19th centuries, under both the Mughal nawabs and the British and in spite of frequent famines, heavy floods and earthquakes (the most tragic one in 1897). The durability of the saris - achieved by using only high quality pure silk - (all the weavers were Hindus from the *tantuvāya* caste, illiterate and hence anonymous) and a unique design which maintained constantly high standard while also allowing for variations in motifs, secured for the Baluchari saris a ready market.

The saris measured approximately 457 cm in length by 107 cm in width. Their main ground is covered mostly by flowerets (*būṭī*) arranged in horizontal or diagonal rows, while along the edged runs a narrow border with floral, and very occasionally animal or bird, motifs. The most remarkable and characteristic feature of the Baluchari saris is its *āncala*, the end piece worn over the breast. Over the whole width it occupies a rectangle of about 60 - 100 cm in length, usually divided into regular rows of repeated oblongs or squares with woven secular and European motifs running both horizontally and vertically around the central design - much the same in fact as the division of the frontal panels on the terracotta temples.

The last known exponent of this traditional art named Dubraj (from the village of Bahadurpur) died sometime early in this century. He belonged, however, to another caste and was only an extremely talented artist who learned the art from the genuine Baluchari weavers. With him died the secret of the original būṭīdār saris. Several unsuccessful attempts were made to revive it. The remaining Baluchari saris are still treasured in old Bengali families and other precious pieces adorn the museum collections in India and abroad. The particularly rich collection of Lady Ranu Mookherjee, consisting of 75 saris, with one initialled even before Dubraj, was exhibited in Calcutta in 1961.

So far there is no existing monograph which in a scholarly way evaluates the available information on the making of Baluchari saris, with its intricate weaving technique and analyzes a representative selection of the existing saris. Fortunately we have an almost contemporary detailed treatment on Bengal and especially the Murshidabad silk fabrics left at the turn of the century by the then deputy collector Baboo Nitya Gopal Mookerji (also Mukerji)[9] in which the būṭīdār saris are given due attention. From later authors who were attracted either by the aesthetic or the historical value of these masterpieces of Indian traditional art, let us mention T. N. Mukherji[10], Ajit Ghose[11], S. K. Saraswati[12], Rustam J. Mehta[13] and Kamala Devi Chattopadhyay[14]. More recently Dr. Sukla Das has written with insight on the subject.[15]

The European element in the *ãncala* part of the saris is well represented, although the weavers seemed to be rather ill at ease with the portraits of British ladies and gentlemen. They certainly look dignified, important and serious,[16] quite in the hitherto accepted stylistic tradition. While the artists originally depicted Mughal nobles and courtly figures riding on horses and elephants, smoking hookah, holding hawks or roses (all Indian dignitaries appearing on saris were Muslims) and exceptionally dancing girls, for the East India Company officers and their ladies an adequate pose and milieu had to be found. At least some of the saris must have been ordered by British officials as gifts, but the majority passed into Indian hands and were worn by Hindu and muslim women from the distinguished Bengali families and the foreign motifs on the saris, however 'modern' and curious, could never express any degree of frivolity.

So we find Company officers in proper dress and European ladies posing in framed niches, engaged in conversation and drinking from goblets, smoking hookah or travelling in coaches drawn by horses. On a great number of the preserved saris the British alone or with Indians are to be seen seated in compartments of railway waggons of the oldest kind, constructed as double-deckers and reminiscent sometimes of the luxury double-decker saloon used by the Governor and the highest officials. The fascination for railway train and engine resulted in a recurrent use of these motifs in variations, depicting British engine-drivers and showing smoking chimneys. Particularly these and waggon wheels were presented in a stylized and highly ornamental form.

Much favoured means of transport used by Europeans and appearing on the saris were double-decker chariots (shown with British ladies and gentlemen and even dogs in the lower section), double-decker steam launchees and other paddle steamers. In the various interior scenes typical Western chairs and other furniture are visible. Outdoor scenes with Europeans again include hunting motifs while the martial aspect is represented by gunners whose cannons are shown in panels.

The artistic relics of all the above-mentioned genres of traditional bengali art reflected, each in its own characteristic way, certain specific aspects of the advance and impact of the European element on the ordinary rural and urban indigenous population. The results of the mutual interaction were intercepted by the artists quite casually, but nevertheless they succeeded in catching and expressing them as an eloquent symptom of the contemporary reality. However limited the medium, the artist left us an unintentional message, an immediate source from which to study the past - not so much in order to learn new facts but rather so as to understand the old ones better.

The Kalighat paintings, the terracotta sculptures and the woven portraits on Baluchari saris speak through their contents, their style and their actual communicative sense. Looking at them, we can somehow penetrate deeper behind the hidden planes of both the human mind and socio-cultural consciousness. When examining written historical sources there is always, relatively speaking, considerable scope for subjective interpretation. Here the sources reveal history in its very identity.

Picture 1: Bengali babu playing the sitar (1860')
The British Library (IOL collection), London
Reproduced in: H. Knížková, Drawings of the Kālīghāt Style, Prague 1975, pl. 36

Picture 2: Damaged scene with a European chair (1786)
Radhe-Govinda temple, Atpur, Hooghly district (author's photograph)
Picture 3: Europeans travelling in train (19th century)
Anchara of a Baluchari sari. Náprstek Museum, Prag (author's photograph)

## Notes

1 E. G. Archer, Kalighat Paintings. In: Marg, Bombay *5*(1952)4, pp. 22-29; id., Bazaar Paintings of Calcutta. The Style of Kalighat, London 1953; H. Knížková, The Drawings of the Kalig at Style. Secular Themes, Prague 1975.

2 Bharater citrakala (Indian painting), Calcutta 1363 (1956), quoted by: H. Knížková, A Contribution to the Study of Drawings in Kalighat Style with Special Allowences for Secular Themes, unpublished dissertation, Oriental Institute, Prague 1968, p. 20 (in Czech).

3 In more detail see H. Knížková/D. Zbavitel, Come and Hear the Story (The Drama of a Hypocritical Brahman). In: New Orient Bimonthly, Prague *6*(1967)5, pp. 142-145.

4 Terracotta Decorations of Late Mediaeval Bengal. Portrayal of a Society, Dacca 1980.

5 Brick Temples of Bengal. From the Archives of David McCutchion, Princeton-New Jersey 1983 (for select bibliography see pp. 187-193).

6 Miloslav Krása, History and Art in the Terracotta Temples of Bengal. In: New Orient Bimonthly, Prague *5*(1966)4, pp. 111-112.

7 See Michell, p. 118.

8 Michell, p. 113.

9 The Silk Industries of Moorshedabad. In: The Journal of Indian Art and Industry, Calcutta *5*(1892)38, pp. 1-8; A Monograph of the Silk Fabrics of Bengal, Calcutta 1903.

10 Art Manufacture of India, Calcutta 1888.

11 Figural Fabrics of Old Bengal. In: Marg, Bombay *3*(1947)1, pp. 38-44.

12 In the catalogue Baluchar Saris, Exhibition from the collection of Sm Ranu Mookherjee. Academy of Fine Arts, Calcutta 1961, pp. 3-5.

13 Masterpieces of Indian Textiles, Bombay 1970.

14 Handicrafts of India, New Delhi 1975.

15 Indian Fabric Art: Baluchari. In: Professor S. C. Sarkar Commemoration Volume, ed. by S. K. Maity. Journal of History, Vol. 3, Jadavpur University, Calcutta 1982, pp. 39-50.

16 'European men and women, dressed in circular hats and bonnets and holding the conventional flower or some indefinable object, probably intended for a wine glass, look quaintly stiff and amusing. In one sari several Europeans are shown standing on a ratha!' Ghose, p. 42.

# African Identities: Ethnicity, Nationality and History. The Case of Matabeleland, 1893 - 1993

Terence Ranger

## Introduction

The papers presented to the Berlin Conference on 'Changing Identities Under Colonialism' gave an oddly distorted impression of Indian and African historical studies and of the interaction between them. There were papers by Indianists on nationalism (Barun De and Bipan Chandra); on reform and resistance as responses to colonialism (Chandra again and J. V. Naik); on class identities (Erik Komarov and Annemarie Hafner); on religious identities and communalism (Tapan Raychaudhury, Jürgen Lütt and Dick Kooiman); and on indigenous artistic representations of identity (Miloslav Krasa). There were no papers by Africanists on any of these topics.

On the other hand, the great majority of the Africanist papers dealt with ethnicity (Bierschenk, Deutsch, Lentz, Ranger and von Oppen), while only one of the Indianists (Dietrich Reetz) did so, gaining for himself some magisterial rebukes from Indian scholars present. It seemed as if Indianists and Africanists occupied totally different worlds of historical discourse and that there was no possibility of interaction between them.

Moreover, all these Africanists (and once again only Reetz among the Indianists) invoked the idea of the invention of tradition. Yet the opening address, by Professor Anouar Abdel-Malek, attacked this concept as part of a concerted neo-colonial counter-offensive, a deconstructionist new wave (in fact, the aggiornamento of neo-positivist structuralism-functionalism) to deride the 'invention' of tradition. National identity, the mainstay of the maintenance of identity-through-transformation faced reductionism and hegemonism. Yet in reality, he insisted, tradition was a living legacy of endogenous creativity in all fields essential to the maintenance of identity.[1] Perhaps - since most of the Indianists were Indian and none of the Africanists were African - the contrast was not, after all, between Indianists and Africanists but between indigenous and expatriate scholarship!

To my mind these were largely false oppositions. There may have been no Africanist papers at Berlin on nationalism, reform and resistance, class, religion, indigenous artistic representation, but there has of course been an abundance of Africanist work on these topics, both by African and expatriate scholars. The whole of the first decade of modern African historiography, indeed, has been characterised as nationalist historiography, and after a long period in which the nationalist problematic was discredited scholars are now returning to the history of African nationalism.[2] There has been a long Africanist tradition of resistance studies,[3] and there is now a striking development of work on African reformers rather than resisters.[4] Much work has been done on the emergence of African worker consciousness and proletarian identity[5] and some on peasant consciousness in the rural areas.[6] Religious identities - whether traditional, Christian, or Islamic - have been and still are abundantly studied.[7] Indigenous artistic representations of Europeans have been analysed in a fascinating recent study by a German Africanist.[8] Hence nationalist, class and religious identities have been deeply explored by Africanists and the examples I have cited - mainly taken from work on southern Africa - could be multiplied a hundred times and for all parts of the continent. What remained to confront was what the Indian scholar, Vivek Dhareswar, calls the return of the repressed, in his case caste and in ours ethnic identity.

Moreover, so far from Africanist and Indianist work on identity being unable to communicate to each other, my own experience has been one of increasing interaction and exchange. Many Indian scholars have been working on the construction of identity and even on the invention of tradition. Thus I can give a list of recent occasions on which my own and other Africanist work has been received by Indian and Indianist scholars as a part of their own debates. I attended the Subaltern Studies Conference in Calcutta on Power, Religion and Community in December 1989 and my own paper on religion and community in Matabeleland has been published alongside Sudipta Kavirajs on the imaginary institution of India and Partha Chatterjees on domestic religion.[9] In April 1991 at the University of Essex my re-examination of the invention of tradition was given in the same session as Polly OHanlons Histories in Transition: Colonialism and Culture in India, in which she made some stimulating criticisms both of Edward Said and of the Hobsbawm and Ranger volume.[10] In May 1993 I attended a conference at Sandbjerg Manor in Denmark where presentations on nationalism and ethnicity by Africanists were accompanied by Sudipta Kaviraj on Religion, Modernity and Politics and by Vivek Dhareswar on Caste and the Secular Self. Kaviraj stressed that despite differences in style and detail the two bodies of work were closely related. Finally, in London in December 1993 at the conference on Empire, Nation and Language, Kaviraj and I again appeared together, he on fashioning a language of patriotism in Modern Bengal and I on Language, Ethnicity and Nationalism: the Case of Matabeleland, a paper closely related to the one I gave at the Berlin conference.

It will have been seen already that many of the Indian works I have cited deal with concepts like institution, fashioning, imagination, etc. Gyanendra Pandeys splendid recent book is entitled The Construction of Communalism in Colonial North India.[11] Other Indianist work makes direct reference to The Invention of Tradition, describing itself as studying newly created traditions, or invoking African models in order to explore Indian Histories.[12] Chris Baylys brilliant Indian Society and the Making of the British Empire contains a chapter on Consolidating 'Traditional' Society, which strikes many echoes for the Africanist historian of colonial ethnicity. The consolidation of peasant society, Bayly writes, and the defeat of the nomad [and] the soldier ... set the scene for the emergence of a more stratified and rigid system.[13] An Africanist writing about the invention of tribalism might set the scene in much the same words. But it is hard to believe that Pandey and Kaviraj and Chatterjee and Dhareswar - or come to that OHanlon and Washbrook and Cohn and Bayly - are part of a neo-colonial reductionist conspiracy against essential identities. If these scholars had been in Berlin (and if there had been time for discussion) the apparent gulf between the two historiographies would have disappeared.

And yet when the false oppositions have been dispelled, there nevertheless remains a real contrast between the two historiographies. In the passage I have quoted above, Bayly writes: a more stratified and rigid system of castes, where an Africanist would write: a more stratified and rigid system of tribes. The Indian work on construction, imagination and invention which I have cited above deals with caste, nationality and communalism but not with ethnicity. Pandey, indeed, asserts that in India colonial constructions of communalism played the same role as colonial inventions of ethnicity in Africa: 'Communalism was, like the term tribalism - which has been widely employed in writings on African politics and history - a statement on the nature of particular, primitive societies. Communalism captured for the colonialists what they had conceptualized as a basic feature of Indian identity - its fundamentally irrational character - long before the term actually came to be used in its Indian sense. Like tribalism, communalism is given, endemic, inborn. Like them, it denies consciousness and agency to the subjected peoples of the colonized world.'[14]

Hence, Pandey would say, the need to deconstruct the notion of communalism, and in Africa to deconstruct the notion of tribalism.

For Vivek Dhareswar, it is caste rather than communalism which most needs deconstructing. The continuing and indeed increasing significance of caste, he writes, represents the return of the repressed, of what has been left out of the narrative of nation and of the secular self. Caste seems to represent a primordial irrationality. Yet, says Dhareswar, caste rather than being a 'primitive' and 'traditional' thing is an extremely modern thing.[15] Just so might Africanists describe the increasing importance of ethnicity as the return of the repressed; just so might they seek to show its extreme modernity rather than its primordiality.

I am not entirely persuaded that ethnicity can be left out of the Indian historiography, just as I am not persuaded that communalism, or even caste, can be left out of the African.[16]

But for the purposes of this Introduction I shall assume that what we Africanists are doing with ethnicity is the same that Pandey is doing with communalism and Dahreswar with caste. This being so, then, it can be seen that while it was distorting and unfortunate that virtually all the Africanists at the Berlin conference were dealing with ethnicity in rural regions of Africa, it was not an accident that this was so. As I said above, having already so extensively discussed national and class identities, when Africanists are invited to write about identity they naturally turn to the repressed question of the tribe.

**Why Africanists need to Deconstruct Ethnicity**

The thrust of most of the chapters in The Invention of Tradition, including my own chapter on colonial Africa, was to deconstruct distorting imperial inventions. To this extent, the book was comparable to Saids Orientalism, and presumably does not fall under Abdel-Maleks lash. Things become more complex when we turn to ethnicity, however, since its creation was clearly something in which Africans were involved as well as Europeans. Indeed, in much of Africa today people passionately believe in the primacy of tribal identities so that the deconstructionist literature might seem at first sight to seek to deprive them of the traditions by which they live.[17]

I don't myself believe this to be true. No-one engaged in work on African ethnicity disputes its power and its significance today. Indeed this emerges much more strongly from recent work on the imaginative construction of ethnic identity than from work which merely assumes traditional continuity.[18] But there are three main reasons why it is important to show that ethnic identity has been constructed, and constructed recently, as an extremely modern thing.

The first is that this construction has been one of the key historical processes of the last hundred years and as such should be a major topic of historical inquiry. There is nothing of the de-historicising effect of post-modernism in Africanist discussion of ethnicity.

The second is that it is one of the characteristics of ethnicity that once it has been constructed no other sort of primary identity seems imaginable. Modern tribal entities are thus stretched back into the past in a way that does serious violence to African historical realities and to the range of possible and actual ways of organising social solidarity. Imperialists believed that Africa had always been a backward continent of innumerable, bounded and warring tribes; at the same time they needed tribes as the constituent elements of a colonial political economy. The tribe, wrote a Northern Rhodesian Provincial Commissioner, is at once the only bulwark we have against anarchy and the only foundation on which to build progress in local government.[19] Countering such colonial myths requires us to try to reconstruct the reality of precolonial Africa.

This is a difficult task because, as Bernard Cohn has pointed out, Africa is very different from India as an object of historical study: 'The societies of India offer a much different situation from that of the African to study long-term social change... Indian society and political development were recognized by Europeans in the eighteenth century as being at relatively the same level as European society.

In India there was ... a legal system based partially on written law, taxation based on regular assessment, with record-keeping... Many of the political and economic roles familiar to Europeans: clerks, judges, tax officials, bankers and traders, existed. In addition, there was a multiple cultural- religious system based on sacred texts.'[20]

Cohns implied contrast overlooks numbers of bureaucratically organised - and literate - African kingdoms. But it is true that in large areas of Africa the coming of literacy and the invention of ethnicity were simultaneous and linked processes. Whereas in India the current patterns of caste and communalism can be contrasted to what emerges from a very long written record, in much of Africa writing in the vernacular provides a charter for ethnic identity.

Many recent studies have shown how critical to defining ethnicity was the creation of written vernaculars.[21] Administrators and missionaries, fresh from the cultural nationalisms of nineteenth century Europe, assumed that language, culture and identity were synonymous. They selected particular languages and dialects, gave them alphabets and grammars, and made them into touchstones of tribal identity. In reality very many Africans thought and communicated in several languages, and within large language zones there existed many distinct political, economic and cultural identities. Nevertheless, the process of alphabetization produced African imaginers of ethnicity to work alongside European inventors. As John Janzen has emphasised, one of the genres of early writing by African Christian converts was what he calls the ethnographic. This rather new use of language produced comparative studies of culture, comparisons of the past with the present, and eventually tribal histories and anthropologies. Literate African Christians were the organic intellectuals[22] who did most to imagine ethnicity and to adapt tradition. These imaginations were by no means mere collaborations with the whites. They were an innovative response to the colonial consolidation of peasant society and to the creation of bounded social and administrative units in place of the mobility and interactive networks of the pre-colonial past. But they gave a misleading appearance of primordial antiquity to tribalism and ethnicity, making it hard to imagine alternative principles of organisation and identity.

So work like Achim von Oppen's contribution to the Berlin conference - included in this volume - is extremely important in the contrast it draws between network and locality concepts of moral economy. Von Oppen enables us to understand how the apparently looser and less developed network was in fact a more favourable environment for market integration than the colonially created bounded local territories - more modern in some senses. It also enables us to understand that while newly defined ethnic identities drew on some aspects of 'tradition', there continued to exist practices and attitudes drawn from the traditions of the network. Jan-Georg Deutschs paper pointed to a different sort of alternative to ethnicity, the pan-ethnic urban societies of the Swahili coast. It pointed, too, towards twentieth century contradictions between a continued urbane Swahili self-identity, proudly contrasted to the tribalism of the interior, and the development of a specific Swahili ethnicity.

The third reason why ethnicity needs to be deconstructed, indeed, is this realisation that it is an arena of debate rather than an embodiment of consensus. John Lonsdale makes a series of important distinctions. The first is his distinction between Political Tribalism and Moral Ethnicity. Political Tribalism refers to the process of inventing tribes as administrative units and thereafter to the process of central government playing one tribe off against another. Moral Ethnicity refers to the process of imagining the meaning of ethnic identity once the tribe has been invented. In Kenya, as in many other parts of Africa, the colonial state was minimalist in its demands. It wanted labour and agricultural products and law and order. It did not want to educate everyone, or convert everyone, or to mediate between sexes and generations and classes. It was in fact a-moral.

Questions of moral economy were left to African societies themselves and above all to the new tribal ethnicities.

This is what Lonsdale means by Moral Ethnicity; not of course that ethnicity is always moral but that it provides the arena for debate about morality. Hence understanding the construction of ethnicity also means understanding gender and class relations.[23] Moreover, the balance of the debate about identity and morality determines the Potential of ethnicity and its relationship to other identities, including the national. Ethnic identities can be defined in narrow, exclusive ways. They can also be defined in broad, inclusive ways. They can be made so primary that they virtually exclude combining them also with a sense of national identity. Or they can be part of a hierarchy of belonging. If ethnicity has been repressed until recently in modern African studies it has been because of the fear that it was necessarily antithetical to the project of nationhood. But an understanding of how inclusive ethnicity can relate to the nation state and of how the project of the nation state can itself be defined as one of mediating between ethnic and other society.

Writing about ethnicity was at first confined to expatriate Africanists,[24] but these three reasons for writing the history of ethnicity are so compelling that more and more African scholars are turning to the topic. Outstanding among these are the Nigerian, Peter Ekeh,[25] the Kenyan, E.S.Atieno-Odhiambo,[26] and the Zambian, Chipasha Luchembe.[27] African novelists have reflected on the relation of their ethnic and national identities; African linguists have studied the creation of sub-ethnicities by means of missionary language work on dialects. African philosophers have pondered the significance of the concepts of invention and imagination.[28]

The reason why so many Africanist papers at Berlin dealt with ethnicity, then, may be readily understood. It was also the reason why I chose the topic myself, though I am currently writing books about nationalism and about class. In the account that follows - which in view of this long general introduction I have not enlarged from its Berlin form - I have been concerned with exactly the three general questions defined above. I have been concerned to show ethnicity in

Matabeleland as historical process; to construct some sort of model of a pre-colonial and non-ethnic society; and to show how important is the continuing argument within Ndebele moral ethnicity. To demonstrate that all this is not merely academic in the perjorative sense, I have set it in the context of contemporary Zimbabwe.

## The Expectations of 1992

This year is the hundredth anniversary of the conquest of the Ndebele state by white settler armies. Historians and political commentators confidently expected a flurry of commemorative activity, if not initiated by the Zimbabwean state, at least organised by its critics in Matabeleland. Everything that had happened in 1992 had supported this expectation. 1992, a year of devastating drought, was also a year of widespread disillusionment with and denunciation of the ZANU/PF Government and while not confined to Matabeleland, this unrest was particularly strong there.

The great Mwali rain-shrines, which constitute a natural forum for diagnosis and analysis in a year of drought, are all situated in Matabeleland. In 1992 their priests concurred in blaming the unprecedented lack of rain on the illegitimacy of the State. Robert Mugabe, they said, had not come to the shrines to report the ultimate success of the guerrilla war of the 1960s and 1970s, nor to seek cleansing for the inevitable crimes of violence. Indeed, the violence not only of two decades but of a century remained unresolved; no-one had carried out rituals of repentance and remembrance for the violence of the 1890s, let alone that of the 1970s. This analysis linked the overthrow of the Ndebele state to an asserted failure to establish a legitimate national order after 1980.

Thus there was an attempt in 1992 to establish a memorial to the fallen heroes of ZAPUs guerrilla army, ZIPRA, at Pu Pu in Lupane District, Northern Matabeleland. ZIPRAs role in the liberation war had been largely written out of the post 1980 historiography, which gave almost all credit to Robert Mugabes ZANLA. Pu Pu was chosen to proclaim ZIPRAs heroism because it had been the site of the final battle between the armies of the Ndebele state and the white invaders in December 1893; it had been the setting for the Rhodesian epic of the Alan Wilson patrol, wiped out to a man by the retreating Ndebele; it was the last occasion that Lobengula, the Ndebele King, was publicly seen alive. During colonial times a memorial to the Alan Wilson patrol had been erected there: this had been damaged by guerrillas in the 1970s. When the local representative of the Mwali shrines was consulted, he insisted that no memorial could be erected to ZIPRA until the whole century of violence had been atoned for. The Alan Wilson obelisk should be repaired; a monument to Lobengula must be erected; national leaders, black and white, should attend to repent of violence. So a preliminary ceremony took place on Heroes Day in August 1992 at which the spirits of the Ndebele kings were invoked; royal Ndebele praise-poems were performed; ex-guerrillas attended together with thousands of locals.

Government watched these events at Pu Pu in 1992 with an anxious eye. It feared that they would mobilise a purely Ndebele constituency and undercut the national mourning which should characterise Heroes Day. Everyone expected that the August 1993 celebrations at Pu Pu would be bigger and bolder; that the downfall of the Ndebele state would be brought into the present and linked with the heroism of the largely Ndebele ZIPRA guerrilla army.[29]

Moreover, Government had other things to fear from Matabeleland in 1992. Violence there had not ended in 1980. Clashes between ex-ZIPRA dissidents and the Zimbabwean army, particularly the notorious Fifth Brigade, had led to very many civilian deaths in the mid 1980s.[30] Even after Joshua Nkomo and Robert Mugabe arrived at their Unity Accord and the dissidents surrendered under a presidential amnesty, the memory of state repression was bitterly cherished in Matabeleland. In 1992 all this came to a head. A flooded mine-shaft at the abandoned Antelope Mine at Kezi in Southern Matabeleland was opened up so as to obtain water for reprocessing gold waste; the white miners discovered the skeletons of civilians whose bodies had been dumped there by the Fifth Brigade. The photographs of the bones which even appeared on the front-page of the government-supporting Herald newspaper - provided forensic evidence of the atrocities which hitherto had depended on oral testimony. A great outcry arose, both from people in Matabeleland and from the opposition press, for reparation and confession by the state. It was confidently expected that this clamour would increase in intensity in 1993. Some commentators urged that Robert Mugabe take advantage of a 1993 ceremony at Pu Pu to include repentance for the state repression of the 1980s in a general cleansing of a hundred years of violence.

So far as formal politics were concerned, there were also some alarming developments for Government in 1992. In Bulawayo successor city to Lobengulas capital - Ndebele intellectuals were active in the Open Forum movement which openly demanded federal autonomy for Matabeleland. An Ndebele cultural society, Vukani, seemed to be appealing to narrowly defined aristocratic Ndebele values. Now that Joshua Nkomo was serving in government as Vice President to Mugabe even his massive popularity in Matabeleland was under challenge. There were those ready to insist that Nkomo was not really Ndebele at all, but a descendant of the conquered Kalanga. Some political analysts predicted that in 1993 these urban political opponents of the ZANU/PF Government would make use of the anniversary to establish themselves securely in rural Matabeleland. Revived Ndebele ethnicity seemed on the point of using history to challenge hegemonic nationalism.[31]

## The Dog That Did Not Bark in the Night: Matabeleland in 1993

In one of Conan Doyles famous Sherlock Holmes stories, the decisive clue was that the dog did not bark in the night. In the same way, one might say that the most significant things about Matabeleland in 1993 have been the events that have not taken place.

I returned to Pu Pu on Heroes Day (11 August) with three friends but we were the only people there; nothing has been done since last year; the Alan Wilson obelisk remains in ruins; no monument has been erected to Lobengula; no memorial has been built to ZIPRA. The only signs of development were two placards, one identifying Pu Pu as the site of the last battle of 1893, and the other saying that it is hoped to have a ZIPRA memorial there. In Harare I was told that there would be a ceremony at Pu Pu on the actual anniversary of the 1893 battle in December; but in Matabeleland it became clear that nothing would happen in December either. It seems a sad anti-climax after the expectations of 1992.

Moreover, the clamour for the admission by Government of its crimes during the dissident period has died down, though certainly not vanished. The opposition has failed to make any impact in the Matabeleland countryside. Indeed, there are clear signs that not only Nkomo but even Mugabe now enjoy some popularity in rural Matabeleland - at any rate there were cheering crowds on Mugabes recent tour of Southern Matabeleland.

Government has held no ceremony to commemorate the 1893 War, norhas there been any large-scale commemoration by anybody else.[32] Instead there are elaborate official plans to celebrate the founding of modern Bulawayo in 1894, it evidently being safer to call to mind the origins of a colonial city than the downfall of an African state. As part of these Bulawayo celebrations, it has been announced that Government will finance the rebuilding of Lobengulas Old Bulawayo as a theme park, on the model of the Yorvik exhibition in York. Lobengulas town will become, it is hoped, a major tourist attraction, along with Great Zimbabwe and the Victoria Falls. And even this does not recall 1893, since the town to be reconstructed is the Old Bulawayo abandoned by Lobengula ten years earlier in 1883, his subsequent capital now being under the concrete of the modern city. To my mind, the rebuilding of Old Bulawayo, complete with ox-wagons and men and women dressed in the costumes of the 1880s and the performance of traditional rituals (which Ndebele elders are going down to KwaZulu to learn), is a poor substitute for the repentance of violence at Pu Pu. But there are some indications that the scheme has been received with enthusiasm in Matabaleland. The Kumalo royal family has welcomed it and has sent representatives to live at the site; when I met various local historians in Northern Matabeleland this summer they were all ready to accept the project as a belated official recognition that the Ndebele past was, after all, part of national history. It seems possible that 1893 may have been successfully shuffled away to one side.[33]

So, how are to we to account for these non-events ? Why did the Ndebele dog not bark in the night ? How has the nationalist state been able to use history to undercut an ethnic challenge? To my mind the answer lies partly in the changed atmosphere of 1993 but partly in the ambiguities of Ndebele identity.

**Explanations**

Let us begin with the changed atmosphere of 1993. To put it briefly - 1992 was a year of drought and hunger; 1993 is a year of rain and plenty. A cult metaphysic which seeks out explanations for drought and finds them in state illegitimacy becomes less plausible when the rains arrive. The government claims credit for having fed the people during the drought; in Matabeleland, as elsewhere in Zimbabwe, most feel that this was its minimum obligation. But they do give credit for the free distribution of seed by the state and for free tractor ploughing, both of which are thought of as positive acts of grace and generosity. In Inyathi Communal Area in Northern Matabeleland, which I visited in August, I was told that land had been ploughed last planting season which had never been ploughed before. They had had a bumper crop. Free seed and free ploughing have been promised again for this years planting. In a Communal Area like Inyathi, moreover, Mugabe and Nkomos current rhetoric of land redistribution is also popular, since Inyathi is compressed on all sides by commercial farms and ranches, each the size of half a county. In this atmosphere, learned local historians were ready enough to express pleasure at the reconstruction of Old Bulawayo. In this atmosphere, too, Joshua Nkomos hold on rural loyalties has been renewed and a mere indication from the state that a second ceremony at Pu Pu would not be welcome seems to have been enough to ensure that nothing happened.

But in addition to these immediate factors, there are also longer term ambiguities which help to explain why 1993 has not after all been a year of revived Ndebele ethnicity or of repudiation of Zimbabwean national identity. To put it simply, no-one in Matabeleland is quite sure who or what represents Ndebele identity. Leadership of any single significant Ndebele ceremony to commemorate 1893 would certainly have been contested. Rather than have the wrong leadership take advantage of the 1893 anniversary to advance the wrong sort of Ndebele identity, many people would prefer to have no commemoration at all. Moreover, one very important - and perhaps dominant - strand in Ndebele ethnic thinking has been, and remains, very anxious to combine both Ndebele and national personalities in a hierarchy of belonging. Rather than an assertion of Ndebeleness which came into open conflict with being Zimbabwean, many people would prefer to avoid any ethnic assertion at all. I take this to be the main reason for Joshua Nkomos enduring popularity since he has always represented a combined Ndebele/national identity. I take this to be the reason why Dumiso Dabengwa, ex-intelligence chief of ZIPRA, now Minister for Home Affairs, and the moving influence behind the Pu Pu ceremony of 1992, did not press for a second ceremony this year. Dabengwa has been instead the main protagonist of the Old Bulawayo rebuilding.

As we shall see, even my statement of the events of 1992 and my description of the first Pu Pu ceremony were deliberately simplified so as to present an apparently unproblematic ethnic revival. In fact even in 1992 there were clear signs of the fractured and contested character of Ndebele identity.

**Ndebele Identity: a historical retrospect**

Over the last eight years I have written extensively about the invention and imagination of Ndebele identity.[34] To summarise:

(a) It is often assumed that the Ndebele were originally an offshoot of the Zulu; that the Ndebele state was modelled on the Zulu state; that the Sindebele language in its pure state was identical with Zulu; and that the Ndebele aristocracy were a Zulu elite. Hence, it is often said, there was a core of Zulu ethnicity at the heart of the Ndebele state. But none of these things are true. Mzilikazi, founder and first ruler of the Ndebele state, was never incorporated into Shakas kingdom; the innovations by which he constructed his own state derived from pre-Shakan Nguni practices; he and his followers broke away before the Zulu language was consciously created by means of the privileging of dialects and the development of a new royal terminology.

The most that can be said is that the leading figures in the emergent Ndebele polity were Nguni. However, by the time of their entry into what is now Zimbabwe in 1829 people of Nguni descent were in a minority; many Nguni men had married Kwena or Tlokwa or Hurutshe wives; Ndebele society had been profoundly Sotho-ised; and a significant percentage of the Ndebele aristocracy north of the Limpopo had Sotho ancestry. In short, the Zulu state did develop an ethnic identity, but the Ndebele state was a mechanism for multi-ethnic incorporation.[35]

(b) Once Mzilikazis followers had arrived in what is today central Matabeleland there were many different patterns of incorporation of the peoples they found there. Even at the core of the state groups of Rozvi, Kalanga, Nyubi and Sotho lived side by side with the newcomers. Most of these were incorporated politically, governed by Ndebele izindunas ... [sending] their children into Ndebele amabutho and whilst remembering their pasts, [coming] proudly to answer to the name of Ndebele. Most came to speak Sindebele as their first language, but they contributed many idioms and words to it in the process. Some, however, retained an effective political autonomy; all continued with pre-Ndebele religious observations. As Julian Cobbing remarks: The majority of Ndebele-speakers today are the descendants either of captives or of those autocthonous peoples whom the Ndebele found on their arrival.[36]

The core state was surrounded by a ring of tributary areas in which at least the political elites spoke Sindebele as a second language while retaining their own basic organisations. Further out still were groups in irregular contact with the Ndebele state and often resistant to it.

(c) It could certainly be argued that the incorporative mechanisms of the Ndebele state had the potential to create an ethnicity. Some Soviet scholars have argued, on the other hand, that the incorporative state had become what they call a nationality, bringing together numerous ethnicities in a formation which had the potential of growing into a nation. However, by the time of the white conquest in 1893 these processes of incorporation and assimilation were both too recent and too continuous for either an ethnicity or a nation to have emerged. Ndebele identity, though expressed in a shared language, remained largely a political project. It was therefore threatened by the colonial conquest which enabled both individuals and groups to break away from Ndebele authority.

(d) In the twentieth century, however, a number of distinct and often conflicting processes had the effect of ethnicising Ndebele consciousness. In rough chronological order these were:

(i) The contradictory impact of the colonial administration
The white conquerors were determined to destroy the Ndebele state. They abolished the kingship and divided up those political entities which had grown out of the regimental system. On the other hand, white administrators thought ethnically and were incapable of thinking in any other way. Many of them, particularly those who had been recruited from Natal, assumed that the Ndebele were a sort of lapsed Zulu. They devoted a good deal of time and energy to trying to restore Zulu discipline; they used the Zulu language in their formal addresses to the indunas; they even thought of introducing Zulu customary law.[37]

(ii) The influence of the mission aries
Missionaries were divided between those who came from the south, spoke Zulu and shared many of the administrations assumptions, and those who came into Matabeleland without any sort of Zulu experience and who tried to understand its society on its own terms. The latter began to develop Sindebele as a written language, which contributed to a sense of separate ethnic identity. However, what Benedict Anderson calls the imperative of print capitalism operated in Matabeleland.[38] Most missionaries - and most government educationalists - favoured the use of Zulu as a language of instruction and made use of Zulu

scriptures and school-books. In its own way this also contributed to a process of ethnicisation because congregations and school pupils were instructed in Zulu/Ndebele even in those areas which had preserved their own languages for public and religious discourse in the nineteenth century.

(iii) The impact of colonial evictions

As Julian Cobbing writes, the colonial period saw a white land-grab in Central Matabeleland and the eviction of Ndebele indunas and their peoples into the outlying tributary areas. There was a thorough mixing of peoples.[39] In the various Reserves and Special Native Areas into which people were moved, there had to be new processes of interaction and identity formation. These processes underlie a good deal of twentieth century ethnicisation - and also underlie a good deal of its contradictions.

The attempt to resist evictions often took the form of appealing back to the identity of the Ndebele state, to whose leaders Cecil Rhodes had promised security on their arcestral lands at the indabas which ended the 1896 risings.[40] This brought Ndebele history into the present. But Creating new communities once the evictions had been carried through took different forms. In some places - as in Matopos Reserve - it took the form of everyone accepting Sindebele as their primary language but accepting the pre and supra-Ndebele Mwali, rain-shrine cult as the source of ecological and social norms.[41] In other places - as in Wenlock Special Native Area - it took the form of re-inventing the solidarities of a nineteenth century regimental unit.[42] Further south, in what had been Kalanga, Sotho and Venda tributary areas in the nineteenth century, a sort of composite identity developed; in the north, where large Ndebele-speaking communities were dumped among Tonga autochthones, there was no such interaction. The newcomers asserted the superiority of their Ndebele identity over the Tonga both in traditional and in modern progressive terms. In short, all sorts of redefinitions of being Ndebele took place, some asserting an exclusive and narrow ethnic identity, and others developing a compositive and inclusive ethnicity.

(iv) The effect of labour migration and of urban society

These rural upheavals were accompanied by the movement of thousands of primary and secondary Ndebele-speakers to the mines and towns. Developments in Bulawayo were particularly important for the rise of Ndebele ethnicity. Bulawayo could be regarded as essentially an Ndebele town, where Ndebele-speakers ought to have a competitive advantage over Shona-speakers and other incoming labour migrants. The result was the emergence of what anthropologists call urban ethnicity - i.e. the coming together of migrants from one very large region under the ethnic label of one privileged group. Thus in Northern Rhodesia migrants from the north-east called themselves Bemba whether they had been part of the Bemba polity or not. In the same way, migrants from most parts of Matabeleland called themselves Ndebele whether they had originated from the area of the old central state, or from the Ndebele-ised periphery, or from the resistant fringes. Southern Kalanga were particularly prominent among the Bulawayo Ndebele. Ndebele football teams, boxing squads, etc developed. So too did the Matabele Home Society, which sought to speak for the extended Ndebele identity, often to the disgust of aristocratic indunas with a more limited definition.

During the evictions of the late 1940s and early 1950s the Matabele Home Society made common cause with local resistance associations, thereby linking the new urban ethnicity with the makers of new identities in the countryside.

(v) The emergence of urban and rural nationalism

In the 1940s and 1950s nationalist ideas developed both among urban intellectuals and in the rural areas of Matabeleland. In the towns this was a time of cultural nationalist assertion. It began to be assumed that language was critically important to identity. But in Matabeleland this had complicated results. There was, for example, the struggle between Zulu and Sindebele as a literary language. Although there were advocates of Zulu who were motivated by Pan-Africanist considerations, in general this was a struggle among the imaginers of Ndebele ethnicity. Those who favoured the use of Zulu wanted to appropriate the prestige of the Zulu kingdom; those who favoured Sindebele wanted to assert the uniqueness of Ndebele identity. In general the protagonists of Zulu appealed to a traditionalist nineteenth century vision of ethnicity; those who favoured bastardised Sindebele favoured the inclusive twentieth century version. But then there was a further division. If language was crucial, then what about Kalanga? Many men who spoke Sindebele in Bulawayo spoke Kalanga in their rural homes. Many leading Bulawayo Ndebele intellectuals, including Joshua Nkomo and his brother Stephen, were simultaneously Kalanga cultural entrepreneurs.[43]

The notion of simultaneity became critical. The Bulawayo spokesmen for an extended Ndebele identity worked out a doctrine of hierarchical loyalties. For purely local and family matters one could be Kalanga; for Bulawayo and provincial matters one must be Ndebele; for territorial matters one had to be a nationalist. These ideas made a natural connection with many developments in the rural areas. The bitter evictees no longer appealed to the promises of Cecil Rhodes but asserted their rights to all land as indigenous; they joined territorial nationalist parties so soon as these were formed. Nationalist leaders were drawn out into the rural areas of Matabeleland by local demand. In this way there grew up a genuine territorial nationalism, though with a strong Matabeleland flavour.[44]

The rhetorical themes of rural Matabeleland nationalism reflected the rich and ambiguous mix of twentieth century Ndebele identity formation: an appeal to the warrior tradition of the Ndebele state, side by side with an appeal to the superiority of the Mwali shrines over Christianity, even though the Mwali cult preceded the Ndebele state. A great deal of imaginative work has gone on so as to link these two originally separate traditions, so that it is today held that Mzilikazi was summoned into the country by Mwali, and that the spirit of the cult possessed and inspired one of the main Ndebele military commanders during the 1896 risings. When I visited Inyathi Communal Area this August my hosts produced the oldest local man to act as historical informant. This elder began by claiming that his family had come from the south with Mzilikazi and were part of the original Nguni; he could tell me of all the regiments and battles. But when he began to bemoan the loss of Ndebele tradition it turned out that what he meant was that too few people any longer observed the prescriptions of the Mwali cult!

Joshua Nkomo was the master choreographer of nationalist rhetoric. He was an enthusiast for Kalanga revival; he was a member of the Matabele Home Society and a collector of royal praise-poems; he began to visit the Mwali shrines as early as 1953 and later took his nationalist colleagues from Mashonaland on pilgrimages to the caves. He was the adored spokesman of Matabeleland rural nationalism but he was also the elected leader of the African National Congress, when it was revived in 1957; of the National Democratic Party; and of the Zimbabwe Peoples Union. He was the leader of the Ndebele, in the widest and most inclusive sense, but he was also leader of the nation in waiting. He was opposed by spokesmen for a narrower, exclusive definition of Ndebele identity, who warned against territorial nationalism and argued for an anti-nationalist bargain with the whites which might result in a revived Ndebele monarchy and an autonomous homeland.

## Conclusion

This summary narrative gives some idea of the complexities of imagining Ndebele ethnic identity in the twentieth century and helps to explain some of the difficulties inherent in remembering 1893 a hundred years later. Let us go back to the ceremonies at Pu Pu on 11 August, 1992. In my earlier description I made the 1992 Pu Pu ceremonies seem unequivocally and straightforwardly a glorification of the nineteenth century Ndebele state and of late twentieth century Ndebele guerrilla prowess. In fact things were more complicated than that. Many of the people who live round Pu Pu are descendants of pre-Ndebele populations; at the ceremony there were not only praise songs for Mzilikazi and Lobengula but also demands that pre-Ndebele kings be honoured. When the Mwali priest at Pu Pu demanded that a hundred years of violence be atoned for, he implied the illegitimacy of Ndebele violence as well as of colonial conquest. Representatives of the Khumalo royal family were at Pu Pu; so also were mediums of Rozvi and Kalanga spirits.

This was one complexity of the 1992 Pu Pu commemoration. Another lay in Joshua Nkomos participation. So far from rejoicing in a celebration of Ndebele heroism, Nkomo was determined to suppress any ethnic manifestation which threatened national unity. So far from speaking as leader of ZAPU and commander of ZIPRA, Nkomo presented himself as Vice President in the national government. It was clearly his judgement that while in the 1950s it was possible to celebrate Ndebele identity and still plainly be a territorial nationalist, in the 1990s the balance requires to be struck differently. The events of the 1980s and the operations of the Fifth Brigade in Matabeleland cast dreadful doubt on the nationalist option and greatly strengthened those spokesmen of Ndebele identity who repudiate it. At Pu Pu Nkomo chose to present himself solely as a nationalist and to hope that people would remember that he was also spokesman for the inclusive Matabeleland imagination.

A 1993 Pu Pu ceremony would have been more contested still. But the governments preference of a rebuilt Old Bulawayo, while immediately safer, carries with it some odd consequences. Although Lobengula was the hero of the spokesmen of the inclusive Ndebele identity - who often contrasted his readiness to reward ability in any of his subjects with Mzilikazis supposed preference for the Nguni - nevertheless the rebuilding of the royal capital is bound to celebrate a traditionalist version of Ndebele history. As for the idea of a journey by indunas to Kwazulu in order to re-learn rituals, this is a strange recurrence of the old idea that the Ndebele are really Zulu. Plainly this excludes all those Ndebele-speakers who are obviously not descendants of the Zulu; it also falsifies the history of the nineteenth century state and undervalues its creativity. Moreover, the Kwazulu of Inkatha has spent enormous time and energy in the invention of some rituals and the elaboration of others. (Delegates from Inkatha have visited Matabeleland to recruit support from their brothers, although ZAPU/ZIPRAs links were always with the ANC). In short, Old Bulawayo may give support to the narrow, Nguni definition of Ndebele identity, which in the short run is less challenging to a government that the province-wide inclusive Ndebele definition, but in the long run threatens secession and tribalism. It is possible that though the dog did not bark in 1993, there was a dangerous growl at the back of its throat.

## Notes

1 Anouar Abdel-Malek, Identity, Alterity, Reductionism. An Essay on the perspectives of the dialectics of maintenance through tranformation, Berlin, October 1993, pp. 12-13.
2 See, for instance, the statement by the Zimbabwean scholar, Brian Raftopolous, Race and Nationalism in a Post-Colonial State, Conference on Ethnicity and Nationalism, Sandbjerg Manor, May 1993, and Shula Marks' presentation at the same conference, Black and White Nationalisms in South Africa. I myself spoke at Humboldt University on the night before the Berlin Conference began on changing interpretations of African nationalism.
3 For a summary of the development of this historiography see Terence Ranger, Resistance in Africa: From Nationalist Revolt to Agrarian Protest. In: Gary Okihiro (ed.), In Resistance. Studies in African, Caribbean, and Afro-American History, Amherst 1986.
4 An admirable example is the work of the Afro-American historian Michael West, African Middle-Class Formation in Colonial Zimbabwe, 1890-1965, Ph. D. thesis, Harvard University 1990.
5 Charles van Onselen, Worker Consciousness in Black Miners: Southern Rhodesia, 1900-1920, and Ian Phimister, African Worker Consciousness: Origins and Aspects to 1953. In: Phimister/Van Onselen (eds.), Studies in the History of African Mine Labour in Colonial Zimbabwe, Gweru 1978; this topic has been the subject of repeated debate and examination in the Journal of Southern African Studies. The tendency has been to move from the search for proletarian consciousness to studies of 'worker moral economy' and 'urban culture'.
6 For example, Terence Ranger, Peasant Consciousness and Guerrilla War, London and Harare 1985.
7 See, for instance, the chapters by Felix Ekechi, Owen Kalu, John Peel, Murray Last and Terence Ranger in: Toyin Falola (ed.), African Historiography. Essays in honour of Jacob Ade Ajayi, Ikeja-London 1993. For a recent and dynamic example of the long anthropological fascination with religious identities, see Jean and John Comaroff (eds.), Modernity and its Malcontents, Ritual and Power in Postcolonial Africa, Chicago-London 1993.
8 Fritz Kramer, Der Rote Fes, first published in 1987 and now published in English as: The Red Fez. Art and Spirit Possession in Africa, London-New York 1933. Kramer argues that while for Europeans identity involves setting 'the Other' apart, for Africans it involves literally possessing the other.
9 These papers are included in Partha Chatterjee and Gyanendra Pandey (eds.), Subaltern Studies. VII, New Delhi 1992. After attending the conference I drew the attention of Africanists to Indian work on working-class identity, popular religion and eco-history in: Terence Ranger, Subaltern Studies and Social History, Southern African Review of Books, February/May 1990.
10 A subsequent development of her argument in O'Hanlon and David Washbrook, Approaches to the Study of Colonialism and Culture in India, History Workshop, 32, Autumn 1991, influenced my own 'The Invention of Tradition Revisited: the case of Colonial Africa', in: Terence Ranger/Olufemi Vaughan (eds.), Legitimacy and the State in Twentieth Century Africa, St Antony's/Macmillan 1993.
11 G. Pandey, The Construction of Communalism, New Delhi 1990.
12 Rosalind O'Hanlon, Caste, Conflict and Ideology, Cambridge 1985, p. 304; Bernard Cohn, An Anthropologist Among the Historians, New Delhi 1987. Cohn includes in this collection his chapter from The Invention of Tradition, Representing Authority in Victorian India.
13 C. Bayly, Indian Society and the Making of the British Empire, Cambridge 1988, p. 155.

14 Pandey, The Construction..., p. 10.

15 Vivek Dhaneswar, Caste and the Secular Self, Sandbjerg, May 1993.

16 The formation of 'Islamic' and 'Christian' identities in Nigeria, for instance, (and even in hitherto easy-going Tanzania), seems to demand Africanist studies of 'communalism'. Caste has in the past been used as a way of analysing Ndebele society. In Indian studies, so it seems to the uninitiated, 'ethnicity' seems to be restricted to analyses of the 'tribals', though some of Cohn's discussions of 'networks and centres' or of 'regions subjective and objective' seem to come close to fusing the ideas of caste and ethnicity. Cohn, An Anthropologist..., chapters 4 and 6.

17 There is an apparent parallel here with the debate about 'kastom' in the Pacific, where scholars seem to have ignored colonial inventions and concentrated on the innovations of cultural nationalists. They have been roundly denounced as a result. Because a special issue of Mankind on 'Reinventing Traditional Culture' came out in 1982, a year before the publication of The Invention of Tradition, Hobsbwam and Ranger's collection has inevitably been seen in this context by participants in the Pacific debate. See R. Keesing, 'Creating the Past: Custom and Identity in the Contemporary Pacific, Honolulu 1990. I owe these and many other references to my student, Melanie Chait, whose 'Creation and Imagination in the Pacific', ms., November 1993, is an extremely useful introduction to the Pacific literature.

18 By far the most compelling account of the varying meanings of 'being Kikuyu' is John Lonsdale's The Moral Economy of Mau Mau: Wealth, Poverty and Civic Virtue in Kikuyu Political Thought, in: Bruce Berman and John Lonsdale, Unhappy Valley. Conflict in Kenya and Africa: Book Two: Violence and Ethnicity, London-Nairobi 1992. A similar depth and complexity is communicated in Thomas Spear/Richard Walter (eds.), Being Maasai. Ethnicity and Identity in East Africa, London-Nairobi 1993.

19 Annual Report on African Affairs, North-Western Province, 1951/52, cited in: Kate Crehan, Tribes and the People Who Read Books, draft chapter in her forthcoming study of North-Western Zambia.

20 Cohn, An Anthropologist, p. 137.

21 Patrick Harries, The Roots of Ethnicity: Discourse and the Politics of Language Construction in South-East Africa. In: African Affairs *87*(1988)346; Terence Ranger, Missionaries, Migrants and the Manyika: The Invention of Ethnicity in Zimbabwe. In: Leroy Vail (ed.), The Creation of Tribalism in Southern Africa, London 1989.

22 John Janzen, The Consequences of literacy in African Religion. In: Wim Van Binsbergen/Matthew Schoffeleers (eds.), Theoretical Explorations in African Religion, London 1985; for the work of African 'organic intellectuals' see Steven Feierman, Peasant Intellectuals. Anthropology and History in Tanzania, Madison 1900.

23 Lonsdale, The moral economy... For an exploration of gender contestations expressed in terms of 'moral ethnicity', see D.W.Cohen/E.S.Atieno-Odhiambo, Burying SM. The Politics of Knowledge and the Sociology of Power in Africa, London-Portsmouth 1992.

24 When Leroy Vail called the conference which led to the publication of The Creation of Tribalism in Southern Africa, he extended invitations to all the History Departments of Universities in independent southern Africa. No African scholars attended.

25 Peter Ekeh, Social Anthropology and Two Contrasting Uses of Tribalism in Africa, Comparative Studies in Society and History, *32*(1990)4.

26 E.S.Atieno-Odhiambo/David Cohen, Siaya. The Historical Anthropology of an African Landscape, London 1989; E.S.Atieno-Odhiambo, From the Kenya State to the Civil Society of the Luo Nation, Conference on the State and Civil Society in Africa and Eastern Europe, Bellagio, February 1990.

27 Lipashe Luchembe, Ethnic Stereotypes, violence and labour in early colonial Zambia, 1889-1924. In: Samuel Chipungu (ed.), Guardians in Their Time. Experiences of Zambians Under Colonial Rule, 1890-1964, London 1992. See also Chipungu's own African Leadership under Indirect Rule in Colonial Zambia, and Ackson Kanduza's Towards a History of Ideas in Zambia, which deals with just such 'organic intellectuals' working in the written vernacular as I have described. In his introduction, Chipungu, while stressing that the book represents indigenous Zambian scholarship, nevertheless compares Luchembe's chapter to the work of several contributors to the recently published volume The Creation of Tribalism in Southern Africa, and his own work to Shula Marks' study of the Zulu.

28 V.Y.Mudimbe, The Invention of Africa. Gnosis, Philosophy, and the Order of Knowledge, Bloomington 1988.

29 For an account and analysis of what happened at Pu Pu see Horizon, October 1992. In addition to a description of the ceremony itself, Horizon carried pieces by Jeremy Brickhill and Terence Ranger which set the occasion in the whole context of violence and healing.

30 The most authoritative scholarly treatment of these events and of their impact on memory and identity is Richard Werbner's Tears of the Dead. The Social Biography of an African Family, Edinburgh 1991 and Harare 1992. See also Werbner's The Making of Moral Knowledge: Local-Global Displacements, Anthropology Association, IV Decennial Conference, Oxford 1993.

31 The atmosphere and rhetoric of Matabeleland in 1992 is described in Terence Ranger, Accounting for Drought, Making Rain and Healing History in Matabeleland, Oxford, 15 October 1992.

32 The sole commemoration of 1893 so far took place in Bulawayo in March. It was organised by the Vukani Mahlabezulu Cultural Society 'to commemorate the 100 years of the fall of the Ndebele state' and addressed by Sydney Malunga, m.p., who denied that Vukani was 'a subversive organisation'. 'Some people think this gathering is a rebellion', he added. But if it was a rebellion against any one, it was a rising against historians who 'had long distorted the history of this country in order to promote tribalism and hatred among the people'. Malunga announced that the ceremony was 'the beginning of a series of events that will take place in this city to commemorate the defeat of our first politicians. Every Zimbabwean should therefore identify with them'. His speech was followed by 'traditional songs and dances in praise of the heroes who died trying to defend Zimbabwe's independence in 1893'. I have not heard of any other of the 'series of events'.

33 The Britain Zimbabwe Society's annual research day in June 1993 was on the theme '1893 - 1993' and concerned the various ways in which use had been made of the history of 'states' in Zimbabwe. The opening session concerned archaelogy and included an account of the Old Bulawayo project. A summary of the day's discussions, 'History, Memory and the State, 1893 - 1993' is obtainable from the Britain Zimbabwe Society.

34 A review of these various writings and a summary of my current views on Ndebele ethnicity can be found in my 'The Invention of Tradition Revisited'. In: T.O.Ranger/O.Vaughan (eds.), Legitimacy and the State in Twentieth Century Africa, St Antony's/Macmillan 1993. An article entitled 'Ethnicity and Nationality: the case of Matabeleland' is appearing in the next issue of the South African Historical Journal.

35 For the best treatment of the early history of the Ndebele see Julian Cobbing, The Ndebele Under the Khumalos, 1820-1896, Ph.d thesis, Lancester 1976. For the emergence of Zulu enthnicity and language see especially John Wright/Caroline Hamilton, The Making of the Amalala: Ethnicity, Ideology and Relations of Subordination in a Precolonial Context. In: South African Historical Journal, 22 November 1990.

36 Cobbing, The Ndebele..., p. 115, 124, 125.
37 Terence Ranger, The Invention of Tribalism in Zimbabwe, Gweru 1985.
38 Benedict Anderson, Imagined Communities. Reflections on the Origin and Spread of Nationalism, London 1983.
39 Cobbing, The Ndebele..., p. 115.
40 Terence Ranger, Whose Heritage? The Case of the Matobo National Park. In: Journal of Southern African Studies *15*(1989)2.
41 Terence Ranger, Power, Religion and Community: the Matobo Case. In: Partha Chatterjee/ Gyanendra Pandey (eds.), Subaltern Studies VII, Delhi 1992.
42 Terence Ranger, Tradition, Collaboration and Resistance: the Nqameni Chiefs of Wenlock, Oxford 1993.
43 Terence Ranger, Language, Law and Nationalism. Ethnicity and Nationality: the case of Matabeleland, Institute of Commonwealth Studies, May 1991.
44 Terence Ranger, The Origins of Nationalism in Rural Matabeleland, Oxford 1990.

# Mobile Practice and Local Identity. Changing Market Moralities in Rural Northern Rhodesia (Zambia), 1930s to 1960s

Achim von Oppen

## 'Balovale' Identities

When interviewing ex-district officers of the former colony of Northern Rhodesia (now Zambia) and reading through their reports, I was struck by the remarkably strong personal identification of these men with 'their' areas. For those who have served in remote districts such as the one where I did most of my fieldwork, this identification is probably stronger than among most of their post-colonial successors.[1] Officers once stationed in that District, which was then called 'Balovale' (later sub-divided into the Zambezi and Kabompo Districts, now in Zambia's Northwestern Province) seem to have developed during their years of service a kind of local identity that had strong territorial connotations. It referred to a particular geographical space as well as to its human inhabitants. These came to be classed together as 'Balovale peoples', glossing over their various social divisions and different ethnic identities,[2] as long as they had chosen permanent residence within the district boundaries.[3] These borders, determined by politicians and surveyors from both the British and the Portuguese side, where obviously the ones that counted most for the administrators. Below the district level, to be sure, colonial officers tended to see the population primarily as members of particular 'tribes' and, at a still lower level, of villages, each with its economic and political characteristics. In the course of the later colonial period, however, with a growing 'development'-orientation, the administration increasingly tried to draw, mentally and administratively, fixed boundaries around these, in their view 'traditional', social units.[4] In this way, and as part of the introduction of local-based 'Indirect Rule' (which happened here, for particular reasons, only in 1946)[5], territorial subdivisions of the district were formed. Three 'Senior Chiefs' were appointed as heads of respective 'Native Authority Areas', which were each divided into several 'Native Districts' under different 'Sub-Chiefs' or 'Divisional Headmen', and these again into 'Villages' or 'Village Areas' under 'Area' or 'Village Headmen'[6]. Each of these administrative 'Villages' included a sometimes substantial number of 'traditional' family settlements, usually small hamlets which are called membo or nyikala (singular limbo, mukala) in Luvale and Lunda, respectively.[7]

There were, in other words, marked attempts to strengthen territoriality as a principle of political and social organization. On the one hand, these attempts drew on the overall ideology of 'Indirect Rule' which assumed a fixed hierarchy of local rulers and leaders, to whom their 'subjects' were tied through 'customary' bonds of descent and personal loyalty. On the other hand, and more implicitly, the territorial organization of state power undermined precisely this concept of hierarchical personal relations. In effect, territorial administration presupposes communities of proto-'citizens', linked by actual residence and bureaucratic rule, rather than social relations, to particular geographical spaces. This contradiction resulted from heterogeneous ideas about social and political order on the one hand, and real interests and experiences of the colonial administration on the other. These included, at a more general level, mainstream ideas about localized subsistence economy, kinship-based society, and lineage or 'tribal' authority, which appealed to both anthropologists and 'enlightened' government officials of the time. There were also, in the background, European historical experiences of control over land being the decisive basis of power over people, and of territorial control being the site where 'modern government' originated.[8] More specifically, there was the quest for near-to-absolute control by the colonial state, embodied by local administrators, notably the 'District Commissioner'. The officers' personal identification with particular areas was further enhanced by their special position in the colonial service, notably a relative autonomy from Central Government Departments, their being required to acquire command of some local language, and a tendency to be posted for longer periods or more often in the same area than their post-colonial successors. In addition, district officers, especially the post-war generation, were usually quite young men who found some of their first professional challenges in rural Africa.

Other members of the tiny European community in remote districts such as Balovale had to some extent parallel views and experiences, competing with, and sometimes cross-cutting, the grid of the emerging colonial state: Missionaries, labour recruiters and, as will be seen further below, businessmen also aspired for a new spatial order, with a hierarchy between local centres and out-stations in the bush. Instead of going further into the European emphasis on territory, however, the contrasting perspective(s) of the African population should come into the focus now.

In fact, neither the 'traditionalist' nor the 'modernist' version of territoriality, related to concepts of 'indirect' and 'direct' rule, respectively, appealed very much to ordinary villagers. Both concepts often enough clashed with very different popular understandings of geographical space. They differed so much that, in fact, large areas within Balovale never became subject to 'proper' 'native administration' nor to sustainable boundaries.[9] At the same time, however, it must be acknowledged that these local views were not homogenous, and far less fixed than - in theory - the European ones.

One of the fairly constant features of societies around the Upper Zambezi, throughout their history, has been a remarkable spatial mobility. Entire hamlets (membo) and individual members, both men and women, regularly used, and still use, to move to other sites several times in a lifetime. The reason is a variety, often a combination, of economic and social factors, such as exhaustion of soil, water and game resources; trade; initiation; marriage; death; authority conflicts and other, often violent tensions. A particular combination of matrilineal rules of descent, virilocal rules of residence and frequent divorce/remarriage favoured the considerable spatial mobility of individuals, including women, and often over considerable distances. Population density was, and is, remarkably low, allowing for relatively open access to natural resources. The physical landscape is fairly uniform over hundreds of kilometers, with its combination of basically two typical elements - dry, sandy, wooded uplands, and seasonally flooded treeless plains. The consequence is a scattered, generally very sparse population, and a relatively small size of settlements. This required, in turn, always an active 'foreign policy' between the residence units, to secure marriages, labour assistance, alliances, trade exchanges, and peace. A multitude of relationships, again often spanning enormous distances, were (and are) constantly constructed and renegotiated between 'villages' and individuals. Both kinship and friendship idioms are used in the process, but they regularly include a strong element of negotiation and contract.[10]

This situation seems to have provided, on the whole, a very favourable environment for pre-colonial market production, with a strong demand for products of the gathering economy (beeswax, ivory, rubber), resulting in decentral forms of marketing along caravan routes, reallocation of labour through slave trade and voluntary migration, and need for long-distance communication and security. After colonial 'pacification', older forms of production for exchange continued, complemented rather than substituted by new market-oriented activities, notably labour migration to the mining centres of Southern Africa.. In consequence, settlement fragmentation and mobility if anything increased even further during the colonial period.

Another aspect of mobility was the ability to resist political centralization or state formation. Spatial movement often meant to relinquish loyalty to one local leader, and attempt to establish another. Local leaders themselves - variously calling themselves 'headmen' (vilolo) or 'chiefs' (vamyangana) - were constantly trying to attract followers to build up power positions. Their success was often meagre, or not lasting longer than one generation. In consequence, jurisdictions of individual leaders changed very rapidly and had no sharp geographical boundaries; they were, at any rate, defined more in terms of personal allegiance than territory.

This does not mean that location had no importance for the inhabitants of the region in constructing their identity before colonial administrators tried to impose this criterion on them. For instance, ethnic terminology such as Luvale or Lwena, Luchazi and Mbunda, which was in use even before the colonial period, but more or less divorced from political rule, often derived from particular ecological environments (plants, rivers or soil qualities). Also, every freeborne villager did, and still does, retain a lifelong emotional attachment to what he or she would call 'our (or: my) village' (limbo lyetu or lyami). But on closer inspection, both concepts hardly relate to fixed segments of geographical space. Ecological names point first of all at the productive specializations which are related to particular ecosystems; and as mentioned before, the same elements of the 'savannah-woodland-mosaic' appear in continuous repetition across vast stretches of land. 'Our village', on the other hand, denotes more precisely the group of closest kin residing together, most often matrilineally related men with their mother, unmarried sisters, and wives, that make up the core of a neighbourhood; and such neighbourhoods change frequently in composition and location. In tune with the persistent mobility of settlements, also the shrines of important land-related cults are remarkably mobile; the most important ritual site of every village, the 'ancestor tree' (muyombo) in the public space at its centre, is left unattended when the inhabitants move away, after an offshoot is taken from it and planted at the new site.[11]

In short, there was very little identification with particular localities among the wider population on which colonial efforts towards establishing local identity in territorial terms could build. The landscape in which villagers tended to anchor themselves was first of all a social one, structured by multiple networks of personal obligations, carefully constructed through a variety of moral concepts and languages.[12]

Having thus outlined the wider context of my case study, I now go a bit deeper into the implications of these two types of identity, territory- and network-based. The empirical axis along which I will pursue this question, is the morality of peasant marketing, notably of food products. As will be seen, the production and sale of rural products in and from Balovale District was an area of central concern for both villagers and administrators in the area, and it was one of the fields in which their different concepts of identity clashed.

I start from the general assumption, following Polanyi's 'substantive' school in economic anthropology, that economic transactions in any society never function on the basis of the utilitarian motives of individuals alone, but are always and necessarily 'embedded' in institutional contexts.[13] The important aspect of these arrangements is, in my view, that they involve particular 'moralities of exchange'.[14] These contexts, however, are not simply given, e.g. by stages of societal development, but constructed and changed through continuous social interaction. E.P. Thompson, referring to the same example of food marketing, has coined the famous term 'moral economy' for the set of rules invoked by food rioters in early modern Britain. This term, however, has often been used in an evolutionist and sometimes inflationary way, reducing it to a pre- or 'anti-market' ideology.[15] In contrast, I start from the assumption that any transactional order, including the one of 'the' market, has its own morality.[16]

More correctly, we should speak of 'moralities' in plural, since there are often competing interpretations by the different social groups involved.[17] These usually involve not only ideas about 'just' terms of exchange and and 'correct' modes of negotiating these terms, but, at a more implicit level, also some concept of social balance between exchange partners, embedded in a context of 'legitimate' community. At this point, social identity becomes directly relevant for economic transactions.

In this paper, I concentrate on the contrast between network and territory as notions of market morality in their importance for Balovale history, mainly between the 1930s and the early 1960s. I will explore how these different understandings emerged from particular interest groups and experiences, how they confronted each other, and what resulted from this confrontation. In doing so, I draw on a cross-section of data, both oral and archival, which I collected during a series of research stays in Zambia and Britain between 1979 and 1986. Some of the material requires further analysis or validation and leads, therefore, to conclusions of a more tentative character.

## Constructing Market as Territory

Interests in tapping local economic resources for the wider world economy were never very strong in this district. The only regional products with some officially recognized export value were 'traditional' ones with little scope for capital investment (initially wild rubber, beeswax throughout the period). As in the other rural peripheries of Northern Rhodesia, the export of migrant labour through recruitment agencies and individual movement was supported by administrators; but they had to realize that enthusiasm for wage labour was remarkably low among the male population. It may be said that economic policies were - and to a large extent still are - intended to serve two rather political concerns: The viability of the administration itself; and the establishment and maintenance of what was called 'peace and stability' and the like, i.e. tranquility and loyalty among the inhabitants of this remote area adjacent to the international border. The idea of sharply bounded local territories - notably the District, 'Native Authority' and Village Areas - with distinct 'local communities' was not only instrumental in the establishment of the colonial political order, but pervaded also the administrators' concepts of the economy.

After the establishment of the station or Boma in 1907, one of the first worries of district officers was to secure the food needs of their own employees (labourers, messengers, clerks), on which the latters' loyalty hinged to some extent.[18] In addition, labour recruitment agencies had their own food demand. Until the 1940s, food rations in kind were an important, perhaps particularly motivating, part of the payment of district workers and labour recruitees waiting for departure. To provide these rations often turned out to be a tricky problem. Transport distances from the major farming areas developing along the main railway line were enormous; pre-colonial food trade, that once had successfully supplied the numerous slave and goods' caravans crossing the area, had collapsed; and problems were aggravated by the spatial concentration of food demand around the Boma, while the producing population remained highly scattered. The few European businessmen who had settled in the area were taken under contract to buy up the quantities required in their shops, and gradually developed a network of subsidiary shops and buying stations throughout the district. The response of village producers, eager to regain access to markets for their customary cash-and-staple crops (mainly cassava, some millet, groundnuts and beans), was so positive that soon these traders were also able to serve 'meal contracts' for neighbouring districts.[19]

Despite obligations of solidarity with their fellow officers, and although they had to recognize the value of local income generation for the rural population (see below), the rapidly rising food sales met with decreasing enthusiasm among the administrators of Balovale. They were apprehensive for the risk of diminishing quantities becoming available for domestic needs and/or increasing price pressure as a result of regional exports, mainly of cassava meal.[20] From around 1940, measures were taken, with limited success, to curb or ban regional exports in years of scarcity and to prohibit 'extensive' cultivation practices allegedly endangering food production.[21] After the war, rations in kind for government employees were abolished while at the same time District and 'Native Authority' staff expanded considerably. To make staple food for them more readily available, public market places were established at their centres.[22] Localized markets also helped to exact levies on food transactions charged in growing amounts by the 'Native Authorities' as their own revenue base, and to control prices. Throughout the colonial period, the fixing of producer prices for foodstuffs applicable to the whole district territory (later also at N.A. Area level) was one core activity of district administrators.[23]

These regulations reflected also a deeper distrust among colonial administrators in ways of finding the 'right' terms of exchange through negotiation among market partners, which were central elements in both older 'indigenous' and 'liberal' market moralities.[24] Instead, officers tended to be adherents of an idea of authoritarian political regulation of market activities following political priorities.[25] These priorities were not dictated by self-interest, i.e. the build-up and reproduction of their own administration, alone. At least as strong was a paternalist and in some ways mercantilist idea of having to care for the welfare and economic progress of the region under their jurisdiction and its inhabitants.[26] There was also a historical shift in priorities. In the early period, the intention to ensure a reliable food supply at low and stable prices for local government employees (in a nutshell the same food policies as at the territorial/national level[27]) was made quite explicit. From the Great Depression, such arguments were increasingly blended with a developmental discourse that reflected the growing weight of the second concern of district administrators: to secure a certain degree of economic welfare as a precondition of loyalty of the regional population.

Labour migration from Balovale was never as high as from other remote rural areas in Northern Rhodesia.[28] This had clearly to do with the underpriviledged position of 'North-Westerners' at urban labour markets due to particularly low impact of school education (until the 1950s mainly by missionaries) (Papstein 1978:3; Wilkin 1983),[29] but also with an entrenched preference for peasant commodity production, rather than wage labour, due to a long-pre-history of successful experience. Problems with the recruitment of migrant labour from both the supply and demand side, the latter culminating in the years of Depression, instilled fears in district administrators that a lack of access to extra-district markets could cause unrest among the local population. They had definite ideas, however, where these markets should be found, namely in the growing towns of the Northern Rhodesian 'Copperbelt'.[30] Several measures, such as the completion of a first road connection in 1942, increased border patrolling, the repression of older, pre-colonial currencies such as cloth and salt in favour of coined money (also aimed at facilitating poll tax collection), and the introduction of new standard measurements helped to establish the regional market more firmly as a periphery of the Northern Rhodesian economy and to sever customary ties with adjacent areas in Angola and 'Barotseland'.

After some attempts to stimulate production for Britain's war needs (notably the revitalization of wild rubber collection), a number of initiatives were started from 1948 to develop new 'economic crops' with an urban demand such as groundnuts, maize, rice and Turkish tobacco. These consisted first in village extension and input distribution campaigns, and were subsequently more concentrated on 'progressive farmers' for some of whom 'peasant farming schemes' outside the villages were established.[31] Also price and marketing controls were increasingly justified by 'welfare and development' arguments. When, for instance, price ranges instead of fixed prices were introduced in 1957, the upper limit was explained as making regional products competitive at outside markets, while the lower limit was to guarantee a minimum return to producers.[32] When private trader-buyers, in periods of high production or slack demand, began to lower their prices or stop buying produce in the remoter parts of the district alltogether, meetings were held by district administrators which proposed the setting up of a public, cooperative marketing system which foreshadowed the parastatal experiments of the post-colonial era.[33]

Despite these 'encouragements' of certain forms of integration with wider markets, however, the image of economy adopted by the majority of post-war colonial officers in Balovale/Kabompo was firmly framed by administrative borders. What should happen within these borders, at various levels, exhibited a notable degree of 'public welfare' thinking, and could be described as a 'subsistence plus' model. In other words, food exports from the region - a source of income that was by the 1950s (at the time of peak labour migration) definitely more important than remittances from extra-district wages[34] - were regarded as legitimate only when they represented a surplus beyond local subsistence.[35] Food self-sufficiency of the district, now in terms of the whole of its population, was the primary concern of administrators. Food scarcity, sometimes amounting to famine (well-known as periodical events mainly in the western low-lands of the district as a result of unusually high floods), put material and political strains on the administration to organize relief supplies. In such years, or when to officers self-sufficiency appeared threatened in other ways, bans on food exports were imposed and - in principle - effected by levy collectors and messengers posted along the most important transport routes. Social and locational distribution of food within the district, in contrast, was only a secondary consideration. Nonetheless, price ceilings were also brought into effect at 'Native authority Area' level for sales of rural products, be they at local markets (mainly to government employees), or even - at least in theory - in the villages. Their aim was, allegedly, to protect poorer strata of villagers such as single women who also relied to some extent on food purchases.[36]

## Defending Market as Network

The restrictions and regulations mentioned so far were clearly facets in the colonial state's unresolved quest for territorial rule. They were attempts of the central government to get a grip on largely autonomous (yet market-related) economic and social processes among the local population. Not very surprisingly, peasants and traders in Balovale constantly, and often successfully, tried to defy or find ways round these measures. The struggles over marketing that ensued always included, beyond diverging interests, an aspect of struggle over meaning and identity, in which the different sides, implicitly or explicitly, tried to defend their moral views on 'just' exchange and legitimate community, or to actively impose them on each other.

There was a considerable element of not understanding (and refusing to understand) the 'rules of the game' on each side. A glimpse at the historical background of the 'indigenous' morality of exchange, with which the colonial interventions in marketing mentioned before unavoidably clashed, therefore seems in order here. It must be stressed, first of all, that this local morality was not 'indigenous' in the sense of purely 'internal' origin, and it was precisely not 'local' in the sense of presupposing spatial boundaries for its application. It had developed in this area prior to the colonial conquest out of attempts to accomodate new kinds of exchange in older institutional forms which, however, had probably been reshaped or even 'invented' to a considerable extent in the process.[37] An ideology of establishing, redressing or reconfirming social balance (not equality) through reciprocal relationships had been an important underpinning of any act of transfer of material products and resources. The relevance of this idea becomes evident in the specific historical context of this highly fractured, mobile society without strong central political authority. The proneness to conflict in inter- and intra-village relationships was, if anything, aggravated by pre-colonial market expansion. To be sure, these models of balanced social relations should not be mistaken for reality but seen rather as contra-factual blueprints, directed against emerging forms of unequality in a society in which class formation and political hierarchy were not stable and sustainable enough to find justification in corresponding cultural expressions.

At least two distinguishable understandings of reciprocal exchange had emerged in the region until the 19th century, which pervaded negotiations among villagers themselves as well as with foreign traders: A 'barter' type, applied to direct exchanges of goods according to fixed material equivalents (kulanda); and a 'gift' type, applied to transfers with less emphasis on material equivalence which usually involved an element of deferred reciprocation or 'credit' (mukuli). These types were relevant for different social groups and situations: the first for day-to-day transactions between complementary groups within the existing division of labour (archetypally women vs. men and fishermen-hunters vs. cultivators; extended to export producers vs. traders bringing import goods); and the second usually for major transfers between individuals regarding each other as equals (even though perhaps distinguished by rank) and eager to establish some kind of more permanent, personal alliance, e.g. between chiefs, headmen and elders, but also any other adult persons from different residence units. The two concepts often overlapped each other in empirical exchange acts. 'Gifts' or bonuses, for examples, were usually transferred on top of nominally equivalent barter exchange, to seal a more permanent 'business relationship' and also to accomodate market fluctuations. Both elements were negotiable; but while in barter exchanges, bargaining concerned more the measures and quality, in 'gifts' or bonuses also the quantity was subject to intense negotiation.

There were other, more general similarities in these understandings of exchange which apparently facilitated their active adaptation to the particular conditions of pre-colonial market integration in this area considerably (and distinguished them profoundly from the ones of colonial administrators). Firstly, these understandings did not presuppose any kind of corporate 'moral community', but rather mobile individuals or specialized groups intrinsically open towards others or 'strangers'. Secondly, they did not regard balance and trust between market participants as something simply given by 'public interest' or superior powers, but as something to be systematically built in negotiations among exchange partners themselves. This is not the place to go into the details of a multitude of institutional arrangements for economic exchange, developed and adapted with enormous creativity by various social groups in the region when they entered relations with foreign traders, both African and European, during the 19th century.

The question is rather, how these inhabitants, grown up in a very different economic morality, responded to the colonial administrator's (and their local

European allies') attempts to impose a new, territorial, order of exchange on them. In doing so, I will concentrate on the later colonial period, since the end of the 'Great Depression' and the beginning of more deliberate attempts for colonial 'development'. A first striking result of such exploration is that these attempts, despite their power aspect, and although they were obviously in contradiction to both 'indigenous' and 'free market' moralities of exchange, were not as unequivocally rejected as one would have assumed. A second result is that the responses clearly differed between different social groups in the district.

It is probably least surprising that Chiefs, Headmen and their clients (including some local businessmen) were more than ready to embark upon the new, territorial order of the economy. The newly created 'Native Authorities' were not only responsible to control and implement the measures of the district administration, they began to fix additional prices in their jurisdictions; established permanent markets at their 'capitals' and checkpoints along their 'borders' at which levies on old and new market products were collected; issued calls and organized staff to propagate new 'economic crops' and cultivation methods; and competed for the first 'Peasant Farming Schemes'.[38] Below the chiefdom level, 'Subchiefs', 'Area' and 'Village Headmen' had to supervise and facilitate the implementation of the new regulations. The local elites carrying the newly created institutions of 'Indirect Rule' obviously tried to use here the powers delegated to them by the colonial administration for very similar ends, to improve their own tax base and to set up a territorial type of control.

But the process was not as smooth as that. Frequently, tensions arose from the contradiction between aspirations for territorial rule (extended to the entire population of the area), and the ideology of ethnic identity that was the basis of 'Native Administration'.[39] An implication of any ideology of personal association is that all members, in return for their loyalty, have legitimate claims for attention to their demands by their leaders. Such 'clientelist' interpretations of power relations were particularly compelling in an area like this, where political rule had always been fairly weak. Not common descent or group identity, but networks of personal allegiance had provided the model for this morality of power well before the colonial period. Not only the limitations placed on them by the District, but also the need to respect their 'subjects' demands for income and autonomy effectively hampered the efforts of 'Native Authorities' to improve their position and give the local economy a territorial framework. Some groups among these 'subjects' were undoubtedly more successful in their claims than others. One symptom, in the field of market production, may have been the growing tendency to channel new government funds for 'improved farming' away from the existing villages, into new settlements that involved pioneer businessmen-farmers who were closely related to chiefly power, including one Senior Chief himself.[40]

Businessmen with established shops and depots, however, the strongest agents of 'the market' in the area, seem to have had a fairly ambivalent attitude vis-a-vis the District and 'Native' Governments' attempt to establish a territorial economic order at the local level. On the one hand, they resented restrictions on prices and movements of local products, but could not influence them as much as they may have liked to, because local decision-makers followed a variety of (political) considerations and were subject to instructions from higher authorities. On the other hand, these restrictions could be useful for bigger businessmen to achieve or cement quasi-monopsonistic positions, against the much larger number of petty traders and transporters. In pursuit of such positions, in addition, they themselves started to build territories. In major local centres and villages, there were usually several shops at the same location, both European and African owned, who competed for customers and suppliers of agricultural produce. But out in the remoter parts of the district, a clear spatial division between catchment areas of particular buying stations, mostly owned by Non-Africans, developed.[41]

These catchment areas began to replace the older personal networks, on which especially African traders continued to rely: Scattered over the area, they had contract producers (fishermen, beekeepers, cultivators), called 'trusted men' (vakufwelela in Luvale), whom they gave credit in kind, often foodstuffs; after the harvest, the trader came back to collect fish, wax or crops. Vakufwelela also acted as buying agents for other producers. The advantage of this system from the trader's point of view was often, but not necessarily, the possibility to negotiate a lower producer-price (effectively 'interest' on his credit, but termed as 'friendship price' and the like). The main motive, however, seems to have been a greater security of supply; it saved him or her long searching or waiting for finished products in this sparsely populated area, and lowered the risk of inferior quality. From the producers' point of view, there was no material pressure to become the client of a particular trader as long as there was competition among a variety of petty traders. But clientage had the advantage of guaranteeing them the supply of basic consumer goods and an outlet for their products at specified times of the year, something particularly precious in the remoter areas.

It seems, nevertheless, that petty producers flocked to the European-owned buying stations and shops where they opened.[42] The main reason seems to have been that it offered them the possibility to sell and buy throughout the year, at least throughout the season. Also the fact that European buyers tended to stick more closely to the standard prices set by the administration, despite their being kept at a low level, seems to have appealed to poorer male and female crop producers who had no direct access to other markets and were in a weak position to bargain 'friendship prices' with African traders. They may have been also willing to accept the new standard measurements by weight, in which European businessmen sometimes took pride to educate their peasant suppliers as proof of the 'objectiveness' of their payment. Older villagers, however, who were used to very different, more negotiable standards of value, both material and social, found it very difficult to trust weighing scales and what appeared to them as unintelligible figurework.[43]

The emerging class of local African businessmen, understandably, saw this effective competition by relatively capital-rich Europeans as a threat. Encouraged initially by a missionary (who had trading interests of his own), they began to organize themselves in a professional association, the Balovale African Traders Cooperative Society.[44] After a promising start during which they managed to collect several thousand pounds to buy a lorry, the cooperative effort began to fade. Nevertheless, the initiative was to some extent successful in attracting public, i.e. the administration's, attention and supporting a more favourable official attitude towards their advance. Implicitly, however, was this on their part a giving in to a territorial (district) organization of economic interests, a symptom of a growing new type of local identity at one level. Still, at another level, it contrasted considerably with the real range of their business operations, not always legal and based on personal networks of 'trust' and 'friendship', which extended as far as adjacent parts of Angola, Barotseland (now Western Province) and the Copperbelt.

Also on the side of petty producers and traders, there was in reality little enthusiasm for the territorial morality of administrators and chiefs. As long as, and where, possibilities existed to bypass the bigger traders and businessmen and reach potential markets directly, they cared little about distances, boundaries and official restrictions. This concerned first of all the long-standing, substantial exchanges of forest products (cassava meal, wooden articles, and honey) for mainly fish and livestock with the flood plains to the west of the Zambezi river which continued virtually unabated until around the end of the colonial period in 1964. They stretched far into the neighbouring Barotseland (to the South) and into adjacent parts of Angola, where there was, in addition, an established market for beeswax. The preference for these exchanges were, in the first place, very 'market-rational' responses to the much better margins that could be realized in this way. There was a customary, but increasing, demand for 'traditional' products of the area, and there were less (monetary) costs for transport involved, which was done mostly by dugout canoe. In addition, these products were much more compatible with the established cultivation system and work calendar, and had a higher surplus potential, than the 'modern' agricultural crops, such as maize, that were demanded in the urban areas to the East. Considerable efforts were made by scores of petty traders and producers (the latter including many women) to supply these markets, and to avoid checkpoints, revenue collectors, customs patrols and the like as much as possible.[45]

Another attraction of these 'traditional' markets, however, were the customary types of exchange relationships and morality that were involved here. They continued to be based on the older ideologies of fixed unit prices and/or 'personal relationships' between buyers and sellers. These rules offered not only the older advantages of spatial flexibility and security, but were also useful as a defence against new pressures, such as local government intervention and increasing market price fluctuation. In barter exchanges, price fluctuations were largely excluded, or disguised under varying amounts of 'gifts' given on top of the price proper. The same applied to local transactions, as long as they were not based on the 'modern' money of the wider 'territorial' market of the colony. Interestingly, village producers, especially women, clung as long as possible to the older, pre-colonial currency of cloth-lengths as payment for their products, and district officers, in the late 1930s, took deliberate action to enforce coined money.[46] The main motive seems to have been here to protect local exchanges against inflationary pressure from the outside, although an additional one may have been the interest of wives to prevent their income being used by husbands for the poll tax, payable in cash. Inflationary pressure was (and is) greater on agricultural crops, according to older divisions of labour the mainstay of poorer villagers and women, than on 'male' off-farm products (fish, meat, wooden and bee products). In the context of 'indigenous morality of exchange', a relative loss of value of agricultural compared to off-farm products meant not only an economic, but also social devaluation for women and other crop producers. To prevent this was easier as long as the circulation of new, 'territorial' money could be contained or even banned from the local economy, and the older morality of stable, reciprocal exchange rates between fixed barter units (archetypally a certain basket of cassava meal against a certain plate of fish or meat) maintained.[47]

Coined money, however, did enter intra-village exchanges from the 1930s, probably less because of the district officer's intervention than due to increasing remittances from migrant workers after the years of Depression.[48] Monetary prices for local products had to be accepted as basis of negotiations, also by poorer male and female producers. In their extra-village transactions, villagers had shown that they never saw prices as being really unchangeable; they were conversant with both real market fluctuations and the political character of many of the prices imposed on them. At least the major commodity producers among them were very outspoken against the low prices imposed by the administrators, and tried to negotiate increases through an idiom of patron-client-relations.[49] For the mentioned poorer strata of (mainly agricultural) producers, however, in their effort to maintain their position in the intra-village economy, the administrators' attempts to keep food prices stable over long periods must have had some appeal.

These differentiated interests converged, however, in popular protest erupting when prices were actually lowered or marketing opportunities ceased to exist alltogether. Such a point was reached in 1956. A substantial crowd of men and women from a particular remote part of the district, led by a number of local headmen loyal to a deposed junior chieftainess (calling themselves vakakayi, approximately 'children of worldliness'), attacked the District Commissioner on one of his tours with 'a hail of stones and sticks'. According to a detailed report by the latter, demands for increased crop prices and for the removal of newly introduced

Native Authority taxation had been one aspect of this conflict.[50] Other contemporary sources suggest that popular anger about these material burdens had been mounting also as result of a collapse of 'relations of trust'. Peasant producers had been 'encouraged' by N.A. agricultural advisors (one of them incidentally being the later 'Luvale historian' Mose Kaputungu Sangambo) to grow rice and other new 'economic crops', which was then marketed through a (white) trader/businessman, an area monopolist with whom the peasants had believed to be in good relations.[51] Shortly afterwards, however, urban prices for these crops collapsed, and the trader stopped buying produce in the area. What protesters had wanted from the District Commissioner (and felt frustrated about, when he initially refused) was not only protection from market fluctuations, but also a political intervention to redress the balance between the parties involved.

**A New Morality in the Making?**

One possible way of looking at such strategies and protests is that a 'traditional' morality was invoked or perhaps even invented in defence against the advancing a-moral market.[52] But what advanced here was not just 'the' market, but a particular 'real market' (Maureen Mackintosh),[53] strongly shaped by political interventions of local administrators under a territorial morality, and partly supported by businessmen.

This seems to suggest another, but equally misleading conclusion: That an authoritarian administration, increasingly under socialist orientation which foreshadowed the post-colonial 'moral economy' of a benevolent father state, was ranging obstacles against a real drive for 'free market' accumulation.[54] But the administrators' blueprint of a new economic order was, at any rate, not very effective, and was mitigated by wider market influences as well as the local moralities of different strata of villagers. These were, at any rate, certainly not options for a 'free market' model.

The question remains whether these clashes and interactions between different 'moral economies' favoured the formation of something like a new concept of 'moral' economic relationships. Some of the examples cited in this paper suggest that a distinction between 'local' and 'wider' market rules, involving an increasingly territorial understanding of economy, was gradually creeping in not only from the administrators' side, but also 'from below'. Such an understanding seems to have been an element in the struggle for the maintenance of intra-village exchange rates; the rebellion of the vakakayi (based on one particularly remote sub-chieftainess' area); and in the formation of the 'Balovale African Traders Association'. In all these cases, a 'local identity' seems to have emerged somewhat in defence against the effects of both territorial power and market insecurity, in the context of a widening political reference area.

A concept of 'localness' was not indigenous to this particular district, but began to be created in interaction between 'outsiders' and 'locals' as part of the building of colonial society. Until today, however, it has remained only one of the registers used by the inhabitants of the area to define their identity. A multitude of relationships across the boundaries of local territories have remained vital for their inhabitants. For more than a century, these relationships had shown themselves as more capable of adapting to the development of markets and 'modernity' than a territorial order.

## Notes

1 A taste of these feelings can be grasped, for instance, from the memories of a former District Officer on Mwinilunga. See Tony Lawman, The long grass, London 1958, chapter 2.

2 Within the District, four languages were, and are, spoken by five major groups with distinct ethnic identities: Luvale, Lunda, Chokwe, Luchazi and Mbunda.

3 For an attempt to give this term scientific status by 'the' regional anthropologist, see Charles M.N. White, Witchcraft, divination and magic among the Balovale tribes. In: Africa, *18*(1948)2, note 1. In subsequent publications, White tended to speak of 'Luvale people(s)', comprising the same group minus the relatively most distinct among them, the (Southern) Lunda.

4 For a historical overview of these attempts with regard to 'villages', which began in what is now Zambia soon after the colonial conquest, see George Kay, Social aspects of village regrouping, Lusaka 1967.

5 Robert Papstein, From ethnic identity to tribalism: The Upper Zambesi region of Zambia, 1830-1981. In: Leroy Vail (ed.), The creation of tribalism in Southern Africa, Berkeley 1989

6 In the post-war period, there were unsuccessful attempts to reorganize these lowest administrative units into bigger settlement clusters, called 'Parishes' (Kaonde-Lunda Province, 5-Year-Development Plan 1943, NAZ SEC 2/279; Kay 1967).

7 In the following text, indigenous terms will be given, for convenience, only in Luvale, not in the other three languages spoken in the district (Lunda, Chokwe and Luchazi-Mbunda), of which Lunda is the next in importance.

8 The other side of this experience, the close historical connection between territoriality and nationality, tended to be repressed by colonial rulers, only to unfold its full vigour in the policies of nationalist politicians after their victory (see Benedict Anderson, Imagined Communities. Reflections on the origin and spread of nationalism, London-New York 1991, 163ff.). For a recent summary of general relations between territoriality, social community, and power see Smith 1990.

9 High population mobility and a deadlock between competing headmen and chiefs caused both the Chavuma and the Kabompo-Manyinga area to be excised from the rest of Balovale and to be placed under non-'tribal' administration. See Papstein, From ethnic identity..., 385ff.; Art Hansen, When the running stops: The social and economic incorporation of Angolan refugees into Zambian border villages (unpublished PhD Diss. Cornell University), Ithaca,

N.Y. 1976; Charles M.N. White, Notes on the political organization of the Kabompo District and its inhabitants. In: African Studies 9(1950).

10 Achim von Oppen, Terms of trade and terms of trust. The history and contexts of pre-colonial market production around the upper Zambezi and Kasai, Hamburg-Münster 1994.

11 Wim M. J. van Binsbergen, Explorations in the history and sociology of territorial cults in Zambia. In: J.M. Schoffeleers (ed.), Guardians of the land, Gwelo (Zimbabwe) 1979.

12 The 'landscape' paradigm is borrowed from David William Cohen/E.S. Atieno Odhiambo, Siaya. The historical anthropology of an African landscape, London-Nairobi 1988, 9ff.

13 Karl Polanyi, The economy as instituted process. In: Karl Polanyi/Conrad M. Arensberg/Harry W. Pearson (eds.), T&rade and Market in the Early Empires, New York 1957.

14 Maurice Bloch/Jonathan P. Parry (eds.), Money and the morality of exchange, Cambridge 1989.

15 An example for Africa is Michael J. Watts, The demise of the moral economy: food and famine in a Sudano-Sahelian region in historical perspective. In: E.P. Scott (ed.), Life before the drought, Winchester, Mass. 1984; see also the clarifications by Thompson himself. Edward P. Thompson, The moral economy reviewed. In: Id., Customs in Common, Harmondsworth 1993, p. 259-351.

16 Against Bloch/Parry, Money and the morality..., who still tend to distinguish 'moral' (i.e. social) transactions from essentially a-moral, economic ones. For a collection of brillant essays on the morality of 'the market' in cross-cultural perspective see Roy Dilley (ed.), Contesting markets. Analyses of ideology, discourse and practice, Edinburgh 1992.

17 For an attempt to reconstruct the 'moral economies of the peasant', paraphrasing Scott, Life before the drought..., in their impact on marketing in Balovale see Achim von Oppen, "Wer Nahrung liefert, hat auch Hunger". Getreidemarkt und moralische Ökonomie der Bauern - ein Kontrastbeispiel aus dem südlichen Afrika (ca. 1950-1990). In: Manfred Gailus/Heinrich Volkmann (eds.), Der Kampf um das tägliche Brot. Nahrungsmangel, Versorgungspolitik und Protest 1770-1990, Opladen 1994.

18 E.g. Annual Report D.C. Barotse District 1911/12, NAZ KDE 8/1/2; Annual Report Balovale 1916/17, NAZ KDE 8/1/8.

19 E.g. District Annual Report Balovale 1922/23, NAZ KDE 8/1/14; Annual Reports 1935ff. (NAZ SEC 2/71).

20 Extensive statement, for instance, in Annual Report Balovale District 1951, NAZ SEC2/135.

21 Legally based on the 'Native Foodstuffs (Control of Acquisition) Ordinance' of 1940; Annual Reports Balovale 1948 and Kabompo 1948, NAZ SEC2/155.

22 Newsletter Kaonde-Lunda-Province No. 14, Sept. 1943, NAZ SEC 2/193; Annual Report Balovale 1951 (NAZ SEC 2/135).

23 See table in: von Oppen, "Wer Nahrung liefert...

24 E.g. Annual Reports Balovale 1935, 1947; Kabompo 1951 (NAZ SEC 2/135; SEC 2/71, vol.I).

25 Douglas Rimmer, The economic imprint of colonialism and domestic food supplies in British Tropical Africa. In: Robert I. Rotberg (ed.), Imperialism, colonialism and hunger: East and Central Africa, Lexington, Mass. 1983.

26 Interview O.E., 2/11/87.

27 See Jadwiga Lukanty/Adrian P. Wood, Agricultural policy in the colonial period. In: Adrian P. Wood/Stuart A. Kean/John T. Milimo/Denis M. Warren (eds.), The dynamics of agricultural policy and reform in Zambia, Ames, Iowa 1990, p. 3ff.

28 Charles M. N. White, A Preliminary survey of Luvale rural economy (Rhodes-Livingstone-Papers 29), Manchester 1959, p. 48ff.

29 Robert J. Papstein, The Upper Zambezi: A history of the Luvale people, 1000-1900 (unpublished PhD Diss., University of California), Los Angeles 1978, p. 3; Paul D. Wilkin, To the bottom of the heap. Educational deprivation and its social implications in the North Western Province of Zambia, 1906-1945 (unpublished PhD Thesis), Syracuse University 1983.
30 The idea of revaluating the region as a supplier for urban food markets had been looming since the end of the First World War. See Annual Reports Balovale 1917 and 1923, NAZ KDE 8/1/8+14.
31 For details see Achim von Oppen, Reluctance, trust and worldly demands. Peasant modes of negotiating agricultural development in the history of NW-Zambia, c. 1915-1975. Paper read at the 14th European Congress of Rural Sociology, Giessen 1990, p. 21ff.
32 Kabompo District Notebook, vol. II, p. 248f. (NAZ KTV 1/1).
33 Minutes of a Meeting held at the Provincial Commissioner's office, Solwezi, 11/06/1963 (NAZ MA 169/3).
34 White, A Preliminary survey..., p. 42f.
35 Similarly, for Malawi Megan Vaughan, The story of an African famine. Gender and famine in 20th century Malawi, Cambridge 1987.
36 Interview Advisors to Chief Ishinde, 25/10/1986.
27 The following paragraphs summarize findings much more fully developed in von Oppen, Terms of trade...
38 See von Oppen, Reluctance, trust..., p. 26f.
39 See footnote 9, above.
40 Annual Report Balovale 1959; interview Mr. Kabobola, 25/10/1986.
41 Annual Reports Balovale 1947 and 1951, NAZ SEC2/154+135.
42 Interview Charles Geddis, Nov. 1986.
43 Interview Yowena Samakayi, 24/10/1986.
44 Newsletter Kaonde-Lunda-Province, No.22 (1945), SEC2/193.
45 See also von Oppen, Reluctance, trust..., p. 13f.
46 Annual Reports Balovale District 1935 and 1940, NAZ SEC 2/71 vol.1, SEC 2/7 vol.9.
47 von Oppen, Terms of trade..., p. 409ff.
48 E.g. Interview Lazaro Chinzombo 30/10/86.
49 E.g. Minutes of the African Provincial Council Kaonde-Lunda-Province 1946/47, NAZ SEC2/230.
50 Report by the D.C. Balovale, dated 8/5/1956, in the Kabompo District Notebook, NAZ KTW 1.
51 Annual Report Balovale 1951 and 1955, SEC 2/135+137.
52 Cf. e.g. Watts, The demise of the moral...
53 See Cynthia Hewitt de Alcántara, Introduction: Markets in principle and praxis. In: European Journal of Development Research, Special Issue "Real markets", *4*(1992)2, footnote 1.
54 Cf. Rimmer, The economic imprint...

# Slavery, Coastal Identity and the End of Slavery in German and British East Africa

Jan-Georg Deutsch

When in the mid-1920s the League of Nations made enquiries about slavery to its member governments, the British government reported back, that as far as the Mandated Territory of Tanganyika was concerned, slavery did not constitute a real problem, and that the recently enacted Involuntary Servitude Ordinance of 1922 would effect a speedy decline of an already dying institution.[1] Yet, only thirty years earlier - under German colonial rule -, slavery was a pervasive feature of most East African societies. Very conservatively estimated, it appears that in the 1890s at least 220,000 people were legally classified as slaves, the majority of whom were women; their actual numbers were probably much higher.[2] Thus in the period concerned, a social transformation process of both slavery itself and of society as a whole seems to have taken place, whose even rudimentary outline appears to be unknown.

There is certainly no lack of secondary literature on the question of slavery in Africa or even East Africa. Cooper's and Morton's monographs on slavery in British East Africa, as well as the compilations of articles by Inikori, Miers, Watson, Robertson, Willis, Lovejoy and Clarence-Smith, provide a whole array of material and ideas about the subject.[3] Yet, not one of these books deals explicitly with the question of slavery in  or British Tanganyika. Even Marcia Wright's recent book on women and slavery in East Africa touches upon abolition only marginally.[4] As regards unpublished secondary sources the situation is slightly better. Glassman's work on Pangani and Brown's work on Bagamayo contain detailed accounts of pre-colonial coastal slavery, while the recently finished thesis by Sunseri contains a chapter on colonial slavery on Mafia island.[5] However, even the most detailed study of Tanzanian history so far, John Iliffe's 'Modern History of Tanganyika', gives the subject only a cursory treatment.[6] Finally, one should mention that despite the fact that the initial engagement of the German Imperial state in East Africa was justified as an anti-slave-trade campaign, Imperial historians have paid little attention to the issue.[7] Apart from a handful of contemporary articles in journals like the *Deutsche Kolonialzeitung* or the *Mittheilungen des Seminars für orientalische Sprachen zu Berlin*, it appears that there are only two studies available which are directly concerned with slavery in : One is a heavily biased German colonial office account by F. Weidner (*Die Haussklaverei in Ostafrika*, Jena 1915), and the other is an obscure UMCA pamphlet (*The Black Slaves of Prussia*, London 1918) by the then Bishop of Zanzibar, F. Weston. The issue of slavery in  seems therefore to have been largely neglected by Imperial and African historians alike.

In this article I want to explore the social history of slavery in just one specific area of the East African littoral.[8] The paper examines the importance of slavery and its subsequent abolition within the context of the historical evolution of 'ethnic' relations in the region.[9] In what follows, I will first shortly outline the history of slavery in nineteenth century Tanganyika before the arrival of the German Colonial Society, and then sketch out what happened afterwards in the coastal region.

**Pre-colonial Slavery**

It is well known, that as result of the declining ivory trade, and in connection with the thriving arms trade, slave-raiding and -trading became more common in Tanganyika in the second half of the nineteenth century. In the 1870s over 20,000 slaves were shipped annually from the coast.[10] How many Africans were enslaved in this period, can only be guessed, since there are few figures available on the death rates of large scale slave caravans, and no figures available on the probably numerically much more important small scale, local slave trade in the region.[11]

Contrary to the powerful nineteenth century European image of large scale 'Arab' slave raiding campaigns, a very large number of slaves, especially women and children, were actually sold into slavery. This happened for a variety of reasons: social and economic marginality in times of famine and social disruption, as a form of repayment of commercial debt, as a fine or form of punishment in judicial cases of theft, murder, witchcraft and adultery, even as a payment of bridewealth. Moreover, slave raiding often meant the abduction of one or two people from isolated villages in remote areas, who would then be sold from one slave owner to the other, often several times.[12] Throughout the century the demand for slaves steadily increased, which had both repercussions on the use of the slaves in commercial and judicial transactions, as well as might have transformed the form of such transactions themselves.

In the same period, the character of slavery in many areas changed. Whereas in the early nineteenth century, servitude was more kinship oriented, i.e. towards an exchange of slaves, especially women, between lineages, the second half of the century saw the rise of market oriented slavery, i.e. slaves became increasingly a means of commercial exchange as opposed to social and political exchange.[13] This partial commodization of slaves was also reflected in the increasing use of slaves in commercial undertakings, be it as porters, agricultural labourers and mercenaries. At the same time, however, older forms of slavery persisted, while the numbers of slaves in servile positions within households and lineages, dramatically increased.

From ethnographic research, especially from the examination of pre-colonial customary law (or what is believed to be pre-colonial customary law), it is clear, that slavery in one form or the other was a widespread social and economic institution, overlapping in many instances with other social institutions of personal dependency, such as the pawning of children and of relatives.[14] The actual social position of slaves, i.e. what it meant to be a slave, greatly varied between locations and societies, even within such in this respect supposedly culturally homogenous group like the Swahili on the coast. This was due to the fact that slavery in East Africa was an intensely local affair. Lacking the (state) power to completely impose their will on their slaves, owners had to a varying extend to compromise with their slaves. Living conditions, social status, working patterns, and such like were thus the result of a series of contested, renegotiated and ever changing local bargains between slaves and their owners. These bargains were struck on the basis of a variety of elements, whose importance greatly differed between locations. These elements included factors such as the relative numerical strength of slaves and slave owners, the dominant local ideology like, for example, the teachings of Islam, the locally dominant forms of production and exchange, like, for example, the market oriented production of food crops for regional consumption or geographic factors, which, for example, in the case of the islands of Mafia, Unguja and Pemba greatly weakened the bargaining position of slaves, because escape was so much more difficult than on the mainland.[15] Despite these extreme local variances, it is probably no exaggeration to suggest that in late nineteenth century slaves were the universally most accepted form of currency within the moral and commercial economies of most pre-colonial Tanganyikan societies.

The use of slaves for commercial purposes was most pronounced on the coast. Yet it is important to note that even in this area the transformation to plantation slavery or other forms of commercial exploitation was far from complete. Moreover, few plantation slaves, and indeed many of their owners, accepted moral attitudes which reduced slaves to a mere chattel. Nevertheless, as an extension of the rise of Zanzibar's political and economic power in the region, coconut and sugar plantations were established in the vicinity of Dar es Salaam, Bagamoyo and Pangani to serve the growing regional, especially Zanzibar food market, which made use of large numbers of slaves. Thus, for example, it was officially estimated that in 1897 about half of the population of the then largest town on the coast, Bagamoyo, were slaves.[16] It may be also significant that run-away slaves apparently only established sizeable communities in the adjacent hinterland of the coast.[17]

Slavery, the rising commercial importance of the coast within the region, and the imposition of Zanzibar political agents in almost all coastal towns redefined its relationship with other mainland societies in the course of the century.[18] While the links between the hinterland and the coast increased and communication between coastal people improved, a distinct, though locally varied, 'coastal identity' emerged.[19] This identity was largely based on its commercial success and to some extend on the racialist notion of the cultural difference between free coastal people and up-country, potentially servile, people. Moreover, its at least partial acceptance of the teachings of Islam linked the coast through trade and Islamic scholarship to the Indian Ocean network and the Middle East. This enabled coastal people, and especially their urban elite, to make the claim that their lifestyle was not only distinct, but also inherently superior to those of other mainland societies. During the course of the century, however, social tensions within coastal society increased, as the effects of commercial success, Zanzibari rule and market oriented slavery increasingly threatened to undermine the established social order.[20]

Enslavement and, especially, slavery on the coast had a strong gender bias.[21] Particularly recently enslaved, up-country women experienced severe discrimination on account of their gender, class and 'ethnic' position. Moreover, due to islamic notions about the unequal legal and social ranking of men and women, female slaves, especially concubines, occupied distinct social and economic positions within society, and thus followed very different strategies and avenues to improve their lowly status. Lastly, the growth of market oriented slavery on the coast arguably further marginalised the already precarious social position of slave women as agricultural labourers and servants in general.[22]

## A Social History of Slavery and its Abolition

As a result of government policy, economic change, and the initiative of slaves and owners, the institution of slavery withered away in the early decades of colonial rule. This effected coastal society in two fundamental ways. First, it changed the 'ethnic' relationship between coastal society and inland societies, since it redefined the distinctions and supposed ranking between them.[23] Secondly, the gradual decline of slavery redefined coastal self-identity, since much of it was based on the hierarchical distinctions between free persons and slaves, providing the most important points of references for social identification and status.[24]

'Ethnic' and social boundaries "define who is playing the same game according to the same set of rules and who is not", often signifying to the players their differential access to critical material and immaterial, especially spiritual, resources.[25] Obviously, the abolition of slavery changed those rules and thus the game. What has therefore to be described is how the 'game' of changing modes of social and 'ethnic' identification was played out under the particular historical circumstances of the abolition of slavery.

When the German administration arrived on the coast, they encountered a highly stratified society, in which its members were classified according to their 'ethnic', social, and supposed racial origin, their wealth, their personal status of freedom, the recency or antiquity of their arrival on the coast, and their adherence to certain aspects of Islam.[26] The top position of this society was occupied by a small number of wealthy land- and/or slave- owning families, many of whom claimed to be of 'pure' Omani or Arab descent. Members of these families also often occupied the most prestigious public offices in the towns. The middling strata was occupied by artisans, sailors, and traders, some of whom also owned slaves. Some members of this middling strata were of slave origin or were still slaves themselves. The bottom strata consisted of the urban poor and destitute slaves.

The slaves were in themselves further stratified. At the top were skilled slaves, such as wood carvers, metal- and leather workers, whose social position was not radically different from that of free artisans, and governmental slaves, especially those in clerical positions. The middling strata was occupied by agricultural slaves, who paid only tribute to their owners. The bottom strata consisted of 'shamba' slaves, who worked the fields for their owners, and of manual workers. The position of servants varied according to their position within the household. Furthermore, slave strata were divided into those slaves who had only recently arrived on the coast, those who had lived there for a number of years and those who were born on the coast.

This stratification was not rigid, but allowed for upward (and downward) social mobility. Thus within a lifetime, slaves could occupy various positions in the social hierarchy, each of which encompassed rather different social realities. Moreover, even if the parents of slaves who had recently arrived on the coast were denied social recognition by the free born members of coastal society, their sons and daughters usually occupied a higher social position on account of their acculturation to coastal social values. Lastly, stratification was heavily gender biased. Due to some extent to the influence of the teachings of Islam, the social honour of women was generally regarded to be lower than the honour of men. It was also believed that certain types of work, especially those involving skills, should be exclusively done by men. Male domination and female slavery merged at several points, but probably most starkly in the institution of concubinage, which more or less forced female slaves into intimate relationships with their male owners.[27] For many women, becoming a concubine was the only accessible route to manumission, since, according to Islamic law and local practice, it was deemed to be a particularly pious act to free concubines, if they had given birth, on the deathbed of their owners.

Social conflict between slaves and owners largely centred around the aspirations of slaves to participate fully in coastal society, particularly in its culture and economy. This was eagerly denied by other coastal strata, especially by the slave holding commercial and religious elites. Apart from flight and other forms of resistance, their principal strategies to improve their lowly social position within coastal society was outward conformity to coastal culture and religious practices, marriage into free-born families, and obtaining manumission through various means. Slaves seem to have collectively very rarely challenged the social order as such, but appear to have been in agreement with their owners about the worth of its basic institutions, including the institution of slavery. Those who nurtured social aspirations and could not pretend to be of Arab or Omani origin would often call themselves 'Mswahili'.[28]

During the German and early British colonial period, the bargaining position of slaves vis à vis their owners considerably improved. First, they were now able to purchase their freedom - with or without agreement of their owners. Furthermore, slaves were at least to some extent protected against maltreatment from their owners. After the occupation of the coastal areas by British troops, slavery was moreover no longer recognised as a legal institution by the colonial courts. Escape from bondage was thus no longer a punishable offence.[29] Secondly, during the periods of political and social upheaval, like the period of colonial conquest, the Maji Maji War, and the First World War, many slaves were able to cut the ties which bound them to their owners, since escape in those periods was so much easier. Thirdly, in the early colonial period, the missions specifically directed their efforts towards slaves, and thus redeemed ex-slaves were among the first group of Africans who received mission education. This later helped some of them to obtain employment as clerks and even teachers in the colonial administration and in the mission organisation itself. Fourthly, a small number of ex-slaves made political careers in the administration, becoming local government officials in areas in which the German and later the British, administration could not find - in their view - suitable local collaborators. Finally, since the coast was the most economically active region in Tanganyika in the German and early British colonial period, temporary employment in the emerging urban centres and in the European owned plantation sector, as well as self-employment as independent small-scale farmers and as artisans, allowed a large number of ex-slaves to escape from clientilist subordination to their previous owners.

It is, however, important to note that the end of slavery had a different meaning for women and men. Gradual abolition affected men and women in different ways, since women faced different obstacles in their endeavour to improve their often exceedingly low social positions. For example, the disadvantaged access to land made it more difficult for women to leave their owners than for men. Thus, as they had done under slavery, women had to employ different strategies than men to improve their specific position in the emancipation period. As Marcia Wright pointed out: 'The divergence between male and female carrier lines persisted and widened, when the commercial economy of the late nineteenth century merged into the colonial economy of the early twentieth century. While men became employees with the possibility of advancing in education, skills and prestige in the new order, women continued to be assigned reproductive roles in the economic, biological and cultural senses.'[30] Though emancipation freed women from direct personal dependency, they did not obtain equal status to men in coastal society.

The transformation and subsequent decline of slavery removed one of the crucial points of reference for social identification and orientation on the coast. It appears that as a result social distinctions on the coast became increasingly blurred. At the same time larger social groupings emerged, for example those, who by various means, including small scale farming and casual work in the towns, managed to avoid formal employment in the emerging plantation sector of the coastal economy with its appalling conditions of work. The fight for equal participation in the coastal economy and society seems thus to have become a fight to resist the pressures of proletarization. This subject, however, needs much further research.

The shift in the focus of the struggle came also about as a result of the decline of the economic and political power of the coastal elite, which up to the colonial period had been the basis of their social power and of slavery. Though in the first decade of colonial rule the social and political position of parts of the elite were to some extent preserved by the German administration, their economic position subsequently steadily declined. The coastal merchants lost their most lucrative lines of trade, since the ivory, slave and gun trade was either forbidden or monopolised by the administration. In other lines they faced stiff competition from Asian and European traders. In addition, most of the indigenous plantations owners were ruined already by the turn of the century, since they could not compete with European plantations in the wage labour market and slave labour was no longer available in sufficient quantities. For some time, the coastal elite managed to sustain their previous lifestyle by selling off their plantations and their urban property, but once those assets were gone, there was little left for them to convincingly back up their claim to 'ethnic' and social superiority. Moreover, since lowly social strata increasingly became drawn to Islam by proselytising brotherhoods, claims to social superiority could also no longer be based on religion.[31] This also facilitated the blurring of social distinctions between the various strata on the coast.

With the decline in the relevance of the old social points of reference, 'ethnic' claims of superiority equally became increasingly meaningless. Since these claims were largely based on slavery, commerce and Islam, the decline of the former two weakened 'ethnic' pretensions.[32] Even the privileged access to spiritual resources was challenged, as in the German colonial period Islamisation of neighbouring 'ethnic' groups increased to an unprecedented degree.[33] Moreover, migration to the coast by people, who insisted on maintaining their 'ethnic', social and cultural separateness from the coastal people, further diversified coastal culture and identity. This further helped to alleviate and obfuscate the supposedly rigid 'ethnic' and social distinctions between the coastal people and inland people, which probably explains why in the period between 1890 and 1930 the category 'Waswahili' vanished from ethnographic German and British census returns.[34] Finally, the peculiar 'imposition of neo-traditional inventions' by European administrators, missionaries and anthropologists, which in the early colonial period had led to a strengthening of ethnicity and 'ethnic' claims in other areas, did not work on the coast. Lacking centralised political institutions or local hereditary rulers, as well as easily recognisable cultural homogeneity, the coastal people were not considered to be a proper 'tribe', and were thus particularly badly suited to the imposition of the

British system of 'indirect rule'. Moreover, coastal people themselves also strongly refused to 'invent' themselves as a 'tribe'. Part of their identity was arguably based on a notion of racial and cultural difference to 'ethnic' East African peoples, and this made such an 'invention' inconceivable. The coastal people were thus the first "detribalised" Africans in Tanganyikan social ethnography.[35]

The end of slavery had a dramatic effect on coastal society. In some places, particularly around Bagamoyo and Dar es Salaam, and on the island of Mafia, it was a socially and economically highly disruptive event. In other place, specifically in rural areas further away from the towns and colonial administrative centres, the transition to freedom was apparently a much smoother process. The end of slavery in Africa has been rightly called 'a quiet social revolution'[36]. In as much as the social history of the end of slavery in East Africa is concerned, it appears that in some places it was a quiet 'ethnic' revolution as well.

## Notes

1 TNA 11193, League of Nations, Doc. A 25 (a), Letters from the British Government, 20 May 1924. This position certainly overstates the extent to which slavery as an institution had declined. Yet, that such a decline had happened in the period concerned is undisputed.

2 In 1914, it was estimated that the number of slaves in  amounted to 165,000. Given that about 52,000 certificates of freedom had been issued by the German government, the minimum estimate of the number of slaves in  amounts to about 220,000. For these figures, see J. Iliffe, A Modern History of Tanganyika, Cambridge 1979, p. 131. See also O. F. Raum, German East Africa - Changes in African Life under German Administration, 1892-1914. In: V. Harlow/E. M. Chilver (eds.), Cambridge History of East Africa, vol.II, Oxford 1965, p. 168. My own ongoing research shows that the number of slaves in  certainly exceeded 500,000, amounting to about 15% of the population.

3 F.L. Cooper, Plantation Slavery on the East Coast of Africa, New Haven 1977; id., From Slaves to Squatters: Plantation Labour and Agriculture in Zanzibar and Coastal Kenya, 1890-1925, New Haven 1981; F. Morton, Children of Ham. Freed Slaves & Fugitive Slaves on the Kenya Coast, 1873-1907, Boulder 1990; A.G.B. Fisher/H.J. Fisher, Slavery and Muslim Society in Africa, London 1970; J.E. Inikori (ed.), Forced Migration. The Impact of the Export Slave Trade on African Societies, London 1982; S. Miers/D. Kopytoff, Slavery in Africa, Madison 1977; S. Miers/R. Roberts (eds.), The End of Slavery in Africa, Madison/Wis. 1988; J.L. Watson (ed.), Asian and African Systems of Slavery, London 1980; C.C. Robertson/M.A. Klein (eds.), Women and Slavery in Africa, Madison/Wis. 1983; J.R. Willis (ed.), Slaves and Slavery in Muslim Africa, 2 vols., London 1985; P. Lovejoy (ed.), The Ideology of Slavery in Africa, Beverly Hills 1981; Africans in Bondage: Studies in Slavery and the Slave Trade, Madison/Wis. 1986; id. (with J.S. Hogendorn), Slow Death for Slavery: The Course of Abolition in Northern Nigeria, 1897-1936, Cambridge 1993; id. (with A. S. Kanya-Forstner), Slavery and its Abolition in French West Africa, Michigan 1993. See also C.M. Eastman, Women, Slaves and Foreigners: African Cultural Influences

and Group Processes in the Formation of the Swahili Coastal Society. In: International Journal of African Historical Studies *XXI*(1988)1, pp. 1-20; M. Strobel, Muslim Women in Mombasa, 1890-1975, New Haven 1979.

4 M. Wright, Strategies of Slaves & Women. Life-Stories from East/Central Africa, New York 1993.

5 J.P. Glassman, Social Rebellion and Swahili Culture: The Response to German Conquest of the Northern Mrima, 1888-1890, University of Wisconsin Ph.D. thesis, Madison 1988; see also his article 'The Bondsman.s New Clothes: The Contradictory Consciousness of Slave Resistance on the Swahili Coast'. In: Journal of African History *XXXII*(1991)2, pp. 277-312; W.T. Brown, A Pre-Colonial History of Bagamoyo: Aspects of the Growth of an East African Coastal Town, University of Boston Ph.D. thesis, Boston 1971; T. Sunseri, A Social History of Cotton Production in , 1884-1915, University of Minnesota Ph.D. thesis, Minneapolis 1993.

6 Iliffe, A Modern History..., p. 161.

7 See, for example, A.J. Knoll/L.H. Gann (eds.), Germans in the Tropics: Essays in German Colonial History, New York 1987; R. Nestvogel/R. Tetzlaff (eds.), Afrika und der Deutsche Kolonialismus: Zivilisierung zwischen Schnapshandel und Bibelstunde, Berlin 1987. The anti-slavery movement in Germany, however, has been examined by the Imperial historians K. J. Bade, Zwischen Mission und Kolonialbewegung, Kolonialwirtschaft und Kolonialpolitik in der Bismarckzeit: der Fall Friedrich Fabri. In: K.J. Bade (ed.), Imperialismus und Kolonialmission, Wiesbaden 1982, pp. 103-141, and H. Gründer, Christliche Mission und deutscher Imperialismus, Paderborn 1982, chap. 4.

8 This article is part of a wider study, which was financed by the Deutsche Forschungsgemeinschaft. See J.-G. Deutsch, Slavery and its Abolition, Habil. Schrift, Universität Düsseldorf, forthcoming.

9 The word 'ethnic' has been put in inverted commas throughout this paper in order to emphasize that the construction of ethnicities is a historical process. See T.O. Ranger, The Invention of Tradition Revisited: The Case of Colonial Africa. In: T.O. Ranger/O. Vaughan (eds.), Legitimacy and the State in Twentieth Century Africa: Essays in Honour of A. M. H. Kirk-Greene, London 1993, p. 62-111.

10 Iliffe, A Modern History..., p. 51.

11 This argument is based on life histories of slaves, some of which were recorded by the German authorities. See, for example, ZNA G2/47/2, Record of Court Proceedings, Bezirksamt Pangani, 22-24 November 1892.

12 Wright, Strategies..., pp. 7-8.

13 For a more general elaboration of this idea as regards trade, see R. Gray, R./D. Birmingham (eds.), Pre-Colonial African Trade in Central and Eastern Africa before 1900, London 1970, pp. 2-3.

14 See the Introduction to P.E. Lovejoy/T. Falola (eds.), Pawnship in Africa: Debt Bondage in Historical Perspective, Boulder 1993.

15 For a detailed description of pre-colonial customary law and the role of slavery within this law, see for example, Rhodes House, Micr. Afr. 297, Vol.II, Mikindani District Book ('Makonde and Makua tribes') and Pangani District Book ('Wabonde tribe'). See also Iliffe, A Modern History..., p. 73.

16 Amtliche Jahresberichte über die Entwicklung der deutschen Schutzgebiete in Afrika und Übersee (nebst Denkschriften und Statistiken, 1897/98, p. 74. My own research shows, that this figure is also fairly representative for other coastal towns, for example Kilwa and Lindi.

17 See, for example, Rhodes House, Micr. Afr. 297, Kilwa District Book, 'Wamatumbi Tribe'.

18 W.T. Brown, The Politics of Business: The Relationship between Zanzibar and Bagamoyo in the Late Nineteenth Century. In: International Journal African Historical Studies *IV*(1971)3, p. 631-643.

19 The most recent general books on the subject are J. de V. Allen, Swahili Origins, London 1993, und J. Middleton, The World of the Swahili: An African Mercantile Society, New Haven 1991. Many useful ideas can also be found in W. Arens, The Waswahili: The Social History of an Ethnic Group. In: Africa *XXXXV*(1975)4, pp. 426-438.

20 Glassman, Social Rebellion..., pp. 172-175.

21 Wright, Strategies..., p. 2.

22 This paragraph relies heavily on the Introduction in Robertson/Klein, Women and Slavery..., op.cit.

23 It is here not the place to discuss the tricky problem to what extent Swahili society represents an 'ethnic' group. At the end of the 19th century, the Swahili elite presented itself largely as a socially and culturally defined group (a 'civilization'). This claim defined other mainland societies as backward almost 'primordial' ethnicities. Arguably, Swahili identity can thus be seen as a form of dissenting or negative ethnicity, which by its very claim takes on board ethnic pretensions.

24 This and the following paragraph draws on D. Parkin, Swahili Mijikenda: Facing Both Ways in Kenya. In: Africa *LIX*(1989)2, pp. 161-175; F. Constantin, Social Stratification on the Swahili Coast: From Race to Class?. In: Africa *LIX*(1989)2, pp. 145-159; Ranger, The Invention...

25 T. Spear/R. Waller (eds.), Being Maasai, London 1993, p. 16.

26 J. Maw/D. Parkin, Introduction. In: J. Maw/D. Parkin (eds.), Swahili Language and Society, Beiträge zur Afrikanistik no. 23, Wien 1985, pp. 1-13.

27 Strobel, Muslim Women..., p. 48.

28 This and the preceding paragraphs are largely based on Glassman, Social Rebellion, chap. 3-5.

29 TNA 11193, League of Nations, Doc. A 25 (a), Letters from the British Government, 20 May 1924. I have not seen any evidence yet which suggests that slave cases were dealt with in Islamic courts or tribunals in the 1920s or 1930s. This aspect needs much further research.

30 Wright, Strategies..., p. 2.

31 Iliffe, Modern History..., pp. 368-369.

32 For the problem of Swahili 'ethnicity', see endnote 23.

33 Iliffe, Modern History..., p. 211.

34 See, for example, Rhodes House (Oxford), Micr. Afr. 472, Pangani District Books, sheet 3, Pangani District Census 1928 and 1932. For the rather differed development in British East Africa, see J. Willis, Mombasa, the Swahili and the Making of the Mijikenda, Oxford 1993.

35 Raum, German East Africa..., pp. 166-168.

36 Miers/Roberts, The End of Slavery in Africa, p. 28.

# Die Entstehung der Unabhängigen Afrikanischen Kirchen in Südafrika - kirchliche Emanzipationsbestrebungen oder Ausdruck eines frühen Nationalismus?

Ulrich van der Heyden

"Der Aethiopismus ist die richtige Sozialdemokratie in Südafrika." Unter dieser Überschrift setzte sich der Missionar der Berliner Missionsgesellschaft Carl Prozesky mit den Anfängen des für die meisten europäischen Missionare noch kaum faßbaren Phänomens der rasch an Einfluß gewinnenden Separation schwarzafrikanischer Christen, die als äthiopische Bewegung in die Literatur eingegangen ist, auf einer Tagung der Kapsynode im Jahre 1905 auseinander.[1]

Wie dieser Missionar standen auch die anderen Mitarbeiter europäischer Missionsgesellschaften und deren Leitungen um die Jahrhundertwende ziemlich ratlos vor der für sie völlig neuen Erscheinung der zunehmenden Artikulation einer für sie noch nicht genau zu definierenden Protesthaltung einer nicht geringen Anzahl afrikanischer Christen. Auf Grund ihrer paternalistischen Sicht fiel es den Missionaren zunächst äußerst schwer, die Ursachen für diese als "Widerspenstigkeit", "Undankbarkeit" oder "Aufruhr" betitelte Abkehr von den europäischen Missionskirchen zu erkennen, zumal sich nach der so gut wie vollständigen Brechung des bewaffneten Widerstandes der afrikanischen Ethnien gegen ihre koloniale Unterjochung gegen Ende des 19. Jahrhunderts in Südafrika dieser in neuen Formen ausgetragen wurde. Und die neuen Widerstandsformen wandelten sich zudem im Verlaufe nur weniger Jahre.

Kann man zunächst von einer ausgesprochen religiösen Zielrichtung des Widerstandes sprechen, hatten die Inhalte und Formen des Protestes nach einigen Jahren schon einen ausdrücklich politisch motivierten Charakter angenommen. Wesentlichen Anteil daran hatte der mit militärischen Mitteln ausgetragene burisch-britische Konflikt, der sogenannte Burenkrieg von 1899 bis 1902. Dieser übte auf die Transformierung des Charakters des Widerstandes eine Art Katalysatorfunktion aus.[2] Der Missionsinspektor der Berliner Missionsgesellschaft Karl Axenfeld dessen besondere Aufmerksamkeit den neu entstandenen äthiopischen Kirchen und Sekten galt, stellte schon kurz nach Beendigung des Burenkrieges fest: "Wie er das gesamte Leben Südafrikas umgestaltet hat, so hat (der Burenkrieg, U.v.d.H.) auch der Eingeborenenbewegung eine neue, beachtenswerte, gefährliche, ja vielleicht verhängnisvolle Richtung gegeben... Durch den Krieg ist aus der ehemals kirchlichen Selbstständigkeitsbewegung eine politisch-soziale geworden."[3]

In der Tat war es schon bald nach Friedensschluß verstärkt zu Erscheinungen von durchaus als deutliche Anzeichen eines frühen Nationalismus einzuschätzenden

Äußerungen und Handlungen von Anhängern verschiedener Afrikanischer Unabhängiger Kirchen gekommen. Kritische Beobachter aus Missionskreisen scheuten sich aufgrund der Inhalte dieser Äußerungen deshalb nicht, diese Entwicklung mit der nordamerikanischen Unabhängigkeitsbewegung im 18. Jahrhundert oder mit westeuropäischen Emanzipations- bzw. panslawistischen Bestrebungen zu Beginn des 20. Jahrhunderts zu vergleichen.[4] Theoretische Köpfe aus dem Umfeld der deutschen Missionsgesellschaften, die ohne Zweifel zu den bestinformierten Europäern über die südafrikanischen Vorgänge, nicht nur auf kirchlichem Gebiet, gehörten, machten schon relativ frühzeitig darauf aufmerksam, daß die äthiopische Kirche hinter den von ihnen mißtrauisch registrierten "Äußerungen des Freiheitsdranges" stand. Die Herausbildung selbständiger Kirchen der Schwarzen hätte ihre Ursachen vornehmlich in der wirtschaftlichen Depression, in die Südafrika nach Beendigung des Burenkrieges gekommen sei. Die äthiopische Bewegung, unter der die über fast das gesamte Gebiet der heutigen Republik Südafrika zu jener Zeit sich separierenden und emanzipierenden afrikanischen Kirchen zusammengefaßt werden, stünde hinter den Forderungen nach gleichen Rechten zwischen den Schwarzen und Weißen, sei Inspirator der "Freiheitsbewegung" im und nach dem Burenkrieg geworden, analysierte im Jahre 1905 ein Hermannsburger Missionar.[5] In der ersten deutschsprachigen Publikation über den Äthiopismus verweist er ausdrücklich auf den Zusammenhang zwischen "äthiopischer Kirche und damit den Unabhängigkeitsbestrebungen der Farbigen Südafrikas"[6].

Der Berliner Missionsinspektor Karl Axenfeld kommt in einer 1907 veröffentlichten Studie über den Äthiopismus zu genau derselben Erkenntnis, wenn er schreibt: "Daß die Bewegung ... mit schnellen Schritten das Gebiet (der kirchlich-missionarischen Protestebene, U.v.d.H.) verließ und ins politisch-soziale hinüberschritt, ist wesentlich eine Folge des englisch-burischen Krieges gewesen."[7] In der Tat hatte der militärisch ausgetragene Konflikt zwischen Buren und Briten zu einer Art Ernüchterung bei den Afrikanern geführt. Bei Axenfeld ist es auf die Formel gebracht: "Der Respekt vor den Weißen sank, und die Furcht wich."[8] Ein anderer Missionar resümierte: "Das Ansehen des weißen Mannes unter den Farbigen hat durch den Krieg erheblich gelitten."[9]

Mit diesen richtigen Einschätzungen der Bedeutung des Burenkrieges für die Herausbildung eines explizit politischen, vielleicht auch nationalistischen Charakters der sogenannten äthiopischen Bewegung stand der Missionar nicht allein da. Auch andere kritische und skeptische Beobachter der äthiopischen Bewegung - die nebenbei bemerkt nicht nur aus missionarischen, sondern auch aus kolonialadministrativen Kreisen stammten - kamen zu ähnlichen Schlußfolgerungen.[10]

Die erste Separation schwarzer Christen von europäischen Missionsgesellschaften begann, wie gemeinhin angenommen wird, im Süden Afrikas im Jahre 1892 mit der Abspaltung des ehemals wesleyanischen Geistlichen Moses Mangena Mokone. Inzwischen dürfte nach neueren Erkenntnissen der Forschung davon ausgegangen werden, daß die Vorläufer des Äthiopismus in Südafrika einige Jahrzehnte älter sind. Verdeutlichen läßt sich dies vor allem an der Analyse der sogenannten Dinkoanyan'schen Separation von 1873, die als ideologischer Wegbereiter der siebzehn Jahre später entstandenen Bapedi-Nationalkirche im nördlichen Transvaal betrachtet werden kann.[11]

Und diese auch als Ba-luther bezeichnete Kirchenabspaltung schwarzer Christen von der Berliner Missionsgesellschaft gilt als eine der ersten und meines Erachtens bedeutendsten äthiopischen Kirchen Südafrikas, was jedoch in der Forschung bislang nicht reflektiert wurde. Weder der Erforschung der Geschichte der Bapedi-Nationalkirche und schon gar nicht ihre Vorgeschichte wandten sich bis dato Ethnologen, Missions- oder Kirchenhistoriker in ausführlichen Forschungen zu, wenngleich in Überblicksdarstellungen zur Geschichte der Herausbildung von Nationalismus oder der sogenannten jungen Kirchen Afrikas gern auf dieses Beispiel zurückgegriffen wird. Dabei dürfte unbestritten sein, daß gerade den ersten Abspaltungen schwarzer Christen von einer europäischen Missionsgesellschaft in dieser Region des afrikanischen Kontinents eine besondere Bedeutung für die Missions-, Kirchen- und Nationalgeschichte zukommt. Außerdem ist die Abspaltung eines konvertierten einflußreichen Angehörigen des Häuptlingsgeschlechts von der damals wie heute in Südafrika nicht unbedeutenden Berliner Missionsgesellschaft, die als die Dinkoanyan'sche Separation in die Geschichte Transvaals einging, ein durchaus nicht unwesentlicher, hingegen kaum beachteter Bestandteil der Vorgeschichte der britischen Annexion der Buren-Republik in den Jahren 1877 bis 1881. Dieser Schritt wird bis heute in der Geschichtsschreibung als ein wichtiges, das Verhältnis zwischen burischstämmigen Südafrikanern und den Bewohnern mit englischsprachiger Abstammung beeinflussendes Ereignis angesehen.

Im Oktober 1873 verließ nämlich der in Transvaal, am Rande des sogenannten Sekukunilandes lebende Bruder des Oberhäuptlings der Pedi, Dinkoanyane, mit zunächst 334 Stammesangehörigen die größte Gemeinde der Berliner Station Botshabelo, nördlich von Middelburg gelegen.[12] Von dem damals in Südafrika hoch geachteten und einflußreichen Missionar der Berliner Missionsgesellschaft Alexander Merensky getauft, war Johannes Dinkoanyane - wie nunmehr sein Name lautete - diesem "mit kindlicher Anhänglichkeit ergeben" und arbeitete daran, wie es in der ersten Mitteilung über die "Dinkoanyane'sche Separation" heißt, "daß unser Volk (gemeint ist die afrikanische Gemeinde der Berliner Missionsgesellschaft, U.v.d.H.) in christlicher Zucht und Sitte erhalten werde"[13]. Der Häuptlingsbruder hatte sich besonders eng an die Berliner Missionare angelehnt und wurde deshalb im allgemeinen als uneigennütziger Helfer der Mission betrachtet.

Der Anlaß der Lostrennung von Mitgliedern der afrikanischen Gemeinde war auch wie bei späteren Anlässen bei anderen europäischen Missionsgesellschaften in Südafrika relativ belanglos. In einen Streit der afrikanischen Gemeinde über die Sitte der weiblichen Haartracht nach der Eheschließung, in dem Dinkoanyane als Angehöriger des Häuptlingsgeschlechts entscheiden sollte, mischten sich die

Berliner Missionare ein. Sie berichteten an die Missionszentrale: "Von unserer Seite ward ihm gesagt, daß er dergleichen Gesetze ohne unsere Zustimmung hier nicht machen dürfe."[14] Zur Einmischung in diese eigentlich banale Angelegenheit kam ohne Zweifel der Druck der Transvaal-Administration mit Paß- und Contract-Gesetzen auf die afrikanische Bevölkerung hinzu,[15] so daß sich hier eine explosive politische Situation herausgebildet hatte.

Nur zu gern versuchten zunächst die betroffenen Missionare, die Trennung eines beträchtlichen Teils der afrikanischen Gemeinde von der größten Berliner Missionsstation damit zu begründen, daß die äußeren Faktoren die ausschlaggebenden für diesen Entschluß waren. Unterzieht man hingegen die damalige Berichterstattung einer genauen Analyse, so dürfte die in allen Lebensbereichen für die Afrikaner spürbare paternalistische Einflußnahme durch die europäischen Missionare wenigstens ebenso gravierend für ihren Entschluß gewesen sein. Das Ergebnis der Untersuchung von Werner van der Merwe in der einzig existierenden Biographie von Dinkoanyane ist voll zu unterstreichen, denn er urteilt, daß Dinkoanyane "have the station in order to free himself from the authority of both Merensky and the South African Republic"[16].

Nach einiger Zeit des Zögerns, in der es die Missionare versäumt hatten, die angestauten Probleme mit den betroffenen Personen offen zu diskutieren, verließ Dinkoanyane mit seinen Anhängern endgültig die Station Botshabelo. Sie suchten einen geeigneten Platz in Transvaal, wo sie zwar von der staatlichen Administration und von der Aufsichtsgewalt der Missionare weitgehend unabhängig leben, aber nach wie vor von den Missionaren auf geistigem Gebiet betreut werden konnten. Dieser Schritt sei durch das "ungebrochene Heidentum" oder "nationales Selbstwertgefühl" motiviert gewesen, wurde in europäischen Missionskreisen kommentiert. In der Tat paßte die von Mut und Selbstbewußtsein zeugende Handlung nicht ins Muster der ihrer ethnischen Identität beraubten, sich ihrer militärischen Unterlegenheit bewußten und die neue Herrschaft mehr oder minder vollständig akzeptierenden afrikanische Elite. Die abgewanderten Pedi lehnten die Mission oder das von ihr repräsentierte Christentum nicht als solches ab, sondern nur den Missionar, dem der Grund und Boden nach der burischen Gesetzgebung gehörte und der dadurch "Macht und Polizeigewalt" ausüben konnte.[17]

Den Wunsch nach weiterer geistiger Betreuung erfüllten die Berliner Missionare den Weggezogenen jedoch nicht. Denn sie betrachteten die Separation über deren gesamten Dauer sehr mißtrauisch. Als Rechtfertigung für sich oder auch gegenüber ihren Vorgesetzten suchten sie die Ursachen für die Separation selbstverständlich bei vornehmlicher oder zumindest gleichberechtigter Anerkennung der äußeren politischen Gründe dann natürlich bei den Afrikanern. Sie nutzten, wenn sie schon nicht zu verhindern war, die Wirrungen um diesen ungewöhnlichen Schritt aus, um noch vehementer gegen die erhalten gebliebenen traditionellen Sitten und Gebräuche der afrikanischen Christen vorzugehen. In der Berichterstattung liest sich das dann wie folgt: "Uns selbst war die Bewegung ja auch ein Anlaß, in Predigt- und

Bibelstunden die oben zu Tage getretenen Fehler der Basutho häufiger als sonst durch Gottes Wort zu richten."[18]

Um dem für sie "fremden" Einfluß auf Sitten und Bräuche, ja auf das alltägliche Leben zu entgehen, der so weit führte, daß die Berliner Missionare quasi schon die Apartheid-Gesetzgebung in ihrer Stationsordnung in Ansätzen (getrennte Wohngebiete, unterschiedliche Badestellen u. dgl. m.) vorwegnahmen, suchte sich Dinkoanyane mit seiner Schar nach der Trennung von der Mission ein offensichtlich von niemandem direkt beanspruchtes und von den benachbarten burischen Farmern isoliertes Stück Land zur Siedlung aus.

Sie fanden es in einer sehr schwer zugänglichen Felsenschlucht am Spekboom River. Hier errichteten sie ein Dorf und machten den Boden, soweit es der felsige Untergrund zuließ, urbar. Ihre Hütten versteckten sie so vorteilhaft in den Felsen, daß sich ihre Siedlung, wie es in einer in Deutschland um die Jahrhundertwende weit verbreiteten Darstellung der Geschichte Südafrikas heißt, "in eine fast uneinnehmbare Felsenburg verwandelte"[19]. Dieser Ort erhielt die Bezeichnung "Mafolofolo".

Die Berliner Missionare waren erstaunt und erbost darüber, daß die von der Mission losgesagten Stammesangehörigen und ihr Häuptling Dinkoanyane "den Bauern (also Buren, U.v.d.H.) offen Hohn" sprachen, ja ein "erwachender Nationalgeist" nach ihren Beobachtungen deutlich zutage trete. Völliges Unverständnis spricht aus den missionarischen Berichten, als festgestellt wurde, daß sich die Afrikaner in ihren Handlungen und Äußerungen gegen die weitere burische Expansion wandten und dazu sogar eine Allianz mit den unter Oberhäuptling Sekukuni stehenden noch nicht unterjochten Pedi eingingen, von denen sie sich vor Jahren getrennt hatten.[20] Somit verlief die kirchliche Separation zu einem Zeitpunkt, zu dem sich die politischen Widersprüche zwischen burischer Administration und Siedlern einerseits und den noch in relativer Freiheit und weitgehend traditionellen Lebensformen lebenden Pedi andererseits immer stärker zuspitzten und diese allein deshalb schon dem Anschein einer politisch motivierten Handlung ausgesetzt waren.

Dinkoanyane beteuerte indes von Anfang an, daß er "durchaus nicht beabsichtige, von Gottes Wort sich zu trennen,"[21] was von den Missionaren allerdings als taktisches Vorgehen gewertet wurde, um auch die übrige Gemeinde zum Abfall von der europäischen Mission zu bewegen. Dabei mußten sie jedoch eingestehen, daß "er selbst und die christlich Ernsten seines Volkes predigen, sie hielten Schule und tägliche Erbauungen, und Dinkoanyane schickte Gesandtschaft über Gesandtschaft nach Botschabelo, ob er nicht wieder in die Gemeinde aufgenommen werden oder wenigstens einen eigenen Lehrer (also Missionar, U.v.d.H.) bekommen könne"[22]. Er erhielt von Alexander Merensky jedoch zur Antwort, daß eine Aufnahme in die Gemeinde en bloc nicht zu realisieren sei und daß auch ein Missionar als Pastor nicht zu ihnen kommen werde, solange Dinkoanyane nicht "auf eigenem oder gemietetem Grund und Boden in rechtssicheren Verhältnissen lebe" und dann auch nur, "wenn er sich verpflichte, einen bedeutenden Teil des Gehaltes für den Missionar aufzubringen"[23]. Diese Bedingungen waren selbst bei gutem Willen für die separierten Pedi nicht zu erfüllen. Das Festhalten an den unerfüllbaren Forderungen resultierte nicht allein aus Merenskys Überlegungen, sondern widerspiegelte den Geist der zuständigen Synode. Deren Mitglieder waren der Meinung, daß sich die Dinkoanyane'schen "in offener Auflehnung gegen die Landesobrigkeit ... befanden"[24].

Die Missionare Albert Nachtigal und Hermann Düring besuchten die "Abtrünnigen" noch einige Male, die kontinuierlich ihre Anhängerschaft vergrößern konnten. Die europäischen Besucher brachten in der Berichterstattung immer wieder ihr Erstaunen darüber zum Ausdruck, daß Dinkoanyane dem christlichen Glauben nicht abschwor, ja sogar beachtenswerte Predigten hielt. In den "Berliner Missionsberichten" aus dem Jahre 1876 heißt es dazu: "Dinkoanyane richtet sich inzwischen je länger je mehr als ein kleiner Fürst ein, der sein Volk nach alten nationalen Gesetzen regiert, das Christenthum beibehalten will, auch dringend und wiederholt um einen eigenen Lehrer (also Missionar, U.v.d.H.) bittet, aber sich dabei in dem Glauben versteift, die Lehrer, welche die Farbigen unter das Gesetz der Bauern zwingen wollten, seien nicht ihre Freunde, sondern auch nur darauf bedacht, sie zu beherrschen, ihnen Arbeiten und Lasten aufzuerlegen... Unsere Missionare nehmen den Abgesonderten gegenüber die Haltung ein, daß sie alle diejenigen, welche sich der christlichen Ordnung auf unseren Stationen nicht unterordnen wollen, als unter Kirchenzucht stehend behandeln, also auch die Weggezogenen nicht mit Wort und Sakrament bedienen, so lange bis sie einzeln gekommen sind, die Verkehrtheit ihres Weges eingesehen und Kirchenbuße gethan haben."[25] Versuche der Missionare, die Dinkoanyane'schen zur Rückkehr zu den Stationen zu bewegen, schlugen fehl, wenngleich sie selbst freudig aufgenommen wurden "und so lange von allgemeinen Dingen gesprochen wurde, hat man sich gegenseitig aneinander erfreut und erquickt"[26]. Aber der bei jedem Besuch wiederholte Wunsch an die Berliner Missionare, man möge ihnen einen Missionar senden, der auf ihrem Land leben sollte, wurde als "unausführbar" zurückgewiesen. Missionar Hermann Düring, der wohl am häufigsten Kontakt zu Dinkoanyane hatte, vermerkte in seinem Tagebuch, daß Dinkoanyane großes Herzeleid plage, weil er noch immer "ohne Lehrer sitze", aber schon viele Kinder vorhanden seien, die ohne das Sakrament der heiligen Taufe aufwüchsen.[27]

Die ablehnende Haltung der Berliner Missionare änderte sich auch in der folgenden Zeit nicht. Im Gegenteil, immer mehr steigerten sich die Missionare, da die "Abtrünnigen" nicht reumütig zurückkamen und sich sogar mit den noch von den Buren unabhängigen Stammesgenossen verbündeten, in heftige Ablehnung. Als wieder einmal an die Berliner Missionsgesellschaft die Bitte nach Entsendung eines Missionars herangetragen wurde, reagierte man äußerst empört: "Die Durchführung eines solchen Unternehmens wäre einfach Revolution und Landesverrat gewesen und wurde vom Missionar Merensky dem Dinkoanyane ausdrücklich als solcher bezeichnet."[28] Es ist also kein Wunder, wenn Dinkoanyane versuchte, das in der missionarischen Betreuung entstandene Defizit aus eigenen Mitteln, mit eigenen Anstrengungen zu beheben. Man praktizierte nunmehr ein von der europäischen Mission unabhängiges Christenleben, das Synkretismen aufwies. Daß diese nicht stärker zur Ausprägung gelangte, liegt wohl nur in der kurzen Existenz der Dinkoanyane'schen Separation begründet. Selbst Alexander Merensky, der diese mit heraufbeschworen hatte, mußte eingestehen: "Johannes (also Dinkoanyane, U.v.d.H.) und seine Leute sind Christen geblieben! ... In der Felsenburg des Johannes hat ... das Wort Gottes und mit ihm christliche Zucht und Sitte geherrscht."[29]

Aber welche Elemente der von den Missionaren übermittelten "christlichen Zucht und Sitte" wurden beibehalten? Exakte Auskunft gibt es darüber nicht. Außer Berliner Missionaren besuchten keine anderen Weißen die als Felsenburg bezeichnete Siedlung von Dinkoanyane. Und diese hatten nicht eben großes Interesse daran, den Abtrünnigen lobende Einschätzungen zu geben. Dennoch sind einige wichtige Fakten aus deren Berichterstattung zu entnehmen. So scheinen sich die Dinkoanyane'schen an die Monogamie gehalten zu haben und praktizierten keine "Zauberei". Auch die von den Missionaren aufs heftigste bekämpften Beschneidungsriten wurden nicht praktiziert. Des weiteren wurden "offenbare Sünden, wie Trunkenheit und Unzucht" bestraft. Jeden Sonntag wurde Gottesdienst gehalten, oft von Dinkoanyane selbst. Gebetsstunden wurden durchgeführt, und man "sammelte sich auch sonst um Gottes Wort". Sie errichteten eine Kirche. Aus dem Kreise der am Spekboom River siedelnden Afrikaner wurde gar ein Lehrer bestimmt, der den Kindern das Lesen und Schreiben beibringen sollte und "am Sonntage die Kinder zu einem besonderen Gottesdienste versammelte". Das Abendmahl wurde anscheinend nicht gefeiert. Jedoch wurden Kinder getauft. In der Berichterstattung darüber wird allerdings behauptet, daß es sich hierbei nur um "Todkranke" gehandelt haben soll. Die Pedi, die, soweit es ihnen möglich war, am christlichen Glauben festhielten, nutzten gar den sich ständig verbessernden Kontakt zu ihren "heidnischen" Stammesbrüdern unter Sekukunis Führung aus, um unter diesen in der Art ihrer ehemaligen europäischen Vorbilder zu "missionieren".[30]

Ob die Dinkoanyane'sche Separation zu einer die typischen Kriterien aufweisenden äthiopischen Kirche gekommen wäre, muß dahingestellt bleiben. Auf alle Fälle gibt es für diese Entwicklung eine ganze Reihe von Anzeichen und Indizien. Es muß eingehenderen Forschungen vorbehalten bleiben, ob die Einschätzung von Erhard Kamphausen auch auf die geschilderte Missionsabspaltung zutrifft, denn er resümiert: "Die frühen Sezessionsbewegungen sind damit als Ausdruck des Widerstandes gegen die Vormachtstellung der europäischen Missionare und als Protest gegen die politische Entmachtung zu begreifen. Es läßt sich aber nicht nachweisen, daß die Forderungen und Zielsetzungen der Sezessionisten bereits die Formen des Äthiopismus, d. h. theologisch begründete und die Stammesgegensätze transzendierende Vorstellungen angenommen haben."[31]

Abgebrochen wurde die m. E. deutlich sichtbare Entwicklung hin zu einer äthiopischen Kirche abrupt im Juli 1876. Im Rahmen der Planung eines für die damaligen Verhältnisse in Transvaal gigantischen Feldzuges gegen die Pedi Sekukunis griff auch ein aus 200 Mann bestehendes burisches Kommando die Siedlung Dinkoanyanes an. Die Angreifer erhielten Unterstützung von einigen Tausend Kriegern der Swazi.[32] Die Eröffnung eines Kriegsnebenschauplatzes verwundert schon, wenn man allein aus militärstrategischen Gesichtspunkten die Operationen der Transvaal-Buren zu erklären versucht. Neben dem Feldzug gegen Sekukunis Hauptsiedlung in Thaba Mosego bestand der ganze "Pedi-Krieg", der immerhin von Großbritannien offiziell zum Anlaß genommen wurde, um die Südafrikanische Republik (Transvaal) zu annektieren, fast nur noch aus dem Feldzug zur Unterwerfung der Dinkoanyane'schen in der Felsenfestung Mafolofolo. Deutlicher werden die Motive für diesen Kriegszug, wenn in Betracht gezogen wird, daß sich hier ein recht erfolgreiches Gemeinwesen der Afrikaner entwickelte, unabhängig von der Bevormundung europäischer Missionare, unabhängig und selbstbewußt gegenüber den benachbarten burischen Siedlern und frei in der Wahl seiner Verbündeten. Und zudem waren die Dinkoanyan'schen nicht in die "Barbarei" oder das "Heidentum" zurückgefallen, sondern sie hielten am Christentum und an damit verbundenen bestimmten Formen der "Zivilisation" fest. Daß die blutige Niederschlagung der Dinkoanyan'schen Separation nicht nur - wenn überhaupt - militärische Gründe hatte, sondern vor allem politisch motiviert war, darauf verweist auch der südafrikanische Historiker Peter Delius in seiner ausführlichen Untersuchung über die Politik der Pedi gegenüber Buren und Briten im 19. Jahrhundert: "Mafolofolo offered the possibility of a Christian life without the attendant heavy demands for tithe, labour and tax."[33] In der Tat hier liegt der wirkliche Grund für die gewaltsame Beendigung der Dinkoanyane'schen Separation. Die "Dinkoanyane'schen Verlockungen"[34] waren sowohl für die "heidnischen" als auch für die christianisierten und auf den Missionsstationen lebenden Pedi und darüber hinaus auch für die anderen afrikanischen Ethnien in Transvaal attraktiv und somit für die burische Administration gefährlich geworden. Sie mußten beseitigt werden.

Es ist eine Ironie der Geschichte, daß die Separation schwarzer Christen von einer deutschen Missionsgesellschaft schließlich mit deutscher Hilfe gewaltsam ihr Ende fand. Deutsche Krupp-Kanonen unter dem Befehl eines deutschen Hauptmanns erledigten im Bündnis mit Swazi-Kriegern und Buren-Kämpfern die Aufgabe. Dinkoanyane und viele seiner Anhänger fanden den Tod. Die Überlebenden begaben sich in den Schutz der Berliner Missionsstationen oder flüchteten zu Sekukuni.

Noch lange beschäftigte die Missionare aus Berlin die Dinkoanyane'sche Separation in der Auseinandersetzung mit "aufsässigen" Gemeindemitgliedern, bis etwa 15 Jahre später die Pedi-Nationalkirche entstand. Trotz allen Unvermögens, die "Schuld" in den eigenen Reihen zu suchen, sowie bei aller Ablehnung der

Separation von Dinkoanyane kam der damalige Missionsdirektor Hermann Theodor Wangemann bei deren Analyse zu der beachtenswerten Erkenntnis: "Dinkoanyane hat den Buren viel Schaden getan und ist endlich in seiner Rebellion untergegangen, aber die Schuld an der ganzen Rebellion tragen die Buren, die selbst den christlich Getauften unter den Farbigen nicht das Recht zugestehen wollten, welches einem jeden Menschen von Gottes wegen zusteht, das Recht einer freien Persönlichkeit."[35]

Weitere Beispiele der Separation oder auch nur Versuche, eine solche von den europäischen Missionsgemeinden durchzuführen, die jedoch in der historischen wie religionsgeschichtlichen Forschung bislang keine Beachtung gefunden haben, ließen sich anführen.

Schon in den häufig auch als "vorätiopisch"[36] bezeichneten kirchlichen Selbständigkeitsbewegungen von schwarzen Christen vor 1890 wurden - wie in den Ausführungen deutlich wurde - unter dem Deckmantel des religiösen Protestes politische Forderungen, mehr oder minder ausgeprägt formuliert, vorgebracht. Dies geschah sicherlich nicht bewußt, sondern war vermutlich eher spontaner Ausdruck der Unzufriedenheit mit der auf allen Ebenen sicht- und spürbaren weißen Vorherrschaft; vor allem in der Kirche, wo zwar die Gleichheit des Menschen vor Gott gepredigt wurde, jedoch selbst im täglichen Leben der Gemeinde rassistische Vorurteile in der Praxis dominierten. Und dabei galten gerade die Kirche bzw. die Missionare für nicht wenige Afrikaner als moralische Stützen in einer in sich zusammenbrechenden traditionellen Welt. Denn die noch bis in die Mitte des 19. Jahrhunderts hinein von den kolonialen Verwaltungen in relativer Unabhängigkeit lebenden afrikanischen Ethnien in Südafrika hatten durch den Expansionismus der Buren ihre ethnische und politische Selbstständigkeit verloren. Durch den nunmehr einsetzenden Proletarisierungsprozeß und das sich etablierende Wanderarbeitersystem waren die sozialen und tribalen Grenzen ins Wanken geraten. Durch die damit einhergehenden Wertezerstörungen und die Vernichtung der kulturellen wie der ethnischen Identität existierte kein funktionierender Rahmen mehr für die bisher üblichen Formen des Protestes. Als starke, allseits anerkannte oder zumindest akzeptierte Institution mit relativ langer historischer Verwurzelung war aber immer noch die christliche Kirche, vornehmlich in Gestalt der europäischen Missionskirchen, vorhanden. Wenn auch die christliche Missionierung zum Teil erst seit einigen Jahrzehnten, im Norden der heutigen Republik Südafrika gar erst seit einigen Jahren einige Erfolge zu verzeichnen hatte, so erwiesen sich doch die europäischen Missionsgesellschaften für den Afrikaner als relativ kontinuierliche und stabile Institutionen, die den Zusammenbruch des eigenen ethnischen und sozial-ökonomischen Systems augenscheinlich unbeschadet überstanden. Sie gaben Wertmaßstäbe vor, definierten moralische und politische Normen und hatten im großen und ganzen - trotz personeller Veränderungen sowie qualitativ unterschiedlicher Verhältnisse und Beziehungen zur kolonialen Administration bzw. zur schwarzen Bevölkerung - ein gleichbleibendes Interesse an der Aufrechterhaltung des status quo. Demzufolge waren die konservativen Werte der Missionare in den Augen der Afrikaner ruhige Pole in der sich ansonsten rasch verändernden gesellschaftlichen Situation in Südafrika. Indes konnten diese konservativen, starren Modelle der Missionen auf die Herausforderungen der neuen Zeit mit dem vehementen Übergang zur Industrieproduktion, der Mechanisierung der Landwirtschaft und dem damit verbundenen Proletarisierungsprozeß breiter Massen der Afrikaner sowie deren erwachendem politischem Bewußtsein - das sich zunächst in noch völlig nebulösen Frühformen eines schwarzen Nationalismus ausdrückte -, keine befriedigenden Antworten geben. Und es gelang den mit den kirchlichen und politischen Verhältnissen unzufriedenen Afrikanern, durch die Gründung von eigenen, selbstständigen Kirchen aus den nicht gerade reform- und widerstandswilligen Missionskirchen auszubrechen und sich auf diese Art und Weise öffentliche Aufmerksamkeit zu verschaffen.

Somit hatten die Afrikaner die Möglichkeit, soziale und politische Forderungen in relativ geschütztem Rahmen zu artikulieren.

Wurden bis zu Beginn des Burenkrieges in der Diskussion in Südafrika, aber auch in Europa und Nordamerika über die Ursachen der Entstehung und des anfänglichen Erfolges der äthiopischen Kirchen im Süden Afrikas - sicherlich nicht zu Unrecht - vornehmlich innerkirchliche Gründe angegeben, wie die paternalistische Haltung der europäischen Missionare gegenüber ihren schwarzen Gemeinden - wie auch das Beispiel der Dinkoanyan'schen Seperation zeigt - oder die Unzufriedenheit ordinierter afrikanischer Pfarrer oder sogenannter Nationalhelfer mit der Ungleichbehandlung im Verhältnis zu ihren weißen Kollegen, so änderte sich dies nach Beendigung des Krieges. Dies gilt in der südafrikanischen Historiographie als weithin feststehende Tatsache. Stärker sollte in der zukünftigen Forschung - wenn mir erlaubt ist, diesen Wunsch auszudrücken - Berücksichtigung finden, daß es auch schon in den sogenannten voräthiopischen Kirchen die Artikulierung von politischen Forderungen gab. Denn es ist weit weniger bekannt, darauf verwies Horst Gründer in seinem kürzlich erschienenen Handbuch zur Geschichte der Neuzeit, daß die äthiopischen Kirchen schon bald nach ihrer Entstehung unter dem Slogan "Afrika den Afrikanern" zugleich "Zellen eines schwarzen Protonationalismus" bildeten.[37] Von anderen Historikern wurde der entstehende Äthiopismus ausdrücklich als "Frühform des religiösen Nationalismus"[38] oder als "embryonaler Nationalismus"[39] bezeichnet.

In der Tat stellten schon im Jahre 1875 Missionare der Berliner Missionsgesellschaft fest, als sie ihrer Missionsleitung in der deutschen Hauptstadt über die Dinkoanyan'sche Separation Bericht erstatteten, daß "sich je länger je mehr der erwachende Nationalgeist der Basuto geltend" mache.[40]

Die Bedeutung des Äthiopismus als Manifestation des afrikanischen Nationalismus wurde von der Wissenschaft schon in den dreißiger Jahren, vor allem zunächst von E. H. Brookes[41], erkannt und dann auch in weiteren Untersuchungen bewiesen. Deshalb sollte meines Erachtens mit Einschätzungen, wie sie jüngst von

Jörg Fisch in der ansonsten lesenswerten Geschichte Südafrikas vorgenommen wurde, vorsichtig umgegangen werden, der schreibt, daß in Südafrika "der schwarze Nationalismus ... erst ein Produkt des 20. Jahrhunderts" sei.[42]

Wenn auch noch nicht ausdrücklich als Nationalismus definiert, so gab es diesen mit den typischen Inhalten doch schon seit Entstehung der äthiopischen Kirchen. Karl Axenfeld meinte in einem Vortrag: "Der Aethiopismus ist das Erwachen der schwarzen Rasse zu dem Anspruche, kulturell, eventuell auch politisch der weißen Rasse nachzukommen, gleichzukommen und sie vielleicht aus dem schwarzen Erdteile zu verdrängen."[43]

Hauptthemen des Äthiopismus waren - und damit gehen seine Forderungen über die des frühen Nationalismus oder Protonationalismus weit hinaus - das Bewußtsein von Menschenwürde, persönliche Freiheit, soziale Gerechtigkeit und Streben nach politischer und sozialer Gleichheit.[44] Von Anfang an galt die besondere Aufmerksamkeit der Äthiopisten der Land- und Bildungsfrage.[45] Im übrigen sind das alles Forderungen, die mit der Gründung des African National Congress 1912 auf die Tagesordnung der Befreiungsbewegung im Süden Afrikas gesetzt wurden.[46]

Daß die äthiopische Bewegung darüber hinaus auch keine unwesentliche Bedeutung für den Panafrikanismus besaß, darauf hat schon Imanuel Geiss in seiner umfangreichen Untersuchung über den Beitrag des Pananfrikanismus zur Dekolonisation des schwarzen Kontinents hingewiesen. Er hob hervor, daß "'Aethiopismus' und unabhängige afrikanische Kirchen ... teils zum historischen Hintergrund, teils zur Substanz des Panafrikanismus" gehören.[47]

Besonders deutlich wird der Zusammenhang zwischen Unabhängigen Afrikanischen Kirchen und Nationalismus bzw. Panafrikanismus, wenn die aus dieser Bewegung - wenn man sie denn als solche bezeichnen will - hervorgegangene soziale Gruppe betrachtet. Es läßt sich nicht übersehen - und darin unterscheidet sich die Entwicklung in Südafrika nicht von ähnlichen in anderen Regionen des Kontinents -, daß es eine sich in Anfängen entwickelnde afrikanische Bourgeoisie und Kleinbourgeoisie war, die bei gleichzeitiger Unmöglichkeit politischen Kampfes ihren Freiheits- und Gleichheitsanspruch durch die Gründung und vor allem dann Entwicklung von Kirchen formulierte, die somit ein Moment des frühen afrikanischen Nationalismus darstellen.[48]

Hinweisen möchte ich an dieser Stelle auf ein gravierendes Desiderat in der Forschung. So gab es in den siebziger Jahren des 19. Jahrhunderts in Südafrika auch außerhalb der Kirchen Bestrebungen zu einem nationalen Bewußtsein, zu einem - tribale Grenzen überschreitenden - Wir-Gefühl zu kommen. Nachweisen läßt sich dies vor allem an den Bestrebungen der Eliten, also an den paramount chiefs und ihrer unmittelbaren Umgebung der Pedi, Zulu und Southern Sotho. Dies ist ein besonderes, sehr interessantes Forschungsfeld.

Zum Abschluß meiner Ausführungen möchte ich ausdrücklich auf den im Entstehungsprozeß der Unabhängigen Afrikanischen Kirchen in Südafrika sichtbaren engen Zusammenhang zwischen den Bestrebungen zur politischen Emanzipation und dem aufkeimenden Nationalismus, der m.E. noch nicht in jedem Falle die engen Ketten des Tribalismus gesprengt hat,[49] hinweisen. Mit dem zuletzt genannten Sachverhalt ist eine neue, gewichtige Problematik, eine für Südafrika sehr relevante, in der Wissenschaft bislang jedoch weitgehend unbearbeitete Thematik angesprochen, die indes Gegenstand einer anderen Tagung sein sollte.

## Anmerkungen

1 Zitiert in: Martin Gensichen, Das Auftreten des Aethiopismus in der Kapkolonie, in: Missionsberichte der Gesellschaft zur Beförderung der evangelischen Missionen unter den Heiden zu Berlin für das Jahr 1907 (zitiert als Berliner Missionsberichte), Berlin 1907, 155.

2 Vgl. die einzig sich der Thematik explizit annehmende Fallstudie von Greg Cuthbertson, "Cave of Adullam": Missionary reaction to Ethiopianism at Lovedale, 1898-1902. In: Missionalia, Bd. 19, Pretoria 1991, 57ff.

3 Karl Axenfeld, Die Schlange im Grase. Blicke in die äthiopische Bewegung in Südafrika. In: Die Evangelischen Missionen. Illustriertes Familienblatt, hg. von J. Richter, Gütersloh *1*(1905), 59.

4 Vgl. T. Becher, Unabhängigkeitsbewegungen der Farbigen in Südafrika, Basel 1905, 4.

5 Vgl. ebenda, 10ff.

6 Ebenda, 35.

7 Karl Axenfeld, Der Aethiopismus in Südafrika, Berlin 1907, 7.

8 Ebenda.

9 Gabriel Sauberzweig-Schmidt, Der Einfluß des südafrikanischen Krieges auf den äußeren und inneren Zustand der Berliner Mission in Südafrika. In: Allgemeine Missions-Zeitschrift. Monatshefte für geschichtliche und theoretische Missionskunde, Berlin *31*(1904), 445.

10 So etwa Gabriel Sauberzweig-Schmidt, Der Aethiopismus. Die kirchliche Selbständigkeitsbewegung unter den Eingeborenen Südafrikas. In: Die Reformation, Berlin 1904, Nr. 43, 680, wo es heißt: "Die Bewegung, wie sie sich in den wenigen Jahren ihres Bestehens herausgebildet hat, stellt sich dar als eine sozial-politische in kirchlichem Gewande."

11 Vgl. Ulrich van der Heyden, Vom innerkirchlichen zum politischen Protest. Die Vorgeschichte der Bapedi-Nationalkirche im südafrikanischen Transvaal. In: Materialien des Dritten Internationalen Kolonialgeschichtlichen Symposiums in Bremen 1993 (im Druck).

12 Vgl. Eduard Kratzenstein, Kurze Geschichte der Berliner Mission in Süd- und Ostafrika, Berlin [4]1893, 219.

13 Berliner Missionsberichte 1875, Berlin 1875, 135.

14 Ebenda, 136.

15 Vgl. Ulrich van der Heyden, Die letzten kolonialen Eroberungskriege in Südafrika. Die Unterjochung der Pedi und Venda Transvaals in den Jahren 1875 bis 1898, vornehmlich anhand deutschsprachiger Quellen, Diss., Berlin 1984, 78.

16 Werner van der Merwe, Johannes Dinkwanyane, 1842-1876. In: South African Historical Journal, Bloemfontein (1976)8, 15.

17 Kratzenstein, Kurze Geschichte..., 217.

18 Berliner Missionsberichte 1875, Berlin 1875, 142.

19 J. Scheibert, Der Freiheitskampf der Buren und die Geschichte ihres Landes, Bd. 1, Berlin 1903, 323.
20 Berliner Missionsberichte 1875, Berlin 1875, 144; vgl. auch B.V. Lambaard, Bydreas tot bronne vor Johannes Dinkwanyane. In: Historia, Pretoria *10*(1965)1, 4ff.
21 Berliner Missionsberichte 1875, 145.
22 Ebenda.
23 Alexander Merensky, Erinnerungen aus dem Missionsleben in Südost-Afrika (Transvaal) 1859-1882, Bielefeld-Leipzig 1888, 358.
24 Kratzenstein, Kurze Geschichte..., 219.
25 Berliner Missionsberichte 1876, 304.
26 Ebenda.
27 Vgl. Archiv der Berliner Missionsgesellschaft: Acta Korrespondenz mit den Missionaren auf Botschabelo, Abt. III, Fach 4, No. 6, 1875-1885, Bd. 2, ohne Paginierung.
28 Berliner Missionsberichte 1876, 326.
29 Merensky, Erinnerungen..., 359.
30 Vgl. ebenda.
31 Erhard Kamphausen, Anfänge der kirchlichen Unabhängigkeitsbewegung in Südafrika. Geschichte und Theologie der Äthiopischen Bewegung 1872-1912, Bern-Frankfurt/M. 1976, 78.
32 Vgl. D. R.Hunt, An Account of the Bapedi. In: Bantu Studies, Johannesburg 1931, 297.
33 Peter Delius, The Land Belongs To Us. The Pedi Polity, the Boers and the British in the Nineteenth-Century Transvaal, Berkeley-Los Angeles 1984, 175.
34 Christliche Missionsgeschichte, hg. vom Evangelischen Bücherverein zu Berlin, Berlin 1879, 73.
35 Hermann Theodor Wangemann, Südafrika und seine Bewohner nach den Beziehungen der Geschichte, Geographie, Ethnologie, Staaten- und Kirchen-Bildung, Mission und des Racen-Kampfes, 4. Aufsatz, Berlin 1881, 57.
36 Hans-Jürgen Greschat, Eine "voräthiopische" südafrikanische Kirche. Die Sezession der Ba-Luther in Pediland im Jahre 1890. In: Glaube - Geist - Geschichte. Festschrift für Ernst Benz, hg. von G. Müller und W. Zeller, Leiden 1976, 536ff.
37 Horst Gründer, Welteroberung und Christentum. Ein Handbuch zur Geschichte der Neuzeit, Gütersloh 1992, 557.
38 Heinrich Loth, Kolonialismus und Antikolonialismus in Südafrika unter religiösen Formen. In: asien, afrika, lateinamerika *4*(1976)4, Berlin 1976, 590.
39 Werner Korte, Wir sind die Kirchen der unteren Klassen. Entstehung, Organisation und gesellschaftliche Funktion unabhängiger Kirchen in Afrika, Frankfurt/M.-Bern-Las Vegas 1978, 25.
40 Berliner Missionsberichte 1875, 144.
41 E.H. Brookes, The Colour Problems in South Africa, London 1933, 35; vgl auch Bingham Tembe, Methodische Grundlagen der Erforschung afrikanischer unabhängiger Kirchen in Südafrika. Eine Bewertung ausgewählter Literatur. In: Zeitschrift für Missionswissenschaft und Religionswissenschaft, Münster *68*(1984), 192ff. und 257ff.
42 Jörg Fisch, Geschichte Südafrikas, München 1990, 182.
43 Axenfeld, Der Aethiopismus..., 3.
44 Vgl. beispielsweise Kamphausen, Anfänge..., 58.
45 Vgl. Bingham Tembe, Integrationismus und Afrikanismus. Zur Rolle der kirchlichen Unabhängigkeitsbewegung in der Auseinandersetzung um die Landfrage und die Bildung der Afrikaner in Südafrika, 1880-1960, Frankfurt/M.-Bern-New York 1985.

46 Vgl. Francis Meli, South Africa belongs to Us. A History of the ANC, Harare/Bloomington-Indianapolis/London 1989.

47 Imanuel Geiss, Panafrikanismus. Zur Geschichte der Dekolonisation, Frankfurt/M. 1968, 109.

48 Korte, Wir sind die Kirchen..., 25 und 33ff.

49 Vgl. Meli, South Africa..., 1.

# Indidenous Premises, Change and Modes of Response

# Intellectual Basis and Ideological Premises of Maharashtrian Response to British Colonial Rule

J. V. Naik

## I

Cultural imperialism invariably operates as an auxiliary of economic imperialism. So it was with British colonial rule in India. Macaulay in his famous Minute on Education (1835) said that the primary aim of English education in India, was to raise up an English-educated middle class 'who may be interpreters between us and the millions we govern - a class of persons Indian in colour and blood, but English in tastes, in opinions, in morals, and in intellect'[1]. Macaulay's was not an empty rhetoric but a well calculated move, fully supported by 'the great bulk of the Calcutta merchantile community', for the westernization of Indian intellectual elite.[2] Two decades later, this policy was reiterated in the celebrated Education Despatch (1854), often called the 'Magna Carta of Indian education', which could 'only think of the India to come as the supplier of raw materials for the British Industries and as the consumer of the finished products of England'.[3]

Such and similar odius aspects of colonialism notwithstanding, the nineteenth century English-educated Indian intellectuals, with a few bright exceptions,[4] responded to British rule positively, and even regarded it as 'Divine Providence' until at a later stage. This was because the British, regardless of whatever else they did in India, served as a potent instrument firstly in the induction of progressive Western ideas, at a time when the country was passing through a kind of intellectual and spiritual coma, which were conducive to a rational reordering of the whole traditional thought-structure and social outlook; and secondly in the creation of a pan-Indian modern state which, in turn, fulfilled an essential pre-condition for nationhood. It was for this reason that the whole Moderate school of Indian politics, from Raja Rammohun Roy to G. K. Gokhale, came to think that the 'British connection was ordained, in the inscrutable dispensation of Providence for India's good'[5]. Inherent in this belief of dispensation, was a vision of a new life and society - humane, democratic, secular - to be achieved through the instrumentality of British rule. None of the major Votaries of this so-called theory of 'Divine Providence', however, expected, or wanted, British rule to be permanent; the British were to hold India in trust until such time as she became fit to reclaim her independence.[6]

Such a benign view of British colonial rule was, however, repugnant to a few rebels in the English-educated camp right from the start. For, on the basis of the ground reality, they were quick to percieve the central contradiction between colonial rule and the interests of the Indian people. To them the sedulous idea of 'civilising mission' of Great Britain appeared to be a myth, for they asserted that there was no such thing as beneficent imperialism and that there could not be anything altruistic about colonial rule. While they did not fail to appreciate the secular-scientific ideas that came in the wake of British rule, their main concern was the alien political subjugation and the consequent economic ruination of the country. To such critics, British colonial rule was not a divine dispensation, but 'The most bitter curse India has ever been visited with'.[7] The same view of British rule was even more forcefully, though uncritically, held by the traditionalists and revivalists, for the fear of the Hindus becoming 'denationalized'. While the traditionalists were prone to reject everything Western - human, mechanical, intellectual -, for the fear of the destruction of the existing traditions, the revivalists looked for some 'golden age' of the antiquity, rather than reason, to combat western influences and to restore order in the disarray and confusion caused by the dawn of the Kaliyuga, which made it difficult for them to fall in line with progress and evolution.[8] The latter hostile reaction to British rule gave rise to a tendency to idealise the past, rationalise religion, custom, caste-system and everything that went with the traditional thought structure and institutions, which the reformers of the liberal school found extremely hard to fight.

The conflict that ensued between these diverse reactions is the essence of the social history of India under the British rule. In no other part of India, perhaps not even Bengal, the conflict was so articulate as it was in Maharashtra. It was with the overthrow of the Maratha power in 1818, that the British had succeeded in securing their political supremacy and paramount authority in the sub-continent, which not only placed vast resources at their command but also freed them to conduct their educational and utilitarian experiments on a firm footing. Although for the time being the Marathas submitted to the inevitable, given their latent memory of the Swaraj, the unconscious ethos of the old ruling elite in Maharashtra never accepted the transfer of power in 1818 as anything more than a tactical retreat. There was a sullen resentment amongst them. The tables had to be turned and the lost ground recovered. For the achievement of this end, much that was efficient in the British administrative system had to be learnt without, however, abandoning the traditional values. This being their prime objectives, the idea of total reorganization of society on rational principles never became 'an item of fundamental faith among the main stream of Maharashtrian thought'.[9]

No one knew this better than Mountstuart Elphinstone, the first Governor (1819 - 1827) of the newly constituted Bombay Presidency, who was also a keen student of the Maratha history.[10] To assuage the feelings of the old ruling class as well as the general populace, Elphinstone followed a policy of studied Conservatism in matters both political and social which, in no small measure, shaped the thought-process in post-1818 Maharashtra. His formal effort, after the fall of the Peshwas, was 'to leave as much and influence with the old ruling classes as was consistent with overall English supremacy'[11]. He also did not take so dim and dark view of the Hindu life and culture as, for instance, James Mill did in his *The History of British India*. Nor was he in favour of the Evangelicals enforcing Christian doctrines on the conquered population; he would rather leave it to the recipients of the new liberal education to discover the fallacies of popular Hinduism. The basic aim of his administration was not to destroy any of the traditional institutions, but rather to make use of them, and transform them for the benefit of both the ruler and the ruled, on the basis of evolutionary and utilitarian principles. For this purpose he introduced liberal education.He recognised that the diffusion of knowledge would lead to a demand for independence in some distant future. But that did not deter him from doing his duty to the people under his charge. He had made his intentions clear in a letter which he wrote to Sir James Mackintosh, on 2 July 1819, in which he said: 'The most desirable death for us to die should be the improvement of the natives reaching such a pitch as would render it impossible for a foreign power to retain the government.'[12]

Favourably impressed by the benevolent regime of Mountstuart Elphinstone, the initial Maharashtrian response to British rule was one of enthusiasm and hope. In a Public Address presented to Elphinstone on the eve of his departure to England in 1837, the local leaders of the Bombay Presidency, said in part: '... we are led to consider the influence of the British Government as the most desirable blessing which the Supreme Being could have bestowed on our native land.'[13] Bal Shastri Jambhekar (1812 - 1846), the first brilliant product of English education in Western India and the pioneer of modern social reform movement in Maharashtra, was so deeply impressed by the conservative liberalism of Elphinstone, that he wrote in the *Bombay Durpun* of 13 April, 1832: 'India has not seen a greater statesman or a more enlightened and liberal-minded man than Elphinstone'[14], an opinion which was generally shared even by the later-day militant nationalists and Extremists such as B. G. Tilak.[15]

Later British administrators, however, did not and could not live up to Elphinstone's ideal. For imperialism has its own inner logic and it runs its own course. As the fuller impact of the British colonial policies, especially in their economic implications, began to be more keenly felt in the conquered territories, the earlier views on British rule underwent a radical change at least in the more discerning section of Indian intelligentsia brought up on English education. Perhaps the earliest and easily the most determined intellectual resistance to British rule came from Maharashtra. This is revealed by a spate of anti-British political and economic literature, albeit journalistic, both in English and Marathi, produced by a small band of Maharashtrian intellectuals in the city of Bombay in the early 1840s. Prominent among these early critics of British rule, were: Bhaskar Pandurang Tarkhadkar (1816 - 1847), an early product of the Elphinstone Institution, who wrote his 'eloquent epistles', whith the pseudonym 'A Hindoo', in the *Bombay Gazette* of the year 1841, in which he made a studied criticism of almost all aspects of the British colonial rule, and thereby earned for himself the sobriquet 'A Second Junius'[16], Govind Vithal Kunte alias Bhau Mahajan (1815 - 1890), another brilliant Elphinstonian, who consistently and thoroughly exposed the seamy side of the British colonial rule through the columns of his powerful Marathi newspaper, the *Prabhakar* started on 24 October, 1841[17], and Ramakrishna Vishwanath, the unknown author of a remarkable Marathi book, written in 1843 and dedicated to 'The People of India', entitled *Hindusthānchi Prāchin va Sampratchi Sthiti Āni Pundhen kāi Tyāchā Parinām Honār Hyā Vishayi Vichār* ('Thoughts on India's past and present conditions and their impact on the future') which contained a severe indictment of the British economic policies.[18] These critics together made a penetrative analysis of the British rule, especially in regard to 'draining India of its wealth and reducing it to poverty', and arrived at a conclusion that it was not a divine dispensation, but 'the most bitter curse India has ever been visited with'. These Marathi writers were forerunners of Dadabhai Naoroji's Drain Theory, a fact acknowledged by Dadabhai himself in his opening lecture on Drain, entitled *England's Duties to India* delivered before the East India Association, London, on 2 May, 1867.[19]

It seems surprising that, by mid 1840s, some of these critics had read some of the influential European thinkers and essayists such as the philosophers of the French Revolution, Volney, Thomas Paine, Adam Smith, David Ricardo, Edmund Burke and Edward Gibbon to whom they made pointed references. The point is, the initial inspiration in their quest for liberty and equitable social order, was almost exclusively Western. It is not merely the exploitative nature of British rule that came in for the lash of their bitter attack, they were even more severe in their criticism of the fossilised Indian religious and social tradition which, they held, was primarily responsible for India's downfall. In this regard they wrote: 'It is the priest craft of the Brahmins that have so far lowered the national character of the Hindoos as to be easily governed and even tyrannised over the handful of foreigners which is to be greatly lamented, but it is political craft of the latter that has now impoverished them, which is still more to be lamented.'[20] They also did not fail to give due credit to the British rulers for the humanitarian work such as abolition of the practice of Sati and infanticide and the suppression of Thugee, which the British did, but said that 'all these acts of common humanity vanish away in the vortex of your (British) political cruelty.'[21]

This stinging criticism was at once challenged by a group of pro-British writers who wrote, under the pen-names of 'A Parsee Boy' and ' Fourth Hindoo', in the *United Service Gazette*. They lavished high praise on 'the moderation, clemency and excellence of the British Government'. Their tribute to the British rulers runs as follows:[22] 'There is neither tyranny nor injustice in the countries, where the British flag is flying. To use an Oriental idiom, in the countries under the protection, the Lion and the Lamb drink from the same fountain. - May the Almigthy ever be its supporter, may its army be always successful in every country, where they direct their marches. This is the humble prayer of ... its loyal subjects.'

The critics treated this eulogy as nothing but 'shameless flattery'. Marshalling the facts of history to their aid, they demolished the arguments of the pro-British writers in a manner which was at once condemnatory and convincing. They admonished the 'Parsee Boy' for his un-Indian attitude born out of gross ignorance of the true nature of things and dismissed his pro-British writings heavily loaded with quotes from Janes Mill's *The History of British India*, as downright nonsense. They especially pitied the man who called himself 'A Fourth Hindoo' for being 'so base and shallow-minded' as to support the 'Parsee Boy' in his justification of colonial rule.[23]

Such was the first debate in Maharashtra for and against the British rule. Though it lasted barely six months from July to December, 1841, it marked the beginning of two contrasting trends of thought which, in the years to come, were to dominate in varying degrees the two principal schools of Indian politics: the Moderates and the Extremists. It should, however, be emphasised that the early nationalist critics of British rule, unlike the later-day Extremists, were radical not only in matters political but social as well, for they had realised that for the achievement of national emancipation the various aspects of reform - political, economic, social, religious - were inseparable and had to be pursued simultaneously. In fact, in 1847, some of these radicals, under the leadership of Dadaba Pandurang Tarkhadkar (1814 - 1882), a noted scholar and a serious student of comparative religion, formed a secret society called the Paramahansa Sabha with the object of demolishing caste and its attendant vils. Its members rejected idol-worship, abjured the narrow sanctions of caste, swore to regard each other with feeling of real brotherhood and resolved to work for the creation of an equitable society on the basis of rationality. By the abolition of the distinctions of caste, creed and custom, the Sabha aimed at uniting all in one fraternity, and in the worship of one God. Although the Paramahansa Sabha did not last long, it gave rise to two important reformist bodies in Maharashtra, the one named Prarthana Samaj (1867) which, though lofty in its religious and social principles, remained confined mostly to English-educated high caste Hindus, and the other called the Satya Shodhak Samaj (1873) which led the low caste protest movement.[24]

By the middle of the nineteenth century there arose a group of reformers in Maharashtra who firmly held the view that social reform was a condition precedent to political reform: 'Our social institutions must improve and become rational and just. There can be no advance politically without social and moral advancement.'[25] To them 'the British conquest of India was not a calamity to be lamented, but an opportunity to be seized'[26]. The new social order was to be achieved through the instrumentality of god-sent British rule. The first and foremost exponent of this concept of divine dispensation in Maharashtra was Lokahitawadi Gopal Hari Deshmukh (1823 - 1892), a high ranking Brahmin official in the

British judicial service. His celebrated *Shatpatre* ('Hundred Letters') contributed to the Marathi weekly, the *Prabhakar* during the period 1848 - 1850, contained not only an outspoken, impatient, penetrative analysis of the social and intellectual slavery of the caste-ridden Hindu society but also suggestion for its improvement. In one of his letters, he wrote, 'English owed their conquest to the stupidity of the Hindus. God sent these Gurus (English) to this country from a distant land. In fact, God wisely planned British rule to awaken the people from their deep slumber. There was no other alternative. The evil customs such as Sati, infanticide practised by the people aroused God's wrath. It was to bring the people to their proper senses that God helped British take over'[27]. Lokahitawadi held the Brahminical culture responsible for the pitiable condition of the lower caste people, and vehemently attacked the Brahmins for their 'extreme conceit, their faulty education, their exaggerated sense of self-importance, and their attitude of holding all others in total disdain', and said that, 'in order to demolish these stupid notions and bring sanity to the people, there was no other alternative but to bring them into contact with the civilised foreigners. And it was this purpose God planted rule in India'[28].

The English, he said, were to hold India in trust. If the British misused this divine trust by doing things which are detrimental to the people's interests, 'the people will declare themselves independent and the English to quit'. It would take, he said, more than two hundred years for Indians to free themselves from British domination, 'but there was no doubt about the ultimate end, and the transfer of power was inevitable'[29].

Similar views on British rule were held by R. G. Bhandarkar (1837 - 1925), the well known Indologist and social reformer. So much pleased he was with 'all the benefits of higher civilization' gained by India under the British rule, that he wrote, 'I believe it to be an act of Divine Providence that English alone of all the candidates who appeared about the same time for the empire of India should have succeeded. The Marathas, the Portuguese, the Dutch and the French were all weighed in balance and found wanting and the Empire was given to the English.'[30] As an ardent social reformer, he pressed for the removal of social distinctions, and said: 'If we ask England to remove our disabilities, we must as a necessary preliminary show that we are worthy of the favour by removing the disabilities of the oppressed classes of our society.'[31]

M. G. Ranade (1842 - 1901), one of the ablest and sagacious thinkers and social reformers of the nineteenth century India, also welcomed the Indo-British connection for the sake of national reconstruction on a higher and 'more elevating' lines. In this he saw 'the guiding hand of God in History'[32]. He had a high regard for the British nation whose character, he said, 'had been formed by ages of struggle and self-discipline which illustrates better than any other contemporary power the supremacy of the reign of law'[33]. Similar sentiments about the British rule were expressed by Dadabhai Naoroji and Phirozeshah Mehta the leaders of the Bombay Liberal School, in their presidential Addresses to the Indian National Congress.[34]

Easily the most pragmatic and sociologically the most appealing view of British rule as divine dispensation is to be found in the writings of Jyotirao Phule (1827 - 1890), a non-Brahmin social revolutionary and the chief ideologue of the low caste protest movement in Maharashtra. The idea prominently and poignantly appears in three of his books: *Gulamgiri* ('Slavery'), *Ishara* ('warming') and *Chattrapati Shivaji Raje Bhonsle Yancha Pawada* ('Ballad on Chhatrapati Shivaji Raje Bhonsle').[35] The British Rule of Law, implying equality before law with its natural corollary of human rights, provided the hope of liberation to the millions of downtrodden whose cause Phule earnestly espoused. Phule was deeply influenced by the writings of Thomas Paine and Theodore Parker. His approach was not nationalistic but humanistic. The Shudras and Ati-Shudras lived for centuries together in a state of utter social degradation, and there was absolutely no hope of securing any kind of social justice under the Brahmanical culture system. For the first time in Indian history British rule brought a glimmer of hope to the socially enslaved. It was, therefore, quite natural for Phule to offer thanks to God for sending the British to rescue the oppressed humanity 'from the clutches of the Brahmin demons'[36]. It was this reason that Phule hailed the failure of the Revolt of 1857, and made it obligatory on the part of every member of the *Satya Shodhak Samaj* ('Truth Seekind Society') to take 'an oath of in the name of God Khandero and declare his allegiance to British rule'[37].

## II

Even though the intellectual basis and ideological premises of Maharashtrian response to British rule differed from individual to individual, an urge to create a new life and new society was felt by the intellectual class as a whole. The prime question before them was: in what manner and method the desired reform was to be brought about? Except for a few notable rationalists - J. R. Phule, the founder of revolutionary low-caste protest movement, G. G. Agarkar (1856 - 1895), a thoroughgoing disciple of J. S. Mill - who rebelled against the whole traditional thought-structure and social outlook with the intention of replacing it with a new social order based to rationality and equality, the reformers of the liberal school in Maharashtra, by and large, wished to see the new India built on its old foundations, but excluding no light coming from any quarter. It was, however, mainly through English education and the other forces which came in the wake of British rule, that the reformers discovered new ideas. They were prone to accept them not because they were 'Western' but because they were best suited to meet the ends of truth justice and humanity. They wished to graft the new values on the old stock through the process of kind of osmosis.

It was in tune with this ideal that Bal Shastri Jambhekar, a fine scholar of the eighteenth century European enlightenment and the pioneer of liberal thought in

Maharashtra, advocated reform to come from within, on evolutionary lines, conforming as far as possible to the Hindu *Shastras* and tradition.[38] The first serious attempt to graft Western values on the indigenous religious tradition was made with the founding of the Prarthana Samaj, a modified version of the Brahmo Samaj of Bengal, in Bombay in 1867. This was the first major socio-religious reform movement to come up in Maharashtra after the advent of British rule. Its creed was formulated by R.G. Bhandarkar (1837 - 1925) and M.G. Ranade (1842 - 1901), the first two graduates of the Bombay University who had studied Joseph Butler's *Analogy and Fifteen* Sermons for their B. A. Examination in 1862 and were deeply influenced by his religious ideas. Butler was a standard author of moral philosophy in the Bombay University since its establishment in 1857.[39]

The theology and philosophy of the Prarthana Samaj was embodied in the six cardinal principles of its faith. The main ideas contained in the principles are: monotheism and spiritual worship of one true God who is the creator of the Universe, rejection of idolatry, non-belief in incarnations and revelations, non-acceptance of any book as revealed word of God. The most fundamental and the guiding principal of the Prarthana Samaj was Fatherhood of God and brotherhood of man. This principle according to Bhandarkar, implied not only obliteration of caste, but also 'levelling down of all social distinctions'.[40] Admittedly, the initial inspiration to the movement came from the Western sources.[41] But the originality of the leaders of the Prarthana Samaj lay in their reconciling the Western rationalism to Indian religious and spiritual tradition. In formulating liberal faith of the Prarthana Samaj they acknowledged their debt to the Western influences, but in promoting its creed they drew mainly on Indian religious and devotional literature, especially of the Bhakti school of thought in Maharashtra. In fact, Ranade in his zeal to give Indian ancestry to the Prarthana Samaj movement called it 'only a faint reflection and humble offshoot of the ancient Bhagwat Dharma' which he described as 'Protestant Hinduism'.[42] Bhandarkar was more candid in his explanation of the 'position of the Prarthana Samaj in the Religious world'. He said that it had accepted the *Upanishads*, in the *Bhagvadgita*, in Buddhism, in the teachings of medieval saints like Tukaram, in the Bible, and the other religious literature of the world.[43] Under their leadership the Prarthana Samaj, unlike the Brahmo Samaj, never became a sect outside the Hindu fold. For, they believed that social reform cannot but come through religious reform, religious reform must come from the country's essential past.

The overwhelming majority of the orthodox Hindus, who were predisposed to reject Western influences, reacted violently against the Prarthana Samajists, alleging that their whole religious and social programme was subversive of the traditional order. They dubbed the Prarthana Samajists as 'imposters, cheats and converts' and charge that they were 'deceiving Hindus and, therefore, should be ostracised'. In Vishnushastri Chiplunkar (1850 - 1882), an English educated militant nationalist and irreconcilable foe of British rule, the Hindu orthodoxy found its chief spokesman. Through the columns of his extremely popular Marathi magazine, the *Nibandhamala*, and the nationalist newspaper, the *Kesari*, Chiplunkar launched a vitriolic attack on the social reformers in general and the Prarthana Samaj of slavishly imitating Christianity and destroying the Hindu tradition. B.G. Tilak (1856 - 1920), a close associate of Chiplunkar and the 'father of Indian Unrest' against British rule, who had a large following in Maharashtra, commended Chiplunkar for attacking what he called 'the newfangled, half-baked reformers' and said'he (Chiplunkar) knew that every society requires certain bonds and ties, and these could be forged or kept intact by being proud of ancient institutions. In the absence of this consciousness all efforts at reform could be futile... It was natural that these people who talked of shattering a traditional social and religious system within, no time should deserve the ridicule of all.'[44]

The reformers of Bhandarkar - Ranade school of reform never had any quarrel with Tilak's proposition.[45] But they were totally against the 'bonds and ties' turning into chains and fetters thwarting the healthy development of society and keeping it in a state of perpetual bondage. The object of social reform, they explained, is 'to eradicate such evil customs as have undermined the energies of the Indian people and prevent the free expansion of their powers and capacities'[46]. They despaired of seeing India becoming a united nation so long as divisions of caste and other social evils prevailed. Denial of education to women and not giving them their rightful place in society, they said, had resulted in the waste of half of the moral and intellectual resources of the country; early marriage cannot but lead to the degeneration of the Hindu race; enforced girl widowhood condemns life to misery and often immorality; the ban on social travel cannot but thwart the enterprising spirit of the people.[47] The purpose of social reform they said, is to 'render the nation vigorous and free from social obstructions and restrictions'[48], and to achieve a 'high standard of social efficiency'[49].

The Christian Missionary's argument that Christianity alone could be saviour of India, though accepted by a few Hindu highcaste converts - Baba Padmanji, the Rev. Waman Narain Tilak, Pandita Ramabai, - was totally repugnant to Bhandarkar-Ranade school of reformers.[50] Nor did they, unlike the social revolutionaries such as J.R. Phule, advocate 'headlong action' but said that 'The motive forces of reform should be powerful in our hearts, but they must be tempered in a manner not to lead us to cut ourselves from the vital connection with the past'. They were Conservatives à la Burke and were against adopting 'the procedure of the French Revolution' for bringing about change.[51] The change which they sought was 'a change from constraint to freedom, from credulity to faith, from status to contract, from authority to reason, from unorganised to organised life, from bigotry to toleration, from blind fatalism to a sense of human dignity'[52].

These socio-religious reformers held that the tradition and modernity are not wholly incompatible. Not all elements in tradition are inimical to progress. Those features of tradition which are rational and healthy could be taken as a starting points for a further advance. A departure from the past and the attitudes that it represents, however, inevitable at some point, but the break need not necessarily be abrupt or total. 'By seeking the several reforms that we have in view', wrote Bhandarkar, 'we certainly shall not be taking a leap in the dark, for the condition of our society once was what we are now endeavouring to make it. This is the spirit in which we should approach the question of sweeping away from our institutions the corruption of the later ages.'[53] Citing evidence from the ancient texts, he sought to prove that in the olden days the people of India followed more rational practices which latterly became corrupt for some means of penalties imposed by the caste or by the State with the proviso that 'Legislation steps in only when the other methods fail'[54]. They were, however, totally against Revolutionary method, or the method of breaking the continuity.[55]

Critics of the Bhandarkar-Ranade school of reform, were quick to expose the hollowness of invoking texts for reform. The rationalist reformers disdained this strategy altogether. Jyotirao Phule, who pinned his faith in British law for ameliorating condition of the depressed Classes, held that the whole corpus of Brahmanical literature - Shruti, Smriti, Puranas and even Bhagvadgita - was specially designed to enforce obedience of lower classes to the Brahmanical hegemony and to keep the oppressed and the depressed in a state of perpetual slavery.[56] Dr. B. R. Ambedkar, the architect of the Indian Constitution, who regarded Phule as one of his Gurus, held more or less the same view. Agarkar's rational objection for having recourse to authorities for reform, was that 'once the principle, say, of the equal rights of women is found acceptable rationally, it was the same thing ... whether the scriptural crutches are available or not. After all it is easy to find authority and precedents for contradictory propositions and any debate that relies on authority is bound to be sterile'.[57] He, like his 'revered Guru', J. S. Mill, did not think it essential to have a shining historical tradition in order to have the right to freedom.

The futility of the method of interpretation old texts for social reform was best illustrated by the famous controversy over the Age of Consent Bill. Since the Revolt of 1857, the British Government was reluctant to pass any social legislation, lest ist would hurt the religious susceptibilities of the Indian people. It was under the pressure from the social reformers that the Government introduced the Bill in the Imperial legislative Council, seeking to change the marriage by a simple revision the Indian Penal Code making twelve, not ten, the minimum age of consumation. The orthodox party, led by Tilak, declared that the proposed legislation was against the *Dharmashastras*, and raised the usual cry, 'Hinduism-in-danger'. The Tilakites sought to politicise the whole issue by injecting religious and national sentiments. They had long been arguing that the foreign government has no right to interfere in the intimate personal and religious matters of the People. In the process, secular approaches to the problem advocated by men such as B. M. Malabari, a Parsee reformer, were relegated to background and the whole controversy came to be centred round the religious injunctions regarding the prepuberty marriage of Hindu girls.[58]

To meet the Orthodox challenge, the reformers led by Bhandarkar produced copious evidence from the ancient authorities in support of proposed reform.[59] But Tilak would not agree. He took a firm stand that the Hindu *Shastras* enjoin the Garbhadhan on the occasion of the first menstruation after having performed the home sacrifice. This, he claimed, has been the practice for 'at least 2500 years since the era of the Sutras'.[60] He accused Bhandarkar, K. T. Telang (1854 - 1893) and others of misinterpreting ancient authorities on the Hindu marriage law. Pandit Tarkachudamani, the well-known Bengali Sanskrit scholar, reiterated Tilak's interpretation of the rites of Garbhadhana, and Sir Romesh Chandra Mitter represented the cause of the anti-reformers in the Legislative Council. Despite the opposition from the Hindu orthodoxy, the Government passed the bill in 1891.

At the beginning of this controversy, in 1884, Ranade, responding to B. M. Malabari's Notes in the *Times of India* advocating legislative and executive sanction against the Hindu custom of child marriage and enforced widowhood had very poignantly expressed his views on the complexities of reform in the traditional Hindu Society, so spell bound with custom and authority, which he said, was beyond comprehension of either Parsee or European philanthropists. He wrote in part:[61] '... Our people feel and feel earnestly, that some of our social customs are fraught with evil, but as this evil is of temporal character, they think that it does not justify a breach of commands divine, for each breach involves higher penalty. The truth is, the orthodox society has lost its power of life, it can initiate no reform, nor sympathise with it. Only a religious revival, a revival not of forms, but of sincere earnestness which constitute religion can effect the desired end... The European nations are not aware of this difficulty; they have passed through the metaphysical stage, and consideration of positive good or evil here below have with them a force which suffices to carry them through, when a majority is secured on the side of change. It is this conviction of the hard conditions of the problem which retards our progress. People find fault with us, even abuse us for half-heartedness, for our apparent want of fire and enthusiasm. God alone knows that in our households we are perpetually at war with our dearest and nearest, we struggle and strive to do our best, and have perforce to stop at many points when we fear the strain will cause rupture. This is our present situation.'

Such, indeed, was the moral dilemma, a kind of identity crisis faced by most reformers of the liberal school. One, therefore, notices a certain dichotomy between their precepts and practices. Justice M. G. Ranade in his memorial speech on Mr. Justice K. T. Telang (1854 - 1893), a noted scholar and reformer who could not live up to his professed ideals, made a perceptive observation. He said that 'the moral interest of the chequered career' of Mr. Telang, 'lay in the divided and conflicting life we have to live in the midst of two civilizations'[62]. In the given situation the reformers had, perforce, to wage a dual struggle: against cultural imperialism and the hegemonic influences of the colonial values on the one hand, and on the other, against the ideological basis of the traditional order. The importance of this struggle, which could but meet with a partial success, lay in the making of the Indian intellectual attitudes and cultural norms in the colonial era, which continue to persist to this day.

## Notes

1 Macaulay, Minute on Education, 2 February 1835, cited in: Eric Stokes, The English Utilitarians and India, Delhi 1982, reprint, p. 46.

2 Ibid.

3 S. Nurullah/J.P. Naik, A History of Education in India, Bombay 1951, p. 87; cf. Stokes, p. 252.

4 See J.V. Naik, An Early Appraisal of the British Colonial Policy, Journal of the University of Bombay, Arts No., *XLIV-XLV*(1975/76)80-81, pp. 243-270.

5 This phrase was incorporated in the Preamble to the Constitution of the Servants of India Society founded by Gokhale in 1906. For the full original text of the Preamble and the rules of the Servants of India Society, see R. P. Paranjpye, Gopal Krishna Gokhale, Poona [2]1985, pp. 64-68.

6 For a fuller discussion of the concept see J.V. Naik, British Rule as 'Divine Providence': Myth and Reality. In: J. Kaiser/S.P. Gupta (ed.), Art and Society II (Prof. Mohammad Habib Commemoration Volume), Centre of Advanced Study, Muslim Aligarh University, Aligarh 1993; cf. K.N. Panikkar, Presidential Address. In: Proceedings of the Thirth-sixth Session of the Indian History Congress, Modern India Section, Aligarh 1975, p. 377.

7 Naik, An early Appraisal...

8 Matthew Lederle, Philosophical Trends in Maharashtra, Bombay 1976, p. 185.

9 K. Mukerji, The Renaissance in Bengal and Maharashtrian Thought from 1850 to 1920, Artha Vijnan (Gokhale Institute of Economics, Pune), December 1962. Vol. 4, No. 4, p. 337.

10 A. R. Kulkarni (ed.), History in Practice: Historians and Sources or Medieval Deccan - Marathas, New Delhi 1993, pp. 17-20.

11 Mukerji, p. 34; Kenneth Ballhatchet, Social Policy and Social Change in Western India, London 1957, p. 171.

12 Cited by Lederle, p. 32, (Source: Sir T.E. Colebrooke, Life of the Honourable Mountstuart Elphinstone, Vol.II, p. 72).

13 Cited by Colebrooke, II, p. 199.

14 The Bombay Durpun, 13 April 1832.

15 B.G. Tilak, Mountstuart Elphinstone Yānchi Kārkirda. In: Kesari, 12 March 1895 (Marath)i, reproduced in Lok Tilakāche Kesarintil Lekha, Bhag I (Rajakiya Khand), p. 437.

16 For the career and writings of B.P. Tarkhadkar ('A Hindoo') see Naik, An Appraisal...

17 See. J.V. Naik, Bhau Mahajan and his Prabhakar, Dhumketu and Dnyan Darshan: A Study of Maharashtrian Response to British Rule. In: The Indian Historical Review (ICHR) *XIII*, Nos. 1 & 2 (July 1986 and January 1987), pp. 135-152.

18 This book is republished in: D.K. Bedekar (ed.), Chār June Arthashastriya Grantha, 1843-1853, Pune 1969 (in Marathi). Ramakrishna was the Maharashtrian to attempt an analysis of the Hindu society from the economic point of view.
19 Dadabhai Naroji, Essays, Speeches and Writings, ed. by C.L. Parekh, Bombay 1987, pp. 32-33.
20 Letter of 'Philatropy', Bombay Gazette, 7 July 1841, pp. 22-23.
21 Cited by Naik, An Early Appraisal..., p. 268.
22 Ibid., n. 16a, p. 246.
23 Ibid., p. 247.
24 For fuller details, see J.V. Naik, Early Anti-caste Movement in Western India: The Paramahansa Sabha. In: Journal of the Asiatic Society of Bombay, *49, 50, 51*(1974); *75, 76*(new series)(1979), pp. 136-161.
25 Collected works of Sir R.G. Bhandarkar, ed. by N.B. Utgikar, Bhandarkar Oriental Research Institute, Pune 1928-1933, II, p. 513.
26 B.R. Nanda, Gokhale: The Indian Moderates and the British Raj, Delhi 1977, p. 22.
27 Lokahitawadinchi Shatpatren, ed. by P.G. Sahastrabuddhe, Pune [3]1963, Letter No. 46, p. 317 (Marathi).
28 Ibid., Letter No. 54, p. 327.
29 For a general discussion on 'Divine Dispensation' and Lokahitawadi's idea on it, see K.N. Panikkar's Presidential Address to the Modern India Section, Proceeding of the Indian History Congress, 36th Session, Aligarh 1975, p. 379.
30 Collected Works of Sir R.G. Bhandarkar, Vol. I, pp. 358-359.
31 Ibid, Vol. II, pp. 501-502.
32 Miscellaneous writings of the late Hon'ble Mr. Justice Ranade (with an introduction by Mr. D.E. Wache), Bombay 1915, p. 126.
33 Quoted by Nanda, p. 22.
34 See the Presidential Address of Dadabhai Naoroji and Pherozeshah Mehta to the Indian National Congress for the years 1888 and 1890 respectively.
35 Mahatma Phule: Samagra Vangmaya, ed. by S.G. Malshe and Dhananjay Keer, Bombay 1969, pp. 7, 90, 136 and 315 (Marathi).
36 Ibid., p. 7.
37 Dhananjay Keer, Mahatma Jyotirao Phule: Father of Our Social Revolution, Bombay 1964, p. 126.
38 Memoirs and writings of Archarya Bal Gangadhar Shastri Jambhekar, ed. by G.G. Jambhekar, Pune 1950, II, p. XXXVII.
39 For a perceptive analysis of the connection between the prescribed text books in the University of Bombay and the reformist ideas of the prominent 19th century social reformers in Western India, see Ellen McDonald, English Education and Social Reform in the late Nineteenth Century Bombay. In: Journal of Asian Studies *XXV*(May 1966), pp. 502-511.
40 Collected Works of Sir R.G. Bhandarkar, II, p. 480; see also J.V. Naik, Social Composition of the Prarthana Samaj: A Statistical Analysis, Proceedings of the Indian History Congress, 48th Session, Goa 1988, pp. 502-511.
41 Official Report of the Prarthana Samaj of Bombay for its first seventeen years, dated 26 December 1883. In: The Prarthana Samaj Minute Book, Vol. I, 1883, pp. 1-2.
42 M.G. Ranade, Religious and Social Reform. In: Id., Essays and Speeches, collected and compiled by M.B. Kolaskar, Bombay 1902, pp. 198-199.
43 Collected works of Sir R.G. Bhandarkar, p. 623.
44 Quoted in: G.P. Pradhan/A.K. Bhagwat, Lokmanya Tilak, Bombay 1959, pp. 136-137.

45 For details see J.V. Naik, R.G. Bhandarkar's concept of a Social Reformer. In: India Past and Present, A Biannual Journal of Historical Research, Bombay *IV*(1987)1, pp. 51-64.

46 Collected works of Sir R.G. Bhandarkar, II, p. 527.

47 Ibid., p. 528.

48 Ibid., p. 520.

49 Ibid., p. 501.

50 The Subodha Patrika (Organ of the Prarthana Samaj), 20 September 1925.

51 Collected works of Sir R.G. Bhandarkar, II, pp. 513-514.

52 Miscellaneous Writings of the late Hon'ble..., Bombay 1915, p. 116.

53 Collected works of Sir R.G. Bhandarkar, II, pp. 513-514.

54 Ibid.

55 Miscellaneous writings of the late Hon'ble..., pp. 112-113.

56 Mahatma Phule Samagra Vangmaya, pp. 281-84, 296, 405; see also Tarkateertha Laxman Shastri Joshi, Jyotirao Phule: Rebel and Rationalist, Rationalists of Maharashtra, Renaissance Institute, Dehradun 1962, pp. 15-28; Gail Omvedt, Cultural Revolt in Colonial Society. The non-Brahman Movement in Western India, 1873-1930, Bombay 1976.

57 Pradhan, Gopal Ganesh Agarkar..., p. 40.

58 Cf. Charles Heimsath, Indian Nationalism and Hindu Social reform, Bombay 1964, pp. 147-175; also Richard Tucker, Ranade and the Roots of Indian Nationalism, Bombay 1977.

59 See A note on the Age of Marriage and its consumation according to Hindu Religious Law with four Appendices, Collected Works Sir R.G. Bhandarkar, II, p. 545.

60 Cited in: H.A. Phadke, R.G. Bhandarkar, New Delhi 1968, p. 69.

61 The Times of India, 22 August 1884.

62 Cited by: Sir Narayan Chandavarkar, The Speeches and writings of Sir Narayan Chandavarkar, ed. by L.V. Kaikini, Bombay 1911, p. 29.

# Separate Electorates: Separate Identities? Experiences from Colonial India

Dick Kooiman

## The Problem of Communal Identities

Communal identities are always in the process of changing. They have changed in the past and they will change in the future. Nobody will care to challenge these truisms. What remains to be discussed, and that is complicated enough, is what we actually mean by communal identities - the definition problem - and what the factors are that make them change, and for what purpose - the historical question. This contribution will address the change of communal identities in India under British colonialism, especially in relation to the gradual introduction of systems of election and representation.

The provision of separate electorates for religious minorities has often been put forward as a powerful factor in the formation of communal identities. This distribution of political privilege along lines of religion is alleged to have divided people in mutually exclusive, often hostile, if not openly fighting social groups, culminating in regular outbursts of communal violence. Since these hotly disputed separate electorates were a phenomenon peculiar to the provinces under direct colonial rule, a comparison will be made between constitutional developments in British India and those in one of the major indirectly administered areas, the Princely State of Travancore which was largely left free to make its own electoral arrangements. Such a comparative analysis may serve to improve our understanding of the emergence and change of communal identities and also contribute to the mapping out of the uneven geographical spread of communalism in India, the need of which was recently expressed by Ian Copland.[1]

Any attempt to define a community is in fact an attempt to draw a boundary line demarcating one particular community from another. These boundaries are defined by one or more attributes shared by all those who together make up that community. People belonging to a national community are defined by a shared history and a common destiny for the future and strive for that reason after the establishment or maintenance of their own independent state. Other communities can be identified by the application of religion or caste as the defining lines of demarcation. Such communities are not territorial but comprise the faithful or caste-fellows who live scattered over a wider area or in the midst of people belonging to other religions or castes. In the same way, we may discern linguistic, cultural, tribal or racial communities.

Another important observation to make is that the boundary lines demarcating communities seldom or never coincide. All Malayalam speakers may belong to one linguistic group that transcends the territory of Travancore but at the same time they are clearly distinct from Tamil speakers within the same state. Hindu *Nayars* and Syrian Christians in Travancore are serious rivals in many respects, but they both share a ritual contempt for the lowest Hindu castes. The point is clear. The more communal boundaries concur, the stronger the resulting communal cohesion will be, but this optimum result may be approximated but is never achieved. In actual practice, the culturally defined shared attributes represent competing criteria and do not define one single group.[2] One individual can belong to several communities at the same time and can be mobilised along different, mutually exclusive lines of communal identity. According to David Washbrook, this lack of correspondence between territory, religion, language etc. is the reason why communal politics in India have been so remarkably ineffective.[3]

The inevitable result of this argument must be that a community is never a socially homogeneous unit. Nevertheless, the distinctive characteristic of the phenomenon called communalism is the belief that a group of people, because they have one ascriptive identity in common (religion, language), also share common interests in all other fields (political, economic). By placing all emphasis on one shared cultural attribute, an earnest attempt is made to overcome a disturbing internal diversity by a higher but largely 'imagined unity'. That imagined unity may refer to a nation, as studied by Anderson[4] but also to a religious, caste or linguistic community.

A collective communal identity is not a pre-given primordial social fact, even though it has often been thought useful to seek the sanction of history. Therefore, communal identity is not like the proverbial sleeping beauty who only waits for the magic touch to be awakened and mobilized into social consciousness. Communal distinctions, however, are indeed pre-given. They exist, even where people are not inclined to attach much importance to them. Activation of these boundaries takes place in a process of social identification, in what de Swaan has called the dialectics of inclusion and exclusion. In mass politics communities emerge in a dynamics of competitive group solidarities, when political entrepreneurs operate to mobilize one or another structure of identification.[5] Following this line of reasoning, the emergence of communalism means that one particular set of social boundaries is deliberately activated and imparted with a new meaning at the cost of other possible identities.

Language offers an important structure of identification. In an attempt to bring its political message home to all people the Indian National Congress re-organised its branches on a linguistic basis (Nagpur Constitution 1920) and recommended that India should be a federation of linguistic provinces (Nehru Report 1928). However, the political use of language with its tremendous potential for group mobilisation was not free from danger. After Independence an official States Re-organisation Commission reported (1955) that culture-based regionalism, centering on language communities, represented values more easily intelligible to the average Indian, than did Indian nationalism. In line with this finding the Indian Union was eventually reorganized by drawing the boundaries of each state so that they conformed with the region of a dominant language. The whole process was accompanied by widespread rioting and violence. Yet, regional leaders are still raising the demand for linguistic reorganisation, not seldom with a view to the local power and employment structure.[6]

Religion is another variable of communal identity. The decision of the Indian colonial government to introduce religion and caste as categories for administrative and electoral classification infused political meaning into concepts like Hindu vs. Muslim and Brahmin vs. non-Brahmin. Under colonialism, the religious definition of community has become so pre-dominant that in common parlance communalism has become more or less synonymous with communalism of the religion and caste variety only. Pandey has noted that in popular, and academic usage, the term has sometimes been narrowed even further to refer to 'Muslim' communalism only.[7]

The problem of communalism, however, is not something peculiar to Indian Muslims or even to India, although the terminology used seems to suggest such a geographical limitation. Elsewhere, similar social phenomena are studied under different terms like ethnic policies, religious fundamentalism, tribalism or Balkanization. What we urgently need is a new social science vocabulary to lift these social movements out of their narrow regional and cultural confines and see them as sharing the same basic structure. What I propose, in the absence of such a new vocabulary, is to expand the term communalism to cover all group formations where social and cultural pluralism is subsumed under one single factor of identity, in India as well as in Northern Ireland or former Yugoslavia.

Speaking about communal identities under colonialism, two noteworthy trends in the historiography of modern India can be discerned. One school of historians, attributing a natural quality to the unity of India and accepting the official archives as the primary source of historical information, is strongly inclined to adopt the national community as the final end-in-view. Gyanendra Pandey has recently pointed out, that this approach tends to represent the history of India since the early nineteenth century as the biography of the emerging nation-state, relegating all references to other communal controversies to the shadow of the sidelines.[8]

A second, not less noteworthy historiographical trend however, is the tendency among historians to place much emphasis upon the construction of caste and religious identities under colonial rule with the result that the history of modern India tends to become the history of emerging communalism. In a recent book, the same Gyanendra Pandey has taken the well-known stand that the attempts of the colonial power to classify the people of India in categories of caste and religion and to rule them accordingly has largely contributed to the present conflicts between Hindus and Muslims in India.[9] To argue that religious communalism is an outcome of the colonial age, however, relies too much on the implicit assumption of an 'unspoilt past of inter-communal harmony', which was questioned by Dipankar

Gupta in a review of this book.[10] It may also tend to overestimate the impact of colonial rule on Indian society.

The Indian national movement and the Government of independent India have not succeeded in establishing a territorially integrated and consolidated nation-state. It would have been too much to ask. India is still struggling to build a national community out of the diverse and often discordant elements of a population that was once forcefully brought together under British paramountcy. In the same way, communal diversity or even communalism is not the dubious achievement of a malign colonial power seeking to impose its political dominance over the subcontinent. Cultural pluriformity has always been the hall-mark of the subcontinent's history and the origin of many cultural attributes that communities now cherish as their particular identity can be traced to pre-colonial times.

## Communalism and the Electoral System

The equation of communalism with caste and religion may be seen as part of the colonial heritage. Many writers have tried to establish a direct connection between colonial policies and present-day religious communalism. Even if we assume that many laws and regulations by the Raj were taken solely for reasons of bureaucratic and administrative efficiency, the allotment of political rights along lines of caste and religion was less innocent and open for more diverse interpretation.

The potentially most divisive means for the distribution of political privilege were the systems of nomination and election to the representative councils that were gradually introduced from the end of the 19th century. It was a long and arduous way that led from nomination by the Government to election by a fully enfranchised population with reserved seats and separate electorates as important intermediate stages. In the case of reservation, seats were reserved in one or more constituencies for which only members of one particular community could stand as candidate. In case of separate electorates, voters belonging to a certain community were placed in a separate constituency in which only members of that particular community were entitled to vote and to stand as candidate.

The institution of separate electorates has come in for wide-spread criticism, especially in nationalist quarters and handbooks of history. Bipan Chandra views the separate electorates as a particularly strong instrument of British divide-and-rule and is definitely of the opinion that colonial policies bear special responsibility for the growth of communalism in India.[11] Sumit Sarkar observes that nationalists have tended to exaggerate the element of conscious British responsibility in dividing Indian elite groups along communal lines. Yet, he also agrees that communal consciousness was bred and often directly fostered by colonialism. Separate electorates inevitably hardened the lines of division by forcing community leaders to cultivate their own religious followings alone.[12] Both authors agree, however, that British policy of divide-and-rule could only succeed because of the many social divisions existing within Indian society.

We have to recognize, however, that these internal divisions have not disappeared with the departure of the British. After Independence the Constitutional Assembly introduced adult suffrage unqualified by separate electorates, proportional representation or religious identity. Only the reservation of seats for Scheduled Castes and Scheduled Tribes has remained as well as the preferential treatment of a large number of backward or otherwise disprivileged communities in educational institutions and governmental services. Yet, communal tensions and conflicts persist, recently culminating in disastrous mass violence after the demolition of Ayodhya's Babri Masjid by militant Hindus.

It may seem tempting to attribute the persistence of HinduMuslim conflict to the lingering effects of a mischievous colonial policy. However, after more than 45 years of independence and the complete disappearance of separate electorates one might have expected that this unfortunate colonial heritage is at last gradually disappearing from the Indian scene. Nevertheless, communalism of the caste and religion variety has become a recurrent feature of Indian public life. The conclusion must be that a pluralist theory of society was not only a valuable aid to the maintenance of imperial rule but also an effective tool for the administration of the independent state. The organisation of the Indian Union is such that it remains rewarding for communal and other interest groups to mobilize themselves in a contest for particular favours which places them in competition to each other more than in common opposition to the national government. There is even a political logic to the use and continuance of preferential policies which build a vested interest in their own perpetuation and have become virtually irreversible, since policy-makers have redefined the disprivileged to encompass the majority.[13]

This continuity between colonial past and independent present will help us to reduce the strong emphasis on the relation between religious communalism and colonial divideand-rule policies exemplified in separate electorates. To extend this argument, we may also try to make a synchronic comparison between political developments in British India and the semi-autonomous Princely States. The state of Travancore with its rich diversity of castes and religions may offer interesting material for a comparative analysis. In 1901 its population numbered 70 per cent Hindus, 23,5 per cent Christians and 6,5 per cent Muslims, and the state was famous for its high rate of literacy, flourishing local press and active political participation.

As an Indian Kingdom, Travancore on the south-western tip of the Indian peninsula, was forced to recognize British paramount power. In exchange, it was allowed to retain its own administration on the condition only that the *Maharaja* and his Dewan agreed to rule in accordance with the advice that a British Resident might occasionally think it necessary to offer. During the second half of the 19th century, outside interference through British Residents was increasingly losing importance as an instrument of imperial policy and Travancore was in fact left free to manage its own internal affairs. In the next section we will briefly discuss the major constitutional reforms that have been introduced in British India and Travancore with special attention to provisions of communal representation.

## A Short History of Constitutional Reform

The Indian Councils Acts of 1892 did not yet provide for any constitutional safeguard of minority interests. There was a strong body of opinion in favour of some form of communal representation, but the small size of the Provincial Councils made implementation impracticable. Membership was by nomination only. Yet, there was indirect election in so far as most of the non-official members were nominated on recommendation by non-religious bodies like local boards and chambers of commerce. The functions of the new Councils were more than merely legislative, as they had also the powers to discuss the budget and address questions to the Executive.[14]

In 1888 Travancore was the first Princely State to introduce a Legislative Council, a deliberative body for purposes of legislation and without administrative functions.[15] To afford his people a more direct opportunity of expressing their wants and wishes, the Maharaja granted them also a Popular Assembly (1904). This Assembly was primarily aimed at promoting good understanding between Travancore's many castes and communities whose growing antagonisms were causing the state much trouble. Membership of Council and Assembly was by nomination, but the Assembly obtained the right to recommend, and thus indirectly elect, the non-official members of the Legislative Council.[16]

Political safeguards to minorities in British India were first elaborated in the Morley-Minto reforms of 1909. These safeguards gave statutory recognition to communal representation by providing for separate electorates for the Muslim minority. For the nationalists the emphasis on religious identity as an important political consideration was a clear case of divide-and-rule and the available evidence seems to prove them right.[17]

One of the major aims behind the political reforms was the rallying of the loyal elements as a counterpoise to the Congress. The most effective counterpoise at that moment were the Muslims. But another useful ally were the Rulers of the Indian Princely States who were cultivated as the most trusted pillars supporting the imperial edifice in the face of nationalist danger. Therefore, the Viceroy, Lord Minto, stressed a policy of non-interference and stated that administrative reforms in the states should not be imposed from outside, but had to emanate from the State governments themselves in harmony with their own traditions.[18] Political reform might not be part of that tradition and accordingly, Travancore confined itself to an increase in the number of Assembly members including the nominations from backward castes.

Under the Government of India Act (1919), initiated by their Lordships Montague and Chelmsford, the principle of communal representation was extended more widely both in the centre and the province. Separate electorates were also provided for Indian Christians, Sikhs, Anlo-Indians and Europeans. As far as election was concerned, the subdivision of the electorate did not stop at the separation of Hindus from Muslims, Sikhs and Christians. Among the Hindus, non-Brahmins had been asking for a greater share of political representation and during the massive anti-imperialist upsurge after World War I their demand was recognised by the British with the same suspicious ease as the Muslim demand was in 1909. Within the general body of non-Muslims a minimum of seats was reserved and allotted to the non-Brahmins who, although majority communities, might otherwise remain underrepresented.

Besides elected and official members there remained a third category of members, those nominated by the Governor out of non-officials. These nominations were meant to secure a spokesman for a class or community which would otherwise go unrepresented or to fill up an undesirable gap. Thus the Depressed Classes or untouchables achieved representation, not by reservation but by nomination, in the same way as the Pulayas and others were nominated to the Travancore Assembly.

Asked for their opinion on the proposed legislation, the Travancore *Darbar* noted with grateful approval the explicit assurances that the rights and dignities of the Indian Rulers would be respected and maintained. It expressed only a warning that what it called 'the popular element' in the proposed reconstitution 'may not be ... quite in harmony with the political relationship between the Government of India and the Princes'[19]. There was not the slightest reason for uneasiness, however, and all remaining doubts were finally removed by the Secretary of State who pointed out in the House of Commons that measures of political reform suitable for British India might not be equally suitable for the different conditions in Indian states.[20]

Travancore used this freedom to remodel its Legislative Council in several stages till it got its final shape in 1921. The franchise was considerably broadened and extended to women, yet the number of people entitled to vote was only somewhere between 2,5 per cent and 3 per cent of the population.[21] With the right to discuss the budget, move resolutions and ask questions the Travancore Council had much less powers than the Montford Councils in British India. The most important difference was the absence of any provision for communal electorates or seat reservation. The only comfort for communities who felt unjustly deprived of representation was the possibility that the Government might nominate one of their number to the remaining seats.

As the franchise qualification was mainly based on landed property, it was especially favourable to a community like the Nayars. In consequence, the Travancore Legislative Council after 1921 was controlled by the Nayars who numbered 16 per cent of the population but held the large majority of the 23 elected seats. Christians, including Syrians and the new converts of the Catholic and Protestant mission, numbered 32 per cent of the population but held only between four and seven seats and the other communities none or only one. As Nayars had also come to dominate the administrative services, this imbalance in the opportunity structure was greatly resented by the Christians, Ezhavas and Muslims. Therefore, prominent members of these communities articulated this resentment by appealing to ascriptive identities of caste and religion to mobilise support. From the 1920s the main thrust of this struggle was leveled at the question of legislative reform.

In response to a growing agitation all over the state the Travancore Government announced its reform proposals in October 1932. The reforms introduced a bi-cameral system consisting of an Assembly and State Council which both had the power to initiate and pass legislation. Franchise for both Houses was on the same footing but at higher rates for the Council. In all, only about 3 per cent of the population was enfranchised which was hardly an increase compared to the 1921 reforms.[22]

These reforms fell far short of the political aspirations that had been coming up among the many disadvantaged communities. The main disillusionment for the politically conscious Christians, Ezhavas and Muslims was the government's forthright rejection of communal electorates and even reserved seats. From the outset, the Government made it perfectly clear that it considered such measures to be unsuited to conditions in Travancore, where they could only contribute to the creation and multiplication of existing communal cleavages and to the promotion of sectional interests, endangering the larger interests of the state. In its stead the Government preferred direct election combined with the compensatory principle of nomination.

The communal organisations of Christians, Ezhavas and Muslims, which had joined forces in a Joint Political Conference (JPC), rejected representation by government nomination as an inadequate compensation for representation by election. The demand for communal electorates was dropped but the JPC argued instead with increased vigour for reservation of seats in joint electorates (or multi-member constituencies) for the major communities in proportion to their share in the population. A few weeks later the JPC passed the important abstention resolution, saying that the Christian, Ezhava and Muslim communities were determined to abstain from taking any part in the forthcoming elections so long as Government did not make provision for communal representation in the legislature.[23] The Abstentionists contended that the reforms proposed by the government in fact placed all other communities under the dominance of one group, the Nayars, and that this unequal distribution of power was the basic cause of the present intensification of communal strife and division. Apart from these fundamental differences, there was the practical problem of how the territorial extent of constituencies could be so arranged as to secure exact proportional representation between all sections of the population. These and other reasons made the Government conclude that the proposed electoral reforms should first be given a fair trial before alterations could be taken up for consideration. The Travancore elections of 1933, however, turned out to be a poor show. Only a quarter of the general electorate voted and in most constituencies candidates were returned unopposed. The British Resident reported grudgingly that the Abstentionist Movement had achieved a considerable measure of success.[24]

In the meantime the long drawn-out process started by the installation of the Indian Statutory Commission had finally resulted in the Government of India Act of 1935. In this constitution communal representation was accepted as a regular feature, both in the legislature and in the public services. Seperate electorates for Muslims and other minority communities were maintained and extended, whereas the untouchables (Scheduled Castes) received reserved seats as agreed upon after Gandhi's Epic Fast.

In the same year 1935 the Government of Travancore decided to reconsider the thorny question of the revision of the electorates in order to to bring about a just and equitable representation in the legislature.[25] When the reforms were made publicly known, the Government explained that it could not conceive of a legislature in which the elected seats were parcelled out in strictly mathematical proportions among no less than 12 to 14 communities, as had been done shortly before in the administrative service. Therefore, the major contingent of seats remained to be filled in open competition which would involve a trial of strength between the major rivals, the Navars and the Syrian Christians.

The Travancore Government also thought it necessary to introduce seat reservation for those communities who were 14 numerically strong and politically conscious and yet by the manner of the distribution of their population in the state unable to command a majority in any constituency. Accordingly, Ezhayas, Muslims and Latin Catholics lost virtually all their nominated seats, but were given an increased number of reserved seats in the general constituencies. Finally, the Government appointed a Special Commissioner and instructed him to make detailed proposals regarding the principles of franchise and the delimitation of constituencies.[26]

On the strength of this Commissioner's recommendations the Government passed Orders (1936) widening the franchise and regrouping the constituencies. The enfranchised percentage of the population was raised to 10-12 per cent, about a sixth of the adult population, and a proportion similar to that in British India following the Government of India Act. The 43 existing electoral divisions were dissolved and the state was divided into 17 new multi-member constituencies returning 43 members to the Assembly and 10 similar divisions returning 16 members to the Council. These multi-member joint electorates included a number of seats having a reserved qualification.[27] The new delimitation was such that, in view of their voting strength, ten of the 29 general seats were likely to go to the

Nayars, ten to the Syrian Christians and four to other Hindu castes, leaving only five seats for really open competition. That meant that especially the Nayars had to face a painful loss of influence, which they accepted, at least for the moment, 'with remarkable good grace'[28].

The 1937 elections took place in a quiet atmosphere that was free of the more extreme manifestations of communal tension. The JPC captured 25 of the 48 elected seats in the new Assembly and became the largest single party. The protected communities gratefully secured their reserved seats and both Nayars and Syrian Christians succeeded in sending 12 of their number to the Assembly. However, there was no change in the constitutional set-up of the state. The powers of the legislature remained restricted and the executive offices of the Government remained firmly in the hands of the Maharaja and his Dewan, Sir C.P. Ramaswamy Iyer.

## Concluding Observations

From this short history of constitutional reform we may conclude that systems of political participation, election and communal representation were introduced in British India much earlier and on a much larger scale than in the highly literate and politically conscious Princely State of Travancore. Separate electorates were granted in British India as early as 1909 along with the first cautious steps towards direct election. They were easily conceded to Muslims who as the former ruling minority feared that constitutional reforms might reduce them into insignificance, and in 1919 extended to other minority groups like the Sikhs, Indian Christians and Anglo-Indians. There was no struggle needed to get separate electorates and Indian Christians even had serious misgivings about them.[29] In Travancore, on the other hand, no separate electorates were ever granted, although several communities joined in a desperate campaign to wrest them from a reluctant government.

Seat reservation was introduced in British India in 1919, first for the large group of non-Brahmins and later (1935) for the Scheduled Castes. In Travancore seat reservation had to wait for the reforms of 1935 and applied to Muslims, Ezhavas and Latin Christians only.

Nomination, initially the only way to council membership, came later to be used as a principle of distributive justice by allotting seats to groups that might otherwise have no representation. In British India nomination to council membership was finally abolished in 1935, when all seats were elected and non-official. In Travancore, on the other hand, the system of nomination was maintained and even after 1935 nominated members, both official and non-official, constituted a substantial part of council membership.

Although the State of Travancore was never forced to follow the constitutional experiments carried on in British India and the important fact that no separate electorates were ever introduced, the reports by British Residents abound with complaints that the population was 'unhappily stricken with the plague of communal animosities' and that communalism had intruded into every government department.[30] The Dewan, Sir C.P. Ramaswamy Iyer, was even of the opinion that people in Travancore were much more inclined to think and act in terms of a specific communal identity than was usual in British India.[31]

After Independence Travancore was first merged with the Princely State of Cochin and finally, together with the directly administered district of Malabar, incorporated into the new Malayalam-speaking state of Kerala. This new state, made up for the larger part of former Princedoms, has been more or less free from the violent communal outbursts that have plagued large parts of northern India. Yet, less overt but deeply ingrained, Kerala politics are marked by community-based political parties and votebanks. Some scholars even contend that Kerala politics should be understood as the extension of caste and religion to the public domain. There may be elements of each community in all political parties (with the exception of the Muslim League), yet all parties have come to be associated with particular communities and within each party factionalism expresses the deeper divisions of religion and caste.[32]

Communalism of religion and caste does not seem to have been a phenomenon that could be contained within the boundaries of the directly administered provinces, at least not in the southern part of the peninsula. If that conclusion is correct, electoral safeguards for religious groups or castes may have had less influence on the formation of communal identities than has generally been assumed. The emergence of communal identity feeling with all its concomitant strife and conflict is part of a large and complicated process in which many factors play a role. In conclusion we will have a look at the particular circumstances that prevailed in Travancore.

As the north of India the south-western part of the subcontinent also accomodated a Muslim minority. These Muslims had not come overland as part of a Muslim conquest, but had peacefully settled as traders on the coast, especially in Malabar at a much earlier date. After the arrival of the European trading companies they had been ousted from their commercial strongholds and driven inland where they eked out a marginal existence as small traders and land labourers. Travancore accounted only for a small number of these Muslims (about 6 per cent). They cherished no memories of a glorious past as former rulers like their co-religionists in north India and had made no contribution to local state formations to boast of. When in the 18th century, Travancore rose as the single most powerful political force on this coast, it were the Syrian Christians who moved into the centre of the new political order. As Susan Baily[33] has shown, they proved to be trusted allies of the state as commercial agents, warriors and office-holders. In the 19th century the old political order collapsed under the restrictions imposed by British paramountcy and as part of the resulting disintegration the Syrians lost much of their privileged position. Supported by British Residents and Christian missionaries, who mistook Syrian decline as caused by age-long heathen suppression, they were able to exploit the new opportunities and emerged as the state's most literate and enterprising community. However, as non-Hindus they were ritually excluded from the most important offices of the state.

With a variation on the sanskritisation model, one may say that Syrians fitted a 'participation model' by their attempts to translate educational and economic achievement into political participation. Resenting their lack of influence, it was this group that started to clamour for political representation and government office. Their demands found no favourable response from the Travancore Government. The 19th century Census figures showed a steady increase in the number of Christians in the state. This increase was almost exclusively due to an inflow of converts from the lower Hindu ranks to Latin Catholicism and Protestantism, but it created an atmosphere of distrust and fear that (Syrian) Christians were going to take over the kingdom. Therefore, Government was not inclined to offer many concessions. Whereas in British India electoral safeguards to Muslims might help to sustain the empire, in Travancore political concessions to Syrians, the most prominent Christian community, were viewed as threatening the kingdom that became increasingly connected with Hindu orthodoxy.

Another important difference between British India and Travancore lay in the orientation of the political movement. In British India politics were dominated by the overarching theme of nationalism. Supported by a rising, educated middle class, the national movement aimed first at an Indianisation of the services and later at responsible government within the empire and full independence. The emphasis on a common struggle of the national community against colonial domination deferred the internal distribution of power to a later date. In spite of that, the national movement was continually threatened by newly emerging groups like the Non-Brahmins in Madras who feared that the political dominance of the Tamil Brahmins might continue even after independence. They demanded a larger share in the management of their own country right away and could depend on a favourable response on the part of the colonial government.

In Travancore, ruled by the Maharaja's government with all power vested in the Dewan, nationalism was much less effective as a rallying cry for the political movement. From the end of the 19th century Nayars had been able to monopolise most key positions in the centre of power alongside the small group of foreign Brahmins. Their preponderance in the state's representative institutions and administrative services was threatened by other aspiring groups, first the Syrian Christians and later also the Ezhavas and the Muslims. These groups were pressing for a redistribution of political privilege within an already largely Indian bureaucracy. In this internal power struggle the role of political parties was taken up by communal organisations. In British India, separate electorates were granted by a Government that could pose as an impartial arbiter between warring communities and at the same time serve its imperial interests by a selective conferment of political rights to those who deserved. In Travancore, with only a handful of British officials, the administration itself had become the property of a few high caste communities who were the Maharaja's most loyal supporters and here the struggle for power assumed almost inevitably a more directly communal character.

There is still another point that might be relevant to our discussion. The Report of the Indian Statutory Commission did not merely explain Hindu-Muslim tension away by the usual reference to 'religious practices which are only too likely to provoke mutual ill-feeling'[34]. It also pointed at a deeper cause: so long as people had no part in the conduct of their own government, there was little for members of one community to fear from the predominance of the other. The gradual introduction of constitutional reforms, however, had greatly stimulated communal tension as it aroused anxieties and ambitions among many communities by the prospect of their place in India's future political set-up. In the same vein the report concluded that the comparative absence of communal strife in the Indian States might be explained by political retardation.[35]

The observation that a devolution of political power, however modest, might arouse communal rivalry should not be confined to British India. As we have seen in the case of Travancore, the mere announcement of political reform in 1932 sparked off a wave of communal unrest. The relative progressive pattern of socio-economic development in this Indian State had given rise to great expectations of political participation. The resentment harboured by groups who felt left out, still reinforced by large-scale educated unemployment, created a climate suitable to the rise of communal animosities. Compared to Travancore, Hyderabad State stands out much more clearly as a case of political retardation. Until the 1930s it had remained a feudal preserve with a low level of literacy and no representative institutions worth the name. But in spite of this conspicuous contrast in existing conditions, communal tensions in Hyderabad also rose to fever-pitch immediately after the appointment of an official committee for constitutional reforms in 1937 with political leaders starting to build parties and mobilise support to get their share in the new structure of power.[36]

However, the introduction of constitutional reforms was not the only clue to the emergence of communalism, and the directly administered districts were not always the obvious scene of communal strife. Also needed was an internal social structure where local people considered the reforms sufficiently valuable to compete for their prospective benefits. In case of Malabar District the most important thing to note was the absence of enterprising communities and an elaborate bureaucracy. In this rather backward agrarian society almost all sections of the agrarian population felt the oppressive exploitation of the agrarian system. The political movement that came into existence here was secular in nature and largely bent on questions of tenancy reform.[37] This brief exposition will make it sufficiently clear that there is still much research to be done before we can draw with some confidence a chronological and geographical map of communalism in India.

It has been argued, and quoted above, that the introduction of separate electorates in British India has greatly contributed to the communal tensions and conflicts that still haunt Indian public life. The institution of this electoral system made it politically rewarding for aspiring leaders to emphasize ascriptive similarities to the extent that people have come to perceive themselves primarily as part of a particular community rather than as citizens of a larger national state. Yet, one might wonder how far this reasoning really holds true.

In case of separate electorates people are indeed grouped together as one constituency on the basis of religion, and religious distinctions might harden and change into much broader antagonisms. There is however no compelling need to appeal to religious values and interests in this electoral system, as both voter and candidate belong to the same creed and there are no rival communities competing for the same seats. In general constituencies with open competition the invocation of religious or caste affiliation is a risky and ambiguous venture, as it might attract some and alienate others. However, the system introduced in Travancore in 1935 had an inherent need to mobilise sentiments of religion and caste. The constituencies were delimited in such a way that major communities like Syrians and Nayars might gain a number of seats commensurate to their population ratio, if only all Syrians and Nayars in their respective majority constituencies would vote for a candidate from their own community. The results of the 1937 elections proved that this message was not lost on the enfranchised members of these communities. Maybe, we touch here on one of the major reasons for the prevailing communalism in this part of India: no separate electorates were granted but the specific delimitation of constituencies meant a clear invitation to political leaders to build their own communal votebanks as a kind of informal electorate.

The absence of communal electorates and the late introduction of seat reservation do not mean that the Travancore Government, personified by an all-powerful Dewan, was averse to the idea of divide-and-rule. It took only different forms and was less institutional in nature. During the Abstention movement the Government made streneous efforts to isolate the Syrian Christians as the main adversaries and to woo the non-caste Hindus. The Temple Entry 1935 was not only, and most probably not in the first place, meant to proclaim the universality of the Hindu faith and to remove a wrongful disability from a great mass of the population, as C.P. Ramwaswamy Iyer would have it,[38] but also a deliberate move to detach the Ezhavas from the forces of political opposition. At the same time the Government lent overt and less overt support to organisations that showed solicitude for the Depressed Classes who had not joined the Abstention movement. There is also a strong suspicion that the political movement among the Tamil-speakers in South Travancore received official encouragement, as this linguistic minority rejected responsible government in Travancore as another guise for the continued dominance of the Malayalam-speaking Nayars, Syrian Christians and Ezhavas from the north.[39]

Divide-and-rule was also used on an individual basis. As politics in Travancore were still largely based on personal networks and status considerations, the Government could by a calculating distribution of high appointments appease certain opponents, buy them over or split them. Just to quote one example, support to the Abstention movement from Syrian Catholics and Latin Catholics was considerably weakened, when two of their most prominent leaders were appointed to the State Council. This reveals that the existence of nominated seats in the legislature could also serve as an extremely useful device in the hands of the Government to reward loyalty and to divide the ranks of the opposition. An astute Dewan like C.P. Ramaswamy Iyer could, by a judicious use of the patronage under his command, succeed in carrying through much of his controversial policies. In the end the opposition combined in the Abstention movement fell victim to his clever tactics.

Finally, having an elaborate and largely Indian bureaucracy, the state of Travancore had its subjects much to offer in the field of educated employment. In 1931 no less than 60 per cent of all educated people worked in Government service. However, the benefits of official service were far from equally shared by all interested communities. Therefore, the internal power struggle was not only about seats in the legislature, which though prestigious were small in number, but also about the much more numerous positions in the administrative service. A first breach in this high caste bastion was made in 1922 when, under pressure from especially Catholic Syrians and Ezhavas, temple management was separated from the Revenue Department, thus removing the ritual barriers that had until then prevented all but the high caste Hindus from entering this most important government department. After that, the demand was raised that all communities should have proportional representation not only in the legislatives but also in the administration. In the 1930s the principle of communal representation in the services was accepted by the Government, at least in the lower grades of the service, whereas in the higher and intermediate grades efficiency as the primary criterion for recruitment was combined with certain safeguards against communal underrepresentation.[40] However, entrance to the services remained a highly contested issue and kept the flame of communal fervour burning, even after Independence when there was no question any more of communal electorates.

## Notes

1 Ian Copland, 'Communalism' in Princely India: the case of Hyderabad, 1930-1940. In: Modern Asian Studies, *XXII*(1988)4, p. 814.
2 Hamza Alavi/John Harris (eds.), Sociology of 'Developing Societies': South Asia, Houndmills 1989, p. 223.
3 David Washbrook, Ethnicity in Contemporary Indian Politics. In: Hamza Alavi/John Harris (eds.), Sociology of 'Developing Societies': South Asia, Houndmills 1989, p. 174. Washbrook, in fact, speaks of ethnicity instead of community.
4 Benedict R.O.G. Anderson, Imagined Communities, London 1991 (rev. ed.).
5 Abram de Swaan, Widening Circles of Identification: emotional concerns in sociogenetic perspective. In: Papers in Progress, Amsterdam *37*(1992)1, p. 11.
6 Robert Hardgrave, India: government and politics in a developing nation, Delhi 1979, p. 87ff.; Urmila Phadnis, Ethnicity and Nation-building in South Asia, New Delhi 1989, p. 89ff.
7 Gyanendra Pandey, The Construction of Communalism in Colonial North India, Delhi 1990, p. 9, note 13.
8 Gyanendra Pandey, In Defence of the Fragment: writing about Hindu-Muslim riots in India today. In: Economic and Political Weekly, *XXVI*(1991)11,12, p. 560.
9 Pandey, The Construction of Communalism.
10 Dipankar Gupta, Communalism and Nationalism in Colonial Indian. In: Economic and Political Weekly, *XXVIII*(1993)8-9, p. 339.
11 Bipan Chandra, India's Struggle for Independence 1857-1947, New Delhi 1988, p. 142, 409-409.
12 Sumit Sarkar, Modern India 1885-1947, Delhi e.a. 1983, p. 20-21, 59.
13 Washbrook, Ethnicity in Contemporary..., p. 175; Lelah Dushkin, Scheduled Castes Politicsn. In: J. Michael Mahar (ed.), The Untouchables in Contemporary India, Tucson 1972, p. 169-170; Myron Weiner/May F. Katzenstein, India's Preferential Policiesn. In: Alavi/Harris (eds.), Sociolovy of 'Developing Societies'..., Houndmills 1989, p. 202-203.
14 Report on Indian Constitutional Reforms, Calcutta 1918, p. 147; Report of the Indian Statutory Commission, vol.I, London 1930, p. 116.
15 Report on the Administration of Travancore, Trivandrum 1887-1888, p. 1.
16 M.J. Koshy, Constitutionalism in Travancore and Cochin, Trivandrum 1972, p. 18.
17 See Tara Chand, History of the Freedom Movement in India, vol.III, New Delhi 1972, p. 366, 398; Sarkar, Modern India, p. 141.
18 Sarkar, Modern India, p. 139.
19 Letter from Dewan M. Krishnan Nair 24-8-1918 in India Office Records (IOR), R/2(882/128).
20 Letter from Government of India, Foreign and Political Department 10-7-1919, in IOR, R/2(883/136).
21 Report on the Administration of Travancore, 1921-1922, p. 39; Travancore: The Present Political Problem, the All-Travancore Joint Political Congress, Calicut 1934, chapt. 1.
22 Travancore: The Present Political Problem, 1934, appendix: p. 64ff.
23 Text in: ibid., p. 36-37.
24 Resident's Fortnightly Report on the political situation in the Madras States for the second half of june 1933, IOR, R/1/1/2338.
25 Fortnightly Report for the first half of June 1935, IOR, R/1/1/2645; text of Government Press Communique in IOR, R/2(888/212).

26 Travancore Government Press Communique 17-8-1935, IOR, L/P&S/13,1283.
27 Travancore Government Orders 20-8-1936, IOR, R/2(888/217); Report on the Administration of Travancore, 1935-1936, p. 100-101; Louise Ouwerkerk, 'No Elephants for the Maharaja', unpublished ms, no date, p. 96, IOR, Mss.Eur.F 232.
28 Letter by Resident Garstin, 28-8-1936, IOR, VP&S/13,1283.
29 N. Austin John Manohar, The History of South India United Church 1908-1947, Unpublished Ph.D.Thesis University of Kerala, Thiruvananthapuram 1992, p. 153-155.
30 Quotation from A.G.G.'s Confidential Memorandum 26-11-1935, IOR, R/2(888/207). See also Colonel Field's Confidential Report to the Government of India 2-1-1935, IOR, R/2(888/210).
31 IOR, VP&S/13,1283.
32 K.V. Varughese, Growth of Communal Parties and Vote-banks: a challenge to secular democracy. In: Religion and Society *XXXIV*(1987)1; Robert L.Hardgrave, Essays in the Political Sociology of South India, New Delhi 1979, p. 209, 211.
33 Susan Baily, Saints, Goddesses and Kings: Muslims and Christians in South Indian society, 1700-1900, Cambridge 1989.
34 Indian Statutory Commission, vol.I, 1930, p. 26.
35 Ibid., p. 29.
36 Copland, 'Communalism' in Princely India, 1988, p. 801, 813.
37 P.K. Michael Tharakan, Communal Influence in Politics: historical background pertaining to Kerala, Religion and Society *XXXIV*(1987)1.
38 Sir C.P.Ramaswamy Iyer, Selections from the Writings and Speeches of Sachivottama Sir C.P. Ramaswami Aiyar, ewan of Travancore, Trivandrum 1945, p. 323-324.
39 Ouwerkerk Collection, File 47, IOR, Mss. Eur. F 232.
40 Dick Kooiman, Political Rivalry among Religious Communities: a ease study of communal reservations in India. In: Economic and Political Weekly *XXVIII*(1993)7, p. 287-295.

# Gab es eine Arbeiterkultur im kolonialen Indien?

Annemarie Hafner

In Europa ist die Arbeiterkulturforschung in Mode gekommen. In Südasien dagegen ist das bisher nur in Ansätzen der Fall. In seiner Ansprache als Präsident der Sektion Moderne Geschichte des Indischen Historikerkongresses 1982, in der Sabyasachi Bhattacharya den Forschungsstand zur indischen Arbeitergeschichte resümierte, erwähnte er den Begriff "Arbeiterkultur" als historiographische Kategorie noch nicht, wies aber auf die Notwendigkeit hin, dem bis dahin kaum untersuchten Problem der proletarischen Mentalität größere Aufmerksamkeit zu widmen.[1] In jüngster Zeit ist im Zusammenhang mit der Entwicklung der Stadtgeschichte in Indien auch die Erforschung der Kultur der "niederen Klassen" ausdrücklich als Aufgabe benannt worden.[2] Schon seit längerem haben jedoch die sogenannten "Unterschichten-Studien" eine Wendung weg von der bisher überwiegenden organisationsgeschichtlichen Sicht bei der Beschreibung der Arbeiterbewegung gefordert und eingeleitet. Man wandte sich statt dessen den Arbeitern selbst zu, um der zentralen Frage nach den Ursachen und Bedingungen für das Entstehen sozialer Bewegungen im industriell-städtischen Milieu nachzugehen.[3] Damit zeichnet sich in der südasiatischen Geschichtswissenschaft die gleiche "zentrifugale" Tendenz ab wie in der europäischen.[4] Sie lenkt ihre Aufmerksamkeit vom Zentrum hin zur Peripherie, von der Politik zur Gesellschaft und hier wieder zu den Rändern und Gruppen, von den Taten und Ereignissen zu Mentalitäten und Verhaltensweisen.

Die vorliegende Studie verwendet einen weitgefaßten Kulturbegriff, der sich an der britischen sozialgeschichtlichen Tradition orientiert, der aber auch in der deutschen Geschichtsschreibung breite Akzeptanz gefunden hat.[5] "Arbeiterkultur" wird als die Gesamtheit der proletarischen Lebensweise verstanden, d.h. es geht vor allem um den Lebensstil von Arbeitern, um ihre klassen- bzw. gruppenspezifischen Normen und Verhaltensweisen, Wertvorstellungen und Institutionen, mit denen sie ihr Zusammenleben, aber auch ihr Verhältnis zu anderen Klassen und Schichten gestalten. Dieser theoretische Ansatz schließt "Arbeiterkultur" im engeren Sinne, d.h. den kreativen Beitrag von Arbeitern auf den Gebieten der Dichtung, des Theaters usw. ein. Die Aktivitäten der kollektiven Interessenvertretungen der Arbeiter (Parteien und Gewerkschaften) im gesamten Konsum-, Freizeit-, Wohnungs- oder Bildungsbereich werden mit dem Begriff "Arbeiterbewegungskultur" erfaßt.[6]

Angesichts der thematischen Breite des beschriebenen Forschungsgegenstandes werden hier nur einige ausgewählte Aspekte der Arbeiterkultur im kolonialen Indien behandelt. Zunächst geht es um die Metamorphose des Bauern zum Industriearbeiter. Es wird untersucht, ob und auf welche Weise sich auf dem Weg "vom Feld in die Fabrik" eine soziokulturelle Identität herausbildete und wie sie sich in den Lebenswelten inner- und außerhalb der Fabrik manifestierte. Danach wird das Weiterwirken vorindustrieller Traditionen betrachtet. Dabei ist vor allem die Interaktion von traditionellen Strukturen (Kaste, religiöse Gemeinschaft, ethnisch-nationale Gruppierung) und dem neuen klassen- bzw. produktionsbedingten Beziehungsgeflecht im städtisch-industriellen Milieu von Interesse. Schließlich spielen auch Formen des sozialen Protests sowie sich neu herausbildende Traditionen der indischen Arbeiterbewegung für die aufgeworfene Fragestellung eine Rolle.

## Migrationswege

In der zweiten Hälfte des 19. Jahrhunderts prosperierten in Großbritannien Produktion und Handel. Für die britischen Unternehmer war die Sicherung der Rohstoffquellen und der Absatzmärkte von existentieller Bedeutung. Gleichzeitig veranlaßten die Verwertungsbedürfnisse des Kapitals die Bourgeoisie der Metropole, die Kronkolonie Indien in die kapitalistische Produktion einzubeziehen. Mit der Implantation industrieller Produktionsformen in Gestalt eines Eisenbahnnetzes, einer wachsenden Zahl von Kohlegruben und Goldminen sowie von Teeplantagen und industriellen Anlagen zur Verarbeitung von Rohstoffen (Jute, Wolle, Leder) schlugen in einer bislang traditionellen Gesellschaft kapitalistische Eigentums- und Ausbeutungsverhältnisse Wurzeln. Entsprechende Klassenkräfte - u.a. auch ein industrielles Proletariat - bildeten sich heraus.

Im Zusammenhang mit ihren spezifischen ökonomischen Funktionen gewannen einige städtische Siedlungen im späten 19. und frühen 20. Jahrhundert ein neues sozioökologisches Profil. Einige Küstenorte wurden zu modernen Produktions- und Handelsplätzen. Neben Industriezentren waren sie Hafenstädte, in denen sowohl die Fertigwaren aus Übersee anlandeten als auch die agrarischen Erzeugnisse und Rohstoffe ihren Weg zu den internationalen Märkten antraten. Bombay, Kalkutta und Madras beherbergten den Großteil der indischen Proletarier, die in Häfen, bei den Eisenbahnen oder in Fabriken ihre Arbeitskraft verkauften.

Im Kontext abhängiger Wirtschaften kam der Textilindustrie - vornehmlich der Baumwoll- und Juteindustrie - besondere Bedeutung zu. Im Jahre 1855 gründete George Acland die erste Jutefabrik in Rischra nahe Kalkutta. Damit nahm eine der großen Fabrikindustrien, in der Kapital eingesetzt wurde, um Rohstoffe zu verarbeiten, in Indien ihren Anfang. Sie stellte bis zum Ende der Kolonialzeit im wesentlichen eine Domäne des britischen, vor allem des schottischen, Unternehmertums dar und war auf den Raum Kalkutta und Umgebung begrenzt.[7] Die Jutefabriken Bengalens hatten für ihre Produkte quasi ein Monopol. Die Situation auf dem Weltmarkt bestimmte dementsprechend nicht nur ihren Wachstumsrhythmus, sondern entschied auch über das Wohl und Wehe der Jutearbeiter. Zwei Funktionäre der Jutearbeitergewerkschaft von Dundee, die 1924/25 die Arbeits- und Lebensbedingungen der Beschäftigten in den Kalkuttaer Jutefabriken studierten, zeigten sich schockiert über die "skandalös niedrigen" Löhne und die "einfach überwältigenden" Profite.[8] Dieser im Interesse der Metropole initiierte und ausschließlich exportorientierte Industriezweig ließ keinerlei industriellen Ableger aus sich hervorgehen.[9] Seine historisch bedeutsame Wirkung bestand in der Schaffung einer industriellen Arbeiterschaft. Seit 1879 wurde die Zahl der Jutearbeiter systematisch erfaßt. Sie betrug damals 27 494. 1939 wurden knapp 300 000 Jutearbeiter gezählt.[10]

Während die Juteindustrie in den ersten vier Dekaden, zwischen 1850 und 1890, die notwendigen Arbeitskräfte im wesentlichen in der lokalen Bevölkerung fand,[11] ging im Laufe der neunziger Jahre des 19. Jahrhunderts eine Veränderung vor sich. Diese Periode der raschen Expansion der Juteindustrie korrespondierte mit einem zahlenmäßigen Wachstum der Arbeiterschaft und war mit einem zunehmenden Migrantenstrom aus Bihar, den Vereinigten Provinzen und Orissa verbunden. 1906 stellte ein bengalischer Regierungsbericht fest: "Twenty years ago all the hands were Bengalis. These have gradually been replaced by Hindustanis from the United Provinces and Behar. These men have been found more regular, stronger, steadier and more satisfactory generally, so that at present in most of the mills two-thirds of the hands are composed of up-countrymen."[12] Das heißt: Ende des 19. und zu Beginn des 20. Jahrhunderts wurden mit der zunehmenden Nachfrage nach Arbeitskräften die Entfernungen, aus denen die Arbeiter angeworben wurden, immer größer. Schon der bereits angeführte Regierungsbericht von 1906 erwähnte Arbeiter aus Madras in Jutefabriken.[13] Der Bericht der Königlichen Kommission zu Arbeiterfragen von 1931 bestätigte diese Tendenz: "The bulk of the jute mill labour comes from the west of Bihar and the east of the United Provinces, a tract lying from 300 to 500 Miles away. Other important recruiting grounds are the equally distant districts in the north of the Madras Presidency and the east of the Central Provinces, while Orissa, which supplies labour of many kinds to Calcutta ... is also represented in the factories."[14] Es scheint, als hätten sich regelrechte "Migrationswege" herausgebildet. In dieser Weise läßt sich auch eine Aussage des schon zitierten bengalischen Regierungsberichts von 1906 interpretieren: "It looks probable that each mill has formed connections with certain districts, although these connections were not deliberately formed by the managers."[15]

Was wurde aus den bengalischen Arbeitern? Häufig wurde behauptet, daß Bengalis für Fabrikarbeit physisch nicht geeignet seien oder eine Aversion gegen körperliche Arbeit hätten. Der Bericht der Königlichen Kommission zu Arbeiterfragen von 1931 gab eine andere Antwort: "In recent years they, more than most Indian peoples, have been realising the possibilities which industry offers to skill, and their numbers are increasingly steadily in the skilled ranks and in the lighter types of factory labour."[16] Der Census von 1921 beinhaltete Daten, die dieser Aussage eine relativ sichere Grundlage gaben. Sie belegten, daß der Anteil der Bengalis unter den Facharbeitern mit 31 Prozent weit höher war als unter den nichtqualifizierten Arbeitern mit 17 Prozent.[17] Diese Ansicht hat sich durchgesetzt. Sie wird auch von der Cambridge Economic History of India geteilt: "And evidence suggests that the reduced importance of Bengali workers in the jute industry may be better explained by taking into account the response of urbanized groups to the advantages offered by the expanding occupational structure of Calcutta and its environs than by attributing unchanging cultural characteristics to Bengalis."[18] In den Juteunternehmen galt die gleiche Personalpolitik, wie sie von den kolonialen Eisenbahnverwaltungen gehandhabt wurde. Sie beschäftigten keine Inder in gehobenen Positionen. Leitende Tätigkeiten wurden ausschließlich von Europäern ausgeübt, "almost invariably Scotsmen, poor boys from the farms and towns about Dundee, who have learned their business in that mother of jute manufacture", wie Daniel Houston Buchanan schrieb.[19]

Im Bombay City Gazetteer von 1909 lesen wir: "Although to Bengal belongs the honour of opening the first factory for spinning cotton by steam-power in India, it is to the Bombay Presidency that we must turn for the home of the industry and to the island of Bombay for its highest development."[20] 1854 nahm die von dem Parsen Cowasjee Nanabhoy Davar gegründete Baumwolltextilfabrik als erste in Bombay die Produktion auf. Weitere folgten. Dieser Industriezweig wurde im wesentlichen vom einheimischen Unternehmertum in Gang gebracht und kontrolliert.[21] Sunil Kumar Sen meint: "If Calcutta was the capital of British capital, Bombay emerged as the capital of the rising Indian *bourgeoisie*."[22]

Zunächst stellten Spinnereien Garn für Handweber her, exportierten es aber auch nach China. Gegen Ende des 19. Jahrhunderts kamen Webereien hinzu. Damals wuchs die Baumwolltextilindustrie auch über Bombay hinaus. Das zweitgrößte Zentrum war Ahmedabad. Bedeutende Textilstandorte waren außerdem Kanpur, Nagpur und Madras. Besonders interessant verlief die Entwicklung der Stadt Scholapur. Sie war zunächst - am Endpunkt einer Eisenbahnlinie gelegen - ein wichtiger Sammel- und Umschlagplatz im Baumwolltransport und wandelte sich dann zur Industriestadt. Am Ende der Kolonialperiode wurde in Indien in 423 Fabriken mit etwa 10 Millionen Spindeln und 203 000 Webstühlen Baumwolle maschinell verarbeitet.[23] Daran waren etwa 650 000 Arbeiter beteiligt, die ein Viertel des gesamten Fabrikproletariats darstellten.[24] Etwa die Hälfte davon befand sich in der Provinz Bombay. Trotz ihres wirtschaftlichen Gewichts und ihrer massiven Konzentration in wenigen Zentren im Westen Indiens konnte die Baumwolltextilindustrie keine Impulse für eine weitergehende Industrialisierung aussenden. Weder ließ die Nachfrage nach industriellen Ausrüstungen eine Maschinenindustrie in Indien selbst entstehen, noch konnte sich durch den technologisch relativ einfachen Produktionsprozeß eine Facharbeiterschaft herausbilden. Die indigenen Besitzverhältnisse in diesem Industriezweig wirkten sich auf die Arbeitsbedingungen der Beschäftigten nicht positiv aus. Die internationale Konkurrenz sowie der Wettbewerb der einheimischen Industriellen untereinander wurde auf dem Rücken der Arbeiter ausgetragen. Das Ergebnis war eine gnadenlose Ausbeutung der un- oder angelernten, in ihrer Mehrheit migratorischen Arbeiterschaft. Die Maxime war "to substitute labor for capital wherever possible"[25]. Der Beweis dafür: Die Lohnkosten betrugen in den zwanziger und dreißiger Jahren zwischen 15 und 20 Prozent der Gesamtkosten.[26] Soziale Leistungen fehlten völlig.

Die Beschaffung der Arbeitskräfte überließen die Unternehmer dem "Jobber". Das war eine Art Vorarbeiter, dessen Aufgabe darin bestand, die erforderliche Anzahl von Arbeitern zu verpflichten und anzulernen.[27] Mangel an Arbeitskräften gab es nicht. Mit einer Ausnahme. Das war 1896, als die Einwohner Bombays, darunter auch die Fabrikarbeiter, die Stadt wegen einer Pestepidemie fluchtartig verließen. In der zweiten Hälfte des 19. Jahrhunderts holten sich die Jobber Leute aus entfernteren Gegenden. Nach dem 1. Weltkrieg warteten die Arbeitsuchenden schon vor den Fabriktoren. Wie andernorts bildeten sich im Lauf der Jahrzehnte regelrechte Migrationswege aus dem Landesinneren auch in Richtung Bombay heraus. Die Hafen- und Industriestadt bezog ihre Arbeitskräfte im wesentlichen aus ihrem Hinterland, d.h. aus Maharaschtra, und hier insbesondere aus dem Konkan und Dekan. Der sich auf diese Weise vergleichsweise einheitliche ethnisch-nationale Charakter der Arbeiterschaft[28] war von Konsequenz für die sich entwickelnde Arbeiterbewegung.

**Auf der Suche nach einer soziokulturellen Identität**

Im Zusammenhang mit der wirtschaftlichen Entwicklung entstanden im Verlauf des 19. und 20. Jahrhunderts in einigen indischen Städten Viertel mit einem ausgeprägten industriell-proletarischen Charakter. In Bombay z.B. siedelte sich die Mehrheit der Fabriken in drei Bezirken nördlich der alten "Eingeborenenstadt" an. Immer dichter bevölkerten die hier Beschäftigten dieses Gebiet. Um die Mitte der zwanziger Jahre brauchten etwa 90 Prozent der Textilarbeiter von ihrer Wohnung zu ihrem Arbeitsplatz nur etwa 15 Minuten Fußweg zurückzulegen. Die Bewohner nannten ihren Stadtteil "Girangaon", das bedeutet "Fabrikdorf".[29] Hier befand sich die Wiege der Bombayer Arbeiterkultur. Ähnliches vollzog sich auch in anderen Großstädten. Auch dort bildeten sich auf einem relativ deutlich abgegrenzten geographischen Terrain Industrie- und Arbeiterbezirke mit einem spezifischen städtisch-proletarischen Milieu und einer entsprechenden Lebensweise heraus.

Im Laufe etwa eines Jahrhunderts formierte sich in Indien ein permanentes Proletariat. Es stellte zwar nur einen Bruchteil der gesamten erwerbstätigen Bevölkerung dar,[30] übte aber durch seine Konzentration in den ökonomischen und politischen Zentren des Landes eine gesellschaftsverändernde und geschichtsgestaltende Wirkung aus. Der Verstetigungsprozeß der industriellen Arbeiterschaft läßt sich anhand der in unregelmäßigen Zeitabständen aufeinanderfolgenden Berichte von Untersuchungskommissionen zur Arbeiterfrage recht gut belegen. Noch 1908 stellte eine solche Kommission fest: "The habits of the Indian factory operative are determined by the fact that he is primarily an agriculturist, or a labourer on the land. ...his home is in the village from which he comes, not in the city in which he labours. ...There is as yet practically no factory population, such as exists in European countries, consisting of a large number of operatives trained from their youth to one particular class of work, and dependent upon employment at that work for their livelihood." Doch schon damals deutete sich eine Tendenz zur Verfestigung an. Der Bericht vermerkte: "...there are some indications that a class of factory operatives, detached from agriculture and village life, and depending largely or solely upon industrial employment, is beginning to be formed."[31] Die Königliche Kommission zur Untersuchung der Arbeiterfrage warf 1931 Unternehmern vor, den Mythos vom Landarbeiter zu pflegen, der nur zeitweise Hacke und Pflug verließ, um sein Einkommen durch kurzzeitige Industriearbeit in der Stadt aufzubessern. Aus dieser falschen Darstellung der Lage resultiere gelegentlich eine irrige Auffassung von der Arbeiterfrage. Nein, meinte die Königliche Komission, "the factory worker (is) not an agriculturist", aber durch Herkommen und Fühlen "villager at heart". Allerdings mache die Schicht, die keine Beziehungen zum Dorf pflege und die Stadt als ihr Zuhause betrachte nur einen kleinen Teil der gesamten Arbeiterschaft aus. Arbeiter dieser Art seien relativ zahlreich in Zentren der Baumwolltextilindustrie vertreten. Hier gehöre eine beträchtliche Zahl der Beschäftigten zur permanenten städtischen Bevölkerung.[32] Schließlich hob das Arbeitsuntersuchungskomitee 1946 seine Ergebniss deutlich von denen seiner Vorläufer ab, indem es feststellte: "In recent years ... there has been a greater concentration of the working-class population in industrial areas and this has led to a rise of an industrial proletariat in most cities, which is prepared to stick to the town to a greater extent than before, to fight for its legitimate rights, and to seek its livelihood in urban rather than rural areas."[33]

Die Industriearbeiter *in spe* entstammten drei Schichten der ländlichen Bevölkerung. Erstens hielten Angehörige der unteren Schichten der Bauernschaft, darunter vor allem Pächter, dem zunehmenden ökonomischen Druck nicht stand und wanderten in die Städte ab. Zweitens kamen Angehörige niedriger Dienstleistungskasten und Unberührbare, die traditionell vom Landbesitz ausgeschlossen waren. Und drittens waren es Nachkommen städtischer, unter der Herrschaft der Ostindien-Kompanie aufs Land zurückgedrängter, wie auch dörfliche, durch die Konkurrenz mit billigeren Industriewaren ruinierte Handwerker.[34]

Regierungsbeamten und Sozialwissenschaftlern fielen die jahrzehntelangen engen Beziehungen von Industriearbeitern zum Dorf auf. Unterschiedliche Erklärungen und Schlußfolgerungen wurden angeboten. Einige sahen die Ursache in den menschenunwürdigen Arbeits- und Lebensbedingungen in den Städten, andere betonten soziopsychologische Gründe. Der indische Arbeiter liebe die Veränderung, hieß es, oder, er sei im Herzen ein Bauer. Wahrscheinlich stimmte es, daß Dörfler, die eine Beschäftigung in der Industrie annahmen, die Hoffnung hegten, eines Tages für immer die Stadt zu verlassen und ein Stück Land ihr eigen nennen zu können.[35]

Konnte ein Mensch in einer überwiegend agrarischen Gesellschaft anders empfinden? Welchen Traum träumte ein Arbeiter, der keine Sicherheit des Arbeitsplatzes kannte, der seine Familie nicht um sich haben und seinen Kindern keine Ausbildung zukommen lassen konnte, und dem selbst in der Fabrik ein beruflicher Aufstieg verwehrt war?[36] Die Klagen über die häufige Abwesenheit der Arbeiter haben aber zu einer Fehlinterpretation ihrer Bindungen an das Dorf geführt und mündeten in der idyllischen Vorstellung von einer Arbeiter- cum Bauern-Existenz, deren Seiten beliebig gewechselt werden konnten. Dabei hatten Analysen nachgewiesen, daß nur einige wenige städtische Arbeiter selbst ein Einkommen aus der agrarischen Produktion bezogen. Die Mehrheit hatte durch die dörfliche Verwandtschaft, die Landstücke besaß oder bearbeitete, nur ein indirektes Verhältnis zu Grund und Boden.[37] Die periodische Rückkehr des städtischen Arbeiters aufs Land bzw. seine dauerhafte Bindung ans Dorf gaben aber dem Kolonialstaat sowie den ausländischen und einheimischen Unternehmern Argumente in die Hand, mit denen sie ihre Niedriglohnpolitik verteidigten. Mit dem Hinweis auf die Funktion des Dorfes als "soziales Auffangnetz" werteten offizielle Beobachter den ununterbrochenen Kontakt des Industrieproletariats zum Land positiv. Sie empfahlen, diese Verbindung nicht zu unterminieren, sondern zu unterstützen und nach Möglichkeit zu regulieren.[38]

Heute hat sich die Erkenntnis durchgesetzt, daß die intakten Verbindungen des Industriearbeiters zum Dorf einen Überlebensmechanismus darstellten, der aus dem System der kolonialkapitalistischen Ausbeutung erwuchs. Der Industriearbeiter erhielt nur einen Lohn, der die "Verewigung der Arbeitskraft"[39], d.h. die Ersetzung der verschlissenen Arbeitskräfte durch neue, nicht berücksichtigte und gerade ausreichte, ihn selbst zu erhalten. Wenn er arbeitslos oder arbeitsunfähig wurde, war er gezwungen, ins Dorf zurückzukehren.

Das Pendeln zwischen Dorf und Stadt war ein Charakteristikum der Industriearbeit im kolonialen Indien. Sie erhielt dadurch einen zyklischen Charakter. Arbeiter hielten Kontakt zu ihren Familien, die im Dorf zurückgeblieben waren. Wie oft sie eine Reise ins Heimatdorf unternahmen, hing von ihren finanziellen Möglichkeiten ab. Vorzugsweise legten sie ihre Besuche in die Erntezeit. "The most predominant cause of workers' visits to their homes in villages does not appear to be cultivation of land so much as seeing relatives and friends, attending marriages and festivals, although such visits often coincide with the festival season such as Holi, Pujas, etc.", stellte das Arbeitsuntersuchungskomitee 1946 fest.[40] So reflektierten die periodischen Aufenthalte im Dorf auch "a strong emotional attachment and sense of belonging to the kin group back home", resümierte Chitra Joshi ihre Betrachtungen zum sozialen Milieu der Textilarbeiter in Kanpur.[41] Der Vollzug religiöser Riten bei Geburten, Hochzeiten oder Totenfeiern hielt die überlieferte Erlebnis- und Gedankenwelt in den Köpfen der städtischen Arbeiter am Leben. Sie bot Halt und Zuflucht in einer bedrohlichen Umwelt.

Nicht nur die fortdauernden Beziehungen zum Dorf verliehen den sogenannten primordialen Loyalitäten Bestand. Auch das sich neu entwickelnde soziale Beziehungsgeflecht in der Stadt, sowohl in der Arbeitswelt als auch im Wohnbereich, wurde durch Bedingungen geprägt, die traditionelle Strukturen und entsprechende Verhaltensweisen konservierten. Ursächliche Bedeutung kam dabei der Methode der Anwerbung von Arbeitskräften - dem sogenannten Jobber-System - zu.[42] Jobber - die Mittelsmänner zwischen Arbeiter und Manager - rekrutierten die Arbeitskräfte für bestimmte Produktionsaufgaben bzw. Betriebseinheiten entsprechend ihrer regionalen oder Kastenherkunft bzw. aufgrund von Verwandtschaftsbeziehungen im weitesten Sinne. Auf diese Weise ergaben sich auf der untersten Produktionsebene sozial relativ homogene Strukturen. Gleichzeitig reproduzierte die strategische Rolle, die das soziale und familiäre Netzwerk sowie das solidarische Kastenverhalten für den Zugang zu industriellen Arbeitsplätzen spielten, die traditionelle Segmentation.

Die Industriezentren erwiesen sich nicht als die großen "Schmelztiegel" der Kultur. Die Zwänge der gemeinsamen Fabrikarbeit sowie des städtischen Wohnens modifizierten aber die strenge Kastentrennung und schliffen die scharfen Grate der Diskriminierung ab, denen die Angehörigen der Unberührbarenkasten in den Dörfern ausgesetzt waren.[43] Dennoch: Die Tendenz der Absonderung zwischen den verschiedenen Gemeinschaften im privaten Bereich blieb erhalten. Die räumliche Ordnung der Wohnviertel zeigte ein allgemeines Muster: zum einen erfolgte die Trennung zwischen Hindus und Muslims, zum anderen zwischen Hindus der oberen und der unteren Kasten. Kastenvorurteile hielten sich am hartnäckigsten im privaten und Freizeitbereich. Kommensalitätsregeln wurden nach Möglichkeit befolgt, und ihre arbeitsfreie Zeit verbrachten die Angehörigen unterschiedlicher Gemeinschaften in der Regel getrennt voneinander.[44]

Die fortdauernde Existenz primordialer Loyalitäten bei Industriearbeitern wurde in den letzten Jahren in der geschichtswissenschaftlichen Literatur untersucht. Das Problem ist umstritten und findet unterschiedliche Erklärungen. Zum einen wird ihr Fortbestand aus der Eigenart der indischen Zivilisation hergeleitet. Man ist der Ansicht, das das Endziel der "Moderne" in Indien nicht die säkulare Arbeiterklasse in einem säkularen Staat sein könne, sondern Gemeinschaftsidentitäten mit den ihnen innenwohnenden Engherzigkeiten und Ungleichheiten ihren Platz behaupten werden. Für die Kolonialperiode gilt die Auffassung, daß vorkapitalistische Strukturen und feudale Verhaltensweisen in das industrielle Milieu transferiert wurden, wo sie sich reproduzierten. Eine andere Interpretation betont den Übergangscharakter der Gesellschaft. Sie legt Wert auf den Umstand, daß kapitalistische Verhältnisse und bürgerliche Normen in Indien Fuß faßten, unter kolonialen Bedingungen aber die vorindustriellen Verhaltensweisen nicht aufhoben, sondern modifizierten und sich mit neuen gesellschaftlichen Strukturen und Verhaltensmustern verbanden. So schloß - im Falle der industriellen Arbeiterschaft - partikularistisches, d.h. auf die Kaste oder religiöse Gemeinschaft orientiertes Bewußtsein ein neues, auf die Klasse bezogenes Verhalten nicht aus.[45]

## Alltagskultur

Der weite Problemkreis des Alltagslebens von Industriearbeitern im kolonialen Indien wurde bisher kaum thematisiert. Es fehlen zusammenfassende Darstellungen ihres Freizeit- und Geselligkeitsverhaltens, ihrer Wohn-, Eß- und Trinkkultur, ihrer Art, Feste und Feiern zu begehen sowie zu ihren Vorstellungen Frauen, die Familie und die Generationen betreffend. Nur verstreut finden wir Bemerkungen, daß Fabrikarbeiter es liebten, Drachen steigen zu lassen[46] oder in Sportklubs Ringen und eine Art "Stockkampf" trainierten. Fast nichts wissen wir darüber, wie und in welchem Maße die sogenannten europäischen Einflüsse wie Kino usw. ihre Freizeitgestaltung veränderten. An diesem Punkt ist notwendigerweise die Frage nach der Massenkultur aufzuwerfen. Sicherlich begingen die Industriearbeiter die gleichen religiösen Feste wie die anderen Stadtbewohner, d.h. sie feierten Divali und Holi und anderes, je nach hinduistischer, islamischer oder anderer Religionszugehörigkeit.[47] Dennoch bleibt die Frage unbeantwortet, welchen Stellenwert alle diese Dinge in einem Arbeiterleben einnahmen und ob sie im proletarischen Milieu eine spezifische Ausprägung fanden.[48]

Die Gestaltung des Alltagslebens hängt zweifellos eng mit dem Lebensstandard zusammen. Generell konnten die Industriearbeiter im kolonialen Indien ihre materiellen Grundbedürfnisse nur unzureichend befriedigen. Der indische Ökonom Ahmad Mukhtar faßte ihre Lage aus eigener Anschauung mit den Worten zusammen: "The Indian factory-labourer lives in an atmosphere which stinks destitution, disease and ignorance. He is under-fed, under-clothed and badly housed. His life is a continuous struggle against poverty."[49] Am augenfälligsten trat die Misere des kolonialen Proletariats in den Wohnbedingungen zutage. Die Elendsbeschreibungen sowohl von Chawls als von Bustees aus der Feder von Kolonialbeamten sowie in- und ausländischer Gewerkschafter sind bekannt. Sie besagen, daß die Arbeiter in engen, dunklen und unzureichend gelüfteten Behausungen ohne ausreichende Strom- und Wasserversorgung mit mangelnden sanitären Anlagen in Elendshütten oder Mietskasernen lebten. Fast alle Arbeiterfamilien konnten sich nur einen Raum leisten, in dem sie wohnten, aßen, schliefen, sich fortpflanzten, starben. Die im Jahre 1928 nach Indien entsandte Delegation des britischen Gewerkschaftskongresses faßte ihre Eindrücke mit den Worten zusammen: "We visited the workers' quarters wherever we stayed, and had we not seen them we could not have believed that such evil places existed."[50]

Dennoch reicht es nicht aus, den Alltag der indischen Industriearbeiter unter dem Begriff "Kultur der Armut" zu subsumieren. Hinter vielen Erscheinungen des städtisch-proletarischen Milieus, die fremde aber auch einheimische Beobachter als

Ergebnis entweder von Armut und Rückständigkeit oder auch von unerklärbarer Exotik deuteten, steckt mehr. Häufig verbergen sich hinter ihnen kulturelle Werte, die bisher noch nicht erhellt bzw. im Zusammenhang mit Arbeiterkultur problematisiert wurden. Nur ein Beispiel soll dafür angeführt werden. Seit Jahrzehnten fällt Beobachtern das scheinbar unerklärliche Paradoxon ins Auge, daß auch die ärmste Arbeiterbehausung innen erstaunlich ordentlich und sauber gehalten wird, während auf gemeinsam benutzten Treppen, Gängen und Höfen sich der Unrat häuft. [51]Erst in letzter Zeit wurde der Versuch unternommen, dieses Phänomen zu erklären und es in ein Kulturkonzept einzuordnen.[52]

## Zwang und Widerstand

Im Spannungsfeld von Zwang und Widerstand entwickelten die indischen Industriearbeiter Formen des sozialen Protests und Organisationen zur kollektiven Interessenvertretung. Die historische Forschung hat versucht, Licht ins Dunkel der organisatorischen Anfänge der indischen Arbeiterbewegung zu bringen. Dabei ist die vom Jobber dominierte Produktionseinheit in den Mittelpunkt der Aufmerksamkeit gerückt. Heute stößt die These von Richard Newman, "the jobbers' gang forms a crucial link between the new institutional expressions of workforce solidarity and the primordial relationships that the millhands brought with them into industry,"[53] kaum mehr auf Widerspruch. Es war der Jobber, der in den ersten sechs Jahrzehnten industrieller Produktion in Indien sowohl die Wohlfahrtsfunktionen einer Gewerkschaft ausübte, mit den Unternehmern verhandelte, als auch die Arbeiter zum Protest motivierte. Arbeiter engagierten sich, wenn es um Lohnfragen ging, wenn das Management ungerechtfertigt Geldstrafen für angeblich verdorbenes Material verhängte, und sie setzten sich für die Verkürzung des Arbeitstages ein. Die Protestformen waren kurzzeitige Arbeitsniederlegungen der einzelnen Arbeitertrupps oder Werksabteilungen.[54] Häufig wurden gar keine konkreten Beschwerden vorgebracht oder Forderungen gestellt, und es gab keine Anzeichen für eine Mißstimmung, bis Arbeiter in Gruppen oder noch häufiger einzeln ohne Erklärung ihren Arbeitsplatz verließen.[55] Individueller Protest wurde vor allem durch das Fehlen am Arbeitsplatz (Absentismus), durch Bummeln während der Arbeit und das mutwillige Produzieren von Ausschuß deutlich. Gerade diesen Protestformen wandten Sozialhistoriker im Zusammenhang mit Fragen der Alltagskultur seit kurzem ihre Aufmerksamkeit zu und bewerteten sie neu.[56]

Als Klasse gerieten die Fabrikarbeiter in Gegensatz zur Bourgeoisie, als sie vom individuellen zum gemeinschaftlichen Protest übergingen. Ursachen für Streiks waren meist Lohnfragen; Arbeitsniederlegungen erfolgten aber auch aus anderen Gründen wie z.B. seit Ende der zwanziger Jahre zunehmend als Reaktion auf Rationalisierungsmaßnahmen durch Unternehmer. Die meisten der Streiks ereigneten sich spontan. Trotzdem lassen sie ein gewisses Maß koordinierten Handelns erkennen. Meist entschlossen sich Arbeiter, aus einem bestimmten Anlaß ihren Widersachern die Stirn zu bieten. Sie legten die Arbeit nieder, waren dann aber aufgrund unzureichender Kenntnisse nicht in der Lage, selbst Verhandlungen zur Lösung der Probleme zu führen. Sie wandten sich an Vertreter der nationalen und demokratischen Intelligenz, die bereit waren, sich für soziale Belange zu engagieren.

Die Arbeiterbewegung nahm in Indien unmittelbar nach dem ersten Weltkrieg organisierte Formen an. Sozialökonomische Faktoren und politische Ereignisse nationalen und internationalen Ranges versetzten die Werktätigen in Bewegung. Im Winter 1918/1919 erkämpften 125 000 Bombayer Textilarbeiter, ohne auf Streikfonds, materielle Unterstützung durch andere oder auf eigene Ersparnisse zurückgreifen zu können, eine zehnprozentige Lohnerhöhung. Ihr Streik setzte hinsichtlich seiner Dauer und seines Umfangs neue Maßstäbe. Die Arbeitsniederlegungen der indischen Industriearbeiter wurden in der Folgezeit in der Regel im Rahmen des gesamten Unternehmens geführt, ja, sie sprangen auf andere über und erfaßten vielfach ganze Industriezweige einzelner Städte und Regionen. Die Streikbewegung der zwanziger Jahre veranlaßte die Königliche Kommission zu Arbeiterfragen 1931 zu folgender Einschätzung: "The world-wide uprising of labour consciousness extended to India, where for the first time the mass of industrial workers awoke to their disabilties, particularly in the matter of wages and hours and of the possibility of combination. The effect of this surge was enhanced by political turmoil which added to the prevailing feeling of unrest and assisted to provide willing leaders of a trade union movement."[57]

Die Streiks wurden seit den zwanziger Jahren von Anstrengungen begleitet, Gewerkschaften ins Leben zu rufen. Arbeitervereinigungen wurden aber häufig nicht vor, sondern während und nach Arbeitsniederlegungen gegründet. Viele von ihnen waren nicht viel mehr als Streikkomitees, die sich nach Beendigung eines Ausstandes wieder auflösten. Dennoch faßten Gewerkschaften als umfassendste Organisation der Werktätigen in Indien Fuß. Generell waren sie bestrebt, die Arbeits- und Lebensbedingungen der Industriearbeiter zu verbessern und deren Rolle im gesellschaftlichen Leben durch die Wahrnehmung demokratischer Rechte und Mittel stärker zur Geltung zu bringen. Insgesamt gesehen blieb der Organisationsgrad der indischen Industriearbeiter aber gering und die Wirksamkeit dauerhafter Arbeiterverbände relativ schwach. Ihnen standen viele Hemmnisse entgegen. Unwissenheit und Armut gehörten dazu. In dem Bericht einer Delegation des Internationalen Textilarbeiterverbandes von 1927 werden als Ursachen für die geringe Verbreitung arbeitsfähiger Arbeitervereinigungen der Mangel an Bildung, traditionelle Voreingenommenheiten gegenüber Arbeitskollegen mit einer anderen Kasten- bzw. Religionszugehörigkeit und finanzielle Engpässe genannt.[58] Auch der migratorische Charakter der Industriearbeiter und ihre Beziehungen zum Dorf mögen sich hemmend ausgewirkt haben. Im Widerspruch dazu führen neuere Untersuchungen aus, daß vor allem diejenigen Arbeiter Militanz und Zähigkeit während sozialer Konflikte an den Tag legten, die auf materielle Ressourcen des Dorfes zurückgreifen konnten. Nicht zuletzt müssen die diskriminierende Haltung der Arbeitgeber sowie die Politik der Kolonialregierung als schwerwiegende Ursachen für die anhaltende Schwäche der indischen Gewerkschaftsbewegung in der ersten Hälfte des 20. Jahrhunderts erwähnt werden. Darauf weist Rajnarayan Chandavarkar hin: "The vagaries and weaknesses of trade unions, as the Indian case suggests, should not be interpreted as a reflex of the values, aspirations and consciousness of the workers; rather, it is more consistently explained in terms of the hostility and the politics of employers and the state."[59] Als Folge konnte sich eine organisierte Klassensolidarität nur ansatzweise entwickeln und blieb leicht zerstörbar.

Von besonderer Bedeutung für Aussagen zur politischen Kultur des Industrieproletariats im kolonialen Indien ist das Verhältnis von Führung und Mitgliedschaft. Kaum gebildet, aber vor allem des Englischen nicht mächtig, der Sprache, in der auf höherer Wirtschafts- bzw. staatlicher Ebene verhandelt werden mußte, waren die Industriearbeiter nicht in der Lage, die Leitung ihrer Vereinigungen selbst in die Hände zu nehmen. In der Regel übernahmen patriotische Intellektuelle - häufig als "outsider"[60] bezeichnet - die Führungspositionen. Auch zu dieser Problematik gibt es unterschiedliche Auffassungen. Während einige Historiker im Verhältnis zwischen Funktionär und Mitglied eine vorkapitalistische "Patron-Klient"-Beziehung fortgeführt sehen, bezeichnen andere die Zwangssituation unter kolonialkapitalistischen Verhältnissen als Ursache dafür, daß sich zum einen keine Führungsschicht aus Arbeiterkreisen selbst entwickeln konnte, und sich zum anderen ein spezifischer Arbeitsstil der Organsationen ergab.

Lebensweise, sozialer Protest und die politische Kultur der indischen Industriearbeiter spiegeln auf eindrucksvolle Weise wider, wie Denk- und Verhaltensweisen unterschiedlicher Gesellschaftsformen nebeneinander bestanden und aufeinander einwirkten. Während Kaste, Religion und Dorfleben noch das Fühlen und Handeln der Menschen beeinflußten, führten kolonialkapitalistisch geprägte Verhältnisse in den Industriezentren zusammen mit demokratischen Institutionen wie Parteien und Gewerkschaften das Alte umwälzende Wertmaßstäbe in das Leben der städtischen Lohnarbeiter ein. Seit geraumer Zeit sind Historiker bemüht, den Zusammenhang zwischen der ländlichen, von feudalen Beziehungen dominierten Herkunft und der Lebensweise des indischen Industrieproletariats mit ihren spezifischen Formen gesellschaftlicher Aktivität zu erhellen. So wurde die Frage aufgeworfen, ob die These von der aufsteigenden Linie, wie sie für die europäische Arbeiterbewegung entwickelt wurde, auch für Asien und Afrika gültig sei, oder ob die durch koloniale Unterordnung hervorgebrachten Bedingungen nicht eine neue Typologie erfordern.[61] Als vorläufiges Ergebnis kann festgehalten werden, daß sowohl elementarer sozialer Protest als auch komplexe Aktionsformen in einer Kombination von ökonomischen wie politischen Inhalten in Indien viele Jahrzehnte lang nebeneinander existierten und das Bild der Arbeiterbewegung bestimmten.

## Anmerkungen

1 Sabyasachi Bhattacharya, Presidential Address. Modern Indian History. Indian History Congress 1982, 16ff.

2 Nita Kumar, Urban Culture in Modern India - World of the Lower Classes. In: Indu Banga (Hg.), The City in Indian History. Urban Demography, Society, and Politics, New Delhi 1991, 191ff.

3 Ein hervorragendes Beispiel dafür ist Dipesh Chakrabarty, Rethinking Working-Class History. Bengal 1890-1940, Delhi 1989.

4 Vgl. Ulrich Raulff, Vorwort Mentalitäten-Geschichte. In: Ulrich Raulff (Hg.), Mentalitäten-Geschichte. Zur historischen Rekonstruktion geistiger Prozesse, Berlin 1987, 7.

5 Vgl. Vernon Lidtke, Recent Literatur on Workers' Culture in Germany and England. In: Klaus Tenfelde (Hg.), Arbeiter und Arbeiterbewegung im Vergleich. Berichte zur internationalen historischen Forschung, München 1986, 338.

6 Gerhard A. Ritter erfaßt mit dem Begriff Arbeiterkultur "den Gesamtzusammenhang einer schichtenspezifischen Lebensweise, die ihren Ausdruck nicht nur und nicht vor allem in künstlerischen Manifestationen der Arbeiterschaft und ihren Bildungsbestrebungen, sondern im sozialen und politischen Verhalten, in Wertvorstellungen und eigenen Institutionen findet". Zu ihr "gehören daher neben den Organisationen der Arbeiterschaft, die in ihren Funktionen als kollektive Interessenvertretungen und Instrumente politischer Partizipation auch Aufgaben einer industriegesellschaftlichen Sozialisation der Arbeiterschaft wahrnahmen, auch das Freizeit- und Geselligkeitsverhalten der Arbeiterschaft, ihre Wohn-, Eß- und Trinkkultur, die Gebärden und Gewohnheiten am Arbeitsplatz, das Kommunikationsverhalten der Arbeiter im Betrieb, in Nachbarschaft und Kommune, die Struktur und das Beziehungsgeflecht der Arbeiterfamilie und hier vor allem das Rollenverständnis von Mann und Frau sowie das Verhältnis der Eltern zu den Kindern und zu den sonst zur Wohngemeinschaft gehörenden Personen". Einleitung in: Gerhard A. Ritter (Hg.), Arbeiterkultur, Königstein 1979, 1.

7 "The jute industry's growth was concentrated and localized around Calcutta. All mills were (and still are) located in a thin strip of land - roughly about 55 miles long and 5 miles wide - along both banks of the river Hooghly from Budge Budge in the south and Naihati in the north." Ranajit Das Gupta, Factory Labour in Eastern India: Sources of Supply, 1855-1946. Some Preliminary Findings. In: The Indian Economic and Social History Review (IESHR), New Delhi *13*(1976)3, 281.

8 Berechnungen ergaben, daß die Jutefabriken in der Dekade zwischen 1915 und 1924 jährlich durchschnittlich 90 Prozent Profit gemacht hatten, und daß der "jährliche Durchschnittsgewinn achtmal so hoch war wie die gesamten Lohnkosten". Daniel Houston Buchanan, The Development of Capitalistic Enterprise in India, New York 1934, 252f.

9 "Der Enklavencharakter der marginalen Industrialisierung im kolonialen System machte sich im Osten Indiens mit seiner exportorientierten Industrie besonders bemerkbar. Teeplantagenenklaven, Kohlebergwerksenklaven und die Juteindustrieenklave in Kalkutta standen durch die überall vertretenen Managing Agencies miteinander in Verbindung, hatten aber zu ihrem jeweiligen Hinterland kaum irgendwelche Beziehungen." Dietmar Rothermund, Indiens wirtschaftliche Entwicklung. Von der Kolonialherrschaft bis zur Gegenwart, Paderborn 1985, 76f.

10 Dhananjay Ramachandra Gadgil, The Industrial Evolution of India in Recent Times 1860-1939, New Delhi 1974 (5. Ausgabe/3. Auflage), 78. Amiya Kumar Bagchi, Private Investment in India 1900-1939, Madras 1975, 277.

11 Shyam Rungta, Bowreah Cotton and Fort Gloster Jute Mills, 1872-1900. In: IESHR, *22*(1985)2, S. 116f.

12 B. Foley, Report on Labour in Bengal, Kalkutta 1906, 14.

13 Ebenda, Appendix, 27.

14 Report of the Royal Commission on Labour in India (RRCLI), London 1931, 11.

15 Foley, Report on Labour..., 15.

16 RRCLI, 11.

17 Vgl. Bagchi, Private Investment in India..., 136; Das Gupta, Factory Labour in Eastern India..., 302, 308.

18 Morris David Morris, The Growth of Large-Scale Industry to 1947. In: Dharma Kumar/-Meghnad Desai (Hg.), The Cambridge Economic History of India (CEHI), vol. 2: c. 1757-c. 1970, Cambridge 1983, 657.

19 Buchanan, The Development of Capitalistic Enterprise..., 246.

20 The Gazetteer of Bombay City and Island, Bombay 1909, vol. 1, 486.

21 "...foreign capital never amounted to more than a few per cent of total investment in the industry." Morris David Morris, The Emergence of an Industrial Labor Force in India. A Study of the Bombay Cotton Mills, 1854-1947, Bombay 1965, 27.

22 Sunil Kumar Sen, Studies in Economic Policy and Development of India (1848-1926), Kalkutta 1966, 60.

23 M.R. Chaudhuri, Indian Industries. Development and Location. An Economic-Geographic Appraisal, Kalkutta 1970, 156.

24 Jagdish N. Bhagwati/Padma Desai, India - Planning for Industrialization. Industrialization and Trade Policies since 1951, London 1970, 31.

25 Morris, The Emergence of an Industrial Labor Force..., 32.

26 Ebenda, 33.

27 "The jobber, known in different parts of India and in different industries by different names such as sardar, mistry, mukadam, tindal, chowdhry, kangany, etc. is almost a ubiquitous feature of recruitment and labour administration in India, and usually combines in himself a formidable array of functions. Thus he is not only a recruiting agent, but very often a supervisor or foreman, or even a sub-employer, or a gangman who is both a sub-employer and a worker sharing the income with other workers." Labour Investigation Committee. Report on Labour Conditions (RLC), Main Report, Delhi 1946, 80.

28 Für das Jahr 1925 wird folgende ethnisch-nationale Zusammensetzung der Bombayer Textilarbeiterschaft angegeben: 40 Prozent kamen von Ratnagiri, 15 Prozent von Puna und Satara, 5 Prozent aus dem Kolaba-Distrikt und 11 Prozent aus den Vereinigten Provinzen. S.M. Rutnagur, Bombay Industries. The Cotton Mills, Bombay 1927, 319.

29 Vgl. Rajnarayan Chandavarkar, Workers' Politics and the Mill Districts in Bombay between the Wars. In: Hamza Alavi/John Harriss (Hg.), Sociology of "Developing Societies". South Asia, Basingstoke-London 1989, 261.

30 Das Industieproletariat machte 1910 1,5 Prozent und 1941 3,1 Prozent der gesamten erwerbstätigen Bevölkerung Indiens aus. Die Zahl der Fabrikarbeiter wuchs von 316 000 1891 auf 1 751 000 1939. RLC, 13ff. P.P. Pillai (Hg.), Labour in South East Asia. A Symposium, New Delhi 1947, 7ff.

31 Report of the Indian Factory Labour Commission (RIFLC), 1908. Vol. I - Report and Appendices, London 1908, 18, 23.

32 RRCLI, 12f.

33 RLC, 8.
34 RRCLI, 14-16.
35 Vgl. Gardner Murphy, In the Minds of Men. The Study of human behavior and social tensions in India, New York 1953, 202.
36 Amiya Kumar Bagchi, The Ambiguity of Progress: Indian Society in Transition. In: Social Scientist, New Delhi *13*(1985)3, 11.
37 Ebenda.
38 Ebenda, 19f.
39 Karl Marx, Das Kapital. Erster Band. In: Karl Marx/Friedrich Engels, Werke, 185f.
40 RLC, 71.
41 Chitra Joshi, Bonds of Community, Ties of Religion: Kanpur textile workers in the early twentieth century. In: IESHR *22*(1985)3, 252.
42 Vgl. Dipesh Chakrabarty, The Early 1890s: A Communal Culture Emerges. In: Hamza Alavi/John Harriss (Hg.), Sociology of "Developing Societies". South Asia, Basingstoke-London 1989, 188f.
43 Vgl. Gardner Murphy, In the Minds of Men..., 98f.
44 Chitra Joshi, Kanpur Textile Labour. Some structural features of formative years. In: The Economic and Political Weekly (EPW), Bombay *16*(1981), 44ff.
45 Vgl. Amiya Kumar Bagchi, Working Class Consciousness. Review Article. In: EPW *25*(1990)30, PE-54ff.
46 Vgl. Claude Batley, Bombay's Houses and Homes, Bombay 1949, 38.
47 Jim Masselos, Appropriating Urban Space: Social constructs of Bombay in the time of the Raj. In: South India, N.S. *14*(1991)1, 33ff.
48 Vgl. Nita Kumar, Urban Culture in Modern India..., 197f.
49 Ahmad Mukhtar, Factory Labour in India, Madras 1930, 5f.
50 A.A. Purcell/J. Hallsworth, Report on Labour Conditions in India, London 1928, 8.
51 Vgl. Batley, Bombay's Houses..., 37f.
52 Vgl. Dipesh Chakrabarty, Open Space/Public Place: Garbage, Modernity and India. In: South Asia, Armidale, N.S. 14(1991)1, S. 15ff.
53 Richard Newman, Workers and Unions in Bombay 1918-1929. A Study of Organization in the Cotton Mills, Canberra 1981, 5.
54 Buchanan, The Development of Capitalistic Enterprise..., 416ff.
55 RIFLC, 20.
56 Vgl. Rajnarayan Chandavarkar, Workers' Resistance and the Rationalization of Work in Bombay between the Wars. In: Douglas Haynes/Gyan Prakash (Hg.), Contesting Power. Resistance and Everyday Social Relations in South Asia, Delhi 1991, 135f.
57 RRCLI, 317.
58 Report of the Delegation of the International Federation of Textile Workers' Associations Regarding Conditions of Labour in Textile Works in India. In: National Archives of India, Department of Industries and Labour, File No. L-835/1928, 5, 9.
59 Chandavarkar, Workers' Resistance..., 317.
60 Vgl. Sabyasachi Bhattacharya, The Outsiders: A Historical Note. In: Ashok Mitra (Hg.), The Truth Unites. Essays in Tribute to Samar Sen, Kalkutta 1985, 90ff.
61 Vgl. Sabyasachi Bhattacharya, Capital and Labour in Bombay City, 1928-29. In: EPW *16*(1981)42-43, PE-42.

# N.G. Ranga und Swami Sahajanand Saraswati - Bauernführer zwischen Tradition und Moderne

Petra Heidrich

Im September 1937, in dem Jahr, da der Indische Nationalkongreß im Rahmen der durch die Verfassungsreformen von 1935 gewährten Provinzautonomie erstmalig in einer Reihe von Provinzen die Regierungsgewalt ausüben konnte, erkundigte sich Vallabhbhai Patel besorgt bei Rajendra Prasad über die Situation in dessen Heimatprovinz Bihar: "I read a report in the Press wherein it was said that some District Officer had to order a lathi-charge on some rowdy kisan demonstration. Such kisan demonstrations are being organised in Maharashtra by Indu Lal Yagnik, in your Province by Swami Sahajanand, and in Andhra by Prof. Ranga. They are trying to discredit the Congress Ministry by taking crowds of kisans to the Assembly Chambers with impossible and extravagant demands. They are all working in the name of the All India Kisan Organisation."[1]

Seit der Indische Nationalkongreß sich nach dem ersten Weltkrieg unter Mahatma Gandhis Führung zu einer Massenbewegung entwickelt hatte, verstand er sich in erster Linie als eine Organisation der Bauern. Vallabhbhai Patel und Rajendra Prasad gehörten zu der Generation von nationalen Führern, die maßgeblich dazu beigetragen hatte, daß bäuerliche Schichten eine verläßliche soziale Basis des Indischen Nationalkongresses bildeten. Vallabhbhai Patel hatte auf M. K. Gandhis Initiative teilweise mit beachtlichem Erfolg 1918 in Kheda und 1927 im Kreis Bardoli (Provinz Bombay) den gewaltlosen Widerstand der Bauern gegen von der Kolonialregierung vorgenommene Landsteuererhöhungen organisiert. Rajendra Prasad hatte Gandhi 1917 beim Champaran-Satyagraha in Bihar zur Seite gestanden, als die öffentliche Meinung gegen den von britischen Pflanzern erzwungenen Indigoanbau mobilisiert wurde. Er hatte in der Folgezeit Gandhis konstruktives Programm auf dem Lande unterstützt und sich aktiv um die Einbeziehung von ländlichen Schichten in die nationalen Kampagnen der Nichtzusammenarbeit von 1921 bis 1922 und des bürgerlichen Ungehorsams der Jahre 1930/31 und 1932 bis 1934 bemüht. In diesem Zusammenhang zeigte Rajendra Prasad selbst an der Gründung der Bauernvereinigung (Kisan Sabha) der Provinz Bihar im Jahre 1929 aktives Interesse. Ganz in gandhistischem Sinne sahen jedoch sowohl Patel als auch Prasad ihre Aufgabe in erster Linie in der Mobilisierung der ländlichen Bevölkerung für den nationalen Unabhängigkeitskampf. Wo in ihrer Regie bäuerliche Probleme aufgegriffen wurden, handelte es sich in der Regel um lokale Konflikte, in denen Bauern direkt mit der Kolonialmacht oder deren Vertretern konfrontiert waren. In bezug auf innergesellschaftliche Probleme, z. B. die der Pächter oder Landarbeiter, stand im Namen der nationalen Einheit das Bemühen um Ausgleich und die Harmonisierung widerstreitender Interessen im Vordergrund.

Der direkte Kontakt, der zwischen den Bauern und Kongreß- und Khilafatführern erstmalig in größerem Umfang im Rahmen der Nichtzusammenarbeitsbewegung der Jahre 1921/22 geknüpft worden war, hatte jedoch eine Entwicklung mit eigener Dynamik in Gang gesetzt. Die zumeist jungen Kongreßaktivisten, die auf dem Land die Idee der Nichtzusammenarbeit mit der Kolonialmacht verbreiteten, mußten sich erstmalig mit Interessenkonflikten auf dem Lande und den Forderungen der bäuerlichen Bevölkerung auseinandersetzen. Obwohl sich nach dem Abflauen der nationalen Kampagnen auch das Heer der Kongreßmitarbeiter zumeist wieder in die Städte zurückzog, wurden die einmal geknüpften Kontakte lose fortgeführt. Einige Kongreßaktivisten blieben sogar im Zusammenhang mit Gandhis konstruktivem Programm auf dem Land und waren gezwungen, sich näher mit den unmittelbaren Problemen der Bauern zu befassen. Zum anderen begann die allmähliche kulturelle Umwandlung der indischen Gesellschaft seit dem 19. Jahrhundert, die Idee der Religions- und Sozialreform, auch auf dem Lande zu greifen. Aufstrebende bäuerliche Schichten, die stärker als andere in die sich ausbreitende Warenproduktion einbezogen waren, brachten eigene Führungspersönlichkeiten hervor, die den nationalen Führern alten Stils das Feld der Politik nicht mehr allein überlassen wollten.

Die Führung des Indischen Nationalkongresses wurde auch weiterhin von Vertretern der städtischen Intelligenz, der freien Berufe beherrscht, die zudem vornehmlich den oberen Kastengruppen angehörten. Wo sie - wie Patel und Prasad - einen ländlichen Hintergrund hatten, stammten sie zumeist aus wohlsituierten Familien. Ihre westliche Bildung, ihre Lebensweise, die herausgehobene soziale Position im Rahmen der Kastenhierarchie und häufig auch ihr ökonomischer Hintergrund hatten eine solch tiefe Kluft zwischen ihnen und der Masse des indischen Volkes entstehen lassen, daß es beträchtliche Verständigungsschwierigkeiten gab, als sich der Indische Nationalkongreß eine Massenbasis schaffen wollte. Die unbestreitbar große Kluft, die unter den spezifischen, von der Kolonialherrschaft geprägten Bedingungen zwischen der einheimischen "Elite" und den Volksmassen entstanden war, bewog die Vertreter der Unterschichtenstudien (Subaltern Studies) sogar, von einer "strukturellen Dichotomie" in Kultur und Bewußtsein zwischen den indischen Eliten und den beherrschten Volksmassen zu sprechen.[2] So groß die Kluft aber auch war; als der indische Unabhängigkeitskampf unter der Führung des INK zur Massenbewegung wurde, fanden sich auch Persönlichkeiten, die fruchtbare Kontakte zwischen den einheimischen Eliten und den Volksmassen herstellten.

Auf diese Mittelspersonen, die enge Bindungen zum indischen Dorf aufrechterhielten oder in der praktischen Arbeit herstellten, mußten sich die städtischen Eliten unterschiedlicher politischer und ideologischer Richtungen stützen, wenn sie politischen Einfluß behalten oder neuen gewinnen wollten. Im Prozeß der Zusammenarbeit veränderten sich beide Seiten. Während einerseits die Mittler neue Ideen aufnahmen, sie auf ihre Weise verarbeiteten und in die ländlichen Gebiete trugen, beeinflußten sie andererseits auch die Politik der Eliten. Vertraut mit der Situation auf dem Lande, machten sie es sich zur Aufgabe, ein realistisches Bild von den dörflichen Verhältnissen und den bestehenden Interessenkonflikten zu vermitteln. Sie halfen neuen, aufstrebenden bäuerlichen Schichten, ihre Forderungen zu artikulieren und in die Politik einzubringen, und sie trugen letztlich dazu bei, die politisch dominierenden Eliten von der Notwendigkeit struktureller Veränderungen auf dem Lande zu überzeugen. Swami Sahajanand Saraswati und N.G. Ranga gehörten zu jenen Mittlern, die den Kontakt nationaler Führer unterschiedlicher politischer Ausrichtung mit ökonomisch oder politisch zu aktivierenden bäuerlichen Schichten herstellten. Andererseits ließen sie es sich nicht nehmen, im Rahmen des 1936 gegründeten Allindischen Bauernverbandes selbst aktiv in die Politik einzugreifen.

Der Beitrag beschränkt sich darauf, Herkunft und Werdegang, Wertevorstellungen und geistige Entwicklung dieser beiden äußerst verschiedenen Persönlichkeiten bis in die Zeit ihrer gemeinsamen Arbeit im Allindischen Bauernverband darzustellen. Ist doch ihr so unterschiedliches individuelles Schicksal exemplarisch für die sich in der ersten Hälfte des 20. Jahrhunderts in Indien vollziehende Entwicklung neuer sozialer und geistiger Elemente aus traditionellen Denkmustern und Strukturen. Die relativ gründlich untersuchten organisationsgeschichtlichen und politischen Aspekte der Betätigung beider Bauernführer wie auch die Methoden und Grenzen ihrer Kommunikation mit den Bauern werden hier nicht behandelt.

Swami Sahajanand Saraswati wurde 1889 als Navrang Rai im Dorf Deva des Ghazipur Distrikts der Vereinten Provinzen (U. P.) geboren. Die Situation unterschied sich in diesem östlichen Teil der U. P. kaum von der im angrenzenden Bihar. Es war ein landwirtschaftlich rückständiges, vom Samindari-Steuerveranlagungssystem geprägtes Gebiet. Die Familie des Swami gehörte zu den Jujhautiya-Brahmanen, die mit den Bhumihars Heiratsbeziehungen pflegten. Sie besaß nur ein kleines Samindari, lebte unter bescheidenen Bedingungen von der Landwirtschaft und hatte keine Bildungstradition. Der intelligente Junge wurde jedoch 1899 in die Upper Primary School von Jalalabad geschickt, deren sechs Klassen er in drei Jahren absolvierte. Anders als im Süden und Westen Indiens gab es zu jener Zeit in den landessprachigen Grundschulen der Hindi-Region Nordindiens kaum Modernisierungsbestrebungen. Hier wurde das kulturelle Erbe und die Sicht der oberen Kasten mit Bildungsprivileg an deren Kinder vermittelt.[3] Die Grundschulbildung des Navrang Rai entsprach diesem Muster. Die Lehrer waren Kshatriyas, orthodoxe Hindus und Shiva-Verehrer. Die in der Schulzeit betriebene Shiva-Verehrung machte auf ihn einen so starken Eindruck, daß er - nach seinen eigenen Worten - Zeit seines Lebens ein Sanatani - ein orthodoxer Hindu blieb. Sein anfangs unduldsamer Glaube wurde nur allmählich durch Lebenserfahrung gemildert und abgewandelt.[4] Für die spätere Wandlung eines seiner Lehrer vom orthodoxen Shiva-Verehrer zum Anhänger der religiösen Reformbewegung des Arya Samaj zeigte er wenig Verständnis.[5]

Nach der Upper Primary School besuchte Navrang Rai von 1902 bis 1904 die Hindi Middle School von Ghazipur. Zur Zeit der Abschlußprüfung wurde er als Fünfzehnjähriger mit einem Mädchen verheiratet, das jedoch zwei Jahre später starb. Wegen guter Prüfungsergebnisse und der Aussicht auf ein Stipendium beschloß er, auch Englisch zu lernen. Im Jahre 1904 wurde Navrang Rai in die Sonderklasse der German Mission High English School in Ghazipur aufgenommen, die den Absolventen von landessprachlichen Mittelschulen die Möglichkeit einräumte, nach fünf statt nach zehn Jahren die Reifeprüfung zu machen. Hier nahm er auch Sanskrit-Unterricht und las seine ersten Texte. Die Bibel, die er in der deutschen Missionsschule kennenlernte, machte keinen nachhaltigen Eindruck auf ihn. Stattdessen vertiefte sich seine Shiva-Verehrung. Er besuchte regelmäßig den örtlichen Tempel, begann sich mehr und mehr um seine rituelle Reinheit zu sorgen und entwickelte - wie er selbst meinte - einen außerordentlichen religiösen Dogmatismus.[6] Die Begegnung mit Elementen der westlichen Kultur mobilisierte vor allem seinen Widerstand. So berichtete er von Auseinandersetzungen mit Lehrern, die die Hindu-Religion kritisierten.[7] Gleichzeitig wuchs sein Wunsch, der Welt zu entsagen und Sannyasi - Bettelmönch - zu werden. Als er erfuhr, daß seine Familie heimlich eine zweite Heirat vorbereitete, um ihn an das weltliche Leben zu binden, verließ er 1907 - kurz vor der Reifeprüfung - Familie und Schule und begab sich nach Varanasi.

Die Verhältnisse, unter denen Nidubrolu Gogineni Ranganayakulu - später als N. G. Ranga bekannt - aufwuchs, waren ganz andere. Er wurde am 7. November 1900 in Nidubrolu, im fruchtbaren Krishna Distrikt der damaligen britisch-indischen Provinz Madras, dem heutigen Andhra geboren. Es war vorwiegend ein Raiatwari Gebiet, landwirtschaftlich fortgeschritten, mit sich stabilisierender und diversifizierender Warenproduktion. Hier entstand eine Schicht von der Kommerzialisierung profitierender, aufstrebender Bauern, die unter kolonialen Bedingungen auf dem Lande zwar noch nicht dominierte, aber, nach A. Satyanarayana, die "materielle und soziale Basis für die Entwicklung einer zukünftigen kapitalistischen Klasse"[8] bildete. N. G. Ranga selbst wuchs in einer Familie "erfolgreicher Bauern" auf, die fruchtbares Land sowie zahlreiche Gebäude besaß.[9] Sie hatte eine angesehene soziale Stellung im Dorf und gehörte einer der dominierenden Bauernkasten der Region - den Kammas - an. Die Kammas zeichneten sich durch ein ihrer langen landwirtschaftlichen Tradition entsprechendes Selbstbewußtsein aus. Ranga zitiert seinen Schwiegervater: "We the peasants are ... free and independent. We earn our livelihood, we are the real princes of the land"[10]. Diese Überzeugung sollte auch Rangas gesamte politische Karriere bestimmen.

Die ablehnende Haltung der älteren Bauerngeneration gegenüber der Bildung, die nur Lohnabhängige, seien es Staatsdiener oder Brahmanen, nötig hatten, teilte Ranga jedoch nicht mehr. Wuchs er doch in einer Zeit auf, als im Süden Indiens die sich teils ergänzenden, teils überschneidenden und teils auch widersprechenden Einflüsse religions- und sozialreformerischer Ideen, der aufkommenden Nicht-

Brahmanenbewegung, der nationalen Emanzipationsbestrebungen der Telugu sprechenden Andhras wie auch der gesamtindischen antikolonialen Bewegung auf dem Lande zu wirken begannen. Waren seine Eltern noch Analphabeten, durfte Ranga schon die Dorfschule besuchen. Über eine weiterführende Bildung gab es jedoch Meinungsverschiedenheiten in der Familie. Für zwei Jahre mußte sich der junge Ranga um den Familienbesitz kümmern. Er befaßte sich mit Farmarbeit sowie der Rechnungsführung für Wirtschaft und Haushalt. Ein Gerichtsfall und der Streit mit englischen Steuerbeamten ließen den Vater aber über die Vorzüge einer englischen Schulbildung für seinen Sohn nachdenken. 1914 erlaubte er ihm, die English High School in Ponnur zu besuchen. Hier erlebte Ranga, welche Kluft sich bildungsmäßig zwischen den Brahmanen und den Angehörigen von Bauernkasten aufgetan hatte. Er hielt es fortan für seine Aufgabe, unter den Bauern Bildung zu propagieren, um die Kluft zu verringern.

Rangas Jugend war eindeutig durch das Klima der Nicht- Brahmanenbewegung geprägt. Seine autobiographischen Erinnerungen sprechen für die These, daß sich diese Bewegung nicht nur auf die politischen Aktivitäten einer kleinen Oberschicht reduzieren läßt, sich nicht nur als ein "Mythos" erwies, wie Christopher Baker 1971 meinte,[11] sondern Anteil an einem kulturellen Wertewandel hatte. Die landbesitzenden und -bearbeitenden Bauernkasten der Vellalas, Kapus, Reddis, Kammas und Velamas wollten den Brahmanen, die hier im Süden 1911 nur drei Prozent der Bevölkerung ausmachten,[12] ihre Privilegien streitig machen. Wenn auch diese Kastenbewegungen in erster Linie von privilegierten Oberschichten im Eigeninteresse genutzt wurden, waren sie doch auch mit sozialen und religiösen Reform- sowie Bildungsbestrebungen in den ländlichen Gebieten verbunden. Zum einen ging es um die rituelle Aufwertung der Bauernkasten zu Kshatriyas, dem zweiten angesehenen Varna in der Kastenhierarchie, um das Recht auf direkten, nicht durch die Brahmanen vermittelten Zugang zu den heiligen Schriften, zum anderen kamen auf den Kastenkonferenzen auch soziale Fragen, das Problem der Unberührbarkeit, der Ausgrenzung der Frau durch Purdah und das ruinöse Mitgiftsystem (dowry) zur Sprache. Auf dem Gebiet der Bildung wurden Maßnahmen zur Bekämpfung des Analphabetentums und zur Erwachsenenbildung gefördert und die Einrichtung von ländlichen Bibliotheken propagiert.[13]

Schon bevor sich die Nicht-Brahmanenbewegung mit Gründung der Justice Party 1917 auf politischer Ebene manifestierte, hatte der Bildungsgedanke durch die Andhra Library Movement auf dem Lande Verbreitung gefunden. Auch in Rangas Heimatdorf hatte ein Freund der Familie eine Bibliothek aufgebaut, und der junge Ranga wurde zu ihrem eifrigsten Leser und Propagandisten. Hier machte er sich mit gehobenem (brahmanical) Telugu und den Grundlagen des Sanskrit vertraut, und hier lernte er auch die Werke des Telugu-Schriftstellers und Sozialreformers Veerasalingam, eines Brahmanen, schätzen. Veerasalingams vom Brahmo Samaj beeinflußte Reformideen beeindruckten Ranga so nachhaltig, daß er später auch aus diesem Grund Vorbehalte gegen militante Anti-Brahmanen-Kampagnen hatte. Auch die Schriften des bengalischen Religionsreformers Vivekananda, die er in der Bibliothek in Telugu vorfand, las er mit Interesse. Aufgewachsen war er mit der Dorfreligion, mit dem Ramayana und den Erzählungen über den Gott Krishna. Er erlebte shivaitische und vishnuitische Wanderprediger und lernte die christliche Lehre durch englische Missionare kennen. Rangas Kindheitsglaube wurde jedoch vor allem durch die beißende Kritik der Vertreter der militanten Nicht-Brahmanenbewegung an den nordindischen religiösen Epen erschüttert. Die Vedanta-Auffassungen Vivekanandas und die Lehren Ram Tirthas boten einen Ausweg. Er empfand sie als überzeugende Synthese der vielfältigen und widerstreitenden religiösen Anschauungen. Eng fühlte er sich mit bäuerlichen Strömungen in der Telugu-Kultur verbunden. Wie andere Jugendliche rezitierte er die Gedichte des aus einer Bauernkaste stammenden mittelalterlichen Telugu-Dichters Vemana. Dessen freie religiöse Auffassungen und Lebensweisheiten sprachen ihn an.[14]

Die politischen Bewegungen seiner Zeit ließen Rangas Heimatdorf nicht unberührt. Anjaneyulu, der Begründer der Dorfbibliothek, machte ihn mit den Lehren Tilaks und Bepin Chandra Pals bekannt und führte ihn in die Nationalbewegung ein. Das Streben nach nationaler Selbstbestimmung sah Ranga auch durch westliches kulturelles und politisches Denken gerechtfertigt, mit dem er sich über die Bibliothek und in der Schule vertraut machte. Er informierte sich mit Hilfe der Wochenzeitungen "Andhra Patrika" oder "Krishna Patrika" über das Tagesgeschehen, nahm 1917 lebhaften Anteil an der Bewegung gegen die Verhaftung Annie Besants und verfolgte ihre in einfachem Englisch geschriebene Zeitung "New India". Im gleichen Jahr nahm er auch an der Andhra Conference in Nellore teil. In die Madras Presidency Kamma Conference, deren soziale Anliegen ihn ansprachen, wollte er eine bäuerliche Note einbringen. Seine eigenen Erfahrungen ließen ihn mit der Nicht-Brahmanenbewegung sympathisieren. Er las ihre Zeitungen "Justice" und "Ryot", mißbilligte jedoch die Loyalität der politischen Nicht-Brahmanenbewegung gegenüber den Briten und fühlte sich mehr zur Nationalist Non-Brahmin Conference hingezogen.[15] Im Gegensatz zum Swami verbrachte Ranga seine Kindheit und frühe Jugend auf dem Dorf in einem geistig anregenden Klima. Hier wurde das Fundament für seine späteren sozialen und politischen Auffassungen gelegt.

Der Swami hingegen stand in einer völlig anderen Traditionslinie. Im Jahre 1907 trat der Siebzehnjährige in Varanasi in das Aparnath Kloster (Kashi Aparnath Math) ein, ließ sich die Kopfhaare scheren, rüstete sich mit dem ockerfarbenen Gewand und dem Topf des Bettelmönchs aus, legte seinen Namen Navrang Rai ab und wurde als Sahajanand in den Orden der mit einem Bambusstab (Danda) - dem Vishnu Symbol - ausgerüsteten Danda Sannyasis aufgenommen. Auf der - letzlich vergeblichen - Suche nach einem echten Yogi, der die Yoga-Technik vermitteln konnte, begab er sich mit einem Gefährten auf die Wanderschaft durch das Bundelkhand-Gebiet und die Gangesebene bis zu den heiligen Stätten des Nordens. Er lebte das entbehrungsreiche Leben des Sannyasi und blieb unberührt von weltlichen

Ereignissen wie der Bewegung gegen die Teilung Bengalens, von der er unterwegs hörte. Die Abneigung, die der Swami aus seiner orthodox religiösen Haltung heraus gegen die Engländer empfand, äußerte sich in jener Zeit darin, daß er sie und ihre Sprache vollständig zu vergessen suchte.[16]

Nach anderthalbjähriger Wanderung begab sich der Swami Anfang 1909 wieder nach Varanasi ins Aparnath Kloster. Da er, obwohl an Lebenserfahrung reicher, seinem eigentlichen Ziel - der göttlichen Erleuchtung - in dieser Zeit nicht nähergekommen war, versenkte er sich für die nächsten sieben Jahre in die heiligen Schriften der Hindus, die Shastras. Der brahmanischen Tradition entsprechend strebte er nun Erlösung durch absolutes Wissen an. Mit der ihm eigenen Konsequenz durchlief er den traditionellen religiösen Bildungsweg. Er besuchte verschiedene klösterliche Sanskritschulen, bevorzugte aber das Gespräch mit selbstgewählten Lehrern. Unter ihrer Anleitung beschäftigte er sich intensiv mit Sanskrit-Grammatik, studierte die Kaumudi-Theorie, die philosophischen Systeme Nyaya, Samkhya, Mimansa, Vedanta und Yoga, befaßte sich mit Astrologie und ayurvedischer Medizin. Im Studium fand er nach seinen eigenen Worten grenzenlose Befriedigung.[17] Die mündlichen Kommentare seiner besten Lehrer zu religionsphilosophischen Werken ließ er später drucken. Darüber hinaus erwarb sich der Swami selbst den Ruf eines Sanskrit-Gelehrten. In der 1976 erschienenen Geschichte Bihars fand er z. B. nicht als Bauernführer Erwähnung, sondern als Verfasser seiner Rituallehre "Karmakalap".[18]

Während seines Studiums hörte der Swami von Freunden zum ersten Mal, daß Saryupari- und Kanyakubja-Brahmanen den Bhumihars das Recht absprachen, Danda Sannyasis zu werden. Das Selbstwertgefühl des Swami, der dem Dharma, den speziellen Pflichten des Brahmanen, immer mit besonderem Eifer nachgekommen war, war tief verletzt. Die Empörung, daß Bhumihars, mit denen seine eigenen Jujhautiya-Brahmanen Heiratsbeziehungen pflegten, wegen ihrer ausschließlich landwirtschaftlichen Tätigkeit nicht als Brahmanen anerkannt wurden, bewog ihn, die Weltentrücktheit des Sannyasi aufzugeben.[19] Die Bhumihar-Bewegung weckte sein Interesse für die ihn umgebende Realität. Für die Bhumihars wiederum war sein Redetalent, das er schon auf religiösen Veranstaltungen - Tagungen des Bharat Dharma Mahamandal und der Sanatana Dharma Sabha - erprobt hatte, wie auch sein Wissen als Sanskrit-Gelehrter von großem Nutzen. Sie überredeten ihn, an der Tagung der Kastenvereinigung der Bhumihars, der Bhumihar Brahman Mahasabha, im Dezember 1914 teilzunehmen. Damit begann seine langjährige Arbeit für diese Kastenvereinigung.

In einer Zeit, da sich die Nicht-Brahmanenbewegung im Süden und Westen Indiens anschickte, auf der politischen Ebene aktiv zu werden, kam mit Zeitverzug im Norden auf andere Weise Bewegung in das Kastensystem. Stärker als im Süden und Westen, wo Strömungen im Rahmen der Nicht-Brahmanenbewegung die Kastenhierarchie selbst angriffen, waren im Norden Sanskritisierungsbestrebungen - Bemühungen um Aufstieg im Rahmen des Systems - vorherrschend. Es lag im

Trend der Zeit, daß sich Kastengruppen zu Kastenorganisationen, -assoziationen und -föderationen zusammenschlossen, um über organisierte Bildungsbestrebungen, veränderte Sitten und Gebräuche sowie eine reformierte Religion ihren Status zu erhöhen. Einen ausgeprägt sozialen Aspekt hatten die Bewegungen der unteren Kastengruppen, der Unberührbaren, aber auch der zahlenmäßig zersplitterten Shudra-Kasten, die sich seit Beginn des 20. Jahrhunderts unter dem Einfluß von Religions- und Sozialreformern zu formieren begannen. Sie meldeten Widerstand gegen traditionelle Unterordnungs- und Abhängigkeitsverhältnisse an. In der Kastenorganisation der Bhumihars dagegen rang eine wohlhabende, in der Landwirtschaft verwurzelte Elite mit politischen Ambitionen um soziale Aufwertung durch Anerkennung ihres Brahmanentums.

Um den Brahmanenstatus der Bhumihars zu beweisen, suchte der Swami anfangs in den alten Schriften nach Belegen dafür, daß Brahmanen nicht Priester sein mußten, sondern durchaus auch Land- und Hauswirtschaft betreiben durften,[20] und er wies Verwandtschaftsbeziehungen zu anerkannten Brahmanengruppen nach. Später setzte er all seinen Ehrgeiz darein, Bhumihars für den Priesterberuf zu gewinnen und so zu schulen, daß sie ihrem traditionellen Brahmanen-Dharma gerecht werden konnten. Speziell für die des Sanskrit unkundigen Bhumihars verfaßte er das "Karmakalap", eine Rituallehre und Sternenkunde in Hindi, in der nur die Mantras in Sanskrit verfaßt waren. Er hatte wesentlichen Anteil an der Purohit(Hauspriester)-Bewegung Mitte der zwanziger Jahre.

Während die Veröffentlichung seiner 1915 begonnenen Studien zum Nachweis von Verwandschaftsbeziehungen zwischen Bhumihars und den Maithila-, Saryupari- und Kanyakubja-Brahmanen von der Bhumihar-Elite mit Anerkennung aufgenommen wurden, schoß er nach Meinung einflußreicher Bhumihars mit der Purohit-Bewegung über das Ziel hinaus. Diese Elite, zu der Rajas, große und mittlere Samindare, wohlhabende Landwirte und eine kleine städtische Bildungsschicht gehörten, war an Sozialprestige, nicht aber an wirklicher Sanskritisierung interessiert. Wenn z. B. Sir Ganesh Datta Sinha, bedeutender Samindar und Bhumihar-Führer es als Zumutung empfand, Bhumihar-Söhne zu Almosensammlern und Geschichtenerzählern erziehen zu lassen,[21] ergeben sich Parallelen zur selbstbewußten Haltung der Kamma-Bauern, die sich wegen ihrer landwirtschaftlichen Selbständigkeit jeder anderen Kaste überlegen fühlten. Trotz der Mißstimmigkeiten wurde der Swami 1927 zum Geschäftsführer des Sitaram Ashram in Bihta bei Patna bestellt, wo Bhumihar-Söhnen kostenlos das Studium der heiligen Schriften, insbesondere der Veden ermöglicht werden sollte. Ein Trust, dem auch Sir Ganesh Datta angehörte, führte die Aufsicht und wachte über die Einhaltung der Satzung. Zum Zerwürfnis mit den einflußreichen Bhumihar-Brahmanen führten denn letztlich auch nicht die Meinungsverschiedenheiten über die orthodox religiöse Haltung des Swami, sondern seine Aktivitäten in der Nationalbewegung und sein seit Ende der zwanziger Jahre zunehmendes soziales Engagemenent. Der Ashram, der als

Sanskrit Mahavidyalay gedacht war, entwickelte sich in den dreißiger Jahren zum Zentrum der vom Swami geführten Bauernbewegung in Bihar.

So wie die politische Nicht-Brahmanenbewegung im Süden Indiens auf Kooperation mit der Kolonialmacht setzte, hielten sich auch die Kastenbewegungen im Norden von der Nationalbewegung fern. Seiner Weltentrücktheit entrissen, begann der Swami sich jedoch auch bald für den nationalen Befreiungskampf zu interessieren. Nach dem Wanderleben des Asketen und nach der Versenkung ins Wissen sollte ihn nun der uneigennützige Dienst am Volk seinem eigentlichen Ziel, der Annäherung an Gott, näherbringen. Dem Trend der Zeit entsprechend gewann auch für ihn das Mahabharata und vor allem die Bhagavadgita mit ihrer auf aktives, leidenschaftsloses und pflichtorientiertes Handeln ausgerichteten Grundidee eine völlig neue Bedeutung. Die Gita wurde ihm als geistige Orientierungshilfe so wichtig, daß er sie fortan immer bei sich trug.[22] Seit er für die Bhumihar Sabha tätig war, las er neben Hindi auch wieder Englisch und informierte sich über die politischen Ereignisse.

Zur Leitfigur für den aktiven Einstieg des Swami in die politische Bewegung wurde jedoch Mahatma Gandhi. Gandhis Persönlichkeit, sein asketisches Auftreten, seine tiefe Religiosität und das kritisch positive Verhältnis zur Tradition des eigenen Landes faszinierten den orthodoxen Swami. Das Prinzip der Nichtzusammenarbeit mit der Kolonialregierung sprach wiederum seine antibritischen Gefühle an. Auch ohne politische Bildung empfand der Swami die Fremdherrschaft als nationale Erniedrigung. Ein Gespräch, das er im Dezember 1920 in Patna mit Gandhi führen konnte, als dieser zur Propagierung von Khilafat und Nichtzusammenarbeit das Land bereiste,[23] gab den Ausschlag. Der Swami wurde zum Kongreß-Freiwilligen. Er nahm an der Kongreßtagung 1920 in Nagpur teil und widmete sich anschließend mit vollem Einsatz der Nichtzusammenarbeitsbewegung auf dem Lande. Er sammelte Geld für den Tilak Swaraj Fund, propagierte das Spinnrad und begann selbst zu spinnen. Nach der Teilnahme am Ahmadabad Kongreß Ende 1921 wurde er wie viele andere Kongreß-Freiwillige Anfang 1922 verhaftet und erhielt seine erste Gefängnisstrafe.

Die Arbeit in der Nationalbewegung war der entscheidende Einschnitt im Leben des Swami. Er lernte Menschen aus den unterschiedlichsten Gesellschaftsschichten in ungewöhnlichen Situationen kennen. Reisen zu Kongreßtagungen und später die Arbeit in der Bauernorganisation führten ihn in verschiedene Regionen des Landes. Die Reisen stärkten - wie auch Ranga in seinen Memoiren bemerkte - das Nationalgefühl der Beteiligten. Auch die tief verwurzelten Vorurteile, die der Swami als orthodoxer Hindu gegenüber den Muslims hatte, wurden in der Nichtzusammenarbeitsbewegung abgebaut. Gespräche mit Maulanas, Haftgefährten im Gefängnis, ließen ihn den Islam mit anderen Augen sehen. Im Koran, den er später selbst in der Hindi-Übersetzung las, fand er Gedanken religiöser Toleranz, die er dem Islam ehemals abgesprochen hatte.[24] Obwohl er selbst ein zutiefst religiöser Mensch blieb, die äußerst streng befolgten Reinheitsregeln des Brahmanen gegen spätere

Vorwürfe als Regeln der Hygiene verteidigte und auch seinen Lebensstil nicht änderte, trat die Religion für ihn in dem Maße in den privaten Bereich zurück, wie gesellschaftliche Fragen an Bedeutung gewannen.

Das Engagement des Swami für die Kastenorganisation der Bhumihars hielt bis Ende der zwanziger Jahre an. In dieser Zeit wuchsen die Meinungsverschiedenheiten mit den Führern der Bhumihar-Bewegung. Als der Swami Ende der zwanziger Jahre im Zusammenhang mit der Unabhängigkeitsbewegung begann, die Interessen der hilfesuchenden Bauern und Pächter in der Umgebung seines Bihta-Ashram auch gegenüber wohlhabenden Bhumihar-Samindaren zu vertreten, wurden die Differenzen unüberbrückbar. Ein nicht unerheblicher Teil der Spenden für den Bihta-Ashram blieb fortan aus. Der Swami selbst sorgte im Jahre 1929 für die Auflösung der Bhumihar Brahman Sabha. In seiner Parteinahme für die Bauern - Bhumihars, aber auch Goalas, Kurmis und Koeris - spielte die Kastenzugehörigkeit keine Rolle mehr. Der u.a. auch von Girish Mishra und Braj Kumar Pande gegen den Swami erhobene Vorwurf, eine Doppelrolle gespielt zu haben - die des radikalen Bauernführers und die des Interessenvertreters der Bhumihars[25] - ist nicht gerechtfertigt. Swami Sahajanand Saraswati hatte sich unter dem Einfluß der Nationalbewegung vom weltentrückten Bettelmönch über den Ideologen einer Kastenorganisation bis zum engagierten Bauernführer entwickelt.

N. G. Rangas politisches Weltbild wurde dagegen durch seine bäuerliche Herkunft, seine geistig anregende Jugend, aber auch durch ein Studium in England geprägt. Der nationale Unabhängigkeitskampf bot den Rahmen, in dem er seine Vorstellungen weiterentwickelte. Nach Abschluß der Oberschule im Jahr 1920 besuchte N. G. Ranga für kurze Zeit das Andhra Christian College in Guntur, bevor der Vater sich entschloß, den Sohn zum Studium nach England zu schicken. Mit Hilfe von Freunden konnte Ranga im St. Catherene's College in Oxford unterkommen. Mit wachem Interesse verfolgte er vor allem die soziale Bewegung in England, beobachtete den wachsenden Einfluß der Labour Party und war von sozialistischen Ideen beeindruckt. In seinen Memoiren erwähnt er vor allem den Einfluß, den die Fabian Society und deren Führer Sidney und Beatrice Webb in Universitätskreisen hatten.[26] Er las H.G. Wells und Bertrand Russell, interessierte sich für die Ereignisse in Sowjetrußland, für die französische und amerikanische Revolution und ihre Leitfiguren. Das politische Interesse war so groß, daß er seine anfängliche Absicht, Rechtsanwalt zu werden und sich für den Indian Civil Service zu qualifizieren, aufgab und stattdessen Ökonomie, Politische Wissenschaften und Soziologie studierte. Er setzte sich das Ziel, als Politiker auf die Zukunft Indiens Einfluß zu nehmen.

Trotz all der neuen Eindrücke hatten jedoch die Ereignisse in seinem Heimatland immer Vorrang. Mit Begeisterung verfolgte er wie andere Auslandsinder die Nichtzusammenarbeitsbewegung. Vor allem Gandhis Lösungsansätze für Indiens Probleme gewannen seine Sympathie. Wie Gandhi wollte er an die Traditionen des Landes anknüpfen und dem Bauern einen zentralen Platz im unabhängigen Indien einräumen. Er ging von der Überzeugung aus, daß Indien als Bauernland einen anderen Weg als die Industrienationen des Westens einzuschlagen hätte und begutachtete alle neuen Ideen und Theorien, mit denen er während seines Studiums in England konfrontiert wurde, unter diesem Gesichtspunkt. Er knüpfte intensive Kontakte mit der britischen Arbeiterbewegung. In seinen Semesterferien hatte er Gelegenheit, an einer von der Workers Educational Association (WEA) organisierten dreiwöchigen Sommerschule für junge Gewerkschafter teilzunehmen und war beeindruckt von der solidarischen Atmosphäre. In England gewann er die Überzeugung, daß die Ideen der sozialen Gerechtigkeit und sozialen Demokratie auch bei der Planung des zukünftigen Indien eine Rolle spielen müßten.[27] Durch Freundschaften, die er auf der Sommerschule schloß, erhielt er Einblick in die praktische Arbeit von Gewerkschaften, Arbeiter-Klubs und WEA-Zentren. Die gewerkschaftlichen Bemühungen um die Arbeiterbildung in England beeindruckten ihn so nachhaltig, daß er später mit ähnlichen Methoden die Bildung unter den indischen Bauern befördern wollte.

Rangas aktives Interesse an der Labour-Politik machte ihn zu einem der Mitbegründer des Oxford Labour Clubs wie der International Labour Group. 1922 nahm er an der Sommerschule des Labour Research Department in Scarborough teil und lernte dort führende linke Köpfe jener Zeit kennen - Page Arnot und R. P. Dutt, zu jener Zeit Herausgeber des Labour Monthly, sowie H. N. Brailsford. Als Bauernvertreter aus einem kolonial beherrschten Agrarland befremdete ihn die Ausschließlichkeit, mit der sich Sozialisten und Kommunisten auf das Industrieproletariat orientierten, ebenso wie deren Verurteilung Gandhis als Sozialreaktionär. Großes Interesse brachte er dagegen dem von G. D. H. Cole und Hobson propagierten "Gilden-Sozialismus" entgegen. Er wurde in seiner Hoffnung bestärkt, an indische Traditionen anknüpfen und aus den Überresten von Berufskasten moderne Gilden entwickeln zu können.[28] H.N. Brailsford lenkte sein Interesse zudem auf die Kredit-, Dienstleistungs- und Marktgenossenschaften und ihre mögliche Relevanz für das indische Dorf. Im Jahre 1922 unternahm Ranga eine zweimonatige Tour durch Europa, um das Genossenschaftswesen in Dänemark, Frankreich, Italien, der Schweiz und Deutschland zu studieren. Nach der Rückkehr vertrat er vor der International Labour Group die Ansicht, daß die Bauernvölker Asiens und Afrikas eigene politische und ökonomische Gedanken und Aktionslinien entwickeln müßten. Zu seinem Leitbild machte er einen Sozialismus, der den Bauern wenn nicht vor, so doch zumindest gleichberechtigt neben den Arbeiter stellen und dem Genossenschaftswesen auf dem Lande einen zentralen Platz einräumen sollte. 1926 graduierte Ranga in Wirtschaftswissenschaften als B. Litt (Economics) und erwarb zusätzlich Diplome in Politischer Wissenschaft und Ökonomie.

Nach Indien zurückgekehrt, fand Ranga eine Anstellung als Professor für Geschichte und Ökonomie im Pachaiyappa College der Universität Madras. Nach dem Muster der Fabianer führte er Dorfuntersuchungen fort und veröffentlichte sie unter dem Titel "Economic Organisation of Indian Villages". Er begann, die Hinwendung zum Dorf, Sozialarbeit nach britischem Muster auf dem Lande und die Organisierung der Bauern zu propagieren. Im Jahre 1928 setzte er sich bei der Gründung der Andhra Provincial Ryots Association gegen Gründungsmitglieder durch, die die Bauernvereinigung nach dem Muster der amerikanischen Bauerngewerkschaften gestalten und von der Politik fernhalten wollten.[29] Auf ihrer zweiten Konferenz im Jahre 1929 unterstützte Ranga als Präsident der Vereinigung die Kongreßpolitik und erklärte die Bauernherrschaft zum Ziel der Bewegung.[30] Im Jahre 1930 gab er seine bezahlte Anstellung auf, um sich ganz der Sache der Bauern zu widmen. Es war die Zeit, in der sich die Folgen der Weltwirtschaftskrise auch in der indischen Landwirtschaft bemerkbar zu machen begann, die bäuerlichen Probleme sich zuspitzten und der nationale Unabhängigkeitskampf auf einen neuen Höhepunkt zusteuerte - die Zeit, in der sich auch der Swami den Bauern zuwandte.

Swami Sahajanand Saraswati hatte schon im November 1927 von dem Bihta-Ashram aus eine West Patna Kisan Sabha ins Leben gerufen, die im März 1928 mit einer Verfassung und einem Statut organisatorische Gestalt annahm. Der unmittelbare Anlaß war die Wahl zum Provinzlandtag im Wahlkreis West Patna, wo man die dem INK nahestehenden indischen Vertreter im Interesse der Pächter beeinflussen wollte. Ganz im gandhistischen Sinne sollten die Spannungen zwischen Samindaren und Bauern mit konstitutionellen Mitteln abgebaut werden. Über seine eigene Haltung schrieb der Swami später: "Thus I began the organised Kisan Sabha as a staunch class-collaborator..."[31] Die Bihar Provincial Kisan Conference, die am 27. November 1929 auf dem großen Bauernmarkt in Sonepur die Gründung der Bihar Provincial Kisan Sabha beschloß, kam aus ähnlichen Gründen zustande. Als Initiatoren hatte man Swami Sahajanand Saraswati und Pandit Yamuna Karji gewonnen, zu ihren Gründungsmitgliedern zählten jedoch auch Kongreßführer wie Krishna Singh, der spätere Premierminister von Bihar, und Rajendra Prasad. Die Vertreter der Swaraj Party - Kongreßleute, die sich dem Wahlboykott nicht angeschlossen hatten - wollten mit Hilfe einer Bauernorganisation ihrem Entwurf für eine neue Pachtgesetzgebung im Provinzlandtag größeres Gewicht verleihen. Während der vom Nationalkongreß initiierten Bewegung des bürgerlichen Ungehorsams ruhte die Arbeit der Bihar Provincial Kisan Sabha. Erst im August 1933 wurde sie wiederbelebt, um diesmal den Pachtgesetzgebungsplänen der von Samindaren beherrschten United Party entgegentreten zu können.

Der unmittelbare Kontakt mit den Bauern brachte den Swami jedoch bald in Konflikt mit der offiziellen Kongreßpolitik. Die Arbeit in einem Komitee der Kisan Sabha, das den Beschwerden der Bauern des Gaya Distrikts nachging, erfüllte den Swami mit Erbitterung gegen die Großgrundbesitzer, zum Teil Bhumihars. Weder die Regierung von Bihar noch die vermögenden Samindare waren gewillt, den von den Folgen der Weltwirtschaftskrise gebeutelten Pächtern Nachlaß zu gewähren. Vermittlungsbemühungen der Kommission stießen bei den Grundbesitzern auf taube

Ohren. Die für den Swami bittere Erfahrung, daß die Samindare nicht reformierbar waren, bestätigte sich 1934 bei der Arbeit in einem zur Linderung der Erdbebenfolgen in Bihar gebildeten Notstandskomitee. Angesichts der Tatsache, daß Grundbesitzer erbarmungslos die Pachtrückstände der total ruinierten Bauern eintrieben und sogar die Erdbeben-Beihilfen von ihnen einforderten, wandte sich der Swami vollends von der gandhistischen Linie des Ausgleichs ab. Gandhi verlor für ihn seine Glaubwürdigkeit, als er dem Swami den unrealistischen Rat gab, die dem Kongreß nahestehenden Manager der Samindare um Hilfe zu bitten. Mit der Abkehr von Gandhi als Leitfigur wurde der Swami empfänglich für die Argumente der Kongreß-Sozialisten, die sich in dieser Zeit um Kontakte mit der Bauernbewegung zu bemühen begannen.

N.G. Ranga setzte sich seit 1931 in Andhra für die Linderung der Folgen der Weltwirtschaftskrise auf dem Lande ein. Er war maßgeblich beteiligt an der Gründung eines Andhra Peasant Protection Committee, das ein Moratorium für landwirtschaftliche Schulden forderte. Mit Hilfe von Bauernkomitees in den Dörfern organisierte er den Widerstand gegen Steuererhöhungen in den Godavari und Krishna Distrikten. Er leitete Untersuchungen zur Lage der Bauern in den Samindari Regionen Andhras und wirkte mit an der Gründung der Andhra State Zamindari Ryots Conference in Venkatagiri, die zum ersten Mal die Abschaffung des Samindari Systems durch Gesetz forderte. Als Verteter Andhras brachte Ranga dieses Anliegen 1931 auf der Sitzung des Allindischen Kongreßkomitees in Bombay vor, fand jedoch wenig Resonanz. Unter dem Einfluß der Ideen der Fabianer setzte Ranga stark auf Veränderung der sozialökonomischen Struktur auf dem Lande mit legislativen Mitteln. So ließ er sich trotz des Wahlboykotts durch den INK 1933 in die Zentrale Gesetzgebende Versammlung wählen. Hier regte er die Bildung einer Bauerngruppe von Abgeordneten unterschiedlicher Parteien an. Auch seine Bemühungen um ländliche Entwicklung führte er fort. Er leitete die Dorfräte-Bewegung (Village Panchayat Movement) für ländliche Selbstverwaltung ein und beschäftigte sich, inspiriert von Gandhi, mit der Lage der Unberührbaren, die zumeist Landarbeiter waren. In ihrem Interesse wollte er die Industriegesetzgebung auf das Land ausgeweitet wissen.

Im Jahre 1934 begann Ranga auch eines seiner Hauptanliegen seit früher Jugend - die Bildungsarbeit unter den Bauern - voranzutreiben. In seinem Heimatdorf Nidubrolu eröffnete er das Indian Peasant Institute mit einem kleinen Verlag für Bauern-Literatur, und im gleichen Jahr wirkte er mit an der Gründung der Erwachsenenbildungsgesellschaft von Andhra. Das Bauerninstitut in Nidubrolu wurde zum Ausbildungszentrum von Bauernaktivisten in ganz Andhra. Neben den regelmäßigen Veranstaltungen des Instituts wurden Wochenend- und Sommerkurse für junge Bauern in verschiedenen Distrikten Andhras abgehalten.[32] Um die Kastenschranken zu überwinden, wurde Wert auf gemeinsame Mahlzeiten gelegt. Unterschiedliche politische Gruppierungen konnten sich später bei ihrer Arbeit auf die Absolventen dieser Kurse stützen. Bauernaktivisten wurden auch angeregt, Lieder über ihre Kämpfe zu verfassen. Ranga brachte die Bauernlieder in einer Anthologie (Rytu-Bhajanavali) in Telugu heraus. Sie fanden über die Kurse weite Verbreitung und bereicherten die bäuerliche Kultur Andhras.[33]

Um Bauernanliegen im Nationalkongreß wirksamer vorbringen zu können, begann sich Ranga um einen Zusammenschluß der Bauernaktivisten auf gesamtindischer Ebene zu bemühen. Rückhalt fand er beim linken Flügel des Nationalkongresses, der sich seit 1929 in einzelnen Provinzen herausbildete und im Jahre 1934 auf gesamtindischer Ebene zur Congress Socialist Party (CSP) formierte. Kongreßsozialisten unterstützten ihn bei der Einberufung einer allindischen Konferenz der Bauernaktivisten im Oktober 1935 in Madras. Da die Bauernführer der U. P. und von Bihar, an erster Stelle der Swami, wegen noch vorhandener Vorbehalte gegen eine gesamtindische Bauernvereinigung nicht teilgenommen hatten, wurde in Madras ein Organisationskomitee mit Ranga als Präsidenten gebildet. Es sollte Kisan Sabhas in den Provinzen propagieren und die Provinzorganisationen für eine gesamtindische Vereinigung gewinnen. Im Ergebnis dessen wurde im April 1936 zur Zeit der Jahrestagung des INC in Lakhnau der Allindische Kisan Congress einberufen. Hier wurde ein Allindisches Bauernkomitee mit Ranga, dem Swami und Mohanlal Gautam als Sekretären gewählt, die Veröffentlichung eines allindischen Bauern-Bulletins mit Indulal Yagnik als Herausgeber beschlossen und ein Allindisches Bauern-Manifest mit Forderungen angenommen, die dem INC unterbreitet werden sollten.[34]

Es begann eine Periode fruchtbarer Zusammenarbeit zwischen den Bauernaktivisten der Provinzen. In dem Klima der Einheitsfrontpolitik von 1935-1939, die die Kommunisten entsprechend ihrer damaligen internationalen Linie in Indien verfolgten, fand der Kisan Kongreß, der sich seit 1938 All-India Kisan Sabha nannte, Anregung und Unterstützung bei Sozialisten und Kommunisten sowohl auf theoretischem Gebiet bei der Erarbeitung und Begründung seiner Forderungen als auch in der praktischen Arbeit durch einen Zustrom von engagierten Organisatoren und Helfern. Zum anderen bot die Bauernbewegung den verschiedenen um sie bemühten politischen Kräften die notwendige Massenbasis. Dennoch blieb eine gewisse Distanz zwischen den Bauernführern und ihren jeweiligen politischen Partnern. Die Bauernführer hegten ein durchaus nicht unberechtigtes Mißtrauen, daß es den politischen Parteien mehr um den Masseneinfluß als um die Probleme der Bauern ging. Der Swami, Ranga und andere Bauernführer fühlten sich dagegen durch ihr gemeinsames Engagement für die Bauern enger verbunden. Ranga bemerkte später: "I found in Swami Sahajanand Saraswati a kindred spirit, who was 100 % Kisan-minded..."[35] Dennoch gerieten auch sie und mit ihnen die Kisan Sabha in den Strudel der Ereignisse, die mit dem Ausbruch des zweiten Weltkrieges, mit dem Ende der Einheitsfrontpolitik und der Neuorientierung der nationalen Befreiungsbewegung verbunden waren. In diesem Strudel, der die politische Landschaft veränderte, trieben sie auseinander, und auch die Bauernbewegung veränderte ihr Gesicht.

Vorerst aber, seit Mitte der dreißiger Jahre, erlebte die Bauernbewegung einen ungeahnten Aufschwung. Zum 2. Allindischen Kongreß der Kisan Sabha, der parallel zur INK-Tagung in Faizpur im Dezember 1936 abgehalten wurde, waren 40.000 Bauern teils aus entfernten Dörfern erschienen, und im Jahre 1938 zählte der Verband über eine halbe Million Mitglieder.[36] Auf Kundgebungen, Versammlungen, Demonstrationen und in großen Protestmärschen verlieh er seinen Forderungen Nachdruck. In zahlreichen lokalen Kämpfen verteidigten Pächter ihre Rechte auf den von ihnen bearbeiteten Boden, und Bauern wehrten sich gegen Kanalwassersteuer-, Bodensteuer- und Pachterhöhungen sowie gegen feudale Abgaben. Die größte Leistung der AIKS bestand jedoch darin, daß sie mit ihren Aktivitäten den Boden für notwendige strukturelle Reformen auf dem Lande vorbereitete.

Unter Rangas Einfluß hatte die Andhra Zamindari Ryots Association schon seit 1931 eine Gesetzgebung zur völligen Abschaffung des Samindari Systems gefordert. Sie brachte diesen Gedanken in die im April 1935 gebildete South Indian Federation of Peasants' and Workers' Associations ein, die die "ultimate abolition of Zamindars and all other intermediary institutions between the peasants and the Government"[37] verlangte. Der Swami in Bihar schloß sich dieser Forderung erst nach einigem Zögern an, weil sich die Verhältnisse in seiner Region grundsätzlich von denen in Andhra unterschieden. Im November 1935 nahm aber auch die Bihar Provincial Kisan Sabha eine Resolution zur Abschaffung des Samindari-Systems, und zwar ohne Entschädigung, an. So wurde dann auch die Abschaffung aller Systeme des Großgrundbesitzes und die Übertragung der Rechte am Boden an die Bauern, die ihn bearbeiteten, zu einer Grundforderung des von der AIKS im Jahre 1936 angenommenen All India Kisan Manifesto.[38]

Im Jahre 1937 bildete der Indische Nationalkongreß in einer Reihe von Provinzen die Regierung. Zu seinem Wahlsieg hatten auch die Kisan Sabha und deren Führer mit ihrer uneingeschränkten Unterstützung beigetragen. Die geplante Agrargesetzgebung, die vor allem in den Samindari-Gebieten wie Bihar den Kompromiß mit den Samindaren als einem bedeutenden Teil der begrenzten Wählerschaft suchte, erfüllte jedoch nicht die Versprechungen des INK-Wahlmanifestes und des Agrarprogramms von 1936. Die in Bewegung geratenen Bauern und ihre Führer wurden enttäuscht. Als Reaktion darauf radikalisierte sich die Kisan Sabha. Auf ihrer Jahrestagung im Mai 1938 in Bengalen bestätigte die AIKS eine Resolution zur "Abschaffung des Feudalismus", in der die Kisan Sabhas aufgerufen wurden, "to ... launch forthwith a vigorous campaign for abolishing all systems of landlordism root and branch without paying any compensation"[39]. Der Druck, dem sich die Kongreßregierungen durch die Bauernagitationen ausgesetzt sahen, fand seinen Niederschlag in Sardar Patels eingangs erwähnten ärgerlichen Worten. In Bihar ergriff der Kongreß disziplinarische Maßnahmen gegen den Swami und seine Gefährten. Auf einer Sitzung des Allindischen Kongreßkomitees im September 1938 in Delhi wurden ausdrücklich alle Maßnahmen der Kongreßregierungen "zur Verteidigung von Leben und Eigentum" unterstützt und der "Klassenkrieg mit gewaltsamen Mitteln" verdammt.[40] Die Forderung nach strukturellen Reformen auf dem Lande, die die Kisan Sabha und ihre Führer so nachdrücklich vertreten hatten, war jedoch aus der Planung für ein zukünftiges unabhängiges Indien nicht mehr wegzudenken. 1945 konkretisierte der Arbeitsausschuß des INK in einem Wahlprogramm die geplante "Reform des Landsystems" dahingehend, daß er nun ebenfalls: "the removal of intermediaries between the peasant and the State" forderte.[41]

Die so unterschiedlichen Bauernführer, der streng traditionell-religiös gebildete Bettelmönch Swami Sahajanand Saraswati und der mit moderner Bildung und Auslandserfahrung ausgestattete Bauernpolitiker N. G. Ranga trafen sich auf dem Höhepunkt der Bauernbewegung in der zweiten Hälfte der dreißiger Jahre auf einer gemeinsamen Plattform. Bewirkt hatte dieses Zusammentreffen die Nationalbewegung, in der beide ihre Erfahrungen und Erkenntnisse gesammelt hatten. Als Interessenvertreter der selbständigen Bauern und aufbegehrenden Pächter wurden sie mit den Problemen der Klassendifferenzierung ihrer eigenen Gesellschaft konfrontiert und mußten sich mit der sozialen Frage auseinandersetzen. Über die mit der nationalen Unabhängigkeitsbewegung verbundenen Ideen von nationaler, demokratischer Selbstbestimmung hinaus nahmen sie deshalb die ebenfalls in den Industrieländern des Westens entwickelten Vorstellungen von sozialem Fortschritt in unterschiedlichem Grade in ihr Weltbild auf. Sie bemühten sich beide mehr oder weniger erfolgreich um die Akzeptanz dieser Ideen sowohl unter den Bauern als auch im Nationalkongreß. Ranga versuchte, den Fabianschen Sozialismus abzuwandeln und einem Bauernland wie Indien anzupassen.

Beide Bauernführer waren und blieben fest in der Tradition ihres Landes verwurzelt. Der Swami ließ bis zu seinem Lebensende nicht von seinem brahmanischen Lebensstil ab. Seine asketische Neigung, die Ablehnung irdischen Reichtums, begünstigte jedoch die Aufnahme sozialistischer und kommunistischer Vorstellungen. Er nahm sich der Sache der Bauern mit einer an der Gita orientierten Pflichtauffassung des uneigennützigen Dienstes an. Seine Entwicklung war ungewöhnlich, aber kein Einzelfall, wie der Lebensweg seines zeitweiligen Gefährten in der Bihar Provincial Kisan Sabha, Rahul Sankrityayan, beweist.[42] Bei Ranga waren es dagegen die eigene Abstammung aus einer aufstrebenden, um Anerkennung ringenden Bauernkaste und die damit verbundenen Erfahrungen, die ihn die Sache des selbständigen Bauern zu seiner Lebensaufgabe machen ließen. Eines seiner Hauptanliegen war die Veränderung der antiquierten sozialökonomischen Struktur auf dem Lande. Unter kolonialen Bedingungen erforderte dieses Ziel die aktive Beteiligung an der Nationalbewegung. Darüber hinaus war eine gewisse Radikalität vonnöten, um innergesellschaftliche Widerstände gegen strukturelle Veränderungen zu überwinden. Auf dem Höhepunkt der Bauernbewegung verbündete sich Ranga zeitweilig mit Sozialisten und Kommunisten, obwohl er sich von ihnen in der Bauernfrage grundsätzlich abgrenzte. Im unabhängigen Indien entwickelte sich

Ranga folgerichtig zum engagierten und beredten Verfechter eines Bauernkapitalismus. Auf diesem Weg rückte er von sozialistischen Ideen ab und suchte seine Bündnispartner je nach den Umständen in unterschiedlichen politischen Lagern. Gerade weil er seiner Leitlinie - der Verteidigung und Förderung des selbständigen Bauern - treu blieb, absolvierte er eine äußerst bunte politische Karriere.

Der Lebensverlauf beider Bauernführer - N. G. Rangas wie auch der des Swami - zeugen davon, daß sich die Verwurzelung in der Tradition des eigenen Landes und die Aufnahme moderner, in den Industrienationen des Westens entstandener Ideen durchaus nicht ausschlossen. Wo diese Ideen den indischen Bedingungen nicht entsprachen, wurden sie abgewandelt, angepaßt und qualitativ verändert.

## Anmerkungen

1 Rajendra Prasad, Correspondence and Select Documents, hg. von Valmiki Chowdhary, New Delhi 1984, 106. From Vallabhbhai Patel, 22nd September 1937, 97.
2 Vgl. R. Guha, On Some Aspects of the Historiography of Colonial India. In: R. Guha (Hg.), Subaltern Studies I, Writings on South Asian History and Society, Delhi 1982.
3 Vgl. Krishna Kumar, Quest for Self-Identity. Cultural Consciousness and Education in Hindi Region, 1880-1950. In: Economic and Political Weekly 25(1990)23, 1251.
4 Swami Sahajanand Saraswati, Mera Jivan Sangharsh, Bihta (Patna) 1952, 17 (Hindi).
5 Ebenda, 18.
6 Vgl. ebenda, 37.
7 Ebenda, 37.
8 A. Satyanarayana, Andhra Peasants under British Rule. Agrarian Relations and the Rural Economy 1900-1940, New Delhi 1990, 118.
9 Vgl. N.G. Ranga, Fight for Freedom, Delhi u.a. 1968, 4/5.
10 Ebenda, 37.
11 Vgl. Christopher Baker, Review: Politics and Social Conflict in South India ... by Eugene F. Irschick, Berkeley/Los Angeles 1969. In: Modern South Asian Studies 5(1971)3, 227.
12 Vgl. Census of India, 1931, Bd. I - India, Teil I - Report, Delhi 1933, 465.
13 Vgl. Ranga, Fight for Freedom, 24.
14 Vgl. ebenda, 51.
15 Vgl. ebenda, 28.
16 Ebenda, 61.
17 Ebenda, 134.
18 Vgl. A.L. Thakur, Sanskrit Literature in Bihar (1757-1974). In: Kali Kinkar Datta/Jatashankar Jha (Hg.), The Comprehensive History of Bihar, Bd. III, Teil II, Kap. XXI, A., 464.
19 Vgl. Swami Sahajanand Saraswati, Mera Jiwan Sangharsh, 161-162.
20 Ebenda, 160.
21 Vgl. ebenda, 278-279.
22 Vgl. ebenda, 167-168, 232.
23 Ebenda, 184-185.

24 Vgl. ebenda, 243-244.
25 Vgl. Girish Mishra/Braj Kumar Pandey, Socio-Economic Roots of Casteism in Bihar. In: N.L. Gupta (Hg.), Transition from Capitalism to Socialism & Other Essays, New Delhi 1974, 166.
26 Vgl. Ranga, Fight for Freedom, 82.
27 Vgl. ebenda, 103.
28 Vgl. ebenda, 110-111.
29 Vgl. N.G. Ranga/Swami Sahajanand Saraswati, History of Kisan Movement, Madras 1939, 25-26.
30 Vgl. L.P. Sinha, The Left Wing in India (1919-1947), Muzaffarpur 1965, 303.
31 Swami Sahajanand Saraswati, The origin and growth of the Kisan movement in India, unveröffentlichtes Manuskript, Swami Sahajanand Saraswati Papers (Mikrofilm), Nehru Memorial Museum and Library, 10.
32 Vgl. Ranga, Fight for Freedom, 191ff.
33 Vgl. V. Ramakrishna, Literary and Theatre Movements in Colonial Andhra: Struggle for Left Ideological Legitimacy. In: Social Scientist 236-37, *21*(1993)1-2, 74.
34 Vgl. Ranga/Saraswati, History of Kisan Movement, 62-63.
35 Ranga, Fight for Freedom, 216.
36 Vgl. Ranga/Saraswati, History of Kisan Movement, 64 u. 84.
37 N.G. Ranga, The Indian Peasant, o.O., 1936, 68.
38 The All India Kisan Manifesto. As adopted by the All-India Kisan Committee on 21st Aug. 1936. In: The Indian Annual Register. Juli-Dezember 1936, Bd. II, Kalkutta o.J., 295.
39 N.G. Ranga, Kisan Hand Book, o.O. 1938, 59.
40 Vgl. The All India Congress Committee, Delhi, 24th Sept. to 26th Sept. 1938. In: The Indian Annual Register, Juli-Dezember 1938, Bd. II, Kalkutta o.J., 278f.
41 Vgl. Indian National Congress, Resolutions on Economic Policy Programme and Allied Matters (1924-1969), New Delhi 1969, 15f.
42 Vgl. Arvind N. Das, Peasants and Peasant Organisations: The Kisan Sabha in Bihar. In: The Journal of Peasant Studies *9*(1982)3, 64ff.

# Christliche Hindus - indische Christen? Die "Nationalarbeiter" der Dänisch-Halleschen Mission in Südindien im 18. Jahrhundert

Heike Liebau/Margret Liepach

Das Wirken europäischer Missionen in Indien stellt ein interessantes, komplexes, bisher jedoch überwiegend einseitig ausgewertetes Begegnungsfeld zwischen Angehörigen unterschiedlicher Religionen und Zivilisationen dar. Das nach außen manifestierte Streben einer Mission nach zahlreicher Bekehrung der "Heiden", die Dokumentierung des "Missionserfolges" in statistischen Zahlenangaben sind zwar für die Bewertung der Missionstätigkeit im ursprünglichen Anliegen relevant, sagen aber noch nichts über die veränderten Befindlichkeiten der konkret Betroffenen aus.

Dem vorliegenden Artikel liegen Untersuchungen zu einer zahlenmäßig kleinen Gruppe christianisierter Inder zugrunde, die in der ersten Hälfte des 18. Jahrhunderts als Prediger oder Katecheten im Dienst der Dänisch-Halleschen Mission[1] in Südindien standen. Für diese sogenannten "Nationalarbeiter" war der Übergang von der "heidnischen" zur christlichen Identität nicht mit einem öffentlich dokumentierten Glaubenswechsel abgeschlossen, sie hatten ihre christliche Identität als Missionsdiener darüber hinaus glaubwürdig und überzeugend an die Bevölkerung des Landes zu vermitteln. Ihre indische Herkunft mit der traditionellen Verankerung in Kastensystem und Dorfgemeinde steht in scheinbar unlösbarem Widerspruch zu dem Anspruch, im Rahmen der Mission und damit im Namen des Christentums wirksam zu werden.

Der in der Gestalt der "Nationalarbeiter" verkörperte und von den betreffenden Personen mehr oder weniger bewußt erlebte Konflikt zwischen traditionellen indischen/hinduistischen Lebensformen und europäisch/christlichem Denken spielte in der bisherigen Forschung zur Geschichte der Tranquebar-Mission kaum eine Rolle. In den im 19. Jahrhundert entstandenen biographischen Arbeiten werden die Landprediger in erster Linie als Helfer der europäischen Missionare betrachtet und in dieser Eigenschaft nach ihren unmittelbaren missionarischen Aktivitäten befragt.[2] Auch in neueren Arbeiten war dieser spezielle Personenkreis nie vordergründiger Forschungsgegenstand.[3]

Bisher existieren umfassendere Studien weder zu einzelnen Persönlichkeiten noch zur Problematik insgesamt.[4]

Bei den für die vorliegenden Darlegungen herangezogenen Quellen handelt es sich zunächst um die seit 1710 regelmäßig gedruckten Halleschen Berichte[5] bzw. die Neuen Halleschen Berichte[6]. In den dort publizierten Diarien der Missionare werden die Monats- bzw. Reiseberichte der Landprediger selten in voller Länge, häufig dagegen in Auszügen abgedruckt. Teilweise werden sie auch nur indirekt in den Berichten der Missionare wiedergegeben. Angaben zu besonderen Anlässen, z.B. im Zusammenhang mit der Ordinierung oder dem Tod eines Predigers, sind in den Anhängen zu den einzelnen "Continuarien" bzw. "Stücken"[7] enthalten. Nicht selten werden hier ganze Kapitel zu Nationalarbeitern aufgenommen oder ihre Briefe nach Halle, an das Missionskollegium in Kopenhagen oder das Dänische Königshaus abgedruckt.

In den Berichten finden sich darüber hinaus, meist in den Vorreden oder in Briefen, in unregelmäßigen Abständen Aufstellungen der von der Mission unterhaltenen Nationalarbeiter - Katecheten, Unterkatecheten, später dann auch der Landprediger.

Über das gedruckte Quellenmaterial hinaus existiert eine große Anzahl an handschriftlich vorliegenden Dokumenten, teils im Original (Tamil), teils in deutscher, englischer oder dänischer Übersetzung, die bisher allerdings nur teilweise in die Auswertung einbezogen werden konnten.

Die Autorinnen dieses Beitrages versuchen, Probleme des genannten Personenkreises beim Übergang zum Christentum herauszuarbeiten und Erfahrungen dieser Menschen im Umgang mit der neuen Identität zu rekonstruieren.

Ausgehend von unterschiedlicher religiöser und sozialer Herkunft der Personen sowie unter Berücksichtigung von entsprechend differierenden Bildungsmöglichkeiten und Aufgabenbereichen innerhalb des Missionsdienstes wird danach gefragt, wie sich die veränderte Identität der "Nationalarbeiter" manifestiert und von der indischen Bevölkerung einerseits, von den europäischen Missionaren andererseits aufgenommen wird, bzw. wie die Betreffenden selbst mit ihrem Religionswechsel und der daraus resultierenden neuen Stellung im gesellschaftlichen Leben umgehen.

## Herkunft und Motivation der "Nationalarbeiter"[8]

Nicht für alle der im untersuchten Zeitraum von in den Quellen der Tranquebarmission namentlich genannten Landprediger und Katecheten konnte die soziale Herkunft (Kaste/Beruf) bzw. die religiöse Abstammung eindeutig festgestellt werden. Die bedauerlicherweise lückenhaften Informationen lassen demzufolge auch nur vorläufige bzw. tendenzielle Verallgemeinerungen und Schlußfolgerungen zu.

Im Hinblick auf die Herkunft der "Nationalarbeiter" und damit verbunden ihre Motivation für den Übergang zum Christentum sowie für die Aufnahme des Missionsdienstes scheint eine Unterscheidung folgender Gruppen gerechtfertigt:

1. In der Anfangsphase der Auswahl und Heranbildung von "Nationalarbeitern" gab es einen großen Anteil an Personen, die aus hinduistischen Familien stammten bzw. in unterschiedlichem Maße mit den religiösen Tradition lokaler indischer

Glaubensrichtungen verbunden waren. Für diesen Personenkreis zog der Übergang zum christlichen Glauben meist nicht nur den Verlust des sozialen Umfeldes (Großfamilie, Dorfgemeinschaft, Kastenzugehörigkeit) nach sich, er bedeutete zugleich auch einen entscheidenden Bruch mit dem bisher gelebten und praktizierten Alltag (Namensgebung, Eßgewohnheiten, Kleidung).

Die bisher ausgewerteten Materialien lassen die Schlußfolgerung gerechtfertigt erscheinen, daß unter den von den Missionaren der Tranquebar-Mission bekehrten bzw. in den Missionsdienst aufgenommenen Indern Vertreter niederer Kasten überwiegen[9], obgleich die Angaben zur Kastenherkunft oft verschwommen sind. So ist in einzelnen Fällen aus den Berichten zwar zu erfahren, daß die betreffende Person etwa 'aus hohem heidnischem Geschlecht' stammt. Weitere Angaben bzw. die konkrete Bezeichnung der Kaste fehlen aber. Teilweise sind Hinweise auf die berufliche Herkunft vorhanden.

Für die aus hinduistischen Familien stammenden Konvertiten spielten je nach Kastenzugehörigkeit, Bildungsniveau bzw. sozialer Situation verschiedene Motive für den Übergang zum Christentum eine Rolle. Vertreter höherer Kasten, insbesondere Brahmanen, gelangten nach mehr oder weniger intensiver geistiger Auseinandersetzung bewußt zum Entschluß, Christ zu werden. Materielle Beweggründe sowie die niedrige soziale Stellung im Kastensystem sind bei Vertretern der unteren Kasten zweifellos zu berücksichtigen, können aber nicht isoliert von anderen konkreten Umständen gesehen oder für alle gleichermaßen verallgemeinert werden. Zu vermuten ist, daß der Inder, der sich zunächst einmal in irgendeiner Form dem Christentum als einer fremden Religion zu nähern versuchte, dies aus einem wie auch immer gestalteten Konfliktbewußtsein heraus tat. Der Charakter der Widersprüche sowie der unmittelbare Anlaß des Nachdenkens über die christliche Religion sind individuell verschieden.

2. Zu der zweiten für die Herkunft der "Nationalarbeiter" der Tranquebarmission relevanten Bevölkerungsgruppe gehören die Vertreter unterschiedlicher christlicher Konfessionen, in erster Linie die römisch-katholischen Christen[10], mit denen sich die evangelischen Missionare in ihrer täglichen Arbeit regelmäßig auseinandersetzten. Für diese Personen, die bereits einen Bezug zum christlichen Glauben an sich hatten, stellte die Begegnung mit dem von den Tranquebar-Missionaren gepredigten Christentum einen Widerspruch zu ihren bisherigen christlichen Glaubensvorstellungen dar. Wenn es sich auch in diesen Fällen nicht um einen Religionswechsel, sondern "nur" um einen Wechsel der Konfession handelt, waren doch dessen Auswirkungen für die Betroffenen oftmals schmerzlich.
Christen verschiedener Konfessionen (Thomaschristen, Syrische Christen, Armenische Christen) waren bereits seit Jahrhunderten in Südindien ansässig. Ihre Lebensweise und Traditionen hatten sich unter indischen Verhältnissen gefestigt und weiterentwickelt. Demgegenüber war das von den Missionaren gelehrte evangelische Christentum in der europäischen Lebensweise verwurzelt. Die betreffenden

Personen wechselten also nicht einfach die Konfession, sondern sie verließen ein synkretistisch in Südindien verankertes Christentum zugunsten einer in Indien faktisch fremden Glaubensrichtung. Als Vertreter der in Südindien ansässigen Christen konnte man durchaus eine anerkannte Stellung im gesellschaftlichen Leben einnehmen.[11] Der Wechsel der Konfession hatte individuell unterschiedliche Ursachen und konkrete Anlässe. Nicht unwichtig war dabei auch die Bekanntschaft (persönlich oder indirekt durch Literatur oder Erzählungen) mit einem Vertreter der Tranquebar-Mission als Repräsentant der neuen Glaubensrichtung, seiner Überzeugungskraft, Ausstrahlung und Vorbildwirkung auch im Unterschied zu anderen bisher erlebten Europäern und Christen.

3. Die dritte Gruppe, die im Laufe des betrachteten Zeitraumes zahlenmäßig ständig zunimmt, setzt sich aus evangelischen Christen der zweiten, dritten und folgenden Generationen zusammen. Die Missionare legten mit der Zeit besonderen Wert darauf, Inder aus dieser Personengruppe als Katecheten einzusetzen bzw. zu ordinieren. "Es werden die Catecheten ordentlicher Weise aus denen genommen, die im Seminarion erzogen sind, und in der Schule eine Weile gearbeitet haben. Im Anfange des Wercks hat man auch Erwachsene, die theils von der Römischen Kirche, theils aus dem Heydenthum sich zu uns gewandt, nehmen und hinläglich praepariren müssen: welches auch noch zuweilen im Nothfall geschieht."[12] Einmal in Missionsdiensten stehende Inder ließen ihre Kinder bewußt in derselben Tradition aufwachsen und von frühester Jugend an auch am Missionleben teilnehmen.[13] Für diesen Personenkreis bedeuteten sowohl das Christentum in der von den Missionaren verkörperten evangelisch-pietistischen Prägung als auch das Missionsleben bekannte Elemente des Alltags. Die von den Eltern vorgelebte Frömmigkeit und der aktive Dienst im Namen des Glaubens prägten die Entwicklung der Nachkommen von eingeborenen Landpredigern und Katecheten. In vielen Fällen ist gerade bei diesen Personen eine vehemente Ablehnung "heidnischer" Lebensweise, gepaart mit einem ausdrücklich betonten Überlegenheitsanspruch indischer Christen auffallend.

## Ausbildung der "Nationalarbeiter"

Der Bildungsweg der "Nationalarbeiter" vor ihrem Eintritt in den Missionsdienst stand in unmittelbarem Zusammenhang mit den sich aus Herkunft und Wohnort der Familie ergebenden Möglichkeiten und Anforderungen.

Hindus hatten, je nach Kastenzugehörigkeit und sozialem Status der Familie, entweder keine Schulbildung bzw. eine entsprechende Ausbildung im Rahmen der bestehenden religösen Normen. Während für die Vertreter der oberen Kasten, insbesondere für die Brahmanen, der traditionelle Bildungsweg in seinen einzelnen

Etappen vorgezeichnet war, stellten für Angehörige niederer Kasten die materiellen Voraussetzungen der Familie eine entscheidende Komponente hinsichtlich der Bildungsmöglichkeiten dar. Indische, sogenannte "heidnische" Schulen, die sich innerhalb des Wirkungsbereiches einer Mission befanden, standen z.T. auch unter deren Einfluß. Auf die Tranquebar-Mission bezogen bedeutete dies, daß nationale Schulen regelmäßig von Missionaren aufgesucht wurden, die dort unterrichtenden "heidnischen Schulmeister" über den christlichen Glauben belehrt und evtl. den Kindern kleine Aufträge erteilt wurden. Eingeborene Katecheten, die indische Schulen in ihrem Arbeitsbereich zu betreuen hatten, unterrichteten zeitweise selbst in diesen Schulen.[14] Neben den eigentlichen indischen Schulen gab es direkt von einer Mission gegründete Schulen für verschiedene Bevölkerungsgruppen.

Für die Christen verschiedener Konfessionen erfolgte die frühe schulische Ausbildung oftmals innerhalb einer entsprechenden Missionsschule.[15]

Von den Missionaren der Tranquebar-Mission wurde bereits 1707[16] die erste Schule für indische Kinder errichtet. 1726 berichtet man bereits von 21 Schulen, in denen 575 Kinder unterrichtet wurden.[17] Über die religiöse Zusammensetzung der Schüler wird folgendes mitgeteilt: "Vier von diesen Schulen enthalten nur christliche Kinder, die übrigen 17 bestehen aus heydnischen und Muhammedanischen Kindern; und wiederum vier von diesen 17 haben iegliche so wohl einen christlichen, als einen heydnischen Schulmeister, die beyde ihre Besoldung von den Missionarien empfangen. Die in diesen acht Schulen befindliche Kinder werden, ausser dem, daß sie lesen, schreiben und rechnen lernen, von den christlichen Schulmeistern in ihrem Catechismo und der Erkäntniß der heiligen Schrift unterwiesen, und von den Missionarien, beydes mit Büchern und anderen Nothwendigkeiten versehen."[18]

Die unmittelbare Vorbereitung auf den Missionsdienst bzw. die Ausbildung innerhalb des Missionsdienstes wurden von der Tranquebar-Mission systematisch organisiert. 1716, nachdem Bartholomäus Ziegenbalg (1683-1719) von seiner Europareise zurückgekehrt war, wurde das erste Seminar für die Katecheten-Ausbildung mit acht Schülern eröffnet.

Neben der schulischen Ausbildung nach einem bestimmten Lehrprogramm wurden den angehenden bzw. jungen Katecheten viele Erfahrungen durch die Einbeziehung in die alltägliche Missionspraxis vermittelt. Ausgewählte Schüler durften Katecheten auf deren Wanderungen begleiten, Katecheten begleiteten die Landprediger im Dienst und konnten so ständig von ihnen lernen. Die christlichen Schulmeister wiederum wurden häufig nach einer bestimmten Zeit zu Katecheten.

Ein spezielles Predigerseminar gab es nicht. Die künftigen Landprediger wurden individuell auf ihre Ordinierung vorbereitet und von einem dafür bestimmten Missionar in die Tätigkeit eingeführt. Insgesamt gesehen, kommt in dieser frühen Phase den betreuenden Missionaren eine wichtige Rolle zu. Bereits einer der ersten Missionare, Ernst Gründler (1677-1720), hatte zeitweise Katecheten zu betreuen, für die er eigens ein Aus- und Weiterbildungsprogramm erarbeitet hatte. Für die

Gehilfen von Landkatecheten, die später deren Stelle einnehmen sollten, wurden spezielle Schulungen durchgeführt.[19] Die "Nationalarbeiter" blieben immer "ihren" Missionaren rechenschaftspflichtig. Das traf auch auf die Schulmeister zu. "...Alle diese Catecheten und Schulmeister kommen täglich Abends nach 7 Uhr zum Hn. M. Gründler, und berichten, was den gantzen Tag über in ihren Circulis vorgegangen ist."[20] Der spätere Missionar Christian Friedrich Schwartz (1726-1798) hatte zeitweise bis zu zehn Nationalarbeiter zu betreuen.

## Aufgaben der "Nationalarbeiter"

Europäische Missionare in Indien waren wie alle Fremden in der indischen Geschichte im Interesse der Durchsetzung ihrer Ziele auf die Zusammenarbeit mit und die Unterstützung durch bestimmte einheimische Bevölkerungsschichten angewiesen. Man benötigte die Einheimischen zunächst als Dolmetscher, Reisebegleiter, Schreiber, bzw. im Laufe der Zeit auch zur intensiven und regelmäßigen Betreuung der zum Christentum bekehrten Inder. Die sog. Nationalarbeiter wurden in unterschiedlicher Weise in den Missionsdienst einbezogen. Neben den ordinierten Landpredigern und den verschiedenen Katecheten (Stadtkatechet, Landkatechet, Ober-, Unterkatechet) existierte eine zahlenmäßig größere Gruppe von Gehilfen, Schulmeistern und anderen in irgendeiner Weise in Missionsdiensten stehenden indischen Christen. Die Vertreter beider Gruppen unterschieden sich in erster Linie hinsichtlich ihres Bildungsniveaus und der ihnen im Rahmen der Mission übertragenen Aufgaben.

Die Missionare der Tranquebar-Mission begründeten die Einbeziehung von Einheimischen in ihre missionarische Arbeit zunächst mit deren besserer Sprach- bzw. Ortskenntnis sowie der Klimatauglichkeit der Einheimischen. Aber obwohl sich der erste Missionar Bartholomäus Ziegenbalg[21] bereits im Jahre 1709 nach der Möglichkeit, Eingeborene zu ordinieren, erkundigt hatte, wurde erst 1729 vom Missionskollegium in Dänemark die offizielle Erlaubnis dazu erteilt[22]. Und es dauerte noch einmal 4 Jahre, bis 1733 der erste "Nationalprediger" Aaron[23] ordiniert und damit formal den Missionaren gleichgestellt wurde. Entsprechend dem persönlichen Platz in der Hierarchie der einheimischen Missionsarbeiter hatte jeder einen genau festgeschriebenen Aufgaben- und Pflichtenbereich, der neben den für sein Amt festgelegten allgemeinen Aufgaben in Abhängigkeit vom Wirkungsort, von der zu betreuenden Gemeinde sowie von persönlichen Fähigkeiten auch ganz individuelle Pflichten enthielt. Generell galt für alle die Forderung nach strenger Frömmigkeit, unbedingter Disziplin in der Erfüllung der Aufgaben und regelmäßiger Rechenschaftslegung an den Ranghöheren. Landprediger waren den Missionaren rechenschaftspflichtig, Katecheten den Landpredigern und die Gehilfen ihrerseits den Katecheten. Die Missionare fühlten sich in jeder Hinsicht für die "Nationalarbeiter" verantwortlich, führten mit ihnen Arbeitsberatungen durch und nahmen deren

Berichte entgegen. Auch untereinander führten Katecheten unterschiedlicher Regionen Treffen zum Erfahrungsaustausch durch, z.B. um zu ergründen, was sich "für Hindernisse fänden, daß die Kirche sich nicht vermehrete"[24].

Neben allgemein formulierten Grundsätzen und Richtlinien für die Arbeitsweise von Katecheten erhielt vermutlich jeder Katechet seinen ganz persönlichen Aufgabenkatalog. Auf gemeinsamen Versammlungen wurden den Katecheten Richtlinien für die Arbeit gegeben.[25] Darüber hinaus gab es Lehrveranstaltungen zu speziellen Problemen.[26] 1728 wurden z.B. 16 Arbeitsaufgaben für Sattianäden formuliert, die im Grunde unter zwei große Bereiche zu fassen sind: die Hinführung von "Heiden" zum christlichen Glauben sowie die Betreuung von zum Christentum bekehrten Indern. Unter diese übergeordneten Aufgaben fallen u.a. auch ganz konkrete Anforderungen an den Lebenswandel der Katecheten, der von Indern und Missionaren gleichermaßen kritisch beobachtet wurde. Der Katechet hatte Betstunden in den Dörfern durchzuführen, eventuelle Streitigkeiten unter Christen zu schlichten, hinduistische Zeremonien bei Christen zu unterbinden.[27]

Der ordinierte Landprediger hatte "in Verwaltung seines Amts keine Hinderniß[28]". Er war zur Durchführung bestimmter Amtshandlungen und Zeremonien, wie etwa des heiligen Abendmahls oder der Taufe, berechtigt. Trotzdem kann man nicht von einer eigenverantwortlichen, selbständigen Arbeit sprechen. Die Missionare betrachteten sich durchaus als Vorgesetzte der einheimischen christlichen Missionsangestellten. Selbst erfahrene ordinierte Landprediger wurden regelmäßig belehrt und kontrolliert, "... denn bei den Tamulen ruht vorderhand doch alles auf den Missionaren, und selbst den treuesten eingebornen Gehilfen ... kann nichts selbständig überlassen werden"[29]. Die Frage der Verselbständigung und damit verbunden der eigenverantwortlichen Arbeit der Landprediger stand für die Missionare der Tranquebar-Mission nicht. Erst später in der Leipziger Mission erscheinen Berichte über die Selbständigkeit von Landpredigern: "Einigen unsrer älteren Landprediger sind selbständige Pastorate anvertraut..."[30]

Die Katecheten trugen die Hauptlast der alltäglichen vorbereitenden und betreuenden Arbeit unter Christen und "Heiden" vor Ort. Sie hatten u.a. auch die Orte zu besuchen, die den Missionaren noch unbekannt bzw. die für sie schwer zugänglich waren.[31] In Missionsdiensten stehende Frauen konnten in persönliche Lebensbereiche der einheimischen Frauen vordringen, die von Männern nicht angetastet werden durften. Diese Aufgaben übernahmen z.T. die sogenannten "Bibelfrauen", die Frauen und Mädchen betreuten, ihnen aus der Bibel vorlasen und sie auf die Taufe und andere Ereignisse vorbereiteten.[32]

## "Nationalarbeiter" zwischen indischer Herkunft und christlichem Glauben

Der Entschluß eines Hindus, den christlichen Glauben anzunehmen, führte in den meisten Fällen zum einschneidenden Bruch mit den bisher bestehenden sozialen

Bindungen. Denn es betraf in der Regel zunächst nur eine Einzelperson, die diesen Schritt ging, nicht geschlossene Familien. Durch die Taufe der betreffenden Person, die bei Nachweis entsprechender Kenntnisse der christlichen Religion erfolgte, wurde der Glaubenswechsel formal bestätigt und gleichzeitig nach außen dokumentiert. Während es für einen einfachen Christen leichter war, einen für ihn und seine Umwelt im täglichen Leben tragfähigen und praktikablen Kompromiß zwischen dem neuen Glauben und der bisherigen Lebensweise zu finden, wurde gerade diese Frage zum entscheidenden Punkt für die im Dienste der Mission tätigen Inder. Die unmittelbare Teilnahme am eigentlichen Missionsleben, die z.T. auch das Wohnen auf dem Missionsterritorium beinhaltete, sowie die ständige Kontrolle von Arbeit und Lebenswandel durch die Missionare rissen die Landprediger und Katecheten aus ihrem früheren Lebensrhythmus und verlangten eine der neuen Stellung angepaßte Disziplin. Der radikale und plötzliche Identitätsverlust durch Bruch mit Kaste, Familie, Dorfgemeinde auf der einen Seite konnte nicht kompensiert werden durch die abwartende Beobachtungshaltung und oftmals nur langsam wachsende Anerkennung durch das neue religiöse und soziale Umfeld. Katecheten und Landprediger standen im Niemandsland zwischen zwei einander fremden Religionen und Zivilisationen. "Weil sowohl Heyden als auch Christen ein Auge haben"[33], d.h. die Missionsdiener ständig in der Öffentlichkeit unter der Bevölkerung des Landes agierten, dabei aber von europäischen christlichen Missionaren angewiesen und kontrolliert wurden, befanden sie sich in einem doppelten Konflikt. Die Tätigkeit als Katechet bzw. Prediger erforderte eine Neuorientierung im Denken und Glauben, die sich auch im äußeren Erscheinungsbild und im Handeln der Nationalarbeiter manifestierte. Während die Katecheten in ihrer traditionellen Kleidung arbeiten konnten[34], trugen die Prediger europäische Priestergewänder[35] und waren so unmittelbar als indischer Christ erkennbar. Mit dem Religionswechsel und der christlichen Taufe erhielt der Inder auch seinen Taufnamen, der entweder ein biblischer Name war oder sich aus der Übertragung christlicher Begriffe ins Tamil ergab.

Nicht alle christlichen Normen und Gewohnheiten ließen sich ohne weiteres auf die "Nationalarbeiter" übertragen. Besonders schwierig war es, sich über die früher eingehaltenen Kastenschranken beim Essen hinwegzusetzen. 1792 berichtet der Missionar Christoph Samuel John (1747-1813): "Unser Landprediger Rajappen hat wirklich mit einem vornehmen Europäer auf seiner Landreise gegessen, welches er thun konnte, weil seine Landsleute nichts davon erfuhren; zum Essen des Rindfleisches aber würde er sich selbst nicht haben bringen können, aus Beysorge, es wieder von sich geben zu müssen."[36]

Daneben erforderte das neue Leben als Missionsdiener die Abkehr von Traditionen, rituellen Handlungen und religiösen Festen, die z.T. tief in das Alltagsleben der Hindus eingebettet waren und neben dem religiösen Hintergrund oft auch einen lebensnahen praktischen Sinn hatten. Landprediger und Katecheten mußten nicht nur sich selbst von derartigen Handlungen distanzieren, sie trugen darüber hinaus die Verantwortung dafür, daß sich auch die Christen in ihrem Wirkungsgebiet nicht an traditionellen Aktivitäten beteiligten.[37]

Der Glaubenswechsel und der ständige Umgang mit den europäischen Missionaren blieb sicher nicht ohne Auswirkungen auf das Denken der indischen Missionsdiener. Anhand der von ihnen verfaßten Briefe und Berichte ist zumindest nachvollziehbar, daß sie mit dem gleichen begrifflichen Instrumentarium arbeiteten wie die Missionare. Das mag z.T. auch dem religiösen Inhalt der Dokumente sowie der in den meisten Fällen von den betreuenden Missionaren selbst vorgenommenen Übersetzung geschuldet sein. Anzunehmen ist aber dennoch, daß die Landprediger und Katechten eine loyale Haltung gegenüber den Missionaren einnahmen und sich im Laufe der Zeit daran gewöhnten, in den Kategorien der europäischen Missionare zu denken und mit deren Worten zu reden. Durch Anerkennung und Lob seitens der Missionare fühlten sich die "Nationalarbeiter" in ihrer Sonderstellung gegenüber der einheimischen Bevölkerung bestätigt. Äußerungen von einheimischen Missionsangestellten lassen erkennen, daß sich das christliche Überlegenheitsdenken der europäischen Missionare auch in der Haltung der nationalen Missionsdiener gegenüber den indischen Traditionen widerspiegelte.[38]

Die Haltung der Verwandten und Bekannten zum Übergang eines Inders zum Christentum waren in der Regel ablehnend. In ihrem Empfinden mußte die Abkehr von traditionellen Normen und Lebensformen einem Verrat an Familie und Kaste gleichkommen. Dementsprechend waren auch die Reaktionen gegenüber den Betroffenen selbst. Ihm gingen nicht nur die Rechte innerhalb der Familie und der soziale Halt, der durch Kaste und Dorfgemeinde gegeben war,[39] verloren, teilweise waren die Reaktionen der Umgebung durch offenen Haß bis hin zur Gewalt gekennzeichnet. 1734 heißt es in einem Bericht, "daß die, so Christen worden, ... auch manchen Spott und Hohn leiden müssen, da sie von ihren heydnischen Verwandten und Freunden so gar keinen Beystand und Hylfe haben, sondern als ein Vogel in der freyen Luft, und als ein Haus ohne Stütze und Pfeiler ... seyn müssen."[40] Die Entscheidung, die getroffen werden mußte, lautete in vielen Fällen: Christentum oder soziale Geborgenheit der Familie/Kaste/Dorfgemeinde.

Einer ablehnenden Haltung seitens der Umgebung waren auch diejenigen ausgesetzt, die den römisch-katholischen Glauben aufgaben und zum evangelischen Christentum übertraten. Ausgrenzung, Verfolgung bis hin zu Mord waren die Folge.

Differenzierter und unter anderem Vorzeichen sind die Haltungen der Einheimischen zu den "Nationalarbeitern" zu betrachten. In Gestalt eines indischen Katecheten erschien zwar zunächst jemand, der fremd war, weil er einem anderen Glauben angehörte, man fragte aber gleichzeitig nach der Kastenzugehörigkeit der Person. Die Inder sahen auch in den christlichen Missionsdienern in erster Linie die indische Herkunft und akzeptierten als Verkünder der neuen Religion zunächst nur jemanden aus ihrem unmittelbarem sozialem Umfeld. Dieser Tatsache waren sich die Missionare bewußt und trugen dem in der Verteilung der Arbeitsaufgaben an die Katecheten und Prediger Rechnung. Das Einsatzgebiet eines eingeborenen Missionsdieners erstreckte sich in der Regel auf sein ursprüngliches Herkunftsgebiet. "Denn es kann hierbey angemercket werden, daß man für die Sutirer, das ist, Bürgersleute, und für die Bareier, das ist, Bauersleute, für jede Art Catecheten ihres Standes haben muß, sonderlich im Lande... Denn die Indianer bleiben bey ihrem Stande, es sey einer hoch oder niedrig."[41]

Das Verhältnis eines Missionars zu "seinen Nationalarbeitern" läßt sich mit dem Verhältnis eines Lehrers zu seinen Schülern vergleichen. Er fühlte sich verantwortlich für Ausbildung, Erziehung und Entwicklung der Katecheten und zumindest für die Arbeitsanleitung und Kontrolle der Prediger. Bei der Beurteilung der Fähigkeiten und Fortschritte eines eingeborenen Missionsdieners spielte für den Missionar auch dessen Kastenherkunft eine durchaus zu beachtende Rolle. Die Kastenunterschiede der "Nationalarbeiter" wurden von den Missionaren bewußt beachtet, und diese Personen wurden auch als Christen noch unter dem Kastengesichtspunkt beurteilt, d.h. konkret betrachtete man Vertreter höherer Kasten als sauberer und lernfähiger. Dementsprechend höher waren auch die Ansprüche, die man an diese Personen stellen konnte. Eigenschaften, die man bei Vertretern höherer Kasten als selbstverständlich voraussetzte, wurden, bemerkte man sie ebenso bei Personen aus niedrigen Kasten, umständlich beschrieben und gewürdigt. "Saruwaien und Dewanesen sind Suttirer. Ignasi-Muttu und Soettinaicken aber Parreier. Die beyde Parreier aber halten sich so reinlich, daß sie gar keine Schwierigkeit finden, mit Suttirern umzugehen."[42]

Diese unmittelbare Herleitung der Entwicklungsmöglichkeiten und -erfolge von Missionsdienern aus ihren Kastenverhältnissen steht scheinbar im Gegensatz zum Grundsatz der Gleichheit aller Christen vor Gott. Die Missionare stellen positive Veränderungen (z.B. ebenere Gesichtszüge) an Konvertiten fest und führen das auf das eigene Handeln zurück.

Das regelmäßig wiederkehrende begriffliche Instrumentarium, welches von den Missionaren im Hinblick auf die im Missionsdienst stehenden Inder angewandt wird, resultiert in erster Linie aus lokalen Vergleichen. Dem aus Europa kommenden Gehilfen wird der "eingeborene Gehilfe" gegenübergestellt, dem europäischen Prediger der "Landprediger, Nationalarbeiter". Anthropologische Merkmale spielen kaum eine Rolle.

In der Öffentlichkeit wurden die "Nationalarbeiter" gelobt, wurden ihre Entwicklungen dargestellt, Leistungen hervorgehoben. Sie waren in die Missionsstruktur integriert, hatten ihren Platz in der Hierarchie, waren den Missionaren zu Gehorsam und Rechenschaft verpflichtet. "Solche beständige Rechenschaft und Aufsicht ist ein Mittel, das ganze Werck nach allen seinen Theilen im Schwang zu erhalten, und der Fahrläßigkeit und Vergessenheit, die der Nation anhängt, zu begegnen."[43] Wichtigstes Kriterium der Beurteilung von Nationalarbeitern durch die Missionare war der Wille und die Bereitschaft des Inders, die ihm gestellten Aufgaben zu erfüllen (Fleiß, Gehorsam, Pünktlichkeit, Höflichkeit).

Das hier dargestellte ideelle Abhängigkeitsverhältnis wurde bekräftigt durch die soziale und materielle Abhängigkeit der Landprediger und Katecheten von den Missionaren. Denn im allgemeinen wurden die Nationalarbeiter von den betreuenden Missionaren auch selbst bezahlt. Das sah so aus, daß die Missionare von ihrem Sold einen bestimmten Teil für die Katecheten zur Verfügung stellten. Diese Regelung schloß jedoch nicht aus, daß die Missionare sich an übergeordnete Instanzen wandten mit der Bitte, darüber hinaus zur Besoldung der "Nationalarbeiter" beizutragen. "Ich habe bisher den Katecheten sowohl hier, als in Paleimkottei ihren monatlichen Sold gegeben, sollte die Hochlöbliche Societät zur Besoldung der Katecheten etwas geben, würde es sehr erfreulich seyn."[44] Der von den Missionaren gezahlte Sold mußte oftmals ganze Familien ernähren, die zusammen mit den "Nationalarbeitern" ihren traditionellen sozialen Rahmen verloren hatten. Durch die so entstandene materielle Abhängigkeit war in diesen Fällen der Glaubenswechsel nicht in erster Linie eigene Entscheidung, sondern zwingende Notwendigkeit. "Die Taufe ... führte in den meisten Fällen zu einem radikalen Bruch mit der eigenen Familie. Das aber hatte die Entstehung von neuen christlichen Gemeinschaften zur Folge, in denen die Sozialfürsorge durch die Missionare nicht selten in wirtschaftliche Abhängigkeit von ihnen und sogar Parasitentum ausartete."[45]

## Schlußbemerkungen

Für die seit 1706 in Südindien tätige Dänisch-Hallesche Mission war die Einbeziehung indischer Missionsdiener in Gestalt von Katecheten und Landpredigern eine wichtige Arbeitsmethode. Die Missionare hatten indische Gehilfen von Anfang an dringend benötigt. Eine breite evangelisch-christliche Basis in der Bevölkerung war zunächst nicht vorhanden. Konvertiten, die in den Augen der Missionare die für den Missionsdienst notwendigen Fähigkeiten besaßen, wurden zusätzlich ausgebildet und gefördert. Bei der Mehrzahl der hier betrachteten Personen handelt es sich um Inder, für die die direkte bzw. indirekte Begegnung mit den deutschen Missionaren zum Ausgangspunkt für weitreichende Veränderungen im persönlichen Leben wurde.

Der Glaubens- und Identitätswandel der betrachteten Personen war nicht nur das Ergebnis der Überlegungen und Handlungen der Inder selbst, dieser Prozeß wurde gelenkt und gefördert durch die Missionare. Der im Missionsdienst stehende Inder mußte seinen Persönlichkeitswandel öffentlich vertreten und im Namen des von ihm angenommenen Glaubens unter der Bevölkerung agitieren.

Für die Inder war er ein indischer Christ, im Unterschied zu einem europäischen Christen. Diesem indischen Christen konnte man auf Grund der gleichen Herkunft nahestehen und ihm zuhören, man konnte ihn aber auch wegen seines Glaubenswechsels bedingungslos verachten.

Der historische Rahmen für diesen Beitrag ist bewußt auf den kurzen Zeitraum der ersten Hälfte des 18. Jahrhunderts begrenzt worden.

Allein für die Zusammenstellung des biographischen Faktenmaterials der Landprediger und Katecheten ist ein umfangreiches Quellenstudium in verschiedenen Archiven erforderlich. Zusammenhängende Sammlungen von Dokumenten einzelner Persönlichkeiten existieren nicht.

Die Beschäftigung mit den frühen "Nationalarbeitern" der Dänisch-Halleschen Mission ist insofern eine interessante und besondere Problematik, als die Missionare zunächst nicht auf bereits existierende christliche Gruppierungen zurückgreifen konnten. Die von ihnen eingesetzten ersten Landprediger und Katecheten wurden innerhalb kurzer Zeit aus ihrem ursprünglichen sozialen und religiösen Umfeld heraus in neue Beziehungen und Zwänge gedrückt. Nicht zu allen Fragen geben die Quellen Auskunft. Vieles kann erst in Zukunft auf der Basis umfassenden Faktenmaterials sowie durch vergleichende Betrachtungen eingehend untersucht werden.

## Anmerkungen

Abkürzungen:

ELMB - Evangelisch-Lutherisches Missionsblatt, Dresden, Leipzig, 1,1845- 96/1941 (ELMB)

HB - Der Königlich-Dänischen Missionarien aus Ost-Indien eingesandter ausführlichen Berichten erster Theil, Halle, 1710... bis siebenter Theil, Halle, 1760 (Hallesche Berichte)

MWF - Missionswissenschaftliche Forschungen. Gütersloh 1, 1962ff.

NHB - Neuere Geschichte der Evangelischen Missions-Anstalten zur Bekehrung der Heiden in Ostindien. Halle, 1/1,1770-8/95,1848 (NGEMA) (auch als Neuere Malabarische Nachrichten, Neue Hallesche Berichte, NHB bezeichnet)

1 Die Dänisch-Hallesche Mission war 1704 auf Wunsch des Dänischen Königs ins Leben gerufen worden und bis ca. 1845 in Südindien aktiv. Von Anfang an bestand eine intensive Zusammenarbeit mit den Franckeschen Stiftungen in Halle. Hauptwirkungsgebiet dieser evangelischen Mission war die dänische Handelsniederlassung Tranquebar in Südindien.

2 Vgl. u.a. R. Vormbaum, Benjamin Schultze, evangelischer Missionar in Tranquebar und Madras, und seine Mitarbeiter, Düsseldorf 1850 (Evangelische Missionsgeschichte in Biographien, Band 1, Heft 4); W. Germann, Johann Philipp Fabricius. Seine fünfzigjährige Wirksamkeit im Tamulenlande und das Missionsleben des achtzehnten Jahrhunderts daheim und draußen, Erlangen 1865, 197ff.

3 Vgl. konkret zur Tranquebar-Mission A. Nørgaard, Mission und Obrigkeit. Die Dänisch-Hallesche Mission in Tranquebar 1706-1845, Gütersloh 1988 (MWF, Bd. 22).

4 In neueren Arbeiten zur Wirksamkeit anderer christlicher Missionen in Südindien wird die Problematik der einheimischen Missionsdiener aufgegriffen. Vgl. H. Bugge, Mission and Tamil Society. Sixty years of interaction. Thesis submitted for the degree of Ph. D. at University of Copenhagen, Institute of History, August 1991, 78-106; D. Kooiman, Conver-

sion and social equality in India. The London Missionary Society in South Travancore in the 19th Century, Amsterdam 1989.

5 Der Königlich-Dänischen Missionarien aus Ost-Indien eingesandter ausführlichen Berichten erster Theil, Halle, 1710 ... bis siebenter Theil, Halle 1760 (Hallesche Berichte, HB).

6 Neuere Geschichte der Evangelischen Missions-Anstalten zur Bekehrung der Heiden in Ostindien, Halle, 1/1, 1770 - 8/95, 1848 (NGEMA) (auch als Neuere Malabarische Nachrichten bzw. Neue Hallesche Berichte, NHB bezeichnet).

7 In den HB bzw. NHB verwandte Bezeichnung für die einzelnen Missionsberichte.

8 "Nationalarbeiter" ist der von den deutschen Missionaren am häufigsten gebrauchte Begriff zur Bezeichnung der indischen Missionsangestellten. Die in diesem Beitrag verwendete Schreibweise der indischen Namen für die Landprediger und Katecheten entspricht ebenfalls der vorherrschenden Schreibung in den Missionsberichten.

9 Dasarathi Swaro zeichnet für Orissa ein ganz anderes Bild und stellt den Unterschied zu den in der Region Madras lebenden Indern heraus: "In contrast to Orissa, in the Madras Presidency most of the converts were poor and belonged to low castes who embraced Christianity for economic gain. The low caste Pariah converts were despised by the high caste converts. In Bengal Presidency too, during the same period many low castes were baptised. However, that was not the case with converts of Orissa." Vgl. Dasarathi Swaro. The Christian Missionaries in Orissa. Their Impact on Nineteenth Century Society, Calcutta 1990, 54.

10 1728 spricht der Missionar Pressier in einem Brief an zwei ehemalige Kollegen in Halle nur von der Annahme des Evangeliums durch Römisch-Katholische Christen. Vertreter anderer Konfessionen werden nicht erwähnt. HB 27. Cont., 220.

11 Als ursprünglicher Angehöriger der Pariah-Kaste und römisch-katholischer Christ der dritten Generation hatte z.B. Rajanaiken eine anerkannte Stellung als Offizier in der Tanjorschen Armee.

12 HB 33. Cont., 881, 1731.

13 So war z.B. Gurupadam, der Sohn des Landpredigers Aaron und Schwiegersohn des Landpredigers Diogo, bevor er selbst 1757 Katechet wurde, zunächst als Abschreiber sowie als Gehilfe in einer tamulischen Missionsschule tätig.

14 "Die Schule der heydnischen Kinder wird immer annoch fortgesetzet und fleißig frequentiret. Eine dergleichen Schule haben wir auch, zum Nutz der heydnischen Kinder, aufs neue auf dem volckreichen Flecken Boreiar angerichtet, und schon 7 Monathe continuiret, darinne sich anietzo 16 Kinder befinden. Solche Schule haben wir an dem Hause des daselbst wohnenden Catechetens gebauet, daß er täglich selbige visitiren und selbsten ein bis 2 Stunden täglich darinnen dociren, und dem Preceptor, den wir darzu halten, an die Hand gehen kan." HB 14. Cont., 163-164.

15 So hatte z. B. der 1698 geborene Aaron einige Zeit die 1717 eröffnete englische Schule in Cudelur besucht. Vgl. R. Vormbaum, Evangelische Mission in Biographien. 1. Band, 4. Heft, Düsseldorf 1850.

16 A. Lehmann, Es begann in Tranquebar, 1955, 100f.

17 HB Vorrede zur 22 Cont., § VII.

18 Ebenda.

19 HB 31. Cont., 1. St., 711, Nov. 1730.

20 HB Vorrede zur 17. Cont., 13.

21 Bartholomäus Ziegenbalg war gemeinsam mit Heinrich Plütschau (1676/77-1746/47) im Jahre 1705 als erster Missionar nach Tranquebar gesandt worden.

22 Norgaard, Mission und..., 156-158.

23 Aaron (1698-1745) stammt aus einer wohlhabenden, angesehenen indischen Familie, besuchte eine englische Schule in seinem Heimatort Cudelur, war 1719 Unterkatechet in Tranquebar geworden.

24 HB 37. Cont., 1. St., 65ff., Sept. 1733.

25 HB 39. Cont., Tageregister 1734, 295f., Versammlung mit Landkatecheten, Hinweise für ihre Arbeit.

26 HB 45. Cont., 1. St., 1113, Apr. 1737: Hinweis auf Lektionen für die Landkatecheten über die Irrtümer der Katholischen Kirche; HB 46. Cont., 1. St., 1244, 9.12.1737, Versammlung aller Katecheten und des Landpredigers über das Verhältnis zur Kath. Kirche und die Beichte.

27 "Er hat dahin zu sehen, daß unsere Christen sich nicht mit so genannter heiliger Asche, wie die Heiden beschmieren, oder andere heydnische Ceremonien oder Menschen-Satzungen annehmen und mitmachen." HB 26. Cont., Jan. 1728, 1.

28 HB 37. Cont., 153 ("Nachricht von der Bestellung des ersten National-Predigers bey der Evangelischen Mißion unter den Malabaren in Ost-Indien").

29 Germann, Johann Philipp Fabricius..., 199.

30 ELMB, 1889, 136ff. Bericht von Missionar Räther.

31 Deutliche Grenzen wurden den europäischen Missionaren z.B. gezeigt, als sie den Versuch unternahmen, im Gebiet des Rajas von Tanjore zu missionieren. In den 20er Jahren gelang es zunächst nur, briefliche Kontakten zwischen dem Missionar Benjamin Schultze (1689-1760) und dem Tanjorschen Herrscherhaus herzustellen. Man tauschte Geschenke aus, lernte sich zu dem Zeitpunkt aber noch nicht persönlich kennen."Es wird auch den Lesern der Missions-Berichte schon zur Gnüge bekannt seyn", heißt es in einem Bericht vom 31. Dezember 1733, "daß wir Europäer keine Freyheit haben uns im Tanschaurschen Gebiete niederzulassen... Was ist also mehr zu wünschen, als daß Gott aus der Nation selbst Männer mit seines Heiligen Geistes Gaben zu solchem höchst nöthigen Lehr-Amte ausrüste?" Vgl. HB 37. Cont., 152 ("Andere Beylage des Diarii. Nachricht von der Bestellung des ersten National-Predigers bey der Evanglischen Mißion unter den Malabaren in Ost-Indien"). Erst Jahrzehnte später entwickelte dann Christian Friedrich Schwartz sehr intensive Beziehungen zur königlichen Familie.

32 Der Begriff "Bibelfrauen" taucht erst in den Berichten der Leipziger Mission auf. Im 18. Jahrhundert spielten einheimische Frauen im Missionsdienst eine geringe Rolle, obwohl es vereinzelt aktive weibliche "Nationalarbeiter" gegeben hat.

33 HB 26. Cont., 2 ("Tageregister der Herren Missionarien zu Tranquebar vom Jahr 1728").

34 Vgl. Kupferstich: Ein Malabarischer Catechet; Ein Portugiesischer Soldat. HB 31. Cont., 1730.

35 Vgl. Kupferstich von Aaron, HB III. Theil.

36 NHB 4.Bd., 44.St., 709 (1794).

37 Vgl. Anm. 27.

38 Gleiches stellt Urs Bitterli fest, wenn er schreibt: "Indem man den Neger lobte und vor anderen auszeichnete, hinderte man ihn daran, sich seine Situation bewußt zu machen; er gewöhnte sich an, in den Kategorien seiner weißen Meister zu denken, übernahm im Umgang mit seinesgleichen die Kulturarroganz der Vorgesetzten und erlitt so einen kaum mehr rückgängig zu machenden Identitätsverlust." Urs Bitterli, Die 'Wilden' und die 'Zivilisierten'. Grundzüge einer Geistes- und Kulturgeschichte der europäisch-überseeischen Begegnung, München 1991, 431.

39 "Besonders das Wirken Isaaks, dessen Opferfreudigkeit so groß war, daß er um des Friedens willen mit seinen Verwandten sogar auf sein väterliches Erbteil, um das ihn diese anfochten,

freiwillig verzichtete." Vgl. Ch.W. Gericke. evengel.-luth. Missionar in Kudelur und Madras. Sammlung von Missionsschriften, Nr. 2, 10.

40 HB 39 Cont., 1734, 433.

41 HB 23. Cont., 882 (Bericht vom Jahre 1731).

42 NHB 1.Bd., 2.St., 257 ("Brief an den sel. Herrn Konsistorial Rath D. Franke vom 6. Oct. 1768").

43 HB 33. Cont., 884 (Bericht vom Jahre 1731).

44 NHB 50. St., 175 (Brief von Chr. Fr. Schwartz an Herrn Uebele in London).

45 H. Grafe, Evangelische Kirche in Indien. Auskunft und Einblicke, Erlangen 1981, 82.

# Popularizing Sciences through Arabic Journals in the Late 19th Century: How al-Muqtaṭaf Transformed Western Patterns[1]

Dagmar Glaß

> **Die erstaunlichsten Kombinationen ruft diese Begegnung des Occidents mit dem Orient hervor...**
> **Ignaz Kratshkovsky**

## I. Al-Muqtaṭaf: Yaᶜqūb Ṣarrūf's journal

### *I.1 Introductory Remarks*

*Al-Muqtaṭaf* (The Selection) was founded in Beirut in 1876 by Yaᶜqūb Ṣarrūf (1852-1927)[2] and Fāris Nimr (1856-1951)[3], two Lebanese Christians who were among the first graduates of the Syrian Protestant College (SPC), the later American University (AUB) of Beirut. The journal appeared until 1952, thus - without interruption - covering a 75 year period of socio-cultural change in the Arab world.

*Al-Muqtaṭaf* was by no means only a two-men enterprise. Quite on the contrary, more than one generation of the modern Arab writers gathered around it - among them a number of graduates from the SPC, the first Arab university of Western type. Nevertheless, it is correct to say that *al-Muqtaṭaf* is the lifework of Yaᶜqūb Ṣarrūf. Ṣarrūf was far more connected with *al-Muqtaṭaf* than its co-founder Fāris Nimr who, from 1889 onward, concentrated on publishing the influential political newspaper *al-Muqaṭṭam*[4].

Ṣarrūf was 24 years old when he began to publish *al-Muqtaṭaf* in Beirut. When he died in Cairo, on the 9th of July, 1927, he had spent 50 years of his life editing and writing 70 volumes of the journal equaling about 50,000 octavo-pages[5].

During their studies at the SPC, and later in the framework of the lectures they gave Ṣarrūf and Nimr made experiences which were to become very important for their journalistic life: They realized that the Arabic language, which prided itself of a long tradition of expressing classical scientific thought, is, in principle, able to convey modern (Western) sciences and knowledge, too. Between 1866 and 1882, it was Arabic that served as the language of instruction.[6] During this first period, the SPC had seen "the triumph of Arabic over English", wrote Jabr Ḍūmiṭ (1859-1930)[7], a disciple of Ṣarrūf and Nimr (XXVIII/6, p. 906)[8]. At that time "all (natural) scientific and medical disciplines" (XXVIII/6, p. 906)[9] were taught in Arabic. In the following period, the university saw the exact opposite, namely "the triumph of English over Arabic"[10] which lasted until about 1890. From the 1890s,

Arabic was resurrected, but English remained dominant. Until the turn of the century, *al-Muqtaṭaf* gained a high reputation not only in the East, but in the West, too. "The Muktataf, an enterprising and ably conducted scientific Magazine, is... highly valued among the Arabic students of the Levant and is medium of communication between the best scientific thought of our times, as it appears in the European and American Journals and the awakening mind of the Arabic-speaking East. It also contains earnest and thoughtful original discussions of current topics, and much practical information adapted to local needs. Its mission is a stimulating and timely one among the educated classes in Syria and Egypt."[11] Ten years after this first Western evaluation of the journal, an English observer of the Arabic press, W. Fraser Ray, wrote: "The contents of the first number (of *al-Muqtaṭaf* - D.G.) were very meagre when compared with that of last February (1892 - D.G.), the articles in the one numbering eight, and in the other sixteen, irrespective of notes and queries... and there can be no doubt that such a magazine as *Al Muktataf* exercises a civilising as well as an educational influence."[12] Finally, the journal was described by Martin Hartmann, the first German scholar to deal systematically with the Arabic Press, as a "Journal of Science and Literature; appears on the first of every month; contains a variety of scientific problems, instructive remarks on art and mechanics, inventions, discoveries, etc. etc. It is a magazine of great authority with the readers..."[13].

### *I.2 Ṣarrūf's ambitions*

Until 1927, Ṣarrūf's education and interests[14] obviously characterized the scientific journal's concept and content. Ṣarrūf himself specialized in subjects from physics, chemistry, astronomy, biology, mathematics, and mechanics as well as of history of science and biography. It can be said that the encyclopaedic concept of the journal was decisively indebted to that "great encyclopaedic mind" (LXXII/4, p. 424)[15], as Ṣarrūf has been called by "the Muslim 'radical' Westernizer" Ismāʿīl Maẓhar (1891-1961)[16]. Ṣarrūf was no reporter of daily politics and political events, but a journalist specializing in reporting on science (cf. LXXII/5, p. 571 f)[17]. This is the opinion of another lifetime-companion of Ṣarrūf, the Egyptian publicist Muḥammad Ḥusayn Haykal (1888-1956)[18]. To Shakīb Arslān (1871-1946)[19], the great Lebanese poet, Ṣarrūf commented that he who has acquired a taste for sciences considers political writing as a triviality for which one loses all enthusiasm (cf. XXVIII, p. 9)[20]. Ṣarrūf was not only a journalist, but also a prolific translator[21] and a promoter of modern Arabic literature[22], but it was Ṣarrūf's main ambition in life to popularize sciences by utilizing the means of the press. To Saʿīd Shuqayr, his son-in-law, who was also involved in the *Muqtaṭaf*--enterprise, Ṣarrūf is said to have remarked that "Arabs will not have a say among the nations of the world and will not become really independent if we do not enlighten the mind of the ordinary people (*al-ᶜāmma*) and improve their educational level by utilizing all means of instructing and publishing. This is the purpose we work for..." (LXXI, p. 302)[23].

## II. The lack of studies in 19th century Arabic journals

Up to now there is a deplorable lack of studies dealing with the role played by Arabic periodicals in the process of modernizing Arabic writing and language, although modern (or contemporary) Arabic style and language are indebted to them "far more than to actual literature"[24]. For a long time, these texts had been regarded as subjects not worthy of interest, at least by Western scholars. Even pioneers in the field of studying modern Arabic writings could not stifle remarks expressing a negative attitude towards periodicals which was formerly common. So we read in Hartmann's column "*Zeitschriftenschau*", started by the *Orientalistische Literaturzeitung* (OLZ) in 1898: "Leider sind die ägyptischen Blätter fast sämtlich ziemlich skrupellos in der Verwendung fremden Gutes: die französische und die englische Presse wird unverfrorenst geplündert."[25] Even in an article by Ignaz Kratshkovsky published in 1922, i.e. a quarter of a century later, but which was actually a call for research in the field of modern Arabic literature, we read: "Soweit sie (die neu-arabische Literatur, D.G.) neu ist, steht sie unter europäischem Einfluß, der uns schon im Orginal, aus erster Quelle bekannt ist; soweit sie der Tradition folgt, ist sie eine mehr oder weniger glückliche Nachahmung mehr oder weniger großer Vorbilder der Vergangenheit, die uns gewöhnlich auch bekannt sind. Zuweilen ist hier nur noch die Sprache orientalisch, alles andere stammt aus dem Westen."[26]

More than the Arab press, the language of this press, especially its terminology, was scorned and rejected. So it was, for example, considered as not to be a language in the sense of the word: "... das ist - nun eben eine Zeitungssprache mit allen ihren Eigenheiten, Schwächen und Unarten, eine Sprache, die sich jeder Zeitungsschreiber selber macht... Aber es ist weit davon entfernt, daß sie ein gemeinsames Band aller arabisch Redenden bildete... Sie ist - in gewissem Sinn - Kunstsprache... aber sie kann ebensowenig wie diese auf Geistes- und Kulturgebiet einen bleibenden Wert darstellen, kann keine Zukunft haben."[27]

From the intensive and constant contact with Western sources resulted the fact that the Eastern (Arabic) encyclopaedic journals (including *al-Muqtaṭaf*), which emerged as a new type of periodical in the second half of the 19th century, resembled in content and form the scientific reviews and magazines published at that time in Europe and America. However, does this mean that popularizing sciences in Arabic through journals was a mere translation of Western writing without any creativity on the side of the Arab writers? Did dependence on Western patterns really mean that the Arabic language used to contribute to the press was merely a

Westernized language, without a future? Did Arab journalists merely imitate their Western counterparts, thus forfeiting any claim to attain an indigenous, Arab identity? For several reasons it is not easy to answer such questions, but the basic reason is the lack of studies dealing with 19th century journals as one of the landmarks of the encounter between East and West in the Ottoman Empire before the turn of the century.

Nevertheless, he who wants to investigate this neglected literary genre can find numerous hints in studies dealing with other genres of modern Arabic literature (modern poetry, drama, short story, novel) that have attracted more attention, for example in works by Moreh (1976)[28], Le Gassick (1978)[29], Peled (1979)[30], Badawi (1985)[31] or Somekh (1991)[32]. These works pay much attention to the questions of topics and forms, translation and creation, genre and language. By applying to *al-Muqtaṭaf* lines of research layed out by these and other studies we can ask the following questions: Which topics are selected? Which text types are used? Which references to Western patterns are made? Do the Muqtatafis, indeed, merely imitate? What do they translate? How do they translate? How do they use the Arabic language, especially its vocabulary? Where are outlets for Arab journalistic creativity? In what follows an attempt is made to collect data that allow us to answer such questions.

## III. Analyzing al-Muqtaṭaf's concept: procedures and first results

### *III.1. The corpus under review*

A first step is to limit the text corpus. The corpus which was taken into consideration comprises *al-Muqtaṭaf* I/1 = May 1876 to XIII /6 = March 1889 (about 8,000 pages). It covers the period until the foundation of the political daily *al-Muqaṭṭam* [33]. This period was characterized by searching for a journalistic concept while fighting against instabilities such as the move from Beirut to Cairo in 1884/85, and financial difficulties[34]. Nevertheless, he who studies the journalistic effort made by the Muqtatafis until 1889 will come to the conclusion that it is just this period in which the journal, in principle, became what it then remained until the death of Yaʿqūb Ṣarrūf, in 1927.

### *III.2 The diversity of journalistic texts*

The encyclopaedic *al-Muqtaṭaf*, like other periodicals, contains texts of different types. We are faced with a diversity of journalistic texts. That is why, as a second step, it must be tried to classify the texts e.g. by socio-functional or formal criteria. However, this is a problem which turns out to be more complicate than expected.

Until now, I have not found a final solution. Nevertheless, for the following explanations it should suffice to distinguish seven journalistic sections in the period under review:

(1) editorial notes (*muqaddamāt*[35], *khawātim*, etc.)[36]
(2) articles and serials (*maqālāt* resp. *nubadh*)[37] including contributions written for
*al-Muqtaṭaf*, reprints of contributions to other Arabic periodicals, and extracts from books published in advance of their print

(3) addresses (*khutab*) read on various occasions to various scientific circles[38]
(4) various brief texts (aphorisms, riddles, etc.)
(5) columns (*abwāb*) including entries of various content, size, and form
(6) announcements (*iʿlānāt*) dealing with the academic life at the SPC as well as books and Arabic periodicals to appear[39]
(7) advertisements (*iʿlānāt*)[40]

In what follows it is number (5) that merit our special attention, for several reasons:

**One**, that what has simply been called columns (*abwāb*, sing.: *bāb*) turns out to be, at a closer look, a very polymorphous as well as dynamic, and therefore an outstanding section of *al-Muqtaṭaf*. Until 1889, they can be considered to be something like an experimental section of the journal that in the end proved successful.
**Two**, all historical studies on the journal[41] do not offer precise descriptions of this section. Even the more text-oriented one by Sulaymān (1987)[42] takes only marginal notice of it.
**Three**, more than all other texts it is the columns that typify the journalistic genre. Columns are written for being inserted into journals (and newspapers). So in a certain sense, they are primary journalistic texts.

For these reasons the analysis focuses its efforts on the *abwāb* of *al-Muqtaṭaf*. Between 1876 and 1889, we find twelve *abwāb* which were continued longer than six month from the date of their first occurrence onward[43].

Table 1
**12 *abwāb al-Muqtaṭaf***

| *Headlines* | *First occurrence* |
|---|---|
| (1) /1 Akhbār wa-Iktishāfāt wa-Ikhtirāʿāt (News, Discoveries, and Inventions) /2 Manthūrāt (Notes) | I/1 = May 1876 (pp. 23f.) I/4 = September 1876 (p. 94) |
| (2) Min al-Marṣad al-Sūrī al-Falakī wa-l-Mitīyūrūlūjī (From Syria's Astronomical and Meteorological Observatory) | I/2 = July 1876 (pp. 46f.) |
| (3) Masā'il wa-Ajwibatuhā (Questions and Answers) | I/2 = July 1876 (pp. 47f.) |
| (4) Fawā'id (Benefits) | I/3 = August 1876 (pp. 68f.) |
| (5) Bāb al-Munāẓara wa-l-Murāsala (Disputation and Correspondence) | VI/1 = June 1881 (pp. 44-50, large edition[44]) |
| (6) Bāb Tadbīr al-Manzil (Home Economics) | VI/1 = June 1881 (pp. 51-55, large ed.) |
| (7) Hadāyā wa-Taqārīẓ (Donations and Encomiums) | VI/2 = July 1881 (pp. 127f., large ed.) |
| (8) Bāb al-Riyāḍīyāt (Mathematical Column) | VI/12 = May 1882 (pp. 741f., large ed.) |
| (9) Bāb al-Ṣināʿa (Artisans' Column) | VII/4 = November 1882 (pp. 97-104, small ed.) |
| (10) Bāb al-Zirāʿa (Farmers' Column) | VII/9 = April 1883 (pp. 237f.; s. ed.) |
| (11) Bāb al-Handasa (Engineers' Column) | X/7 = April 1886 (p. 425) |

At a first glance, one might say: similarity with Western journals, hardly any differences. However, by comparing the Arabic *abwāb* with Western counterparts one comes to the conclusion that there are also remarkable differences. Arab journalists, including the Muqtatafis, had to make, without any doubt, many more efforts than only to translate, to imitate Western patterns. To fit the press, a Western medium, to the needs of the Arabic- speaking readers they had to find their own concept, genre and terminology.

### *III.3 Western and Arabic periodicals: Sources of al-Muqtaṭaf*

#### III.3.1 Western journals used by Ṣarrūf and Nimr

From various sources of information[45] we know that, in the period under review, Ṣarrūf and Nimr used to draw from numerous Western periodicals, but it is three journals that were used more frequently than other Western publications: the English "Nature" (N)[46], the American "Popular Science Monthly" (PSM)[47] and the English "Nineteenth Century" (NC)[48].

To get an idea about the impact of the Western journalistic patterns, the similarities and differences between the Arabic *abwāb* and the Western columns, I have consulted N, PSM an NC. By comparing the *abwāb* of *al-Muqtaṭaf* with their Western counterparts one can have a closer look at the interesting relationship between the Western journalistic patterns of column and Eastern contents as well as at rendering Western topics by means of the Arabic language in in the framework of the *abwāb*, or in other words: at the transformation of Western patterns in contact with Eastern, i.e. indigenous literary and linguistic prerequisites. Although, in general, the columns are the Western prototypes of the *abwāb*, it is not correct to say that the latter is a mere imitation of the former. And, in particular, there are cases in which special Western prototypes do not exist. Concerning *al-Muqtaṭaf,* we must state that three columns, namely *bāb* (3) *Masā'il wa-Ajwibatuhā* (Questions and Answers), *bāb* (4) *Fawā'id* (Benefits), and (6) *Bāb Tadbīr al-Manzil* (Home Economics) have no counterparts in the journals consulted.

#### III.3.2 Arab journals used by Ṣarrūf and Nimr

The fact that *al-Muqtaṭaf* did not only draw from Westerns journals, but from Arab journals as well, has rather been neglected until now. Indeed, Ṣarrūf's journal reprinted contributions written for other Arabic (Syrian and Egyptian) periodicals or drew from them as sources of information. This is shown by severals indicators, such as introductory phrases, e.g. *Jā'a fī Thamarāt al-Funūn ᶜan Jamᶜīyat al-Maqāṣid al-Khayrīya fī Bayrūt mā naṣṣuhu...* (IV, p. 277). Among the Eastern periodicals used by *al-Muqtaṭaf* were: *Thamarāt al-Funūn*[49], *al-Ṭabīb*[50] (e.g. I,

p. 24), *al-Nashra al-Usbūʿīya*[51] (e.g. I, 73), *al-Ahrām*[52] (e.g. I, p. 120), *al-Naḥla*[53] (e.g. III, p. 250), *Lisān al-Ḥāl*[54] (e.g. ibid.), *al-Salām*[55] (e.g. IV, p. 127) or *al-Waqā'iʿ al-Miṣrīya*[56] (e.g. VII, p. 340).

However, as far as the *abwāb* are concerned, we may assume that *al-Muqtaṭaf* excelled all others. This is, for the time being, confirmed by two facts:

**One**, a comparison with the first five volumes of *al-Jinān*[57], founded by the famous Lebanese scholar Buṭrus al-Bustānī (1819-1883)[58], the concept and layout of which *al-Muqtaṭaf* had adopted[59], shows that the set of *abwāb* presented by Ṣarrūf and Nimr attained a far wider range than that included in al-Bustānī's journal.

**Two**, Ṣarrūf and Nimr themselves said, when enlarging the *Fawā'id* in June 1878, that no other Arabic periodical of the time published such *abwāb* as *Masā'il wa-Ajwibatuhā*, the *Fawā'id* and *Bāb Tadbīr al-Manzil* before them (cf. III/1, p. 25).

## *III.4. The abwāb of al-Muqtaṭaf*

### III.4.0 General remarks

Table 1 (see III.2) shows that it took Ṣarrūf and Nimr ten years to establish the *abwāb*. This section is, without any doubt, a result of the Muqtatafis' increasing journalistic experience in popularizing sciences. But there is another side to this coin. The *abwāb* are also a response to increased readers' interest in *al-Muqtaṭaf*. Last not least, it is due to the *abwāb* that the journal was considerably enlarged until 1889[60].

The *abwāb* consist of smaller texts of various topics, sizes and forms. They cover between a few lines and a few pages. However, the *abwāb* are so manifold that it is difficult to describe them. So what follows is not more than an attempt to give a survey of the twelve *abwāb* mentioned in table 1.

### III.4.1 Akhbār wa-Iktishāfāt wa-Ikhtirāʿāt/Manthūrāt

*Akhbār wa-Iktishāfāt wa-Ikhtirāʿāt* started with two pages in I/1, pp. 23 f, i.e. May 1876, later comprising more pages (up to eleven, cf. VII/3, pp. 73-84). This *bāb* sometimes alternated with *Manthūrāt*, sometimes both *abwāb* occurred together. Later, the former became the regular feature, whereas the latter disappeared because the information carried by it was devolved upon other *abwāb*. For this reason *Manthūrāt* is only mentioned here.

*Akhbār wa-Iktishāfāt wa-Ikhtirāʿāt* is a set of smaller entries, notes (*akhbār*, sing.: *khabar*), each of them regularly covering a few lines. The notes contain, mostly under short headlines, a multitude of information on Western research as well as the current academic and public scientific activities in the West and the East. The first instance of this *bāb* contained eleven notes.

Among them, we can read the following one (I, p. 24):

*al-Ibar*
**[The Needles]**

*Dakhalat Ibar al-fūlādh* **[steel needles]**[61] *ilā Bilād al-Inklīz* **[England]** *min Isbāniyā* **[Spain]** *wa-Jirmāniyā* **[Germany]** *wa-awwal man ṣanaʿahā fī Lundun* **[London]** *rajul jirmānī* **[German]** *sanata 1565*

The majority of these first *akhbār*, however, dealt with topics from handicrafts and household. Under headlines such as *Klūrid al-ḥadīd li-iṣlāḥ al-mā'* (Purifying Water by Using Ferric Chloride) (I, p. 23), *Wāsiṭa li-ḥifẓ al-laḥm* (A Method to Preserve Meat) (ibid.) and *Maʿjūn li-jalā' al-asnān* (A Paste for Cleaning One's Teeth) (ibid.) they gave the readers instructions for making and using something. From July 1876 onward, such texts were entitled *fawā'id* and used to appear in special columns (*Fawā'id*, see III.4.4 and *Bāb Tadbīr al-Manzil*, see III.4.6). In the 1880s, *Akhbār wa-Iktishāfāt wa-Ikhtirāʿāt* specialized in presenting various scientific news. So it presented numerous biological notes.

So, in April 1879, one could read for example (III, p. 280):

*Kashf al-khamr* [?] *bi-l-fūtūghrāfiyā*
**[The Discovery of Ferments? with the Help of the Photography]**

*Yuqālu innahum ihtadaw hadīthan ilā kashf al-khamr* **[ferments/enzymes ?]** *bi-l-fūtūghrāfiyā* **[photography]** *wa-dhālika bi-an yuṣawwirū āthār nuqaṭ minhu ʿalā lawḥ aw mā ashbah thumma yatafaḥḥaṣū ṣuwaraha bi-l-mikruskūb* **[microscope]** (*al-minẓar al-mukabbir*) **[paraphrased and inserted by Muq.]** *fa-yatabayyanū al-ṣaḥīḥ minhā min al-maghshūsh wa-l-jayyid min al-radī'*

Apart from biological or geographical[62] and astronomical[63] notes, the *bāb* contained many notes on modern technical inventions, for example on the telegraph (*al-tilighrāf*, see point IV.), the telephone (*al-tilifūn*, see point IV.), the balloon (*al-ballūn*, see point IV), the phonograph (*al-fūnūghraf*, e.g. III, p. 56), the electroscope (*al-iliktruskūb*, e.g. VII/10, p. 275, small ed.) as well as inventions in the military sector. So, in April 1883, under the headline *Āla jadīda min ālāt jahannam* (A New Infernal Machine) a *khabar* informed the Arab readers about a new ship gun (midfaʿ jadīd) developed by the German Alfred Krupp (cf. VII/9, p. 254).

Other topics often treated by *al-Muqtaṭaf* in the period under review are that of electicity (*al-kahrabā'īya*) and vehicles operated by steam-engines.

So, in August 1880, the readers could find the following note (V/3, p. 72):

*al-Kahrabā'īya wa-sikkat al-ḥadīd*
**[Electricity and Railroad]**

*Lam yatruk Adīṣun* **[Edison]** *al-mukhtari*ᶜ *al-shahīr mas'alat al-ḍaw'*
*al-kahrabā'ī* **[electric light]** *illā li-yashtaghila fī mas'ala ukhrā laysat*
*aqall nafᶜan minhā li-l-ᶜālam wa-hiya mas'alat istiᶜmāl al-kahrabā'īya*
**[electricity]** *ᶜiwaḍan ᶜan al-bukhār fi l-sikak al-ḥadīdīya* **[railroad]**. *Fa-qad jā'a*
*fī jarīdat al-Sayntifik Amīr/i/kān* **[Scientific American]**[64] *anna baᶜḍ kuttābihā*
[some of its **journalists**] *rakibū maᶜ/a/ arbaᶜata ᶜashara shakhṣan ākharīn*
[Muq. did not use *ākhar*] *fī qiṭār* **[train]** *li-Adīṣun tumashshīhī al-kahrabā'īya bi-surᶜa*
*25 aw 30 mīlan fi l-sāᶜa* [25 or 30 **miles per hour**]. *Wa-inna Adīṣun yu'ammilu* [voc. by Muq.]
*baᶜd itqān dhālika an yuᶜawwala* [voc. by Muq.] *ᶜalā ikhtirāᶜihī fi l-naql wa-l-filāḥa*
*wa-ghayrihimā*

Otherwise, numerous notes on scholars, schools, societies, conferences, etc. were included. Under headlines such as 1) *Mu'tamar al-sharqīyīn* (The Congress of Orientalists) (VI/6 = November 1881, p. 376) and 2) *al-Majmaᶜ al-Brīṭānī* (The British Association) (ibid., pp. 377 f) *al-Muqtaṭaf* reported on activities of Western scientists. Note 1) mentioned participants and programme of the 5th International Congress of Orientalists held at Berlin in September 1881. Note 2) dealt with the British Association for the Advancement of Science that held its 51st meeting at York in August and September 1881. It summarizes a paper on rise and progress of the paleontology (*ᶜilm al-baliyūntūlūjiyā*[65], ibid., p. 377) presented by T. H. Huxley (*al-Ustādh Hakslī*, ibid. 377).

On the other hand, the Muqtatafis also recorded scientific-cultural movements in the East such as the foundations of schools and societies, and their activities. So by reading *al-Muqtaṭaf*, one could get the information that, in 1880, a graduate of the SPC had opened an evening school (*madrasa laylīya*) for teaching English and Arabic in Alexandria (cf. IV, p. 224), furthermore, that Ḥusayn al-Jisr[66], in May 1880, has founded in Tripolis/Lebanon an "Islamic national school" (headline: *Madrasa waṭanīya islāmīya*, cf. IV, p. 278), a *khabar* which the Muqtatafis took from *Thamarāt al-Funūn*, or that the *Madrasa al-Baṭrakīya* of Beirut has celebrated the birthday of its founder (cf. VIII/5 = February 1884, p. 315).

In principle, *Akhbār wa-Iktishāfāt wa-Ikhtirāᶜāt* is a large compilation of pieces taken from periodicals (and other publications[67]) of that time, Western and Eastern ones. It resembles in numerous Western counterparts, for example N's "Notes", "Societies and Academies" (informing the reader about European academic life) as well as "Biological Notes", "Meteorological Notes", "Geological Notes" and "Chemical Notes". But also the PSM's "Popular Miscellany" and "Notes" (with more information on scientific subjects than on scientists and societies etc.) were important items.

III.4.2 Min al-Marṣad al-Sūrī al-Falakī wa-l-Mitiyūrūlūjī

This *bāb* started in I/2 (pp. 46 f), i.e. July 1876, but it did not remain a seperate one during the whole of the time under review. In the 1880s, it was mostly incorporated into *Akhbār wa-Iktishāfāt wa-Ikhtirāᶜāt* or *Manthūrāt*.

It offered information from the Syrian Observatory which was founded and run by the famous missionary and scholar Cornelius van Dyck (1818-1896)[68] containing news about the institution and the staff as well as data referring to meteorological phenomena and astronomical constellations observed in Syria/-Lebanon. In form, it resembles N's "Greenwich as a Meteorological Observatory" and "Our Astronomical Column".

III.4.3 Masa'il wa-Ajwibatuhā

*Masā'il wa-Ajwibatuhā* seems to be an outstanding part of the journal. It is a dialogue between Eastern readers and editors. The readers are questioners (*al-sā'ilun*) asking short questions (*al-masā'il*) to be answered by the editors. When the column was opened in I/2 (pp. 47 f), i.e. July 1876, two questions were asked:

1) a glazier (glassblower) from Hebron asked how carnelian-red glass can be made (*Sa['a*[69]*]lanā zajjāj min al-Khalīl ᶜan kayfīyat ᶜamal al-zujāj al-aḥmar al-ᶜaqīqī*; I/2 p. 47), and
2) a person *Yā'. Ḥā'.* (no more than the initials are given) wanted to know what is meant by "horsepower" and how the capacitiy of an engine is measured (*Sa['a]lanā yā'. ḥā'. Yuqālu inna qūwat hādhihi l-āla al-bukhārīya* **[steam-engine]** mi'atā ḥiṣān **[two hundred horses]** *aw mā ashbah fa-mā huwa al-murād min dhālika wa-kayfa tuᶜarrafu qūwat al-āla* **[engine capacity]**; ibid.).

From that time, the *bāb* appeared regularly, later including up to 30 questions from the most diverse fields of human life, for example questions on

3) dye making (e.g. *Kayfa yuṣnaᶜu al-ṣibāgh al-aṣfar*; I, p. 165),
4) mirror producing (e.g. *Kayfa tuṣnaᶜu al-marayā*; I, p. 186),
5) insect controlling (e.g. *Mā huwa al-ᶜilāj li-mulāshāt al-ḥasharāt al-ṣaghīra allatī ta[']kulu nabāt al-qamḥ*; I, p. 233) or
6) corn cutting (e.g. *Kayfa tuᶜālaju al-masāmīr allatī tatawalladu fī l-arjul*; I, p. 281).

Furthermore, Ṣarrūf and Nimr were asked

7) why they attach *bā' ᶜayn* to their names (*Mā maᶜnā waḍᶜ ḥarfay al-bā' wa-l-ᶜayn baᶜd dhikr ism munshi'yay al-Muqtaṭaf...*; I/12, p. 281)[70],

8) how many believers adhered to each religion of the world (*Narjūkum an tatakarramū ʿalaynā bi-dhikr ʿadad sukkān al-arḍ ḥasab adyānihim*; VI/1, p. 58) or
9) how Islam came to Egypt (*Kayfa dakhala al-Islām Miṣr a-bi-ḥarb am bidūn ḥarb wa-man kāna al-mutasalliṭ ʿalayhā qabl dukhūlihim*; XII, p. 372).
10) Some readers sent chemical substances to Ṣarrūf and Nimr requesting the editors to analyze them (e.g.: II, pp. 142 f). Other readers wanted to know
11) how long a baby should be breastfed (*Mā hiya al-mudda al-kāfiya li-irḍāʿ al-ṭifl*; VI/5, p. 308),
12) what digestives the editors of *al-Muqtaṭaf* could recommend (*Mā hiya ajwad muqawwiyāt al-haḍm*; XI/6, p. 379),
13) whether there is a suitable methode to give up smoking (*Hal min wāsiṭa iʿlājīya tusāʿidu ibṭāl ʿādat al-tadkhīn*; XI/6, p. 378),
14) whether it is correct to say that the skin of dogs has no pores (*Yuqālu inna jild al-kalb khāl/in/ min al-masāmm fa-hal dhālika ṣaḥiḥ*; X/8, p. 504) or
15) whether *al-nafs*, *al-ʿaql* and *al-rūḥ* are one and the same thing (*Hal al-nafs wa-l-ʿaql wa-l-rūḥ wāḥid*, XII, p. 184).

The shortest answers given by Ṣarrūf and Nimr were *naʿam* (yes) (e.g. to *mas'ala* 15) and *kallā* (not at all) (e.g. to *mas'ala* 14), but mostly their answers went into details.

According to the editors, numerous questions refer to topics treated in *al-Muqtaṭaf*, but just as many do not, i.e. they deal with "external" subjects. On the other hand, a remarkable number of the questions were repetitions, i.e. the editors were asked questions about what was already dealt with by the Muqtatafis (cf. IV/5, p. 217). Until October 1879, these repetitions and the "external questions" must have become so numerous that the readers were requested to read the journal closely before asking questions, and to take more notice of the indices attached at the end of each year of publishing (cf. ibid.). It seems - but for the time being, this is not more than a result of cursory reading - that later the dialogue carried by *Masā'il wa-Ajwibatuhā* is closer to the subjects that were treated in the various sections of the journal.

Approximately up to December 1883, *masā'il* were published without mentioning the names of the senders although Ṣarrūf and Nimr had already in I/12 (p. 281), i.e. April 1877, declared that they only accepted questions from those who added their place of residence and their names. From VIII/4 = January 1884 onward, the principle of anonymity was given up. Henceforth, the questioners' names were placed in front.

Until 1889, the majority of questions came from Lebanon/Syria and Egypt. Since *al-Muqtaṭaf* appeared in Cairo[71], the number of *masā'il* was, according to the editors (cf. X/4 = January 1886, p. 256), on the increase.

In some respect, the *mas'ala* can be considered to be the journal's first "letter to the editor". But a comparison between the *masā'il* and the Western letters of N's "Letters to the Editor", PSM's "Correspondence" and NC's "Modern Symposium"[72] shows that these Western patterns cannot be regarded as the prototype of the *masā'il*. *Masā'il wa-Ajwibatuhā* seems to be an independent journalistic phenomenon. For tracing the roots of this *bāb*, one has probably to go back more to the Arab-Islamic history than to Western "originals". However, to evaluate this *bāb* a closer investigation is intended.

III.4.4 Fawā'id

*Fawā'id* (sing.: *fā'ida*) are short instructive texts that centered around handicrafts and household. The first four *fawa'id* appeared in I/3 (pp. 68 f), i.e. August 1876. They were contributed by Anṭūn Nawfal, a graduate of the SPC, who gave under the headwords 1) - 4) hints on the topic of how to remove several kinds of stains from several kinds of cloth:

1) *Izālat dabgh/dibgh* [?] *al-sā'ilāt* [Muq. did not use the plural *al-sawā'il*] *al-hadīdīya ᶜan al-thiyāb al-bayḍā'* (ibid., p. 68 f),
2) *Izālat al-dibgh* [?] *ᶜan al-jūkh ᶜalā ikhtilāf alwānihī* (ibid., p. 69),
3) *Izālat buqaᶜ al-zayt ᶜan al-aṭlas wa-naḥwihī min al-aqmisha wa-ᶜan al-qirṭās* (ibid.), and
4) *Iṣṭināᶜ ṣābūn yuzīlu* [*yuzayyilu* ?] *al-dibgh* [?] (Making soap to remove stains, ibid.).

For example *fā'ida* 2) says (I, p. 69):

*Izālat al-dibgh* [?] *ᶜan al-jūkh ᶜalā ikhtilāf alwānihī* **[How to remove stains from cloths in several colours]**. *Yu'khadhu li-dhalika 250 kirāman* [250 **grammes**] *min al-ᶜasal wa-l-muḥḥ (ṣufrat al-bayḍ)*[paraphrased and inserted by Muq.] *wa-miqdār jawza min milḥ al-nushādir* [**sal ammoniac**/exactly: **ammonium chloride**] *wa-tumzaju kulluhā mazjan jayyidan thumma yūḍaᶜu minhā ᶜala l-dibgh* [?] *wa-yughsalu al-qumāsh baᶜd qalīl fī mā' bārid fa-yazūlu al-dibgh* [?].

To publish such *fawa'id* was, according to Ṣarrūf and Nimr, one of the improvements in the concept of the al-Muqtaṭaf (cf. III/1 = June 1878, p. 25). No other Arabic periodical had published texts of this kind before (cf. ibid.).
However, also the readers themselves were given a hearing. This can be seen in I/7 (p. 161) where a person, who signed with *Kāf. Nūn.*, presents four *fawā'id* (the headlines of which are added in parentheses) on:

5) how to get rid of dandruff (*Tanẓīf al-ra's min al-hibrīya (al-qishra)* [*al-qishra* added by Muq.]; ibid.),

6) how to redye blond hairs (*Radd al-lawn al-dhahabī ila l-sha<sup>c</sup>r al-ashqar al-dhahabī al-shā'ib*; ibid.),
7) how to make almond juice (*Iṣṭinā<sup>c</sup> sharāb al-lawz*; ibid.) and
8) how to make date juice (*Iṣṭinā<sup>c</sup> sharāb tamr al-hindī*; ibid.).

In other places, also those found information who wanted to know e.g.

9) how to make ivory white (*Tabyīḍ al-<sup>c</sup>āj*; II, p. 280)
11) how to make beer (*<sup>c</sup>Amal al-bīrā*; III, p. 151) or
12) how to write without ink (*al-Kitāba bi-lā ḥibr*; ibid., p. 152 ).

For example *fā'ida* 9) says (II, p. 280):

*Tabyīḍ al-<sup>c</sup>āj*
*[How to make ivory white]*

*Yubayyaḍu al-<sup>c</sup>āj bi-mashḥihi bi-mashḥūq ḥajr al-khuffān* **[pumice stone]** *wa-l-mā' ma<sup>c</sup>an thumma bi-waḍ<sup>c</sup>ihī fi l-shams warā' zujāj shubbāk li-'allā yatashaqqaqa wa-yukarraru hādha l-<sup>c</sup>amal ḥattā yabyaḍḍa tamāman. Yubayyaḍu bi-taghṭīsihī fī mā' fīhi qalīl min al-ḥāmiḍ al-kibrītīk* **[sulphuric acid]** *(zayt al-zāj)* **[oil of vitriol]** [*zayt al-zāj* is inserted by Muq.] *aw klūrid al-kils* **[chloride of calcium/calcic chloride/calcium chloride]**.
*Aw bi-ḥarq kibrīt ḥattā yatalaṭṭafa dukhānuhū bi-l-hawā' wa-tadkhīnihī* [voc. by Muq.] *bihī wa-bi-dhalika tubayyaḍu* [or: *tabyaḍḍu* ?] *anṣibat* [Muq. did not use *nuṣub* ?] *al-sakākīn wa-maqābiḍ al-firshāyāt wa-naḥwuhā* [or: *naḥwahā* ?] *min al-ashyā' al-thamīna al-maṣnū<sup>c</sup>a*

After publishing the journal for one year, the editors tried to classify the *fawā'id* into *Fawā'id ṣinā<sup>c</sup>īya* (Benefits to Artisans) (e.g. I/12, p. 273; II, p. 279 f; IV, pp. 189-192, resp. 296 f), *Fawā'id ṣiḥḥīya* (Benefits to Health) (cf. e.g.: II, p. 8; IV, p. 319), *Fawā'id <sup>c</sup>ilmīya* (e.g. II, pp. 278 f), and *Fawā'id zirā<sup>c</sup>īya* (Benefits to Farmers) (e.g.: III, p. 294; IV, pp. 22-24 resp. p. 81). This classification depending on contents was sometimes blurred by entitling the benefits in another way, for example *Fawā'id mujarraba* (Tested Benefits) (e.g. III/1, pp. 39 f; 81 f; 151 f or 219). Especially the last title shows the conceptual aspect not to publish other *fawā'id* than those which had been tested, either by the editors themselves or by other persons (cf. III/1, p. 25).

In November resp. December 1881, *fawā'id* appeared under the headline *Nubadh ṣinā<sup>c</sup>īya* (cf. VI/6, pp. 370 f) resp. *Nubadh zirā<sup>c</sup>īya* (cf. VI/7, pp. 462-464). It seems that the editors were looking for a suitable manner to handle all the practical information. *Nubadh ṣinā<sup>c</sup>īya* (cf. VI/6, pp. 370 f) contained instructions (the headline of which are added in parentheses) e.g. for:

13) making curry (*al-Karī* [voc. by Muq.]); ibid, p. 370),

14) making a "black beauty aid" (*al-Kuzmatīk* [voc. by Muq.] *al-aswad*; ibid., p. 371) which should be of benefit to one's hair (cf. ibid.),
15) imitating gold (*Taqlīd al-dhabab*; ibid.) or
16) making agents to polish metals, e.g. gold and brass (*Munaẓẓif li-l-dhahab* resp. Munaẓẓif li-l-nuḥās al-aṣfar; ibid.).

For example *nubdha* 15) says (VI, p. 371):

*Taqlīd al-dhabab*
**[How to imitate gold]**

*Khudh 16 juz'an min al-nuḥās al-aḥmar* **[copper]** *wa-7 ajzā'*
*min al-b*[?]*latin* **[platinum]** *wa-juz'an min al-zink* **[zinc]** *wa-ișharhā*
**[smelt them]** *ma<sup>c</sup>an. Fa-yaḥṣulu minhā murakkab yushbihu al-dhahab* **[gold]**
*min ʿiyār 16 wa-lā yata[ʾa]ththaru bi-l-ḥāmiḍ al-nitrīk* **[nitric acid]**
*mā lam yakun al-ḥāmiḍ murakkazan jiddan wa-ghāliyan*

*Fawā'id* resp. *nubadh* were opened by the imperative form (see *nubdha* 15) or the passive/imperfect (see *fāwā'id* 2 and 9).

From 1882 onward, *Fawā'id ṣināʿīya* appeared at longer intervals. This decrease, maybe, correlates with the fact that after May 1881, three new columns with information on how to apply scientific knowledge were opened, namely *Bāb Tadbīr al-Manzil* (cf. III.4.6), *Bāb al-Ṣināʿa* (cf. III.4.9 ) and *Bāb al-Zirāʿa* (cf. III.4.10). In the three Western journals consulted counterparts could not be found.

### III.4.5 Bāb al-Munāẓara wa-l-Murāsala

This *bāb* was opened in VI/1 (pp. 44 ff), i.e. June 1881. Though being basically also a form of the dialogue between readers and editors, like *Masā'il wa-Ajwibatuhā* (cf. III.3.3.3), it considerably differs from the latter. Apart from readers' reactions to certain contributions, the *bāb* also contains authors' reactions (respones) to the readers' correspondence.

Since March 1885, when *al-Muqtaṭaf* was published in Cairo, correspondences were, according to the editors, on the increase (cf. X/4 = Jan. 1886, p. 256).

When *Bāb al-Munāẓara wa-l-Murāsala* occurred first, it was introduced by some editorial notes prescribing what was to be published in the framework of it. This introduction became the "label" of this *bāb* because it remained in place whenever the *bāb* appeared later (VI/1, p. 44). The editors wrote: "After examining we regard it nessecary to open such a *bāb*... For what is to be inserted into the *bāb* the contributors alone are responsible. We abstain from making contributions. But we reject contributions that do not refer to *al-Muqtaṭaf*'s contents. We select the subjects to be carried by this *bāb* complying with the following principles:

(1) Opponent and proposer (challenger) dispute on one and the same subject, your opponent is your challenger. (2) The purpose of the disputation is to attain the truth. He who spots mistakes made by others must be respected, but otherwise, one who admits to his own mistakes must be respected more. (3) Brevity is important. Brief contributions are given preference over long-drawn-out articles." (*Qad ra'aynā baᶜd al-ikhtibār wujūb fatḥ hādha l-bāb fa-fataḥnāhū taghrīban fi-l-maᶜārif wa-inhāḍan li-l-himam wa-tashḥīdhan li-l-adhhān. Wa-lakinna al-ᶜuhda fī mā yudraju fīhi ᶜalā aṣḥābihī fa-naḥnu burā' minhū kullihī. Wa-lā nudriju mā kharaja ᶜan mawḍūᶜ al-Muqtaṭaf wa-nurāᶜī fi-l-idrāj wa-ᶜadamihī mā ya*[']*tī*:
*1) al-Munāẓir wa-l-naẓīr mushtaqqān min aṣl wāḥid fa-munāẓiruka naẓīruka*
*2) Innamā al-gharaḍ min al-munāẓara al-tawaṣṣul ila l-ḥaqā'iq. Fa-idhā kāna kāshif aghlāṭ ghayrihī ᶜaẓīman kāna al-muᶜtarif bi-aghlāṭihī aᶜẓam 3) Khayr al-kalām mā qalla wa-dalla. Fa-l-maqālāt al-wāfiya maᶜ al-ijāz tustakhāru ᶜala l-muṭawwala*) (VI, p. 44).

Contributions to this *bāb* cover between two and a few pages. Most of them are opened by phrases of address such as *li-Janāb Munshi'yay al-Muqtaṭaf al-Muḥtaramayn* or *Ḥaḍrat Munshi'yay al-Muqtaṭaf al-Fāḍilayn* although they are responses to what writers (but not the editors) or readers have written.

Contributions to *Bāb al-Munāẓara wa-l-Murāsala* were regularly signed with the authors' names. Among them we find numerous well-known writers of the *Nahḍa*. Apart from the Lebanese physician Shiblī Shumayyil (1850-1917)[74], an exponent of materialst philosophy in that time, we read the names of such important authors as Jurjī Zaydān (1861-1914)[75], Asᶜad Khalīl Dāghir (1860-1935)[76], Jabr Dūmiṭ[77], and Naᶜūm Shuqayr[78]. Even Muslim scholars contributed to the disputation carried by this bāb, e.g. Muḥammad al-Shādhilī Ibn Farḥāt (d. 1892?)[79] (cf. VIII/, 349 ff, 326 ff), the Shiite Shaykh Ḥusayn al-Jisr (1845-1909)[80] (cf. VIII/8 = May 1884, pp. 495-497), and Shaykh Ibrāhīm al-Aḥdab (1826-1891)[81] (cf. VIII/11 = August 1884, 676 ff).

In its form, the *Bāb al-Munāẓara wa-l-Murāsala* can be characterized as an Arabic *pendant* to Western correspondece columns such as N's "Letters to the editor", PSM's "Correspondence" and NC's "Modern Symposium"[82]. They might have stimulated Ṣarrūf and Nimr to establish this *bāb*.

However, when evaluating this *bāb* one must be careful and should also keep in mind at least three other facts:

**One**, the Arab-Islamic history has developed its own method, including texts, of disputation. This goes back to the medieval scholastic methods of *jadal* (dialectic), *khilāf* (divergence of opinion, disagreement in law), *naẓar* and *munāẓara* (disputation)[83].

**Two**, concerning *al-Muqtaṭaf* (Arabic/Eastern periodicals, in general ?), the text type "letter to the editor" and the phenomenon correspondence/dialogue seem more heterogeneous, even more complicate than concerning Western patterns. *Rasā'il,* *masā'il*, and that what in Arabic is called *radd* (pl.: *rudūd*) (reply/response)[84], too - all these various texts are parts of the one journal with special functions in correspondence. They carry dialogues of several kind: so ***Masā'il*** carries a special dialogue between the readers and the editors, whereas the "letters" of ***Bāb al-Munāẓara wa-l-Murāsala*** stimulate the dialogue among the readers, and between the readers and the writers (without the editors). Later, also the ***Bāb Tadbīr al-Manzil*** (see III.4.6) is involved. It is certainly not correct to say that all these texts are Arabic versions of the "Western letter to the editor".

Three, correspondence to *al-Muqtaṭaf* did not begin with the establishment of a special ***bāb***, and it did not end with this. ***Rudūd*** and ***rasā'il***, had already been inserted into the journal before ***Bāb al-Munāẓara wa-l-Murāsala*** occurred first.[85] But, also after opening it in June 1881, letters to Ṣarrūf and Nimr continued to be published apart from the ***bāb*** (e.g. VII/7, = Jun. 1883, pp. 297-315, small ed.). So one must conclude that, until 1889, the correspondence of the readers to their journal as well as the dialogue was still not brought into a stable conceptual order.

## III.4.6 Bāb Tadbīr al-Manzil

This ***bāb*** was opened in VI/1 (pp. 51-55), i.e. June 1881. It aimed at the *ahl al-bayt*, i.e. those who are responsible for domestic economy and the education of children. Ṣarrūf and Nimr introduced this ***bāb*** by the following remarks which also became a "label". The editors wrote: "We have opened this ***bāb*** in order to inform the *ahl al-bayt* about what they should know about child education, food preparation, flat cleaning, dressing, washing, making one's toilet, etc. We want to benefit each family." (*Qad fataḥnā hādha l-bāb li-kay nudrija fīhī kull mā yuhimmu ahl al-bayt maʿrifatahū min tarbiyat al-awlād wa-tadbīr al-ṭaʿām wa-l-libās wa-l-sharāb wa-l-maskan wa-l-zīna wa-naḥwi dhālika mimmā yaʿūdu bi-l-nafʿ ʿalā kull ʿā'ila.*) (ibid., p. 51)

Among the first 16 entries we find for example

1) opinions on instruction and education of childen (headline: *Shadharāt fī tarbiyat al-awlād*, VI, p. 51) and
2) *fawā'id* (*nubadh*) (see III.4.4) on (again) how to take out stains (headline: *Izālat al-buqaʿ wa naḥwihā ʿan al-thiyāb*; ibid.),
3) *fawā'id* on how to make perfume soap (headline: *al-Ṣābūn al-muṭayyab*; ibid., p. 52)
4) recipes for making jam, e.g. of orange juice (headline: *Murabbā ʿaṣīr al-burtuqāl*; ibid., p. 53) as well as
5) *fawā'id* on polishing metals, e.g. silver (headline: *Mashūq li-jalīy al-fiḍḍa*, ibid., p. 54).

**About the subject of the education of children (1), one could read for example (VI, p. 51):**

*Shadharāt fī tarbiyat al-awlād*
**[Several opinions on the education of children]**

*Qāla baʿḍuhum. Tadhhīb al-walad yabtada'u qabl*
*taʿlīmihī fī l-madrasa yabtada'u bi-naẓrat* [?]
*ummihī wa-iltifāt abīhī wa-tabassum ukhtihī*
*wa-ijtihād akhīhī*
*Wa-qāla aḥad al-aṭibbā': inna mā yasmaʿu al-ṭifl wa-yarāhū al-sanatayn*
*al-ūlayayn min ʿumrihī yantabiʿu fī dhihnihī intibāʿan lā yumḥā*
*wa-yu'aththiru fīhī mā dāma ḥayyan. Fa-yajibu al-intibāh al-tāmm ilā*
*kull kalima yasmaʿuhā wa-kull ʿamal yarāhū li-kay lā-yasmaʿa illā*
*al-kalām al-ṣādiq al-muhadhdhab wa-lā yarā illā al-aʿmāl al-ḥasana*
*al-mufīda*
*Wa-qāla ghayruhū: al-ṣidq amass mā yajibu intibāʿuhū fī tarbiyat al-awlād*
*wa-tahdhībihim wa-l-sulūk maʿahum fa-man kadhaba ʿalā waladihī wa-tilmīdhihī*
*wa-law marra wāḥida ʿallamahū al-kidhb wa-nazaʿa haybatahū*
*min ʿaynayhū*

However, the subject of the education of children (like other subjects, too, e.g. the importance of knowledge and education especially for young people) was also treated by quoting the classical Arabic stock of *aqwāl ḥikamīya* (wisdom sentences/aphorisms) and gnomic poetry.

The following pieces were contributed by a person who signed with Anṭūn Ḥaddād (VII, p. 239):

*Aqwāl ḥikamīya*

*Qāla al-hakīm rabbi al-walad fī tarīqihī fa-matā shākha lā yaḥīdu ʿanhā*
*wa-qala al-shāʿir inna al-ghuṣūn idhā qawwamtahā iʿtadalat*
*wa-lā yalīnu wa-law qawwamtahū al-khashab...*

Besides the education of children, also domestic chemistry (later, the term *al-kīmiyā' al-baytīya* is used, e.g. VIII/3, p. 179) remained an important subject in the period under review.

*Fā'ida* 5) says (VI, p. 54):

*Masḥūq li-jalīy al-fiḍḍa*
**[A powder to polish silver]**

*al-Ifranj yabīʿūna masḥūqan asmar yusammūnahū masḥūq al-ṣuḥūn*
*wa-hādhā tarkībuhū: ūqīya min uksīd al-ḥadīd* **[ferric oxide]** *al-masḥūq*
*nāʿiman tashtarī min ʿind al-ṣaydalānī wa-arbaʿa awāqī min al-ṭabāshīr*
*al-mustaḥdar al-masḥūq saḥqan nāʿiman. Tumzaju maʿan jayyidan*
*wa-tufraku al-fiḍḍa bi-mazījihā thumma tujlā bi-jild al-waʿl*

*al-naẓīf thumma bi-mandīl min al-ḥarīr fa-talmaʿu ka-annahā jadīda*

*Bāb Tadbīr al-Manzil* also contained numerous *fawā'id ṣiḥḥīya*. So the readers were e.g. cautioned against drinking too much cold water too quickly in hot days (cf. VI, p. 178).

The *fā'ida* says (VI, p. 178):

*Shurb al-mā' al-bārid*
**[Drinking cold water]**

*Mimmā yajibu al-ḥidhr minhu ayyām al-ḥurr al-shadīd shurb kamīya kabīra min al-mā' al-bārid aw al-mubarrad bi-l-thalj dufʿa wāḥida. Wa-idhā ghasala al-insān ṣudghayhī bi-mā' bārid qallat ḥarārat jasadihī ka-mā law shariba mā' bāridan wa-laysa li-l-ghasl natā'ij muḍirra mithl natā'ij al-shurb*

From 1883/84 at the latest, Ṣarrūf and Nimr opened this *bāb* also to readers' disputation, e.g. on girls' and women's education[86]

In the Western journals consulted, only one pattern could be found that, partly, may have stimulated the Muqtatafis, namely PSM's "Popular Miscellany". However, this column does not include text such as *fawā'id* and recipes.

### III.4.7 Hadāyā wa-Taqārīẓ

This *bāb* was established in VI/2 (pp. 127 f), i.e. July 1881. But already before that time, we can find what later was incorporated into *Hadāyā wa-Taqārīẓ*, namely announcements (*iʿlānāt)* of books and Arabic newspapers/journals as well as brief precursors of what, today, is called *intiqādāt*, book reviews[87]. Until July 1881, these *iʿlānāt* were mainly included in *Manthūrāt* (see point III.4.1) or appeared under headlines such as *Taqārīẓ* and *Maṭbūʿāt jadīda*.

After establishing a special *bāb* for announcements and reviews, it seems that there is a stricter separation between *iʿlānāt* listing books and periodicals and, on the other hand, texts reviewing publications which constitute the stock of the special *bāb*.

Among the first publications reviewed when *Hadāyā wa-Taqārīz* occurred first (cf. VI, p. 127) we find different publications, for example

1) the by-laws of *Bākūrat Sūrīya*[88],
2) Jumayyil Mudawwar's *Tārīkh Bābil wa-Ashūr*[89], and
3) ʿAbdallāh Nadīm's satirical weekly *al-Tankīt wa-l-Tabkīt*[90].

*Fīlān* 3) says (VI, p. 127):

*al-Tankīt wa-l-Tabkīt*

*Ṣaḥīfa waṭanīya usbūʿīya adabīya hazlīya. Ṣāḥibuhā wa-muḥarriruhā al-adīb ʿAbdallāh Nadīm wa-maktab idāratihā maktab jarīdatay al-ʿAṣr al-Jadīd wa-l-Maḥrūsa bi l-Iskandarīya wa-qad ra'aynā fī l-ʿadad al-awwal alladhī warada ʿalaynā minhā min al-maqālāt al-adabīya wa-l-hazlīya al-intiqādīya mā nuqaddiru lahū kabīr al-fā'ida li-anna uslūbahū khayr uslūb yadfaʿu al-waṭanīyīn ila l-iqlāʿ ʿammā bihī ḍayruhum wa-l-tamassuk bi-mā bihī khayruhum. Wa-mimmā sarranā fīhā bi-nawʿ khāṣṣ shurūṭ al-ishtirāk. Waffaqa Allāh muḥarrirahā al-fāḍil ilā bulūgh amānīhī*

As a matter of fact, the Arabic *bāb* for announcements and reviews has numerous Western "originals", including the review-columns in the journals consulted, for example N's "Our Book Shelf" or PSM's "Literary Notices".

III.4.8 Bāb al-Riyāḍīyāt

This *bāb* was established in VI/12 (pp. 741 f), i.e. May 1882. It specialized in mathematical problems and their solutions. This *bāb* resulted from a dialogue between the editors, especially Ṣarrūf, and specialists in the field of mathematics.

III.4.9 Bāb al-Ṣināʿa

This *bāb* was opened in VII/4, (pp. 97-104), i.e. November 1882 addressing those who are called in Arabic *ahl al-ṣināʿa* (artisans). Its first contribution under the headline *al-Fūtūghrāfiyā* (The Photography) (ibid., p. 97) was a part of a serial, as we can see from the subtitle *tābiʿ mā qabluhu* (the succeeding part to what was published earlier) and the concluding phrase *sata* [ ]*tī al-baqīya* (to be continued). This serial was started in August 1882 (cf. VII/1, pp. 47 ff) and finished in January 1883. The contribution in question is written like an article from a book of reference on photography. It gives instructions by describing the right methods and instruments to use for taking and developing photos.

The second contribution (VII/2, pp. 102-104) to this first instance of *Bāb al-Ṣināʿa* bears the headline *al-Maʿādin al-khalīṭa wa-l-liḥām* (Alloys and Welding [?]) (ibid., p. 102). This subject must have attracted the interest of many readers (specialists) in those days because it did not only appear in this place. Some of the *fawā'id* (see III.4.4) also dealt with it.

The contribution begins with a definition of what is meant by *al-maʿādin al-khalīṭa* (VII, p. 102):

*al-Maʿādin al-khalīṭa wa-l-liḥām*

**[Alloys and Welding [?]]**

*Nurīdu bi-l-ma<sup>c</sup>ādin al-khalīṭa* **[mixed metals/alloys]** *mā turakkabu ma<sup>c</sup>an min al-ma<sup>c</sup>ādin maṣhūran* **[by smelting/melting]** *bi-l-ḥarāra...*

**[What follows are four *fawā'id* describing the procedure of how alloys can be produced and which instruments should be used as well as several kinds of alloy (*anwā<sup>c</sup> al-khalīṭ*) (ibid.)].**

The *bāb* specialized in dealing with the needs of the Eastern world of handicrafts, one of the pillars of Eastern economy in those days. By describing new technologies or elementary features of materials, partly new ones, it tried to offer solutions to Arab artisans and to encourage them to use new methods of production.

The Western journals consulted do not include special columns for artisans, but there are other Western publications specialized in technologies which have stimulated Ṣarrūf and Nimr.

III.4.10 Bāb al-Zirā<sup>c</sup>a

Although agriculture, another pillar of the Eastern economy of that time, was among the most important topics treated by *al-Muqtaṭaf* and other Arabic periodicals of the 1870s/80s[91], *Bāb al-Zirā<sup>c</sup>a* was not opened before VII/9 or 10 (pp. 237 f resp. 274 f, small ed.), i.e. April or May 1883. Addressing the *ahl al-zirā<sup>c</sup>a* (farmers), it dealt with subjects such as

1) a cattle disease which had occurred im spring 1882 in Syria/Lebanon (headline: *Ittiqā'wabā' al-mawāshī*) (ibid., p. 274),
2) suitable methods of selecting seeds (headline: *Ikhtiyār al-bidhār*) (ibid.),
3) the dependence of the growth of plants on the use of fertilizers (headline: *Numūw al-judhūr*) (ibid., p. 275), and
4) the negative effects of goat keeping on the cedar woods in Lebanon (headline: Ḍarar *al-mi<sup>c</sup>zā)* (ibid.).

One can see that the subjects treated in this *bab* were of great importance for Arab farmers in those days and had a close relation to the farmers' practical work. Later contributions stressed this dimension, as did the editors' summary on the treatment of cotton worms published under the headline *Khulāṣat al-Khulāṣa* (.) *Fī <sup>c</sup>ilāj dūd al-quṭ(u)n* (XI/2, pp. 97 ff), i.e. in November 1886. This text summarizes the results of tests made by Ṣarrūf and Nimr themselves in Shubrā al-Kabīra, near Cairo[92].

Otherwise, in *Bāb al-Zirā<sup>c</sup>a,* the editors also tried to make Arab readers familiar with Western experience in agriculture. In January 1884, Ṣarrūf and Nimr wrote that they intend to publish several contributions on the Western subject of agrochemistry (*al-Kīmiyā'* *al-zirā*ᶜ*īya).*

At the end of their article, they said (VIII, p. 230):

*Wa-qad* ᶜ*azamnā an naḍa*ᶜ*a fī l-ajzā' al-tāliya fuṣūlan mutawāliya fī l-kīmiyā' al-zirā*ᶜ*īya* **[agrochemistry]** *nuwaḍḍiḥu fīhā ahamm al-mabādi' al-kīmāwīya allatī tadkhulu fī l-a*ᶜ*māl al-zirā*ᶜ*īya jārīn fī dhālika majrā ba*ᶜ*ḍ mu'allifī al-ifranj alladhīn qaranū al-*ᶜ*ilm bi-l-*ᶜ*amal wa-sanatakallamu awwalan* ᶜ*ala l-hawā' wa-l-turāb wa-l-mā'*
*wa-nubayyinu māhīyat al-*ᶜ*anāṣir al-mu'allafa minhā wa-khawāṣṣahā wa-lā siyyamā mā yata*ᶜ*allaqu minhā bi-l-zirā*ᶜ*a thumma natakallamu* ᶜ*alā tarkīb al-nabāt wa-mā yatanāwaluhū min al-turāb wa-l-hawā' wa-l-mā' wa-mā yaḥṣulu fīhī min al-murakkabāt allatī yaghtadhī bi-hā al-insān wa-l-ḥayawān. Wa-nubayyinu al-taghayyurāt al-kathīra allatī taḥduthu fī-l-arḍ bi-l-a*ᶜ*māl al-zirā*ᶜ*īya sawā' kānat makānīkīya* **[mechanical]** *aw kīmāwīya wa-hunāka nuṭīlu al-kalām* ᶜ*alā anwā*ᶜ *al-zibl al-ṭabī*ᶜ*īya wa-l-ṣinā*ᶜ*īya wa-ṭuruq isti*ᶜ*māliha wa-manāfi*ᶜ*ihā al-nisbīya thumma natakallamu* ᶜ*alā kathīr min al-mazrū*ᶜ*āt wa-mā yu'aththiru fī namūwihā wa-nakhtimu al-kalām bi-tatabbu*ᶜ *al-ghidhā' al-nabātī fī taḥawwulihī ilā mawādd ḥayawānīya ka-l-samn wa-l-jubn wa-l-laḥm... Wa-innanā wa-in adrajnā hādhihi l-fuṣūl fī Bāb al-Zirā*ᶜ*a naḍmanuhā fawā'id kathīra taladhdhu ma*ᶜ*rifatuhā li-jumhūr al-qurrā'. Wa-*ᶜ*alā llāh al-ittikāl*

This programme of publishing was started by presenting texts which, in form, resemble in the *fawā'id*, but here, they were called *irshādāt li-ahl al-zirā*ᶜ*a ilā mā yajibu* ᶜ*amaluhū kull shahr min shuhūr al-sana* (directions for farmers about what they are recommended to do every month) (VIII, p. 231). "We have translated them", the editors said in the introduction, "from the [Western -D.G.] book *Zirā*ᶜ*at al-ashjār* Arboriculture by John/Johannes Gregor [?] printed in 1881." (*Wa-qad* ᶜ*arrabnāhā* ᶜ*an kitāb Zirā*ᶜ*at al-ashjār* **Arboriculture** *li-Yuḥannā Krīkūr al-maṭbū*ᶜ *sanat 1881...*) (ibid.).

The Western journals consulted do not contain counterparts to the Arabic *Bab al-Zirā*ᶜ*a*, but, as we have seen, there are others, special Western sources used by the Muqtatafis.

### III.4.11 Bāb al-Handasa

This *bāb* is the last creation of Ṣarrūf and Nimr before 1889. The first instance occurred in X/7 (pp. 425 f), i.e. in April 1886. It reported on

1) mineral oil which was discovered in February 1886 near Suez (headline: *Zayt al-Bitrūl fī Miṣr)* (ibid., p. 425)[93],
2) the German project to built the Baltic Canal (headline: *Tur*ᶜ*a bayn Baḥr Baltīk wa-l-Ūqiyānūs)* (ibid., p. 426),
3) the quantities of minerals extracted in America (headline: *Ma*ᶜ*ādin Amīrikā*) (ibid.), and
4) the construction of the Tay Bridge in Dundee/Scotland[94] (headline: *Binā' jisr Tāy*) (ibid.).

For example, the text 2) on the Baltic Canal says (X, p. 426):

*Turʿa bayn Baḥr Baltīk wa l-Ūqiyānūs*
**[A Canal between the Baltic Sea and the North Sea]**

*ʿAzamat dawlat Jirmāniyā mundhu ʿishrīn sana ʿalā fatḥ turʿa* **[canal]** *bayn Baḥr Baltīk* **[the Baltik Sea]** *wa-l-Ūqiyānūs al-Shamālī* **[the North Sea/German Ocean]** *wa-lākin kāna al-Kūnt Multkī* [*Graf* **Moltke]** *yuʿāriḍuhā wa-yaḥtimu bi-wujūb badhl nafaqāt fatḥ al-turʿa al-madhkūra fī binā' al-mudarraʿāt* **[armored cruisers]** *ammā al-ān wa-qad banat dawlat Jirmāniyā al-mudarraʿāt al-ʿaẓīma fa-kaffa hādhā l-Kūnt ʿan muʿāraḍatihā. Fa-iqtaraʿat bi-l-amsi ʿalā fatḥ al-turʿa al-madhkūra wa-qaddarat anna nafaqatahā* [here singular] *satablughu 156 malyūn Mārk* **[156 million Mark]** *ay naḥwa thamāniyat malāyīn min al-Līrāt al-Inklīzīya* **[English Pounds]**. *Wa-satantaffiʿu Jirmāniyā min hādhihi l-turʿa siyāsīyan wa-tijārīyan*

Later texts dated from 1889 described e.g.

5) various sorts of dynamite and gunpowder resp. the methods to produce them (headlines: *Anwāʿ al-dīnāmīt wa-l-bārūd*, XIII, p. 321; *al-Dīnāmīt*, ibid., p. 323) and
6) one special method of the synthesis of nitroglycerin[e] as their main ingredient (headline: *Ṭarīqat M....*[?] *li-ʿamal al-nītrūghlīsirīn*) (ibid., pp. 321f.)

Concerning this *bāb* we can say in a word that it confronted the Arab readers with the beginnings of Western industrialization.

*Bāb al-Handasa* as well as *Bāb al-Ṣināʿa* and *Bāb al-Zirāʿa* have their roots in Western patterns. But none of the three has a single counterpart in the journals consulted. Also concerning these *abwāb* the basic concept of the Muqtatafis is a creative compilation.

### III.4.12 Abwāb: postscript

Until 1889, Ṣarrūf and Nimr had not opened the pages of their journal to literature, although there was a growing and persistent demand for literary works in Egypt and Syria/Lebanon. This is confirmed by an *iʿlān* dated from October 1886 (XI/1, p. alif) which said that many readers requested from the editors to include literary works *(al-riwāyāt al-adabīya)* from which educated and ordinary people *(al-khāṣṣa wa-l-ʿāmma)* could benefit. At that time, however, Ṣarrūf and Nimr could not meet these requests of their readers for the reason of the size of the journal. That is why they suggested another way: We intend, they said, to print literary works seperately and attach them to the journal's volume as supplements. For the subscribers this was going to be a free offer.

From then onwards, they did no longer set aside the readers's interests in modern literature of their readers and included works by Arab authors, e.g. *qaṣā'id* by Aḥmad Shawqī (1868-1932)[95] and Ḥāfiẓ Ibrāhīm (1871-1932)[96], several works by Muṣṭafā Luṭfī al-Manfalūṭī (1872-1924)[97], and later, by Mayy Ziyāda (1886-1941)[98].

## IV Analyzing al-Muqtaṭaf's terminology: procedures and first results

### *IV.0 General remarks*

Arab journalists of the 19th century, not only those who popularized sciences, were confronted with immense difficulties to fit Arabic to the needs of modern writing. One of the problems which ranked first (if not the main difficulty ) was that of how to coin terms able to transmit scientific messages. Mainly because of its deficient vocabulary, Arabic, always the pride of its users, became suddenly a "handicapped" language[99]. "'The Arabic idiom'", Buṭrus al-Bustānī said, "'while abundantly rich in expressing old ideas is in dire want of terms to suit modern needs'"[100].

Journalists had to coin the necessary phrases nearly half a century before any Arab Academy could make a corporate effort to remodel the ancient linguistic structure of Arabic. "This individual, often extemporaneous effort", wrote Stetkevych, "has its roots in the early movement of translation which began in Egypt under Muhammad ᶜAli (reg. 1805-1848), as well as in the rapidly developing periodical press, centered in Egypt and in Lebanon. The translators and the journalists, taken together, have thus far produced and fixed in live usage many more neologisms than the academies."[101]

The problem of how to coin a modern scientific vocabulary was *in nuce* the question of how to adopt foreign, Western terms. Bearing in mind what was said about the journal's references to Western patterns, the contents and the diverse texts, one can see that *al-Muqtaṭaf* were destined to have the strongest influence on modernizing the Arabic scientific vocabulary[102]. But one can certainly imagine that the linguistic solutions offered by them gave more rise to criticism than to praise, at at the beginning. One of the persistent Arab critics was Ibrāhīm al-Yāzijī (1874-1906)[103]. But, on the other hand, it was Arab writers of no less reputation, namely Anastās Mārī al-Karmalī (1866-1947)[104], Muḥammad Kurd ᶜAlī (1876-1953)[105] or Muṣṭafā Ṣādiq al-Rāfiᶜī (1881-1937)[106] who witnessed that among the journal's merits was also its language.

To all his critics, Yaᶜqūb Ṣarrūf replied: "The mode of *al-Muqtaṭaf* is to adhere to the rules of the Arabic language, but its rules comprise that any topic is worth being described by its own mode" *(Al-lugha fī qawāᶜidihā ᶜarabīya wa-lākin min qawāᶜidihā anna li-kull maqām maqālan*) (LXXII, p. 25).

Nevertheless, we may assume that numerous terms were difficult to understand. And often, as Jabr Ḍūmiṭ admitted, only someone familiar with foreign, European languages, first of all English, was able to realize what a message really meant (cf. LXXII, p. 291)[107].

*IV.1 Loan translation and arabicization*

The problems of how to adopt the foreign, Western vocabulary centered mainly around the question of loan translation and arabicization (*tarjama wa-taʿrīb*). Until 1889, it seems that above all, it was this method that was applied by Muqtatafis to express what they wanted to transmit. As a consequence, the readers were flooded with neologismens, *muʿarrabāt* (arabicized terms).

However, from the beginning, the editors were aware of the fact that on the reader's side there was a strong demand for receiving terminological explanation. That is why they explained and paraphrased terms in several ways, e.g. by

(1) vocalizing terms,
(2) adding Arabic substitutes (neologisms, classical terms, ordinary explanations),
(3) adding foreign terms, and
(4) giving complete definitions.

So we have seen that:

1) various foreign terms, used in *akhabār*, *fawā'id*, etc., were vocalized by the Muqtatafis, e.g. **curry** *al-karī* in *fā'ida* 13) (see III.4.4),
2/1) the foreign term "**microscope**", used in a *khabar*, was rendered by *al-mikruskūb* and paraphrased by *al-minẓar al-mukabbir* (see III.4.1; cf. III, p. 280), i.e. by an Arabic neologism,
2/2) the foreign term "**sulphuric acid**", used in a *fā'ida* 9) (see III.4.4; cf. II, p. 280), was rendered by *al-ḥāmiḍ al-kibrītīk* and paraphrased by *zayt al-zāj*, i.e. by adding a classical Arabic chemical term[108],
2/3) the foreign term "**paleontology**", used in another *khabar*, was rendered by *ʿilm al-baliyūntūlūjiyā* and paraphrased by *wa-huwa ʿilm dafā'in al-arḍ* (this is the scientific study of treasures hidden in the earth) (see III.4.1; cf. VI, p. 377). i.e. by an ordinary Arabic explanation which could not give more than a vague idea of the subject[109],
3) the foreign term "**arboriculture**", used in *Bāb al-Zirāʿa* (see III.4.10), was rendered by *zirāʿat al-ashjār*, but paraphrased by adding the Western term itself (VIII, p. 231), and

4/1) the foreign term "**alloys**", used in the first instance of *Bāb al-Ṣināᶜa* (see III.4.9), was rendered by *al-maᶜādin al-khalīṭa* and explained by a definition: *Nurīdu bi-l-maᶜādin al-khalīṭa mā turakkabu maᶜan min al-maᶜādin maṣhūran bi-l-ḥarāra*... (By mixed metals/alloys, we mean that what emerged when metals are smelted/melted at a high temperature for mixing them together..., VII, p. 102).

And in this context, one must finally add that in the other sections of *al-Muqtaṭaf*, e.g. the articles, arabicized terms were also paraphrased:

4/2) when the foreign term "**biology**" occurred for the first time in the journal, it was rendered by *al-biyūlūjiyā*, and paraphrased by a complete definition:... *al-biyūlūjiyā ayy ᶜilm al-ḥayāt wa-lafẓa biyūlūjiyā murakkaba min kalimatayn yūnānīyatayn βιος al-ḥayāt wa λογος al-sharḥ*... (biology, i.e. the scientific study of life. The term biology is composed of two Greek words: *βιος* life and λογος explanation...) (I, p. 79) So we have to conclude that the linguistic phenomenon of paraphrasing terms is not restricted to the *abwāb*.

However, the editors obviously felt that paraphrasing or defining only once or occasionally, and sometimes in different ways, did not suffice. So, between November 1883 and December 1884, they began to publish a "Glossary of Arabicized Terms" (*Muᶜjam al-Muᶜarrabāt*) in serial (cf. VIII/2, pp. 107-112; VIII/3, pp. 166-169; VIII/4, pp. 212-216; VIII/5, pp. 294-296; VIII/6, pp. 341-346; VIII/7, pp. 401f; IX/3, pp. 142-145). They made the attempt to give a systematic survey of the *muᶜarrabāt* used by them. But for several reasons[110] it was to remain incompletly: it ended with the letter *kāf*. As far as it was published, this glossary lists more than 280 transliterated borrowings with their definitions and their first occurrences in the journal.

### *IV.2 On al-Muqtaṭaf's Muᶜjam al-Muᶜarrabāt*

#### IV.2.1 Special terms

Apart from a few ordinary words designating things of modern everyday life[111], the glossary mainly contains special terms (the majority of them nouns) from several scientific fields: above all chemistry, but also physics, biology, medicine, and mechanics, etc. So, we find e.g. the following ten special *muᶜarrabāt:*

(1) *al-uksujīn* (oxygen) (VIII/2, p. 110)
(2) *al-ballūn* (balloon) (VIII/4, p. 214)
(3) *al-bīsīkil/al-baysīkil* (bicycle) (ibid., p. 215)

(4) *al-biyūlūjiyā* (biology) (ibid., p. 216)
(5) *al-tilighrāf* (telegraph) (VIII/5, p. 294)
(6) *al-tilifūn* (telephone) (ibid.)
(7) *al-jiyūlūjiyā* (geology) (ibid., p. 296)
(8) *al-ḥāmiḍ al-kibrītīk* (sulphuric acid) (VIII/6, p. 343)
(9) *al-difthīriyā* (diphtheria) (ibid., p. 344)
(10) *al-sbiktruskūb* (spectroscope) (VIII/7, p. 402)

The fortunes of these ten, and all other, *muʿarrabāt* varied in the course of time, and also the arguments used by Ṣarrūf and Nimr to accept one term and reject the other. Both, the words themselves and the discussion about them, illustrate basic lines from the modern history of the Arabic language, the development of Modern Standard Arabic. For tracing the fortunes of the ten *muʿarrabāt* mentioned several sources have been consulted: contributions to *al-Muqtaṭaf* referring to the language problem, some secondary sources, and contemporary Arabic dictionaries[112].

IV.2.2 Fortunes of the ten muʿarrabāt

IV.2.2.1 Revitalizing classical Arabic

Various efforts were made to substitute these and other *muʿarrabāt* that had been coined and (or only) spread by *al-Muqtaṭaf*. For this purpose it was tried to revitalize and activate classical Arabic vocabulary (incl. old *muʿarrabāt*). It was Yaʿqub Ṣarrūf himself as well as other Muqtatafis and journalists, and, later, the Arab academicians of Cairo and Damascus who made their proposals.

Table 2
**Substitution by revitalizing classical Arabic**

| **No.** | **Arabicized terms introduced by** *al-Muqtaṭaf* | **Arabic sub-stitutes (AS)** | **The AS was coined/introduced by** |
|---|---|---|---|
| (1) | *al-uksujīn* | *al-muṣdi'* | Aḥmad ʿAlī al-Iskandarī[113] |
| (2) | *al-ballūn* | *al-munṭād* | Ibrāhīm al-Yāzijī[114] |

| | | | |
|---|---|---|---|
| (3) | *al-bīsīkil/*<br>*al-baysīkil* | *al-darrāja* | Yaᶜqūb Ṣarrūf/<br>Faris Nimr<br>(cf. XXXIII,<br>p. 562)[115] |
| (4) | *al-biyūlūjiyā* | *ᶜilm al-ḥayāt*<br><br><br>*ᶜilm al-aḥyā'* | William van Dyck[116]<br>(cf. I/4 = Sept. 1876,<br>p. 79)<br><br>Yaᶜqūb Ṣarrūf<br>(cf. LXXII, p. 159)[117] |
| (6) | *al-tilifūn* | *al-miqwal*<br>*al-nadī*<br>*al-misarra*<br>*al-hātif*[118] | ?<br>?<br>?<br>? |
| (10) | *al-sbiktruskūb* | *minẓār al-ṭayf*<br><br><br>*al-miṭyāf* | Yaᶜqūb Ṣarrūf[119]<br><br><br>Fu'ād Ṣarrūf[120] |

IV. 2.2.2 Muᶜarrabāt which are still in use today

As everyone familiar with Modern Standard Arabic knows: Arabic substitutes have not always or not exclusively survived. Sometimes the borrowings withstood all arabicization efforts aiming at substitution, the early non-corporate and the far stronger later corporate ones. In any case, of the ten *muᶜarrabāt* mentioned in IV.2.1 the following ones are still in use today, if sometimes spelled differently. Those *muᶜarrabāt* that have become duplicates of the Arabic substitutes are marked by [d].

(1) *al-uksujīn* (Wehr 1985, 5th ed.)
(2) *al-ballūn* (Wehr 1985, 5th ed.: *balon*) [d]
(4) *al-biyūlūjiyā* (ibid.) [d]
(5) *al-tilighrāf* (Krahl 1984: *tillighrāf*)
(6) *al-tilifūn* (ibid., *tilīfūn*) [d]

(7) *al-jiyūlūjiyā* (Wehr 1985)
(8) *al-ḥāmiḍ al-kibrītīk* (ibid.)
(9) *al-difthīriyā* (ibid., *diftiriyā*; Wehr 1976: *difteriyā*) [d]

*IV.3 Al-Muqtaṭaf's principles of arabicization*

In July 1908, *al-Muqtaṭaf* published an article in which Sarruf and Nimr explained their principles of arabicization: *Uslūbunā fi-l-taᶜrīb* (cf. XXXIII, pp. 559-565, reprint in: LXX, pp. 481-487). This was a response alike to readers and critics, and a delayed explanation for what journalistic life had required of them to do as well. Here, they explained e.g. how they had adopted Western proper names, geographical terms, etc. In our context, it is five principles in arabicizing Western scientific terms that are especially important.

IV.3.1 Principle One

If we know, the editors of *al-Muqtaṭaf* wrote, of Arabic terms (genuine Arabic terms, old *muᶜarrabāt* included) that can precisely transmit the meaning intended, we use them instead of the foreign terms (cf. XXXIII, p. 559).

Term **(3)** above, ***al-bīsīkil/al-baysīkil*** substituted by *al-darrāja* [121], exemplify principle one. But in numerous other (the majority ? of) cases, Ṣarrūf and Nimr obviously deviated from principle one and made exceptions. This is shown by the principles two and three.

IV.3.2 Principle Two

We make exceptions, the editors said, and give the foreign term in Arabic transcription preference over an old (classical) Arabic one if the existing Arabic term, to our mind, is not unambiguous enough (cf. ibid., p. 560). When foreign terms are arabicized, Ṣarrūf and Nimr added, they often become less precise (cf. ibid., p. 563).

Several scientific terminologies exemplify substitutions based on these arguments, e.g. the medical and the chemical ones. The foreign medical designation ***al-difthīriyā***, example **(9)** above, was used by the Muqtatafis instead of the classical Arabic term: *al-khānūq* (cf. VI/10, = March 1882, p. 592)[122]. And also the chemical terminology was changed by them. Parts of the classical Arabic terminology were successively displaced and substituted by modern borrowings. So at the end, ***al-ḥāmiḍ al-kibrītīk***, see example **(8)** above, triumphed over (*zayt*) *al-zāj* (see IV.1, 1/2), *al-ammūniyā* (ammonia) over (*milḥ*) *al-nūshādir* (sal ammoniak, exactly: ammonium chloride[123]) (see III.4.4, 2; cf. XXXIII, p. 560), *al-zink* over *al-tūtiyā* (see III.4.4; cf. XXXIII, p. 560), ***al-uksujīn*** over *al-muṣdī'*, see example **(1)** above, etc.

Ṣarrūf and Nimr argued that it is essential not only to adopt modern scientific ideas but the terms created by the contemporary scientists, too. In the opinion of *al-Muqtaṭaf*'s editors, the modern scientific terms are primarily international, not Western ones. And they are more suitable in order to introduce the Arab reader to modern, current scientific research than old Arabic ones, if existing.

Arabicized terms, they added, can be more precise than the existing classical Arabic terms (cf. XXXIII, pp. 560 resp. 563). So modern chemistry requires to differentiate e.g. between "sulphuric acid" and "sulphureous acid". As the specialists know, the two terms mean two things, namely two different chemical compounds. In consequence, modern Arab authors who want to write in Arabic on problems related to the subject also have to use two different terms. Ṣarrūf and Nimr used ***al-ḥāmiḍ al-kibrītīk*** and *al-ḥāmiḍ al-kibrītūs* (cf. VIII, p. 343 and XXXIII, p. 563) making the necessary difference by deriving two terms from *kibrīt* (sulfur), the one with the suffix *-īk* and the other with the suffix *-ūs*. In reply to all critics who voted for using only *al-ḥāmiḍ al-kibrīti* Ṣarrūf and Nimr said: "He who uses *al-ḥāmiḍ al-kibrītī* instead of *al-ḥāmiḍ al-kibrītīk* is like one who calls a horse a donkey because both animals have a head and a tail." (*Fa-man yusammī al-ḥāmiḍ al-kibrītīk bi-l-ḥāmiḍ al-kibrītī ka-man yusammī al-faras ḥimāran li-anna li-kull minhumā ra'san wa-dhanaban*) (XXXIII, p. 563).

Sometimes, however, the foreign term was given preference over an old Arabic one for other exceptional reasons, as the next principle shows.

IV.3.3 Principle Three

We make exceptions, Ṣarrūf and Nimr continued, and prefer the foreign term in Arabic transcription to an old Arabic term if the existing Arabic word, to our mind, is not widely known or not in use (cf. ibid., p. 565).

So to designate a balloon in Arabic another suggestion was made than ***al-ballūn***, example (2) above, namely *al-munṭād* by Ibrāhīm al-Yāzijī (see table 2). But Ṣarrūf and Nimr rejected it. The main reason was that the old word *inṭāda* (to rise in the air), as they argued, is not in use, but remained only an item in dictionaries (cf. ibid.).

However, what did they do in cases where suitable classical terms did not exist?

IV.3.4 Principle Four

If old Arabic words do not exist, Ṣarrūf and Nimr replied, we prefer those borrowings which have already been introduced (cf. ibid., p. 562).

This should be illustrated by the two *muʿarrabāt*: ***al-uksujīn***, example (1) above, and ***al-tilighrāf***, example (5) above. ***Al-Uksujīn*** was coined by Cornelius van Dyck (cf. LXXIV, 7)[124]. In this and other cases, Ṣarrūf and Nimr copied what he and other teachers of the SPC had proposed, whereas in the case of ***al-tilighrāf*** - a neologism which, maybe, was introduced into Arabic by *al-Jinān* about 1871[125], but in any case, before *al-Muqtaṭaf* was started - they copied the usage of other Arabic journals of the time.

### IV.3.5 Principle Five

Here, the editors of *al-Muqtaṭaf* said, what they did when a classical Arabic term did not exist, and a neologism had not been introduced: We coin, they explained, the terms which are needed ourselves.

One of the neologisms coined by Ṣarrūf and Nimr is ***al-tilifūn***, example (6) above. To defend their creation, Ṣarrūf and Nimr argued: By coining ***al-tilifūn***, and adhering to it, we have not fallen behind the nations of this world, at least, when competing with them for a name designating this important invention of the 19th century (cf. XXXIII, p. 562). And even if we had found an old Arabic word that would have suited to derive a modern term from it, the Arabic substitute, to our belief, would never have been accepted (ibid.). However, the user of Modern Standard Arabic knows that in this respect, Ṣarrūf and Nimr were wrong. As a matter of fact, in Modern Standard Arabic there is a term which is as well accepted as ***al-tilifūn***, namely: *al-hātif* (see table 2).

## V. Conclusions

**One**, *al-Muqtaṭaf* challenged its readers by confronting them with the scientific knowledge of that time. It played a leading role in bridging culture, although its editors did not uncritically accept all Western ideas[126].

**Two**, the Western pattern of the columns is a (if not the) basic one in popularizing siences through this Eastern encyclopaedic journal. The Arabic equivalents of the columns are the *abwāb*.

**Three**, they are not a mere translation or imitation of their Western counterparts. The *abwāb* are a result of transforming Western textual and terminological patterns by adopting suitable foreign ones, by activating, changing resp. substituting classical Arabic ones and by creating new ones.

**Four**, when comparing *al-Muqtaṭaf* with Western scientific journals of the late 19th century one cannot only find similarities, but remarkable differences, too. For the time being, we safely can state that *al-Muqtaṭaf* contains a wider-ranging set of texts than the Western journals consulted, and probably many others, too. Another striking feature is that, until 1889, the Muqtatafis established through *Masā'il wa-Ajwibatuhā*, *Fawā'id*, *Bāb al-Munāẓara wa-l-Murāsala*, and *Bāb Tadbīr al-Manzil* many more forms of dialogue with their readers than their Western colleagues did in a single journal.

**Five**, the transformation of the Western patterns into Arabic journalistic patterns required an Eastern journalistic concept. To find a suitable one was the result of a process of gathering journalistic experience over years. It took Ṣarrūf and Nimr more than ten years to succeed.
**Six**, the journalistic concept of *al-Muqtaṭaf* included a linguistic one. The one did not function without the other. So the Muqtatafis made their own decisions to arabicize foreign terms. By applying different methods, they introduced their readers not only into the terminology used by them, but into the problem of modernizing the Arabic language, too. In the mind of the Muqtatafis, language was a living organism that had to be remodelled continuously to fit the communication needs of the time (*al-Lugha jism ḥayy nam/in/*, cf. XXXIII, p. 565). Their writings were much more ruled by criteria such as live usage, precision and international connotation than by ambiguity, classical exclusiveness or even national linguistic purism. The journal was written in a language which has proved its capacity to survive. The fact that Modern Standard Arabic exists is, without any doubt, also due to the journalistic linguistic patterns transformed and spread by *al-Muqtaṭaf* and its "life and soul", Yaᶜqūb Ṣarrūf.
**Seven**, to get a closer insight into this journalistic transformation of Western patterns for the purpose of popularizing sciences in Arabic further investigations are intended. They have especially to deal with its creative side, e.g. the forms of dialogue, the terms, the style, etc. In general, they must pay attention to the process of defining the distance from classical forms, styles, and terminologies in the framework of the Eastern press.
**Eight**, before writers of Arabic short stories and novels came to make their contributions, it was, besides the translators, the journalists who initiated the changes of writing Arabic prose, and enabled the Arabic language to fulfill a new social function, namely to popularize sciences by the means of the press. Of this new literary Arabic genre is also true what Kratshkovsky has once said about the whole of the "*neu-arabische Literatur*": "Und doch ist (sie, D.G.) interessant, vielleicht nicht weniger als die alte, da sie uns Seiten aufdeckt, für die wir in letzterer nicht die Möglichkeit der Beobachtung haben...Vor unseren Augen vollzieht sich die Schöpfung eines neuen Geistes, die Durchdringung europäischer Formen vom arabischen Sein; nicht selten zeigt dieses sich stärker, als man es nach den Nach-ahmungen, mit denen die neu-arabische Literatur einsetzte, hätte glauben wollen."[127]

## Notes

1 This article is the enlarged and revised version of two papers. The one dealing with al-Muqtaṭaf's contribution to the modernization of the Arabic language I read at the 34th ICANAS, in August 1993 in Hong Kong. The other paper dealing with the journal as a literary result of the encounter between East and West in the late 19th century I presented at a symposium on "Changing Identities" which was held in Oktober 1993 in Berlin, organized by the Center for Modern Oriental Studies. I would like to thank Prof. A. A. Ambros from Vienna with whom I discussed a few passages of the manuscript, and whose remarks have been most useful and enlightening. Thanks are also due to Prof. D. Bellmann from Leipzig for the help he offered me. Furthermore, I wish to express my thanks to Prof. H. Finger from Freiburg who was so kind as to read a version of the manuscript and to advise on writing it in English.

2 For Yaᶜqūb Ṣarrūf's vita see al-Muqtaṭaf, esp.:F. Ṣarrūf, al-Duktūr Yaᶜqūb Ṣarrūf. Maraḍuhū al-akhīr wa-wafātuhū. In: LXXI/2 = August 1927, pp. 121-124; Kh. Thābit, Sīrat Yaᶜqūb Ṣarrūf. Ibid., pp. 192-199; S. Shuqayr et al., Ta'bīn al-Duktūr Ṣarrūf. In: LXXII/5 = May 1928, pp. 555-565; Ḥ. Khabbāz, al-Duktūr Ṣarrūf wa-l-Muqtaṭaf, mādhā aᶜṭāhū wa-mādhā akhadha minhū. In: LXXIII/4 = December 1928, pp. 429-439; F. d. Ṭarrāzī, al-Ṣaḥāfa al-ᶜarabīya, vol. II, Beirut 1913 (reprint), pp. 124-129; D.S. Margoliouth, Ya'kub Sarruf. In: JRAS 1927, pp. 937-939; Y.A. Dāghir, Maṣādir al-dirāsa al-ᶜarabīya, vol. II, Beirut 1955, pp. 540-518; N. Farag, al-Muqtataf 1876-1900. A Study of the Influence of Victorian Thought on Modern Arabic Thought. (Unpublished Thesis), Oxford 1969, pp. 12-41; ᶜI.M. Sābā, Yaᶜqūb Ṣarrūf. Cairo n.d. (= Nawābigh al-fikr al-ᶜarabī, 37), and F. Ṣarrūf, Yaᶜqūb Ṣarrūf, Beirut 1960.

3 For Fāris Nimr's vita see al-Muqtaṭaf, esp.: S. Jisrī, al-Duktūr Fāris Nimr Bāshā. In: CXX/1 = January 1952, pp. 1-12; Ṭarrāzī 1913, op. cit., vol. II, pp. 138-142; Farag 1969, op. cit., pp. 42-47; and Y.A. Dāghir, Maṣādir al-dirāsa al-ᶜarabīya, vol. III/2, Beirut 1972, pp. 1352-1354.

4 Al-Muqaṭṭam was founded on the 14th of February, 1889. It was to become an important and influential British-oriented newspaper as well as an opponent of al-Ahrām. Fāris Nimr concentrated on editing al-Muqaṭṭam while Ṣarrūf remained editing al-Muqtaṭaf. The political daily al-Muqaṭṭam put an end to the financial difficulties the scientific monthly al-Muqtaṭaf was confronted with until 1889. For details see Farag 1969, op. cit., p. 22. For information on the historical background of al-Muqaṭṭam see also Ṭarrāzī 1913, op. cit., vol. II, pp. 138-142; Farag 1969, op. cit., pp. 96-102; and S. ᶜAzīz, al-Ṣiḥāfa al-miṣrīya wa-mawqifuhā min al-iḥtilāl al-injlīzī, Cairo 1968, pp. 96-110. For al-Ahrām see note 52.

5 The whole of the journal comprises 121 volumes with about 81,000 pages. Page format (octavo): 15cm x 24 cm. For other features concerning size and layout of the journal see D. Glaß, Die Zeitschrift al-Muqtaṭaf (1876-1952) und die Erneuerung der arabischen Sprache. Notizen zur Primärquelle eines Forschungsprojektes. In: D. Bellmann (ed.), Gedenkschrift Wolfgang Reuschel. Akten des III. Arabistischen Kolloquiums, Leipzig, 21.-22. November 1991 (in print).

6 In July 1881, al-Muqtaṭaf published an announcement from which can be seen that Arabic was to be no longer the language of instruction at the SPC (cf. VI/2, p. 128).

7 For the vita of Dūmiṭ, later Professor of Arabic at the AUB, see Dāghir 1955, II, op. cit., pp. 553-556.

8 See J. Dūmiṭ, al-ᶜArabīya wa-l-Madrasa al-Kullīya. In: al-Muqtaṭaf XXVIII, pp. 905-912.

9 Pattern of reference to al-Muqtaṭaf, for example XXVIII/6, p. 906. Read al-Muqtaṭaf volume XXVIII, issue 6, p. 906. Sometimes, supplementary data are given.

10 Ibid.

11 Trübner's American, European, and Oriental Literary Record, 1882, p. 129, quoted in: X/7 = May 1883, p. 273.

12 W. Fraser Rae, The Egyptian Newspaper Press. In: The Nineteenth Century, No. 186 (August 1892), p. 222.

13 M. Hartmann, The Arabic Press of Egypt, London 1899, pp. 69f.

14 For the student Ṣarrūf, who had graduated with the degree of Bachelor of Arts (B.A.) in 1870, "studying science, maths, geometry, algebra, chemistry, astronomy, etc., was like reading novels. He solved problems so quickly and so painlessly that one thought he was doing it for fun rather than anything else." (Farag 1969, op. cit., p. 14; cf. also LXXII, p. 417). And about the lecturer Ṣarrūf, it was said: "There was no experiment mentioned in the text-books of chemistry which he did not demonstrate to his class, however dangerous it might be." (Margoliouth 1927, op. cit., pp. 937f.)

15 I. Maẓhar, al-Duktūr Ṣarrūf ʿaliman. In: LXXII/4 = April 1928, pp. 420-427.

16 For Ismāʿīl Maẓhar see I.A. Ibrahim, Isma'il Maẓhar and Husayn Fawzi: Two Muslim 'Radical' Westernizers. In: MES, vol. IX/1 (January 1973), pp. 35-41.

17 M.Ḥ. Haykal, in: S. Shuqayr et al., Ta'bīn al-Duktūr Ṣarrūf. In: LXXII/5 = May 1928, pp. 571f.

18 For M. Ḥ. Haykal see C. Brockelmann, GAL, supplement III, pp. 202ff.; EI², vol. VII, s.v. Muḥammad Ḥusayn Haykal; B. Johansen, Muḥammad Ḥusain Haikal. Europa und der Orient im Weltbild eines ägyptischen Liberalen, Beirut 1967; and Ch.D. Smith, Islam and the Search for Social Order in Modern Egypt: A Biography of Muḥammad Ḥusayn Haykal, Albany 1983; and Ḥ.F. Najjār, Al-Duktūr Haykal wa-tārīkh jīl 1888-1956, Cairo 1988. For Haykal as a journalist see ʿA. al-ʿAzīz Sharaf, Fann al-maqāl al-ṣuḥufī fī adab Muḥammad Ḥusayn Haykal, Cairo 1989.

19 For Sh. Arslān see C. Brockelmann, GAL, supplement III, pp. 394ff.; Dāghir 1955, op. cit., vol. II, pp. 96-101; and A. al-Sharabāṣī, Amīr al-bayān Shakīb Arslān. Maʿhad al-dirāsāt al-ʿarabīya, (1963)2.

20 Sh. Arslān, Arā' fī l-adab wa-l-ʿumrān li-l-marḥūm al-Duktūr Ṣarrūf. In: LXXIII/1 = July 1928, pp. 8-13.

21 Ṣarrūf translated e.g. Samuel Smiles' famous "Self-Help" (appeared in 1880 with the Arabic title Sirr al-Najāḥ) and Walter Scott's "Talisman" (appeared in 1886 with the Arabic title Riwāyat Qalb al-Asad). For Ṣarrūf as a translator see M. Peled, Creative Translation: Towards the Study of Arabic Translation of Western Literature Since the 19th Century. In: JAL, *X*(1979), pp. 128-150 (esp. pp. 138f).

22 For Ṣarrūf as a promoter of modern Arabic poetry see S. Moreh, Modern Arabic Poetry 1800-1970, Leiden 1976, pp. 47f. and 55. Moreh ascribes to him a "catalyst function...in the poetic revolutionary movements in Egypt" (ibid., p. 55).

23 S. Shuqayr, Dhikrā ʿamīd al-Muqtaṭaf al-marḥūm al-Duktūr Ṣarrūf fī Lubnān. In: LXXI/3 = November 1927, pp. 302-305.

24 EI², s.v. Djarīda, vol. II, p. 472.

25 M. Hartmann, in: OLZ, (1898)7, p. 226.

26 I. Kratshkovsky, Entstehung und Entwicklung der neu-arabischen Literatur. (Transl. by G. von Mende). In: Die Welt des Islams, vol. *XI*(1928)3,4, p. 198.

27 J. Boehmer, Zum Problem der neuarabischen Sprache. In: Anthropos, 4 (1909)4, p. 171. Maybe, Western scholars were strongly influenced by Schoenhauer's negative attitude towards the language of the 19th century European press. See e.g. H. Paul, Deutsches Wörterbuch,

9th rev. and enl. ed., Tübingen 1972, s.v. Zeitungsdeutsch. However, the negative attitude towards the Arab (Eastern) press and its language is no longer as strong as it was. After the works of Washington-Serruys 1897 (L'Arab Moderne étudié dans les journeaux et les pièses officielles, Beirut), Sheringham 1927 (Modern Arabic Sentences on Practical Subjects being Selections from Newspapers of Iraq, Palestine, and Egypt, London), E. Mainz, 1931 (Zur Grammatik des modernen Schriftarabisch. Leipzig), and Wehr 1934 (Die Besonderheiten des heutigen Hocharabischen. Mit Berücksichtigung der Einwirkung der europäischen Sprachen. In: Mitteilungen des Seminars für Orientalische Sprachen (MSOS), Zweite Abteilung: Westasiatische Studien, 37, pp. 1-64) have paved the way for further studies in the language of the Arab press also by Western arabists.

28 Ibid.

29 T.J. Le Gassick, Major Themes in Modern Arabic Thought: An Anthology, Ann Arbor 1978.

30 Ibid.

31 M.M. Badawi, Modern Arabic Literature and the West, London 1985.

32 S. Somekh, Genre and Language in Modern Arabic Literature, Wiesbaden 1991.

33 For this newspaper see note 4. al-Muqtaṭaf announced it in XIII/6 = March 1889, p. 432.

34 See note 4.

35 All Arabic phrases put in (parentheses) are drawn from al-Muqtaṭaf, with the vocalization given there.

36 Editorial notes are inserted in several places. We distinguish: 1) preliminary notes to a volume (muqaddamāt) or to a single issue with various titles (both do not occur regularly), 2) brief epilogues to each volume (khāwātim), 3) occasional notes showing several positions, and 4) footnotes to contributions containing explanations of terms, references, biographical information, etc.

37 The articles (resp. serials) cover between two and twelve pages. An article is often divided in several parts (nubdha, pl.: nubadh) which appear either in one issue or in successive issues. Articles have regularly been signed with the author's name, with exception of those which were written by Ṣarrūf and Nimr. Until 1888, there are no formal indicators as to who of the two is the author of an article (see Fihris al-Muqtaṭaf 1876-1952, vol. I, Beirut 1967, muqaddama, p. sīn). Typical topics of the articles, etc. are: 1) history of sciences, arts and culture, knowledge and education, 2) history of mechanics, 3) biographies of scholars from earlier periods of history (e.g. Konfuzius, al-Ṭabarī, Ibn Rushd, Ibn Khaldūn, Galilei, Newton) and contemporary scholars (e.g. Louis Pasteur, Dimitri I. Mendeleyev) as well as obituaries (e.g. Charles Darwin , cf. VII/1, pp. 2-6; Buṭrus al-Bustānī, cf. VIII/1, pp. 1-7; Muḥammad Sharīf Bāshā, cf. XI/9, pp. 506-509 or Victor Hugo, cf. IX/10, pp. 586-591), 4) special subjects from the natural and social sciences (e.g. descriptions of planets, physical phenomena, chemical elements, etc. resp. scientific theories, etc.), 5) studies in philology and linguistics, 6) studies in agriculture, economics, and trade, 7) description of single scientific disciplines (e.g. biology, physiology, paleontology, psychology, etc.), 8) description of discoveries and inventions of the time (e.g. the steam-engine, lithography, the microscope, the thermometer, the telegraph, the telephone, dynamite, etc.), and 9) descriptions of (raw) materials (e.g. glass, rubber, horn, rubies, etc.).

38 For example to such Arab societies as Jamʿīyat Shams al-Birr, founded in 1870, al-Majmaʿ al-ʿIlmī al-Sharqī, founded in 1882, and Jamʿīyat al-Ṣināʿa founded in 1882 or to the graduates of the SPC. So VII/3 = August 1882, pp. 158-167 (large ed.; for the two editions of VII see note 44) contains the famous speech read by Dr. Edwin Lewis, Professor of Chemistry and Geology in the SPC, on the occasion of the commencement July 19, 1882 which caused a lot of trouble and led to Lewis' resignation. This speech, originally delivered in Arabic, was later translated into English. A full English version can be found in Farag 1969, op. cit., pp. 406-

415. For the historical background of this case see ibid., pp. 24-31 resp. 254-262, and N. Farag, The Lewis Affair and the Fortunes of al-Muqtataf (The late Nadia Farag). In: MES, *VIII*(1972), pp. 73-83.

39 However, in some cases, it is not quite clear whether these announcements are appendices to the column Akhbār wa-Iktishāfāt wa-Ikhtirāʿāt or an independent section of the journal.

40 Advertisements appeared either in the last section of the journal or, later, at a few pages in front of an issue. The first advertisements appeared in XI (1886/87). The one, published in front of XI/1 = October 1886, offered to buy remedies from a chemist's shop, newly opend in Cairo under the name Ajzākhānat al-Muqtaṭaf, and advised the people to benefit from the consultation hours held by the Lebanese physician Shiblī Shumayyil at this place (for Shumayyil see note 74). The second ad, written in English (!), appeared in January 1887 (cf. XI/4, between pp. 256 and 257). It was an offer by the "Muktataf Printing Office" in Cairo to print papers, such as "commercial and financial circulars ... prospectuses, visiting cards...", etc. in "Arabic, Turkish, Persian, and all European Languages".

41 Apart from Farag 1969, op. cit., mention must be made of L.M. Kenny, East versus West in al-Muqtataf, 1875-1900. Image and Self-Image. In: D. P. Little (ed.), Essays on Islamic Civilization. Presented to Niyazi Berkes, Leiden 1976, pp. 140-154; and ʿA. al-ʿUmar et al., Majallat al-Muqtaṭaf. Rāʾidat al-ʿilm al-ḥadīth fi-l-ʿālam al-ʿarabī. In: the same author et al.: al-Majallāt al-thaqāfiya wa-l-taḥaddiyāt al-muʿāṣira. Dirāsāt wa-munāqashāt, Kuweit 1984, pp. 9-53.

42 S.Z. Sulaymān, Taṭawwur al-thaqāfa al-ʿilmīya fī Lubnān wa-Miṣr fī ʿaṣr al-nahḍa (1905-1950), Beirut 1987. This valuable study compares al-Muqtaṭaf, in character, content, and style, with eight other Lebanese scientific, literary and political journals. These are:
al-Jawāʾib, founded by Aḥmad Fāris al-Shidyāq in 1861 in Istanbul (see ibid., esp. pp. 88-102),
al-Jinān, founded by Buṭrus al-Bustānī in 1870 in Beirut (see ibid., esp. 102-139),
al-Ṭabīb (cf. ibid., esp. pp. 146-209), founded by George Post, Professor of Botany in the SPC,
al-Hilāl, founded by Jurjī Zaydān in 1892 in Cairo (see ibid., esp. pp. 278-303),
al-Bayān, founded by I. al-Yāzijī and Bashāra Zalzal in 1897 in Cairo, (see ibid., pp. 303f-310 and 323-343)
al-Ḍiyāʾ, founded by I. al-Yāzijī in 1898 in Cairo, too (see ibid., pp. 304 f and 310-343), and
al-Jāmiʿa, founded by Faraḥ Anṭūn in 1899 in Alexandria, since 1906 published in New York (see ibid., esp. pp. 344-363).

43 I have left out those abwāb which appeared in less than six issues such as *Maṭbūʿāt Jadīda* (New Publications) (cf. e.g. IV/5 = October 1879, p. 143) and Akhbār Waṭanīya (literally: National News) (cf. e.g. IV/10 = March 1880, pp. 277ff. and IV/12 = May 1880, p. 335). Maṭbūʿāt Jadīda, a predecessor of Hadāyā wa-Taqārīẓ, includes information on books and periodicals newly published. Akhbār Waṭanīya reported on the foundation of schools and other efforts made by Syrian (Christian and Muslim) scholars to spread out education. In al-Jinān, there was a similar column, entitled: Wilāyat Sūrīya.

44 Al-Muqtaṭaf VI (1881/82) and VII (1882/83) exist in two editions of different size, the large one consist of 760 pages, the small one of 344 pages. Concerning VI I have used the large edition, concerning VII the small edition and the large one.

45 From Farag 1969, Kenny 1976, and al-ʿUmar et al. 1984, all op. cit.. Furthermore, Margoliouth 1927, op. cit., as well as from the contributions to the journals themselves, e.g. from introductory remarks to articles, etc.

46 An illustrated scientific weekly, published in London since 1869.

47 A scientific monthly, published in New York since 1872.
48 A scientific monthly, published in London since 1877.
49 A Muslim political and literary weekly, voice of the scientific society Jamʿīyat al-Funūn, founded by ʿAbd al-Qādir Al-Qabbānī in 1875 in Beirut, the first Beirutian journal, founded by Muslim scholars. For details see Ṭarrāzī 1913, op. cit., vol. II, p. 25.
50 For this Arabic journal see note 41.
51 This periodical, the voice of the Amercian Mission in Beirut, was founded by Cornelius van Dyck in 1866 in Beirut under the name al-Nashra al-Shahrīya. Since 1871, it was published under the name mentioned above. See Ṭarrāzī 1913 resp. 1933, op. cit., vol.s II and IV, pp. 20f. resp. 5.
52 The well-known Egyptian newspaper, founded by Salīm and Bashāra Taqlā in December 1875 in Alexandria, the first number appeared on the 5 August 1876. For details see M. Adham, Jarīdat al-Ahrām wa-fann al-taḥqīq al-ṣuḥufī, Cairo 1985.
53 An influential journal as well (bilingual, in Arabic and English), founded by Lūīs Ṣābūnjī in 1877 in Beirut. Since 1884, it was published in London. See Ṭarrāzī 1913, op. cit., vol. II, pp. 248-251 and 253.
54 A not less important encyclopaedic journal, founded by Khalīl Sarkīs in 1877 in Beirut. See Ṭarrāzī 1913, op. cit., vol. II, pp. 27-33.
55 A political and literary weekly, founded by Jibrā'īl Dallāl in 1879 in Istanbul, see Ṭarrāzī 1913, op. cit., vol. II, p. 193.
56 The first Arab newspaper in Arabic, founded by Muḥammad ʿAlī in 1828 in Cairo. In the 19th century, it remained the official newspaper of the Egyptian governments. For details see I. ʿAbduh, Tārīkh al-Waqā'iʿ al-Miṣrīya, (Cairo) 1983.
57 For al-Bustānī's al-Jinān see note 42.
58 For B. al-Bustānī see C. Brockelmann, GAL, G II, pp. 646f. and GAL, supplement II, pp. 767f.; EI[2], supplement 3-4, s.v. Buṭrus al-Bustānī; Daghir 1955, op. cit., vol. II, pp. 180-185. Furthermore, F.A. al-Bustānī (ed.): al-Muʿallim Buṭrus al-Bustānī, Beirut 1929; B. Abu-Manneh, The Christians between Ottomanism and Syrian Nationalism: the Ideas of Butrus al-Bustani. In: IJMES *XI*(1980), pp. 287-304; and M.I. Lázaro Durán, Aproximación a la "nahda" siro-libanesa: la familia al-Bustānī. El pensamiento reformista del maestro Buṭrus. (Thesis), Granada 1986.
59 See also Sulaymān 1987, op. cit., p. 20.
60 Number of pages: I/1 = May 1876: 24 pp., I (1876/77): 288 pp., XIII/6 = March 1889: 71 pp., XIII (1888/89): 856 pp.
61 For the limitation of the number of pages in this publication it is not possible to give complete English translations of all Arabic texts quoted. That is why I have decided to translate not more than the to insert not more than the arabicized as well as some special terms. The English translation and some additional remarks are given in [brackets].
62 E.g. al-Hind wa-sukkānuhā (India and Its Inhabitents) (I, p. 214), ʿAdad sukkān Miṣr (The Number of Inhabitents of Egypt) (III, p. 164), Ṭaqs Ūrubbā (The Weather in Europe) (IV, p. 253) or Faṣl al-shitā' fī ṣaḥrā' Ifrīqīya (The Winter Season in Africa's Desert) (VII/3, p. 75, small ed.).
63 E.g. ʿUbūr al-zuhara (The Movement of the Venus) (VII/3, p. 76) and Kalaf al-shams (Sunspots) (ibid.).
64 A weekly journal of practical information about art, science and mechanics, published since 1845 in New York.
65 The bā' is written like the Persian p, i.e. with three diacritical points.
66 See note 80.
67 For example transactions of learned societies, statistical directories, year books, etc.

68 C. van Dyck was a prolific scholar and the spiritus rector of the SPC - at least until the 1880s. The teacher van Dyck, who mastered Arabic and other Eastern languages, gave lectures, i.a. on pathology, chemistry, and astronomy, was admired by his students for his universal knowledge and his manifold scientific activities. He had a deep influence on them, as well on Ṣarrūf and Nimr. It was he who promoted the foundation of their journal and suggested its name: al-Muqtaṭaf, see Ṭarrāzī 1913, op. cit., vol. II, p. 54. For the vita of C. van Dyck cf. XIX/2 = Dec. 1895, pp. 881-888, XX/1 = Jan. 1896, pp. 1-5, and XX/2, = Feb. 1896, pp. 97-108, and Ṭarrāzī 1913, op. cit., vol. I, pp. 144-150. For the journalist C. van Dyck see note 51.

69 Without hamza in al-Muqtaṭaf.

70 Bā'ᶜayn stood for the foreign academic degree Bachelor of Arts (Bakalawriyūs ᶜulūm; cf. I/4, p. 94).

71 IX/6 = March 1885 was the first number to be published in Cairo (cf. IX/6, pp. 321-384).

72 One should also mention here, that the NC-column "Modern Symposium" was not opened before April 1877 (cf. NC Vol.I/No. 2, pp. 331-358), i.e. after the Arabic Masā'il wa-Ajwibatuhā had been established.

73 For the spelling of bā' see note 65.

74 For Shiblī Shumayyil see J. Lecerf, Shibli Shumayyil, métaphysien et moraliste contemporain. In: Bulletin des Études Orientales, *I*(1931), pp. 153-186; C. Brockelmann, GAL, supplement III, pp. 212f.; Dāghir (1955) II, op. cit., pp. 497-500; and G.C. Anawati, Shiblī Shumayyil: Medical Philosopher and Scientist. In: E. C. Bosworth et al. (eds.): The Islamic World. From Classical to Modern Times. Essays in Honor of Bernard Lewis, Princeton 1989, pp. 637-650.

75 Zaydān had contributed to editing al-Muqtaṭaf between 1886 and 1892, before he founded his own journal al-Hilāl. For this modern writer and historian see i.a. C. Brockelmann, GAL, supplement III, pp. 186-190; Dāghir 1955, op. cit., vol. II, pp. 442-448; and Phillip, Th.: Ğurgī Zaidān, his Life and Thought. (Beiruter Texte und Studien, 3), Wiesbaden 1979.

76 For Asaᶜd Khalīl Dāghir, the brother-in-law of Ṣarrūf see Dāghir 1955, op. cit., vol. II, pp. 351-354. Farag (1969, op. cit., p. 21) has characterized him as "perhaps the most prolific single contributor to al-Muqtataf". Until the 1930s, he made more than 80 contributions to the journal.

77 See note 7.

78 For Naᶜūm Shuqayr, a historian and intelligence officer in the Brithish army in the Sudan, see Th. Philipp, The Syrians in Egypt 1725-1975, Stuttgart 1985, pp. 112, 117 and 152.

79 Muḥammad al-Shādhilī Ibn Farḥāt's vita is relatively unknown. He was the son of a Mamluk who had entered the services of the Bey of Tunis. Ibn Farḥat became the *qā'id* of Le Kef and an intimate friend of Muḥammad al-Sanūsī. In 1885, he took part in revolts of Tunisian notabilities against the French protectorate administration (cf. M. Al-Sanūsī, Khulāṣat al-nāzila al-tūnisīya, ed. by Muḥammad al-Ṣādiq Busayyis, Tunis, MTE, 1976, pp. 331-335; and M. Chenoufi, Les deux séjours de Muhammad ᶜAbduh en Tunisie. In: Les Cahiers de Tunisie *XVI*(1968), p. 68). For these informations I am grateful to my colleague at Freiburg, Andreas Tunger-Zanetti.

80 For Ḥusayn al-Jisr see Dāghir (1955), II, op. cit., pp. 270-272; and A.A. Ziadat, Western Science in the Arab World. The Impact of Darwinism, 1860-1930. Houndmills-Basingstoke-Hampshire-London 1986, pp. 16, 91-95.

81 For Ibrāhīm al-Aḥdab see Dāghir (1955), II, op. cit., pp. 84-87. Al-Aḥdab had relations with the Muslim journal Thamarāt al-Funūn (see note 49).

82 For the latter see note 72.

83 See i.a. G. Makdisi, The Rise of Colleges. Institutions of Learning in the Islam and the West, Edinburgh 1981, esp. pp. 109f.

84 The first contribution to the disputation carried by Bāb al-Munāẓara wa-l-Murāsala was a reader's reaction to articles about the Damascene people. The one, under the headline Fī Akhlāq al-Dimashqīyīn (On Morals of the Damascene People) was written by Bashāra Zalzal (IV, pp. 210-213 and 243-246), the other, under the headline Dimashq wa-ahluhā (Damascus and Its People) was written by Ẓāhir Khayrallāh al-Shuwayrī (IV, pp. 300-303). But both publications must have aroused vehement feelings, because both authors appended rudūd to what they had written before. For Zalal's Akhlāq al-Dimashqīyīn. Radd cf. IV, p. 321-323. For al-Shuwayrī's Dimashq wa-ahluhā. Radd cf. (V/1, pp. 49ff.).

85 The first brief letters to Ṣarrūf and Nimr, irrespective of the masā'il (cf. III.3.3.3), appeared in May/June 1877 under the headline Thimār al-Muqtaṭaf (Fruits of al-Muqtaṭaf) (II, p. 24). They contained readers' reactions to fawā'id (cf. III. 3.3.4). The senders informed the editors about the positive results achieved when testing them. These first readers' reactions lacked phrases of address. Otherwise, mention must here also be made of an early contribution to disuptation by Shiblī Shumayyil under the headline Iᶜtirāḍ (An Objection) (III/7 = October 1878, pp. 174f.). This was Shumayyil's famous reaction to a brief comment by Ṣarrūf and Nimr on the dispute between the English professors Tyndall and Huxley about the origin of life, entitled Bi-yadihī al-ḥayāt wa-l-mawt (III/1 = June 1879, p. 15). It was this correspondence that urged the editors of al-Muqtaṭaf to give a response: Radd al-Muqtaṭaf (III, pp. 245f.). Here, we are faced with the beginnings of the Arab debate on Darwinism. For this problem see Farag 1969, op. cit., esp. pp. 245-306, Farag 1972, op. cit.; and Ziadat 1986, op. cit..

86 The first contribution was a letter to the editors by the writer Salmā Ṭannūs, published under the headline Taᶜlīm al-nisā' wa-tarbiyatuhunna in VIII/4 = Jan. 1884, pp. 233-236.

87 Among the first books announced/reviewed by al-Muqtaṭaf, before the Taqārīz-bāb was opened, was Amin Shumayyil's Tārīkh al-mas'ala al-sharqīya (published in Beirut in 1877) (cf. III/2 = July 1878, p. 56).

88 A womens's literary society founded in 1880 by Miriyam Makāriyūs (the sister of Fāris Nimr and the first wife of Shāhīn Makāriyūs, the partner of Ṣarrūf and Nimr in publishing al-Muqtaṭaf and founder of the journal al-Laṭā'if) and Yāqūt Ṣarrūf (the wife of Yaᶜqūb Ṣarruf). For this society see i.a. Farag 1969, op. cit., p. 83.

89 Mudawwar's book was published by al-Muqtaṭaf in advance of its print. Cf. III (1878/79) and IV (1879/80).

90 This weekly, one of the first satirical periodicals in Arabic, helped to prepare the ground for the ᶜUrābī-revolt 1880/82 in Egypt. Its eloquent founder, ᶜAbdallāh Nadīm, was given the surname "Khaṭīb al-thawra".

91 This can be read in the introduction of the article al-Zirāᶜa (Agriculture), by Ṣarrūf and Nimr (II/1 = May 1877, pp. 13-15) where they say that Arabic periodicals often selected agricultural topics (cf. ibid., p. 13).

92 On behalf of the Egyptian newspaper al-Ahrām, Ṣarrūf and other Muqtatafis had been sent to Shubrā al-Kabīra to make tests for controlling the cotton worm. Their full report was published in al-Ahrām of the 29 July, 1885; cf. XI/2, p. 97.

93 This contribution is a summary of what was published in an official Egyptian newspaper (al-Ahrām ?) (...nulakhkhiṣu mā jā'at bihī al-jarīda al-rasmīya al-miṣrīya fī hādha l-maᶜnā qālat inna ..., X, p. 425).

94 One of the most important steel bridges built in the 19th century. The construction was finished in 1887.

95 For Aḥmad Shawqī, the Amīr al-Shuᶜarā' of the Nahḍa, see i.a. C. Brockelmann, GAL, supplement III, op. cit., pp. 21ff.; Dāghir 1955, op. cit., vol. II, pp. 504-514; A. Boudot-Lamotte, Aḥmad Šawqī. L'homme et l'oeuvre, Damascus 1977; ᶜI. Shahīd, Al-ᶜawda ilā Shawqī, aw baᶜd khamsīn ᶜāman, Beirut 1986.

96 For Ḥāfiẓ Ibrāhīm, the "poet of the Nile", see C. Brockelmann, GAL, supplement III, op. cit., pp. 57ff.; Dāghir 1955, vol. II, op. cit., pp. 285-291; Kh. al-Hindāwī, Ḥāfiẓ Ibrāhīm. Shāᶜir al-Nīl, Beirut 1973; and Z. Mubārak, Ḥāfiẓ Ibrāhīm, Beirut 1991.

97 For Muṣṭafā Luṭfī al-Manfalūṭī see C. Brockelmann, GAL, Supplement III, op. cit., pp. 196 ff.; and Dāghir 1955, vol. II, op. cit., pp. 730-733.

98 For the vita of Mayy Ziyāda and her works see i.a. E. Rossi, Una scrittrice araba cattolica Mayy (Marie Ziyādah). In: Oriente Moderno, *V*(1925), pp. 604-613; Dāghir 1955, vol. II, op. cit., pp. 435-441; M. Fahmī, Muḥāḍarāt ᶜan Mayy Ziyāda. (Jāmiᶜat al-duwal al-ᶜarabīya. Maᶜhad al-dirāsāt al-ᶜarabīya al-ᶜāliya), Cairo 1955; J. Jabr, Mayy Ziyāda fī hayātiha wa-adabihā, Beirut 1960 (= Nuṣūṣ wa-durūs, 13); Ḥ. M. ᶜA. al-Ghannī, Mayy: adībat al-sharq, Cairo 1985. EI² vol. VI, s.v. Mayy Ziyāda; for her critical studies on modern Arabic literature, partly published in al-Muqtaṭaf, see M. Booth, Biography and Feminist rhetoric in early 20th century Egypt: Mayy Ziyada's studies of three women's lives. In: Journal of Women's History, vol. *III*(1991)1, pp. 38-64.

99 Ami Ayalon, Language and Change in the Middle East. The Evolution of Modern Political Discourse, New York-Oxford 1987, p. 4.

100 Ayalon 1987, ibid., p. 4f.

101 J. Stetkevych, The Modern Arabic Literary Language. Lexical and Stylistic Developments, Chicago-London 1970, pp.13f.

102 For the development of scientific vocabulary in Modern Standard Arabic see G. Krahl, Die technischen und wissenschaftlichen Termini im modernen Arabisch - eine Untersuchung zur arabischen Wortbildung (unpublished Thesis), Leipzig 1967; and A.S. Ali, Development of Scientific Vocabulary in Standard Arabic, London- New York 1987. Krahl's traces the efforts of word formation made by the Arab Academies of Damascus and Cairo. He analyses their results and compares them with data of the live usage of Arabic. Ali compares patterns of word formation in classical and modern scientific Arabic. Both works, however, exclude the linguistic contribution to modern scientific Arabic made by Arabic journals of the 19th century.

103 Ibrāhīm al-Yāzijī is known for founding the two scientific-cultural journals al-Bayān and al-Ḍiyā' (see note 42), but he is famous for its "Lughat al-jarā'id", a collection of articles, first published in al-Ḍiyā', which appeared as a book in 1901 in Cairo. In this book (I have used the edition by N. cAbbud, Beirut 1984), al-Yāzijī, an advocate of the idea that al-Ishtiqāq (derivation) is the only method to modernize the Arabic language, fought against the Arabic of the press which was in his opinion incorrect. The book caused a lot of trouble among Arab scholars because it contained numerous exaggerations. For the *vita* of I. al-Yāzijī and his works see C. Brockelmann, GAL 2, p. 646, and GAL, supplement II, p. 766; and M. Ṣawāyā, Ibrāhīm al-Yāzijī. Ḥayātuhū wa-athāruhū. Beirut 1960 (= Aᶜlām al-fikr al-ᶜarabī, p. 11).

104 For the vita of this important philologist see Dāghir 1955, op. cit., vol. II, pp. 663-671; and H.A.M. Allawi, El Padre Anastās Mārī al-Karmalī: vida y obras (Abstract of Doctoral Thesis), Granada 1984. For the philologist's evaluation of Yaᶜqūb Ṣarrūf as a modernizer of the Arabic language see A.M. al-Karmalī, Al-Duktūr Ṣarrūf wa-l-tajdīd fi-l-lugha al-ᶜarabīya. In: LXXII/2 = Februar 1928, pp. 155-165.

105 For the vita of Kurd ᶜAlī, the founder of the Arab Academy of Damascus, and his life work see Dāghir 1955, op. cit., vol. II, pp. 655-660; EI², vol. V, s.v. Kurd ᶜAlī, Muḥammad Farīd; and R. Hermann, Kulturkrise und konservative Erneuerung. Muḥammad Kurd ᶜAlī (1876-1953) und das geistige Leben in Damaskus zu Beginn des 20. Jahrhunderts, Frankfurt/M.-Bern-New York-Paris 1990. For Kurd ᶜAlī's evaluation of Ṣarrūf and the language of al-Muqtaṭaf see M.K. ᶜAlī, Al-ᶜAllāma al-Duktūr Yaᶜqūb Ṣarrūf. In: Majallat al-majmaᶜ al-ᶜilmī al-ᶜarabī (RAAD), *VIII*(1928), no. 1, pp. 57-60.

106 For this Arab writer see Dāghir 1955, op. cit., vol. II, pp. 375-381; ᶜA.B. ᶜAjlān, Min adab al-Rāfiᶜī wa-maᶜārikihī,. Alexandria 1989; and M.N. Badrī, Al-Rāfiᶜī: al-kātib bayn al-muḥāfaẓa wa-l-tajdīd, ᶜAmmān 1991.

107 J. Ḍūmiṭ, Al-Duktūr Ṣarrūf muᶜalliman. In: LXXII/3 = March 1928, p. 291. For Ḍūmiṭ see note 7.

108 See E. Wiedemann, Beiträge zur Geschichte der Naturwissenschaften. In: Gesammelte Schriften, vol. I, Hildesheim 1970, p. 340. Here, the author says: "Daß diesselbe [i.e. Schwefelsäure/sulphuric acid - D.G.] aber doch den Arabern bekannt war, geht aus Ausführungen bei Qazwînî hervor über die Vitriole [vitriols - D.G.] (Sing. Zâğ Plur. Zâğâğ)..."

109 The case of paraphrasing al-baliyūntūlūjiyā [voc. by Muq.] also shows that the Muqtatafis did not always paraphrase foreign terms in one and the same way. Apart from the expression ᶜilm dafā'in al-arḍ (see text above), we can find two other variants in the journal: 1) when paleontology was introduced by al-Muqtaṭaf the author used ᶜilm dhawāt al-ḥayāt al-qadīma ᶜala-l-arḍ (the scientific study of living beings existing in former periods on earth) (VI, p. 92), whereas 2) the Muᶜjam al-Muᶜarrabāt (see IV.1/IV.2 above) recorded ᶜilm al-mutaḥajjirāt (VIII, p. 214). That the adoption of the foreign terms was really difficult is also shown by the following example: Shiblī Shumayyil (see note 74), who also dealt with paleontology, spellt the arabicized term in a way which differed from that of the Muqtatafis. Shumayyil wrote: al-bāluntūlūjiyā (with the "normal" Arabic *bā'*) also paraphrasing it in a different way: ᶜilm al-aḥāfīr (scientific study of the fossils). See Shumayyil's Sharḥ Bukhnir ᶜalā madhab Dārwin, the Arabic translation (appeared 1884) of Ludwig Buechner's Commentary on the Darwinian Theory (translated from the French version of 1869).

110 X/8 = May 1886 (p. 504) contains a mas'ala in which a certain Muḥam-mad Darwīsh from Baghdad inquired after the rest of the "Glossary of Arabicized Terms". Ṣarrūf and Nimr replied that they were not able to continue it because they had lost "the unpublished rest" during their removal from Beirut to Cairo. In the following time, they did not found an opportunity to collect materials once again (cf. X, p. 504). When in IX/9 = June 1890 (p. 640) a similar mas'ala was asked again, the editors added that they intend to publish a general scientific glossary comprising many more scientific terms than those included in al-Muqtaṭaf.

111 Such as al-bīra (beer) (VIII/4, p. 215), al-flānillā (flanelle) (IX/3, p. 143), *al-rūj* (rouge) (VIII/6, p. 345) and al-b[pers. p]ūmādah (pomade) (VIII/4, p. 215)).

112 H. Wehr, A Dictionary of Modern Written Arabic. Edited by J. Milton Cowan. Third Edition, New York 1976; H. Wehr, Arabisches Wörterbuch für die Schriftsprache der Gegenwart. Arabisch-Deutsch. Fifth edition, revised and enlarged by Lorenz Kropfitsch, Wiesbaden 1985; and G. Krahl/M.Gh. Gharieb, Wörterbuch Arabisch-Deutsch, Leipzig 1984.

113 Proposals to substitute al-uksujīn and many other chemical terms introduced by van Dyck or other scholars from the SPC and spread by the Muqtatafis, were made by the Azhar Shaykh Aḥmad ᶜAlī al-Iskandarī and other members of the Academy of the Arabic Language in Cairo (founded in 1932, see EI², vol. V, s.v. Majmaᶜ ᶜIlmī). However, al-muṣdi' and other terms

proposed by the Egyptians (e.g. al-nassāk for al-blāṭīn) remained not more than artificial solutions. See i.a. M.H. ᶜAbdul ᶜAzīz, al-Taᶜrīb al-qadīm wa-l-hadīth, Cairo 1990, pp. 207f.

114 See Ṣawāyā 1960, op. cit., p. 39. For I. al-Yāzijī see note 103.

115 That is was Y. Ṣarrūf and Nimr who have coined darrāja in the meaning of bycicle is mentioned by the editors themselves in their article about their principles of arabicization (see point IV.3 above).

116 The term was introduced in an early article on physiology (headline: Taḥdīd al-fisiyūlūjiyā al-ḥayawānīya wa-tamyīz dhawāt al-ḥayāt ᶜamma siwāhā) in September 1876 (I/4, pp. 79-81). The author, the third son of Cornelius van Dyck, was, at that time, a student of medicine at the Medical School of the SPC. See Farag 1972, op. cit., p. 75.

117 That ᶜilm al-ḥayāt in the meaning biology was coined by Y. Ṣarrūf is mentioned by A. Mārī al-Karmalī. See note 104.

118 See Wehr 1934, op. cit. (note 27)., p. 38.

119 See F. Ṣarrūf, Siyar alfāẓ ᶜarabīya mustaḥdatha. In: al-Abhath, XII (1963)/3, p. 289.

120 Ibid., p. 286. Fu'ād Ṣarrūf (1900-1985), the nephew of Yaᶜqūb Ṣarrūf, was an prolific scientific publicist. He edited al-Muqtaṭaf after the death of his uncle from 1927 to 1945. For his vita see C. Brockelmann, GAL, supplement III, op. cit., pp. 215-217 (if there are some slight mistakes); and Sulaymān 1987, op. cit., pp. 392-394.

121 Al-darrāja has become the written standard, whereas the foreign word "biskelitt" has remained in dialect (see Wehr 1934, op. cit., p. 54/footnote 1).

122 See Ali 1987, op. cit., p. 36. But, in his opinion, the classical term is al-khunāq instead of al-khānūq.

123 See Wiedemann 1970, op. cit., p. 341.

124 The article quoted was written by Ṣarruf, under the headline: al-Lugha al-ᶜarabīya wa-l-muṣṭalaḥāt al-ᶜilmīya (LXXIV/1 = January 1929, pp. 6-8). However, it was published after his death. The chemical terminology coined by van Dyck can be traced in his book "Uṣūl al-kīmiyā'". Some extracts appeared in Buṭrus al-Bustānī's *al-Jinān*, e.g. in vol. I/5 (March 1870), pp. 140f. For the term al-uksujīn see also note 113. For Cornelius van Dyck see note 68.

125 See Sulaymān 1987, op. cit., pp. 111f.

126 For the attitude of Ṣarrūf and Nimr towards the defects of the Western civilization see especially Kenny 1976, op. cit.

127 Kratshkovsky 1928, op. cit., p. 199.

# The Concept of 'shura' as an Example of Islam's Response to the Impact of European Values

Miloš Mendel

In this contribution I would like to pay attention to one of numerous pillars of Islamic classical political theory - the concept of shura or 'the principle of consultation'. This principle - as well as some other key political concepts and instruments of early Islam - was during the 19th and 20th century renewed and rebuilt in a new political context of European colonial impact accompanied by the infiltration of a set of non-Islamic values. First, let me remind of some characteristics of classical Islamic political theory and imaginations of functioning of state body, state law and the social interaction. Islam's political ambitions which had been clearly manifested from the starting point of 'Islamic revelation' found their practical reflection in a dogmatic system. Its practical and 'prosaic' character accentuating religious and legal standards rather than ethical or spiritual ones has led to the construction of a good number of belittling assessments that originated in the European civilisational background.

The basic feature integrating Islam with practical politics is an organic linkage between spiritual and secular (profane) principles. The purely theoretical concept of classical Islam does not recognize such categories which could be comparable to the political imaginations of Christianity. In Islam the state and religion are a single inseparable entity. There is no church as an institution, Islam has neither a Pope nor patriarchs in the Christian sense or a hierarchy of priests. Islam developed from the very outset not only as a religious doctrine or a theological-ethical concept, but as an all-embracing instruction regarding a 'correct' social and political practice. Islam defines the relationship among believers in everyday life as well as their approach to the external 'non-Islamic' or 'alien' environment. Islam was always during its almost 14 hundred years of history known as a religious system which was able to absorb and to interpret - using its own instruments - the whole range of new realities brought about by everyday social life and to change them into original or semi-original legal and economic norms and rules. It is therefore quite legitimate to regard Islam as an ideology - as ideological framework of the political and social practice of society or its concrete political power machine.

Fundamental among the pillars of Islamic political theory is the concept of umma - the society of equal individuals connected together by the obedience to one God. Criteria based on personal ambitions, kinship, nationality or the colour of skin, ceased to be relevant and this was basically true at least for the early Islam. But the initial umma as the community of new monotheist believers could not avoid utilising old and naturally integrated norms of pre-Islamic ethical and 'legal' values, the majority of which was not simply abandoned by the 'divine reformer'

Muhammad Ibn ᶜAbdallah, but was reinterpreted or even saved to be fructified and practised in a new context. Among the values that were not strictly abandoned, although not enthusiastically enforced in Muhammad's umma, is the above mentioned concept of shura. In the initial umma - the community of believers - Muhammad enjoyed the status of a divine envoy through whom God had revealed his message to the people. He was at the same time the spiritual and political head of umma. The way he lived, the views he communicated to the people were seen as an ideal code of conduct and - what is relevant here - a clearly defined approach to the political functions of the community. Nevertheless, the Prophet's sudden death in 632 A.D. confronted Muslims with the need to solve the problem of succession and the future model of government, if the umma was expected to survive. They had to tackle a serious dilemma, since the only tradition they could rely on was the pre-Islamic and tribal laws and principle of 'council of elders' - shura - under which the most respected individual was elected, usually by consensus, from among their number.[1] The umma abolished tribal laws and supplanted them by a homogenous expression of self-identity based on the common monotheistic faith. Nevertheless the pre-Islamic concept of shura, reinterpreted by Muhammad in his teachings, had to be respected as an integral part of God's revelation.

Although there was no doubt about the theoretical premises, the principle of shura deteriorated because of the political behaviour of Muhammad's orphans immediately after his death.[2] The effort to assert the old tribal principle of shura in the new conditions of umma, i. e. election of any commonly respected member of community, caused one of the dramatic splits in the umma and the creation of the radical splinter group (and later sect) of kharidjiya. The rule of 'tribal democracy' was replaced by much more effective ways of rule - especially after the seizing of power by the Umayyad dynasty. However 'immoral' and 'non-legitimate' the dynastic principle of power might have appeared from the point of view of original Islamic doctrine, this principle was applied on the level of practical politics. But during the period when the growing Islamic state - khilafa - was developing within the framework of Islamic religious ideology, it was simply impossible to eliminate the concept of shura from the Qur'an, from the authentic divine revelation. Shura was enshrined in the Qur'an[3] (but only in one place - 42:38) to consult each other in conducting all relevant affairs. But from the very beginnings of Islamic statehood the professional group of law-makers and, so to say, regime ideologues - ᶜulama - was extremely active in reinterpreting the concept of shura according to the real political demands of the authorities. In their exegetic works and while determining the foundations of the Islamic code of law the ᶜulama established their firm attitude towards the shura by declaring that affairs of the umma cover a wide range of activities, which could be solved by applying the shura principle. But at the same time there were a number of activities which should be excluded from the range of shura, because the Qur'an contained a clear-cut divine guidance that could not be made the object of any discussion by human beings.[4] Moreover, there was another kind of umma's conduct which was to be excluded from the sphere of shura, because of the guidance provided by sunna - prophetic traditions. Likewise, many Islamic scholars further restrict the scope of the shura in case of practices of the early Companions of the Prophet or the conduct of the first four 'rightly guided' caliphs (al-khulafa ar-rashidun) and even some decisions of the early ᶜulama, who had codified the shariᶜa. In this way, the principle of the shura could be admired and highly praised as an instrument of political life, but its importance in political practice was considerably minimized.[5] Thus we see that all the problems which faced the umma during its very emergence and early development, were concerned with the struggle for political power rather than with questions of doctrine or spiritual issues. In order to enable the umma to survive as a unified political body, it became necessary to effect a change towards a more complex sociopolitical mechanism and to outline an ad hoc law-of-the-state theory as necessitated by everyday practical problems, because the umma suffered from the absence of a strong centralised government. We, therefore, need to realise that the pre-Islamic principle of the shura was not appropriate for ensuring political unity, economic prosperity and military capability of the new umma = state = Islamic empire. Nevertheless, the idea of free 'democratic' choice of the leader and consensual decisions on some key legal issues was preserved and in the reality was replaced by the ceremony of bayᶜa - the formal acknowledgement of a new caliph and pledge of loyalty to him by the notables of the umma. But after the early stage of Islamic civilisation it became a mere formality and even in theory there was no process of election or 'collective choice' in the full sense. It was rather a humble recognition than a choice, not to speak about the choice by the masses of the population. By implication the first duty of the umma towards the ruler or leader was just an unconditional obedience because the unity of the umma was always considered to be the highest ideological imperative. Of course, according to the general perception, the ruler should consult the umma and subordinate to its 'common sense', and the umma should inspire him, support him morally and assist him with advices and exhortations, although there was never a clear concept about how and through which social structures should the ruler receive advice and support.

Later, after the final disintegration of the caliphate into various states and semi-independent provinces with more and more secular regimes political conditions required an ever greater degree of speculative ideology which justified the shift towards purely secular practices in religious categories. As the concept of shura was permanently utilised by opponents of the dynastical power during the Umayyad and later the Abbasid period as an argument of criticism of the despotic rule, caliphs and sultans were accordingly forced to create the vague concept of 'council of authorities' (ahl al-hall wa'l-ᶜaqd, those, who dissolve and bind). This body was the compensation of the abandoned principle of the shura. It should consist of loyal ᶜulama and its task was to secure the spiritual or ideological legitimacy of every caliph and later of all sorts of secular rulers. This council was never defined in clear-cut terms. Nobody outlined theoretically its relationship to the umma or the mode of selecting its members. This, in the course of centuries, frequently led to political tensions, which were defused by increasingly despotic secular means. The umma's role was reduced to that of a passive outlooker and it was made to accept the 'fait accompli' in regard to the problem of succession or legitimacy of power.[6] This somewhat detailed explanation of the wide range of the classical approach to the shura and its fate during the history of Islamic civilisation seemed to be necessary in view of the fact that this term like many other terms of Islamic political theory have been permanently mentioned, stressed and reinterpreted by generations of Muslim scholars and thinkers in the era of Islamic reformism from the late 19th century till the present. The main focus of this interest in the concept of shura is, of course, on the shaping of a new self-identity by rationalizing the ever growing need for some kind of democracy in Muslim societies through the use of own or genuine terms taken from the 'authentic revelation'. The protagonists of Islamic reformism take an attitude as narrow as possible and they raise the subject usually in the broader context of a discussion of such issues like umma, khilafa or idjtihad - free interpretation of divine texts, or even in such a crucial context as the divine predestination (al-qada 'wa 'l-qadar). From this point of view we can distinguish three major attitudes: a) intellectual eclectic reformism of the Egyptian 'salafiya', b) Islamic modernism which aims at the separation of the state and religion, c) various shades of Islamic fundamentalism that try more or less to revive the ideal of original umma.

Among the first thinkers who tackled the reinterpretation of Islamic political terms was the Egyptian Muhammad ᶜAbduh (1849-1905) who very accurately and systematically defended Islam as the religion which is fully compatible with alien values and the requirements of the functioning of a modern and flexible state mechanism. ᶜAbduh carried further a process of Islamic reform started by Rifaᶜa Rafiᶜ at-Tahtawi and Jamal ad-Din al-Afghani by equating certain traditional concepts of Islamic thought with the dominant ideas of capitalist Europe. From his point of view the shura is the proof of a humanism deeply rooted in Islam, a part of a major psychological revolution in the structure of Arab society which brought about a new quality of social interaction. Therefore, the shura would be the best response to those opponents of Islamic religion from among Christian, i.e. colonialist enemies, who do not recognize Islam's interest in happiness and wealth of the individual and who deride Islam as a crude collectivist and despotic religion. On the contrary - says Muhammad ᶜAbduh - the concept of the shura is fully compatible with European 'invention' of parliamentary democracy, and even more, its validity is multiplied because of its divine origin being part of God's revelation. The concept of the shura is interpreted by ᶜAbduh in the context of the charismatic character of the umma as reflected in prophetic traditions. The umma is infallible, because the Prophet clearly said: 'My umma will never agree on an error'. But why could he express this famous sentence? Because the everlasting success of Islamic umma is based on its democratic milieu, on a perennial sense of consultation, of discussing the problems jointly and solving them by collective experience. And that is true authentic democracy, that is one of the most fruitful contributions of Islam to the world civilisation.[7]

Frankly, Muhammad $^{c}$Abduh did not deal with the shura as deeply as many of his followers and other reformists during the first half of the 20th century. One of $^{c}$Abduh's followers who developed the thought of salafiya was Rashid Rida (1865-1935) who recast the open-minded heritage of his teacher towards a more conservative and xenophobic direction. Rida was deeply affected by the increasing impact of colonialism and alien values on the Egyptian and Muslim civilisation. Rida was much more inclined to reject than $^{c}$Abduh. He especially blamed the $^{c}$ulama who do not obey God and do not have in their mind the wealth of umma. According to Rida's view, the umma consists largely of people who were estranged from Islam, because they considered it inferior to the Western civilisation, and, by blindly imitating the West, forgot that all that is good in European government can be found already in its divine purity and perfection in 'true Islam'. He refers in particular to the concept of the shura and to the above mentioned institution of ahl al-$^{c}$aqd wa'l-hall. But this institution should not be based on the ruler's will or even on his dictatorial practices as is presently the case. The principle of shura and the consultative committee must be analyzed and interpreted afresh and in accordance with 'the authentic shari$^{c}$a'. Rida claims that Islam itself grants legislative power in administrative, military and financial matters, i.e. in everything outside the cult in the widest sense of the term. This legislative power is entrusted to the umma and is to be exercised through 'consultation' - the shura by all who possess knowledge and judgement, presumably the ahl al-$^{c}$aqd wa'l-hall. Their complete accord as the representatives of the umma to which in reality all the power belongs, must be provided by the third principle of the Islamic law system - by idjma$^{c}$ (consensus of $^{c}$ulama). But the main precondition for the just and pure safeguarding of authentic Islamic practice is the proper choice of representatives from among the umma. Only the implementation of this precondition would guarantee the application of the shura, which is to be applied by elected representatives who use the instrument of consensus.[8]

Let us stay a little bit more in Egypt where the Islamic modernism took its root, when some younger scholars and thinkers started to question very seriously the unchanging, although almost completely formal, unity between state and religion. The separation of both phenomena - comparable to developments in Christianity and more recently in republican Turkey - was viewed by them as a strategic goal and the only way to the salvation of Islam as an ethical and theological system. The most important personality representing this stream was $^{c}$Ali $^{c}$Abd ar-Raziq (1888-1966), whose main intention was to establish that Islam and politics are words that do not go together well. He attempted to demonstrate that khilafa is a betrayal of the mission and message of Muhammad and that Muslims should follow the Prophet in their faith but build a modern polity on modern principles. It can hardly be said that he succeeded in demolishing the traditional theory of the khilafa or the imama. His importance lies in the fact that he instilled into constitutional terms taken from the European political system different accurate and systematic meanings which were more acceptable to Muslim society. He, in fact, provided the new contemporary contents to such classical Islamic terms as Idjtihad and especially shura. He seems to have abandoned almost completely the Islamic law - the shariᶜa as the central instrument of legislation and this was indeed his main purpose in demolishing the old-fashioned concept of the khilafa, because khilafa is practically synonymous with shariᶜa. He emphasized that the Prophet's state was not a state in the usual sense of the term and his political ordinances and actions should not be understood as a frozen dogma. The author further argues that the shariᶜa need not be overestimated because it does not embody Muhammad's practice, since during the time of his prophecy there was no discussion of something like 'shariᶜa'. He asks: Why should we consider the orthodox shariᶜatic explanations as something fixed that cannot be touched or questioned when the umma - the really existing organism of believers - currently faces crucial changes accompanied by the danger of European colonialism that could prove fatal to it? And that is why ᶜAli ᶜAbd ar-Raziq perceived the shura as merely a synonym for parliamentary democracy and explained the term madjlis ash-shura (consultative committee) is semantically the same as the parliament.[9]

At the other end of the spectrum of reformist attitudes towards the shura we come across views which can be called 'fundamentalist'. The origin of such attitudes can undoubtedly be traced to the approach of the Pakistani reformist thinker Abu'l-Aᶜla al-Mawdudi (1903-1979), who was instrumental in raising Islamic fundamentalism and himself influenced many fundamentalist ideologues, such as Sayyid Qutb or ᶜUmar at-Tilimsani. Mawdudi defined the purpose of the Executive in an Islamic state as 'to enforce the directives of God ... and to bring about a society ready to accept and adopt these directives for practical application in its life'[10]. He further refers to the precedent of al-khulafa ar-rashidun who initiated the Prophet in order to substantiate his contention that in an Islamic executive the legislature and judiciary act under the authority of the head of state yet function 'separately and independently of one another'. While earlier and originally the ahl al-ᶜaqd wa'l-hall presented the legislators, they constitute now only a body of advisors to the head of state in matters of law, administration and state-policy. That is, they merely enjoy a consultative status, which is very formal and humiliating. Mawdudi puts the question regarding the position of legislature in Islam and answers it by stating that while consultation is laid down in the Qur'an - shura - it is not clear from the Qur'an and Traditions whether the head of the state is bound to accept recommendations or not. He demands that in the absence of a consultative assembly with the qualifications necessary in an Islamic state, the Executive must be subordinated to the decisions of Legislature. But in his view it is only the temporary measure until the true and authentic 'Islamic state' comes into being. And this means that his 'Islamic power' (al-hukuma al-islamiya) should be based on true theocracy, on the government of madjlis ash-shura, which is considered as the rule of the ᶜulama who are not responsible to anybody but the umma and establish their laws and decisions in the spontaneous climate of mutual consultation - the shura. But he does not directly compare the shura and Western democracy. He does express his views whether the shura constitutes an Islamic type of democracy or whether the Western democracy is merely a false interpretation of the Islamic one. He just states that the 'Islamic power' or the 'Islamic order' represents an ideal of human organisation and that the rule of the 'outspoken and faithful ᶜulama' provides the basic precondition of such an organisation. The shura is recognized as a natural and the only acceptable method of rule.

As is well known Egyptian contemporaries of al-Mawdudi were Hasan al-Banna (1906-1949) - founder and chief ideologue of the Association of Muslim Brothers - and his followers Hasan al-Hudaybi and Abd al-Qadir ᶜAwda. The heterogenous and often even contradictory views held by these fundamentalist thinkers payed much more attention to the concept of the shura than any of their predecessors. That is because they evolved a comparatively detailed concept of the 'Islamic state', which constitutes the main pillar of their broader concept of 'Islamic order'.[11] Al-Banna singles out the umma, i.e. society, as the sole source of power and of all the ruler's authority. Bowing to the will of the umma is the ruler's basic religious obligation. The ruler has no legal authority and no loyalty of his own, as 'he reflects the spirit of the umma and is in harmony with its goals'. Since the ruler is 'the agent contracted for' by the umma, he is 'elected' by it. As for the details of such elections, al-Banna does not describe any procedure, because 'the Qur'an designated no specific ways of holding elections'. Both al-Hudaybi and ᶜAwda claim that elections could be held in any way considered fit by the people concerned, 'perhaps even directly by the people'. ᶜAwda also emphasizes that it could be done by ahl ash-shura (people of consultation), which forms some kind of representative assembly of the umma - something similar to the ahl al-ᶜaqd wa'l-hall, but constituted only from among the 'masses of believers'. The ruler swears to the umma through the institution of ahl ash-shura to govern according to the Qur'an and the 'right' Traditions and the umma swears to obey him as long as he rules by God's laws. In the opinion of the founders of Islamic fundamentalism the practice of 'consultation' - ash-shura - is a mandatory and fundamental part of the Islamic state. They frequently stress in their pamphlets and booklets that 'He (God) commanded consultation among themselves' (the Qur'an 42:38). The institution through which the shura operates is the ahl ash-shura (or ahl al-ᶜaqd wa'l-hall). It alone is invested with the real power of the state, it alone commands and observes the obedience of both ruler and ruled. Since its members represent the people, they too would be 'elected', but the question regarding the procedure and numbers is a 'secondary' matter not defined by Islam and is, therefore, left to the circumstances of each age and place. Who should be eligible to the ahl ash-shura? Al-Banna felt it should consist of two types of people: a) men of the legal profession with a background of 'general knowledge', and b) men experienced in political leadership - heads of families, tribes and other organized groups. Unlike Hasan al-Banna, his Brotherhood-fellow ᶜAbd al-Qadir ᶜAwda was a little less specific: the ahl ash-shura should comprise of people most of whom are knowledgeable of the law. The requirements of the modern scientific world would make it desirable to add some specialists and technicians, but the final word would rest with the law experts. Precise arrangements regarding this matter could be left to time and place. As the 'true rulers of the Islamic state' the ahl ash-shura would have the right to expect all matters to be submitted to them for deliberation and decision. A majority opinion would be required for a decision after a period of free debates on any issue and the minority should support the majority's decision. This is the only valid procedure, because - as we know from above - the Prophet has already said: 'My umma cannot agree on error'.

Thus, we could cite and analyze dozens of other variants of the principle of shura which may differ in some details but are based on the same fundamentals. They are deeply rooted in the very beginnings of Islamic religion. As I said before, Muslim scholars and thinkers like to play with this principle to rationalize more and more the preferred trend towards some kind of democracy or some kind of 'non-totalitarian' rule. These thinkers were fed up with the 'tyranny' of military or 'one-party' secular regimes and even with the despotism and arrogance of 'oil-monarchies', both of which exposed their 'hypocricy', because while they all the time use religious and even fundamentalist phrases, in everyday life and practical politics they behave in accordance with the 'Western moral decadence and rough materialism'.

I am convinced that the path of Islamic societies towards some kind of democracy will be very intricate - if it will be gone at all. Let us not forget that the model of parliamentary democracy was historically a peculiar phenomenon of some parts of Western Europe. Of course, we like democracy and some central European nations relished and enjoyed it during recent years with enthusiasm. But let us not prescribe to non-European societies which kind of humanism or social justice they should introduce and apply. Maybe these societies are tired of the secularism and Western-style mode of life, maybe they live in some kind of ideological vacuum that they would like to fill up with a more familiar and comprehensible set of ideas. Such ideas provided hitherto a major section of these societies with a feeling of self-sufficiency and self-identity, a feeling of originality and the possibility to keep aloof - if necessary - from the strong, dangerous, arrogant, cold-hearted and atheistic West. Leave them alone in their struggle for the self-identity, for their own path toward a just society, which need not be necessarily called 'democratic', but perhaps 'ash-shurawi'. Let us not disturb these societies with our 'experienced' advices and let us allow them to make their own tests of non-totalitarian political models. How the concept of shura would be put into practice in various Islamic societies and whether this will be a realistic proposition at all should be an issue for discussion. But perhaps some political institution called ash-shura or madjlis ash-shura could in the future - in certain circumstances - turn out to be much more democratic than some of today's institutions in Islamic world, proudly called al-barlamán.

## Notes

1 Miloš Mendel, Classical Islam as an Ideological Framework of Policy. In: Ex pede pontis. Papers presented on the occasion of the 70th anniversary of the foundation of the Oriental Institute Prague, Prague 1992, p. 166.

2 Muslims eventually adapted the temporary principle of electing of the Prophet's successor from among the ranks of his closest followers. The first of them was Abu Bakr who assumed the title of caliph (the Prophet's deputy). This fact already embodied Islam's fundamental permanent conflict - that over the legitimacy of power - which in 632-661 crystallised in a conflict of schismatic proportions. Abu Bakr was nominated by a small privileged group of venerable Muslims from Mecca (muhadjirun). For their part Muslims from Medina (ansar) initially sought to assert the tribal electoral principle of the shura. Not even the caliph cUmar Ibn al-Khattab was elected, he was nominated without the community's knowledge. And although the third caliph cUthman Ibn al-cAffan was elected by the shura its members were first nominated by cUmar. After 661 (assassinating of caliph CAli) the principle of shura was rolled back from politics by the dynastic one. The Umayyads stressed the internal stability of caliphate by asserting their hegemony over the principle of 'tribal democracy'.

3 al-Qur'an al-karim: surat ash-shura (42:38).

4 Ahmed Mazrooddin, Islamic Political System in the Modern Age, Karachi 1991, p. 37.

5 The Companions of the Prophet were called ahl ash-ashura and they were those whom the Prophet had consulted during the battle of al-Badr. For this reason some Muslim historians speak of them as ahl al-Badr.

6 Mendel, Classical Islam..., p. 174.

7 For more details on Muhammad cAbduh and his concept of shura see, for example, A. Hourani, Arabic Thought in the Liberal Age 1798-1939, London 1970, pp. 144-145.

8 For more details on Rashid Rida and his views on shura see, for example, E.I.J. Rosenthal, Islam in the Modern National State, Cambridge 1965, pp. 70-72.

9 For more details on CAli CAbd ar-Raziq see his main book al-Islam wa usul al-hukm, Beirut 1966, and, for example, Bassam Tibi, Arab Nationalism - A Critical Enquiry, New York 1981.

10 Abu'l-Acla al-Mawdudi, al-Hukuma al-islamiya, Cairo 1986, pp. 138-139.

11 For more details on Muslim brotherhood and fundamentalist thinkers of the first generation see an excellent monograph of R.P. Mitchell, The Society of Muslim Brothers, London 1969, and a huge number of recent studies on Islamic fundamentalism.

# Le droit pénal colonial et les réactions soudanaises

Hervé Bleuchot

Le problème des "identités en mouvement sous la colonisation" se présente tout d'abord, dans le cas particulier des identités juridiques du Soudan comme un changement de système juridique, un basculement. On trouve manifestement un changement de l'identité juridique du Soudan entre le début et la fin de la colonisation, entre 1898 et 1956. Avant la période coloniale, les divers droits existants au Soudan, depuis l'époque la plus reculée jusqu'à la fin du mahdisme (1881-1898), pouvaient être considérés comme constituant un système unique, le système traditionnel, dominé par le droit musulman, quoique le système juridique de la période égyptienne (1820-1885) appelle d'importantes nuances. Après la reconquête du Soudan contre le successeur du Mahdî, le calife Abd Allâh, une des premières décisions des autorités anglo-égyptiennes fut de mettre en place un code pénal et un code de procédure pénale (1899). D'autres décisions furent prises dans les quelques années suivantes, en matière civile et administrative, notamment avec la création de tribunaux musulmans, et vers 1905 le système anglais moderne était constitué pour l'essentiel. Dans le détail toutefois le passage ne fut pas aussi brutal, les peuples ne changent pas de système juridique aussi rapidement. Le système anglais fut repris et complété entre 1925 et 1932, notamment avec la création de tribunaux indigènes qui donnèrent une nouvelle vie au droit traditionnel. Ce système fut conservé longtemps après l'indépendance.

Face au changement de système sous la colonisation, les Soudanais ont eu des réactions diverses. Il est intéressant en soi de les explorer pour savoir ce qu'elles furent. Mais la connaissance de ces réactions et attitudes permet de répondre en outre à un questionnement très actuel.

On sait en effet que des codes pénaux islamiques furent adoptés en 1983 et en 1991, et la démarche prioritaire qui s'impose est d'explorer l'histoire juridique du Soudan pour rechercher quelque explication à cette apparition ou réapparition du droit islamique. Une question revient souvent : le droit pénal islamique est-il une restauration du droit islamique traditionnel ou une création idélogique, certes se réclamant du passé, mais radicalement nouvelle ? On ne prétend pas résoudre ici ce problème, mais faire observer que sa solution dépend de la solution donnée à un autre problème, celui de la nature du droit légué par la colonisation. Ici se pose de nouvelles questions : le droit colonial légué constitue-t-il une rupture radicale d'avec le droit traditionnel (musulman et païen), ou au contraire peut-on relever des continuités entre les deux systèmes ? De même le droit colonial est-il resté en marge de la société soudanaise, en sorte que, le colonisateur parti, après un temps relativement court, les Soudanais ont retrouvé leur identité en matière pénale ? Ou au contraire est-il entré en dialogue avec cette société, donnant lieu à la création d'une sorte de synthèse, de manière que, après l'indépendance, les codes de 1983 et 1991 constituraient une irruption, une importation idéologique sans rapport avec le Soudan ?

La réponse à ces questions n'est pas simple. Il faudrait distinguer les réactions du Sud et celles du Nord Soudan, distinguer même les réactions des différents groupes ethniques, sociaux, religieux, etc., dans chacune de ces régions. Il faudrait encore effectuer l'analyse problème par problème : les réactions sont différentes selon qu'il s'agit de l'esclavage, de l'excision, du droit familial, de la compensation, etc. Sans compter l'immense intérêt qu'il y aurait à évoquer des problèmes tels que l'organisation judiciaire, la procedure, la politique indigène et les théories de Lugard, les aspects politiques de la décolonisation, etc. Evidemment, il n'est pas possible d'entrer ici dans tous ces sujets.

Nous sommes donc contraint, pour rester dans les limites raisonnables d'un article de nous concentrer sur l'analyse de l'aspect global, c'est-à-dire essayer de répondre à la question de la continuité et du dialogue des droits en présence sous la colonisation, laissant dans l'ombre ou ne faisant que de brèves allusions aux autres aspects.

Nous présenterons tout d'abord le droit traditionnel dans son parcours historique et dans ses caractéristiques fondamentales (première partie). Nous évoquerons ensuite l'introduction des codes indiens au Soudan (deuxième partie). Puis nous décrirons les principales réactions soudanaises à cette introduction d'une philosophie pénale nouvelle pour eux, au moins en partie, en distinguant nettement le cas du Sud (troisième partie) de celui du Nord (quatrième partie). Enfin, à l'aide des résultats de cette double enquête, nous nous efforcerons de donner des éléments de réponse au questionnement posé dans cette introduction.

## Le système traditionnel

### *Trajectoire de la société traditionnelle*[1]

On observe tout d'abord dans l'histoire des royaumes Fung et Fûr, un passage lent d'Etats païens à royautés divinisées à des Etats islamiques très orthodoxes. Il semble que le mouvement naturel de l'islam soit de tolérer chez les peuples convertis des conceptions antérieures, personnelles ou coutumières, mystiques ou superstitieuses, et de ne déployer la rigueur d'une orthodoxie plus étroite que dans les générations suivantes. Au Darfur, le fait est qu'une coexistence pacifique du paganisme et d'un islam laxiste s'observe au XVIe et XVIIe siècles, qu'il y a une vague orthodoxe à la fin du XVIIIe, puis à la fin du XIXe avec Ali Dinar. Dans le Dar Fung, la trajectoire est interrompue par l'occupation égyptienne, mais les mouvement de fond se continuent à travers les confréries à visée politiques

(Majdhubiya, Khatmiya, Sammaniya). Le résultat est bien connu, c'est la vague mahdiste qui refoula la colonisation égyptienne tout à fait superficielle.

Sur le plan juridique, ces royaumes avaient un système traditionnel pluraliste. Le droit musulman acquit progressivement une prééminence sur le plan intellectuel et religieux, mais il était divisé en rites, et plusieurs instances (qâdî, chaych de confréries, gouverneurs, etc.), plus ou moins bien coordonnées lui donnaient une souplesse certaine. Surtout il devait composer avec un droit coutumier et un droit régalien, dont on ne sait presque rien, mais dont l'existence et la prééminence sur le plan procédural concret (en première et dernière instance) est hors de doute. Dans cette combinaison, il n'y a rien que de très ordinaire dans le système traditionnel musulman et cela depuis les premiers califes, si l'on consent à regarder les faits et non la théorie pure du *fiqh*.[2]

Sur le plan pénal il est remarquable que les droits coutumier et régalien, que ce soit chez les Fung ou les Fûr, corrigeaient le droit pénal islamique et que la peine d'amputation pour vol n'était pas employée. Le système de la compensation était universel dans le droit coutumier. Dans le droit régalien c'étaient les amendes qui jouaient le premier rôle. Selon Nachtigal[3], qui résume le Ktab Dali[4], on ne trouvait pas de châtiments corporels ni de peine de mort au Darfur. A l'inverse chez les Fung, la courbache (fouet de cuir d'hippopotame) et la peine de mort en appel étaient fort employées.

Pour confirmer ces affirmations, nous ne donnerons qu'un exemple, tiré d'Al Mufti, pourtant hostile à tout ce qui n'est pas conforme à la théorie du *fiqh*. Il ne pouvait pas ne pas évoquer la coutume à propos des Fûr, tant elle est importante. Il en donne un résumé[5] que nous traduisons en entier, car il peut avoir une certaine valeur, l'auteur ayant fait une enquête orale :

"1. Les femmes sont privées d'héritage.
2. Quiconque vole est condamné à une amende (gharâma) de 7 vaches ou l'équivalent.
3. Quiconque fornique avec une femme mariée est condamné à une amende de 7 vaches; avec une femme non mariée l'amende est d'une vache seulement.
4. La sanction (jazâ') pour le meurtrier est de payer une diya de 100 vaches pour les vachers et de 100 chameaux pour les chameliers.
5. Quiconque frappe violemment quelqu'un en cassant l'os ou en fendant la chair est condamné à une amende d'un damûr[6] et, si le coup n'est pas violent, à une amende de la moitié.
6. Quiconque insulte gravement paiera une amende d'un damûr, mais si l'insulte n'est pas grave, il paiera la moitié.
7. Il n'y a pas de punition pour les infractions entre enfants (crime dits en langue fûr farâcha).

8. Il n'y a pas de punition pour celui qui s'empare du bétail d'autrui[7] pour le tuer en vue d'un banquet de noces, à condition que le nombre des bêtes prises soit raisonnable."

Quoiqu'il en soit de la valeur de ce texte, on peut dire que le système du Darfur est le même système pluraliste que celui du Sennar, le droit musulman étant encadré, en première et dernière instance par le droit coutumier.

A partir de 1820-1822, on le sait, les forces égyptiennes occupèrent le Soudan ou du moins sa partie nord, inaugurant la période dite de la Turkiya. On a dit et répété avec raison que le système juridique égyptien était fort mal connu[8]. Nous avons essayé de combler les lacunes ou du moins de préciser ce qu'il faut chercher en utilisant les ressources de l'histoire du droit égyptien au XIXe siècle[9]. Le système égyptien au Soudan nous est apparu comme un système traditionnel musulman qui cherche les voies de la modernité. Traditionnel musulman puisqu'on retrouve les trois niveaux dans la justice et le droit : coutumier, musulman, et régalien, ce dernier ne séparant pas ou peu la justice pénale de l'administration militaire. C'est donc toujours un système pluraliste. En voie de modernisation, c'est évident, puisque le droit régalien égyptien produisit divers codes et réformes de l'organisation administrative et judiciaire pour rattraper le retard égyptien et se mettre au niveau de l'Occident. Nous n'avons pas pu trouver une confirmation directe de l'application au Soudan des codes pénaux égyptiens. Il semble assuré toutefois, par divers recoupements, que la peine d'amputation pour vol ait été écartée.

Mais la modernité parvint au Soudan à travers un colonisateur égyptien qui était loin de la maîtriser, ni même convaincu de son utilité, surtout aux échelons inférieurs. Les scrupules de Sa'îd, et plus tard l'esprit réformiste d'Isma'îl ne furent jamais bien compris, ni son engouement pour les Européens. Comme on l'a dit ailleurs, les pachas et khédives d'Egypte ressentirent parmi les premiers la faille qui s'était introduite entre la morale et la religion. Le proconsulat de Moussa Pacha Hamdi au Soudan fut par exemple une réaction à l'humanisme de Sa'îd. La part de l'anarchie, du non-droit, resta considérable. Il existe aussi indubitablement, au Soudan, un refus de l'occupant, ne serait-ce que par la fuite des populations hors du système. Munzinger avait observé qu'un chef de confrérie aurait pu déclencher, dès 1865, contre les Egyptiens qui auraient été balayés, un formidable mouvement religieux.[10].

Le mahdisme peut être considéré comme cette réaction, qui couvait depuis longtemps au Soudan. Réaction contre une administration corrompue et incompétente, contre une modernisation mal conduite, mais aussi réaction de type islamiste contre une mise en accusation indirecte de l'islam (très nette à propos de l'esclavage), le mahdisme est aussi une rupture puisqu'il est l'enfant tardif de la vague d'orthodoxie et de mysticisme de la fin du XVIIIe et du début du XIXe siècle (par la Sammaniya). Il établit un système traditionnel parvenu au stade terminal de l'islamisation, celui de l'orthodoxie[11]. Sous la Mahdiya comme dans les régimes précédents, on trouvait les trois niveaux, droit coutumier, droit musulman, et droit régalien. Quoique ce dernier prétendait constamment ne s'inspirer que de l'islam le plus orthodoxe, il s'écartait de l'orthodoxie, faisait appel à des polices multiples qui avaient commencé, semble-t-il un travail de confinement du *qâdî* aux affaires civiles.

L'histoire du droit dans le monde traditionnel païen est presque totalement inconnue avant l'arrivée des colonisateurs. La documentation pousse à réduire cette histoire à celle de l'islamisation. L'oralité des coutumes est évidemment responsable de cette occultation/déformation. Il est certain que le droit païen a une histoire. On en a la preuve chez les Azandé, où l'on sait que le cannibalisme a disparu, que les monarques interdirent la circoncision puis les sociétés secrètes. Mais la zone d'ignorance est immense.

## Aspects du droit traditionnel

Le concept de légalité n'existe pas dans le droit traditionnel, du moins pas sous la forme sous laquelle nous le connaissons. Pour bien saisir ce que nous entendons par là, nous proposons une approche par la fameuse formule d'Evans-Pritchard "in a strict sense, Nuer have no law"[12]. Il ne faut pas se précipiter sur le second membre de la phrase pour démontrer le contraire. Le droit "au sens rigoureux", signifie le droit compris à la manière des positivistes. Dès lors Evans-Pritchard a raison : il n'y a ni parlement, ni code, ni lois, ni jurisprudence, ni tribunaux chez les Nuer, parce qu'il n'y a pas d'Etat législateur et que, selon les positivistes, pas d'Etat, pas de droit. Mais Evans-Pritchard démontre lui-même qu'il existe chez les Nuer un droit qu'il définit ainsi : "une obligation morale de régler des différends par des moyens convenus"[13].

Cette définition implique qu'il existe différentes conceptions de la légalité. Dans les sociétés actuelles occidentales où le droit est codifié, le droit doit s'appliquer strictement à tous, et tout écart entre le droit et le fait est considéré comme un défaut, qui, en principe, doit être sanctionné, mais où rien ne peut être sanctionné en dehors de ce cadre (*nulla poena sine lege*). Il ne faut pas confondre cette conception de la légalité, qui est stricte, avec les problèmes de l'application du droit, application qui peut être souple. Ainsi, chez nous, le ministère public ne poursuit pas toujours, il ne le fait systématiquement que pour les crimes, et délaisse le reste : bien des vols ne font même pas l'objet d'une enquête (au grand dam des victimes) et la répression des infractions mineures est sporadique, voire fantaisiste (infractions au code de la route par exemple). De même l'application du droit faite par les juges pose différents problèmes, juridiques ou non, qui ne remettent pas en cause cette conception stricte de la légalité. Cette dernière ne doit pas non plus se confondre avec les problèmes de l'effectivité du droit, qui sont sociologiques, mesurant l'écart entre la société voulue par le droit et celle qui existe.

Dans la société traditionnelle l'obéissance au droit a un aspect moral ou religieux. Evans-Pritchard dit bien qu'il est une obligation morale. La loi est un idéal, la conception de la légalité est différente. Par exemple chez les Nuer le prix de la compensation matrimoniale doit être de 40 têtes de bétail, au minimum de 20 têtes. Kelly[14] a montré l'importance de l'existence de ce minimum, qui n'existe pas chez les Dinka, et il décèle là la raison du 'Nuer impetus', cette inextinguible soif de pâturages et de bétail. Mais même ce minimum peut être abaissé[15], car en droit nuer, comme en tout droit traditionnel, tout est négociable entre les parties. En période d'abondance de bétail l'idéal est dépassé et il peut se payer jusqu'à 60 têtes et même plus. On ne peut pas se contenter de dire que le prix de la compensation est libre entre les parties, car la règle des 40 têtes ainsi que le minimum de 20 têtes existent. Force est de dire que le droit traditionnel a une conception différente du rôle de la loi dans la société. L'idéalité de la loi aide grandement le justiciable et souvent tout le monde y trouve son compte. Howell[16] donne l'exemple, chez les Nuer, d'un créancier qui se fit reconnaître sa dette vis-à-vis de son débiteur, sans exiger le paiement effectif. L'un sauva la face, l'autre son bien, tous furent contents.

La conception de la légalité de la société traditionnelle explique aussi le petit nombre d'infractions qui font l'objet de mesures pénales proprement dites. La loi idéale ne saurait entrer dans les détails d'une réglementation de la vie quotidienne, comme la nôtre qui va jusqu'à fixer la hauteur des carrelages dans les cuisines des bars ou interdire les cendriers sur les comptoirs. La loi idéale selon la conception traditionnelle, renvoie le quotidien au civil, et celui-ci n'entre en action que si quelqu'un se plaint.

Le droit musulman ne comporte lui aussi qu'un petit nombre d'infractions pénales. Sa conception de la légalité est-elle alors la même que celle d'une société comme celle des Nuer ? La question est controversée depuis longtemps. Au début du siècle, Kohler s'est opposé à Goldziher et Schnouck-Hurgronje à propos du sens profond du droit musulman. Ces deux derniers tendaient à voir dans le droit musulman un code idéal, une morale, une théorie des devoirs. E. Lambert prit une position moyenne en faisant ressortir avec Kohler que les arguments avancés par Goldziher et Schnouck-Hurgronje pourraient aussi s'appliquer au code civil et faire de lui une théorie des devoirs. Un des meilleurs connaisseurs, G. H. Bousquet écrit : "Le *fiqh* ne veut pas être une image de la réalité. C'est plutôt comme un phare qui doit guider les croyants vers l'idéal religieux"[17]. Dans un autre ouvrage : " nier le caractère obligatoire d'une prescription divine tout en l'accomplissant est chose beaucoup plus grave que de la négliger en pratique pourvu qu'on admette qu'elle s'impose à tous"[18] et encore : "le *fiqh* n'est pas un droit aux yeux de l'islam, mais une déontologie, je dirai volontiers : un catéchisme"[19].

Mais Bousquet ne prend-il pas l'écart entre le droit et le fait, qui peut être important, pour une conception particulière de la légalité ? Ne faudrait-il pas chercher plutôt dans les sources arabes classiques une confirmation de cette conception ? La recherche semble *a priori* difficile. D'abord on ne trouvera rien de certain avant 750. Par la suite, l'existence de pouvoirs politiques forts pourront amener tel uléma à admettre la légitimité d'une entorse à la loi, sans qu'on puisse vraiment en déduire qu'il admet l'idéalité du droit musulman. Le recours aux concepts de "nécessité des temps" (*darûra*) ou de "corruption" (*fasâd*) vient-il de la recherche (*ijtihâd* ) ou de la prudence ? Probablement des deux. A l'inverse une affirmation péremptoire que le droit musulman doit s'appliquer "en tout temps et en tout lieu" peut exprimer aussi bien l'idéal universaliste de la loi islamique qu'une conception occidentale (et positiviste) de la légalité. Elle ne prouvera donc rien quant au problème soulevé. Toutefois, des faits incontestables comme le comportement des monarques ottomans législateurs, somme toute aussi musulmans que les autres; ou bien la reconnaissance de la légalité des ruses, cela dès les origines abbassides du *fiqh*, et surtout la reconnaissance universelle de la légitimité de diverses écoles de droit et de divergences à l'intérieur même des écoles, tendent à prouver que la conception de la légalité en droit musulman n'est pas celle des positivistes, mais plutôt celle de la société traditionnelle, d'où le droit musulman est issu et où il s'appliquait.

Dans le droit traditionnel la plus grande partie de ce que nous appelons droit pénal est traitée par une procédure civile. Le but principal d'un procès civil est de rétablir la paix dans la communauté et pour cela la meilleure voie est de fixer une compensation pour la victime ou ses parents. Les infractions telles que les homicides, les viols, les coups et blessures sont considérées comme des obligations délictuelles, des événements qui ne concernent pas la société dans son ensemble, mais principalement deux familles ou deux groupes ethniques ou autres. La conséquence a été bien soulignée par Evans Pritchard, c'est que "la force du droit varie en fonction de la position des parties dans la structure politique, et (que) (par ensemple) le droit des Nuer est essentiellement relatif, comme la structure elle-même"[20].

Ce point de vue civiliste du droit traditionnel ne signifie pas que le droit ignore les peines. Chez de nombreux groupes ethniques, il existe, à côté de la compensation et éventuellement du sacrifice de purification, différentes sortes de peines, par exemple des coups de fouet pour le voleur ou une surcompensation représentant le "prix de la colère". De même en droit musulman les peines ne sont pas inconnues. L'emprisonnement et sa signification n'était pas ignoré et il existait dans le Djebel Marra une prison d'Etat à l'époque des sultans fûr, de même à l'époque égyptienne et à l'époque mahdiste.

La distance entre la conception de la peine en droit traditionnel et en droit moderne n'est donc pas si grande. Ce n'est que dans le cas des "sociétés acéphales" comme celles des Nuer ou des Dinka que l'on peut s'attendre à des incompréhensions sur la valeur dissuasive des peines. Toutefois, même dans le cas de ces sociétés, comme on le verra plus loin à propos des tribunaux des prophètes, il existait des points de contacts.

Enfin on doit dire aussi que l'homme a toujours, dans n'importe quelle société, une conscience morale, distincte de sa conscience religieuse, et cette conscience cherche toujours à se frayer un chemin dans le droit. Les juristes musulmans (fuqahâ') ont toujours tenté de mettre des limitations dans l'application des hudûd (peines fixées par Dieu), comme l'amputation de la main droite du voleur, la lapidation de l'adultère, etc. Ils mirent des limites à la guerre sainte, donnèrent un statut aux dhimmis, aux esclaves, etc. Le travail des *fuqahâ'* comporte incontestablement une dose de protestation, de correction de l'islam. De plus, dans la tradition islamique on ne trouve pas que des clercs, il y a aussi des humanistes, et cela ne peut pas ne pas transparaître par moments dans le *fiqh* ou dans la pratique de la justice. Les tribunaux d'équité des califes (*mahâkim al matâlîm*) en sont une autre manifestation. Des voies réformistes apparaissent à la fin du siècle : l'islam, même dans sa version mahdiste[21], aspire à autre chose.

La question est plus délicate à prouver en ce qui concerne le monde païen au XIXe siècle. Une précieuse indication nous est fournie par Junker[22] qui nous a rapporté son entrevue avec le roi zandé Badinge. Le monarque ne cessait de lui poser des questions. Junker écrit : "Quelques unes de ses difficultés avaient trait aux victimes de la créance universelle accordée à la sorcellerie, et manifestement il semblait craindre que beaucoup de gens n'en souffrent sans doute innocemment". Cette simple remarque va loin : le roi zandé remet en question toute la croyance zandé (en l'oracle, en la sorcellerie) et cela par une perception fine de l'innocence, nous dirions des droits de l'homme. Il a senti, comme d'autres, la contradiction entre les droits fondamentaux et sa propre culture. Dira-t-on que c'est Junker qui a projeté sa propre problématique ? Rien n'est moins certain, Evans-Pritchard a souligné à la fois l'intelligence des Azandé et leur scepticisme envers certaines croyances et donc le fait rapporté par Junker correspond bien à la mentalité zandé.

On doit faire l'hypothèse de l'existence, au-delà de formules juridiques ou religieuses, d'un bon sens moral, partagé par l'humanité tout entière, et qui, pour ce qui nous concerne, a rendu le dialogue possible à l'époque de la colonisation. Cela d'autant plus que les Britanniques qui arrivaient, très pragmatiques, étaient prêts à faire des concessions[23] et à renoncer à une conception trop étroite, trop victorienne de la moralité.

## L'introduction des codes indiens

Le droit colonial anglais avait traité le droit musulman de différentes manières. En général les Britanniques en reconnaissaient l'applicabilité pour les affaires de statut personnel, mais en Inde il avait été admis pendant longtemps comme applicable en matière criminelle (avec des retouches). En Afrique de l'Ouest, il avait été pris comme une coutume parmi d'autres, sauf au Nigeria où il constituait la seule coutume reconnue. En Afrique de l'Est il avait été considéré comme un droit distinct, mais pas en Ouganda ni en Tanzanie où il était mis au rang d'une coutume. Au Soudan, il fallait tenir compte de l'Egypte qui était, rappelons-le, partie prenante dans le système du Condominium selon le traité de 1899.

C'est Lord Cromer qui fut au premier chef le responsable des choix qui furent faits. Evelyn Baring, né en 1841, avait commencé sa carrière comme soldat dans l'artillerie[24], tout en publiant quelques traductions du grec et de l'allemand. Son oncle, Lord Northbrook, nommé vice-roi en Inde (1872-76) le prit comme secrétaire, et Baring commença ainsi une carrière civile dans l'administration des colonies britanniques. Il fut nommé ensuite commissaire de la dette en Egypte (1876-1880), puis travailla de nouveau en Inde (1880-1883) comme secrétaire financier du Conseil du vice-roi (Lord Ripon). En 1883 il fut nommé consul général et agent anglais dans l'Egypte occupée depuis 1882 par les troupes de Sa Majesté, poste qu'il occupa jusqu'en 1907. C'est dans cette fonction clef qu'il fut étroitement mêlé à tous les événements importants de l'histoire soudanaise : la vague mahdiste, la mort de Gordon Pacha à Khartoum (1885), et, à partir de 1896, la reconquête du Soudan, conduite par le général Kitchener. C'est surtout à E. Baring, devenu Lord Cromer en 1891, que l'on doit les choix essentiels en matière juridique au Soudan.

Mais où en était le droit pénal anglais à cette époque ? Certes, depuis le XVIIIe siècle, depuis Beccaria et Bentham, le droit anglais et en particulier le droit pénal était l'objet de vives critiques[25], mais il avait évolué depuis. Au début du XIXe siècle nombre de réformateurs, plus ou moins inspirés par Jeremy Bentham, s'étaient consacrés à la tâche de le réformer. Une première réforme d'importance eut lieu sous le ministère de Lord Liverpool, Lord Peel étant secrétaire à l'intérieur (1822). Elle eut pour effet de faire passer le nombre des crimes donnant lieu à une peine de mort de 200 à 100. D'autres réformes avaient suivi en 1832-34, en 1837 et en 1841 à la suite des travaux d'une commission de réforme et grâce à Lord Russel[26] et en 1861 encore. Tout un courant d'opinion, dont l'existence remonte au moins aux révolutions du XVIIe siècle, souhaitait la simplification et la codification du droit anglais. Mais les réformes du XIXe siècle n'aboutirent pas à la création d'un code[27].

Pourtant à cette époque, un juriste, historien et homme politique éminent, Lord Thomas B. Macaulay, persuadé lui aussi que le droit anglais, en particulier le droit pénal, était désuet et barbare, fut à l'origine de la rédaction d'un code célèbre. Nommé en 1833 en Inde, comme président de la première commission chargée de réformer le droit indien qui se tint à Calcutta, il y prit une part active. La commission mit en valeur le concept de *lex loci*, de loi applicable à tous sur le territoire ('General Territorial Law'), dont fait partie le droit pénal, par opposition aux autres droits, statuts personnels variés, suivant la religion et droits coutumiers locaux. La rédaction de la partie pénale, due Lord Macaulay, était avancée. Si ce droit empruntait la forme codifiée au droit français, son contenu était un résumé cohérent des solutions de la 'common law' (1840). Pourtant les conclusions de la commission ne furent pas suivies : l'adoption du droit musulman et hindou suscitait de graves objections, autant que le principe de la codification pour le droit anglais.

D'autres commission se réunirent en 1853-61 et 1861-70. Elles rédigèrent entre autres un code de procédure pénale (1859), et un code pénal (1860) lequel reprenait le projet de Macaulay et le travail fut révisé de nombreuses fois[28] jusqu'en 1898. Ce sont ces codes que Lord Cromer demanda en trois exemplaires au Foreign Office en décembre 1898.

Dans le Rapport de 1899, Lord Cromer décrit ainsi ces codes : "(le code pénal) est une adaptation en forme simplifiée du code pénal indien, qui a déjà été employé avec succès à Zanzibar et dans les protectorats de l'Est africain. Le code de procédure pénale est partiellement basé sur le code indien, mais eu égard au fait que les magistrats sont tous des officiers, les formes et les méthodes de la loi militaire qui leur sont familières, et qui sont elles-mêmes une adaptation de la loi militaire anglaise, ont été, dans la mesure du possible, retenues"[29].

C'est W. Brunyate qui effectua ces adaptations. Les caractéristiques originelles demeurèrent. En particulier Brunyate conserva les "illustrations", c'est-à-dire les exemples simples et clairs qui explicitaient l'objectif de la loi. L'idée venait de Bentham et avait été heureusement réalisée par Macaulay. Les codes étaient ainsi extrêmement clairs et faciles d'emploi. Les risques d'erreur étaient réduits au minimum.

Macaulay lui-même a écrit que le code pénal indien était inspiré du code Napoléon et du code de Louisiane. René David reconnaît l'influence française et aussi celle du droit écossais[30]. Gledhill pense au contraire que ces influences sont superficielles et que le code indien est surtout une excellente codification du droit anglais[31]. Quant au code soudanais, Cromer écrit dans le rapport de 1904, qu'il n'est "ni britannique, ni indien, ni français, ni en vérité complètement marqué par les caractéristiques du système en vigueur dans aucun autre pays. C'était un projet qui pouvait être correctement appelé soudanais, dans la mesure où il avait été vraiment établi avec le point de vue d'être adapté aux exigences du Soudan"[32].

Nous ne pouvons pas nous étendre sur le contenu de ce code. Indiquons seulement son sens général à partir de l'exemple de l'esclavage. L'article 11 du traité de Condominium disposait que : "l'importation et l'exportation des esclaves au Soudan sont absolument interdites". Ce texte fut repris dans le code (P.C. 1899, s. 288-290.) (= P.C. 1925, s. 311-315)[33], mais il n'interdisait pas la possession desdits esclaves. De cette disposition on peut déduire d'abord que les Britanniques étaient décidés à transformer les moeurs et usages du Soudan dans le sens qui correspondait à leur conception dominante de la justice et de la civilisation. Ensuite qu'ils entendaient procéder avec souplesse et prudence, puisque la possession d'esclaves n'était pas formellement condamnée. Toute leur politique pénale était là.

Dans le cas du Soudan, de multiples problèmes se posaient et les réponses furent données au fur et à mesure qu'ils se présentaient. Sans détailler tout cela, signalons deux choix non négligeables, mais imposés par les circonstances : le pouvoir législatif fut remis au gouverneur général et l'application du droit pénal à l'administration (militaire dans les débuts).

## Les réactions du sud

### *Les débuts*

L'histoire de la région est celle d'une conquête faite au moyen d'expéditions punitives contre des populations surtout occupées à poursuivre leurs guerres tribales. Le code pénal ne devait pas s'appliquer au Sud dans les débuts. La mise en place d'un droit pénal se fit de manière très anarchique. Par exemple le gouverneur de Mongalla établit sa propre échelle de peines, où la courbache (fouet de cuir d'hippopotame) jouait le premier rôle. Il y eut quelques remous à Khartoum, quand on rapporta qu'une femme avait subi des coups[34]. Les gouverneurs et inspecteurs du Sud Ouest cherchèrent à retrouver le droit coutumier, en particulier le droit dinka. Dès cette époque on note que les chefs locaux se sont vus confirmer des pouvoirs pénaux (avec des limitations variables) anticipant ainsi la 'native policy'.

Mais ce qui importe ici c'est le fait qu'en dépit des guerres et des troubles de l'époque, un dialogue se soit engagé. On assistait à une "nilotisation" de la justice[35], puisque la compensation pour meurtre fut progressivement admise. Pour le vol, ce fut plus difficile : au début les Britanniques ne comprirent pas que certaines formes de vol de bétail n'étaient qu'une manière de poser une contestation civile. Se faire justice soi-même ('self-help') était une nécessité chez les Nuer et les Dinka en l'absence de tribunaux réguliers. En 1909, devant un tribunal coutumier dinka, un homme convaincu de vol se vit accorder ce qu'il avait pris plus un taureau pour sa peine ! L'inspecteur (qu'on appellera plus tard District Commissioner, D.C.) soupçonna un favoritisme, cassa la décision, ordonna la restitution et infligea une amende au voleur. C'était évidemment une erreur, une injustice envers le condamné qui n'était pas un voleur mais un créancier[36]. Par la suite, au fur et à mesure que la logique juridique des Nilotiques était mieux comprise, on laissa faire les tribunaux coutumiers

Dans les monts Nuba, au début, seuls les Arabes vinrent apporter leurs affaires à juger aux inspecteurs. Les Nuba étaient hostiles et les *mekk* (rois) et *kujur* (prêtres) interdisaient tout recours à l'arbitrage des Anglo-Egyptiens. Les Nuba refusèrent de renoncer aux guerres intertribales, de payer l'impôt et même de conclure quelque accord de compensation ou de restitution de prisonniers arabes. Une des causes majeures de leur refus de se soumettre était, qu'après avoir payé l'impôt en échange de la protection promise, ils s'estimaient floués par le gouvernement si quelque tribu les attaquait, et libres de contre-attaquer.

Dans la cuvette du Haut Nil, à l'exception des Shilluk, les rapports des Britanniques avec les populations étaient placés sous le signe des guerres tribales avec les Dinka[37] (et plus tard avec les Nuer[38]), le même malentendu sur le rôle de l'impôt et l'étendue de la protection due par les Britanniques se posa. Les troupes gouvernementales s'efforçaient de punir chaque attaquant par des expéditions punitives, mais elles étaient parfois presque battues, comme ce fut le cas en 1912 pour l'expédition montée contre les Anuak. Les Britanniques se heurtèrent aussi à divers prophètes nuer ou dinka. Il semble que ces personnages avaient entamé un processus de création de pouvoirs politiques dans ces sociétés acéphales. D. Johnson écrit : "Ngundeng en particulier avait adopté un idéal social qui condamnait les guerres entre sections et les raids nuer contre les autres peuples. Sa divinité, Deng, disait-on, interdisait la guerre". Plus loin : "il établit un précédent par lequel une autorité unique pouvait prétendre avoir le droit de régler des conflits sur une zone qui transcendait les limites politiques. Les Nuer modernes ont vu le parallèle et font des comparaisons très explicites entre l'oeuvre de Ngundeng et celle du gouvernement"[39].

Bien sûr, on ne peut parler d'application du code pénal. Localement, comme dans le nord du pays nuer, des inspecteurs effectuaient un travail solitaire, en consultant de manière irrégulière des anciens ou des prêtres (chef à peau de léopard chez les Nuer par exemple), mais ils appliquaient un droit coutumier[40]. De même en pays dinka. En 1920, la situation juridique des pays du Sud était toujours peu différente[41] de ce qu'elle avait été au siècle précédent, mais la paix s'établit à partir de cette date et amena un réel changement de situation avec l'intensification de la 'native policy'.

### *Les tribunaux coutumiers*

Ce n'est qu'en 1931, que les Britanniques officialisèrent les tribunaux coutumiers du Sud ('Chiefs' courts'). La justice pénale avait désormais deux niveaux, celui des tribunaux coutumiers traitant les nombreuses petites affaires, et celui des tribunaux ordinaires pour les affaires graves. Il semble que ces institutions furent bien acceptées dans toute la zone à l'époque, surtout après que, sur les indications des anthropologues, les gouverneurs réussirent mieux à identifier les chefs réels à qui remettre la gestion desdits tribunaux. Les D.C. pouvaient se décharger d'une bonne partie de leur travail, en particulier de toutes les petites affaires civiles ennuyeuses (contestation sur les dettes de bétail), d'autant plus qu'elles devenaient de plus en plus nombreuses : les Nuer jouèrent le jeu et même trop bien. Le D.C. devint un élément des institutions nuer, il reçut un nom de boeuf comme un vrai Nuer, il fut salué par tous, loué (et critiqué) par les chefs[42].

Dans les années 1940 on organisa entre les chefs tribaux et les D.C. des districts[43] nuer diverses réunions pour introduire quelque régularité dans le droit coutumier, en particulier pour uniformiser les taux de compensation. On chercha aussi à rationaliser l'organisation judiciaire et à réunir les tribunaux en des conseils administratifs qui seraient soumis à une assemblée législative de tout le Nuerland. Cet objectif est à replacer dans la politique des années 1940 visant à créer partout au Soudan des conseils consultatifs. Mais ce ne fut qu'après la publication du rapport Marshall (1948) et la mise en route de la politique qui s'en est ensuivie qu'un système de conseils administratifs de district fut entrepris. Cette tâche commença réellement la séparation du judiciaire et de l'administratif.

La rencontre entre le droit anglais et le droit coutumier se fit d'abord et surtout, on ne le remarque jamais assez, dans la condamnation et le refus de la vengeance[44]. Ici les lignes sociales les plus antiques (la coutume substituant la compensation à la guerre), les aspirations religieuses anciennes (prêtre à peau de léopard) et nouvelles (prophétisme, islam), se rejoignaient dans l'acceptation des tribunaux du colonisateur pour refouler la vengeance. Le problème ne fut plus que celui de savoir comment articuler cette compensation (*diya* en droit musulman) avec la peine. Le résultat, tel qu'il apparaît dans les dernières circulaires du Chief Justice, est loin d'être satisfaisant. Quoiqu'il en soit, les deux systèmes de droit, l'anglais et le coutumier, s'ils avaient fait chemin ensemble contre la vendetta, ne se rejoignirent pas vraiment sur la compensation envers les victimes d'infraction. Les deux systèmes avaient des défauts évidents, chacun des deux avait besoin de récupérer chez l'autre ce qui lui manquait, le "sens criminel" pour l'un, le "sens de la victime" pour l'autre.

Un autre aspect de la rencontre entre les deux droits est la fixation des coutumes. Le gouvernement central avait quelquefois mis en garde les administrateurs contre une fixation prématurée de la coutume, mais par la force des besoins les gouverneurs et inspecteurs continuèrent leur mise par écrit[45]. Dans la pensée des tenants de la 'native policy', il ne fallait pas briser cet avantage du droit coutumier traditionnel, sa souplesse. Hamilton écrit : "il n'est pas nécessairement souhaitable de régulariser tout de suite les coutumes non contestables en leur donnant une sanction légale. Cette régularisation peut souvent produire une stabilisation de coutumes qui pourraient évoluer vers quelque chose de mieux d'ici vingt ans"[46]. Le fait est qu'on ne s'est pas empressé de rédiger des coutumiers et qu'on a laissé, surtout dans les années trente, les coutumes se décanter en quelque sorte. Il est remarquable que les études juridiques les plus approfondies sur les coutumes des tribus ne se situent pas entre 1930 et 1940, dans la période de la 'native policy', mais, même dans la revue Sudan Notes and Records, avant 1930 ou après 1940. Toutefois la création de tribunaux coutumiers, l'enregistrement écrit des décisions et le contrôle par les autorités administratives du travail des tribunaux conduisaient nécessairement à une fixation du droit coutumier, si ce n'est à une invention d'un droit prétendument coutumier. Ces deux derniers points (fixation, invention) doivent être examinés.

Howell pense à propos des Nuer[47], en discutant Evans-Pritchard, qu'il est vrai de dire que les tribunaux à l'époque de la colonisation ont appliqué le droit coutumier au-delà de ce qu'il était appliqué dans le passé, en fixant ce qui n'avait pas vocation à être fixé. Ils ont donné force de loi à ce qui n'était qu'idéal, indicatif. Il en donne l'exemple suivant chez les Nuer : la compensation matrimoniale, fut, sur ordre des tribunaux, retournée par les parents au beau-fils dans le cas où leur fille était décédée sans avoir rempli son "contrat" de procréation. Il est certes douteux que cette coutume ait été suivie aussi rigidement dans le passé, mais les tribunaux coutumiers l'ont fait appliquer, et seulement en cas de plainte d'ailleurs. La pratique la plus courante, celle d'autrefois comme celle des temps plus récents, se comprend à partir des liens d'affection existants entre les deux familles, de leur peine commune dans le deuil qui les accablait. Les beaux-parents donnaient (et donnent encore) à leur beau-fils un certain nombre de bêtes, ce qu'ils pouvaient, sans formalisme, eu égard soit à la nécessité de son remariage, soit à celle de l'entretien des enfants (même si donc le "contrat" avait été rempli).

Mais si l'on pense que le droit coutumier développé par les tribunaux coutumiers est sans rapport avec le droit ancien, Howell s'inscrit en faux. D'une part ce droit a sa source dans les principes du droit nuer et il s'agit d'un développement naturel; d'autre part les nouveautés, même suggérées par l'administration anglaise ont été admises par les diverses conférences des chefs nuer, dans les années 1940, pour répondre à des situations précises.

On peut déceler quelques effets de la rigidification du droit. Les nouveaux tribunaux rendirent les dettes plus sûres. Par exemple même les petits paiements dus aux divers prêtres nuer (il y a une petite dizaine de spécialistes outre le prêtre à peau de léopard) furent rendus obligatoires, la coutume ou l'usage devenant droit. Autre effet, la multiplication des procès, car les Nuer ne renoncent jamais : une même affaire était représentée sans cesse, encombrant les tribunaux. Dans d'autre cas, on assista à une augmentation des infractions. L'adultère, par exemple, était jadis rare, parce que l'amant craignait surtout une vengeance; s'il payait la compensation, c'était par crainte d'un mauvais coup. Sous le Condominium, on ne craignait plus le mauvais coup, et l'adultère devint plus fréquent, même si la certitude de devoir payer une compensation devint plus forte.

On peut aussi faire l'hypothèse que les concepts et les solutions du code pénal se sont immiscés dans le droit coutumier. A la fin de la période coloniale d'ailleurs, le code était devenu d'usage courant, quoique non obligatoire, dans les tribunaux coutumiers[48]. Howell parle aussi, à propos des Nuer, de "mélange de concepts juridiques" et évoque l'introduction du code pénal[49], soit par des administrateurs anglais, soit par les chefs nuer, et pas de manière cohérente, mais il ne développe pas. Il est probable encore que les chefs, nuer et autres, n'ont pas toujours eu une perception très nette de la cohérence de leur droit, ni de la nécessité d'éviter les contradictions. Le plus souvent les juges indigènes ne comprenaient pas très à fond la philosophie pénale anglaise. Par exemple, qu'à un même acte on puisse appliquer des peines différentes, en raison des circonstances, les rendait sceptiques. Ils avaient pris l'habitude de donner le tarif maximum, pensant que, s'il y avait injustice, la faute en rejaillirait sur les Britanniques et pas sur eux. Selon Howell[50], ils étaient contre l'application de peines en sus de la compensation, mais son témoignage ne porte que sur la situation au début des années quarante.

La réaction des populations au droit pénal général anglais fut surtout l'incompréhension. Un rapport de B. Carter le signalait dès 1904 : la prison apparaît absurdement douce, de manière générale, aux Soudanais[51]. Les Nuer[52], selon Howell, ne comprirent pas toujours pourquoi, la compensation ayant été payée, il fallait aussi subir la prison. Ils n'attachèrent aucun caractère infamant à la condamnation. Certaines peines pour meurtre intra-familial leur apparaissaient absurdes : le mari n'avait-il pas commis une sorte de suicide ? Selon F.M. Deng, la réaction des Dinka à la police, aux peines de fouet et à l'emprisonnement fut l'indignation[53]. La résistance à l'action de la police était normale, une question d'honneur. Mais au moment de l'indépendance, les peines infligées par le gouvernement[54] étaient admises comme ne pouvant donner lieu à vengeance, et il fallait les supporter avec courage, mais sans honte, la honte ne pouvant venir que du viol des valeurs traditionnelles. L'effet dissuasif de la peine de prison resta faible, même en matière de meurtre. Encore récemment un condamné à mort dinka, au reçu de sa sentence, se mit à chanter des chants de guerre dans le prétoire[55].

On a quelques documents intéressants à placer dans le contexte de la controverse des années 1950 à propos de la *diya*, mais qui se répondent sur la question de savoir si les tribunaux coutumiers savaient distinguer compensation et peine[56]. Dans une lettre, Abu Rannat, alors inspecteur des tribunaux coutumiers (dits 'Local Courts', le mot 'local' remplaçant 'native'), dans le but de rappeler que la compétence desdits tribunaux ne s'étendait pas aux affaires d'homicide[57], écrivit, en 1949, une circulaire aux gouverneurs et D.C. , où il s'appuyait sur l'idée que les membres des 'Chiefs' Courts' ne pouvaient "vraiment mesurer la force de la dissuasion si leur idée de la peine est principalement soucieuse de régler le paiement de la compensation". Les gouverneurs n'étaient pas de cet avis. T.R.H. Owen, le gouverneur du Bahr Al Ghazal, écrivait que "les tribunaux (coutumiers) sont en train de perdre rapidement leur tradition et d'acquérir un "sens criminel". Toujours en 1949, H.A. Nicholson, gouverneur d'Equatoria, avait écrit : "C'est devenu une pratique commune pour les tribunaux indigènes, quand ils jugent des affaires où des personnes ont été tuées, d'infliger une peine d'emprisonnement en sus du paiement du prix du sang (on devrait dire à côté du paiement). Cette peine est infligée à l'individu ou aux individus qui ont réellement commis l'infraction et constitue leur punition pour le rôle qu'ils ont joué, tandis que le paiement du prix du sang est une expiation payée par le groupe. Ceci est un développement naturel de la reconnaissance de la responsabilité individuelle, et comme vous le savez bien, il n'y a pas de réduction proportionnelle du montant du prix du sang pour contrebalancer la période d'emprisonnement attribuée..."

Ainsi les derniers gouverneurs britanniques témoignaient que l'essentiel du droit pénal général britannique avait été admis au Sud Soudan, du moins au niveau des chefs chargés de leur application. Il semble d'ailleurs tout à fait général qu'un écart subsiste entre le juge et le justiciable sur la compréhension d'une philosophie pénale : peut-on dire en Occident que tout le monde comprend bien ce que font nos juges ?

## Les réactions du nord

### *Le droit pénal musulman*

Quand Lord Cromer promit en 1899 qu'aucune atteinte ne serait portée contre la religion islamique, un des notables présent demanda si la garantie de la liberté religieuse incluait l'application de la loi islamique et Lord Cromer assura que c'était bien le cas[58]. Etait-ce un mensonge, alors qu'il avait demandé au Foreign Office quelques mois plus tôt qu'on lui fournisse les codes indiens ? Il ne semble pas. Il faut revenir un peu sur ce que nous avons déjà souligné et bien se replacer dans les conditions de l'époque.

Dans l'ensemble de l'islam ou presque, en tout cas dans ses deux pays phares, la Turquie et l'Egypte, le droit pénal musulman n'existait plus et parler du maintien de la *charî'a* signifiait très précisément maintenir le statut personnel. On a eu l'occasion d'évoquer la situation du droit pénal dans le monde musulman, et notamment en Egypte du XIXe siècle[59]. Une longue tradition existait et en particulier dans l'Empire ottoman, tendant à refouler l'application du droit pénal islamique, non pour des motifs humanitaires, mais parce qu'il était lacunaire et reposait sur un système de police et de tribunaux inefficaces dans une société complexe. Au XIXe siècle, en Egypte, un droit pénal autochtone s'était développé sous l'impulsion de Muhammad Alî et de ses successeurs. On avait déja admis la réception du droit français pour les tribunaux mixtes, lors de la réforme de 1876. Dans l'Empire ottoman, le droit français fut aussi reçu en 1858. Mais le fait essentiel est qu'aucune tentative de codification ou de réforme du droit pénal musulman classique ne fut faite, ce qui n'était pas le cas pour le droit civil où plusieurs codifications furent réalisées. En Egypte, quand il fut question de rédiger le code pénal indigène, les ulémas furent consultés par le khédive Tawfîq, mais ils refusèrent de rédiger ce code[60], c'est pourquoi on copia bravement le code pénal mixte, d'inspiration française. A la fin du XIXe siècle, ni en Egypte, ni dans l'Empire ottoman il n'était possible de trouver le moindre juge de droit musulman compétent en matière pénale. Quant aux réformistes, ils étaient pour l'heure incapables de proposer quoi que ce soit et encore moins en matière pénale. Dans la terminologie juridique égyptienne, et toujours à l'heure actuelle, le terme "droit musulman" renvoyait essentiellement au droit du statut personnel des musulmans[61].

Donc Lord Cromer ne mentait pas, il se conformait à l'usage égyptien. Si l'on ajoute son expérience indienne, on comprend mieux encore le refus du droit musulman. En Inde en effet, les Britanniques avaient longuement respecté les coutumes. Leurs craintes vis-à-vis de l'interdiction de la coutume indienne dite du *suttee*, où la veuve était quasiment contrainte par son entourage de se jeter dans le bûcher funéraire du mari décédé, se révélèrent sans fondement, en dépit des avis des orientalistes[62] qui se bousculaient pour les retenir. En effet, quand ils interdirent le *suttee* (en 1829-1830), ils eurent affaire certes à une opposition conservatrice, mais aussi à l'appui d'hindouistes réformateurs. La population ne manifesta aucun sentiment hostile, comme si elle était satisfaite de la décision ou indifférente. Cela, Lord Cromer le savait, par son expérience indienne.

En matière de droit pénal musulman, la même politique avait été suivie. Les tribunaux dits *mofassal*, c'est-à-dire ceux de la Compagnie des Indes avant la réforme de 1860, devaient appliquer le droit musulman, y compris en matière pénale. Mais, ils devaient se conformer aussi à la "justice, à l'équité et à la bonne conscience"[63], et ils écartèrent donc les peines corporelles barbares (lapidation, mutilations) ainsi que le système de la compensation pécuniaire pour un meurtre. En cela ils furent appuyés par divers règlements et textes plus généraux (comme le "code Cornwallis" de 1793), dont la majeure partie avait été faite au XVIIIe siècle. Quand le code pénal indien remplaça le droit pénal musulman dans les zones mofassal, ledit droit pénal musulman n'était que l'ombre de lui-même[64].

Au Soudan pourtant, le droit pénal musulman avait été appliqué jusqu'au dernier jours du calife Abd Allâh. Le droit musulman avait été réformé par le Mahdî, et cette réforme ne pouvait avoir un grand avenir, en raison du système de légitimation musulman par le Coran et la sunna, système que le Mahdî avait conservé[65]. De toute façon, la reprise du droit mahdiste par Lord Cromer était impossible parce que toute la philosophie de la reconquête anglo-égyptienne était anti-mahdiste. La propagande anglaise, et en particulier R. Wingate et son subordonné Slatin Pacha, présentait le mahdisme comme un épisode barbare, comme une régression, même vis-à-vis de la colonisation égyptienne. Du point de vue des Egyptiens, associés dans le Condominium, le mahdisme était une hérésie, et c'est au nom de la lutte contre l'hérésie que la reconquête avait été entreprise. Politiquement, l'adoption du droit mahdiste était totalement impossible : une rupture était nécessaire. Cromer écrira dans son rapport de 1904: "Quand se produisit l'occupation du pays, aucun système de justice civile ou criminelle, digne de ce nom, n'existait, ni non plus aucun Soudanais n'avait une formation juridique de quelque nature que ce soit."[66]

Ce phénomène de la disparition du droit pénal musulman est très important. Il explique pourquoi les partisans de la *charî'a* n'ont pu proposer, à la fin du XXe que des solutions moyennâgeuses, alors qu'en matière civile le droit islamique que l'on propose est plus travaillé et peut même être au niveau des droits occidentaux (cf le code civil de Sanhûri par exemple).

Le Nord était la zone où les Anglo-Egyptiens craignaient surtout des révoltes mahdistes. Il y en eut environ une dizaine, d'importance variable, toutes tuées dans l'oeuf. Il est difficile de les considérer autrement que comme des réactions individuelles ou marginales, puisque la Mahdiya en tant que telle ne s'engagea jamais au côté d'aucune d'entre elles. Les expéditions militaires furent assez nombreuses, non seulement contre les mahdistes, mais contre les tribus ou fractions de tribu qui s'agitaient, par exemple Misîrîya, Kabâbish, Hadendowa[67]. Slatin Pacha poussait à une politique dure, avec châtiments collectifs, arrestations ou pendaisons des chefs[68]. A l'inverse du Sud, le Nord fut parfaitement dominé.

Les populations sédentaires entrèrent dans le système judiciaire très naturellement. Le rapport de 1902 constata que les sédentaires rapportaient très vite l'existence d'un crime, à l'inverse des nomades qui réglaient leurs affaires selon des voies traditionnelles[69]. Mais il est certain aussi, que, en milieu sédentaire, pour nombre d'affaires mineures, les Soudanais cherchaient à régler leurs affaires par des voies traditionnelles[70]. En 1904, B. Carter soulignait que "le même crime, s'il est commis par un noir soudanais, un Arabe ja'aliyîn, un nomade Kabâbish ne sera probablement pas équitablement puni par la même punition"[71]. Dans les prisons, les condamnés pouvaient faire des comparaisons et on enregistrait des plaintes sur l'injustice du système[72]. Au Kordofan et au Darfur les autorités avaient officiellement renoncé à appliquer le code pénal, et la justice se faisait suivant des voies coutumières, ce qui était déja une 'native policy'. Il en fut de même au Dâr Masalit quand la convention anglo-française le rattacha au Soudan anglo-égyptien en 1919. Il est certain que très tôt, quoiqu'on n'en puisse pas préciser la date[73], le système pénal ordinaire lui-même, en matière de meurtre et de vol en particulier, faisait droit aux coutumes et à la compensation dans les tribus[74]. Une "bédouinisation" de la justice en quelque sorte, parallèle à sa "nilotisation" dans le Sud.

On peut donc dire que le code pénal a été appliqué dans le Nord au niveau supérieur de la justice (dans les tribunaux réguliers). Au niveau inférieur, avant l'intervention de la police, la coutume s'est largement maintenue, surtout dans les campagnes et plus encore chez les nomades. Cette coutume tendait même à refouler le droit régulier, nombre d'affaires graves ayant été retenues par le niveau coutumier. Toutefois le droit pénal musulman n'étant pas reconnu, les ulémas et chefs de confréries semblant eux aussi l'oublier, la question de sa mise à jour et de sa conciliation avec le droit anglais ne fut jamais posée. Il y a eu certes un dialogue au Nord, essentiellement entre les coutumes bédouines et le droit anglais, mais aussi sur deux autres questions, l'esclavage et l'excision.

Les Britanniques, au début du Condominium, étaient absolument persuadés que le Mahdisme était la conséquence directe de la suppression de l'esclavage et que, s'ils libéraient brutalement tous les esclaves, ils ne manqueraient pas d'avoir à faire face à un mouvement de fond de même nature. Ce raisonnement est net encore quand, dans l'affaire de Talodi, en 1906, une révolte des Arabes eut lieu après la libération d'une centaine d'esclaves, et que les responsables locaux voulurent justifier[75] la répression qui fut faite.

En 1922, le département de lutte contre l'esclavage fut supprimé[76]. On le sut plus tard, cette suppression relança le trafic. Mais parmi les administrateurs britanniques, tout le monde n'était pas d'accord sur la politique trop conciliante de Khartoum. En 1923-1924, P.G.W. Diggle, inspecteur agricole à Berber, et T. P. Creed, A.D.C. de Berber, farouchement hostiles à l'esclavage, après avoir en vain averti leurs supérieurs, prévinrent l'honorable 'Anti-Slavery Society'. On était alors en pleine crise égypto-britannique, et ce fut le scandale. Avant la fin de l'année le gouvernement dut prendre des mesures, et "rappeler" que les esclaves en fuite n'avaient pas à être ramenés à leurs maîtres. La Chambre des Lords débattit de l'affaire en décembre 1924, et au début de 1925, le 'Legal Secretary', Wasey Sterry, dans une circulaire énonça que le droit à la liberté des esclaves était absolu. La réaction du 'Grand Kadi' et des trois sayyids fut négative, au nom de l'islam[77]. A l'extérieur, la campagne s'intensifiait et débouchait à la S.D.N. sur la convention de Genève (1926) que le gouvernement soudanais dut signer en 1927. Diverses révélations furent faites sur le trafic qui continuait au Soudan. Il ne restait plus au gouvernement soudanais qu'à lancer une campagne de répression active. Les Ruf'a Al Hoi par exemple furent restreints dans leurs mouvements, et sommés de rendre leurs esclaves : ils en remirent 532 et presque tous quittèrent les Rufa'a[78]. On signala des mécontentements chez les Misîrîya et les Hamar. Il n'y eut pas de soulèvement général. En 1930, il était possible de dire que l'esclavage avait pratiquement disparu du Soudan.

Dans le monde islamique[79] tous les Etats, sauf l'Arabie séoudite et le Yémen, adhérèrent à la convention de Genève dans les années 1930. L'Arabie séoudite tout en maintenant la licéité du principe interdisait partiellement l'importation. Le congrès panislamique de la Mecque, en 1936, condamna l'esclavage. On observe la même relecture de l'islam à propos de l'excision.

Encore dans les années 1920, presque tous les Soudanais et Soudanaises pensaient que la circoncision pharaonique était une nécessité religieuse. Les *hadîth* (dires du Prophète) soutenant la tradition sont faibles[80], mais on sait que cela n'empêche pas une institution de se maintenir, tant que la volonté de l'abolir ne prédomine pas. Voici ces *hadîth*[81] : "La circoncision est ma voie pour l'homme, mais elle ennoblit la femme". "La circoncision est douloureuse pour la femme, mais elle plaît à l'homme". "Circoncis, mais ne va pas trop loin, parce que c'est mieux pour l'apparence et que cela donne du plaisir à l'homme". Comme pour l'esclavage, la coutume est constatée, admise sans plus, mais pas interdite. Le Prophète, si tant est qu'il ait prononcé ces paroles, aurait cherché à la limiter, mais dans une mesure imprécise et par une simple recommandation. Comme pour l'esclavage, une seconde lecture de l'islam était nécessaire.

Les autorités britanniques à l'époque de la 'native policy' furent timides, elles étaient prêtes à admettre la coutume, par souci de conciliation, quoiqu'elles pensaient que ladite coutume était barbare. On peut leur reprocher d'avoir trop cédé à l'esprit local. Ce sont les femmes, anglaises d'abord et soudanaises ensuite et surtout, qui ont mené le combat pour ce droit de la femme. Elles ont forcé les musulmans à faire une relecture de l'islam pour l'accommoder avec une vision nouvelle de la morale, puisqu'à la fin des années quarante on trouve les autorités religieuses avec le gouvernement contre l'excision "pharaonique" (la plus dangereuse).

## Conclusion

Le droit traditionnel et le droit colonial, en dépit des quelques éléments de continuité que nous avons soulignés, constituent bien des systèmes juridiques de nature différente. Mais ces éléments de continuité, pour mineurs qu'ils soient, ont permis une acceptation assez large du droit colonial anglais, au point d'ailleurs que l'expression même que nous utilisons pour le désigner "droit colonial anglais" apparaîtra critiquable aux juristes soudanais.

Les critiques soudanaises contre le système juridique légué par les Anglais sont rares. On en souligne le caractère importé et impérialiste, surtout pour justifier l'adoption d'autres systèmes, système arabe unioniste et socialiste (Babiker Awadallah) ou système néo-islamique. Pour l'historien du droit l'argument a peu de poids, tous les systèmes sont importés, peu ou prou, plus ou moins anciennement[82]. La quasi-totalité du système arabo-égyptien qu'on a voulu en 1971 est importée aussi, et plus des trois quarts du code pénal néo-islamique (versions 1983 ou 1991) sont aussi d'origine étrangère. Quant à l'étiquette d' "impérialiste", elle vise une situation générale incontestable, mais son application à la question proprement juridique est cependant trop imprécise.

A l'inverse les louanges envers le système légué ne manquent pas. On se bornera aux plus célèbres, Zaki Mustafa et F.M. Deng. Le premier réagit vertement aux tentatives de 1971 d'arabiser le droit civil et pénal. Il écrit à propos de ce dernier[83] : "En adoptant un système légal d'origine française[84] ... nous allons enterrer un héritage juridique qui a été construit à travers un processus continuel d'expérimentation tout au long des 73 dernières années et laisser un système de droit qui nous a servi de manière assez ('fairly') satisfaisante pendant cette période et dont les défauts et les insuffisances que nous connaissons peuvent être facilement corrigés... Nous allons trahir la possibilité de jamais développer un jeu de règles légales vraiment soudanaises, processus qui a déjà accompli un départ assez ('fairly') impressionnant dans le cadre du système de la 'common law' qui existait avant l'introduction de ces codes..." Pour Zaki Mustafa le système légué a surtout l'avantage d'être issu de l'expérience, d'être modifiable et adaptable aux réalités soudanaises.

Le second auteur, plus sensible aux aspirations du Sud, réagit aussi contre le mouvement d'arabisation et d'islamisation. Il écrit : "Le système légal du Soudan, tel qu'il est actuellement[85], a les fondations faites par un ingénieux architecte. Il l'a soigneusement conçu pour que cohabitent amicalement le droit islamique, le droit coutumier et le droit général importé. Cette structure fournit les principaux éléments nécessaires pour un développement vers une fusion harmonieuse. Savoir si ce système atteindra correctement ces buts dépend du peuple qui le fera fonctionner." Pour F.M. Deng, le système est surtout un équilibre honnête entre les composantes du Soudan (islamique et non islamique) et la modernité, équilibre qui offre à l'avenir toutes les perspectives d'une "fusion harmonieuse".

En dépit des aléas politiques, des "bavures", et de diverses insuffisances, le système anglais s'est toujours efforcé de tenir compte et des droits de l'homme et des cultures juridiques soudanaises. Depuis Brunyate et Cromer, il n'est question que d'adapter, de rejoindre le "sentiment indigène de la justice". On admet la polygamie, on admet le prix du sang, on admet même longtemps l'esclavage et la circoncision pharaonique. L'esprit victorien ne préside pas au système légué. Mais il a une limite : on ne peut pas admettre ce qui est 'repugnant'. Les coutumes ont été admises tant qu'elles n'allaient pas contre l'ordre public, la moralité, la justice, conçus d'ailleurs de manière large. Certes ces concepts sont vagues, comme l'est aussi la formule "justice, equity and good conscience", vagues comme le sens moral que s'efforcent d'exprimer les droits de l'homme et qui n'est pas absent de la société traditionnelle. Ce vague a pour but de préserver les droits de la réalité concrète des hommes autant que les droits de l'avenir. C'est peut-être ce qu'il y a d'essentiel dans le système anglais et qui n'est pas inscrit dans les textes : le respect des réalités allié à une certaine affection envers les hommes et leur vie quotidienne. Plus d'une fois les historiens qui sont entrés dans le détail des faits locaux ont souligné que chaque D.C. réagissait avec "sa" tribu contre Khartoum, comme Gordon avec "ses" noirs contre Le Caire ou Londres. Paternalisme, bien sûr. Mais ce concret des attitudes paternalistes fait problème, il n'est pas réductible à une théorie simple. Que révèlent et que cachent ces "liens de soie" entre Anglais et Soudanais[86] ? Seulement exploitation et profit capitaliste ?

La méfiance envers les théories, envers les 'lawyers', envers les déclarations de principe, est une composante essentielle du système anglais, ce qui nous a amené à penser que le refus des 'reports' avait été voulu. L'organisation judiciaire fut complexe, et là encore, il est possible que le dédale ait été institué pour préserver les droits du cas particulier. Cette souplesse avait certes ses inconvénients. Le droit était imprévisible, en matière civile surtout, et plus d'un juge ou d'un avocat a pesté de se voir opposer un 'unreported case'. Cette situation était beaucoup moins préoccupante en matière pénale, puisque qu'un code était là pour les affaires graves. Ici d'ailleurs, l'activité législative n'a pas joué le rôle qui aurait du être le sien selon Macaulay[87], au point que l'on a dû avoir recours à des circulaires et à une jurisprudence. Mais peut-être est-il possible de penser que l'idéal de Macaulay était irréalisable et que la jurisprudence est le meilleur moyen de mettre la loi à jour. Une jurisprudence se renverse, une circulaire chasse l'autre, au point d'ailleurs qu'on ne retrouve plus les anciennes. Le recours constant à la législation a aussi l'immense inconvénient de faire du droit un enjeu politique, ou pire un prêche, situations malsaines pour ce qui doit être avant tout une technique de règlement des conflits, dans l'intérêt commun.

## Notes

1 Il n'existe dans la bibliographie qu'un seul ouvrage traitant de l'histoire des institutions judiciaires. Il s'agit de Hasân Sayyid Ahmad al Mufti, Tatawwur nizâmi l-qadâ' fî s-sûdân (Histoire du système judiciaire au Soudan), chez l'auteur, t. 1, 1959. L'ouvrage est déparé par divers partis pris dont le plus gênant est d'occulter ce qui n'est pas conforme à la théorie du *fiqh*. En revanche les articles de R.S. O'Fahey, The office of qâdî in Dâr Fûr : a preliminary enquiry. In : Bulletin of The School of Oriental and African Studies *XL*(1977)1, p. 110-124, et de J. Spaulding, The Evolution of the Islamic Judiciary in Sinnar. In : The International Journal of African History Studies *10*(1977)3, p. 406-426. offrent toutes les garanties. Il faut ajouter le mémoire de Olaf Köndgen, Das islamisierte Strafrecht des Sudan von seiner Einführung 1983 bis Dezember 1991; mémoire de magistère sous la direction du prof. Baber Johansen, Université libre de Berlin, 1992, qui offre un texte bref, dense et sûr pour sa partie historique. Des notations intéressantes aussi dans la partie historique de Carolyn Fluer-Lobban, Islamic Law an Society in the Sudan, Londres 1989. A ces travaux nous avons rajouté : Hervé Bleuchot, Cultures juridiques soudanaises et droits fondamentaux. Pour une anthropologie du droit musulman à travers l'histoire du droit pénal soudanais, Université d'Aix-Marseille 1993.

2 E. Tyan, Histoire de l'organisation judiciaire en pays d'islam, Amsterdam 1960.

3 Gustav Nachtigal, Sahara and Sudan, t. 4, Waddai and Darfur, traduit de l'allemand, Londres 1971. Le texte original date de 1889 pour la partie concernant le Darfour.

4 Livre ou écrit promulgué par Dali, un des premier monarque du Darfûr. Le Ktab Dali est réputé perdu. Toutefois, il est curieux qu'un des textes fournis à Arkell comme étant le Ktab Dali soit une mauvaise version du Mukhtasar de Khalîl. O'Fahey, The office..., p. 113, note 18. Si l'on tente quelque conjecture sur ce Ktab Dali, on peut avancer deux idées. En admettant qu'il n'ait pas été influencé par l'islam, ce ne pouvait être qu'un tarif de compensations et d'amendes, plus ou moins distribuées en face d'un petit nombre d'infractions, à l'image des coutumiers africains du Sud Soudan. Or on a remis à O'Fahey un tel tarif. C'est d'ailleurs peut être le texte que nous citons plus loin. Si au contraire l'influence de l'islam s'est faite sentir, le rédacteur a dû prendre pour modèle "le livre", c'est-à-dire non pas le Coran, mais le Mukhtasar de Khalil, dont on sait l'influence considérable qu'il a eu dans l'Afrique musulmane. Or on a remis aussi à O'Fahey un manuscrit altéré de Khalil. On peut

faire alors l'hypothèse que les deux testes remis à O' Fahey sont authentiques et constituent deux états du Ktab Dali. Evidemment c'est aux spécialistes de juger.

5 Al Mufti, op.cit., p. 60-61. Mais ce résumé peut avoir été contaminé par l'image qu'ont les musulmans de tout droit préislamique, image modelée sur le droit préislamique de l'Arabie.

6 Pièce de calicot qui servait de monnaie.

7 Coutume attestée par ailleurs, mais il doit s'agir de parents.

8 Les quelques pages assez vagues de Richard Hill, Egypt in the Sudan, Oxford 1959, p. 42-46. Sur le droit soudanais au XIXe sont toujours reprises par les auteurs. On y ajoute aussi la page 34-38 de Mustafa Zaki, The Common Law in the Sudan, Oxford 1971, qui reprend Hill mais rajoute quelques traits tirés de Gordon Pacha et décrit l'organisation judiciaire sous Isma'îl.

9 Hervé Bleuchot, Le droit pénal et les réformes en Egypte au XIXe siècle. In : Revue tunisienne de droit, *1-2*(1990) (paru en 1993), p. 117-147, et Cultures juridiques soudanaises, op. cit., p. 151-177.

10 Georges Douin, Histoire du règne de Moulay Isma'îl, t. III, L'empire africain, 1er vol. (1863-69), Le Caire 1936, p. 194.

11 Hervé Bleuchot, Signification de la réforme mahdiste du droit islamique, Second International Sudan Studies Conférence Papers, Durham 1991, p. 103-113.

12 "Les Nuer n'ont pas de droit au sens rigoureux du mot". E.E. Evans-Pritchard, Les Nuer, op. cit., p. 190, de l'édition française qui traduit à tort "law" par "lois".

13 Ibid., p. 198.

14 Raymond Kelly, The Nuer Conquest, The Structure and Development of an Expansionist System, Ann Arbor 1988, chapitre 3.

15 P.P. Howell, A Manual of Nuer Law, being an account of Customary Law, its Evolution and Development in the Courts established by the Sudan Government, Oxford 1954, reed. 1970, spécialement p. 99.

16 Howell, A Manual..., op. cit., p. 26.

17 G.H.Bousquet, Précis de droit musulman principalement malékite et algérien, Alger s.d. (1940 ?), p. 50.

18 G.H. Bousquet, Le droit musulman, Paris 1963, p. 38.

19 Ibid., p. 37.

20 Evans-Pritchard, The Nuer of the Southern Soudan. In: African Political System, ed. Evans-Pritchard/Fortes, Oxford 1940, p. 272-297, spécialement p. 294.

21 Le mahdisme est d'abord un réformisme, même si ses procédés de légitimation font qu'il anéantit toute réforme à terme. Bleuchot, Signification..., op. cit.

22 Travels in Africa 1875, Londres 1891, cité in: Evans-Pritchard, Rois et princes azandé, Les Anthropologues, op. cit., p. 118.

23 En raison de leur expérience coloniale. Voir Bleuchot, Cultures juridiques..., p. 263 sq. et Olawale Elias, British Colonial Law. A Comparative Study of the Interaction between English and Local Laws in Britain Dependencies, London 1962.

24 The Dictionary of National Biography, 1912-1921, Oxford University Press, p. 20-28.

25 A.V. Dicey, Lectures on the Relation between Law and the Public Opinion in England during the Nineteth Century, London 1920, p. 88sq.; L. Radzinowicz, A History of English Criminal Law and its Administration, vol. 1, London 1948.

26 Le nombre de crimes passibles de la peine de mort était réduit à huit à cette date. Radzinovicz, A History..., op. cit., vol. 4, p. 330. Sur la réforme de Peel, ibid., vol. 1, p. 567.

27 J.H. Baker, An Introduction to English Legal History, London 1971, chap. 23. Radzinowicz, A history..., vol. 5, p. 731, sur l'échec de la codification.

28 H.H. Dodwell, The Cambridge History of the British Empire, vol. V, The Indian Empire, 1858-1918 and Administration 1818-1858, Cambridge 1932, chap. 21, Law Reform, par Sir Francis Du Pré Olfield, p. 379-394. Lord Stephen était un partisan de la codification du droit anglais et l'auteur de divers projets dont un 'Digest of Criminal Law' qui ne fut jamais adopté par les Chambres anglaises. Radzinowicz, A History..., op. cit., vol. 5, p. 731.

29 Reports by His Majesty's agent and Consul-general on the Finances, Administration and conditions of Egypt and the Sudan, (1899-1919). Ici Rapport général, 1899, p. 52.

30 René David, Les grands systèmes de droit contemporain, Précis Dalloz 1973, spécialement p. 531, note 1.

31 Alan Gledhill, The Penal Codes of Northern Nigeria and the Sudan, London 1963, p. 17.

32 Cité par Guttman, The Reception of the Common Law in the Sudan. In : International and Comparative Law Quarterly, 1957, p. 405.

33 "P.C". signifie Penal Code; "s" signifie "section" (article). Nous n'avons pas à notre disposition le code pénal de 1899, introuvable à Khartoum, ni à la Faculté de droit, ni à la Cour Suprême, ni au Bureau de la Législation. Il n'existe pas non plus à la S.O.A.S. (Londres) ni aux Sudan Archives (Durham).

34 Gabriel Warburg, The Sudan under Wingate, 1899-1916, Londres 1971, p. 135. Le code de 1899 autorisait le fouet et la courbache pour les hommes seulement et pour un maximum de 25 coups. Cf. code 1925, art. 76 et 77.

35 Douglas Johnson, Judicial Regulation ans Administrative Control : Customary Law and the Nuer, 1898-1954. In : Journal of African History, (1986)27, p. 59-78.

36 Johnson, Judicial Regulations..., op. cit., p. 66.

37 G.N. Sanderson, Aspects of Resistance to British Rule in the Southern Sudan, 1900-1928. In : Etudes africaines offertes à Henri Brunschwig, EHESS 1982, p. 347-365.

38 Kelly, op. cit., p. 37 sq.

39 Johnson, op. cit., p. 61 et 77.

40 Howell, A Manual..., op. cit., p. 2.

41 Sanderson, op. cit., p. 348.

42 Howell, A Manual..., op. cit., p. 3.

43 Johnson, Judicial Regulation..., op. cit., p. 75 sq.

44 Ce que nous disons ici de la vengeance est valable aussi pour le Nord.

45 Warburg, op. cit., p. 135-136.

46 J.A. de C. Hamilton, Devolutionary Principles in Native Administration. In : The Anglo-Egyptian Sudan from within, Londres 1935, p. 181-190, spécialement p. 183.

47 Howell, A Manual..., op. cit., p. 226-227.

48 M. Abu Rannat, The relationship between islamic and customary law in the Sudan. In : Journal of African Law *IV*(1960), p. 9-16, spécialement p. 13.

49 Howell, A Manual..., op.cit., p. 236-237.

50 Ibid., p. 236.

51 Rapport spécial, 1904, p. 57.

52 Howell, A Manual..., op. cit., p. 235.

53 Francis Mading Deng, Tradition and Modernization : a Challenge for Law among the Dinka of the Sudan, Yale University Press 1971, reed. 1987, p. 59 sq.

54 Le tribunal coutumier, même composé des chefs de la tribu, était ressenti comme *jur*, étranger. Ibid., p. 58.

55 Ibid., p. 60.

56 R.A. Cook, Blood money and the law of homicide in the Sudan. In: Sudan Law Journal and Reports, 1962, p. 470-484, spécialement p. 479-482.

57 Dans la terminologie du code pénal, le meurtre est intentionnel, l'homicide regroupant les infractions où l'intention de tuer fait défaut.

58 Guttman, p. 404.

59 Hervé Bleuchot, Le droit pénal et les réformes en Egypte au XIXe siècle. In : Revue tunisienne de droit *1-2*(1990) (paru en 1993), p. 117-147.

60 Bernard Botiveau, Sharî'a islamique et droit positif dans le moyen orient contemporain, Egypte et Syrie, Thèse de Science politiques, février 1989, Aix en Provence, p. 100. Selon Rachîd Rida, la responsabilité des ulémas est considérable dans l'acculturation du droit français en Egypte.

61 Pour notre part nous l'employons dans le sens de fiqh, c'est-à-dire renvoyant aux constructions juridiques classiques de l'époque omeyyade.

62 H.H. Dodwell, op.cit. chapitre 7 Social policy, par Sir H.V. Lowett, p. 131 sq.

63 Cette formule était promise à un grand avenir en Inde et au Soudan, où elle servit de fondement au droit civil.

64 A. Gledhill, op. cit., p. 217.

65 Bleuchot, Signification..., op.cit., p. 103-113.

66 Cité par Shirley C. Zabel, Historical Sketch on the Legislative Process in the Early Condominium Period of the Sudan from 1899 to 1912. In : Journal of Islamic and Comparative Law (1968)2, p. 45-53. Faute de place on ne peut analyser ici les raisons du refus du droit égyptien. Voir Bleuchot, Cultures juridiques..., op. cit., p. 283 sq.

67 Nicole Grandin, Le Soudan nilotique et l'administration britannique (1898-1956), Leiden 1982, p. 107-108.

68 Ibid., p. 117.

69 Rapport général, 1904, p. 77.

70 Nous l'inférons à partir de témoignages oraux recueillis par nous sur les Shayqîya.

71 Rapport spécial, 1904, p. 57.

72 Rapport sur les prisons et la police, 1905.

73 Les circulaires criminelles qui auraient pu nous aider dans cette datation sont perdues dans leur forme primitive. En effet, en 1950-1952, le 'Chief Justice' Lindsay, reprit l'ensemble des circulaires criminelles, élimina les circulaires abrogées, réutilisa leurs numéros, modifia, redata, etc. Le résultat est cohérent, mais l'historien est frustré. Nous ne disposons que du recueil Lindsay aimablement communiqué par le Président de la chambre criminelle de la Cour Suprême.

74 Les "détribalisés" exceptés. Voir III. Les réactions au Sud, sur la vengeance.

75 Daly, Empire..., op. cit., p. 106.

76 Ibid., p. 444-445.

77 Ibid., p. 444.

78 Muhammad Ahmad Abd al Ghaffar, Shaykhs ans Followers, Political Struggle in the Rufa 'a Al Hoi Nazirate in the Sudan, Khartoum University Press 1974, p. 56-58. A partir de cette époque, il ne leur fut plus possible de cultiver signale l'auteur.

79 R. Brunschwig, 'Abd. In : Encyclopédie de l'islam, deuxième série, t. 1, p. 25-41.

80 Dans la science islamique du hadîth, on appelle "faible" le hadîth qui n'est pas conforté par une chaîne solide de transmetteurs véraces.

81 Lilian Sanderson-Passmore, Against the Mutilation of Women : the struggle to end unnecessary suffering, London 1981, p. 56 et 81.

82 Masaji CHIBA, Asian Indigenous Law in Interaction with Received Law, London-York 1986, p. 7-9.

83 Zaki Mustafa, Opting out of the Common Law : Recent Developments in the Legal System of the Sudan. In : Journal of African Law, 1973, p. 133-148, spécialement p. 146.

84 Il s'agit du système égyptien que l'auteur se plaît, c'est de bonne guerre, à assimiler au système français. Comme le soudanais, le système égyptien a évolué tout au long du vingtième siècle et s'est beaucoup adapté aux réalités locales.

85 L'auteur écrit en 1969, reproduit sa phrase en 1971 et en 1987. Cf. Francis Mading Deng, The Future of Customary Law in Sudan. In : Malaya Law Review *11*(1969)2, p. 268-286; Tradition and Modernization : a Challenge for Law among the Dinka of the Sudan, Yale University Press 1971, reed. 1987.

86 Allusion au livre de F.M. Deng/M.W. Daly, Bonds of Silk : the Human Factor in the British Administration of the Sudan, Michigan State University Press 1989.

87 Lord Macaulay était hostile à la jurisprudence et pensait que c'était au législateur et non aux juges que devait revenir le soin de faire évoluer la loi pénale.

# Changing or Unknown Identities? The example of the Deutsche Orientbank AG in Cairo and Alexandria (1906-1931)

Wolfgang Schwanitz

This paper seeks to provide a *socio-historical approach* to a part of the history in the German-Egyptian relations in the first half of this century. Using the *Deutsche Orientbank AG* (1906-1931) and the cotton company of *Hugo Lindemann* as points of departure, it serves to elucidate some of the interactions in the bilateral relations alongwith their shifting structures and ideas on industrialisation as a major question in search of identity and as one example - away from the 'industry-metropole / agriculture-periphery'.[1] It has to do with the historical patterns in the German-Egyptian relations. Searching in archives of Berlin, Bonn, Potsdam, and Cairo,[2] I will plumb the depths of the interactions[3] with the help of eight selected historical documents.

In order to discover historically the reasons for German co-responsibility for the today's Egyptian affairs,[4] I raised the following question: How did the *Deutsche Orientbank AG*, *al-Bank ash-Sharqî al-Almânî*, operate on the Nile from 1906 to 1931 - in view of semi-colonial status of the country which was controlled by Great Britain?

It may be mentioned that the Deutsche Orientbank has scarcely been investigated. Not even an article was available.[5] This is remarkable because this bank rose to the number one position amongst the nine German regional banks.[6] I will, therefore, elucidate the bank's history in a first short overview within six steps, in order to then problematise its socio-historical effects.

## A view on the past history before the 20th century

German-Egyptian relations came to fruition after the turn of the century. Before that tme the country on the Nile played a secondary role in German foreign affairs[7] as Egypt's road to statehood under the rule of Muhammed ᶜAlî (1769-1849)[8] failed precisely as a result of West European intervention. However, the cotton monoculture and the plans for the Suez Canal became a millstone on the throat of local agriculture. The period of German statehood (Gruenderzeit) was characterised by new foreign policy interests. Egypt became more significant as a function of the Suez Canal in 1869.

In a handbook Ewald Banse wrote forty years later: 'If Egypt was a corner state ('Winkelstaat') until 1869, if not even a locked country ('Sackland'), its general economic position has shifted completely since then. As a result of its possessions of the Atlantic-Indian international canal it has become one of the most important areas of the earth.'[9] In addition, Egypt's decline within the Ottoman Empire unleashed rivalries amongst the Europeans.[10] A new situation arose as Britain occupied Egypt in 1882 and later declared it to be a protectorate of the Crown.[11]

Germans supplied three percent of passages through the Suez Canal. In 1881 *Glaefke & Hennigs* of Hamburg founded the first German *Orient-Linie* which was granted free passage by the 1888 Canal Convention, and was followed in 1889 by the *Levante-Linie*. Nine hundred Germans on the Nile were not of great significance. In the meantime Bernhard Fuerst von Buelow (1849-1929) was in search of 'our place in the sun', displayed by Emperor Wilhelm II (1859-1941) in 1898 in Jerusalem. In 1884 Berlin received a seat for twenty years to steward the national debt in Cairo, which was assumed by Ottomar von Mohl and Freiherr von Richthofen. They brought the banks in their wake: *Oppenheim*, *Dehlbrueck*, *Rothschild*, *Stern*, *Mendelssohn*, *Bleichroeder*, and *Warschauer*. In 1898 both of them advanced the establishment of Egypt's *National Bank*, *Al-Bank Al-Ahlî*.

In 1895 a German consortium organised by Robert Warschauer received a railroad concession for the first on the Nile. Locomotive companies followed, e.g. *Henschel & Sohn* and the *Friedrich Krupp AG*. The first German-Egyptian commercial treaty was agreed upon in 1892. By 1900 the percentage of German participation in Egyptian trade had grown to three percent. Had Egypt earlier served as a means to disrupt the 'British-French axis', it now attained economic significance in its own right. Freiherr von Richthofen and Graf von Hatzfeld, consul-general as of 1908, supplied some orders.

The AEG[12] laid the Cairo-Alexandria telephone cable. German foreign trade grew to six percent. German orient-groups arose: in 1899 the *Deutsch-Orientalische-Exportgesellschaft*, in 1907 the *Deutsches Orient-Handels-Syndicat*, in 1910 the *Deutsch-Oesterreichischer Orient Verein*, in 1912 the *Deutscher Wirtschaftsverband Balkan/Orient*. Several of them went bankrupt, and others were well established like the *Tropen-Pflanzen-Gesellschaft*, Dresden-Ismaelia and the *Aegyptische Frucht- und Waldfarm-Gesellschaft*, Cairo.

## The establishment of the Deutsche Orientbank AG

For this purpose the Dresden banker Herbert M. Gutman, director of the *Dresdner Bank*, founded in Berlin 1871, invited German banks to a meeting in 1905. Only the *Deutsche Bank*[13] did not send a representative. They were later joined by: Czechs, Austrians, Swiss, the Dutch, Greeks, and the French (see bank's board in document 1).

In Turky some affiliates of the *Banque d'Orient* had been taken over and in Egypt the *Bank Hasan Bâshâ Saʿîd* (see the first banking statement 1906 in document 2).

In addition, Germans assisted by well established German companies in Egypt like the cotton company *Lindemann & Co.*, and, later the *Upper and Lower Egypt Cotton Trading Cy.* in Alexandria. The brothers Hugo and Otto Lindemann operated a press which formed cotton into forms which were ready for shipping. Soon, only a few years later, they provided half of the cotton exports on the Nile. So Hugo Lindemann became a co-founder of the Deutsche Orientbank AG which formed in Berlin and Cairo on 3 January 1906 by the *Dresdner Bank, A. Schaaffhausenscher Bankverein* and *Nationalbank für Deutschland.*

## The Pre-War growth of the Deutsche Orientbank AG

After 1907 branch offices in Constantinople, Brussa, Alexandria, and Cairo belonged, in addition to Berlin and Hamburg, to the Deutsche Orientbank. They were followed by Tanger and Casablanca, Mersina and Dedeagatsch, and al-Minyâ, Tântâ, Mansûra, Banî Suwaif, as well as Damanhûr on the Nile. By doubling its capital to a total of 32 million Marks in 1910 the Deutsche Orientbank advanced to the forefront of all nine German regional banks.

| *The nine German regional banks* | *capital in million Marks* |
|---|---|
| Deutsche Orientbank | 32,0 |
| Deutsch-Ueberseeische Bank | 30,0 |
| Deutsch-Südamerikanische Bank | 20,0 |
| Bank für Chile und Deutschland | 10,0 |
| Brasilianische Bank für Deutschland | 10,0 |
| Deutsch-Asiatische Bank | 7,5 |
| Deutsche Palästina-Bank | 5,0 |
| Deutsch-Ostafrikanische Bank | 2,0 |
| Deutsch-Westafrikanische Bank | 1,0 |

Berliner Börsen-Courier, 21.9.1910; Reichsanzeiger, 5.10.1910.

In 1911 the Khedive ʿAbbâs Hilmî (1874-1944) granted permission for an Deutsche Orientbank subsidiary, the *Egyptische Hypotheken Bank AG,* under Carl Hasselbach, Yûsuf Aslân Bâshâ Qattâwî and Muhammad Talʿat Bey Harb, via the Dresdner Bank, Nationalbank fuer Deutschland, Berliner Handels-Gesellschaft, A. Schaaffhausenscher Bankverein and Schweizer Bankverein.

In 1912 the Deutsche Orientbank established the *Kazan Carpet Co.* in London with offices in Istambul and New York. In 1914 the Deutsche Orientbank took over the *Deutsche Palaestinabank* and its branch offices in Jerusalem and Damascus.[14]

In contrast to the British, it included more Egyptians like Léonidas Zarîfî and Aristoteles Marcarian on its board. But in sharp contrast to this even in 1914 a kind of German antisemitism rosed since the diplomatic envoy in Cairo Graf von Pannwitz noted: civil servants of the Deutsche Orientbank were supposedly Jews in the main.[15]

## The America-Russia-Excursion in the First World War

At those times the Germans were not doing too well on the Nile. In 1915 England confiscated 'enemy property'. Seven hundred private German citizens[16] whose property was confiscated were included on Lord Allenbey's index (as far as the liquidation of the *Egyptische Hypotheken Bank* 1916 and 1918 see document 3). In general, the majority of Germans had to go to Malta. In 1919 some of them resumed their business: with a British stamp in their passports.

Egypt, however, revolted against the British.[17] In 1920 many nationalists went to study in Germany.[18] There influence helped as well so that Sir Lloyd George revoked the trade boycott with the 'German enemy' and the *protectorate* (18 December 1914-28 February 1922), and permitted the *Independent Kingdom of Egypt*. Soon London warned in its reports: the Germans were returning with 'advertising and quality work': *Reidel*, Britz; *Badische Analin & Sodafabrik*, Ludwigshafen; *Wordlich*, Stettin; *Bosch*, *Krupp*, *Borsig* and *Opel*.

The Deutsche Orientbank lost '30 million Gold marks' in Egypt and Turkey during the war. After the increase to 300 million paper Marks Erich Alexander and Henry Nathan made preparations for a new company in New York in 1919, and founded *The Dutch Staheeff Co.* in Den Haag in 1920. Batolin, head of *Ivan Staheeff & Co.*, was a partner of the 'Handels- und Industrie-AG' for two million Gulden. His bank was the *Russisch-Asiatische Bank*, Paris and London, with branch offices in China, Japan, and India.

Erich Alexander and Henry Nathan dined with Mr. Batolin in Berlin's Kaiserhof in 1921. At that time it was recorded that: Batolin heads the *Staheeff* company since 25 years. Formerly in the business of grain, industry, railway interests, and the Russian textile industry belonged to it. Though he is the descendant of peasants, speaks only Russian, Vladimir I. Lenin (1870-1924) asked for him as the new Russian commissioner for nutritional questions. As he was then in so much danger, he left Petersburg and went to America. There he became associated with 'Percy Rockefeller and the Guggenheims'.

In 1921 the Deutsche Orientbank bought then him a villa in Berlin in the Motzstraße for four million Marks. But everything collapsed in 1923: Mr. Batolin finally lost everything he owned in the USSR.

## Bank's growth between the two World Wars

In mid-1925 diplomatic envoy Mertens and Egypt's Prime Minister Ahmad Bâshâ Sîwar concluded a contract in Cairo on the establishment of business. The attorney Fritz Dahm was of the opinion that: before the war Germans had privileges in the Turkish area of sovereignty: freedom of trade, residency protection, and non-applicability of national laws. This was supplanted by the Versailles Treaty. Although privileges became null and void, the treaty on the establishment of business would, nonetheless, be valid. It was now possible to establish business for any purpose and to trade.

On 1 May 1925 Deutsche Orientbank branch offices reopened in Cairo and in Alexandria. Before the diplomatic envoy Graf von Podewils reported: 'government fear of a bolshevist wave' after the March strikes. Advocates like Antûn Marûn allegedly brought seeds, 'which in my opinion makes recognisable the vain attempt to bring about a socialist and communist movement with one jump over thousands of years, whose threads clear point to Moscow.' *Egypt for the Egyptians*, *nationalisation* and *industrialisation* became slogans. But a joint German-Egyptian office for industry, should be formed by *Misr Bank*, founded in 1920 under Muhammad Talᶜat Bey Harb, and Hamburger banks failed because some Egyptians did not like to provoke the British.

On the other hand, Egypt hosted international fairs from 1926 to 1933: industry and agriculture; shipping; automobiles; cotton and statistics; tropical medicine; patent law; journalism; music; railways. The Germans telegraphed that 'the Arab is for the Germans and prefers German commodities to those of the British because of antipathy to the British'[19]. Is it possible that a body of knowledge and ideas was conveyed in this tug-of-war? What significance does this have and the fact that Egyptians studied in Germany for new approaches to Egyptian problems?

Minimum wages obliged the government to subsidise cotton prices. The Deutsche Orientbank advanced four million LE as a consortium, especially since 3 December 1926 was a day of misfortune for the Alexandrian cotton market. A law which was passed required reduction of the useful area. The German-Egyptian commercial treaty took effect as of 1927. Thus the Germans were able to outdo their status from 1914 and became - according to the British - Egypt's second largest trading partner.

The Deutsche Orientbank, with a capital of 10 million Reichsmark, established a *German Coal Depot* in Bûr Saᶜîd. Half of the shares were assumed by the Hamburg Coal Depot (*Hamburger Kohle Depot*) and the remaining shares were assumed by consul Pauling, Hasan Bâshâ Saᶜîd, ex-Interior Minister Ismâᶜil Bâshâ Sidqî, the Suez consul Meinecke, and the Alexandrian Deutsche Orientbank head Erdoes.

## The End of the Deutsche Orientbank AG

'German bank holidays and crises' lead to 'money scarcity and hard currency hoarding' in the Deutsche Orientbank, although it was third amongst 19 foreign banks after the *Al-Bank Al-Ahlî* and the *Bank Misr*. 'with 20 branches for cotton'. The anxiety with the German Mark was imponderable. Commissioner Craig checked out the Deutsche Orientbank. Up to August 1931 for the bank it was not possible to obtain funds from Berlin. Its customers stormed *Barclays Bank*. The bankruptcy judge closed the Deutsche Orientbank once and for all on at the end of August 1931.

The risky cotton business was excluded and the name of the *Dresdner Bank*, of which the German government was a principal share-holder, became accepted as of 1 September 1931 for the former Deutsche Orientbank AG and their Eygyptian branches. But in Turky the Dresdner Bank kept on the original name 'Deutsche Orientbank AG' for some years.

Now business surrounded, on a compensatory basis, 'nitrogen or paints in exchange for cotton', with twelve cotton businesses in Bremen and *IG Farben Co.* [20] The twenty-fifth year of business, 1930, was the last for the Deutsche Orientbank.

Focussing on Egypt Hermann Joseph Abs united several former Orient bankers in the 1930s again as well as in the early 1950s but without using the old name Deutsche Orientbank AG.

The period between the wars[21] was the era of national institutionalisation[22] on the Nile. As the population rose from 1917 to 1937 from 13 million to 16 million, and the multiply used area stagnated though at eight million Faddân[23], the problem grew. In 1936 W. Cleland, professor at the American University of Cairo[24] elucidated the problem with his work *The Population Problem in Egypt*. Grand mufti ᶜAbd al-Magîd Sâlim permitted a temporary period of contraception based on the acquiescence of the husband under Islamic law. In 1937 the first conference on birth control convened in Cairo and recommended population control on the Nile.

In the 1930s the influence of Nazism on the Egyptians rose.[25] In the first Cairo *NSDAP* report in 1935 we read that Alexandria 'is a bastion of Jewishness like no other city in the world'. Germans, according to Mr. Bisse from Cairo, should replace them. The German foreign currency restrictions alone limited exports. In this case the *Dresdner Bank* was at work, for the German proportion of cotton exports was 1.4 percent, compared to the 'Jewish proportion' of 12.9 percent. The pharmaceutical business would be dominated by the *Bayer* and *IG Farben*

*Industries*. Moreover, *Schering-Kahlbaum, Merck, I.D. Riedel, Gehe, Kroll* and *von Heyden* had offices here. However, this *NS* propaganda did not help very much.

On 3 September 1939 Egypt's Prime Minister ᶜAlî Mâhir broke off relations to Germany 'because of the German-Polish crisis' and the obligations arising out of the Anglo-Egyptian Treaty of 1936.

## Conclusions from the example of the Deutsche Orientbank AG

The Deutsche Orientbank illuminated unequal relations. While Germans with an ample capital survived the wars and crises, suffering experienced by the Egyptians was one-sided. Division of the world economy into industrial centres and agrarian peripheries grew hierarchically and asymmetrically. The Deutsche Orientbank was exceptional because it accepted Egyptians on all of its governing bodies. It became multinational, an original form of the joint ventures, which the technology push forty years later so prevalent in Western Europe, the U.S.A, and Japan.

This mixed form also served the upper classes, which were often comprised of minorities. They wanted industry on the Nile.[26] Western Europe's and Germany's industrial model acted as the godfather as far as Muhammad Talᶜat Bey Harb was concerned, advocate of the Deutsche Orientbank subsidiary *Egyptische Hypotheken Bank* and founder of the first national *Bank Misr* in 1920.

As far as the familiar and the foreign make up social history, the question arises: were foreign means of development copied in the British protectorate, under the influence of new powers from Europe, North America, and Japan? For between the wars, as Egypt established itself as a nation, the Germans, Americans, Soviets, and Japanese appeared as young rivals. The Germans considered whether one 'should bring means of production to the Nile', which could have brought them more competition. The envoys and the Deutsche Orientbank were of an affirmative opinion: otherwise it would fall into the hands of others, especially since a German bonus was effective against the British.

Egypt's attempt to find new paths under Muhammad ᶜAlî rebuffed West Europeans. They turned the country to monoculture in the agrarian-industrial division of labour. At the turn of the century it became a net importer of foodstuffs.[27] In the new state after the World War, even without the semi-colonial possessions of the British and with the second global division of labour, a partial industrialisation began at the company level - see the *Lindemann* brothers on this point. This appealed in reverse to the nationalists. But where did the features of the Egyptians lead to who studied in Germany and were interested in discovering their own way; or the other estrangements like the Nazi hate for the Jews,[28] Soviet ideology or the oil interests of the U.S.A?

Are the opinions of some Egyptians correct who today maintain that such influences from Europe inhibited original thinking on the Nile about indigenous alternatives for solving the problems of population and identity for example? Were indigenous solutions suppressed by adaption of Western European concepts and the modelling of the country according to British standards?[29]

It cannot be the task here to contort the 'historical wheel' by assigning any kind of blame. But it should remain in view that the Egyptians who were economically in a world-wide subordinate position had to react to historical processes in Europe, like the War and Erwin Rommel's 'campaign' in al-ᶜAlamain in 1942[30] showed. Thus there was not much energy left over for regulating the problems in searching of identity.

# Aufsichtsrat
der
# Deutschen Orientbank Aktiengesellschaft

Herbert M. Gutmann, Direktor der Dresdner Bank, Berlin, Vorsitzender.
Dr. Jakob Goldschmidt, Geschäftsinhaber der Darmstädter und Nationalbank Kommanditgesellschaft auf Aktien, Berlin, stellvertretender Vorsitzender.
Dr. Paul v. Schwabach, i. Fa. S. Bleichröder, Berlin, stellvertretender Vorsitzender.
Fritz Andreae, i. Fa. Hardy & Co., G. m. b. H., Berlin.
Paul Briske, i. Fa. Briske & Prohl, Berlin.
Kurt Glogowski, i. Fa. Glogowski & Co., Berlin.
Fritz Gutmann, i. Fa. Proehl & Gutmann, Amsterdam.
Carl Hagen, i. Fa. Hagen & Co., Berlin.
Dr. Louis Hagen, Geh. Kommerzienrat, i. Fa. A. Levy, Köln a. Rh.
S. E. Hassan Pascha Said, Kairo.
Dr. Georg Hirschland, i. Fa. Simon Hirschland, Essen.
Arndt v. Holtzendorff, (Hamburg-Amerika-Linie), Gr. Hansdorf bei Hamburg.
Hugo Lindemann, i. Fa. Lindemann & Co. und Upper and Lower Egypt Cotton Trading Cy., Alexandrien.
Dr. Karl Melchior, i. Fa. M. M. Warburg & Co., Hamburg.
Dr. Gottlieb Morawetz, Direktor der Böhmischen Unionbank, Prag.
Freiherr Simon Alfred v. Oppenheim, i. Fa. Sal. Oppenheim jun. & Co., Köln a. Rh.
Samuel Ritscher, Direktor der Reichs-Kredit-Gesellschaft A. G., Berlin.
Curt Sobernheim, Direktor der Commerz- und Privatbank A. G., Berlin.
Dr. Heinrich v. Stein, Konsul, i. Fa. J. H. Stein, Köln a. Rh.

## Generaldirektion

Dr. jur. Erich Alexander    Curt Lebrecht
Stellvertretend: Erich Hanson

## Filialdirektion

**Hamburg**

E. Wilberg    E. Flörke

**Türkei** (Konstantinopel und Smyrna)

C. Lambiki    J. Posth

**Smyrna**

M. Politi    Chahine Zadé Sélaheddine Fevzi

**Egypten** (Kairo und Alexandrien)

Hassan Pascha Said als Delegierter des Aufsichtsrats

A. D. Marcarian    Dr. H. O. Schultz
K. Erdoes

Document 1

# Deutsche Orientbank

## Aktiengesellschaft

**Berlin**

**Hamburg — Constantinopel — Brussa — Alexandrien — Cairo**

## Geschäfts-Bericht

der

## Deutschen Orientbank Aktiengesellschaft

über das

erste Geschäftsjahr vom 1. Januar 1906 bis 31. Dezember 1906.

—

Das erste Geschäftsjahr der am 3. Januar 1906 gegründeten, am 20. Januar in das Handelsregister eingetragenen **Deutschen Orientbank Aktiengesellschaft** war vornehmlich der Organisation und dem Ausbau des Geschäftes gewidmet.

Die von der Banque d'Orient übernommenen Niederlassungen in Hamburg und Constantinopel haben wir weiter ausgestaltet.

Im März 1906 haben wir in Alexandrien und im Juni 1906 in Kairo und Brussa Niederlassungen errichtet, die sich ebenfalls in befriedigender Entwicklung befinden.

Von unserem Aktienkapital von M. 16 000 000.— haben wir am 3. Januar M 4 000 000.—, am 20. März M. 3 000 000.- - und am 1. August M. 3 000 000.- - eingefordert, sodass gegenwärtig M. 10 000 000.— unseres Kapitales eingezahlt sind.

Der Reingewinn hierauf beträgt laut Gewinn- und Verlust-Konto M. 392 814,31. Wir schlagen vor, hiervon M. 19 640,71 der gesetzlichen Reserve zuzuführen, M. 301 666,66 als 4% Dividende auf das Durchschnittskapital von M. 7 541 666,66 zu verteilen und den Rest von M. 71 506,94 auf neue Rechnung vorzutragen.

BERLIN, im März 1907.

DER VORSTAND.

H. M. Gutmann. Zahn. Mosevius. Thomas.

Vorstehender Bericht, sowie die von dem Vorstand vorgelegte Bilanz und Gewinn- und Verlust-Rechnung sind von dem Aufsichtsrat geprüft worden, der nichts dagegen zu erinnern hat und den Anträgen der Direktion zustimmt.

Nach § 19 des Statutes scheiden die gesamten Mitglieder des ersten Aufsichtsrates nach der ordentlichen Generalversammlung aus.

BERLIN, im März 1907. DER AUFSICHTSRAT.

Eugen Gutmann

**Document 2**

58

**Deutsche Orientbank Aktiengesellschaft**

Gegründet von Dresdner Bank, A. Schaaffhausen'scher Bankverein und Nationalbank für Deutschland.
Aktienkapital Mk. 32 000 000.

TELEGRAMM-ADRESSE: DORIBANK. CENTRALE: BERLIN. CODE 5TH EDITION A.B.C. LIEBER'S CODE. PETERSON'S INTERNATIONAL BANKING CODE BAUERS CODE

ZWEIGNIEDERLASSUNGEN:
ADANA
ADRIANOPEL
ALEPPO
ALEXANDRIEN
BENI-SUEF
BRUSSA
CAIRO (DEPOSITENKASSE MOUSKY)
CONSTANTINOPEL GALATA UND STAMBUL DEPOSITENKASSEN PERA UND KADIKEUY
DAMANHOUR
HAMBURG
MANSOURAH
MERSINA AGENTUREN: TARSUS, DJEYHAN, AYASS
MINIEH
TANTAH

Dr.A/Sk. № 30716 5 VIII 16 Berlin, den 4. August 1916

Berliner Handels-Gesellschaft

**Berlin W.**

Wie Ihnen bekannt geworden ist, hat die englische Regierung die Zweigniederlassungen der deutschen Banken in London veranlasst, ihren Hauptniederlassungen mitzuteilen, dass alle in London bei den deutschen Banken hinterlegten Wertpapiere auf den "Public Trustee" übertragen werden.

Die deutschen Banken haben hiergegen unter Unterstützung der deutschen Behörden einen Protest in England eingereicht, mussten jedoch ~~infolgedessen~~ jede Verantwortung für das weitere Schicksal der Papiere ablehnen.

./- Mit Rücksicht darauf, dass die in der Anlage verzeichneten Effekten bei der Dresdner Bank London liegen, müssen wir unsererseits ebenfalls jede Verantwortung für das weitere Schicksal Ihrer Effekten ablehnen.

Hochachtungsvoll
DEUTSCHE ORIENTBANK
AKTIENGESELLSCHAFT

Jeder Bogen dieses Briefes muss, um gültig zu sein, ordnungsmässig gezeichnet sein.
Toutes les feuilles composant cette lettre doivent, pour être valables, être dûment signées.

Document 3

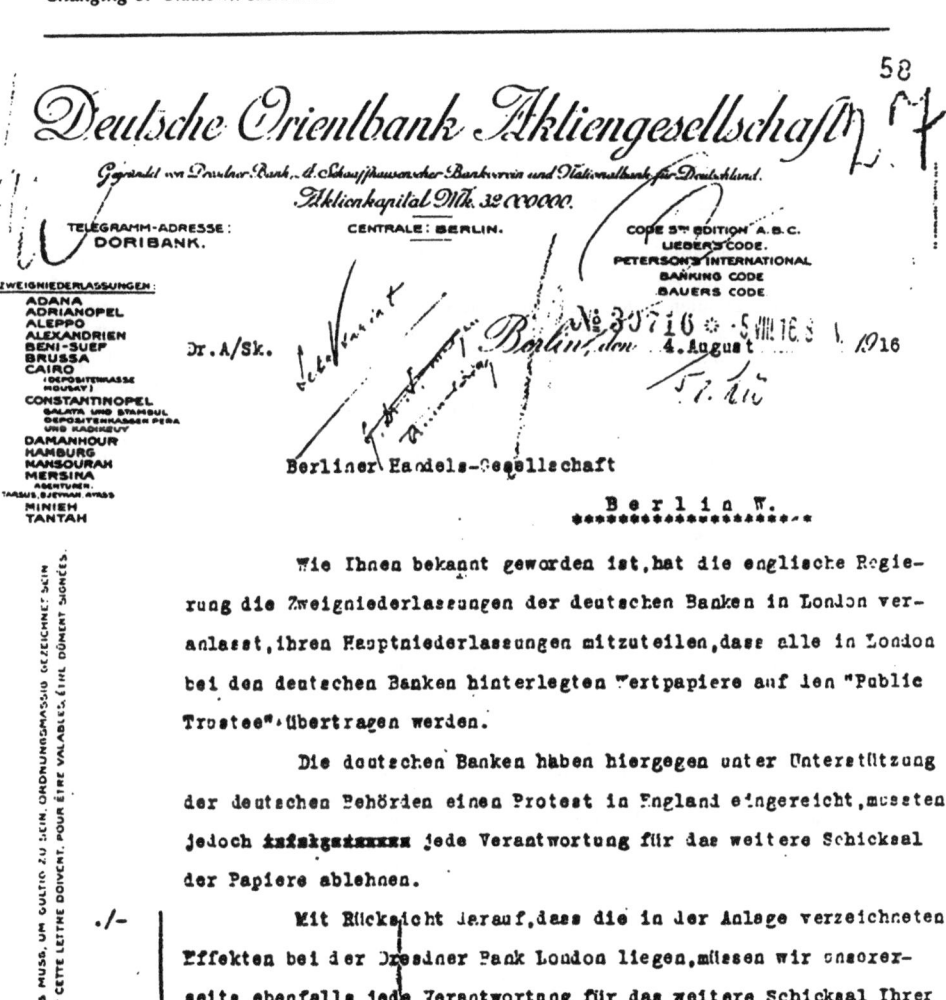

## Notes

1 Thomas W. Kramer, Deutsch-Ägyptische Beziehungen. In: Heinz Schamp (ed.), Ägypten, Tübingen-Basel 1977, p. 553.

2 Historical details are from the Archives: Bundesarchiv Potsdam, Auswärtiges Amt 09.01, Deutsche Reichsbank 25.01, Berliner Handels-Gesellschaft 80 Hal VFII, Bd.1, Kolonialwirtschaftliches Komitee 61 Ko2 und Reichswirtschaftsamt 31.01; Archiv DDR-Ministerium für Auswärtige Angelegenheiten, Berlin, L187; Archiv der Parteien und Massenorganisationen der DDR im Bundesarchiv, Berlin, ZK-Abteilung Internationale Verbindungen IV/2/20, Nachlässe Otto Grotewohl, NL90, Walter Ulbricht, NL182; Politisches Archiv des Auswärtigen Amts, Bonn, Orientalia Generalia 13, Bd. 1-3, Abteilungen I, III, V und VII; Ägyptisches Nationalarchiv Dâr al-Waṯâ'iq al-Qaumîya, Kairo, Bestände Staatssouveränität; see also Wolfgang Schwanitz, SED-Nahostpolitik als Chefsache. Die ZK-Abteilung Internationale Verbindungen 1946-1970 sowie die Nachlässe von Otto Grotewohl und Walter Ulbricht. In: asien, afrika, lateinamerika, Berlin *21*(1993)1, pp. 63-90; Das Niederländische Institut für Ägyptologie und Arabistik sowie das Nationalarchiv in Kairo. In: ibid., *21*(1993)4, pp. 411-415.

3 On Arabs, Jews and Germans: mutual perceptions see also: Wolfgang Schwanitz (ed.), Jenseits der Legenden: Araber, Juden, Deutsche, Berlin 1994.

4 Such as Anita Müller, Schweizer in Alexandrien 1914-1963. Zur ausländischen Präsenz in Ägypten, Stuttgart 1992; see also asien, afrika, lateinamerika, *21*(1993)3, p. 310-313.

5 Behind the Deutsche Orientbank AG: Allgemeine Deutsche Creditanstalt, Leipzig, and Dresdner Bank, Berlin. See Meyers Reisebücher: Ägypten, Leipzig Wien, 1914, p. 211, 238, 333; for an overview on the Deutsche Orientbank AG see: Wie deutsche Gesandte in Kairo und Alexandrien nach Berlin über Ägypter, Amerikaner, Briten, Franzosen, Russen, Japaner und Juden berichteten (1919-1939). In: Schwanitz (ed.), Jenseits der Legenden..., pp. 23-59.

6 Cf. Berliner Börsen-Courier, 21.9.1910; Reichsananzeiger, Berlin, 5.10.1910, 12.11.1910.

7 Graf Ernst zu Reventlow, Deutschlands auswärtige Politik 1888-1914, Berlin 1917; Otto Hammann, Deutsche Weltpolitik 1890-1912, Berlin 1925; Egon Eißmann, Die deutsche Wirtschaftsexpansion in Ägypten 1871-1914 als Komponente des deutsch-englischen Gegensatzes, Leipzig 1958; Martin Kröger, 'Le bâton égyptien': Der ägyptische Knüppel - die Rolle der 'ägyptischen Frage' in der deutschen Außenpolitik von 1875/76 bis zur 'Entente Cordiale', Frankfurt/M.-New York-Paris 1991.

8 Adolf Hasenclever, Geschichte Ägyptens im 19. Jahrhundert: 1789-1914, Halle 1917; Alexander Schölch, Ägypten den Ägyptern!, Zürich-Freiburg 1972; Wolfgang Schwanitz, Der Reformer Muhammad ʿAlî aus ägyptischer Sicht. In: Gerhard Höpp (ed.), Entwicklung durch Reform - Asien und Afrika im 19. Jahrhundert. In: asien, afrika, lateinamerika, (1990) , pp. 225-247.

9 Cf. Ewald Banse, Ägypten - eine Landeskunde, Halle 1909, p. 58.

10 Peter von Sivers, Die europäische Ausdehnung nach Nordafrika (1800-1900). In: Ulrich Haarmann (ed.), Geschichte der arabischen Welt, München 1991, p. 531.

11 Fritz Steppat, Nationalismus und Islam bei Mustafâ Kâmil, Leiden 1956 (Die Welt des Islams *IV*(1956)4].

12 AEG: Allgemeine Elektrizitätsgesellschaft.

13 See moreover Bert Schmiale, Die Deutsche Bank und Philipp Holzmann in Nahost. In: Schwanitz (ed.), Jenseits der Legenden..., pp. 60-82.

14 Peter Thomsen (ed.), Die Palästina-Literatur. Eine internationale Bibliographie in systematischer Ordnung mit Autoren und Sachregister, Leipzig 1927, vol. 4: 1915-1924, pp. 506, 576.

15 See the overview in: Michael M. Laskier, The Jews of Egypt 1920-1970, New York- London 1992.

16 In 'all of Egypt' before the World War there were 1900 Germans belonging to the Reichs-Empire, 7000 Austrians and 700 Swiss, compared to 15,000 French, 21,000 British citizens, 35,000 Italians, 63,000 Greeks. Cf. Meyers Reisebücher: Ägypten, Leipzig-Wien 1914, p. 69; Germans also had to go to Malta during the war, so that for almost ten years there were no Germans on the Nile. They returned as of summer of 1923. In 1928 'Egyptian Germans' included over 1000 belonging to the Reichs-Empire. Cf. Alfred Kaufmann, Ewiges Stromland: Land und Mensch in Ägypten, Stuttgart 1929, p. 84.

17 Reinhard Schulze, Kolonisierung und Widerstand: Die ägyptischen Bauern-Revolten von 1919. In: Alexander Schölch/Helmut Mejcher (ed.), Die ägyptische Gesellschaft im 20. Jahrhundert, Hamburg 1992, pp. 11-54.

18 Gerhard Höpp, Traditionen der ägyptischen Revolution: Ägyptische Nationalisten in Deutschland, 1920-1925. In: Schwanitz (ed.), Berlin-Kairo: Damals und heute. Zur Geschichte deutsch-ägyptischer Beziehungen, Berlin 1991, pp. 72-84.

19 See Kaufmann, Ewiges Stromland..., p. 82.

20 Monika Friedrich, Die Aktivitäten des deutschen Stickstoff-Syndikats in Ägypten 1924-1939. In: Zeitschrift für Unternehmensgeschichte, Stuttgart *38*(1993)1, pp. 26-48; Die Aktivitäten der IG-Farben-Verkaufsgemeinschaft Farben in Ägypten 1925-1939. In: Ibid, *35*(1990)4, pp. 237-254.

21 Linda Schatkowski Schilcher/Claus Scharf (eds.), Der Nahe Osten in der Zwischenkriegszeit 1919-1939, Stuttgart 1989; Sâlim, Latîfat Muhammad Sâlim, Fârûq wa suqût al-malikîya fî misr 1936-1952, Kairo 1989; Camilla Dawletschin-Linder, Die Türkei und Deutschland in der Weltwirtschaftskrise 1929-1933, Stuttgart 1989; Reinhard Schulze, Ägypten 1936-1956: Die Nationalisierung eines kolonialen Staats. In: Wolfgang J. Mommsen (ed.), Das Ende der Kolonialreiche, Frankfurt/M. 1990, pp. 134-156.

22 Wolfgang Schwanitz, Ägyptens historischer Weg zum Technologie-Streit. In: Wissenschaft und Technik im Dienste der Dritten Welt, Berlin 1989, pp. 146-167.

23 Rushdî Sa<sup>c</sup>îd, Nahr an-Nîl, Kairo 1993, p. 233.

24 Silvia Tellenbach, Landesbericht Ägypten. In: Albin Eser/Hans-Georg Koch (ed.), Schwangerschaftsabbruch im internationalen Vergleich - Empirische Grunddaten. Teil 2, Außereuropa, Baden-Baden 1989, p. 28.

25 Stefan Wild, National Socialism in the Arab Near East between 1933 and 1939. In: Die Welt des Islams, Leiden *XXV*(1985), pp. 126-173.

26 Victor Ottman, Das Wunderland am Nil, Berlin 1927, S. 124; Thâbit Thâbit, Misr fî ᶜahd Fû'âd al-auwal, Kairo 1936; Nawâl Qâsim, tatauwur as-sinâᶜa al-misrîya mundhu ᶜahd Muhammad ᶜAlî hata ᶜahd ᶜAbd an-Nâsir, Kairo 1987.

27 Siegmund Schilder, Entwicklungstendenzen der Weltwirtschaft, Berlin 1912, vol. 1, p. 274.

28 Such as the 'Protokolle der Weisen von Zion', which supported Gamâl ᶜAbd an-Nâsir 1958 in an interview with the Indian Magazin Blitz (Cairo Press Review 29.9.1958), and which are available today in central bookshops on the Nile: ᶜAgâg Naûwîhid, brûtûkûlat hukamâ' suhîyûn, Damaskus 1990, vol. 1, 2; see also Umberto Eco, Das Foucaultsche Pendel, München 1992, pp. 563-580.

29 Zakarîyâ Fû'âd, khutâb ila al-ᶜaql al-ᶜarabî, Kairo 1990; Taufîq Ar-Rais, al-ghurabâ' wa tanmîyat at-takhalluf. In: al-Ahrâm al-Iqtisâdî, Kairo, 30.12.1991, pp. 32-34.

30 Heinz Tillmann, Deutschlands Araberpolitik im zweiten Weltkrieg, Berlin 1956.

## Contributors

Professor Dr *Anouar Abdel-Malek*, Special Adviser for Asian Affairs, National Centre for Middle East Studies, Cairo, Directeur de recherche honoraire, C.N.R.S., Paris

Dr *Hervé Bleuchot*, IREMAM, Aix en Provence

Professor Dr *Bipan Chandra*, Professor emeritus, Centre for Historical Studies, Jawaharlal Nehru University, New Delhi

Professor Dr *Barun De*, Director, Maulana Abul Kalam Asad Institute of Asian Studies, Calcutta

Dr *Jan-Georg Deutsch*, Centre for Modern Oriental Studies, Berlin

Dr *Dagmar Glaß*, University of Leipzig

Dr *Annemarie Hafner*, Centre for Modern Oriental Studies, Berlin

Professor Dr *Joachim Heidrich*, Centre for Modern Oriental Studies, Berlin

Dr *Petra Heidrich*, Centre for Modern Oriental Studies, Berlin

Professor Dr *Peter Heine*, Acting Director, Centre for Modern Oriental Studies, Berlin

Dr *Ulrich van der Heyden*, Centre for Modern Oriental Studies, Berlin

Professor Dr *Erik Komarov*, Institute of Oriental Studies, Moscow

Dr *Dick Kooiman*, Faculty of Socio-Cultural Studies, Free University, Amsterdam

Dr *Miloslav Krása*, formerly Institute of Oriental Studies, Prague

Dr *Heike Liebau*, Centre for Modern Oriental Studies, Berlin

*Margret Liepach*, Centre for Modern Oriental Studies, Berlin

Dr *Miloš Mendel*, Institute of Oriental Studies, Prague

Dr *Subrata K. Mitra*, Director, Centre for Indian Studies, Department of Politics, University of Hull

Professor Dr *J. V. Naik*, Department of History, University of Bombay

Dr *Achim von Oppen*, Centre for Modern Oriental Studies, Berlin

Professor Dr *Terence Ranger*, St Antony's College, Oxford

Professor Dr *Tapan Raychaudhuri*, St Antony's College, Oxford

Dr *Dietrich Reetz*, Centre for Modern Oriental Studies, Berlin

Professor Dr *Reinhard Schulze*, Faculty of Linguistics and Literature, Otto Friedrich University, Bamberg

Dr *Wolfgang Schwanitz*, Centre for Modern Oriental Studies, Berlin

Bei Fragen zur Produktsicherheit wenden Sie sich bitte an:
If you have any questions regarding product safety,
please contact:

Walter de Gruyter GmbH
Genthiner Straße 13
10785 Berlin
productsafety@degruyterbrill.com